NATIONAL GEOGRAPHIC

Reach

Language • Literacy • Content

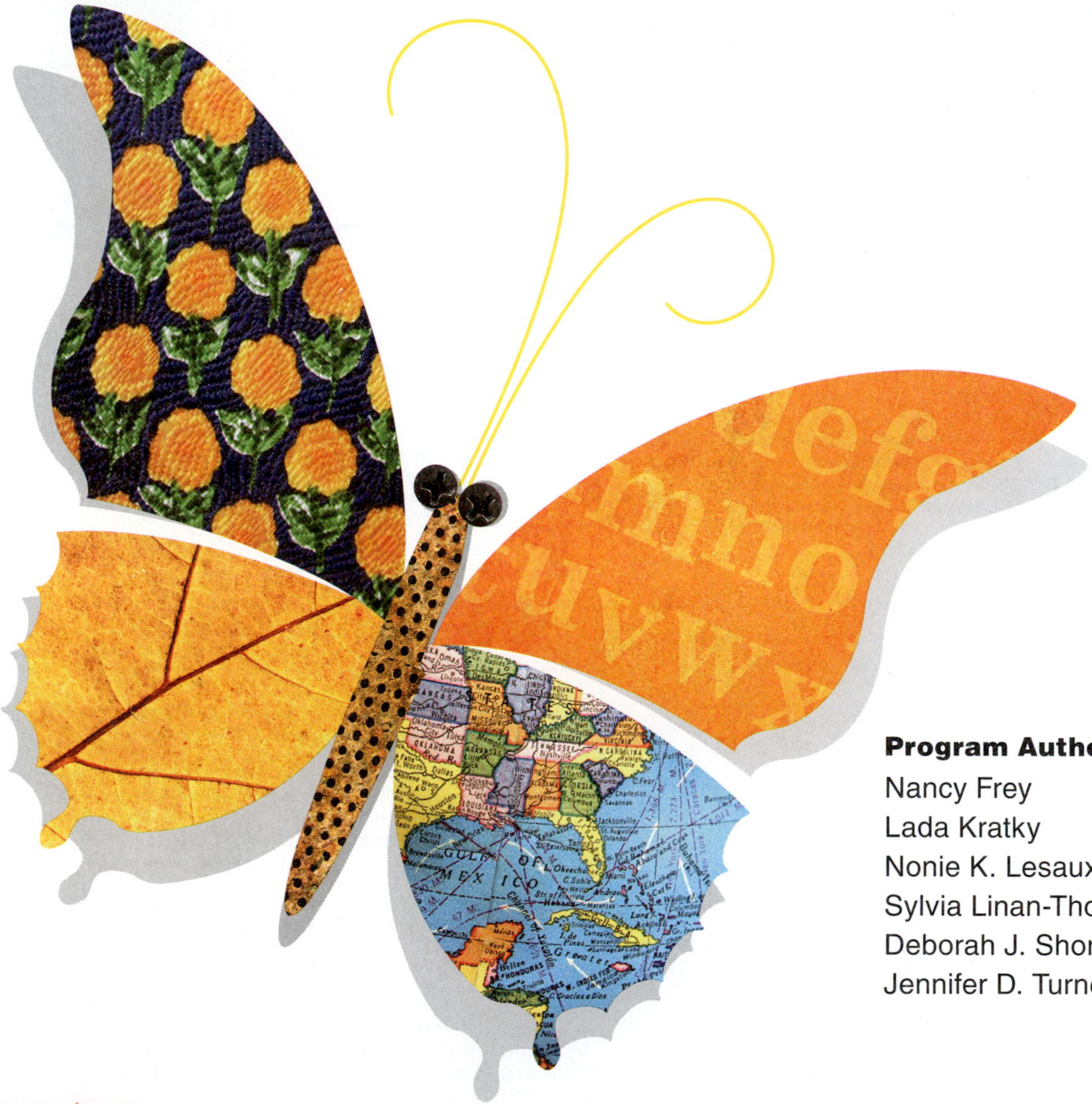

Program Authors

Nancy Frey

Lada Kratky

Nonie K. Lesaux

Sylvia Linan-Thompson

Deborah J. Short

Jennifer D. Turner

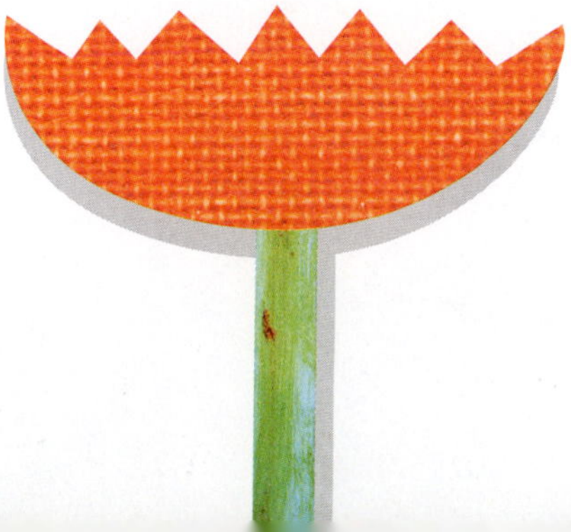

Literature Reviewers

Carmen Agra Deedy, Grace Lin, Jonda C. McNair, Anastasia Suen

Grade 4 Teacher Reviewers

James M. Cleere
Teacher
Donald McKay School
East Boston, MA

Judy H. Kinlaw
ESL Teacher
Southwestern Randolph Middle School
Asheboro, NC

Aimee R. Finley
Bilingual Teacher
C. A. Tatum Jr. Elementary School
Dallas, TX

Laura Hook
Elementary ESOL Resource Teacher
Faulkner Ridge
Catonsville, MD

Michelle Navarro
Teacher on Special Assignment
Orange Unified School District
Orange, CA

Theresa Proctor-Reece
ELL Teacher
Windy River Elementary School
Boardman, OR

Kathy Walcott
Spanish Immersion Specialist
Rockford Public Schools
Rockford, MI

Michelle Williams
ELL & Migrant Programs Director
West Ottawa Public Schools
Holland, MI

Acknowledgments
Grateful acknowledgment is given to the authors, artists, photographers, museums, publishers, and agents for permission to reprint copyrighted material. Every effort has been made to secure the appropriate permission. If any omissions have been made or if corrections are required, please contact the Publisher.

Illustrator Credits:
Front Cover: Joel Sotelo

Acknowledgments and credits continue on page 659.

For product information and technology assistance, contact us at
Customer & Sales Support, 888-915-3276

For permission to use material from this text or product, submit all requests online at **www.cengage.com/permissions**
Further permissions questions can be emailed to
permissionrequest@cengage.com

National Geographic Learning | Cengage Learning
1 Lower Ragsdale Drive
Building 1, Suite 200
Monterey, CA 93940

Cengage Learning is a leading provider of customized learning solutions with office locations around the globe, including Singapore, the United Kingdom, Australia, Mexico, Brazil, and Japan. Locate your local office at **www.cengage.com/global**.

Cengage Learning products are represented in Canada by Nelson Education, Ltd.

Visit National Geographic Learning online at **NGL.Cengage.com**
Visit our corporate website at **www.cengage.com**

Printed in the USA.
RR Donnelley, Willard, OH, USA

ISBN: 978-13054-94589

Printed in the United States of America
16 17 18 19 20 21 22 23 24
13 12 11 10 9 8 7 6 5 4 3 2

Contents at a Glance

Table of Contents

Living Traditions

? BIG QUESTION

How important are traditions?

Read More

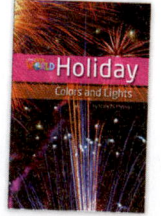
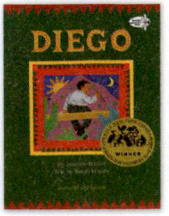

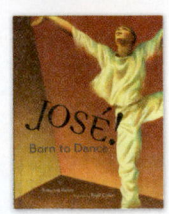
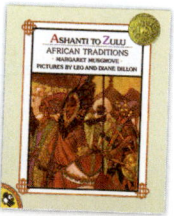
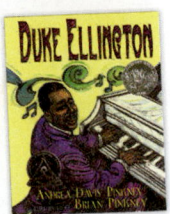

 = Comprehension Coach    = Interactive Whiteboard    = NGReach.com

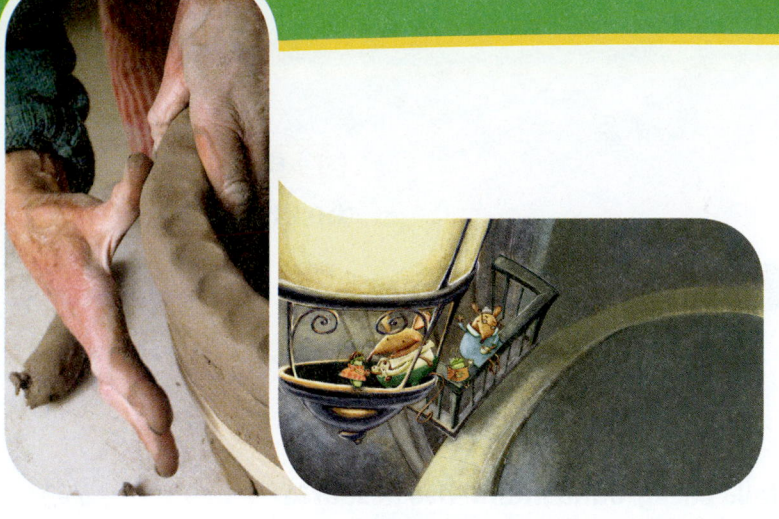

Unit 1

SOCIAL STUDIES

▸ Cultural Traditions, Customs, and Celebrations

Table of Contents

Animal Intelligence

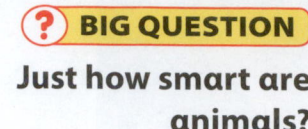

? BIG QUESTION

Just how smart are animals?

Read More

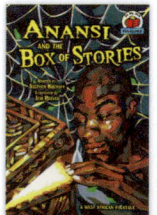

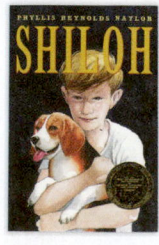
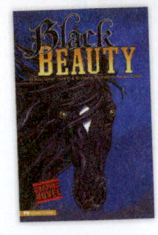

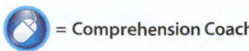 = Comprehension Coach    = Interactive Whiteboard    = NGReach.com

Unit 2

SCIENCE
▶ Animal Behavior

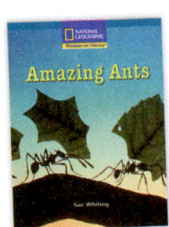
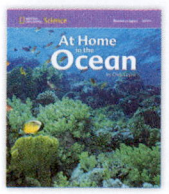

Table of Contents

Amazing Places

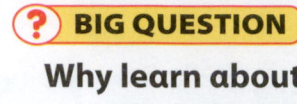 **BIG QUESTION**

Why learn about other places?

Read More

 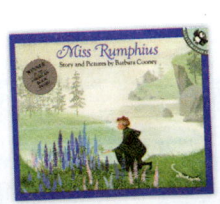 

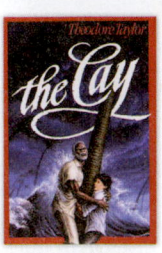 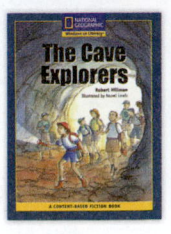 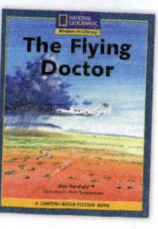

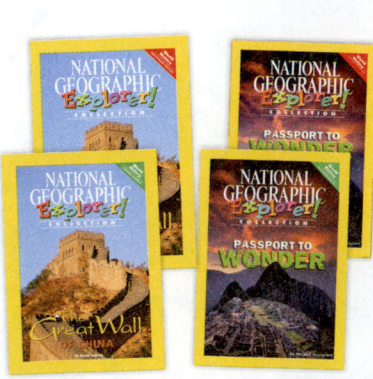

 = Comprehension Coach    = Interactive Whiteboard    = NGReach.com

Unit 3

SOCIAL STUDIES

▶ Geographic Tools and Features

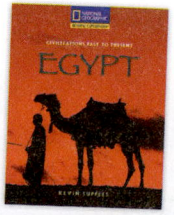
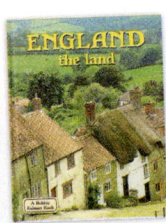
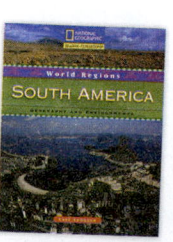

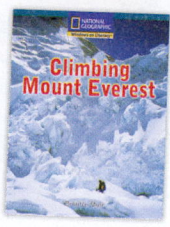

Table of Contents

Power of Nature

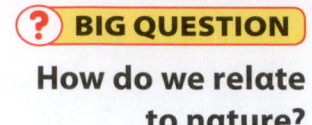

BIG QUESTION

How do we relate to nature?

Read More

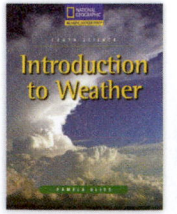
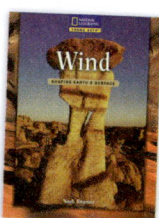
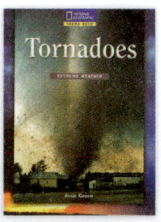
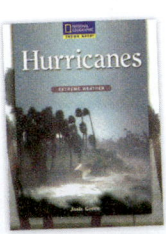
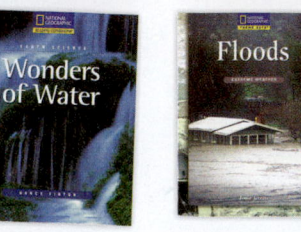
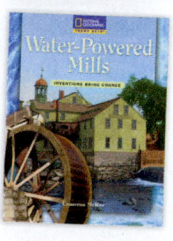

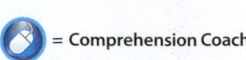 = Comprehension Coach   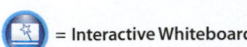 = Interactive Whiteboard    = NGReach.com

SCIENCE

▸ Natural Resources
▸ Wind, Water, Earth, and Air

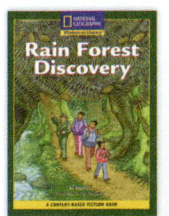

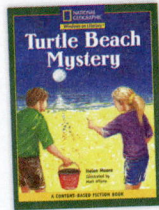

Table of Contents

Invaders!

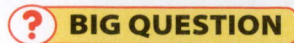 **BIG QUESTION**

When do harmless things become harmful?

Read More

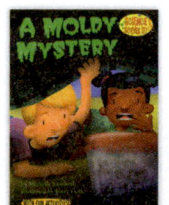 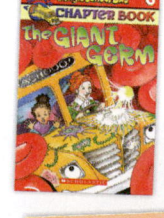 

  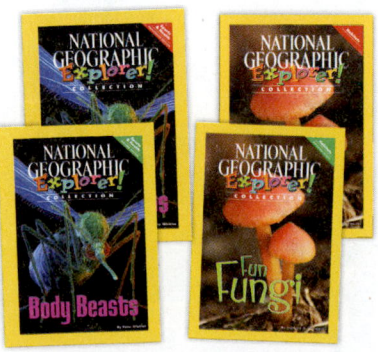

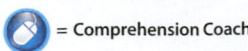 = Comprehension Coach    = Interactive Whiteboard    = NGReach.com

Unit 5

SCIENCE

▸ Science Process: Collect, Record, and Analyze Data
▸ Animal Habitats and Migration

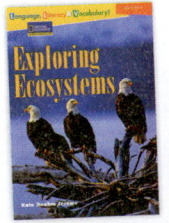
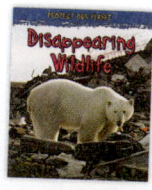

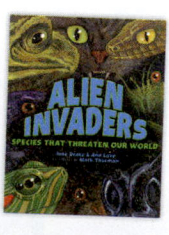

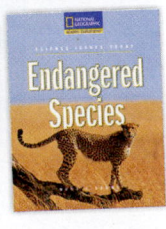

Table of Contents

Treasure Hunters

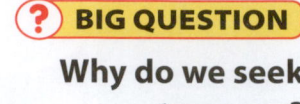 **BIG QUESTION**

Why do we seek treasure?

Read More

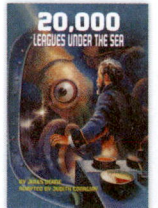 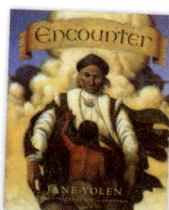 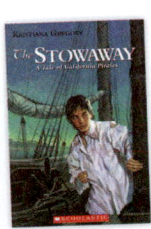

 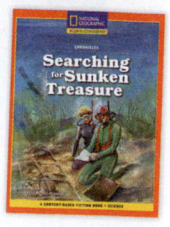 

 = Comprehension Coach    = Interactive Whiteboard    = NGReach.com

SOCIAL STUDIES
▶ Exploration

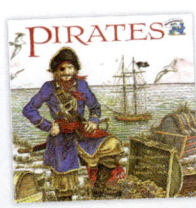

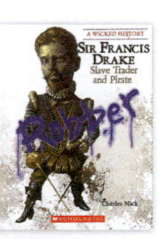
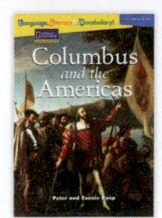
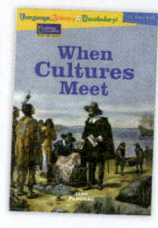
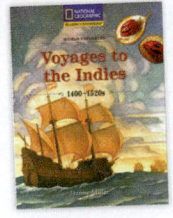
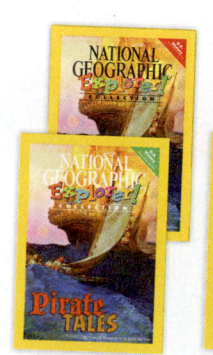
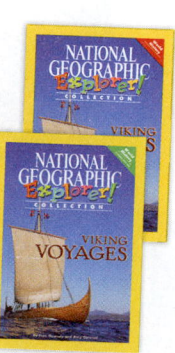

Table of Contents

Moving Through Space

? BIG QUESTION

What does it take to explore space?

Read More

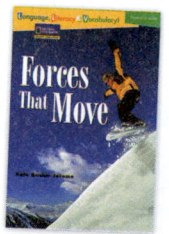

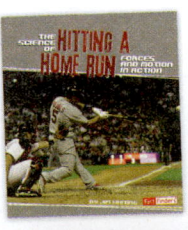

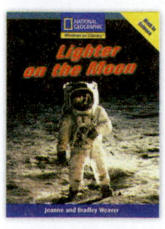
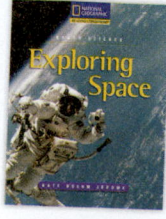
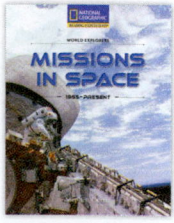
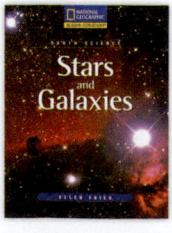

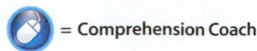 = Comprehension Coach    = Interactive Whiteboard    = NGReach.com

Unit 7

SCIENCE

▸ **Solving Problems**
▸ **Speed**
▸ **Space**

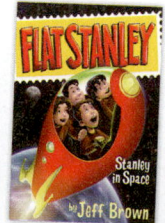

Table of Contents

Saving a Piece of the World

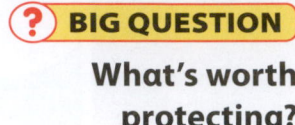

? BIG QUESTION

What's worth protecting?

Read More

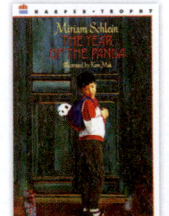
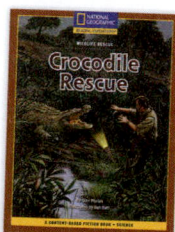
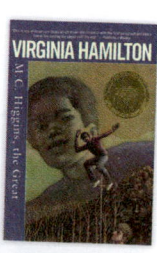
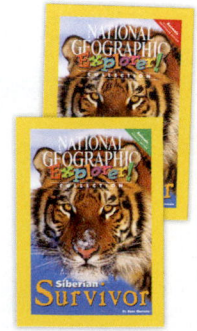

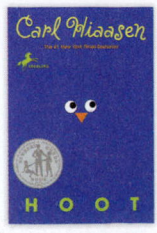
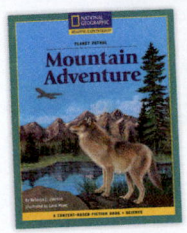

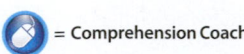 = Comprehension Coach    = Interactive Whiteboard    = NGReach.com

Unit 8

SOCIAL STUDIES
▸ Preserving Species
▸ Preserving Culture

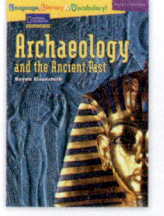

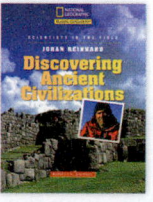
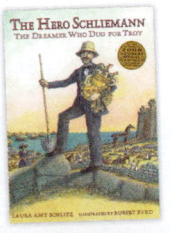
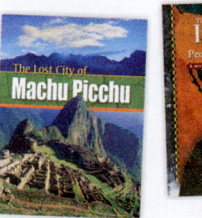
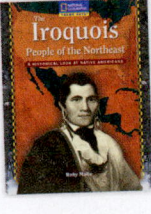
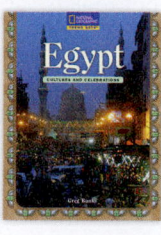
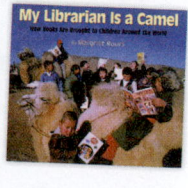

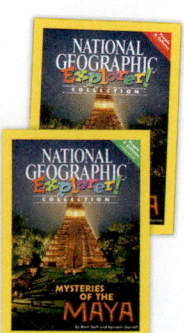

Genres at a Glance

🖥️ = Interactive Whiteboard   ➤ = NGReach.com

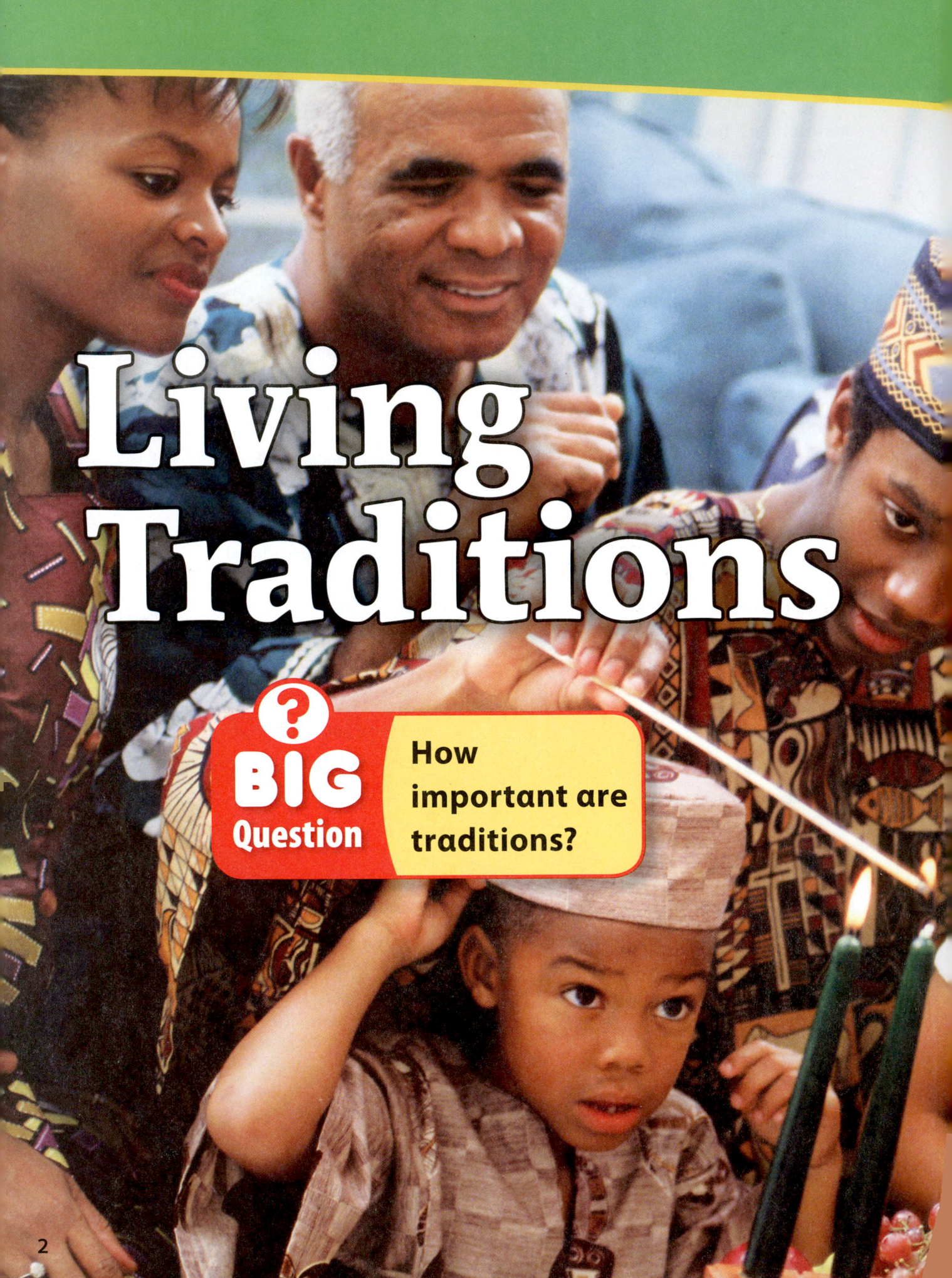

Living Traditions

? BIG Question

How important are traditions?

Unit 1

Share What You Know

Do It!

1 **Think** of your favorite holiday of the year. Draw a picture to show how your family celebrates it. How is the celebration the same every year?

2 **Share** your picture with a partner.

3 **Explain** what makes the holiday special for you.

Build Background: Watch a video about traditions.
 NGReach.com

Express Feelings

Listen to Perla's song. Then use **Language Frames** to express feelings about your own life.

Song ((MP3))

Fresh Hot Corn Tamales

I feel so excited. We're all here today.
We're visiting Abuela. We come every May.
The family is together. It's such a big treat.
Abuela makes tamales for everyone to eat.

Chorus
Oh, fresh hot corn tamales, Abuela makes them right.
Oh, fresh hot corn tamales, we'll eat them day and night.

I see all my cousins, my uncles and aunts.
And then the music starts, so we all sing and dance.
I am very happy. The party is great.
It's one night a year when we all stay up late.

Chorus

Tune: *"A Guanchilopostle"*

Key Words

craft

musical

perform

pottery

tradition

weave

Key Words

Look at this picture. Use **Key Words** and other words to talk about festivals and street fairs. Use the pronunciations in the **Picture Dictionary** to say new words correctly.

Street fairs are a summer **tradition** in many towns. People might **perform** skits. They might play **musical** instruments or dance. At this fair, people walk on stilts!

Artists sell handmade **crafts**. They might **weave** baskets or make **pottery**.

Talk Together

How important are street fairs and other summer festivals? Try to use **Language Frames** from page 4 and **Key Words** to express feelings about summer festivals.

Main Idea and Details

The **main idea** is what something is mostly about. The **details** give more information. When you describe an event, you tell the main idea and details. You focus on the most important information.

Look at the picture of Perla's family.

Map and Talk

You can make a main idea diagram to keep track of what happens. Here's how to make one.

Write the main idea using just a few words. Then list two or three related details.

Main Idea Diagram

Abuela has a party.

- Perla helps with the food.
- Some kids dance.
- Someone plays a guitar.

Talk Together

Look back at page 5. Make a main idea diagram about the street fair. Tell your partner about it. Be sure to focus on what is most important.

More Key Words

Use these words to talk about "Josh Ponte: A Musical Journey" and "Shaped by Tradition."

create
(krē-**āt**) *verb*

To **create** means to make something new. The tiles **create** a pattern on the floor.

culture
(**kul**-chur) *noun*

People's ideas and way of life make up a **culture**. Sports can be part of a **culture**.

express
(ik-**spres**) *verb*

To **express** yourself means to show how you feel. A smile can **express** joy.

medium
(**mē**-dē-um) *noun*

A **medium** is a form of communication. Radio is one **medium** for news.

style
(**stī**-ul) *noun*

A **style** is a special way of doing something. This artist has her own **style** of working.

Talk Together

Tell a partner how each **Key Word** makes you feel. Explain why.

> The word **create** makes me happy. I think about making things.

Add words to My Vocabulary Notebook.
NGReach.com

Learn to Plan and Monitor

Look at the picture. Perla and Abuela are getting ready for a family party. When you prepare for an event, you have to plan. You **preview**, or look ahead to, the event. You **predict** what might happen.

When you read, you also plan. You **preview** the text and **predict** what you will read.

How to Preview and Predict

1. Read the title. Look at the pictures.

I read _____.
I see _____.

2. Begin to read. Stop and make predictions.

I predict that _____.

3. Read on to check your predictions.

My prediction _____.

Talk Together

Read Perla's journal about her trip to Mexico. Read the sample prediction. Then use **Language Frames** as you tell a partner about your own predictions.

Journal

Perla's Journal

Thursday. It's a **tradition** for us to visit our family in Mexico every year. We arrived at Abuela's house today. The car trip wasn't bad, but it was hot! Everyone is here, even my cousin Marta. Marta and I are pen pals, but we never met in person. Will she like me?

Friday. Marta's **style**, her way of acting, is definitely unique! She talks a lot, so I feel shy around her. At least I have my journal. I can **express** myself freely here.

Saturday. Today we made tamales. Abuela got the dough ready. Marta put it on the corn husks, and I added the filling. Then Gustavo tied the tamales. Abuela will cook them tonight. She says that tamales are a big part of Mexican **culture**. I say they are tasty!

Sunday. The party was lots of fun. Abuela showed Gustavo how to dance. Uncle Ramón **created** music. He plays guitar and other **musical** instruments. Marta taught me some new songs. We sang for hours. Live singing is a better **medium** than a CD!

Monday. We're in the car driving home. I miss Marta already. I'll send her an e-mail as soon as we get there!

Sample Prediction

"I read that Perla and Marta have never met.

I predict that they will become good friends.

My prediction is true, but they don't like each other right away."

◄ = A good place to make a prediction

GABON, AFRICA

Read an Interview

Genre

An **interview** gives information and opinions. In an interview, one person asks questions, and another person answers them.

Text Feature

When you read an interview, look for the names of the people who are speaking. Read each **question** and **answer**.

question

Ramona: What role do children play in the music and dance of Gabon?

answer

Mr. Ponte: I learned that children hear music from a very young age. As they get older, children begin to play musical instruments. Girls play some instruments. Others are only played by boys. Music is special to them. People often expect that the child of a great musician will be a great musician, too.

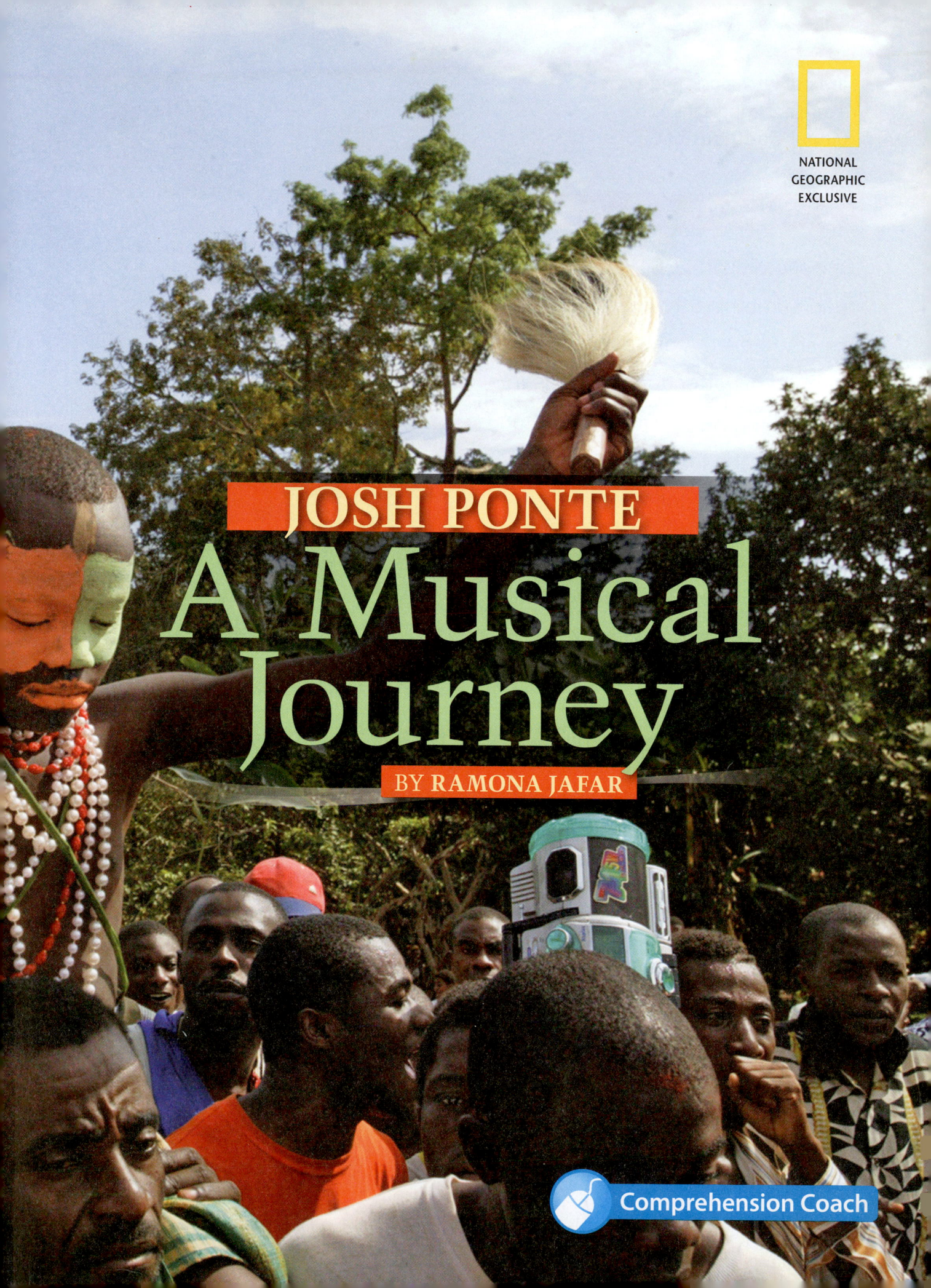

JOSH PONTE

A Musical Journey

BY RAMONA JAFAR

Comprehension Coach

▶ **Set a Purpose**
Find out why music and nature are important to the cultural **traditions** of Gabon.

The Journey Begins

One morning in 2001, Josh Ponte read something that changed his life forever. A newspaper **ad** grabbed his attention: "Gorillas in Africa Need Help." One week later, he was in the forests of Gabon (ga-**bon**) with sixteen gorillas.

Soon, he fell in love with Gabon's unique **culture**. Ponte, who is also a filmmaker and music producer, found that people in Gabon have **traditions** of music that he had never seen or heard. He decided to help share these **rare** cultural traditions with the world.

I spoke with Mr. Ponte to learn about Gabon's music traditions and how those traditions tie to nature.

AFRICA

Gabon

In Other Words
ad advertisement
rare unusual

12

Ramona: Mr. Ponte, tell me why you left your home in England to travel to Gabon, a country in Central Africa.

Mr. Ponte: When I saw the newspaper ad to help Gabon wildlife, I wanted to help. I grew up in England, playing outdoors whenever I could. I have always been interested in nature. I enjoy learning about other places in the world. I wanted to see with my own eyes what was going on in Gabon.

▲ Josh Ponte films people **performing** traditional music and dance in Gabon.

▶ **Before You Move On**

1. **Plan and Monitor** Look at the title and the photos on pages 12 and 13. What do you think this interview will be about?
2. **Use Text Features** Who is interviewing Mr. Ponte? Explain how you know.

13

Music and People

Ramona: After your time with Gabonese wildlife, you traveled around the country. This is where you first saw and heard the music of Gabon. What did you think?

Mr. Ponte: To me, their music sounds perfect. Many sounds work together like the different birds and animals in the forest. For example, one person claps in one **rhythm**, while another hits a can with a stick in a different rhythm. These sounds come together to **create** beautiful songs. It was very different from **what I knew**. I wanted to record this music.

Gabonese musicians ▶

In Other Words
rhythm pattern
what I knew the music I was used to hearing

▲ Children collect water.

Ramona: How did you see music used in daily life in Gabon?

Mr. Ponte: Music is what people do all the time. There is no electricity in the villages. What better thing to do than sing and dance all day and night? The kids sing while they're doing **chores**. The adults sing while they wash their clothes. Music is a tradition that connects them as they work and play. Music helps them to share their lives.

◄ Clapping hands in rhythm

In Other Words
chores work

▶ **Before You Move On**

1. **Main Idea** What did Mr. Ponte want to record, and why?
2. **Clarify** What does Mr. Ponte mean when he says the music is like "different birds and animals in the forest"?

15

Music and Survival

Ramona: The history of Gabonese culture is said to be very old. How has music helped the culture survive?

Mr. Ponte: I learned that their music has a lot of the information they need. Some people in Gabon cannot read and write, so they tell their stories through music. Each **generation** passes these stories to **the next**. Many **musical** ceremonies are about survival in the forest. Most of Gabon is covered with forest.

▲ Gabon's forests are home to many people, plants, and animals.

▲ Gabonese dancers from an ethnic group perform their traditional dance.

Ramona: How important is music in the lives of the people of Gabon today?

Mr. Ponte: I think it's very important. If you ask people in Gabon where they are from, they will tell you their **ethnic group**. Each group has its own <mark>style</mark> of music. So music helps identify people as part of an ethnic group. Music is also used as medicine. When people are ill, they call a musician to **get better**.

◀ Gabonese singers from another ethnic group perform their style of music.

In Other Words
ethnic group culture; family background
get better help them heal

▶ **Before You Move On**
1. **Cause/Effect** How has music helped keep Gabonese <mark>culture</mark> and stories alive?
2. **Paraphrase** Look at the questions the interviewer asks on pages 16 and 17. Now state them in your own words.

Playing Music

Ramona: What role do children play in the music and dance of Gabon?

Mr. Ponte: I learned that children hear music from a very young age. As they get older, children begin to play musical instruments. Girls play some instruments. Others are only played by boys. Music is special to them. People often expect that the child of a great musician will be a great musician, too.

A Gabonese child plays an instrument made from the horn of a forest antelope.

▲ The *mongongo* is an instrument made from a vine stretched across a bent branch.

Ramona: How do you think the forests and nature help people <mark>express</mark> their music?

Mr. Ponte: Gabonese people make instruments from natural resources. People who live in the villages and forests use the natural materials around them, such as trees. There are no stores where they can buy instruments. When you hear their music, it's like listening to the sounds of the forest.

▶ **Before You Move On**

1. **Confirm Prediction** Based on the photos and what you have read so far, was your prediction about the interview correct? Explain.

2. **Analyze** Why is the *mongongo* a good example of a Gabonese instrument?

pluri arc

◀ **A rare musical instrument**

Music Traditions

Ramona: Did you learn about any Gabonese music traditions that are slowly being forgotten?

Mr. Ponte: Yes. Sometimes when we looked for one particular dance, song, or instrument to record, we could not find anyone left alive who knew it. The *pluri arc*, for example, is an instrument that is not seen or played very often.

Ramona: Do you think that new music traditions are replacing older ones?

Mr. Ponte: Traditional music can change every time it is played because nothing is written down.

They say when an **elder** dies in Gabon, it's like a library burning. As time passes, the same songs may be told in different ways.

Also, many young Gabonese people now know about the world through travel and the Internet. The young people start to mix new styles of music with traditional ones. Combining new songs with old songs creates a cultural **melting pot**.

▲ These Gabonese musicians combine traditional styles with modern styles of music.

In Other Words
elder older person
melting pot mixture of many different things

▶ **Before You Move On**

1. **Problem/Solution** What problem did Mr. Ponte sometimes have when trying to record Gabonese music?
2. **Clarify** Why is an elder's death like a library burning? Explain.

Respect for the Natural World

Ramona: In addition to the unique culture, Gabon has unique and amazing wildlife. How important is the natural world to the people of Gabon?

Mr. Ponte: It's very important. In 2002, the government of Gabon created thirteen national parks. They were created to protect Gabon's people and wildlife. Gabon's forests have stayed almost the same for thousands of years. People such as the pygmies (**pig**-mēz) live in the forest. They understand the forest better than anyone. They help scientists keep track of a park's animals to make sure they are safe.

▲ **Loango National Park was one of the thirteen national parks created in 2002.**

Ramona: You've said that the people of Gabon seem to have more time in their daily lives than most people have. What do you mean?

Mr. Ponte: I believe that in the villages of Gabon, life is very simple. I saw children make amazing toys from trash they found in the village. Adults spend much of the day making one hot meal. Watches, computers, and cell phones are not part of their lives. They have time to notice every leaf and every cloud in the sky.

◀ **A handmade toy**

▶ **Before You Move On**

1. **Details** In what year were the national parks of Gabon created? How many parks were **created**?

2. **Clarify** What did Mr. Ponte learn about how people in the villages of Gabon spend their time?

Ramona: Why do you think people in Gabon care so deeply about their natural world?

Mr. Ponte: I think it is because their traditions and lives are connected to the natural world. The village is like a family. The natural world provides them with everything they need to live. They get their food from nature. They build their musical instruments and homes from natural materials.

Caption: ▲ Ponte films a musician playing the *mongongo*, an instrument made from natural materials.

Ramona: What do you think we can learn from the people of Gabon?

Mr. Ponte: We all depend on each other and on nature. In Gabon, I learned that you can have a great life by respecting the world around you. My time in the villages and the forests taught me how important it is to keep our natural world healthy. Twenty-five years from now, I want a world that still has gorillas—and lots of music! ❖

▲ A Gabonese man helps orphaned young gorillas and a chimp.

▶ **Before You Move On**

1. **Clarify** How is a Gabonese village "like a family," according to Mr. Ponte?
2. **Paraphrase** How does Mr. Ponte answer the question on this page? State his answer in your own words.

◀ **Many people in Gabon catch fish for food. Here, a boy in Gabon unloads fish from a boat.**

Talk About It

1. How does this **interview** help you understand Gabon better than another kind of writing might?

   The interview gives _____ .

2. Imagine that you are Josh Ponte, traveling through Gabon and learning about the **traditions** there. **Express feelings** to a partner about your journey.

   This journey made me feel _____ .

3. Name three ways that people in Gabon use music.

   People use music to _____, _____, and _____ .

Learn test-taking strategies.
NGReach.com

Write About It

Josh Ponte went to Gabon because of a newspaper ad he saw. That must have been an exciting ad! **Create** your version of the ad. Think about the **medium** of advertising. How can an ad use words and pictures to make someone want to do something? Use **Key Words** if possible.

Main Idea and Details

Make main idea diagrams to tell about parts of "Josh Ponte: A Musical Journey." Be sure you focus on the most important ideas in each part.

Main Idea Diagram

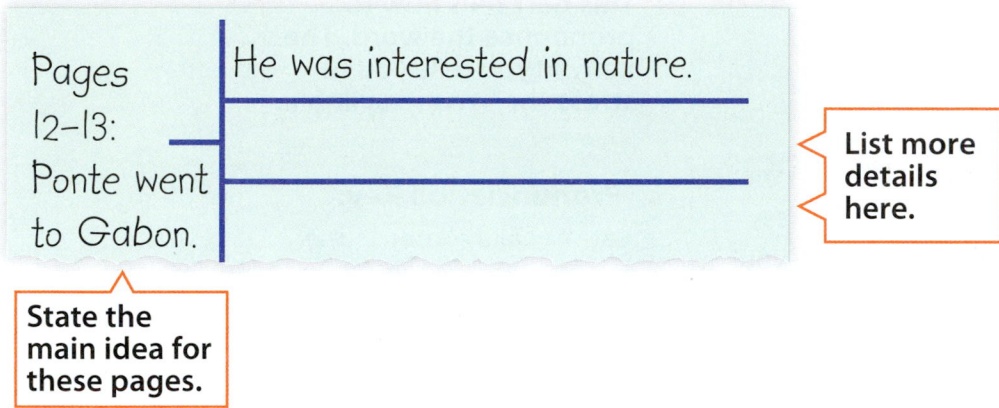

Pages 12–13: Ponte went to Gabon.

He was interested in nature.

List more details here.

State the main idea for these pages.

Now use your diagrams as you retell "Josh Ponte: A Musical Journey" to a partner. Use as many **Key Words** as you can.

This part of the interview is mainly about _____ .

Fluency

Use the Comprehension Coach to practice reading with phrasing. Rate your reading.

Talk Together

Have a talk show. Imagine that the guests on the show are musicians in Gabon. Use **Key Words** as you talk about the importance of **musical traditions** in Gabon.

Use a Dictionary

If you don't know how to say a word, you can use a dictionary to find out. Look at this example of a **dictionary entry**.

> The first part shows how to divide the word into syllables. The word **create** has two syllables.

cre·ate (krē-āt) *verb* To make something

> This part tells how to pronounce the word. The heavy type tells you to stress the second syllable.

You can look up a mark, like ē, in the pronunciation key. It tells you to say the ē in **create** in the same way you say the ē in *me*.

Pronunciation Key:

cat	cāke	met	mē
it	īce	top	up

Try It Together

Read the dictionary entries. Then answer each question.

pot·ter·y (**pot**-ur-ē) *noun* Things made of baked clay, such as plates or vases

tra·di·tion (tru-**di**-shun) *noun* An activity or belief that people share

1. **How many syllables does pottery have?**

   A one

   B two

   C three

   D four

2. **Which syllable of tradition do you stress?**

   A the first

   B the second

   C the third

   D none

Connect Across Texts You read about a filmmaker who is working to keep a **tradition** of African music alive. Now read about an artist who follows a family **tradition** of working with clay.

Genre In a **biography**, an author tells the true story of someone's life. The author may include quotations, or statements, by that person about his or her life.

Shaped by Tradition

BY PATRICIA MILLMAN

▲ **Michael Naranjo with his sculpture, *The Gift***

Michael Naranjo is a Native American and a **veteran of** the Vietnam War. He is also "a sculptor who happens to be blind."

Naranjo grew up in the Tewa (**tā**-wa) **Indian Pueblo** of Santa Clara, New Mexico. His love of sculpting was born at the pueblo community. "My mother **was a potter**. I helped her prepare her clay," he remembers.

▲ **A pueblo in New Mexico**

In Other Words
veteran of soldier who fought in
Indian Pueblo Native American community
was a potter made bowls and pots from clay

▶ **Before You Move On**
1. **Details** What do you know about Michael Naranjo so far?
2. **Explain** How did Michael Naranjo first learn about clay?

Preparing the Clay

Naranjo's mother would put brown clay on a **canvas** cloth and sprinkle white clay on top of it. Next, she would fold the canvas and press the clay into a log shape.

"Then I would take off my shoes and **perform** a little dance on the clay," Naranjo says. "I could feel the **moist** clay between my toes. When I **reached** the other end, I'd step off the canvas."

After the clay is prepared, an artist can mold it. Here, the artist molds the clay to make a pot. ▶

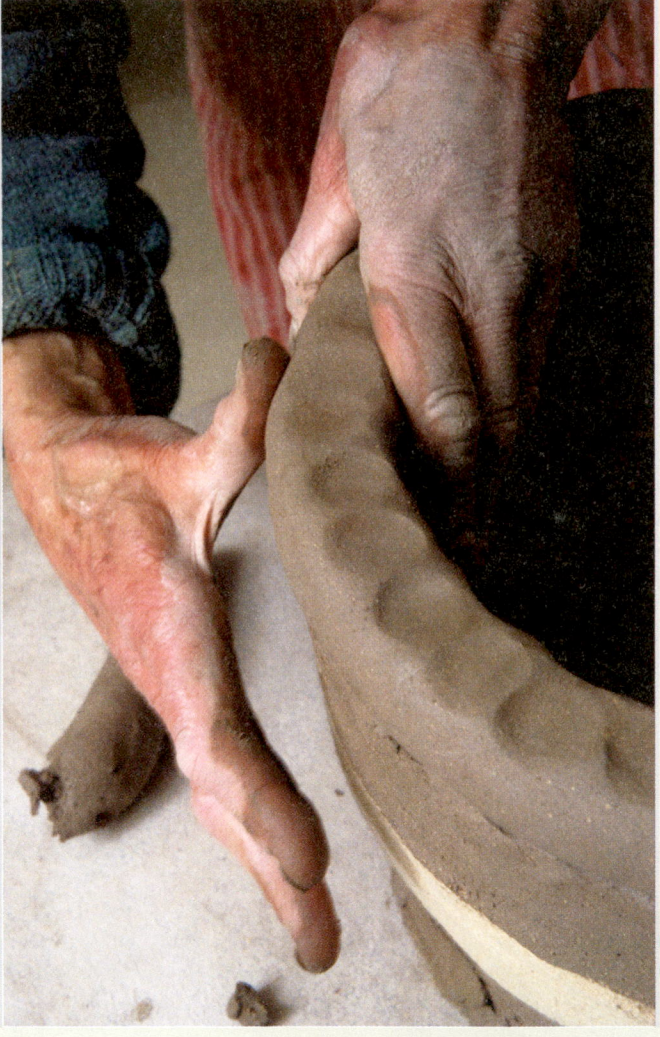

▼ Pressing clay helps prepare it for molding.

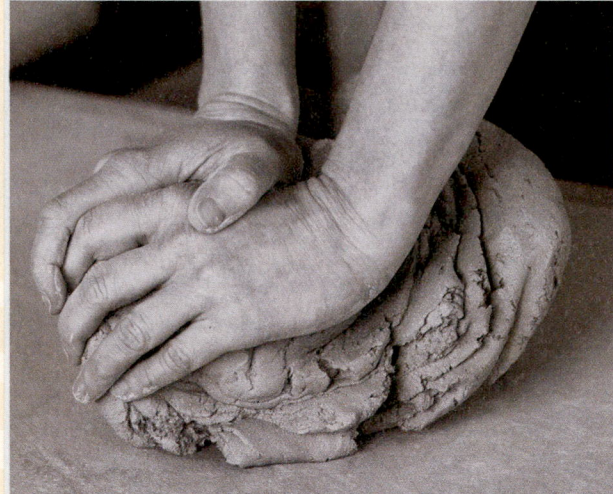

In Other Words
canvas cotton
moist wet
reached danced all the way to

Naranjo's dance served an important purpose. He was **blending** the white clay and the brown clay to make it stronger. With this clay, his mother could make pots that would last a long time.

"Playing with clay—that's probably how I started sculpting," Naranjo says. "Not long after that, I wanted to make **figures** of animals. Even then, I knew that I wanted to be an artist someday."

Rose Naranjo (seated at right) passed along the art of <mark>pottery</mark>-making to her son Michael, her daughter Dolly (seated at left), and her granddaughter Jody (holding her baby). ▶

In Other Words
blending mixing
figures shapes; forms

▶ **Before You Move On**

1. **Describe** How did Naranjo's mother prepare clay?
2. **Make Inferences** What details from the text show what Naranjo means by playing with clay?

Reaching a Goal

Naranjo did not reach his goal easily. While serving with the army in Vietnam, he was badly wounded. He **lost his sight**. He also lost **partial** use of one hand. Naranjo wondered if he could ever be a sculptor.

While he was in the hospital, Naranjo asked for a piece of clay. He made a figure of **an inchworm** from the clay.

Next, Naranjo made a sculpture of a person on a horse. The sculpture was so good that local newspapers photographed it.

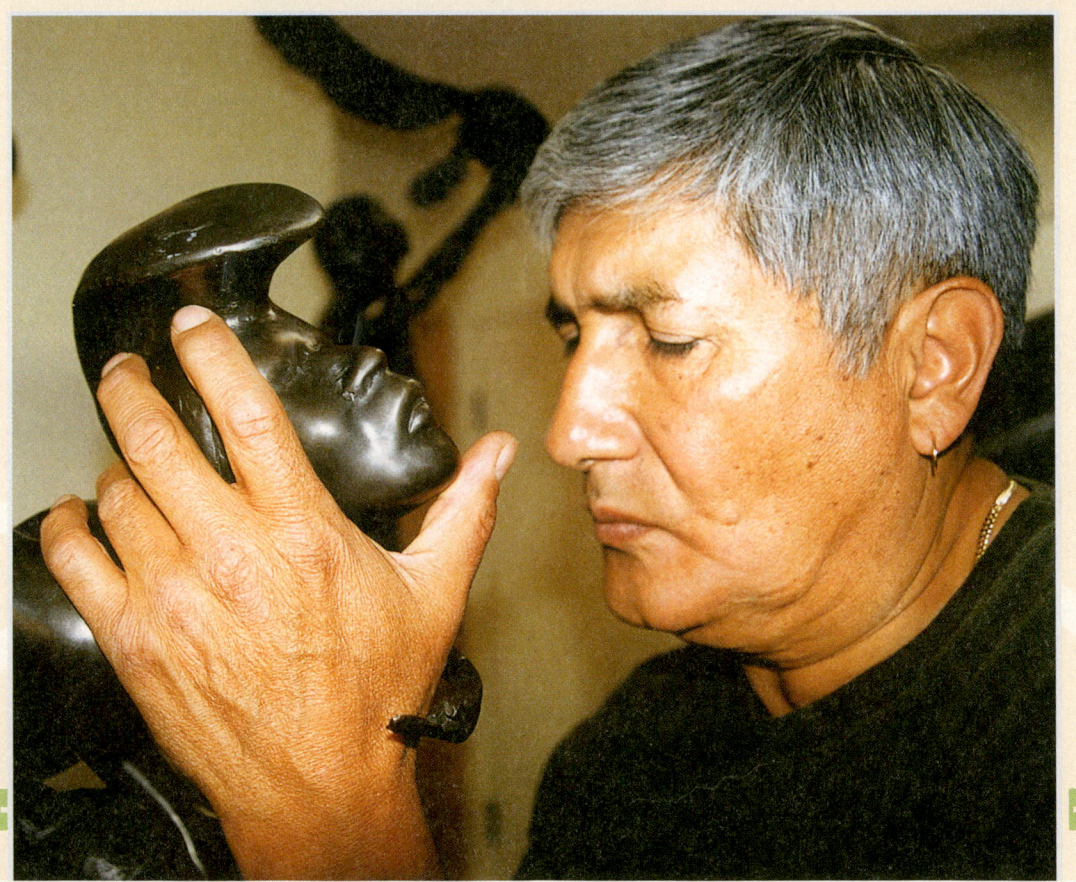

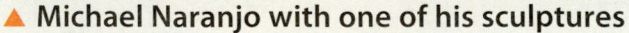 **Michael Naranjo with one of his sculptures**

In Other Words

lost his sight became blind

partial some

an inchworm a very small worm

32

Seeing with His Hands

How does Naranjo sculpt? "I was able to see until age 22, so I know what most things look like," he says. "I get a picture in my mind. Once you have material in your hand that you can mold and shape, you can **carry it over** from your mind to your fingertips."

Today, Naranjo's sculptures are displayed across the United States and in Europe. They are even in the White House. ❖

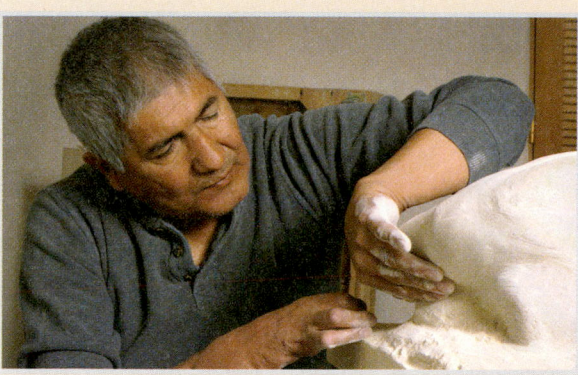

◀ Naranjo "sees with his hands" as he <mark>creates</mark> sculptures.

Sculptures by Michael Naranjo ▶
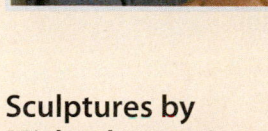

In Other Words

carry it over communicate it

▶ **Before You Move On**

1. **Clarify** What events made Naranjo wonder if he could ever be a sculptor?
2. **Paraphrase** How does Naranjo "see" with his hands? Explain in your own words.

Compare Author's Purpose

Authors write for many different reasons, or purposes. Sometimes they state their purpose. Sometimes you need to figure it out.

- When authors want to entertain, they often write stories, plays, or poems.

- When authors write to inform, they include facts.

- When authors write to **express** ideas or persuade, they give opinions.

Work with a partner to complete the chart.

Comparison Chart

	"Josh Ponte: A Musical Journey"	"Shaped by Tradition"
genre	interview	
author's purpose	to inform about Gabon's musical traditions	
stated? yes/no	yes	
If yes, where? If not, how can you figure it out?		

Talk Together

How important are **traditions** to artists and musicians? Think about the interview and the biography. Use **Key Words** to talk about your ideas.

Complete Sentences

A sentence expresses a complete thought. A **complete sentence** has two parts, a subject and a predicate.

Grammar Rules Complete Sentences

• The **complete subject** tells whom or what the sentence is about. It includes all the words that tell about the subject.	**My older brother**
• The **complete predicate** tells what the subject is, has, or does. It includes all the words in the predicate.	**plays flute in the school band**
• A complete sentence needs both a **complete subject** and a **complete predicate**.	**My older brother plays flute in the school band.**

Read Complete Sentences

Read these sentences with a partner. What is the complete subject in each sentence? What is the complete predicate?

> Many people in Gabon tell their stories through music. Each generation passes these stories to the next. Many musical rituals are about survival in the forest.

Write Complete Sentences

Write a paragraph about Josh Ponte's musical journey. Be sure to include a complete subject and a complete predicate in each sentence. Read your paragraph aloud to a partner.

Ask for and Give Information

Song ((MP3))

Listen to Luka and Peter's song. Then use **Language Frames** to ask for information about a tradition that you know about.

A Tooth Tradition

"I just lost a front tooth, dear brother, dear brother.
How can I replace it? Dear brother, tell me."

"On the roof you can throw it, dear Peter, dear Peter.
A mouse will come get it, dear Peter, a mouse."

"Now my smile looks so funny, dear brother, dear brother.
There's a gap where my tooth was, dear brother, a gap."

"Don't worry, dear Peter, the mouse is a good mouse.
And soon it will send you a shiny new tooth."

Tune: "There's a Hole in My Bucket"

Key Words

ancestor

ceremony

marriage

occasion

ritual

Key Words

Many cultures have traditions for important days in a person's life. Look at the pictures. Use **Key Words** and other words to talk about special **occasions** in different cultures. Use the pronunciations in the **Picture Dictionary** to say new words correctly.

A quinceañera party celebrates a girl's 15th birthday.

Many couples begin their **marriage** with a wedding **ceremony**. This couple has their hands bound together with a cord. This wedding **ritual** began hundreds of years ago.

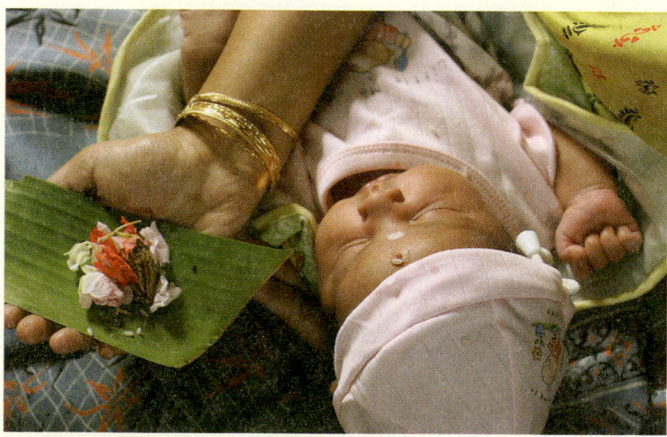

Some families have naming ceremonies for their babies. The baby might be given the name of an **ancestor**. This honors both the family member and the baby.

Talk Together

How important are traditions in weddings? Try to use **Language Frames** from page 36 and **Key Words** to give information to a partner.

Plot

The series of events that make up a story are the **plot**.

- The **beginning** tells who the characters are and how the story starts.

- Most events happen in the **middle**.

- The **end** tells what finally happens.

Look at the pictures. Think about the story they tell.

Map and Talk

You can make a story map to tell the plot. Here's how to make one.

In the first box, tell how the story starts. In the middle box, tell the next events. In the last box, tell how the story ends.

Story Map

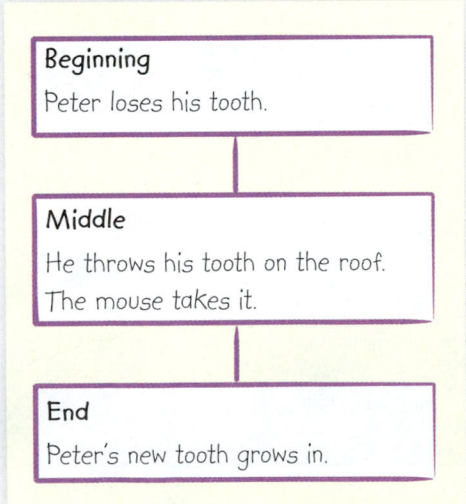

Beginning
Peter loses his tooth.

Middle
He throws his tooth on the roof.
The mouse takes it.

End
Peter's new tooth grows in.

Talk Together

Listen to a story that your partner tells. Make a story map to describe the plot.

More Key Words

Use these words to talk about "Martina, the Beautiful Cockroach" and "Coming of Age."

belief

(bu-**lēf**) *noun*

A **belief** is a feeling that something is true. What is your **belief** about hard work?

custom

(**kus**-tum) *noun*

A **custom** is the usual way of doing something. Their **custom** is to eat cereal for breakfast.

influence

(**in**-flü-unts) *verb*

To **influence** someone is to affect that person. Family members can **influence** your interests.

relationship

(ri-**lā**-shun-ship) *noun*

A **relationship** is the way people or things are connected.

role

(**rōl**) *noun*

A **role** is a part or a purpose. Each actor plays an important **role** in the school play.

Talk Together

Take turns with a partner. Read a **Key Word** and say what it means. Ask your partner to give an example.

A custom is a habit.

I have a custom of reading in bed each night.

Add words to My Vocabulary Notebook.

NGReach.com

Learn to Plan and Monitor

Look at the picture. When you see something you don't understand, you **monitor**, or watch carefully. You look for a way to **clarify**, or make sure you understand, what you see. Soon the meaning may become clear.

You also **monitor** and **clarify** when you read.

How to Monitor and Clarify

1. When you don't understand the text, stop. Think about what the text means.

2. If you do not understand, reread the text. If the meaning still is not clear, read on.

3. Think about how the meaning has become clearer to you.

What does _____ mean?

I will _____.

It means _____.

Talk Together

Read Luka's interview. Read the sample of how to monitor and clarify. Then use **Language Frames** to tell a partner how you monitored your reading.

Interview

Luka's Grandparents

Luka: Tell me about some **customs** related to **marriage**. What **role** did your friends play in your wedding **ceremony**?

Grandma Capeka: Early in the morning, our friends came together. They planted a tree in my family's yard. They put decorations on the tree. They added ribbons and eggshells.

Luka: Then what happened?

Grandpa Jozo: They gave us a traditional gift for the **occasion**.

Grandma Capeka: Yes, they brought us some bread and some salt. The gift shows our **beliefs**. The bread shows our hope for a healthy life. The salt shows that life is sometimes hard. ◄

Grandpa Jozo: Then we had a big feast. At the end, everyone threw their glasses and cups to the ground.

Luka: Why did they do that?

Grandpa Jozo: It's a custom! Breaking glasses brings much luck! Our friends wanted to **influence** our future. ◄

Grandma Capeka: And it worked! Our **relationship** has been a happy one for many years!

Sample

"What does Luka's question mean?

I will read on.

It means, 'What did the friends do at the ceremony?'"

◄ = A good place to monitor and clarify your reading

41

Read a Story

Genre

A **folk tale** is a story that people share and tell again and again. Folk tales usually reflect the culture they come from.

Character and Setting

Characters are the people or animals in a story. Setting is where and when the story takes place.

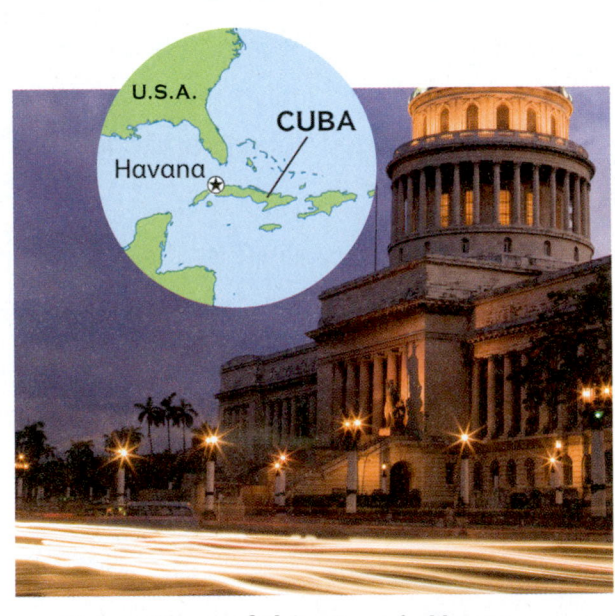

▲ Martina

▲ The setting of this story is Havana, a city in Cuba. The story is set in the past.

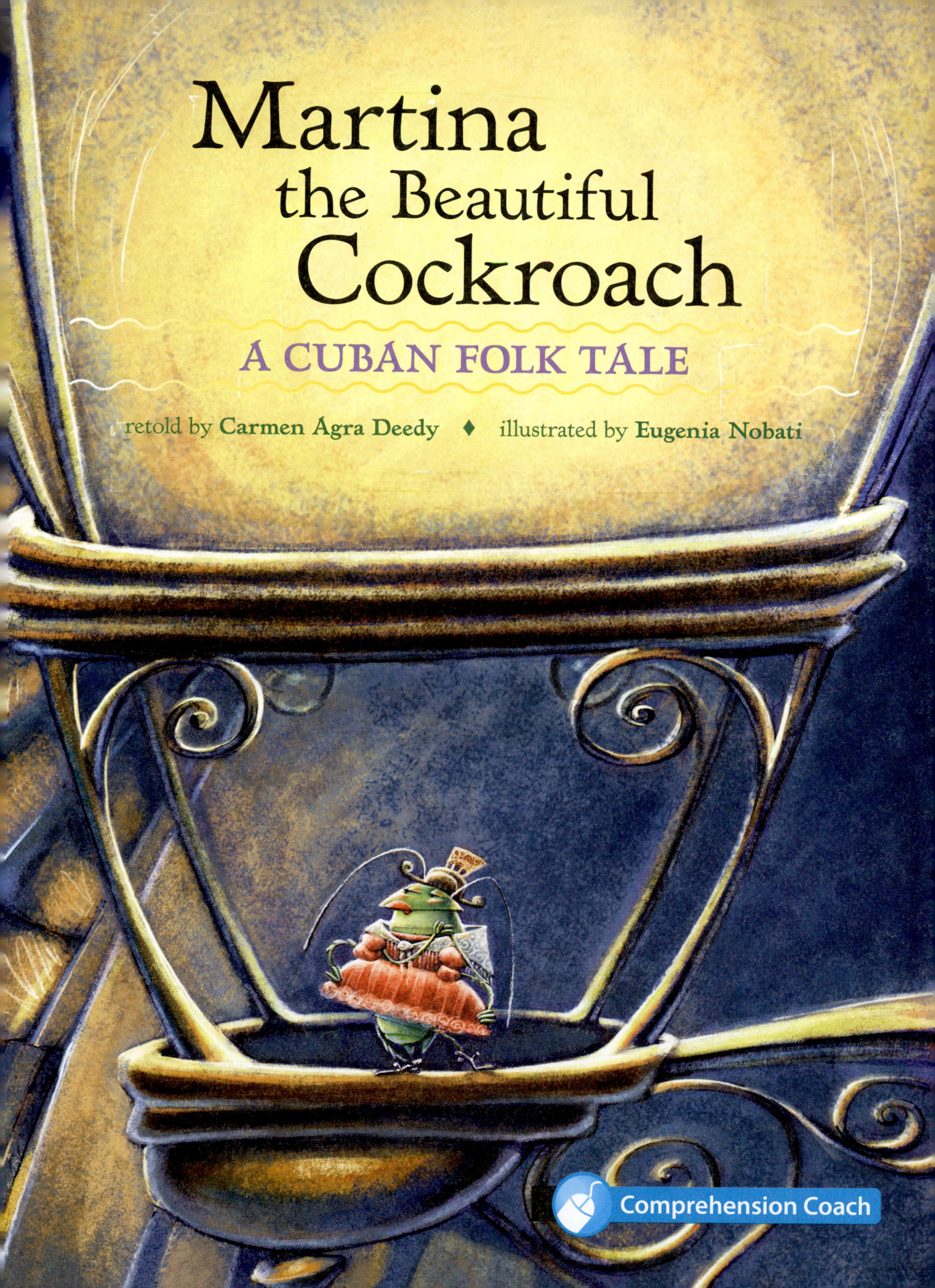

Martina
the Beautiful
Cockroach

A CUBAN FOLK TALE

retold by **Carmen Agra Deedy** ◆ illustrated by **Eugenia Nobati**

▶ **Set a Purpose**
Martina is ready to get married. Find
out how she chooses a husband.

Martina Josefina Catalina Cucaracha was a beautiful
cockroach. She lived in a cozy street lamp in Old Havana with
her big, lovable family.

Now that Martina was 21 days old, she was ready to **give
her leg in marriage**. The Cucaracha household was crawling
with excitement! Every ***señora*** in the family had something
to offer.

Tía *Cuca* gave her *una peineta*, a seashell comb. *Mamá*
gave her *una mantilla*, a lace shawl. But *Abuela*, her Cuban
grandmother, gave her *un consejo increíble*, some shocking advice.

peineta

mantilla

In Other Words
give her leg in marriage get married
    (a joke based on the expression *give
    her hand in marriage*)
señora woman (in Spanish)
Tía Aunt (in Spanish)

"You want me to do WHAT?" Martina was **aghast**.

"You are a beautiful cockroach," said *Abuela*. "Finding husbands to choose from will be easy—picking the right one could be **tricky**."

"B-b-but," stammered Martina, "how will spilling COFFEE on **a suitor's shoes** help me find a good husband?"

Her grandmother smiled. "It will make him angry! Then you'll know how he will speak to you when he **loses his temper**. Trust me, Martina. The Coffee Test never fails."

Martina wasn't so sure.

In Other Words

aghast shocked; amazed

tricky difficult

a suitor's shoes the shoes of a person who wants to marry me

loses his temper gets angry

Meanwhile, *Papá* sent *el perico*, the parrot, to **spread the word**.

Soon all Havana—from the busy sidewalks of El Prado to El Morro castle—was **abuzz with** the news. Martina the beautiful cockroach was ready to choose a husband.

As was the <mark>custom</mark>, Martina would greet her suitors from the balcony, under her family's many watchful eyes.

Daintily, she sat down and crossed her legs, and crossed her legs, and crossed her legs.

She didn't have long to wait.

In Other Words
spread the word tell everyone
abuzz with talking about
Daintily Carefully

Don Gallo, the rooster, strutted up first. Martina tried not to stare at his splendid shoes.

Keeping one eye on his reflection, Don Gallo greeted her with a sweeping bow. "*¡Caramba!* You really are a beautiful cockroach. I will look even more fabulous with you on my wing!"

With that, he leaned forward and crooned,

"Martina Josefina Catalina Cucaracha,

Beautiful **muchacha**,

Won't you be my wife?"

Martina hesitated only for an instant. "Coffee, **señor**?"

In Other Words

¡Caramba! Wow! (in Spanish)

muchacha girl (in Spanish)

señor sir (in Spanish)

▶ **Before You Move On**

1. **Plot** What is *Abuela's* advice to Martina at the beginning of the story?
2. **Character** What is Don Gallo like? How can you tell?

▶ **Predict**
What will the Coffee Test show
Martina about her suitors?

Right on cue, *Abuela* appeared. With a quick glance
at her grandmother, Martina nervously splattered coffee onto the
rooster's spotless shoes.

"Oh my!" she said **with mock dismay**. "I'm **all feelers** today!"

"*¡Ki-ki-ri-kiiii!*" The rooster was furious. "Clumsy cockroach!
I will teach you better manners when you are my wife."

Martina was stunned. The Coffee Test had worked!

"A most humble offer, *señor*," she said coolly, "but I
cannot accept."

In Other Words
Right on cue Just as planned
with mock dismay pretending
  to be sorry
all feelers clumsy

Don Cerdo, the pig, hoofed up next. His smell curled the little hairs on Martina's legs.

"What an **unimaginable** scent," Martina wheezed. "Is it some new pig cologne?"

"Oh, no, **_señorita_**. It's the **sweet aroma** of my **pig sty**. Rotten eggs! Turnip peels! Stinky cheese!" Don Cerdo licked his chops and sang,

"Martina Josefina Catalina Cucaracha,

Beautiful _muchacha_,

Won't you be my wife?"

Martina had already left in search of coffee.

She wasted no time with the pig.

In Other Words
unimaginable awful
señorita Miss (in Spanish)
sweet aroma good smell
pig sty pigpen; home

"*¡Gronc! ¡Gronc!*" squealed Don Cerdo as he dabbed at the coffee on his shoes. "What a tragedy for my poor loafers!"

He really is quite a **ham**, thought Martina.

"Calm yourself, *señor*. I'll clean them for you!"

"I'll say you will!" he snorted. "When you are my wife, there'll be no end to cleaning up after me!"

Martina rolled her eyes in disbelief.

"A most charming offer, *señor*," she said **drily**, "but I must **decline**. You are much too **boorish** for me."

In Other Words
ham bad actor
drily calmly
decline say no
boorish rude (a joke based on the fact that a *boar* is another name for a pig)

The Coffee Test had saved her from yet another **unsuitable** suitor.

The pig was scarcely out of sight when Don Lagarto, the lizard, crept over the railing. His oily fingers brushed the little cockroach's lovely *mantilla*.

"You shouldn't **sneak up on** a lady like that!"

"I don't sneak. I creep," he said, circling Martina.

For some reason this fellow really **bugged** her. "I've had enough of creeps for one day," said Martina. "*Adiós.*"

▶ **Before You Move On**

1. **Plot** What does the Coffee Test show Martina about her first two suitors? How do these characters change?

2. **Clarify** Why is it funny that Martina thinks Don Cerdo is "a ham?"

▶ **Predict**

Will any of the suitors *ever* pass the
Coffee Test?

"**B**ut I need you! Wait!" The lizard fell on one
scaly knee and **warbled**,

"Martina Josefina Catalina Cucaracha,

Beautiful *muchacha*,

Won't you be my wife?"

Martina sighed. "Let me see if there's any coffee left."

This time she **wasn't taking any chances**. Martina returned
with TWO cups for the lizard.

"¡*Psssst! ¡Psssst!*" he spat. Don Lagarto was **livid**. He changed
colors three times before he finally found his true one. "And to
think," he hissed. "I was going to eat—er—MARRY you!"

In Other Words

warbled sang

wasn't taking any chances
 would make sure the test worked

livid very angry

Martina stared at the lizard. You could have heard a breadcrumb drop.

"**Food for thought**, *señor*," Martina said **icily**, "but I must refuse. You are much too cold-blooded for me."

When her grandmother returned to collect the day's coffee cups, Martina was still **fuming**.

"I'm going inside, *Abuela*."

"So soon?"

"*¡Sí!* I'm afraid of whom I might meet next!"

Abuela drew Martina to the railing and pointed to the garden below. "What about him?"

In Other Words

Food for thought That's something to think about
icily in an unfriendly way
fuming very angry
¡Sí! Yes! (in Spanish)

Martina looked down at the tiny brown mouse, and her cockroach heart began to beat faster.

Ti-ki-tin, ti-ki-tan.

"Oh, *Abuela*, he's **adorable**. Where has he been?"

"Right here all along."

"What do I do?"

"Go talk to him . . . and just be yourself."

Martina **handed** *Abuela* her *peineta* and *mantilla*, then **scurried** down to the garden. The mouse was waiting.

Ti-ki-tin, ti-ki-tan.

"*Hola*, hello." His voice was like warm honey. "My name is Pérez."

"*Hola*," she whispered shyly. "I'm Martina—"

"—the beautiful cockroach," he finished for her.

"You think I'm beautiful?"

The little mouse turned pink under his fur. "Well, my eyes are rather weak, but I have excellent EARS. I know you are strong and good, Martina Josefina Catalina Cucaracha." Then he **squinted sweetly**. "Who cares if you are beautiful?"

TI-KI-TIN, TI-KI-TAN.

"Martina-a-a-a-a! Don't forget the coffee!" It was *Abuela*.

No, thought Martina. No coffee for Pérez!

"Martina Josefina Catalina Cucaracha!"

In Other Words

squinted sweetly narrowed his eyes in a cute way, to try to see better

"*Sí, Abuela.*" Martina knew better than to argue with her Cuban grandmother.

With a heavy heart, she reached for the cup.

But Pérez got there first. Quick as a mouse, he splashed **café cubano** onto Martina's shoes.

Now **the coffee was on the other foot**.

Martina was too delighted to be angry. At last, she'd found her perfect match. But she had to ask, "How did you know about the Coffee Test?"

Pérez grinned. "Well, *mi amor*, my love . . . I too have a Cuban grandmother." ❖

In Other Words

café cubano Cuban coffee (in Spanish)

the coffee was on the other foot
they switched places (a joke based on the expression *the shoe was on the other foot*)

▶ **Before You Move On**

1. **Clarify** What does the author mean when she says that Don Lagarto found his true color?
2. **Plot** Which character passes the Coffee Test? Explain.

Carmen Agra Deedy

Carmen Agra Deedy was born in Cuba. When she was young, she moved to the United States. Carmen says the two cultures have taught her that people everywhere are alike.

One example is that people everywhere enjoy funny stories! One day, Carmen was invited to tell a story in Spanish to a gym full of students. Suddenly a huge cockroach flew across the gym. As the students began squealing, Carmen decided to tell one of her favorite Cuban folk tales about a cockroach. That tale became *Martina the Beautiful Cockroach*.

▲ **A Cuban cockroach**

Carmen says that when writing *Martina the Beautiful Cockroach*, "I told it just as I remembered my mother telling it." ▶

Writer's Craft

Find examples of humor in the story. It might be funny things that happen, or the way the author uses funny sayings. Then write a short paragraph that includes humor.

Think and Respond

Talk About It

1. What clues tell you that this story is a **folk tale**?

It is a story that _____ . Also, _____ .

2. Talk with a partner about the **relationship** between Martina and *Abuela*. **Ask for and give information** as you describe the interactions of these characters.

What does Abuela _____ ? Why does Martina _____ ?

Abuela _____ Martina.

3. How does the author use language to make this folk tale funny?

Learn test-taking strategies.
🌐 NGReach.com

Write About It

Would you tell a friend to read this story? Why or why not? Use **Key Words** to write about your ideas in a friendly letter. Include at least one example from the story to explain your opinion.

August 27, 2010

Dear_____,
This story is _____ because _____ .
One example is _____ .

Plot

Make a story map to show what happens in "Martina the Beautiful Cockroach." Notice that some events affect what happens later in the story.

Story Map

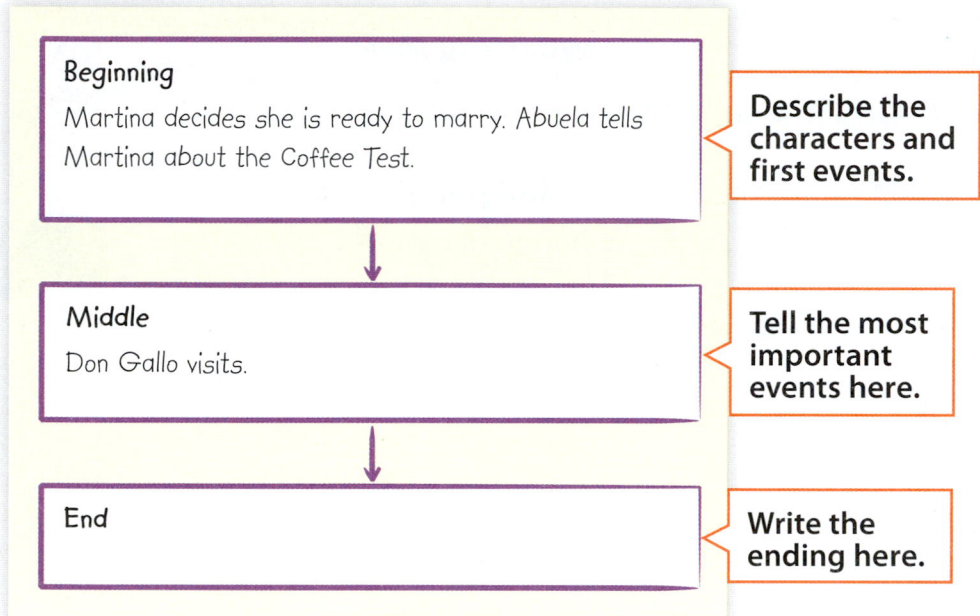

Beginning
Martina decides she is ready to marry. Abuela tells Martina about the Coffee Test.

→ **Describe the characters and first events.**

Middle
Don Gallo visits.

→ **Tell the most important events here.**

End

→ **Write the ending here.**

Now use your story map as you retell the story to a partner. Try to use **Key Words**, too.

First, _____ .
Then, _____ .
At the end, _____ .

Fluency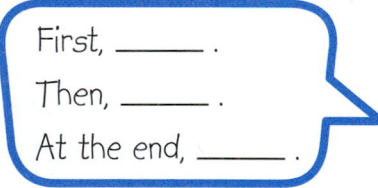

Use the Comprehension Coach to practice reading with expression. Rate your reading.

Talk Together

For Martina and *Abuela*, how important are traditions? Use **Key Words** as you talk about other traditions that may guide the family.

Idioms and Expressions

Idioms and **expressions** are colorful ways to say something. The words that make up an idiom mean something different from what they mean by themselves. Use clues from the sentence to figure out what an idiom or expression means.

What You Say	What You Mean
She will **give her hand in marriage**.	She will **get married**.
I'll **spread the word** about the happy occasion.	I'll **tell people** about the happy occasion.
The room was so quiet **we could hear a pin drop**.	The room was so quiet **we could hear every sound**.

Try It Together

Figure out the meaning of the idioms. Then answer each question.

Lisa was great at most things, but **the shoe was on the other foot** when she started piano lessons. "I'm **all thumbs**!" she complained to her mother at practice time.

1. **The expression the shoe was on the other foot probably means**

   A nothing changed.

   B things were totally different.

   C things were loud.

   D things were on the ground.

2. **The sentence "I'm all thumbs" probably means**

   A I'm very good at this.

   B I'm very confused.

   C I feel sick.

   D I'm not very good at this.

Coming of Age

adapted from *Skipping Stones* · illustrated by Shannon Brady

Connect Across Texts Read about a family **custom** from India that celebrates a girl's coming of age.

Genre A **magazine article** is nonfiction. It gives facts about real people, places, or events.

Many Hindus celebrate important **phases in life** with special **ceremonies** called *samskaras*. For Jyotsna Grandhi, one important *samskara* happened when she **turned** eleven. The ceremony, called a sari ceremony, welcomed her into adulthood. During the ceremony, Jyotsna received her first half sari, or *voni*. In some Indian traditions, this is meant to be the **outfit** worn by young women until **marriage**.

Here is what Jyotsna had to say about her sari ceremony.

full sari

half sari

A sari is a traditional garment worn by some women in India.

In Other Words

phases in life times in a person's growth and development

turned reached the age of

outfit clothing

▶ **Before You Move On**

1. **Use Text Features** How do the title, illustration, and caption help you understand what this article is about?

2. **Main Idea** What does the sari **ceremony** celebrate?

Jyotsna's Sari Ceremony

I celebrated my sari ceremony at my aunt's home in India. I wore my best silk skirt, blouse, and jewelry. I sat on a chair decorated with flowers.

My uncle and his wife presented my first *voni* to me, along with jewelry. I was asked to put on the new clothes and the jewelry.

All our relatives took turns **blessing me** by putting yellow-colored rice grains on my head. They also handed me gifts.

▲ Surrounded by family, Jyotsna Grandhi prepares to celebrate her sari ceremony.

▲ In Jyotsna's sari ceremony, she received her first *voni*, or half sari.

Before the ceremony started, I was excited. I knew that afterwards people would think of me as a young woman. I also was partly sad because I would miss **being pampered** as the **baby of** the house.

During the ceremony, I felt uncomfortable when everybody was looking at me. All I could think of was taking the dress off and changing into my regular outfit. I liked the gift-giving part of the ceremony best!

—Jyotsna Grandhi, 11,
Indian-American, New Jersey ❖

▲ Family and friends gave Jyotsna presents to celebrate her coming of age.

In Other Words
being pampered getting special treatment
baby of youngest person in

▶ **Before You Move On**
1. **Clarify** What parts of the text help you understand why Jyotsna felt uncomfortable during the ceremony?
2. **Details** What special customs are part of the ceremony?

Key Words

ancestor	marriage
belief	occasion
ceremony	relationship
custom	ritual
influence	role

Compare Content

"Martina the Beautiful Cockroach" and "Coming of Age" are two different genres. Yet, they are based on the same big idea. You can compare and contrast the content of the two selections.

Complete the Venn diagram. Think about the time and place described in the folk tale and the article. Notice the types of details the authors use.

Venn Diagram

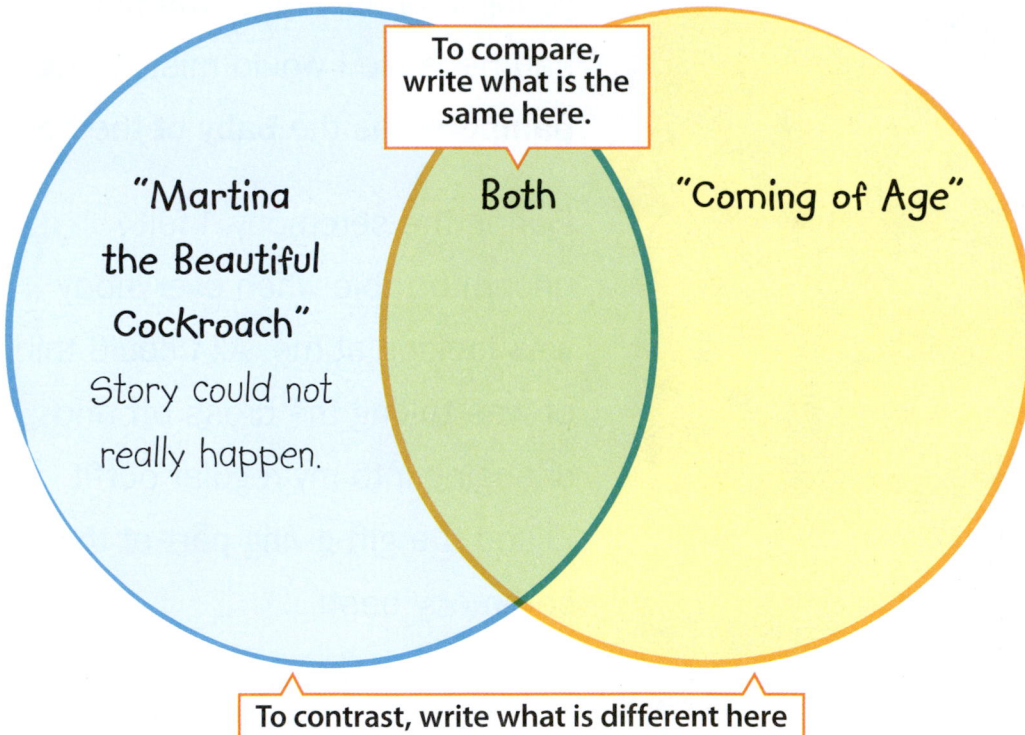

Talk Together

How important are family traditions? Think about the folk tale and the magazine article. Use **Key Words** and examples from the text to talk about your ideas.

Subject-Verb Agreement

The subject and verb of a sentence must agree. A **compound subject** has two **subjects** joined by **and** or **or**.

The **boys** and the **girl** perform at the concert.
The **boys** or the **girl** performs at the concert.

Grammar Rules Subject-Verb Agreement

• Use a **plural verb** with **two subjects** joined by *and*.	**Uncle Leo** and **Aunt Flora sing** at the festival every year.
• If the subjects are joined by *or*, look at the last subject. • If the **last subject** is singular, use a **singular verb**. • If the **last subject** is plural, use a **plural verb**.	Our cousins or **Uncle Leo sings** at the festival every year. **Uncle Leo** or **our cousins sing** at the festival every year.

Read Sentences

Read these sentences with a partner. Find one compound subject. Talk about subject-verb agreement.

Martina and her grandmother sit and talk quietly.
Mamá waits for Martina's choice.

Write Compound Subjects

Write a short paragraph to describe a custom in your family. Use some compound subjects. Check for subject-verb agreement!

Write as a Reporter

Write an Interview

Interview a neighbor or family member about a tradition that interests you. Write an article that tells about the person and describes the tradition.

Study a Model

In an interview, one person gathers information by asking another person questions. Often, the information is presented in a question-and-answer format.

Koko the Storyteller

by Shavon Jackson

Kanoro Lewis is Koko the Storyteller. He travels to schools and fairs all over. I asked him about what he does.

Why did you become a storyteller?

Telling stories is an old tradition. It helps people learn about their heritage.

What kinds of stories do you tell?

All my stories are from the African-American people. Some are folk tales. Others are stories about our history.

What do you do when you tell the stories?

Sometimes I dress up like the characters. My favorite is Anansi the spider. I wear a jacket with eight sleeves!

I really love what I do. I plan to tell stories for as long as people will listen.

The first paragraph introduces the person interviewed and the topic.

Shavon presents **questions in a logical order**. The questions and answers flow smoothly from one to the next.

The answer to each question uses the person's exact words.

Shavon chooses a good quotation to end the interview.

Prewrite

1. **Choose a Topic** Whom will you interview? What tradition will you focus on? Talk with a partner to choose the best ideas.

<table>
<tr><th colspan="2">Language Frames</th></tr>
<tr><td>

Tell Your Ideas

• I'm curious about _____ . _____ could tell me about this tradition.

• _____ is from _____ . I'll ask about the traditions in that country.

</td><td>

Respond to Ideas

• _____ sounds interesting! How will you learn more about it?

• I think most people already know about _____ . Can you choose something else?

</td></tr>
</table>

> Use sentences like these to choose your topic.

2. **Gather Information** Prepare your questions ahead of time in a 5Ws chart. Then set up your interview and ask your questions. Take notes or record the interview.

5Ws Chart

Who?	Who is your favorite character?
What?	What kind of stories do you tell?
Where?	Where do you perform?
When?	
Why?	

> Write a list of questions.

3. **Get Organized** Review your notes or recording. Which questions gave the most important or interesting details? Put those questions in a logical order so they flow smoothly.

Draft

Use your questions and answers to write your article.

• Begin with a few sentences to introduce the person and the topic.

• Clearly label each question and answer.

• Choose the best details to include. Use the person's exact words.

Revise

1. **Read, Revise, Retell** Read your draft aloud to a partner. Use the words "question" and "answer" so your partner will understand what parts you are reading. Then you can both talk about how to improve it.

Language Frames

Retell	Make Suggestions
• You interviewed _____. • The tradition the person talked about was _____. • The most interesting things I learned were _____.	• I'd like to know more about _____. What other details could you include? • The sequence of questions doesn't seem logical. Could you you move _____ to _____?

---

2. **Make Changes** Think about your draft and your partner's suggestions. Use the Revising Marks on page 585 to mark your changes.

   • Are your questions in a logical order?

   > 2. What kinds of stories do you tell?
   >
   > 1. Why did you become a storyteller?  tr
   >
   > 3. What do you do when you tell your stories?

   • Add more details as needed.

   > He travels to schools and fairs all over.
   > Kanoro Lewis is Koko the Storyteller. I asked
   > him about what he does.

Edit and Proofread

Work with a partner to edit and proofread your interview. Check that the subject in each sentence agrees with the verb. Pay special attention to compound subjects.

Publish

On Your Own Make a final copy of your interview. Read it aloud to your classmates. You may want to ask a partner to read the questions or answers for you.

Grammar Tip

 When parts of a compound subject are connected by *or*, make sure the verb agrees with the subject closest to it.

Presentation Tips	
If you are the speaker . . .	**If you are the listener . . .**
When you read a question, make your voice go up slightly at the end of the sentence.	Try to picture the tradition as the speaker describes it.
If you have a picture of the person you interviewed, show it to your listeners.	Make connections to other traditions that you know about.

With a Group Collect all of the interviews and put them together in a binder. Set up listening stations with the recorded interviews. What are some new words and phrases you heard? What did you learn about traditions? Talk with your group about these ideas.

Talk | Together

In this unit, you found lots of answers to the **Big Question**.
Now make a concept map to discuss the **Big Question** with the class.

Concept Map

They help us learn about our culture.

Why are traditions important?

Write a Description

Use your concept map. Write a description of a tradition that is important in your family. Tell what makes it important.

Share Your Ideas

Choose one of these ways to share your ideas about the
Big Question.

Talk About It!

Is there a new tradition you want to start in your family? What is it? What would people do? Tell a partner.

Write It!

Write a Column

How can someone choose a good husband or wife? Write an advice column about it. Give advice for choosing the right person to marry.

You should choose someone you really like, because you will have to spend a lot of time with that person!

Do It!

Share a Game or Song

Share a game or song that you learned from an older family member. Teach it to classmates so they can play or perform it. When you give instructions, be sure you teach the steps in the correct order!

Do It!

Make a Time Capsule

Make a time capsule for younger family members. Write and draw to teach them about your family's most important traditions. Save the capsule to give to them in the future.

Animal Intelligence

?
BIG
Question

Just how smart are animals?

Unit at a Glance
▶ **Language**: Express Ideas, Engage in Conversation, Science Words
▶ **Literacy**: Make Connections
▶ **Content**: Animal Behavior

Unit 2

Share What You Know

Do It!

1. **Think** about a pet you know or a favorite animal from TV. Draw the animal.

2. **Tell** the class about your drawing. What makes the animal special?

3. **Listen** to your classmates tell about their drawings. Ask questions about the animals they drew.

My kitten is tiny and soft.

Build Background: Watch a video about animal behavior.
NGReach.com

Express Ideas

Listen to the dialogue between Gina and Nazario. Then use **Language Frames** to express ideas about an animal you have seen.

Dialogue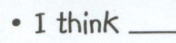

1.

Look! A wild animal.

I think it's a cat.

2.

I know it's a raccoon. It has a *black mask* and a *ringed tail*.

It has sharp *teeth*, too.

3.

I think raccoons are very smart.

I think they are very scary.

4.

Let's take a closer look.

Let's not!

Key Words

adaptation

defend

predator

prey

trait

Key Words

Look at the photos. Use **Key Words** and other words to talk about why animals look and act as they do.

bobcat

A bobcat is a **predator**. Bobcats have many **adaptations** for hunting, such as powerful jaws. A bobcat's **prey** includes rabbits, squirrels, and other small mammals.

raccoon

Raccoons have many **traits** that help them survive. They are intelligent, and they have sharp teeth to **defend** themselves.

Talk Together

Just how smart are bobcats and raccoons? How can you tell? Try to use **Language Frames** from page 74 and **Key Words** to express ideas to a partner.

Analyze Characters

Writers describe **characters**. You can also tell what characters are like by:

- what they say or do

- how they act with each other.

Read the cartoon. Find out more about Nazario and Gina.

Map and Talk

You can make a character chart to analyze characters. Write each name. Then fill in what the character does and says. Tell what these details show about the character.

Character Chart

Character	What the Character Does	What the Character Says	What It Shows
Gina	watches a raccoon	Raccoons are interesting.	She is curious. She is brave.
Nazario	screams, runs away	Raccoons are scary.	He is shy. He is scared.

Talk Together

Tell your partner about another character you have read about. Describe the character's **traits**. Make a character chart with your partner.

More Key Words

Use these words to talk about "Love and Roast Chicken" and "Mouse Deer and Farmer."

behavior
(bi-**hā**-vyur) *noun*

Behavior is how a living thing acts. You can train an animal to learn a new **behavior**.

characteristic
(kair-ik-tu-**ris**-tik) *noun*

A **characteristic** is a feature. White marks are a **characteristic** of this snake.

response
(ri-**spons**) *noun*

A **response** is an answer. These students want to give a **response** to a question.

strategy
(**stra**-tuh-jē) *noun*

A **strategy** is a careful plan. This girl has a **strategy** for winning the game.

survival
(sir-**vī**-vul) *noun*

Survival means living. **Survival** is difficult in very cold places.

Talk Together

Work with a partner. Write a sentence for each **Key Word** showing what the word means.

My strategy for school is to work hard.

Add words to My Vocabulary Notebook.
NGReach.com

Learn to Make Connections

Look at the picture. If it reminds you of something, you have **made a connection** to it

You **make connections** when you read, too.

How to Make Connections

1. Think about what the text is about.

2. As you read, connect the text to yourself. Think about what you know and have seen in the world.

3. Decide how these connections help you understand the text.

> It's about _____.
>
> _____ reminds me of _____.
>
> Now I understand _____.

Talk Together

Read Nazario's story, "Three City Raccoons." Read the sample connection. Then use **Language Frames** as you make connections to the story. Tell your partner about them.

Story

Three City Raccoons

A raccoon family lived in the country. They were Trini, Goyo, and their son Chucho.

"I'm hungry," said Chucho.

Actually, they were all hungry because there was no food. Trini knew their **survival** was in danger. Luckily, she had a good plan. Being smart is a **characteristic** of many raccoons.

"Let's move to the city," she said. "We'll find food there."

"No way," said Goyo. "I like the country."

Chucho's **response** was more positive. "Let's go, Dad," he said. "It will be an adventure!"

Trini and Chucho started walking to the city. Goyo didn't want to go, but he followed them. Why? He didn't want to be alone.

In the city, the family found an exciting new food—garbage!

Trini's **strategy** worked. The raccoons changed their **behavior** in the city. In the country, they were **predators**. They ate bugs and worms. In the city, they looked for garbage at night. Even Goyo was happy.

"People throw away such tasty food," he said, licking some jelly off a paper plate.

The raccoons laughed and went to look for more garbage.

Sample Connection

"It's about raccoons being hungry.

This story reminds me of a TV show I watched about how animals survive.

Now I understand why raccoons have to be smart to survive."

◄ = A good place to make a connection

79

Read a Story

Genre

A **trickster tale** is a story in which the main character tries to outwit, or outsmart, the other characters. The main character is almost always a clever animal.

Characters

Characters are the people or animals in a story.

Cuy the Guinea Pig

Tío Antonio the Fox

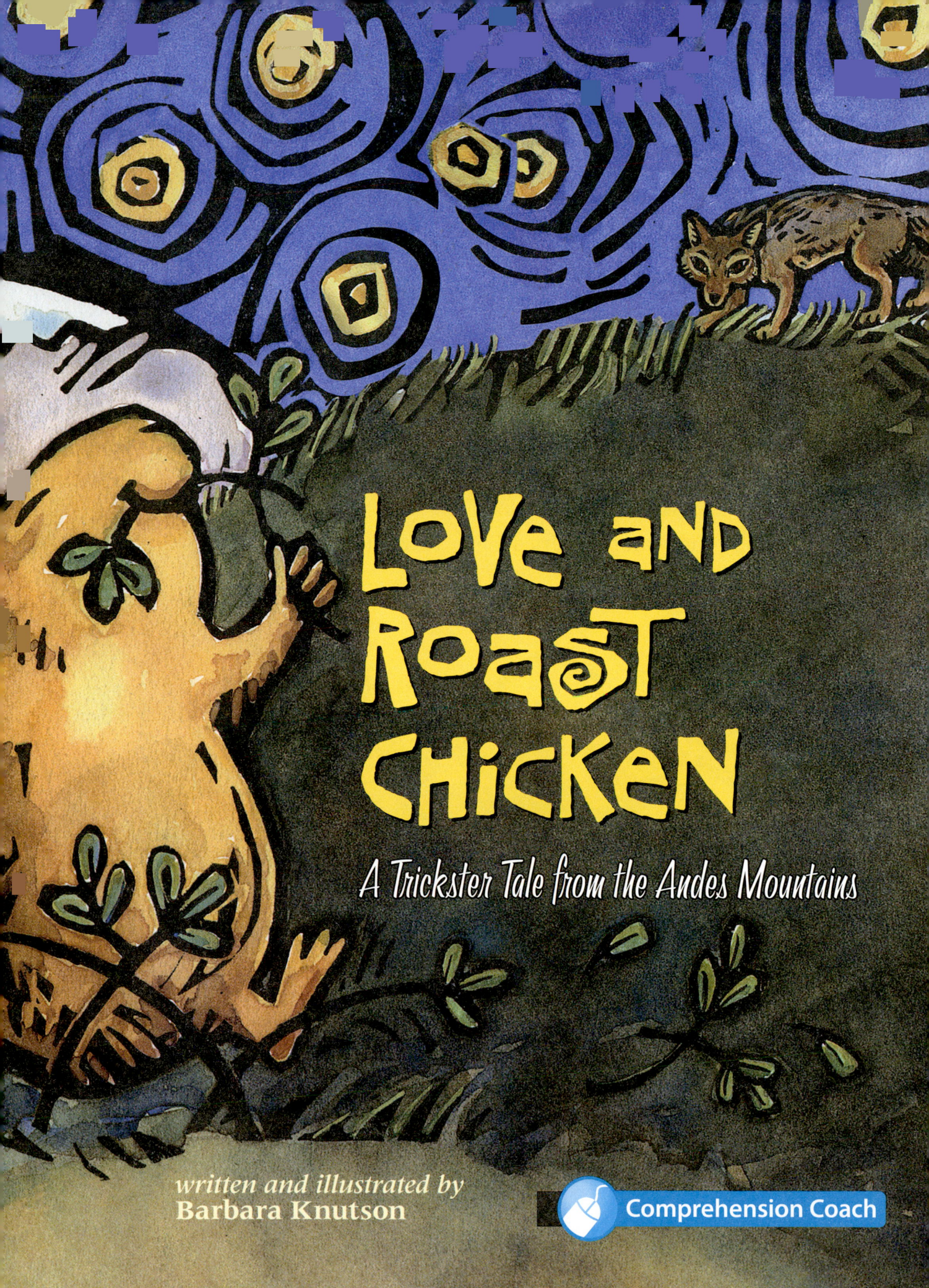

Love and Roast Chicken

A Trickster Tale from the Andes Mountains

written and illustrated by
Barbara Knutson

▶ **Set a Purpose**
A clever guinea pig meets a hungry
fox. Find out how he **defends** himself.

ONE DAY in the high Andes Mountains, Cuy the
Guinea Pig was climbing up and down the paths looking
for something to eat. Suddenly, he saw Tío Antonio the Fox
coming over the rocks right in front of him, and there was
no time to hide.

Cuy **thought fast**. He **squeezed** under the edge of a
great rock and pressed up with his arms.

"Aha! Dinner!" snarled Fox.

"Tío Antonio!" cried Cuy. "Haven't you heard? The sky
is falling!"

In Other Words
thought fast quickly thought of an idea
squeezed pushed himself

82

"**Nonsense!**" growled Tío Antonio, but he **couldn't help looking up**. "It looks the same as always!"

"That's because I'm holding it up with this rock," said Cuy. "I've been here all day, and I need to go to the bathroom. Please, will you hold the rock for just a moment?"

Fox looked up again. It would be terrible if the sky fell. He **crouched** under the rock and pushed up with his front legs.

"Don't let go," warned Cuy, "or we will all be squashed flat." Then he **scurried off** to look for more food.

In Other Words
"Nonsense!" That's not true!
couldn't help looking up looked up anyway
crouched lowered his body
scurried off ran away

▶ **Before You Move On**
1. **Plot** How does Cuy **protect** himself from Tío Antonio?
2. **Character** Which character is a **predator** and which is **prey**? How do you know?

Predict
What will Tío Antonio do?

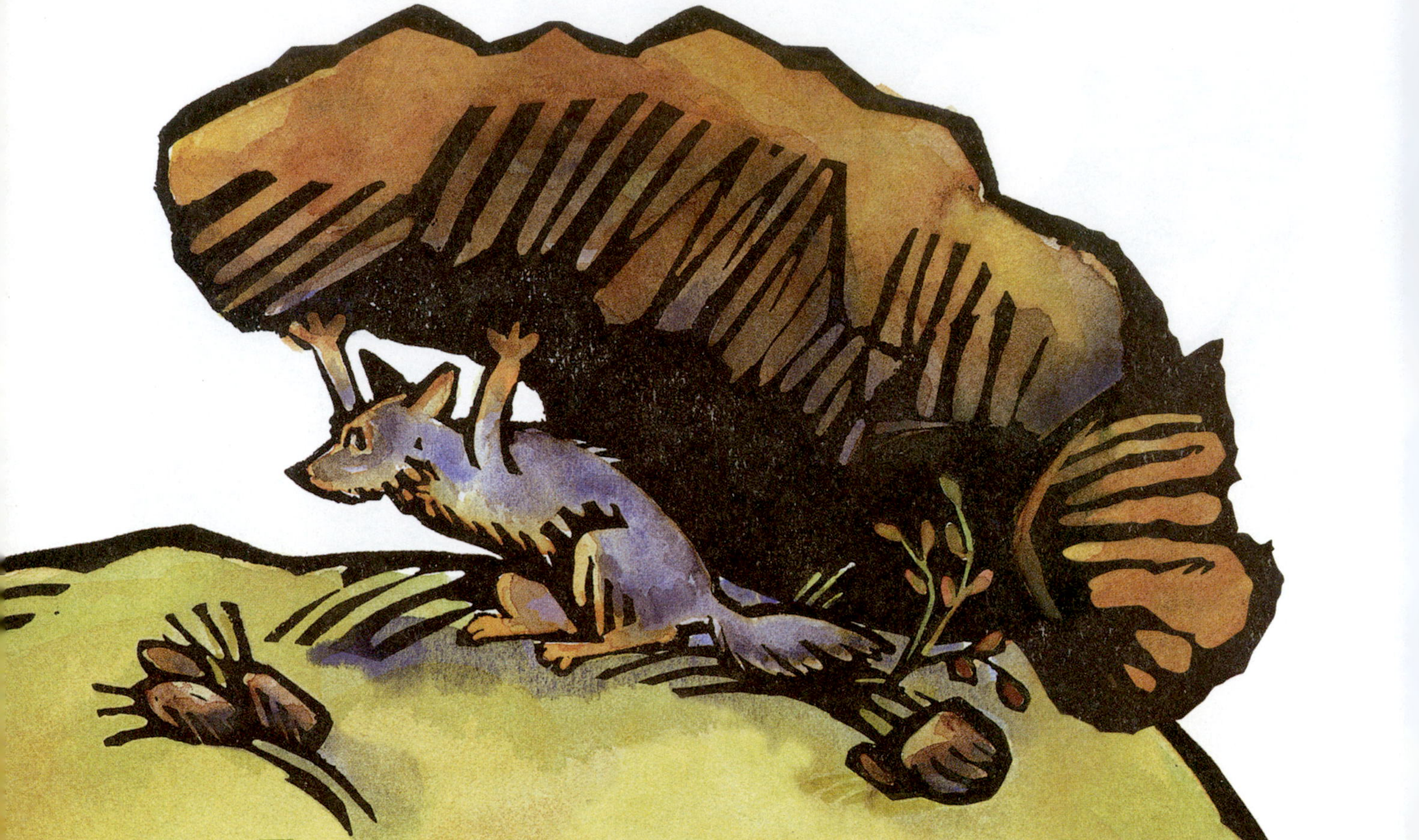

By sunset, Tío Antonio couldn't hold his arms up any longer. "I have to let go, even if the sky falls!" He **ducked**and let go.

Nothing happened. The rock and the sky stayed where they had always been.

"I'll get that guinea pig!" barked Fox as he **bounded** down the trail.

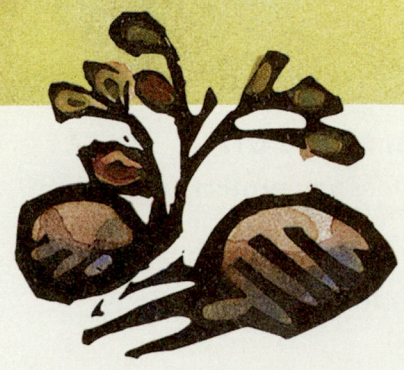

In Other Words
ducked bent down quickly
bounded ran

But Cuy had a plan. "I'm going where there's **plenty** of food and someone who always chases Fox away," he decided.

Cuy knew that a farmer and his daughter lived down in the valley. So he put on a hat and a poncho and went down the mountain to knock on the farmer's door.

▶ **Before You Move On**

1. **Confirm Prediction** What does Tío Antonio do? Was your prediction correct?
2. **Make Connections** How would you feel if you were the fox?

▶ **Predict**
What will happen to Cuy
at the farm?

"**BUENOS DÍAS, _Papay_**," said Cuy.
"Need any help with the alfalfa?"

"What a small man," thought the farmer,
"but I do need help."

"_**Bueno**_," he said. "You can start **right away**."

All day Cuy helped Florinda, the farmer's
daughter, weed and hoe and water the fields. But
all night he feasted on fresh alfalfa.

alfalfa

In Other Words
**Buenos días, Papay** Good morning, Sir (in Spanish)
**Bueno** Good (in Spanish)
right away now

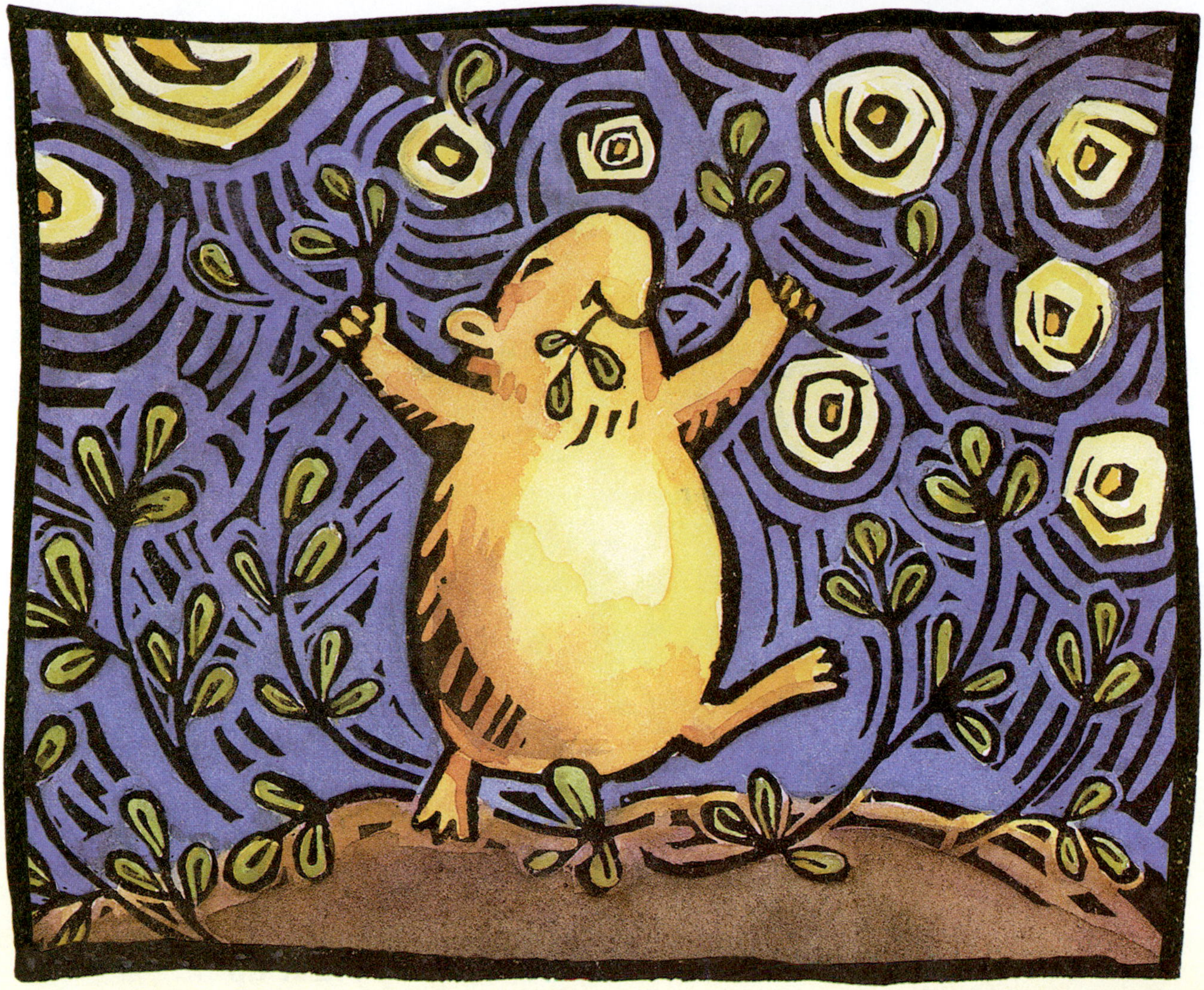

"All this food and **no Fox in sight**. I'm going to stay here **the rest of my life**!" Cuy decided.

By the third day, the farmer noticed something was wrong. "Who is stealing all my alfalfa?" he wondered. "**I'd better** make it look like someone is guarding the field."

In Other Words

no Fox in sight Fox is not here to stop me
the rest of my life forever
I'd better I should

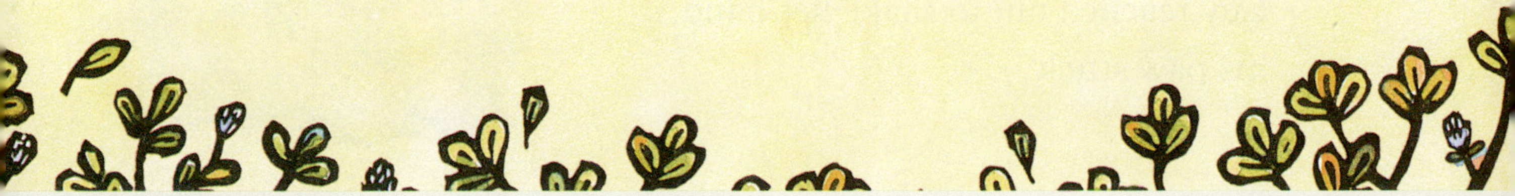

He shaped a little person out of clay and covered it with **sticky sap** from the eucalyptus tree. He **propped it up** in the field and went to bed.

In the middle of the night, Cuy crept out for a snack, but someone had gotten there before him.

"*¡Buenas noches!* Are you a friend of Florinda's?" he said. The visitor said nothing. "I said, hello!" When Cuy reached out to shake her hand, his paw stuck.

"**Oho,** so you want to hold my hand!" said Cuy. He patted her on the shoulder with his other paw, but that one stuck too.

"**¡Caramba!** Let go!" Guinea Pig said. "If you don't let go, I'll kick you!" But the person didn't say a word, and she didn't let go.

Cuy kicked hard with his right foot, which stuck. Then he kicked with his left foot, and that stuck too. "LET ME GO!" shouted Cuy so loudly that the farmer woke up and ran outside.

In Other Words
Oho Oh
¡Caramba! Goodness, stop it! (in Spanish)

▶ **Before You Move On**

1. **Confirm Prediction** Was your prediction correct about what happens to Cuy at the farm? Explain.

2. **Make Connections** Does Cuy remind you of anyone you know? Explain.

▶ **Predict**
How will Cuy save himself from the farmer?

"**¡Qué tramposo!** What a **rascal**! You're not a farmworker, you're a guinea pig!" cried the farmer. "And you've been eating all my alfalfa! Well, Florinda loves to eat roast guinea pig, and tomorrow we will eat YOU!"

He pulled Cuy free from the sticky gum doll. Then he tied him to the eucalyptus tree and went back to bed.

"It can't get any worse than this!" thought Cuy. But here came Tío Antonio sneaking toward the **chicken coop**.

In Other Words
rascal troublemaker
◀ **chicken coop** small house where the chickens live

90

"Well, well!" said Fox. "I was looking for chicken dinner, but here is my **appetizer**!" He came closer, the moonlight **glinting** on his sharp teeth. "Why are you tied up?"

Guinea Pig gulped. "Oh, Tío Antonio!" he cried, thinking fast. "It's all because of love and roast chicken."

Fox **perked up his ears**. "Those are my favorite subjects."

Cuy put his paw over his heart. "You know the farmer's daughter, Florinda? She wants to marry me. But the trouble is, she eats chicken every day. And I **am a vegetarian**!"

In Other Words
appetizer snack
glinting shining
perked up his ears became interested
am a vegetarian don't eat meat

"They've tied me up until I promise to marry Florinda and eat big plates of roast chicken every day! What am I going to do?"

"**Pobrecito**," said Tío Antonio, licking his lips. "I hate to see you suffer. Just to help you, I will take your place."

"Really?" said Cuy. "You are very kind."

So Fox untied Cuy. Then Cuy tied Tío Antonio to the tree and **slipped** back into the alfalfa field for one last feast.

In Other Words
Pobrecito Poor little thing (in Spanish)
slipped went quietly

The next morning, the farmer came out to untie his dinner. To his surprise, he found a fox.

"What now? **Another disguise?**" The farmer picked up a stick.

"Oh no, *Papay*, don't hit me!" said Tío Antonio. "I promise to eat one of your chickens every day of the year!"

"*¿Cómo?*" cried the farmer.

"Of course, *Papay*," Tío Antonio added quickly, "I also plan to marry your daughter."

"*¿CÓMO?*" spat the farmer, and he raised the stick over his head.

In Other Words

Another disguise? Are you pretending to be someone else again?

¿Cómo? What? (in Spanish)

As fast as he could, Tío Antonio explained what Cuy had said.

"You believed a story like that? How foolish!" The farmer laughed until the tears ran down his cheeks. **"¡Qué ridículo!"**

While the farmer laughed, Fox bit **clean** through the rope and scrambled over the field wall. "CUY!" he howled. "You will never trick me again!"

And to make sure that was true, he stayed away from Cuy for a long, long time. ❖

In Other Words
"¡Qué ridículo!" That's ridiculous! (in Spanish)
clean completely

▶ **Before You Move On**

1. **Confirm Prediction** How does Cuy escape the farmer? Was your prediction correct? Explain.
2. **Character** Why is the farmer laughing?

Meet the Author and Illustrator
BaRBaRa KNUTSoN

When Barbara Knutson was young, she loved drawing pictures of animals. When she grew up, she started writing and illustrating books for children.

Barbara also loved to travel. Her adventures around the world gave her many story ideas. No matter where she went, she always brought her sketchbook with her. "I could write and draw what I learned along the way, including many stories about the fox, and one special story about Cuy the Guinea Pig."

◄ Barbara Knutson traveled to many parts of the world. People would often be interested in her sketches.

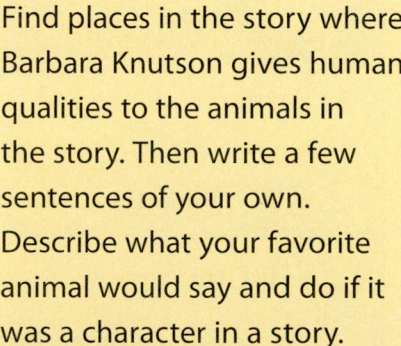

Writer's Craft ✏️

Find places in the story where Barbara Knutson gives human qualities to the animals in the story. Then write a few sentences of your own. Describe what your favorite animal would say and do if it was a character in a story.

Talk About It

1. What tricks do the characters play in this **trickster tale**?

> One trick that Cuy plays is _____ .
> A trick that Tío Antonio plays is _____ .
> One trick that the farmer plays is _____ .

2. Who do you think is smarter, Cuy or the farmer? **Express** your **ideas** about this.

> I think _____ is smarter because _____ .

3. Describe the relationship between Cuy and Tío Antonio. How do these characters interact with each other?

Learn test-taking strategies.
NGReach.com

Write About It

What **traits** do you most admire in Cuy? Why?
Write an e-mail to Cuy to tell him. Use **Key Words**.

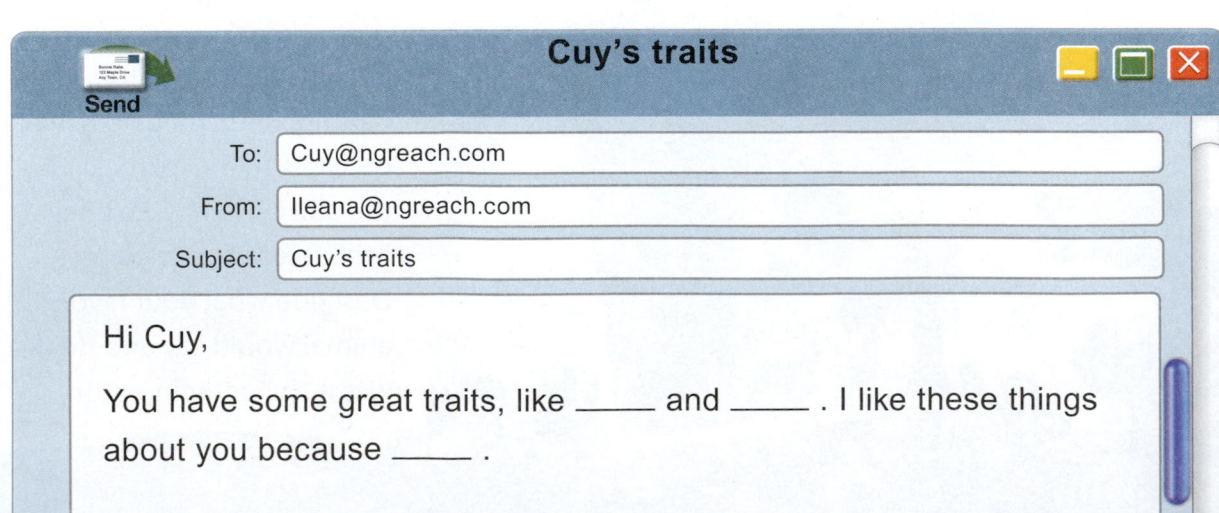

Cuy's traits

Send

To: Cuy@ngreach.com

From: Ileana@ngreach.com

Subject: Cuy's traits

Hi Cuy,

You have some great traits, like _____ and _____ . I like these things about you because _____ .

Analyze Characters

Make a character chart for "Love and Roast Chicken."

Character Chart

Character	What the Character Does	What the Character Says	What It Shows
Cuy	meets a fox	"The sky is falling."	
Tio Antonio			

| In this column, name each character. | Name important things that the character does. | Name important things that the character says. | Explain what the clues tell you about the character. |

Now use your chart as you analyze the characters in the story. Work with a partner. Use as many **Key Words** as you can.

> Cuy is _____ .
> I know because _____ .

Fluency 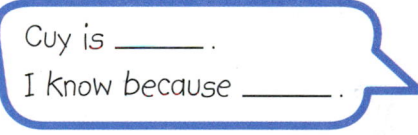 Comprehension Coach

Use the Comprehension Coach to practice reading with expression. Rate your reading.

Talk Together

Just how smart are the animals in "Love and Roast Chicken"? Choose one character and use **Key Words** to describe to a partner how the character is or isn't smart.

Homophones

Homophones are words that sound the same but have different spellings and meanings. When reading, you can use context clues to decide which meaning fits the word. When writing, choose the correct spelling to match the word meaning.

Tale and **tail** are homophones. Read these examples.

She read us a **tale** from long ago that is set in China.

Meaning: a story

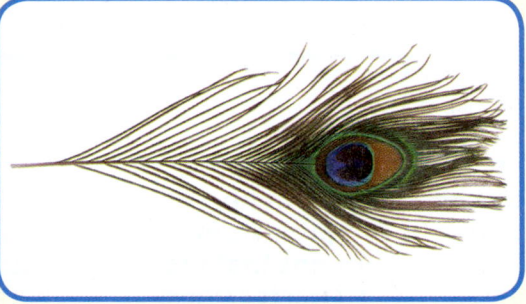

The feather is from a peacock's **tail**.

Meaning: the part that sticks out at the back of an animal's body

Try It Together

Read each sentence. Choose the pair of words that makes the sentence correct.

1. Please _____ a tale about how _____ got spots.
   - **A** write, dear
   - **B** right, deer
   - **C** right, dear
   - **D** write, deer

2. Did you _____ the _____ in the trees last night?
   - **A** here, bare
   - **B** hear, bear
   - **C** here, bear
   - **D** hear, bare

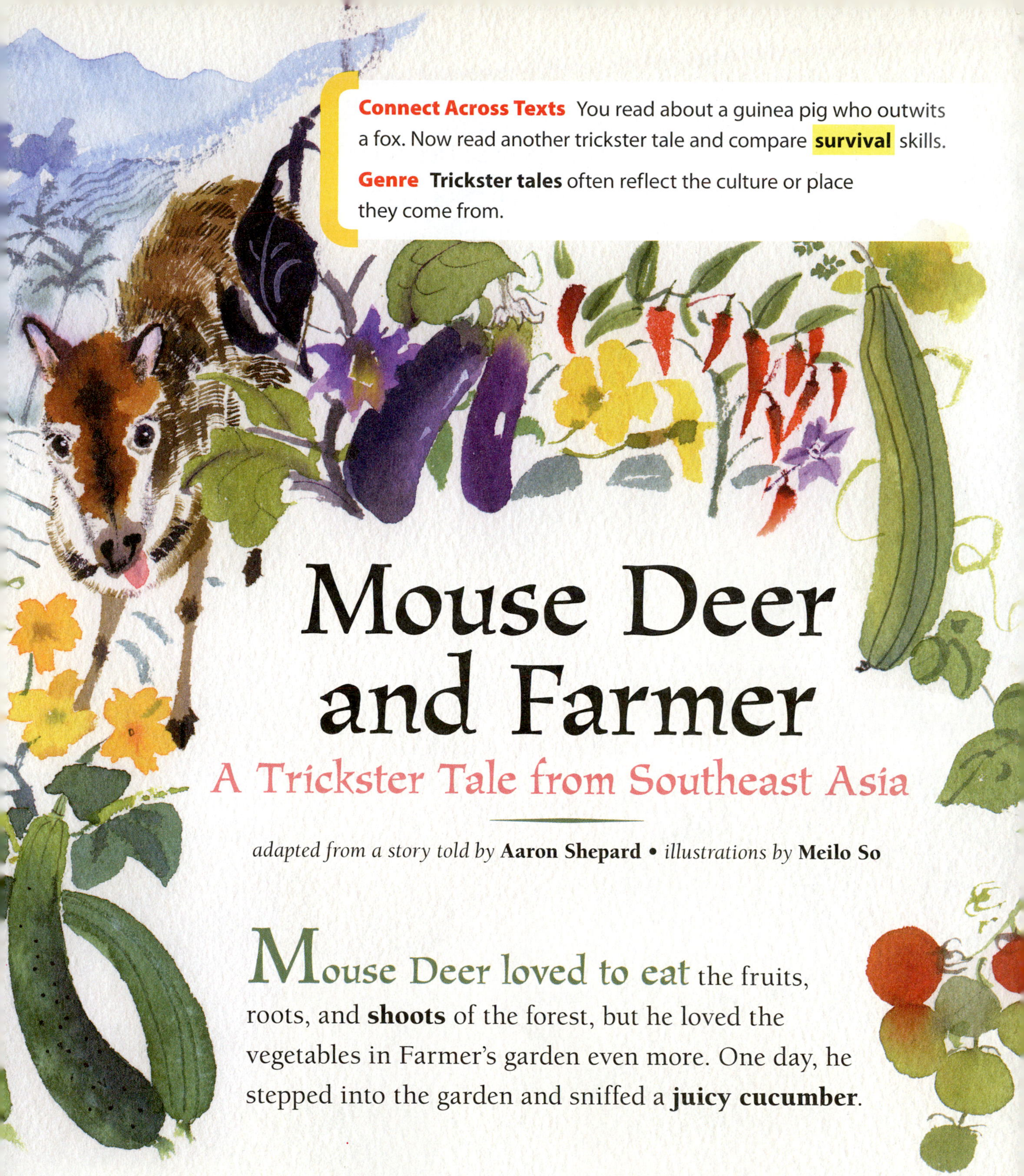

Connect Across Texts You read about a guinea pig who outwits a fox. Now read another trickster tale and compare **survival** skills.

Genre **Trickster tales** often reflect the culture or place they come from.

Mouse Deer and Farmer

A Trickster Tale from Southeast Asia

adapted from a story told by **Aaron Shepard** • *illustrations by* **Meilo So**

Mouse Deer loved to eat the fruits, roots, and **shoots** of the forest, but he loved the vegetables in Farmer's garden even more. One day, he stepped into the garden and sniffed a **juicy cucumber**.

In Other Words

shoots young, soft plants

juicy cucumber tasty green vegetable ▶

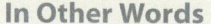

▶ **Before You Move On**

1. **Character's Motive** Why does Mouse Deer step into the vegetable garden?
2. **Setting** Describe Farmer's garden. Use the pictures and text to help you.

Snap! Mouse Deer's leg was caught in a **snare**! When he saw Farmer coming, Mouse Deer lay down and made his body **stiff**.

"Look what I caught," said Farmer. "But this mouse deer looks dead. Maybe he's been dead a long time. I guess we can't eat him."

Farmer freed Mouse Deer from the snare and tossed him back into the forest. Mouse Deer landed with a soft *plop*, then jumped up and ran away.

"Hey! You tricked me!" Farmer yelled, but Mouse Deer just laughed.

snare

In Other Words
snare trap
stiff not move

A few days passed, but Mouse Deer kept thinking about those vegetables. When he went back to the garden, he saw something new. It looked like a man, but its head was a coconut and its body was rubber.

"A scarecrow!" said Mouse Deer. "Farmer can't scare me with that!"

Mouse Deer kicked the scarecrow, but his foot stuck to its body. The scarecrow was covered with sticky sap from a rubber tree!

"Let me go!" Mouse Deer cried.

In Other Words
"A scarecrow!" That isn't a real person!

▶ **Before You Move On**

1. **Character's Motive** Why does Farmer make a scarecrow?
2. **Make Connections** Compare how the farmer in this story and the farmer in "Love and Roast Chicken" outsmart the main character.

Then Farmer appeared. "Welcome back," he said. Then he pulled Mouse Deer off the scarecrow and locked him in a chicken coop.

"You'll stay here tonight," said Farmer, "and tomorrow you'll be our dinner."

That night Mouse Deer couldn't sleep. When the sun **rose**, he just lay there sadly. Then he heard a voice.

"So Farmer finally caught you," said Farmer's dog.

Mouse Deer thought fast. "What do you mean, Dog? Farmer didn't catch me."

In Other Words
rose came up in the morning

102

"Then why are you in the coop?" asked Dog.

"Because there aren't enough beds in the house. You see, tomorrow Farmer is holding a **feast**, and I'm the **guest of honor**."

"That's not fair!" said Dog. "I've been his loyal friend for years, so I should be the guest of honor!"

"You're right. Why don't you take my place?"

So Dog lifted the latch and opened the door. Mouse Deer ran toward the forest, laughing.

"Farmer will have to find a different dinner now, because he can't catch me!" ❖

In Other Words

feast big, special meal
guest of honor most important guest there

▶ **Before You Move On**

1. **Make Connections** How is Mouse Deer like Cuy?
2. **Connect Characters** Why does Dog think he should be the guest of honor?

Compare Characters' Adventures

A trickster tale tells the adventures of the main character. How are the adventures of Cuy and Mouse Deer similar? How are they different? Work with a partner to complete the Venn diagram.

Venn Diagram

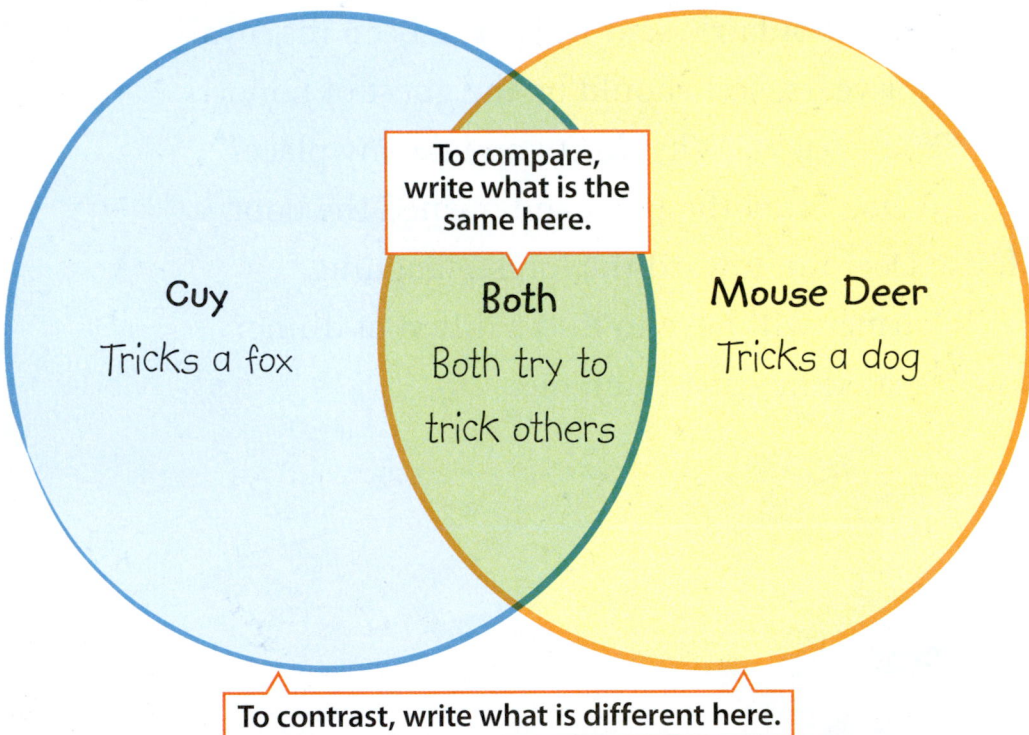

Cuy
Tricks a fox

To compare, write what is the same here.

Both
Both try to trick others

Mouse Deer
Tricks a dog

To contrast, write what is different here.

Talk Together

Just how smart are Cuy and Mouse Deer? Think about the two trickster tales. Use **Key Words** to talk about your ideas.

Kinds of Sentences

There are four different kinds of sentences.

Grammar Rules Kinds of Sentences

• A **statement** tells something.	I am hungry.
• An **exclamation** shows strong feeling.	He can't wait to eat!
• A **command** tells you to do something.	Stop eating that.
• A **question** asks something. You can answer some questions with *yes* or *no*. Other questions ask for more information. They begin with question words.	Aren't you hungry? Doesn't soup smell good? When? What? Why? Who? Where? How?

Read Different Kinds of Sentences

Read these sentences from "Love and Roast Chicken." Find a question. What information does it ask for?

By the third day, the farmer noticed something was wrong. "Who is stealing all my alfalfa?" he wondered. "I'd better make it look like someone is guarding the field."

Write Different Kinds of Sentences ✏️

What would you say to Cuy if you could meet him? Write a short paragraph. Include at least one question. Read your paragraph to a partner.

Engage in Conversation

Listen to the dialogue between Abu, Kirsten, and James. Then use **Language Frames** to have a conversation about pets.

Dialogue (((MP3)))

1.

I think dogs are smarter than cats.

I don't agree. My cat is really smart.

I taught my dog to sit and roll over.

2.

Sit!

3.

Roll over!

4.

You said you taught her to sit and roll over.

I did. But she hasn't learned the difference yet.

Key Words

Key Words

command
imitate
memory
pattern
skill
tool

Look at the photos. Use **Key Words** and other words to talk about dog training. Use the pronunciations in the **Picture Dictionary** to say new words correctly.

A dog uses its **memory** to learn new **skills**.

A whistle is a special **tool** that a trainer uses to call a dog.

A dog jumps over bars of different heights. The dog learns how to follow the **pattern**.

Dogs learn to follow **commands**. Some commands are spoken, and others are signals. Some dogs learn tricks. In some tricks, the dog seems to **imitate**, or copy, its trainer's actions.

Talk Together

Just how smart are dogs? Try to use **Language Frames** from page 106 and **Key Words** to engage in conversation with a partner.

Main Idea and Details

When you want to tell about something, you may start with the **main idea**, or the most important idea. Then you give **details** to share more information.

Look at the pictures of James teaching his dog a new trick.

I taught my dog how to shake hands. She is two years old.

We practiced every day for three weeks. At first, I took her paw.

Later, she learned to give me her paw. I gave her a treat when she got it right.

Map and Talk

You can use a main idea diagram to show important ideas and details. Here's how you make one.

Main Idea Diagram

Main Idea: James taught his dog to shake hands

Write the main idea here.

Detail: They practiced for weeks.
Detail: He gave her a treat when she got it right.

Write details here. Include only the details that support the main idea.

Talk Together

Think of details that support this main idea: Dogs can follow many different **commands**. Make a main idea diagram. Tell your partner about it.

More Key Words

Use these words to talk about "Animal Smarts" and "The Clever Chimps of Fongoli."

ability

(u-**bi**-lu-tē) *noun*

An **ability** is a skill. This girl has the **ability** to play the flute.

communication

(ku-myū-nu-**kā**-shun) *noun*

Communication is the sharing of information.

inherit

(in-**hair**-ut) *verb*

To **inherit** means to get things, usually from parents. A skunk **inherits** its stripes.

language

(**lang**-gwij) *noun*

Language is a way of sharing ideas. Writing is a form of **language**.

learn

(**lirn**) *verb*

To **learn** is to gain new skills and information. This calf must **learn** to walk.

Talk Together

Work with a partner. Make a Word Web for each **Key Word**. Write the **Key Word** in the center. Then write examples for that word.

Word Web of Examples

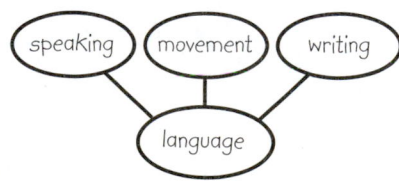

Add words to My Vocabulary Notebook.
NGReach.com

Learn to Make Connections

Look at the picture. Does it remind you of something you have seen or read about? As you think of this, you **make a connection**.

You **make connections** when you read, too.

How to Make Connections

		It's about _____ .
☁	**1.** Think about what the text is about.	
👁	**2.** As you read, think about what you know that connects to the topic.	_____ reminds me of _____ .
▣	**3.** Decide how the connection helps you understand the text.	Now I understand _____ .

Talk Together

Read James's report. Read the sample connection.
Then use **Language Frames** as you make
connections of your own. Tell a partner about them.

Report

Train Your Dog to Be Terrific

by James Harvin

Do you have an uncontrollable dog? Don't give up! Your
dog isn't really bad. It just needs to be trained. Every dog has
the **ability** to **learn**. Training a dog isn't hard, but you need to
follow some rules.

Here's the first rule: Use clear **communication**. Dogs can't
speak your **language**. But they can understand **commands**.
Use the same words every time you train your dog. Dogs will
learn the sounds of the words. To teach your dog to fetch, say
"Fetch" every time. If you sometimes say "Get it" and sometimes say
"Bring me the ball," your dog will get confused.

Here's the second rule: Be patient. Dog training takes time. Your
dog might take a long time to learn a new **skill**. Remember, your dog
did not **inherit** any tricks from its parents. You will need to repeat
things over and over.

Training your dog can be fun.
Your dog will enjoy it, too. But the best
part is the result. Your terrible dog will
be terrific!

Sample Connection

"It's about training
dogs to have better
behavior.

The report reminds
me of an article I read
about pets.

Now I understand you
can help a dog with
training."

◀ = A good place to make a connection

111

Read a Science Article

Genre

A **science article** is nonfiction. It gives facts about a science topic such as animal behavior.

Text Features

Look at **photographs** and **captions** in science articles. They help you understand the text better.

photograph

◄ Koko uses sign language to communicate. Here, she uses the sign for *eat*.

caption

ANIMAL Smarts

by Leslie Hall

NATIONAL GEOGRAPHIC

Comprehension Coach

▶ **Set a Purpose**
Find out how animals
demonstrate their intelligence.

What can animals do? From sharing
information to using **tools** and even
playing tricks on people, **it turns out** that
animals are smarter than we thought.

Cool Tools

Using tools **takes smarts**. When you need to **sort out**
a problem, you have to figure out why it is a problem.
Then you find or make a tool
to help you solve it. Think of
the tools you use every day:
a fork, a pair of scissors,
even a cell phone.

**A fork is a useful tool.
You can use it in many
different ways.** ▶

In Other Words
it turns out we know
takes smarts requires intelligence
sort out solve

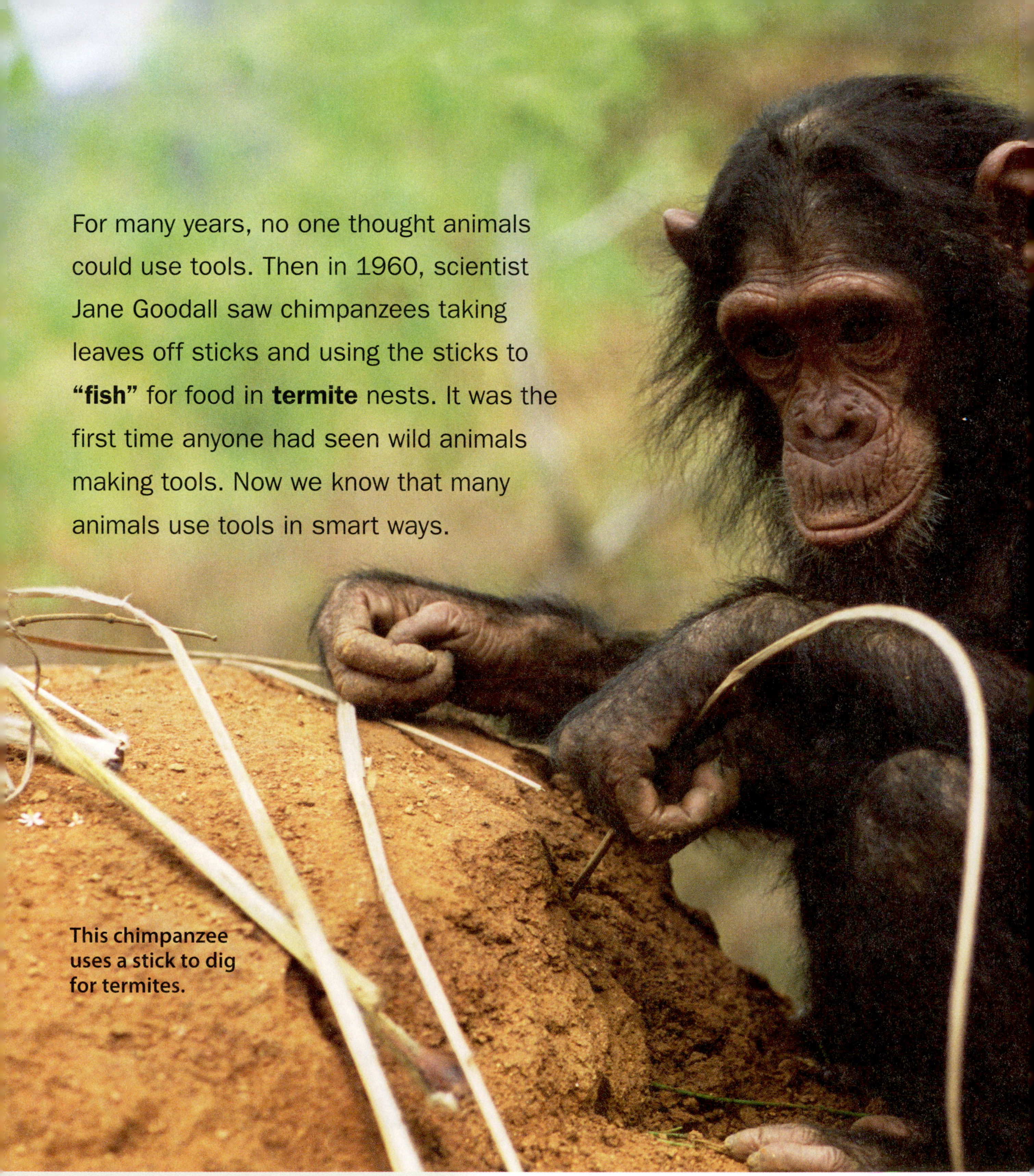

For many years, no one thought animals could use tools. Then in 1960, scientist Jane Goodall saw chimpanzees taking leaves off sticks and using the sticks to **"fish"** for food in **termite** nests. It was the first time anyone had seen wild animals making tools. Now we know that many animals use tools in smart ways.

This chimpanzee uses a stick to dig for termites.

In Other Words

"fish" dig; hunt

termite insect ▶

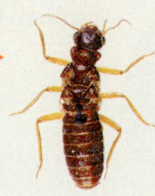

▶ Before You Move On

1. **Main Idea** What was Jane Goodall's discovery?
2. **Make Connections** Compare how you use a fork to how chimpanzees use sticks.

How Animals Learn

Animals already know how to do some things when they are born. For example, a baby orangutan can **grasp** a leaf with its hands. It doesn't need to **learn** how. It **inherits** the **ability**.

Orangutans also learn things from their parents. A young orangutan may see its mother use a leaf as a napkin or a rain hat. It may then copy her actions. The ability to learn shows intelligence.

▼ Young orangutans sometimes copy the actions of their parents.

▼ Orangutans may learn from their parents how to use a leaf as a hat.

In Other Words
◀ **grasp** hold

Memory and Smarts

To remember something also takes smarts. Female poison dart frogs have **incredible memories**. After a frog's eggs hatch, the female carries each tadpole to its own leafy **spot** somewhere in the rainforest.

She returns every few days to bring food to each tadpole. That means the frog has to remember **the location of** as many as 30 tiny tadpoles!

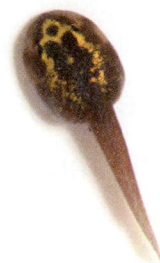

▼ tadpole

A female poison dart frog can remember the location of many tadpoles. ▼

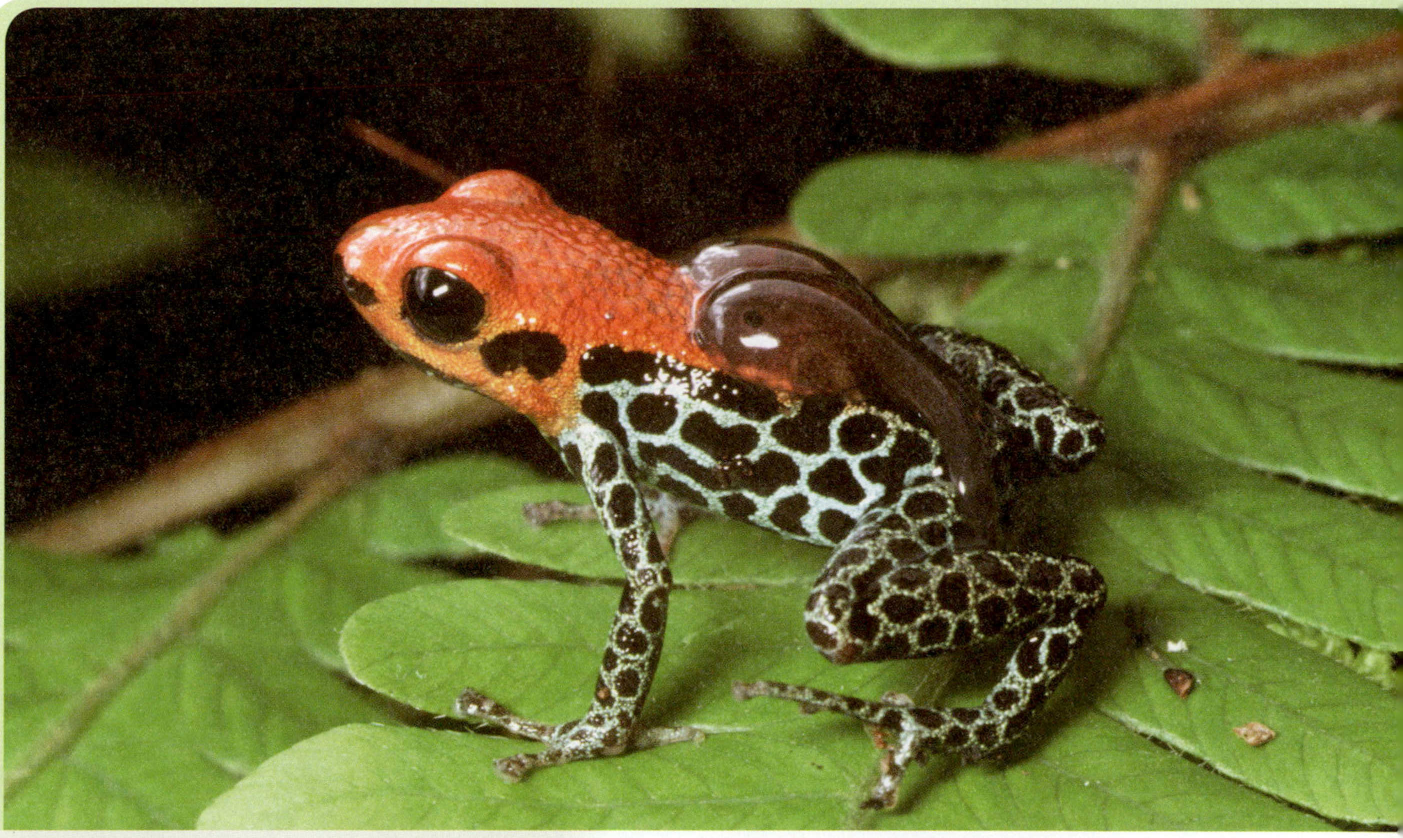

In Other Words

incredible very good

spot place

the location of where she put

Before You Move On

1. **Use Text Features** How do the two orangutan photos show **learned** behavior? Explain.
2. **Details** How does the poison dart frog show intelligence?

A Way with Words

It takes brains to talk. Scientists have found ways to talk with some of Earth's smartest animals. Koko the gorilla was one of the first animals to learn to communicate with human beings.

Scientists taught Koko sign **language** . That is a way to talk with your hands. When people talk, Koko answers in sign language. She can **sign** more than 1,000 words.

Sometimes Koko makes up a new sign. This tells us that Koko can **think on her own**. It also shows that she wants to communicate.

◄ **Koko uses sign language to communicate. Here, she uses the sign for** *eat*.

In Other Words
sign use sign **language** to say
think on her own
 create new signs by herself

Sound Signals

Meerkats don't communicate with people. Yet they do communicate with each other. These **chattering** animals make sounds that mean different things. Meerkats live in groups. While the group looks for food, one meerkat **stands guard**. It makes little peeps to tell the others that everything is safe. When danger is near, the guard meerkat changes the sound. It yelps, barks, or whistles.

▲ When meerkats are in danger, they give a warning. They make sounds when predators are near.

In Other Words
chattering noisy
stands guard watches for danger

▶ Before You Move On

1. **Make Connections** Compare and contrast Koko with another animal you know or have read about. How does each one communicate?

2. **Details** How do meerkats communicate with each other?

Look and Fetch

What can a dog do? It can stay, sit, roll over, and maybe a few other things. A pet dog may seem pretty smart to its owner. Yet some dogs have shown amazing **skill** at understanding language and pictures.

▲ **Many dogs can follow commands.**

Betsy is a clever border collie. She understands 340 **spoken words**. Many dogs can follow **commands**, but Betsy **takes it a step further**. When someone shows her a picture of an object, she goes and **fetches** that object. Betsy can fetch hundreds of different things.

Betsy can understand hundreds of spoken words. ▶

In Other Words

spoken words words that people say to her

takes it a step further does more

fetches gets

A Brainy Bird

Do you think a bird can **recognize** <mark>patterns</mark>? An African gray parrot named Alex could. He amazed scientists by figuring out patterns and then talking about them.

A scientist showed Alex a green cup and a green key. Then she asked the parrot what was the same about the objects. Alex said, "Color." Then the scientist asked what was different. Alex said, "Shape." Now that's a **brainy** bird!

Alex could figure out patterns based on different shapes and colors.

In Other Words
recognize find; notice
brainy smart

▶ **Before You Move On**
1. **Make Connections** Compare another animal you know to Betsy. How does each animal show its intelligence?
2. **Main Idea** How do Alex's actions demonstrate intelligence?

Outsmarting Humans

To play a trick on someone may take some intelligence, too. You have to guess how the person will act. Then you have to find a way to trick the person. Some animals have been terrific tricksters.

An orangutan named Fu Manchu tricked the **zookeepers** at the Omaha Zoo. He escaped from his home by tricking his zookeepers three times. First, he traded food with another orangutan for a piece of wire. Then he hid the wire in his mouth. Finally, he used the wire to **pick the lock** and set himself free!

An orangutan named Fu Manchu used a piece of wire to unlock his cage. ▶

Fu Manchu isn't the only animal to think of an escape plan. In one animal park, an elephant used her trunk to **take bolts off** a locked gate. Then she opened the gate and let all the elephants out.

In Other Words
take bolts off unlock

▶ **Before You Move On**
1. **Details** How did Fu Manchu outsmart people?
2. **Use Text Features** Look at the photo. Explain how an elephant might use its trunk to take a bolt off a locked gate.

Tricking the Trainers

A clever dolphin named Kelly knows how to get what she wants. Her trainers taught her to collect the trash that fell into her pool. When she gave it to a **keeper**, she got **a treat**. In this way, her pool stayed clean. Yet the tricky dolphin figured out how to trick her trainers.

Now when paper drops into her pool, she hides it. When the trainers come, she swims down and tears off a piece of the paper. She gives it to the trainers **in exchange for** a fish treat. Then she goes back and tears off another piece. She gets the same treat for small pieces as she gets for big pieces. So she tears off small pieces to make the paper last longer. That way, **the treats keep coming**!

◀ Dolphins are smart and playful animals. They can also learn tricks.

▶ **Before You Move On**
1. **Details** How does Kelly outsmart her trainers?
2. **Make Connections** Which of Kelly's actions are <mark>learned</mark> behaviors?

Learning About Animals

When scientists **observe** animals, they learn more about their behavior. They learn more about how the animals think and what they think about.

You may be amazed by the memory of a mother poison dart frog. You may be surprised that a parrot can talk about shapes, or that an elephant can plan a clever escape. Yet in the future, these **feats** may seem simple when we know even more about animals. Whether you **chat** with gorillas or **tidy** up with dolphins, it's clear that we have a lot more to learn about animals. ❖

Scientists learn about animals by observing their behavior. ▶

In Other Words
observe study
feats actions
chat talk
tidy clean

▶ **Before You Move On**

1. **Main Idea** What do scientists <mark>learn</mark> by studying animal behavior?

2. **Use Text Features** Describe what is happening in the photo on this page. Use the caption to help you.

Talk About It

Key Words

ability	learn
command	memory
communication	pattern
inherit	skill
language	tool

1. What facts did you **learn** from this **science article**?

   I learned that _____ . I also learned that _____ .

2. Think of an animal you read about in this article. **Engage in conversation** with a partner about what you found out.

3. How is animal **communication** like human communication? How is it different?

   Animals and humans both _____ .
   Some animals _____ , but humans _____ .

Learn test-taking strategies.
🌐 NGReach.com

Write About It

What are some amazing ways animals use **tools**? Make a list. Give examples from the article. Try to use **Key Words**.

Animals use tools to:

1.

2.

Main Idea and Details

Make a main idea diagram for "Animal Smarts."

Main Idea Diagram

Main Idea: Animals are _____ .
Detail:
Detail:

Write the main idea as a complete sentence.

Add details that support the main idea.

Now use your diagram as you explain the ideas in "Animal Smarts" to a partner. Use as many **Key Words** as you can.

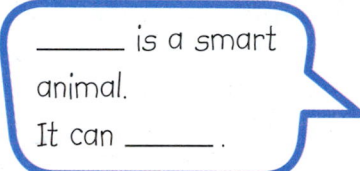

_____ is a smart animal.
It can _____ .

Fluency Comprehension Coach

Use the Comprehension Coach to practice reading with intonation. Rate your reading.

Talk Together

Just how smart are chimpanzees, gorillas, meerkats, parrots, elephants, and dolphins? Choose one animal. Use **Key Words** to explain why you think that animal is so smart.

Use a Dictionary

A **dictionary** is a book with information about words. You might use a dictionary to find out the meaning of a word or to see how a word is spelled or pronounced. Look at these dictionary entries.

> This shows how to say the word. It also shows the syllables.

imitate (im-u-tāt) *verb* To copy someone or something

inherit (in-**hair**-ut) *verb* **1** To receive money or other property from a person who has died **2** To get a particular characteristic passed down from your parents *You inherit eye color from your parents.*

> This word has two different meanings.

Try It Together

Read the dictionary entry. Then answer the questions.

train (trān) *noun* **1** Railroad cars hooked together **2** A long piece of fabric behind a bride's dress *verb* **3** To teach a person or animal how to do something **4** to make a plant grow in a certain way

1. **Which meaning fits this sentence?** *Her white train was made of lace.*

   A meaning 1

   B meaning 2

   C meaning 3

   D meaning 4

2. **Which meaning fits this sentence?** *I want to train my cat to jump through a hoop.*

   A meaning 1

   B meaning 2

   C meaning 3

   D meaning 4

NATIONAL
GEOGRAPHIC
EXCLUSIVE

Connect Across Texts
Read this article to **learn** what one scientist discovered while studying chimpanzees.

Genre A **science article** can tell about a new discovery in science.

THE CLEVER CHIMPS OF
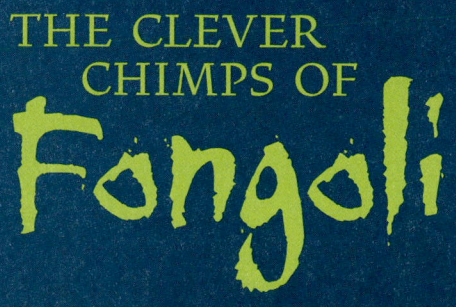

by Elizabeth Sengel

It's hard to get a meal in Fongoli. The **harsh** landscape offers only **patches of greenery**. The sun burns like a 200-watt bulb. By eight o'clock in the morning, the rocky, treeless ground **bakes** in 90-degree heat.

▲ Chimps walk across dry ground in Fongoli.

In Other Words
harsh dry and hot
patches of greenery a few places with trees and plants
bakes gets really hot

▶ **Before You Move On**
1. **Make Connections** What does Fongoli remind you of? Explain.
2. **Use Text Features** What can you tell about this article from the title, the photo, and the caption?

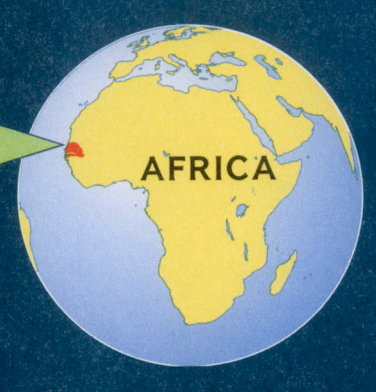
AFRICA

▼ Rainforest chimps live in trees.

▼ In Fongoli, chimps live on the savanna, or dry grassland.

Home on the Range

Fongoli is located in the African country of Senegal. It is the home of a community of savanna-woodland chimpanzees. These animals are different from rainforest chimps, which live among leafy trees. Fongoli chimps spend most of their lives on the ground. At night, they sleep in low trees that surround the open spaces. During the day, they **wander** across the **vast range** looking for food.

In Other Words
wander walk
vast range open land

▲ Jill Pruetz, an anthropologist at Iowa State University, studies the skull of a savanna-woodland chimp.

A Champion Chimp-Watcher

Jill Pruetz knows all about these chimps. She visits Fongoli often to study them. It's hot, **exhausting** work. Six days a week, she **rises at dawn** and steps out of her mud hut. She follows the chimps all day long, observing their behavior and **jotting down** notes. In 2007, Pruetz made big news in the scientific world. She reported something **astounding**. Some Fongoli chimps had invented a new way to find food!

In Other Words
exhausting tiring
rises at dawn gets up early
jotting down writing
astounding surprising

▶ **Before You Move On**

1. **Compare/Contrast** What is the main difference between the Fongoli chimps and rainforest chimps?

2. **Make Connections** The author says Pruetz's work is "exhausting." What sounds exhausting about it?

133

▲ A chimp pushes a sharpened stick into a tree hole.

Whittling Weapons

The clever chimps had figured out how to make a spear-like **tool**. First, they break a branch off a tree and rip away the leaves. Then they **sharpen** one end of the stick with their teeth. They use the spears to hunt bush babies. These are small animals that sleep in **hollow** tree trunks during the day. The chimps look for an opening in a hollow tree **limb**. Then they **jab** the weapon through the opening to try to kill their prey.

▲ A bush baby in a hollow tree trunk

▲ Pruetz holds the sharp tool made by a Fongoli chimp.

In Other Words
sharpen make a sharp point at
hollow holes in
limb branch
jab push

134

Getting Creative

In Fongoli, the chimps **compete for** limited amounts of food. When big males find food, they have very bad manners! Like greedy children, they **refuse to** share. Females and young males have to find their own food. Pruetz believes that this situation has forced them to become creative. That's what led to their tool-making.

Teva is a young chimp in Fongoli. Her mother is one of the best hunters. Will Teva's mother teach her how to make spears? "It will be interesting to see if Teva **picks it up**," Pruetz says.

If Teva learns this skill, she will find it easier to eat in Fongoli. ❖

Teva, a young chimp in Fongoli, learns from her mother. ▶

In Other Words
compete for fight over
refuse to will not
picks it up learns

▶ **Before You Move On**

1. **Problem/Solution** How have the Fongoli chimps solved the problem of finding food? Explain.

2. **Draw Conclusions** Why do the chimps of Fongoli have to be creative?

135

Compare Facts

Both articles give facts about chimps.
Compare the articles. Work with a partner
to complete the comparison chart. Look for more facts in the
articles. Add them to your chart.

Key Words

ability	learn
command	memory
communication	pattern
inherit	skill
language	tool

Comparison Chart

Fact	"Animal Smarts"	"The Clever Chimps of Fongoli"
Chimps walk on the ground.	√	√
Rainforest chimps live in trees.		√
Chimps eat insects.		
Some chimps eat bush babies.		
In 1960, Jane Goodall made an important discovery about chimps.		
Chimps use tools.		

Talk Together

Think about the two articles you read. What are some ways that chimps
are smart? What are some of the reasons they need to be smart? Ask
questions to find out what others believe. Use **Key Words** to talk about
your ideas.

Compound Sentences

A **compound sentence** is made up of two complete sentences. The sentences are joined by *and, but,* or *or* with a comma before the word.

| I like plants. | + | I really love animals. |

I like plants, but I really love animals.

Grammar Rules Compound Sentences

• Use **and** to put together two ideas that are alike.	Some animals can solve problems, **and** they use tools to help them.
• Use **but** to show a difference between two ideas.	Animals know some things at birth, **but** they must learn other things from their parents.
• Use **or** to show a choice between two ideas.	Animals might communicate with sounds, **or** they might use signs.

Read Compound Sentences

Read this passage from "Animal Smarts." Find the compound sentence. What word is used to join the sentences?

Betsy is a clever border collie. She understands 340 spoken words. Many dogs can follow commands, but Betsy takes it a step further.

Write Compound Sentences

Write two compound sentences about the chimps of Fongoli. Use different connecting words. Read your sentences to a partner.

Write as a Researcher

Write a Business Letter ✏️

You want to find out just how smart a certain animal is and how much it can learn. Write a letter to a scientist who studies animal behavior.

Study a Model

A business letter is written to someone you don't know. Read the business letter Mike wrote to ask for information about squirrels.

The **heading**, at the top, shows Mike's address and the date.

134 Oak Street
Stafford, Virginia 22556
October 7, 20—

The **inside address** shows the name and address of the person Mike is writing.

Dr. Anne Velardi
Andrews University
5549 Darian Ave.
Cincinnati, OH 45324

The **greeting** ends with a **colon**.

Dear Dr. Velardi**:**

In the **body**, Mike asks for information and then says "thank you."

My friends and I want to make a funny video about a squirrel that causes trouble. Could you please answer some questions?

First, how smart are squirrels? Can squirrels do tricks, such as jump onto someone's head? How fast can they learn? Thank you very much for your help.

A **formal closing** and **signature** end the letter.

Sincerely,

Mike Wheeler

Prewrite

1. **Choose a Topic** What animal do you want to learn about? Talk with a partner to choose an interesting one.

Language Frames	
Tell Your Ideas	**Respond to Ideas**
• I don't know much about _____ .	• What do you already know about _____ ?
• I've heard that a _____ is smart. I'd like to know just how smart.	• We all know how smart a _____ is. Could you choose a different animal?
• Are _____ smart enough to _____ ?	• I am curious about _____ , too! Great idea!

2. **Gather Information** Brainstorm questions that will help you find out how smart your animal is. Use question words such as *how*, *why*, and *what*.

3. **Get Organized** Use a main idea diagram to help you organize your questions.

Main Idea Diagram

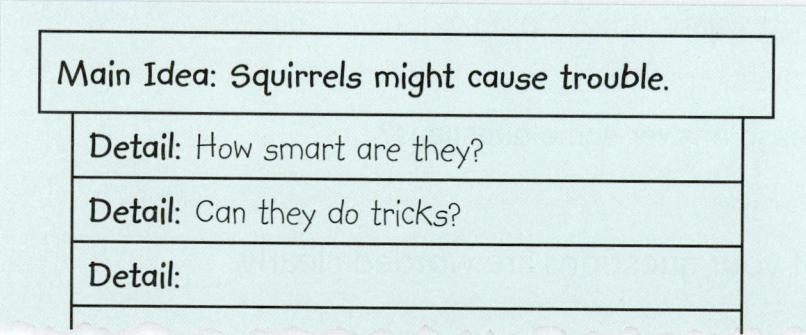

Main Idea: Squirrels might cause trouble.

Detail: How smart are they?

Detail: Can they do tricks?

Detail:

Draft

Use your main idea diagram to write your draft. Include all of the important parts of the letter in the correct order. Remember to be clear about the information you need.

Revise

1. **Read, Retell, Respond** Read your draft aloud to a partner. Your partner listens, and then restates the important information. Next, talk about ways to improve your letter.

Language Frames	
Retell	**Make Suggestions**
• You want to know about _____ .	• The _____ is missing from your letter.
• You want to know if _____ can _____ and _____ .	• I don't understand the question about _____ . Can you ask in a different way?
• You'll use the information to _____ .	• The _____ seems out of order.

2. **Make Changes** Think about your draft and your partner's suggestions. Check that you've included all the parts of a business letter. Use the Revising Marks on page 585 to mark any changes.

   • Is your purpose for writing the letter clear?

   > My friends and I want to make a funny video about a squirrel that causes trouble.
   > ∧Could you please answer some questions?

   • Make sure all of your questions are worded clearly.

   > to do tricks, such as jump on someone's head?
   > Can squirrels learn stuff?

Edit and Proofread

Work with a partner to edit and proofread your business letter. Try using sentences of different lengths and types. This will make your writing more interesting.

Publish

On Your Own Make a clean copy of your letter. Read it aloud to others. See if any of your listeners can answer your questions.

Punctuation Tip

✓ In compound sentences, put a **comma** before the conjunction *and*, *or*, or *but*.

End every question with a **question mark**.

Presentation Tips	
If you are the speaker . . .	**If you are the listener . . .**
Read as if you were speaking to the person that the letter is for.	Listen carefully. Is it clear what information the speaker wants?
When you read a question, make your voice go up slightly at the end.	Jot down notes about the information the speaker is looking for.

In a Group Work together to find the answers to all of the questions in your letters. Post the questions and answers on the bulletin board, or create a Web site that you can add to.

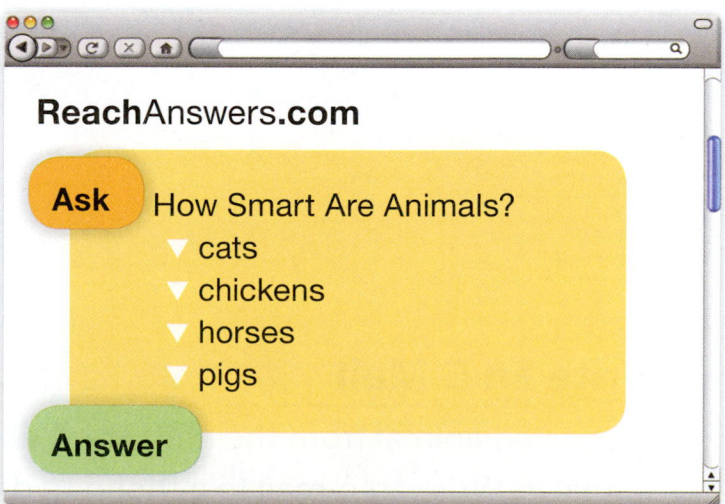

ReachAnswers.com

Ask How Smart Are Animals?
▼ cats
▼ chickens
▼ horses
▼ pigs

Answer

141

Talk Together

In this unit, you found lots of answers to the **Big Question**. Now use your concept map to discuss the **Big Question** with the class.

Concept Map

Smart things animals can do

defend themselves

Write an E-Mail

Choose an animal from the unit. Think about how intelligent this animal is. Write an e-mail to a friend to describe how smart this animal is.

Share Your Ideas

Choose one of these ways to share your ideas about the
Big Question.

Do It!

Design a Maze

Use art materials to design a maze for a mouse. Then display your design for the class. Tell a partner how the maze might be used to test the animal's intelligence.

Write It!

Write a Comic

Write a comic strip that tells a trickster tale. Include a main character that plays tricks on others. Draw pictures to go with your story. Share your comic with the class.

Talk About It!

Discuss Animal Smarts

What is the smartest animal you can think of? Find facts to support your choice. You can use your experiences, too. Which animals do other members in your group choose? See if the group can agree on the smartest animal.

Do It!

Put on a Puppet Show

Make puppets for the characters in "Love and Roast Chicken." Then perform a puppet show to retell the story.

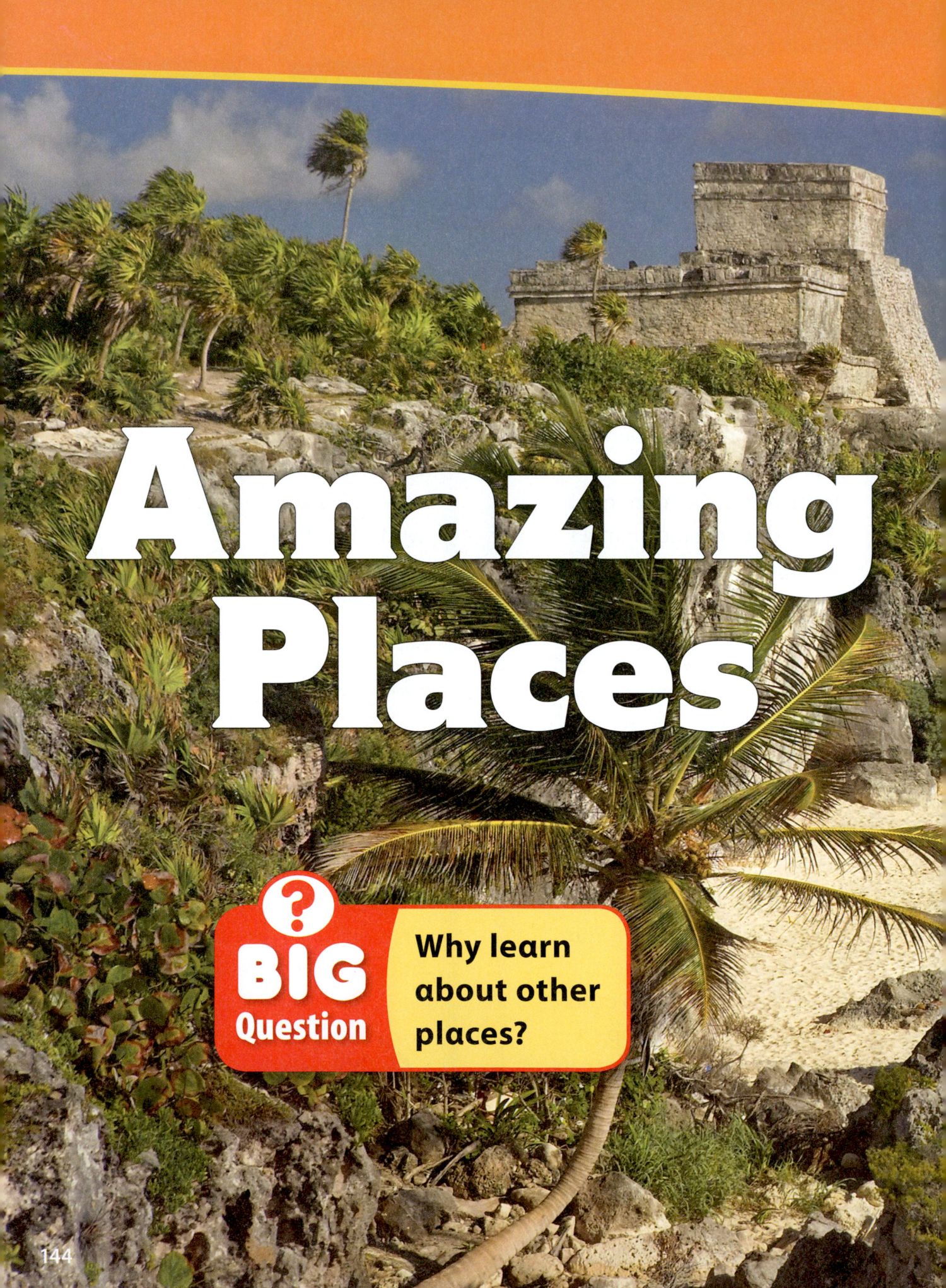

Amazing Places

BIG Question

Why learn about other places?

Unit at a Glance
▶ **Language**: Give and Follow Directions, Describe Places, Social Studies Words
▶ **Literacy**: Visualize
▶ **Content**: Geography

Unit 3

Share What You Know

Do It!

❶ **Make** a story strip about a place you have visited or would like to visit.

❷ **Display** your story strip in the classroom.

❸ **Tell** the class the best things about the place.

Build Background: Watch a video about amazing places.
🌐 NGReach.com

Language Frames

- Go to _____ .
- Look for _____ .
- Follow _____ .

Give and Follow Directions

Listen to Vanita's chant. Then use **Language Frames** to give directions to a place you know.

Chant

A Map to My Home

Go to the corner.
    Turn left at the light.
Look for the bus stop.
    Then turn right.

Follow the road
    to where it ends.
That's where I'll find
    my family and friends.

East or west—
    wherever I roam
Following my map
    will lead me home.

Key Words

Look at the picture. Use **Key Words** and other words to talk about geography.

A **globe** is one kind of **map**.

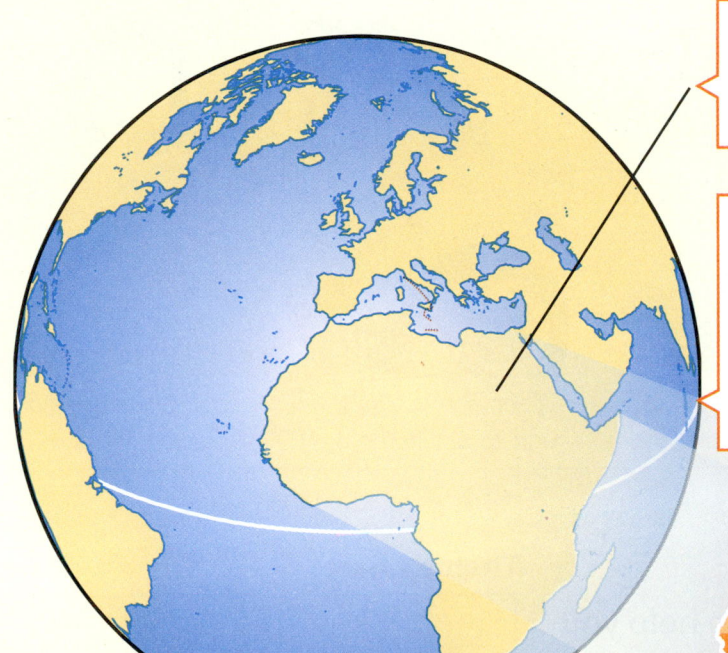

A **continent** is a large mass of land. This is the continent of Africa.

The **equator** is an imaginary line around Earth's middle. It divides the Earth into two **hemispheres**, or halves.

AFRICA

There are many different countries in Africa. The people who live in a **country** are its **inhabitants**.

Talk Together

How does a globe or map help you learn about a place? Use a globe or map to give and follow directions with a partner. Try to use **Language Frames** from page 146 and **Key Words**.

Theme

The main message of a story is its **theme**. Use clues in the story to figure out its theme. Look for clues in the title, the characters, and the plot or events in the story.

Find out about a story that Vanita read.

"What's this about?"

"A girl couldn't wait to see the world."

"Then she couldn't wait to get home."

"It's about why home is good."

Map and Talk

You can make a theme chart to help you identify the message of a story. Write the title, setting, characters, and plot. Think about how these parts work together to give a message. Then write a sentence that tells the theme of the story.

Theme Chart

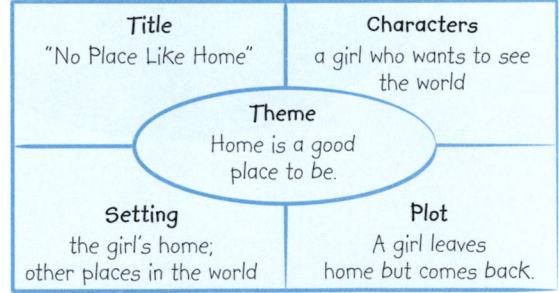

Title	Characters
"No Place Like Home"	a girl who wants to see the world
Theme	
Home is a good place to be.	
Setting	Plot
the girl's home; other places in the world	A girl leaves home but comes back.

Talk Together

Make a theme chart about a story you know. List the title, setting, characters, and plot. Use the chart to explain the theme to a partner.

More Key Words

Use these words to talk about "How I Learned Geography" and "Tortillas Like Africa."

border
(**bor**-dur) *noun*

A **border** is an edge or outline. The frame makes a **border** around the art.

imagine
(i-**ma**-jun) *verb*

To **imagine** something is to picture it in your mind. Your art shows others what you **imagine**.

range
(rānj) *noun*

A **range** is a group of things in a certain order. The Rocky Mountains are a mountain **range**.

suggest
(sug-**jest**) *verb*

To **suggest** is to give someone an idea. These colors **suggest** strong heat.

transport
(trans-**port**) *verb*

To **transport** something is to carry it. Large ships **transport** goods across the ocean.

Talk Together

Use a **Key Word** to ask a question. Your partner uses a different **Key Word** to answer.

Have you ever seen a mountain range?

No, but I can imagine it!

Add words to My Vocabulary Notebook.
NGReach.com

Learn to Visualize

Look at the picture. Imagine, or **visualize**, what Vanita sees from the balloon. Imagine what she hears and feels.

You use all of your senses to **visualize** when you read, too.

How to Visualize

1. Look for details. Find words that tell how things look, sound, smell, taste, and feel to the touch.

2. Use the details to picture things in your mind.

3. Tell how visualizing the story details makes you feel. How does it help you connect to the story?

I read _____ .

I picture _____ .

I feel _____ .

Talk Together

Read Vanita's letter. Read the sample. Then use **Language Frames** as you tell a partner what you visualize.

Letter

November 10, 2010

Dear Vicki,

Hello from Brazil! Remember how we spent last winter looking at your **map** of South America? That really **transported** us to other **countries**. Now I am really here. It is even more beautiful than I **imagined**.

Today we are visiting Iguazú Falls, a waterfall on the **border** between Brazil and Argentina. The paths take you right up to the water. You can feel the cool, wet spray splash your face.

It's very hot. There are lots of bugs, too. But I don't mind. The views are worth some sweating and scratching. Right now, birds are calling to each other. I hope some of them eat bugs.

We have taken many long bus rides here. But the seats are very comfortable.

I have seen a lot of amazing geography from the bus window. We crossed the mountain **range** called the Andes. The bus driver stopped there so we could see the sunset. As the sun sank behind the mountains, the sky turned orange and red.

Love,

Your cousin Vanita

P.S. I **suggest** that you visit Brazil one day!

Sample Visualizing

"I read that you can feel the spray of water on your face.

I picture cool water in the summer.

I feel happy and cool."

◄ = A good place to visualize

151

Read a Story

Genre

A **fictional tale** is an imaginative account of a series of events.

Setting

The setting of a story is where and when the events happen.

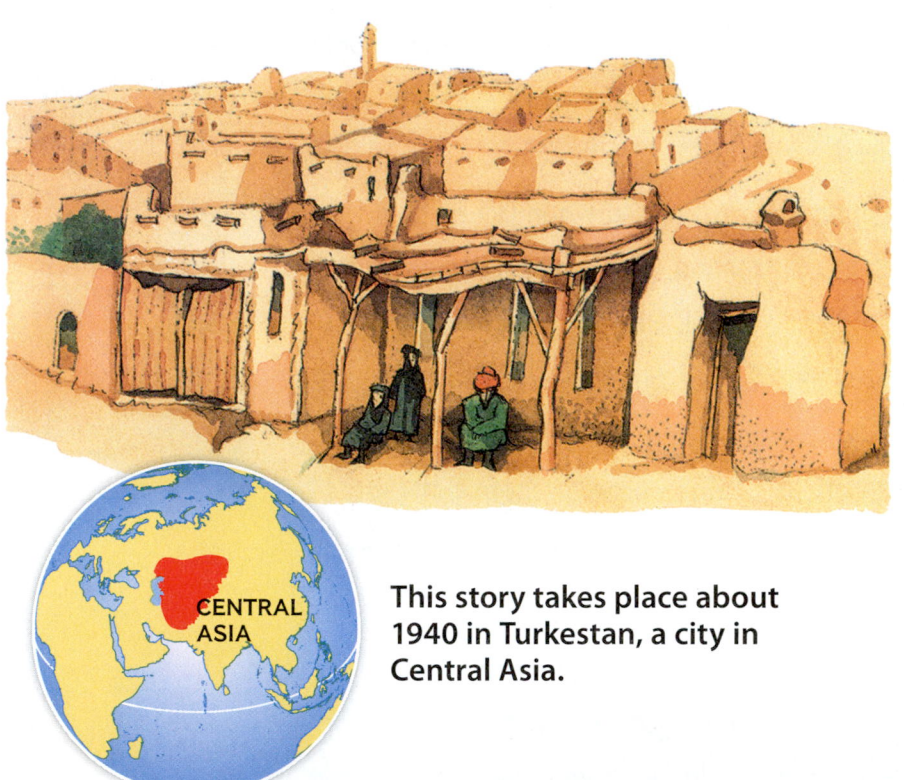

This story takes place about 1940 in Turkestan, a city in Central Asia.

How I Learned
Geography

by Uri Shulevitz

Comprehension Coach

When war **devastated** the land,
buildings crumbled to dust. Everything we had
was **lost**, and we **fled empty-handed**.

In Other Words
devastated destroyed; ruined
lost gone
fled empty-handed left with nothing

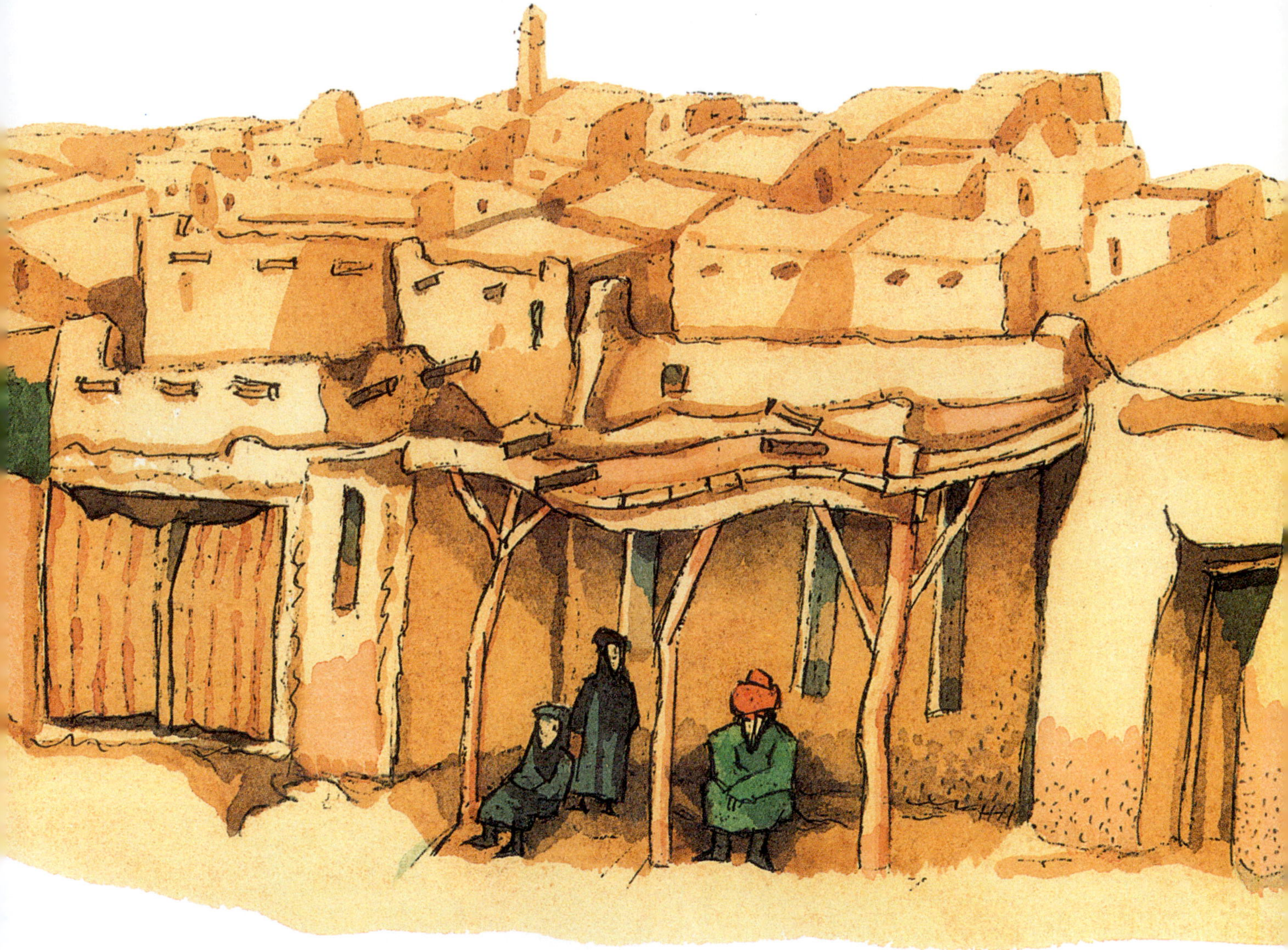

We traveled far, far east to another **country**, where summers were hot and winters were cold, to a city of houses made of clay, straw, and camel dung, surrounded by dusty **steppes**, burned by the sun.

In Other Words

steppes plains; flat lands

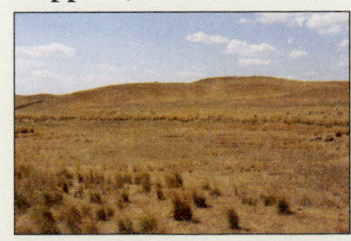

Before You Move On

1. **Setting** Where does the family go after leaving their home?
2. **Figurative Language** What does the author mean by the phrase "burned by the sun"? What would a place like that look like?

▶ **Predict**
What will the family's life be like
in this new <mark>country</mark>?

We lived in a small room with a **couple** we did
not know. We slept on a dirt floor. I had no toys and no
books. Worst of all, **food was scarce**.

In Other Words
couple husband and wife
food was scarce there
was not much food

156

One day, Father went to the **bazaar** to buy bread.
As evening **approached**, he hadn't returned. Mother
and I were worried and hungry.

It was nearly dark when he came home. He carried a long roll of paper under his arm.

"I bought a map," he **announced triumphantly**.

"Where is the bread?" Mother asked.

"I bought a map," he said again.

Mother and I said nothing.

"I had enough money to buy only a tiny piece of bread, and we would still be hungry," he explained apologetically.

"No supper tonight," Mother said **bitterly**. "We'll have the map instead."

In Other Words
announced triumphantly
said proudly
bitterly quietly with anger

I was **furious**. I didn't think I would ever forgive him, and I went to bed hungry, while the couple we lived with ate their **meager supper**.

The husband was a writer. He wrote in silence, but oh how loudly he chewed! He chewed a small crust of bread with such enthusiasm, as if it were the most delicious morsel in the <mark>world</mark>. I **envied him** his bread and wished I were the one chewing it. I covered my head with my blanket so I would not hear him smacking his lips with such noisy delight.

In Other Words
furious very angry
meager supper small dinner
envied him wanted

▶ **Before You Move On**

1. **Confirm Prediction** Was your prediction correct? Describe the family's life in this new place.

2. **Visualize** Imagine you are the boy under the blanket. How does it feel? What do you see and do?

The next day Father hung the map. It **took up** an entire wall. Our cheerless room was **flooded** with color.

I became fascinated by the map and spent long hours looking at it, studying its every detail, and many days drawing it on any scrap of paper that **chanced my way**.

In Other Words
took up covered
flooded filled
chanced my way I found

160

I found strange-sounding names on the map and **savored their exotic sounds**, making a little rhyme out of them:

Fukuoka Takaoka Omsk,

Fukuyama Nagayama Tomsk,

Okazaki Miyazaki Pinsk,

Pennsylvania Transylvania Minsk!

I repeated this rhyme and was **transported** far away without ever leaving our room.

In Other Words
savored their exotic sounds enjoyed
the unusual way they sounded

▶ **Before You Move On**

1. **Theme** What does the **map** mean to the boy?
2. **Visualize** What do you picture when you think of the boy being **transported** by the rhyme?

▶ **Predict**

What will the boy learn from
his father?

I landed in **burning** deserts. I ran on beaches and felt
their sand between my toes. I climbed snowy mountains where
icy winds **licked** my face.

I saw **wondrous temples** where stone carvings danced on
the walls, and birds of all colors sang on the rooftops.

In Other Words
burning very hot
icy very cold
licked blew against
wondrous temples wonderful buildings

I passed through **fruit groves**, eating as many papayas and mangos as I pleased. I drank fresh water and rested in the shade of palm trees.

I came to a city of tall buildings and counted **zillions** of windows, falling asleep before I could finish.

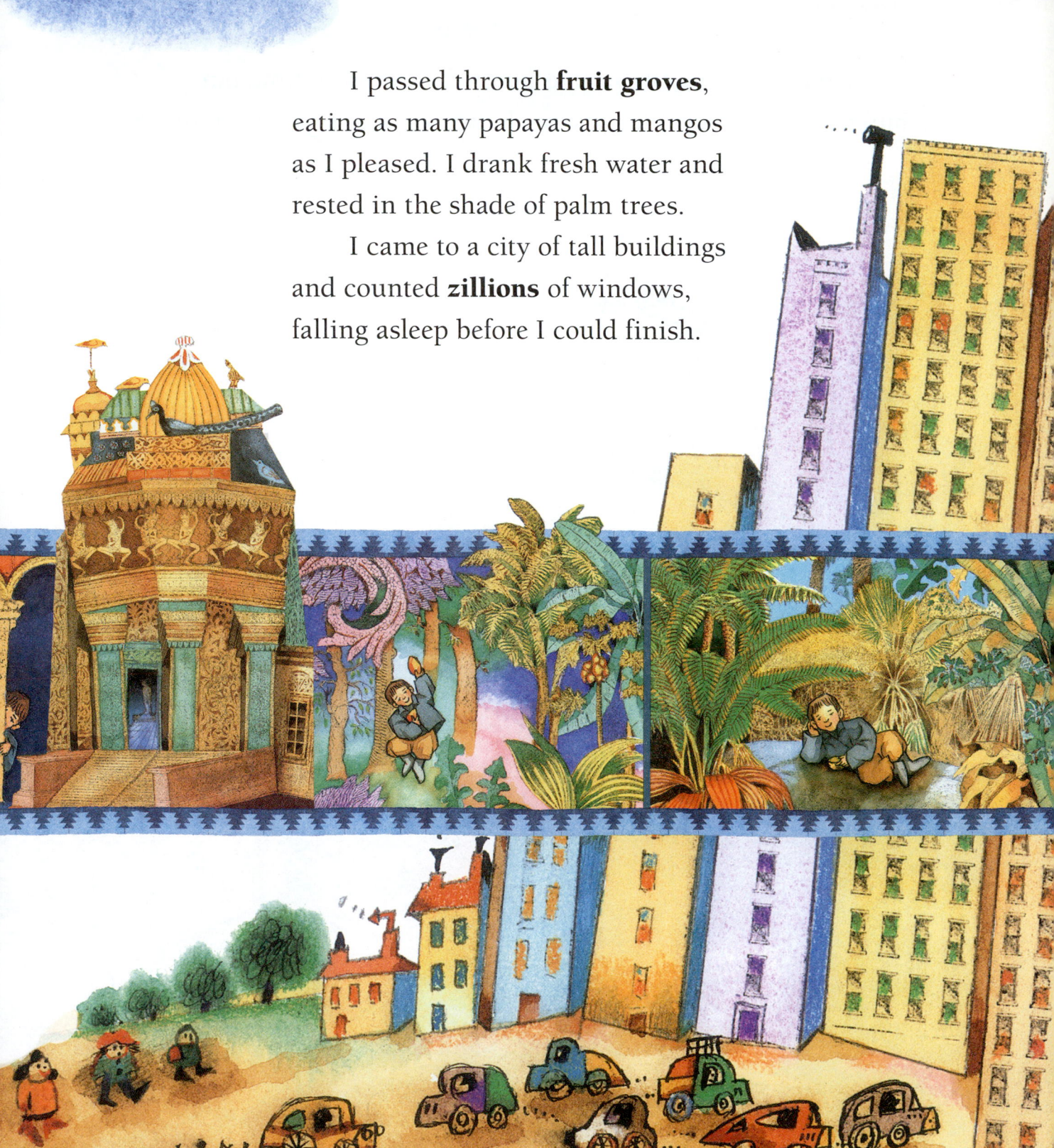

In Other Words

fruit groves areas where fruit trees grow

zillions millions and millions

And so I spent **enchanted hours** far, far away from our hunger and **misery**. I forgave my father. He was right, after all. ❖

In Other Words

enchanted hours
    hours filled with wonder

misery sadness

▶ **Before You Move On**

1. **Confirm Prediction** What does the boy learn from his father? Was your prediction correct?

2. **Theme** What does the boy mean when he says that his father "was right, after all"?

Meet the Author and Illustrator
Uri Shulevitz

Imagine what it would be like to wander for ten years without a real home. That's how Uri Shulevitz spent ten years of his childhood.

Shulevitz was born in Poland in 1935. World War II began when he was just four years old. A bomb fell on his family's apartment. Soon after, the family moved to Central Asia, where this story is set. Later, the family moved to France. Shulevitz explains, "I changed schools and languages frequently because of the war years. The only constant in my life was my drawing."

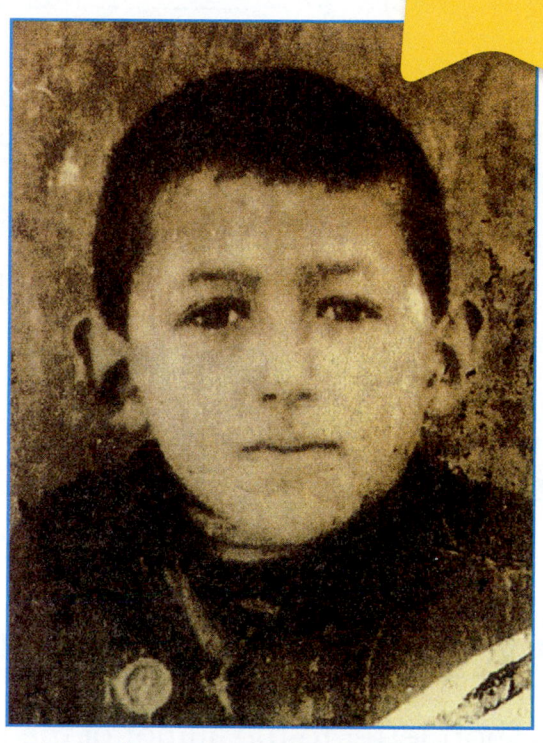

▲ This photograph shows Uri Shulevitz as a boy, when he lived in Central Asia.

Writer's Craft

Look at the way the author describes the places the boy imagines on pages 162 and 163. Now imagine a place you have been or would like to visit. Write a brief paragraph that uses figurative language to describe what this place is like.

Talk About It

Key Words

border	imagine
continent	inhabitant
country	map
equator	range
globe	suggest
hemisphere	transport

1. How do you know that this story is a **fictional tale**?

   The story tells about _____ . It has _____ .

2. With a partner, pretend you are the boy and his dad looking at the **map**. Use it to **give and follow directions**.

3. How do you think the boy felt about leaving his **country**? Tell a partner. Use information from the story and your own experience.

Learn test-taking strategies.
NGReach.com

Write About It

Write a short letter to the author of the story. Use **Key Words** to tell what you liked and what questions you have.

November 10, 2010

Dear Mr. Shulevitz,

   My favorite part of the story was _____ .
I would like to know _____ .

   Sincerely,

Theme

Make a theme chart for "How I Learned Geography." What message does this story have? Look for clues and write them in the chart.

Theme Chart

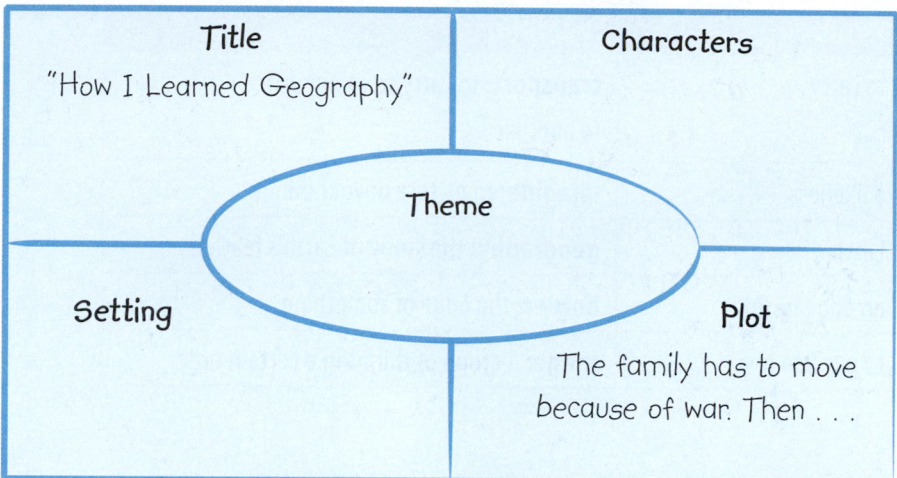

Now use your chart as you summarize the story with a partner. Explain how you decided on the theme. Use as many **Key Words** as you can.

> The story is about _____.
> Important details are _____.
> The theme is _____.

Fluency Comprehension Coach

Use the Comprehension Coach to practice reading with intonation. Rate your reading.

Talk Together

How did learning about other places help the boy? Plan a skit based on the story. Try to include **Key Words**. Act it out for the class.

Word Origins

Many English words have **roots** from other languages. If you know the root, you may be able to figure out the meaning of the word.

Word Origins Chart

Origin	Root	Meaning	Example
Latin	*port*	to carry	**transport:** to carry from one place to another
	imag	a likeness	**imagine:** to picture in your mind
Greek	*geo*	Earth	**geography:** the study of Earth's features
Old French	*bord*	an edge or side	**border:** the edge of something
	rangier	to put in a row	**range:** a group of things in a certain order

Try It Together

Read each item. Choose the best answer.

1. **Which word has something to do with Earth?**

   A gorgeous

   B pigeon

   C geologist

   D gentle

2. **Which word has something to do with carrying an object?**

   A portable

   B pork

   C vapor

   D particle

Connect Across Texts Read this poem about how two boys **imagine** and create the shapes of different **countries** .

Genre **Free verse** is poetry that does not have a regular pattern of rhythm and usually does not rhyme.

Tortillas Like Africa

by Gary Soto   illustrations by Joel Nakamura

When Isaac and I squeezed dough over a mixing bowl,

When we dusted the cutting board with flour,

When we spanked and palmed our balls of dough,

When we said, "Here goes,"

And began rolling out tortillas,

We giggled because ours came out not round, like Mama's,

But in the shapes of faraway lands.

In Other Words
dusted sprinkled
spanked and palmed flattened

▶ **Before You Move On**

1. **Visualize** How do you picture the scene in this poem? Describe what you see, feel, and hear.

2. **Poetry** How can you tell that this poem is written in free verse? Give examples from the poem.

Here was Africa, here were Colombia and Greenland.

Here was Italy, the boot country,

And here was México, our homeland to the south.

Here was Chile, thin as a tie.

Here was France, square as a hat.

Here was Australia, with patches of jumping kangaroos.

We rolled out our tortillas on the board

And laughed when we threw them on the *comal*,

These tortillas that were not round as a pocked moon,

But the twist and stretch of the earth taking shape.

In Other Words

comal flat Mexican frying pan (in Spanish)

◄ **pocked moon** moon that's full of holes

So we made our first batch of tortillas, laughing.

So we wrapped them in a dish towel.

So we buttered and rolled two each

And sat on the front porch—

Butter ran down our arms and our faces shone.

I asked Isaac, "How's yours?"

He cleared his throat and opened his tortilla.

He said, *"¡Bueno!* Greenland tastes like México."

In Other Words

¡Bueno! Good! (in Spanish)

▶ **Before You Move On**

1. **Figurative Language** Which words help you picture the shapes of the <mark>countries</mark>?
2. **Make Inferences** What does Isaac mean when he says that Greenland tastes like Mexico?

Key Words

border	imagine
continent	inhabitant
country	map
equator	range
globe	suggest
hemisphere	transport

Compare Figurative Language

Authors use figurative language to make their writing vivid and interesting. Review these types of figurative language:

- A **simile** compares two things using the words *like* or *as*.

- A **metaphor** compares two things without using *like* or *as*.

- **Personification** gives human traits to animals or things.

Work with a partner to complete the chart. Add more examples of figurative language from the story and the poem. Label each as a simile, a metaphor, or personification.

Figurative Language Chart

"How I Learned Geography"	"Tortillas Like Africa"
Icy winds licked my face. (personification)	"Here was Chile, thin as a tie." (simile)

> The author gives a human trait to the wind.

> The poet compares the shape of Chile to a thin tie.

Talk Together

Think about the characters in the story and the poem. What helped them **imagine** the world? Use **Key Words** to talk about your ideas.

Plural Nouns

A **singular noun** shows "one." A **plural noun** shows "more than one."

Grammar Rules Plural Nouns

	singular noun	plural noun
• Add **-s** to most nouns to show more than one.	map globe	map**s** globe**s**
• Add **-es** to nouns that end in **s**, **z**, **ch**, **sh**, **x**, and sometimes **o**.	beach box	beach**es** box**es**
• For most nouns that end in **y** after a consonant, change the **y** to **i** and then add **-es**. For nouns that end with a vowel and **y**, just add **-s**.	city country journey toy	cit**ies** countr**ies** journey**s** toy**s**

Read Plural Nouns

Read these sentences from "How I Learned Geography." What plural nouns can you find?

> I saw wondrous temples where stone carvings danced on the walls, and birds of all colors sang on the rooftops.

Write Plural Nouns

What do you like to learn from maps? Write a sentence for your partner. Use a plural noun.

Describe Places

Listen to Ethan's song. Then use **Language Frames** to describe a place you know.

My Travels

Song

I travel to China to see the Great Wall.
The wall has stone towers. They're twenty feet tall.

I see Machu Picchu when I'm in Peru.
This city is stunning. The mountains are, too.

I travel to London to visit Big Ben.
This clock rings the hours again and again.

I travel to Egypt and follow the Nile.
It feels warm and peaceful for a young crocodile.

Tune: "On Top of Old Smoky"

Social Studies Vocabulary

Key Words

Key Words

canyon

elevation

landform

ocean

plain

plateau

valley

Look at the picture. Use **Key Words** and other words to talk about different **landforms**.

A **valley** is a low area.

A **plateau** is flat but has a higher **elevation** than a plain.

A **plain** is a large, flat area.

A **canyon** is a deep cut in the earth made by water.

An **ocean** is a very large body of water.

Talk Together

Why learn about landforms? Use **Language Frames** from page 174 and **Key Words** as you describe places with a partner. Share what you know about different landforms.

Main Idea and Details

When you want to describe an experience, you tell about it in a logical order. First, tell the **main idea**. Then add **details** that support it.

Look at the photos from Ethan's trip.

The Great Wall of China has stone towers.

Machu Picchu is an ancient city on a mountain in Peru.

Map and Talk

You can make an outline to show main ideas and details. Here's how to make one. Write the first main idea. Then add details that support it. Repeat for each main idea.

Outline

I. Ethan goes to China.
  A. He sees the Great Wall.
  B. The wall has stone towers.
II. Ethan goes to Peru.
  A. He sees the city of Machu Picchu.
  B. It is on a mountain.

> Use Roman numerals for main ideas.

> Use capital letters for details that support the main idea.

Talk Together

Reread the song on page 174. Make an outline about the last two places Ethan visits.

176

More Key Words

Use these words to talk about "Extreme Earth" and "Photographing the World."

feature
(**fē**-chur) *noun*

A **feature** is part of something. Sharp teeth are **features** that help sharks hunt.

locate
(**lō**-kāt) *verb*

To **locate** is to find. We use maps to **locate** cities and states.

physical
(**fi**-zi-kul) *adjective*

Something you can see and touch is a **physical** object.

region
(**rē**-jun) *noun*

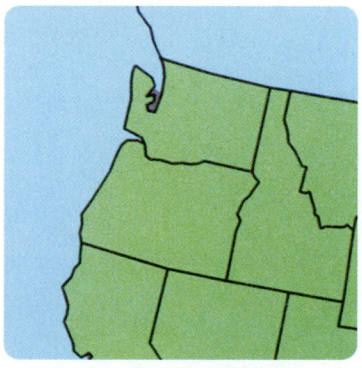

A **region** is an area of land. Oregon is in the northwest **region** of the country.

surface
(**sur**-fus) *noun*

The **surface** of something is its top layer or cover. A table has a flat **surface**.

Talk Together

Make a Vocabulary Example Chart for each **Key Word**. Share your charts with a partner.

Word	Definition	Example from My Life
feature	a characteristic	The best feature of my cat is her soft fur.

Add words to My Vocabulary Notebook.

 **NGReach.com**

Learn to Visualize

Look at the picture. **Visualize** yourself in Ethan's place. What would it be like?

You **visualize** when you read, too.

How to Visualize

 1. As you read, look for words that describe people, places, and events.

 2. Use the words to create pictures in your mind.

 3. Draw what you see in your mind.

 4. Ask yourself, "How does this help me understand?"

I read _____ .

I picture _____ .

I draw _____ .

Now I understand _____ .

Language Frames

👁	I read _____ .
💭	I picture _____ .
✏	I draw _____ .
🧑	Now I understand _____ .

Talk Together

Read Ethan's personal narrative. Read the sample. Then use **Language Frames** as you tell a partner what you visualize as you read about Ethan's trip.

Personal Narrative

My Trip Down

by Ethan Lowe

I'll never forget our trip to the Grand **Canyon**!

Before my trip, I used a map to **locate** the **region** we were going to visit. The map showed the area's **physical features** and the **elevation** of the land.

We woke up at sunrise to begin our hike. We followed the Bright Angel Trail. Native Americans called the Havasupai used this path a long time ago. The trail can't go straight down. It would be much too steep! Instead, the path zigzags back and forth. It looks like the letter Z repeated again and again. It takes a long time to get down to the bottom.

The **surface** of the trail is hard dirt. It has been pounded flat by all the people and mules that go up and down every day. There was a lot of dust because it was hot and dry. Luckily, the Bright Angel Trail does have some shade. Some paths into the canyon have no shade at all.

About 6 miles down, we reached **Plateau** Point. This plateau is a little more than halfway down the canyon. It is flat on top, so you can rest and enjoy the great views. You can see the Colorado River below you and the canyon rim above.

Sample Visualizing

"I <u>read</u> about the shape of the trail. I <u>picture</u> a path that zigzags.

Now I <u>understand</u> why it would take a long time to walk this trail."

◄ = A good place to visualize

Read a Social Studies Article

Genre

A **social studies article** is nonfiction. It gives facts. Some social studies articles give information about different locations around the world.

Text Features

Look for **graphs** and **diagrams**. They can help you understand the text better.

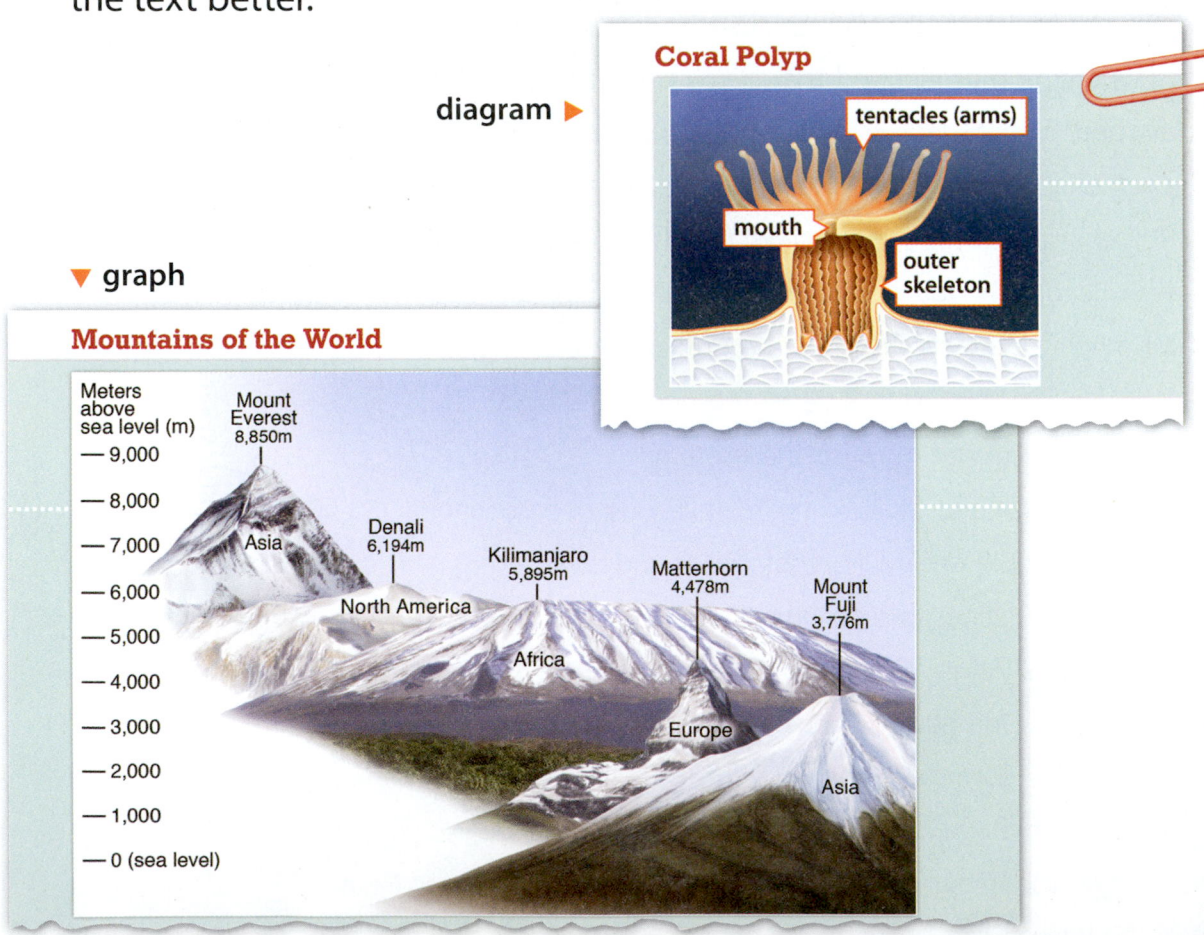

diagram ▶

Coral Polyp

tentacles (arms)

mouth

outer skeleton

▼ graph

Mountains of the World

Meters above sea level (m)

— 9,000
— 8,000
— 7,000
— 6,000
— 5,000
— 4,000
— 3,000
— 2,000
— 1,000
— 0 (sea level)

Mount Everest 8,850m

Asia

Denali 6,194m

North America

Kilimanjaro 5,895m

Africa

Matterhorn 4,478m

Europe

Mount Fuji 3,776m

Asia

Extreme
EARTH

by **Beth Geiger**

Comprehension Coach

▶ **Set a Purpose**
Find out about extreme
places on Earth.

TOP OF THE WORLD

Wicked winds whip across the landscape, and snow and ice **coat** the rocky ground. Temperatures are far below freezing. It's just another summer day at the **top of the world**.

This extreme place is the summit, or top, of Mount Everest. The Asian peak is the tallest mountain on the planet. It rises 8,850 meters (29,035 feet) above sea level. The mountain is still growing.

ASIA

Equator

Mount Everest

▲ **Mount Everest, Asia**

In Other Words

Wicked Strong

coat cover

top of the world
highest place on Earth

Every year, climbers come to this **mighty** mountain. They can spend weeks trying to reach the top. The climb is difficult and lonely. No plants or animals live on Everest. Climbers find only snow, ice, and rock.

People from all around the world travel to Asia to climb the tallest mountain on Earth. ▶

Mountains of the World

Meters above sea level (m)
— 9,000
— 8,000
— 7,000
— 6,000
— 5,000
— 4,000
— 3,000
— 2,000
— 1,000
— 0 (sea level)

Mount Everest 8,850m — Asia
Denali 6,194m — North America
Kilimanjaro 5,895m — Africa
Matterhorn 4,478m — Europe
Mount Fuji 3,776m — Asia

In Other Words
mighty great; very large

▶ **Before You Move On**
1. **Visualize** Which words help you picture what it's like to climb Mount Everest?
2. **Use Text Features** What does the graph help you to understand about the mountains?

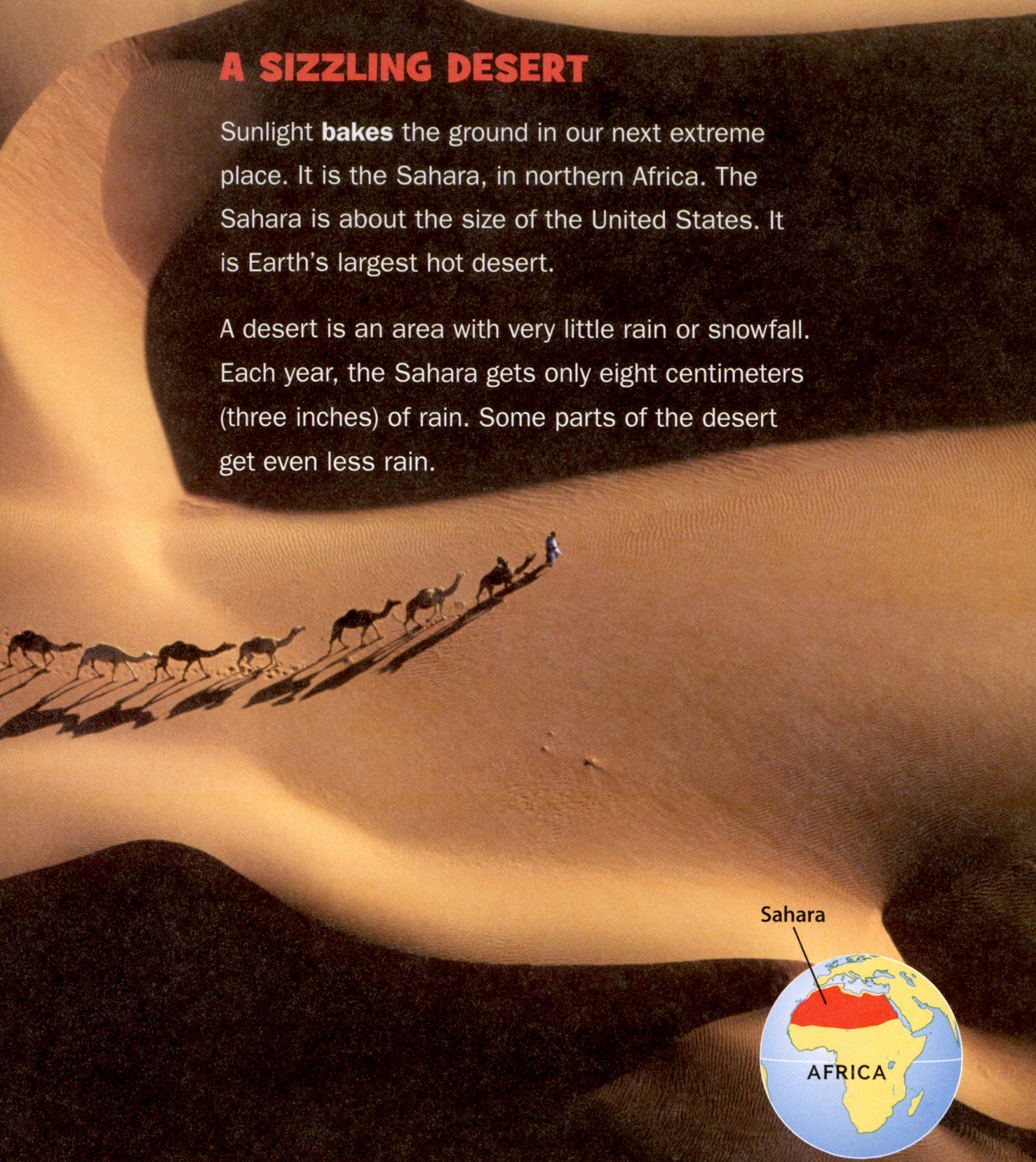

A SIZZLING DESERT

Sunlight **bakes** the ground in our next extreme place. It is the Sahara, in northern Africa. The Sahara is about the size of the United States. It is Earth's largest hot desert.

A desert is an area with very little rain or snowfall. Each year, the Sahara gets only eight centimeters (three inches) of rain. Some parts of the desert get even less rain.

Sahara

AFRICA

▲ Sahara, Africa

In Other Words
bakes heats

HOW HOT IS IT?

With so much sun and so little rain, the Sahara is hot. Summer temperatures here are often more than 32° Celsius (90° Fahrenheit). In fact, Earth's hottest day **on record** was in the Sahara. It was 58° C (136° F). That extreme temperature was in the shade!

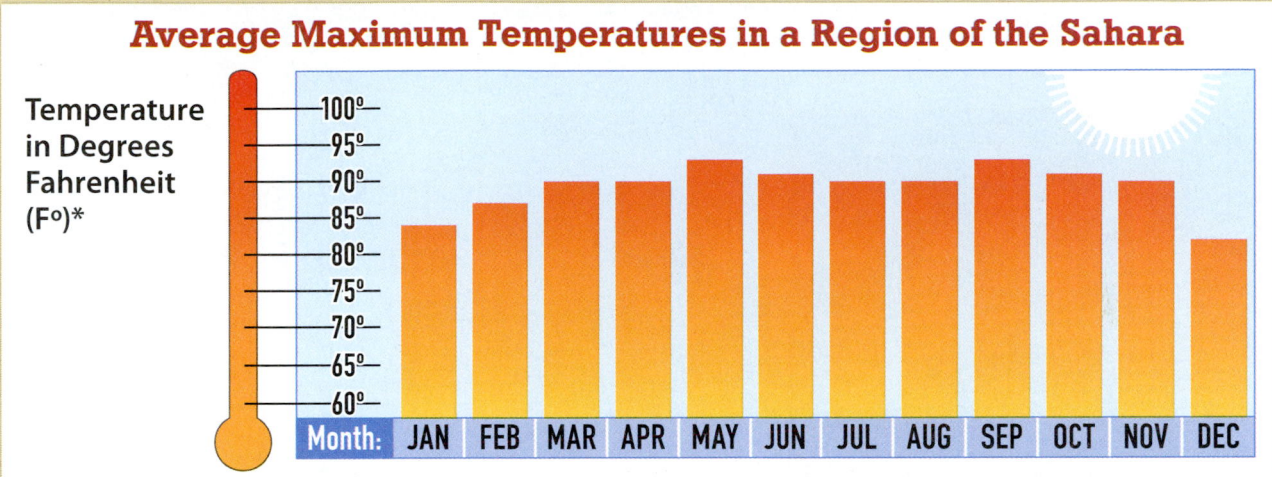

Average Maximum Temperatures in a Region of the Sahara

Temperature in Degrees Fahrenheit (F°)*

*The graph shows temperatures in degrees Fahrenheit to better distinguish the range in temperatures.

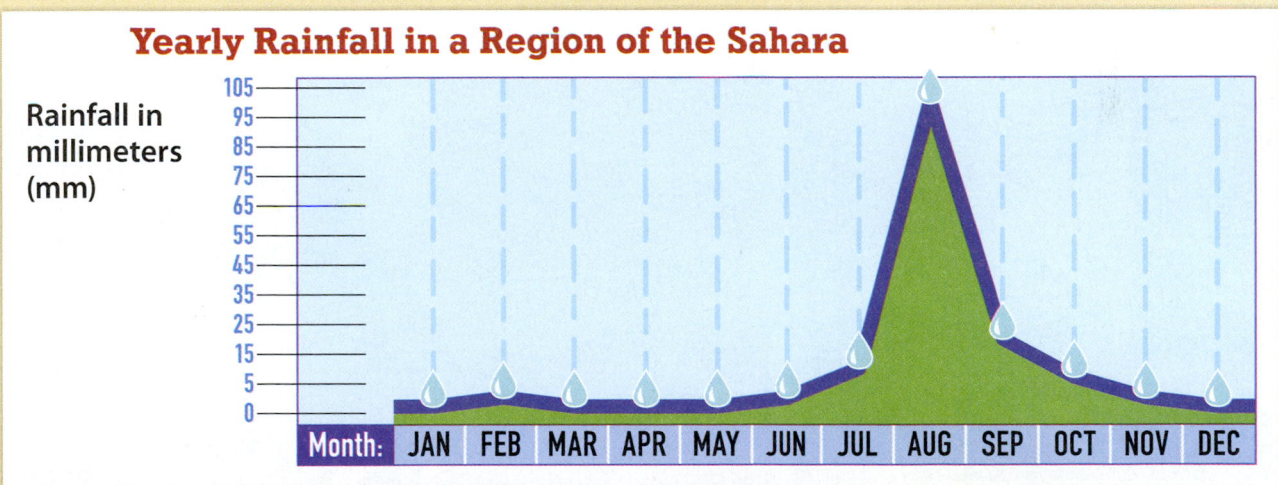

Yearly Rainfall in a Region of the Sahara

Rainfall in millimeters (mm)

▲ These graphs show the average maximum temperatures and rainfall in a **region** of the Sahara over a one-year period.

In Other Words
on record in history

▶ **Before You Move On**

1. **Details** What is the main **feature** of a desert?
2. **Use Text Features** What do the graphs on this page tell you about life in the Sahara? Explain why.

camel

sand viper

fennec

LIFE IN THE DESERT

Few plants grow in such an extreme **climate**. Few animals run, walk, or even crawl here. Yet some animals, such as camels and sand vipers, are **adapted to** the sizzling heat.

The fennec, a kind of fox, is another animal adapted to life in the desert. Huge ears remove heat from the animal's body. Thick fur protects its feet from the hot sand. The fennec sleeps during the hot days and hunts during the cool nights.

In Other Words
climate weather; environment
adapted to able to live in

Some people also live in the Sahara. They are mostly nomads, which means they are always moving from place to place. When water dries up, the nomads **move on**. When food **runs short**, they move again.

Fennec

Large ears remove heat from the fennec's body.

Thick hair protects the fennec's skin from the sun.

Thick fur on the fennec's feet allow it to walk on the hot sand.

Nomads of the Sahara often live in tents.

In Other Words
move on go to a new place
runs short is hard to find

▶ **Before You Move On**

1. **Visualize** What do you think a nomad's life is like in the Sahara? How do you picture it, based on what you read?

2. **Use Text Features** What does the diagram tell you about the fennec?

UNDERWATER KINGDOM

Our next extreme place is under water. It is the Great Barrier Reef, off the coast of Australia. It is the largest **reef** on Earth. It is bigger than New Mexico. In fact, the Great Barrier Reef is the largest thing ever built by living creatures.

The builders are tiny animals called coral polyps. Each polyp takes **chemicals** from the sea. It uses the chemicals to make a hard **outer skeleton** shaped like a cup. This cup protects the polyp's soft body.

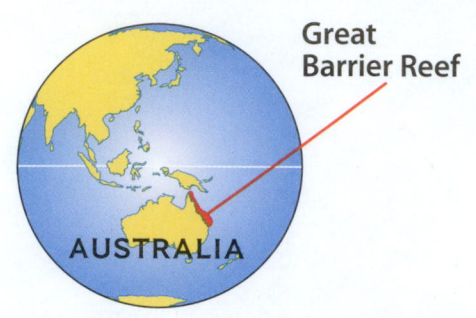

Great Barrier Reef

AUSTRALIA

Coral Polyp

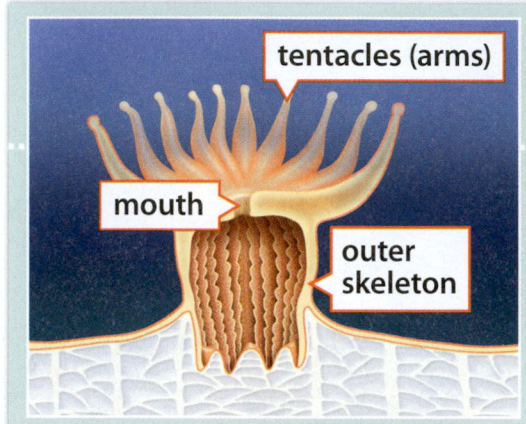

tentacles (arms)

mouth

outer skeleton

polyp

▲ **Each of these tiny polyps will help to form the reef.**

In Other Words

reef underwater structure

chemicals matter; things

outer skeleton
skeleton on the outside of its body

When the polyp dies, the skeleton is left. New polyps build on top of it. Over time, the reef grows and grows.

The Great Barrier Reef isn't just one reef. It is made up of thousands of smaller reefs. There are about 2,800 reefs in all. The reef is so large that astronauts can see it from space.

The Great Barrier Reef is home to many animals. All kinds of fish, turtles, dolphins, and other **marine** life live here. Nearly 2,000 kinds of fish swim in the reef.

Many smaller reefs make up the Great Barrier Reef.

In Other Words
marine ocean

▶ **Before You Move On**

1. **Use Text Features** Use the diagram on page 188 to tell about the body parts of a coral polyp.
2. **Visualize** Draw a picture of what you think the Great Barrier Reef looks like from above. Which words help you draw this?

Amazon River

SOUTH AMERICA

BIG RIVER

Picture all the **fresh water** that flows into oceans around the world. One in five drops comes from a single river. It is the Amazon River in South America.

The Amazon begins in the mountains of Peru. It stretches across the South American continent. The river ends at the Atlantic Ocean on the coast of Brazil.

Where does all the Amazon's water come from? Much of it comes from rain. More than 1,000 centimeters (400 inches) of rain falls into the river each year.

▲ Amazon River, South America

In Other Words
fresh water water that isn't salty

Some rivers are **pretty calm**, but not the Amazon. Storms here sometimes **stir up** waves as high as a house.

As it flows across South America, the Amazon River **winds** through the world's largest rain forest. It is twice the size of all other rain forests combined. More kinds of plants and animals live here than anywhere else on Earth.

Some of the Amazon's animals are pretty extreme. You can find flesh-eating fish and huge snakes. You can also find gentle sloths, monkeys, and even pink dolphins.

sloth

squirrel monkey

pink dolphin

In Other Words
pretty calm slow and quiet
stir up make
winds runs

▶ **Before You Move On**

1. **Visualize** If you were in the boat in the photo, tell how would you feel compared to everything around you.
2. **Details** What <mark>features</mark> make the Amazon and its rain forest "extreme"?

WONDERFUL WATERFALL

Water **races** to the edge of a mountain and dives over it. The water drops 979 meters (3,212 feet). During the long fall, it turns into mist. **Barely a drop makes it to** the ground.

To see this, visit Angel Falls, the world's tallest waterfall. It is 17 times taller than Niagara Falls in the United States. Angel Falls is in Venezuela, a country in South America.

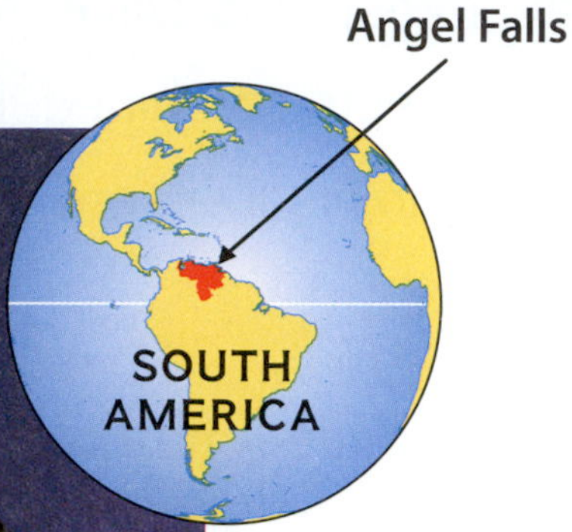

Angel Falls

SOUTH AMERICA

◄ Angel Falls, South America

In Other Words
races flows quickly
Barely a drop makes it to
Almost no water reaches

The falls formed in a special place. Millions of years ago, the land was a large **plateau**. A plateau is an area of flat land that is higher than the land around it.

Over many years, strong wind and water wore away the plateau. They **sliced** the plateau into tall, flat mountains. People call these table mountains because of their flat tops. Angel Falls **plunges** over one of these table mountains.

On average, a plateau that is 1,000 meters (3,280 feet) high would take approximately one to five million years to become a table mountain.

In Other Words
sliced cut
plunges flows

How a Table Mountain Forms

1. A rushing river cuts into the rock at the top of a plateau.

2. Over millions of years, water and wind wear away more and more rock.

3. Eventually, a plateau becomes a table mountain when the rock around it is gone.

▶ **Before You Move On**

1. **Make Inferences** At Angel Falls, why do you think barely a drop makes it to the ground?

2. **Summarize** How is a table mountain formed?

EXTREME EXPLORING

Earth has many more extremes, of course. Two of them are in the southwest region of the United States. The Grand Canyon is one of the world's largest **canyons**. It is **located** in Arizona.

In nearby New Mexico, you can find one of the world's longest and deepest caves. It is called Lechuguilla (le-chü-gē-u) Cave. Explorers from around the world come to see the unusual rock shapes inside the cave.

The inside of Lechuguilla Cave in New Mexico

NORTH AMERICA

Grand Canyon

Lechuguilla Cave

Grand Canyon

▲ Grand Canyon, Arizona

If you're looking for extreme cold, Antarctica is the place for you. This icy continent is the coldest place on Earth. The lowest temperature ever recorded there was -89° C (-129° F)! Then there's the wettest **spot** in the world: Mawsynram, in India. The town gets 1,187 centimeters (467 inches) of rain a year. By any measure—wettest or driest, hottest or coldest—our Earth is extreme. ❖

▼ A community in India during the rainy season.

In Other Words
spot place

▶ **Before You Move On**

1. **Make Comparisons** How are the Grand Canyon and Lechuguilla Cave alike?

2. **Details** Why is the weather in Mawsynram, India, considered extreme?

195

Key Words

canyon	physical
elevation	plain
feature	plateau
landform	region
locate	surface
ocean	valley

Talk About It

1. How did the author organize the information in this **article** so that you can **locate** ideas easily?

   The author included _____ and _____ .

2. What place from "Extreme Earth" would you like to visit? **Describe** the **place**.

3. Use information from the article to help contrast two extreme places on Earth.

   A _____ is _____ , but _____ is _____ .

Learn test-taking strategie.
🌐 **NGReach.com**

Write About It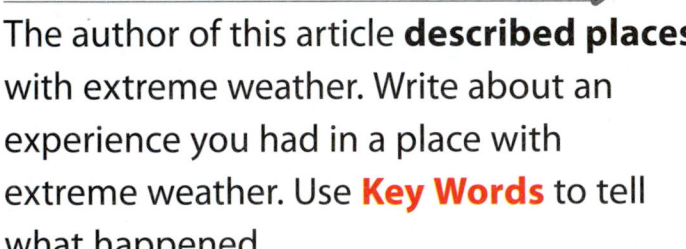

The author of this article **described places** with extreme weather. Write about an experience you had in a place with extreme weather. Use **Key Words** to tell what happened.

I was in _____ . It was so _____ !
One thing we did was _____ .

Main Idea and Details

Make an outline for "Extreme Earth."

Outline

> I.   Mount Everest is the tallest mountain on the planet.   Write the main idea of the first section.
>
>   A. It is 8,850 meters above sea level.   Write details that support the main idea of that section.
>
>   B. No plants or animals live there.
>
> II. The Sahara is the largest hot desert on Earth.
>
>   A. Only 8 centimeters of rain falls each year.
>
>   B.
>
> III.

Now use your outline to summarize "Extreme Earth" with a partner.
Use as many **Key Words** as you can.

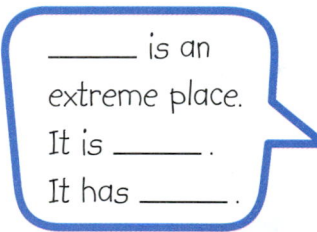

_____ is an extreme place. It is _____ . It has _____ .

Fluency Comprehension Coach

Use the Comprehension Coach to practice reading with intonation.
Rate your reading.

 **Talk Together**

Why did the author of "Extreme Earth" write this article? What does she want readers to learn? Explain to a partner what the purpose of this text is and how you know. Use **Key Words** to explain what readers can learn.

Compound Words

Some longer words are made up of small words put together.
The longer word is called a **compound word**.

landform =
land + form

sunlight =
sun + light

snowfall =
snow + fall

waterfall =
water + fall

Try It Together

Read each item. Choose the best answer.

1. **Which of these is a compound word?**

   A elevation

   B plain

   C mountain

   D seacoast

2. **Which of these is NOT a compound word?**

   A houseboat

   B hilltop

   C surface

   D lighthouse

Connect Across Texts Would you like to visit amazing places? Find out about a person who photographs amazing places.

Genre A **profile** briefly describes a person. It tells what the person does and cares about.

Photographing the
WORLD

by KRISTIN COZORT

▲ **Jimmy Chin**

GROWING UP in the **flatlands** of southern Minnesota, Jimmy Chin dreamed of places with high, snowy mountains and tall rock towers.

He was 12 when he first **fell in love with** the outdoors. Chin explains that after a family trip to Glacier National Park, "I was changed forever. Spending time in the mountains and rock climbing became **my passions**."

In Other Words
flatlands plains
fell in love with began to like
my passions the things I liked the most

▶ **Before You Move On**

1. **Cause/Effect** Why did growing up in Minnesota cause Jimmy Chin to dream of mountains and rock towers?

2. **Analyze** How did a trip to Glacier National Park change Chin? How do you know?

Getting the Shot

Chin is one of the best extreme photographers in the world. He is also a **world-class** athlete. Chin is an expert skier and climber. His athletic skills help him take photos where few people **dare** to go. "I love to bring back photographs that nobody else could have," he says.

▲ Chin's skill as a climber helps him get amazing shots.

In Other Words
world-class very good
dare are brave enough

▲ An extreme shot

Chin photographs the **far corners** of the world. He has survived an avalanche and extreme temperatures. He often puts himself in danger to **get the perfect shot**.

Taking risks is part of an extreme photographer's job. ▶

▶ **Before You Move On**

1. **Cause/Effect** How do Chin's skills as an athlete help him in his job?

2. **Visualize** Imagine where Chin was when he took the top photo. Draw a diagram showing Chin taking the picture of the climber.

Telling the Story

Photography can show the world's landscapes and **document** important events. Three or four times a year, Chin helps photograph major **expeditions**. He compares photographing to filmmaking. "Photographing an expedition is storytelling," he says.

▲ **Chin tells stories using photographs instead of words.**

In Other Words

document show what happened during

expeditions trips to explore faraway places

202

In a distant **region** of Tanzania, Africa, Chin photographed a zebra walking across the dry **plains**.

Raising Awareness

Chin hopes his pictures will **raise awareness** about the beauty of the **physical** world. He says, "I know photography can be a powerful tool." ❖

In Other Words
raise awareness teach people

▶ **Before You Move On**

1. **Interpret** Why does Chin say that photography is like storytelling?
2. **Make Connections** What does Chin mean when he says that photography is a powerful tool?

Key Words

canyon	physical
elevation	plain
feature	plateau
landform	region
locate	surface
ocean	valley

Compare Text Features

A social studies article and a profile each has a title. What other text **features** do they have? Work with a partner to make a comparison chart. List more text features.

Comparison Chart

Features	"Extreme Earth"	"Photographing the World"
title	yes	yes
section headings		
photographs		
captions		
maps		

Write *yes* if it has that text feature. Write *no* if it doesn't.

Talk Together

Why learn about extreme places in the world? Think about the social studies article and the profile. Use **Key Words** to talk about your ideas.

More Plural Nouns

Some nouns do not have regular plural forms. They are called **irregular plurals**.

Grammar Rules Plural Nouns

	singular noun	plural noun
• Some nouns change in different ways to show the plural. • Do not add **-s** or **-es** for irregular plurals.	man woman child tooth foot	men women children teeth feet
• For nouns like these, use the same form to name "one" and "more than one."	moose sheep	moose sheep

Read Plural Nouns

Read these sentences from "Extreme Earth." Find the plural nouns. Which one does not follow regular plural rules?

> Huge ears release heat from the animal's body. Thick fur protects its feet from the hot sand. The fennec sleeps during the hot days and hunts during the cool nights.

Write Plural Nouns

Look at the pictures on pages 194–195. Write a sentence to tell about one of them. Use as many plural nouns as you can. Show your sentence to a partner.

Write Like a Researcher

Write a Research Report

Write a report about one of the most extreme places in the United States. You and your classmates will use what you learn to create a display for others to enjoy.

Study a Model

When you write a research report, you include information from different sources. You organize the facts you find and present them in a new and interesting way.

Read Cheryl's report about Death Valley.

Life in Death Valley

Cheryl Lin

It's hard to imagine a place that's more extreme than Death Valley, in California and Nevada. Death Valley is the hottest and the driest place in North America. It also has the lowest spot in the Western Hemisphere! Yet **Death Valley is full of life**.

Death Valley isn't an easy place to live. It gets less than two inches of rain a year, so there isn't much water. It's hot, too. In July, temperatures often climb to over 115 degrees

The title and introduction tell **what the report is about**. The introduction also gets the reader's attention.

Each paragraph has a **topic sentence** that tells the main idea.

Fahrenheit. The ground is mostly sand and rocks. There is even a dried-up lake that has turned into salt crystals.

None of this stops plants and animals from making Death Valley their home. People have found more than 1,000 types of plants there. It also has 51 types of mammals, 36 kinds of reptiles, 6 types of fish, and more than 300 kinds of birds. The animals aren't all small, either. There are big ones like bighorn sheep, mountain lions, and mule deer.

Water is the biggest challenge for anything that lives in Death Valley. Some plants have roots that go fifty feet beneath the surface to find water. Kangaroo rats get the water they need from the seeds of desert sunflowers. Tiny pupfish can live in water that is 90 degrees Fahrenheit and five times as salty as the ocean!

Sources

"Death Valley." World Book Encyclopedia. 2009. Print.

Death Valley. National Park Service, 11 Jun. 2010. Web. 12 Feb. 2011. <http://www.nps.gov/deva/index.htm>

Hamilton, John. Death Valley National Park. Edina, Minnesota: Abdo Publishing Company, 2009.

Every topic sentence is developed with facts and details.

The report is focused. Every paragraph helps to develop the topic.

A final page lists the sources that Cheryl used for the report.

Prewrite

1. **Choose a Topic** Which extreme place would you like to learn more about? Look in an almanac, or on the Internet to find ideas. Narrow your topic to one that you can cover in a short report.

2. **List Your Research Questions** What do you already know about your topic? What do you want to find out? Think of questions you could use to guide your research.

> ### Research Questions
> • What is Death Valley like?
> • What plants and animals live there?
> • How do living things survive in Death Valley?

3. **Create a Research Plan** A research plan lists your questions and your ideas for how you will answer them. Use different sources to help you with different kinds of questions:

   • Nonfiction books

   • Magazines and newspapers

   • Reference works: encyclopedia, atlas, almanac

   • Web sites and other online sources

   • People: interviews with experts; surveys you create yourself

Gather Information

1. **Identify Sources** Choose your sources carefully. Be sure every source is up to date. Also make sure the information is written by an expert in the area.

2. **Create Source Cards** Keep track of your sources. Use index cards to record important information. Give each card a number.

Source Card for a Book

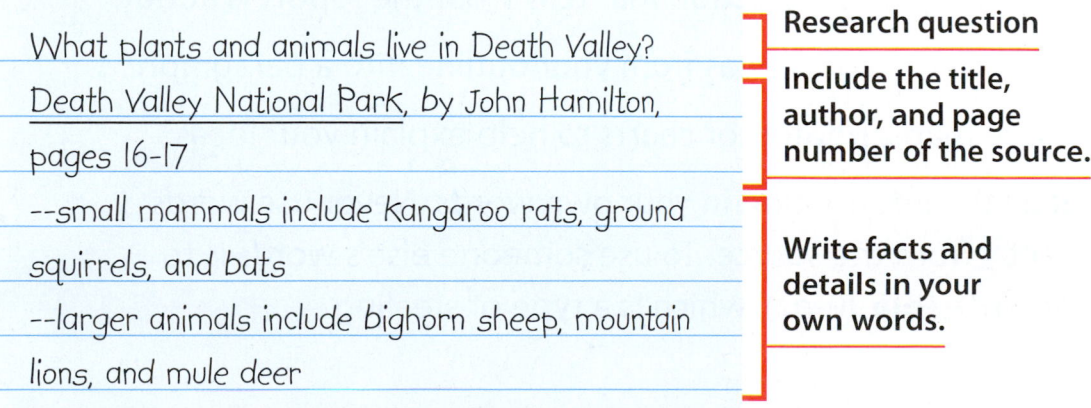

I.	Card number
Death Valley National Park	Title of book
John Hamilton	Author
Abdo Publishing Company, Edina, Minnesota	Publication information
2009	
J917.948	Library call number

3. **Make Note Cards** As you research, record important words, phrases, and ideas onto note cards. Be sure to put all of the information in your own words.

Note Card

What plants and animals live in Death Valley?	Research question
Death Valley National Park, by John Hamilton, pages 16-17	Include the title, author, and page number of the source.
--small mammals include kangaroo rats, ground squirrels, and bats	Write facts and details in your own words.
--larger animals include bighorn sheep, mountain lions, and mule deer	

Get Organized

1. **Sort Your Cards** Begin by grouping your cards according to the research questions. Put the cards in an order that makes sense.

2. **Organize Information** Use an outline or other graphic organizer to help you organize the details. Each group, or category, from your cards can become a main idea. Put the details from those cards under the main idea.

Outline

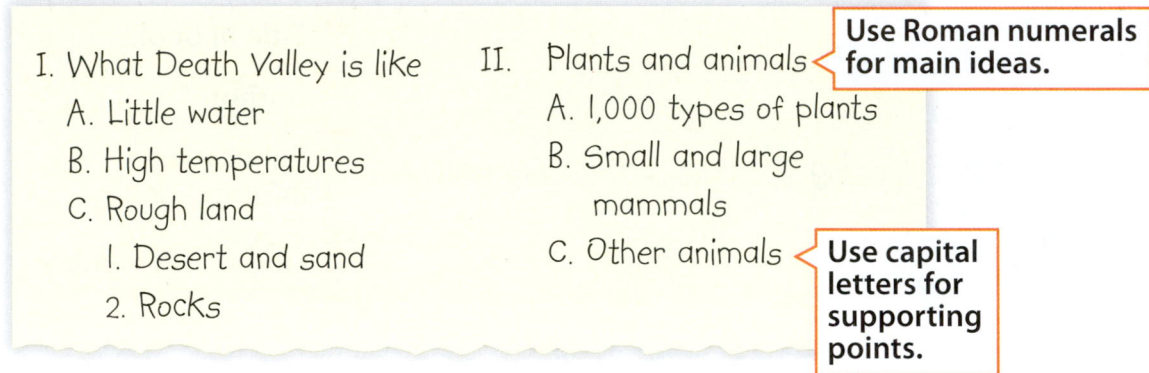

I. What Death Valley is like
   A. Little water
   B. High temperatures
   C. Rough land
      1. Desert and sand
      2. Rocks

II. Plants and animals
   A. 1,000 types of plants
   B. Small and large mammals
   C. Other animals

Use Roman numerals for main ideas.

Use capital letters for supporting points.

Draft

Use your outline to guide you as you write.

- Begin with an introduction that tells what the report is about.

- Turn each group of ideas from your outline into a paragraph.

- Include maps, photos, or charts to help explain your ideas.

- Put all the information in your own words. Never use words directly from the source. To use someone else's words is to plagiarize (**plā**-ju-rīz), which is a type of stealing.

Revise

1. **Read, Retell, Respond** Read your draft aloud to a partner. Your partner listens and then summarizes the main points of the report. Next, talk about ways to improve your draft.

2. **Make Changes** Think about your partner's suggestions. Use the Revising Marks on page 585 to mark your changes.

   - Is your report focused? Delete any facts or details that don't support your topic.

   > In July, temperatures often climb to over <u>115 degrees Fahrenheit.</u> ~~There are places in Africa that get hotter, though.~~

   - Make sure all of the information is in your own words.

   > People have found more than 1,000 types of plants there.
   > ∧ ~~The park supports more than 1,000 plant species.~~

Edit and Proofread

Work with a partner to edit and proofread your reports. Carefully check all your facts. Make sure they are correct.

Publish

3. **Make a Final Copy** Make a final copy of your research report. Add a source list at the end.

4. **Share with Others** With your classmates, create a bulletin board called "Extreme United States." Invite others to see it.

Denali, Alaska

Okefenokee Swamp, Florida and Georgia

? **BIG** **Question**

Why learn about other places?

Talk Together

In this unit, you found lots of answers to the **Big Question**. Now use your concept map to discuss the **Big Question** with the class.

Concept Map

reasons to learn about places

find out about different people

Write a Poem

Write a poem that expresses one reason to learn about places.
Try to include rhyming words and figurative language.

Share Your Ideas

Choose one of these ways to share your ideas about the **Big Question**.

Write It!

Write an Advertisement

Write an advertisement for a place you think is amazing. Describe the place and give reasons people should visit.

Talk About It!

Play a Game

Play a guessing game. Give clues about a famous place. The classmate who guesses correctly can then take a turn giving clues about a different place.

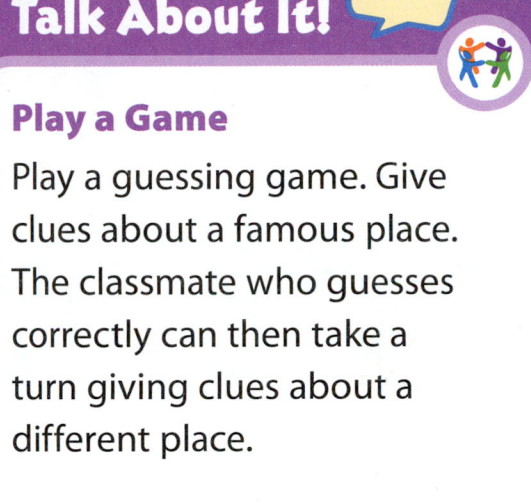

Do It!

Build a Model

Build a model of an amazing place that you have learned about. Use art materials. Display your finished model for the class.

Write It!

Write a Postcard

Imagine you are visiting an amazing place. Create a postcard about it for a friend. Draw a picture for the front of the card, and write the note for the back of it.

Power of Nature

BIG Question How do we relate to nature?

Unit at a Glance

▶ **Language**: Make Comparisons, Express Needs and Wants, Science Words
▶ **Literacy**: Ask Questions
▶ **Content**: Natural Resources

Unit 4

Share What You Know

Do It!

❶ **Make** a list of things in nature that are strong and mighty.

❷ **Sort** your ideas into a class list.

❸ **Draw** a picture of something from the list. Show its strength.

Strong Things in Nature
storms
a tiger
the sun
waves

Build Background: Watch a video about natural resources.
NGReach.com

Make Comparisons

Language Frames

- _____ is _____ .
- But _____ is _____ .
- _____ need _____ .
- And so do _____ .

Listen to Chloe's song. Then use **Language Frames** to talk about different ways people need soil.

Song

A Good Place for a Garden

I could plant my garden on a hilly plot.
It is filled with sunshine. What a lovely spot!
But the hill is high, and the soil is not so deep.
Rain will wash the soil away because the hill's too steep.

So I'll plant my garden somewhere else instead:
A place that's flat to plant my seedlings in a bed.
Carrots need good soil. And so do other plants.
If the soil is rich enough, my garden stands a chance.

Tune: "Sing a Song of Sixpence"

steep hill

bed of soil

plot of ground

Key Words

Key Words

convert

electricity

generate

power

renewable

scarce

Look at the pictures. Use **Key Words** and other words to talk about energy resources.

Wind is a **renewable** resource. It will not run out. It will not become **scarce**, or hard to find.

blade

windmill

We use wind's **power**. Windmills **convert** it for our use.

Windmills can **generate electricity**. The electricity is sent to homes.

Talk Together

How do you use power that comes from nature? Talk with a partner. Make comparisons about how you use power. Try to use **Language Frames** from page 216 and **Key Words**.

Cause and Effect

When something happens, you often look for the reason, or cause. What happens is the effect. When you talk about **cause and effect**:

- tell how the events relate

- use words such as *because*, *since*, *so*, and *as a result* to connect the cause and the effect.

Look at the pictures of Chloe's hill. Read the captions.

Chloe pulls the weeds.

The hill is bare.

Rain washes the soil away.

Map and Talk

You can use a cause-and-effect chart to keep track of how causes and effects are related. Here's how you make one. Write the cause in the first box. Write the effect in the second box.

Cause-and-Effect Chart

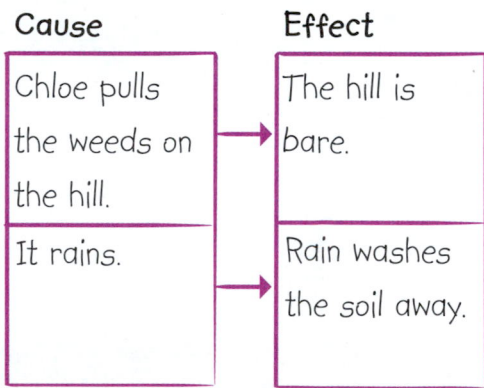

Cause   Effect

Cause	Effect
Chloe pulls the weeds on the hill.	The hill is bare.
It rains.	Rain washes the soil away.

Talk **Together**

Tell your partner something that happens to soil. Have your partner make a cause-and-effect chart.

More Key Words

Use these words to talk about "Wind at Work" and "Water: The Blue Gold."

available

(u-**vā**-lu-bul) *adjective*

When something is **available,** it is ready to take. Fresh fruit is **available** in summer.

conservation

(kon-sir-**vā**-shun) *noun*

Conservation means saving or protecting something.

current

(**kir**-unt) *adjective*

When something is **current,** it is happening now. You can see **current** news stories on TV.

flow

(**flō**) *verb*

To **flow** is to move freely. Water **flows** from a fountain without stopping.

resource

(**rē**-sors) *noun*

A **resource** is something that people need and use. School supplies are **resources** for students.

Talk Together

Work with a partner to complete a Meaning Map for each **Key Word**.

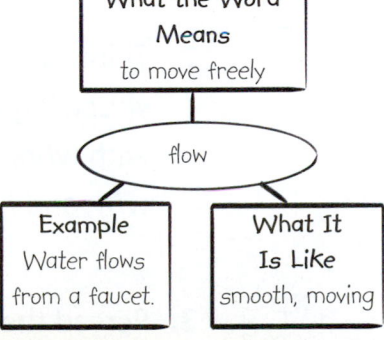

What the Word Means
to move freely

flow

Example
Water flows from a faucet.

What It Is Like
smooth, moving

Add words to My Vocabulary Notebook.
NGReach.com

Learn to Ask Questions

Look at the cartoon. Chloe wants to buy something for her garden, but she doesn't understand what she sees. When you want information at a store, you can **ask questions**.

You can **ask questions** when you read, too. What type of information will help you understand? Look for answers in the text.

How to Ask Questions

	1. As you read, think about what you need to understand better.	I need to understand _____ .
	2. Think about the text. Ask yourself questions that begin with *who, what, when, where, why*, and *how*.	I ask myself, _____ .
	3. Reread the text or read on to find the answers.	I read and find _____ .

Talk Together

Read Chloe's instructions for making a compost bin. Read the sample question. Then use **Language Frames** to tell a partner your questions.

Instructions

How to Make a Compost Bin

Soil is a valuable **resource**. In some areas, rich soil is **scarce**. So a compost bin is a great project for soil **conservation**. With this tool, you can **convert** ordinary kitchen garbage into rich compost.

The basic recipe for compost includes water, brown stuff, and green stuff. Tiny organisms break down the plant materials. As a result, you get rich new soil.

1. To make a compost bin, you start with a small plastic garbage can, one that is larger, a brick, and soil. Punch holes in the bottom of the small garbage can so water and air can **flow** through. Place the brick in the bottom of the bigger can. Put soil around the brick. Set the small can on the brick.

2. Begin filling the small can. Start with a layer of brown stuff. You can use dry leaves, newspaper, sawdust, or pine needles. These things add carbon. Add some water and let it soak in.

3. Then add a layer of green stuff. You can use grass clippings or any **available** food scraps other than meat for nitrogen. Add more water.

4. Keep both garbage cans covered. Keep adding layers until your bin is full. Then wait as your **current** garbage is transformed!

Sample Question

"I need to understand what a compost bin is used for.

I ask myself, 'What does a compost bin do?'

I read and find that it's a container for turning garbage into compost for soil."

◄ = A good place to ask a question

221

Read a Science Article

Genre

A **science article** is nonfiction. It tells facts about a science topic such as forces in nature.

Text Feature

Look for **section headings**. They tell what each section of text is mostly about.

▶ **Set a Purpose**
Find out how wind forms and how it affects people's lives.

section heading

Air on the Move

What is wind? What causes it? Wind is just air **on the move**. When the sun shines on land or water, the land or water warms up, and so does the air above it. As air warms, it becomes lighter and begins to rise. Cooler air **rushes in** underneath to fill the **gap** left by the rising air. That rush of air is wind.

Wind at Work

by **Beth Geiger**

NATIONAL GEOGRAPHIC

Comprehension Coach

▶ **Set a Purpose**
Find out how wind forms and
how it affects people's lives.

Air on the Move

What is wind? What causes it? Wind is just air **on the move**.
When the sun shines on land or water, the land or water
warms up, and so does the air above it. As air warms, it
becomes lighter and begins to rise. Cooler air **rushes in**
underneath to fill the **gap** left by the rising air. That rush of
air is wind.

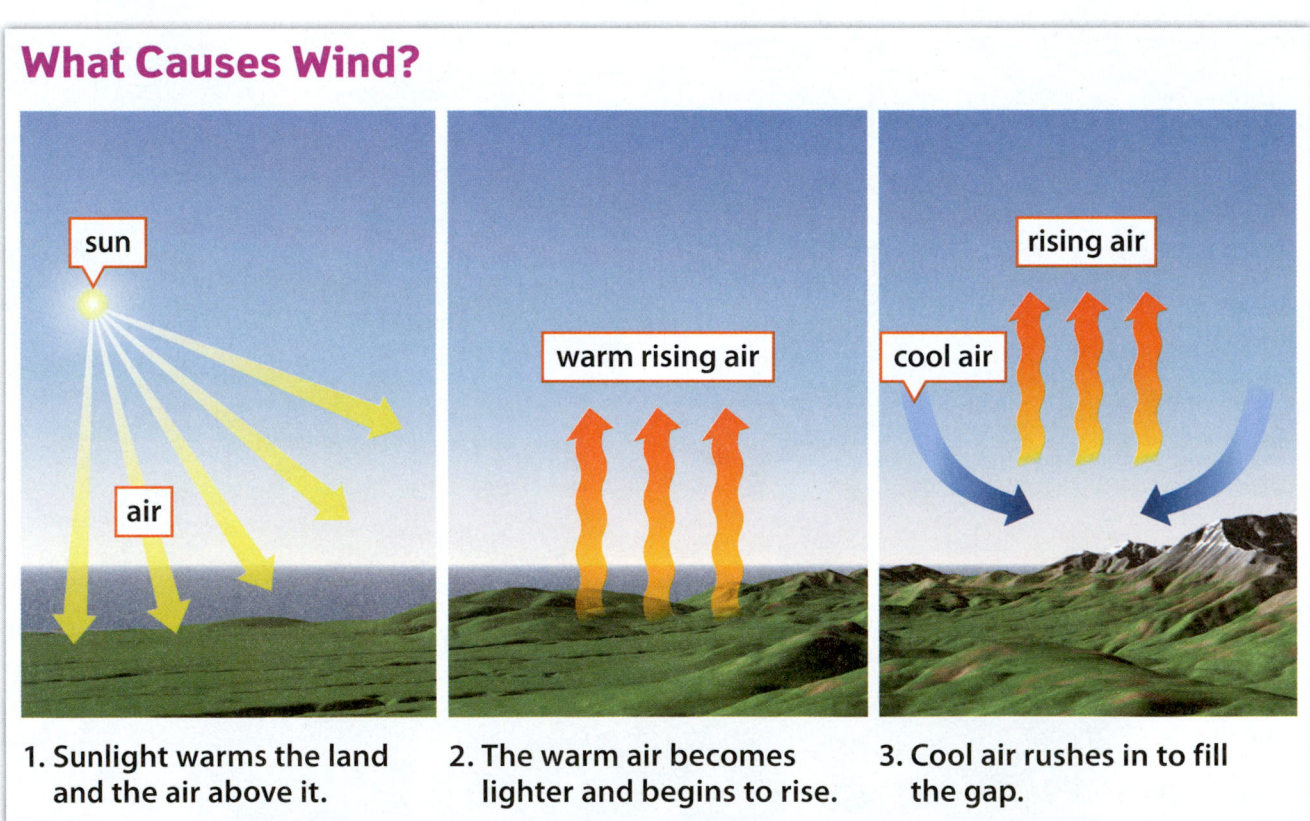

What Causes Wind?

sun

air

warm rising air

rising air

cool air

1. Sunlight warms the land and the air above it.

2. The warm air becomes lighter and begins to rise.

3. Cool air rushes in to fill the gap.

In Other Words

on the move that is moving
rushes in moves quickly
gap space

Wind is always **swirling** around Earth because the planet's surface heats unevenly. For example, water takes longer to heat and cool than land. So air is always rushing between water and land. That's why beaches are often **breezy**!

Different types of places, such as forests, deserts, and prairies, also soak up the sun's heat differently. They cool down at different **rates**, too. Don't forget about the cold places at Earth's North and South Poles and the warm area around the equator, the imaginary line around the planet's middle. Air moves constantly between all these hot and cold spots.

forest

desert

prairie

Forests, deserts, prairies, and other types of places soak up heat differently.

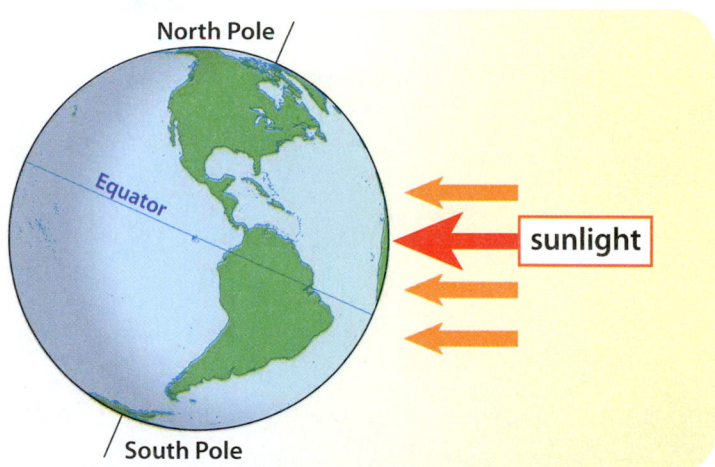

▲ Sunlight usually hits most directly the area near the equator, heating it more than other regions.

In Other Words
swirling moving
breezy windy
rates speeds

▶ **Before You Move On**

1. **Use Text Features** How does the section heading help you understand the text?
2. **Ask Questions** Choose a photo or diagram on page 224 or 225. What else would you like to know about it?

Different Kinds of Winds

Some winds blow in regular patterns across thousands of miles. Other winds, such as gusts in a thunderstorm, are sudden and **local**. Mountains, islands, and even tall buildings affect how wind moves. **No wonder** wind comes in so many varieties. Gales, gusts, breezes, and puffs are just a few kinds of wind.

A Force You Can't See

You can't see wind, but you can see its **handiwork**. Have you seen a tree branch swaying? That's wind. Have you ever watched an umbrella blow inside out? That's wind again.

▲ Tall buildings can change the direction of wind.

In Other Words
local stay in one area
No wonder It's not surprising that
handiwork effect

Wind does more than just **play with** umbrellas. It **sculpts** rocks and landscapes by tearing away tiny pieces off rocks. Piece by tiny piece, wind can erase a whole mountain. This process of wearing away is called erosion.

Bit by bit, over millions of years, wind carves rock into cool new shapes. What happens to all those loose pieces? Wind piles them into graceful sand **dunes**. That's a lot of **power** for something you can't see.

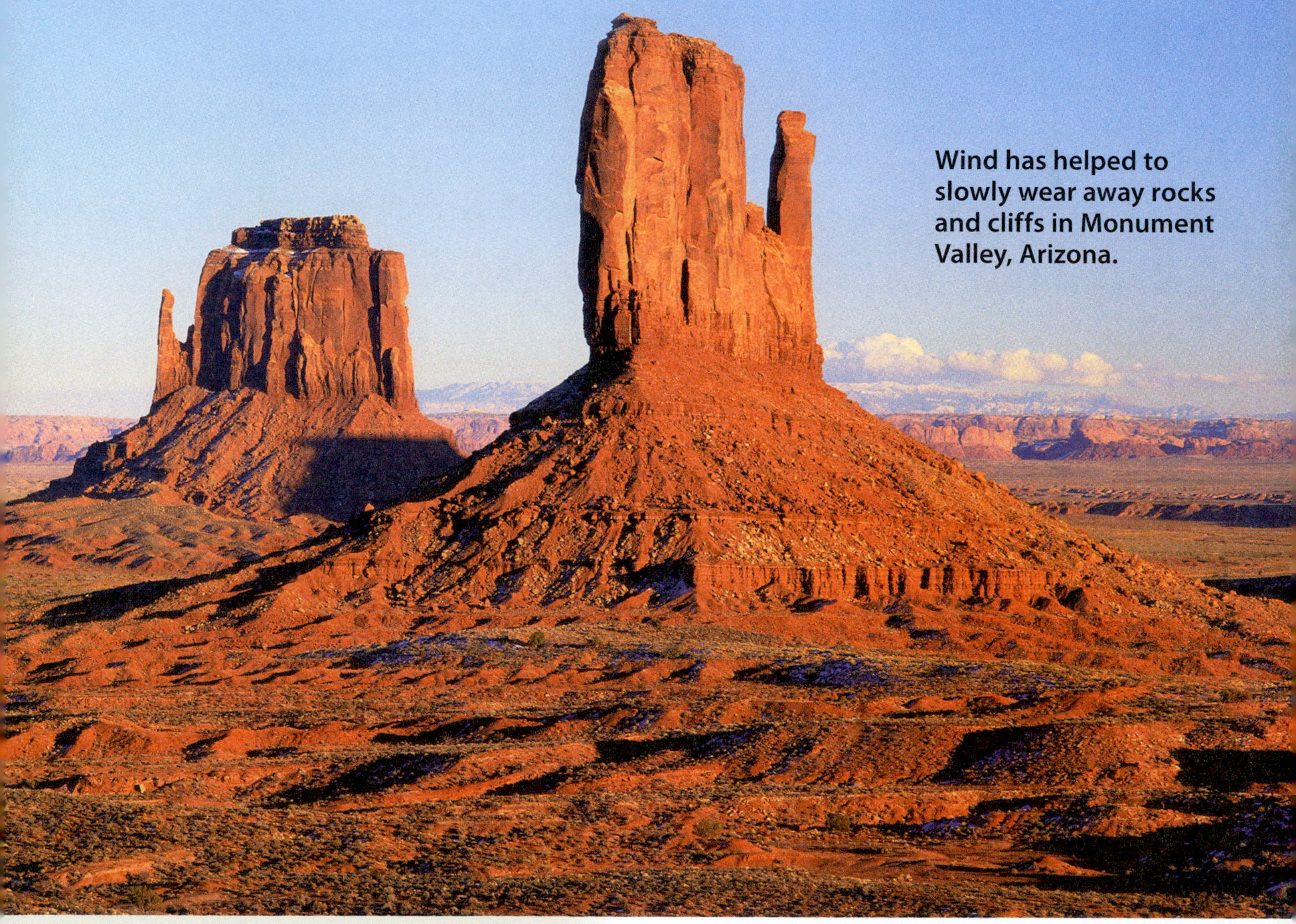

Wind has helped to slowly wear away rocks and cliffs in Monument Valley, Arizona.

In Other Words

play with make trouble for

sculpts shapes; carves

dunes hills ▶

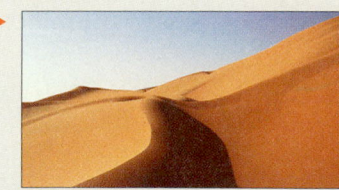

▶ Before You Move On

1. **Cause/Effect** How does the photo on this page show the wind's effect?
2. **Ask Questions** What is one thing you learned about erosion? What do you still want to know?

The Wind in Their Sails ➤

Long ago, people discovered that they could use the wind to go places. Ancient Egyptians **hoisted** sails to travel up and down the Nile River. The Polynesians set sail across the Pacific Ocean at least 3,000 years ago. Wind blew the Vikings on their famous **raids**.

These early sailors were smart. They noticed that Earth's major winds blew in **predictable** patterns. Studying these patterns helped sailors plan their voyages.

Egyptian sailboats

Polynesian longboat

Viking ship

In Other Words
hoisted raised; put up
raids attacks
predictable expected

Some of Earth's most predictable winds blow west near the equator. Trading ships used them to take **goods** around the world. These helpful winds are called trade winds. You could call trade winds the **original fast lanes**.

Other predictable winds called westerlies blow from west to east. These winds are found farther from the equator than trade winds.

People still sail boats today. Modern sailing, however, is mostly for **sport**. Even so, today's sailors still depend on the same wind patterns that pushed trade ships hundreds of years ago.

Planet Patterns

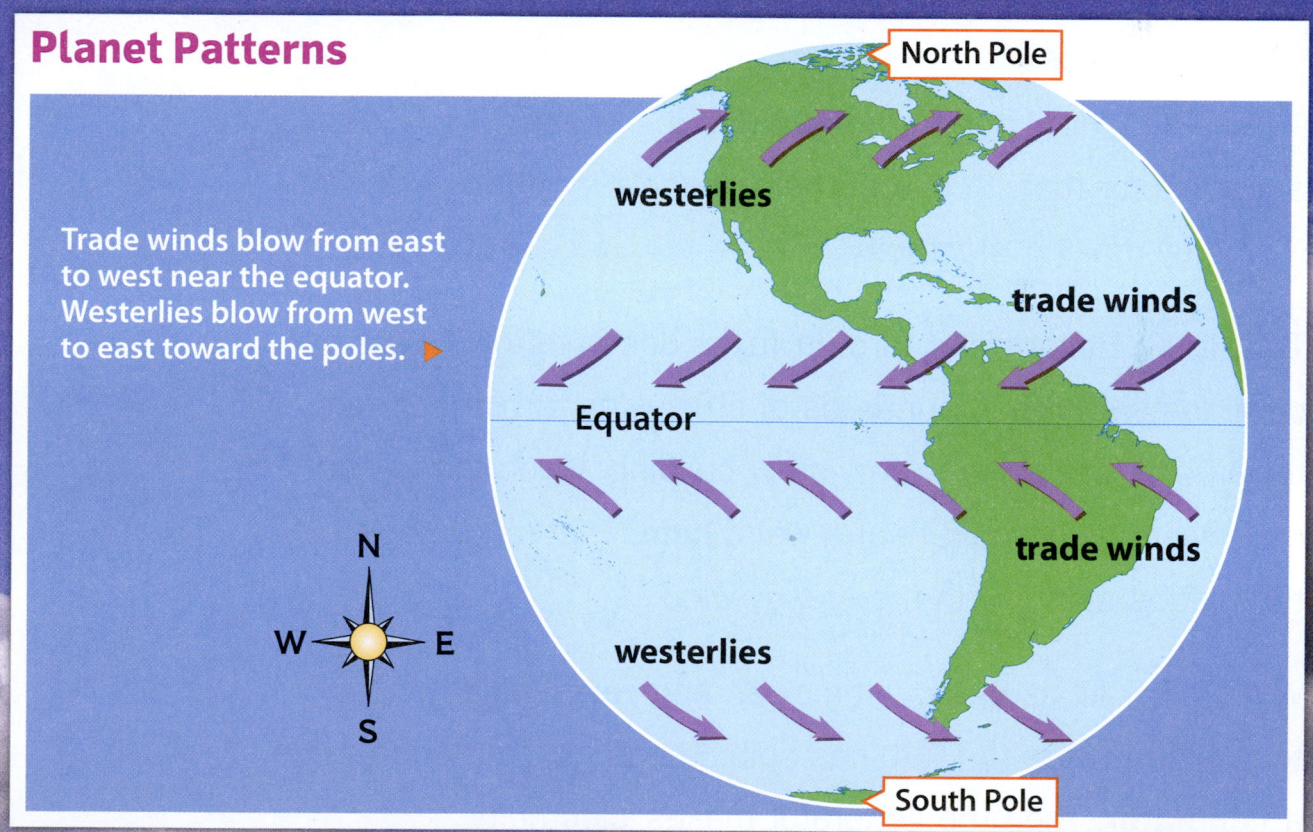

Trade winds blow from east to west near the equator. Westerlies blow from west to east toward the poles. ▶

In Other Words
goods things to trade
original fast lanes first highways
sport fun

▶ **Before You Move On**

1. **Cause/Effect** How did wind patterns help sailors decide on the course they would travel?

2. **Ask Questions** Look at the diagram on this page. What questions do you have about trade winds?

Wind farms use the wind's power to make **electricity**.

blade

turbine

tower

Wind Power

People no longer need wind to cross the ocean. They have airplanes for that. Still, wind helps people in other ways. One way is by making electricity.

The Horse Hollow wind farm in Texas doesn't grow wheat or corn. Instead, it has hundreds of steel wind turbines. Each tower is taller than a twenty-story building. If you stood near the towers, you would hear a weird **hum**. That's the sound of the blades spinning in the steady wind.

Wind, after all, is energy. It's clean and **renewable** energy, too. Wind makes the turbines spin. The spinning motion turns a **generator**. Then the generator makes electricity.

In Other Words
hum noise
generator machine

Wind farms work best in open places where nothing gets in the wind's way. So far, wind farms in the United States capture enough wind to power about 4.5 million homes. That's only about one percent of the electricity we need. Slowly, though, the role of wind power is growing. More wind farms seem to **crop up** every year.

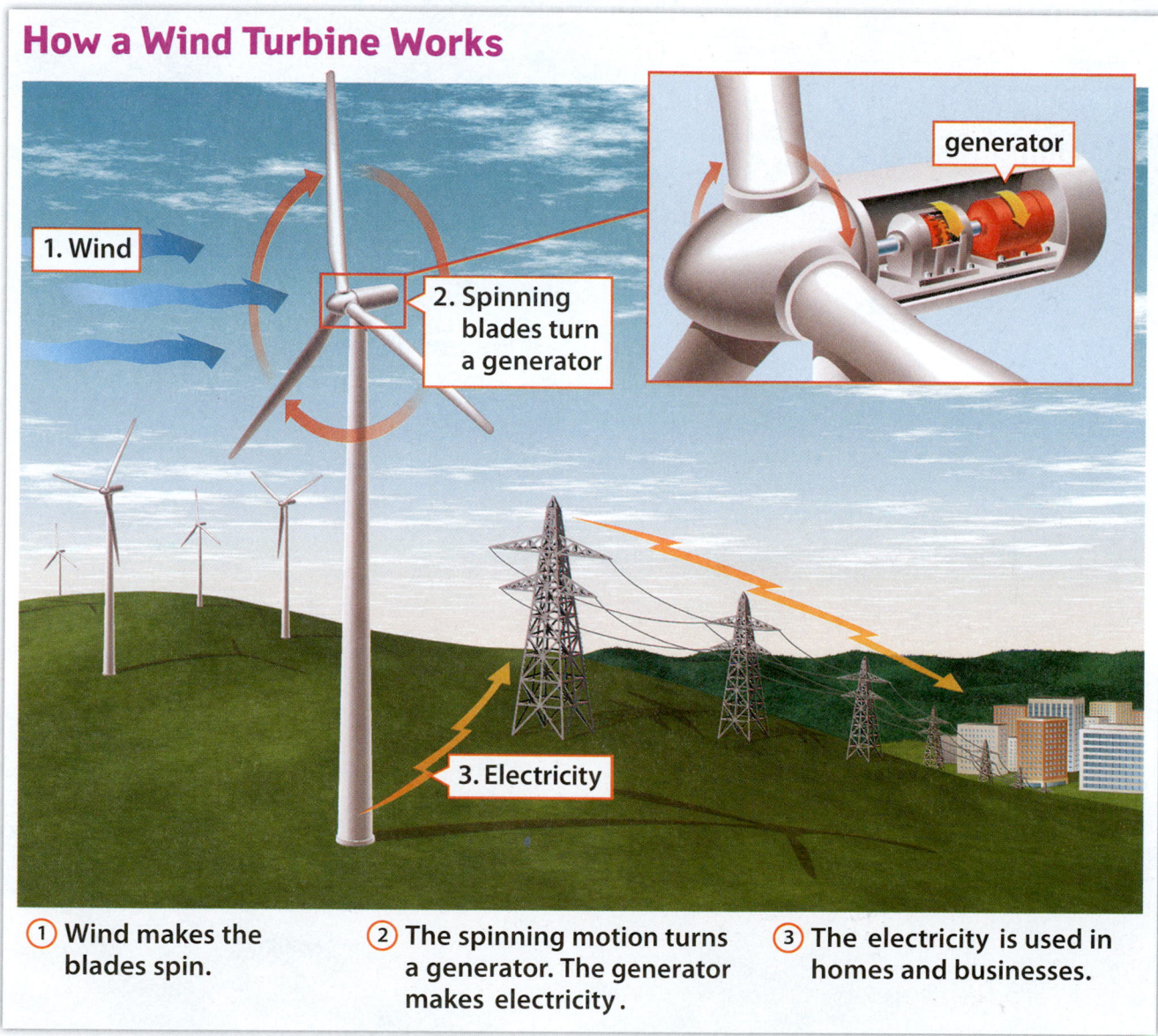

How a Wind Turbine Works

generator

1. Wind

2. Spinning blades turn a generator

3. Electricity

① **Wind makes the blades spin.**

② **The spinning motion turns a generator. The generator makes electricity.**

③ **The electricity is used in homes and businesses.**

In Other Words

crop up appear

▶ **Before You Move On**

1. **Ask Questions** Think of the way **electricity** is made from wind. What questions do you have about the process?

2. **Cause/Effect** How is wind **converted** into **electricity**? Explain.

Tornado Terror

Wind isn't always helpful. It can also be terrifying. Just ask anyone who has seen a tornado. A tornado is a **vertical column** of spinning air.

Tornadoes form in **severe** thunderstorms. They can start when wind above the ground moves faster than wind at ground level. The air in between rolls into a spinning tube.

Sometimes air rising inside a thunderstorm **tilts** the spinning tube **upright**. The result is a tornado.

▲ Tornadoes form in powerful thunderstorms.

In Other Words
vertical column tall tube
severe very strong
tilts pushes
upright until it stands up

Most tornadoes last only a few minutes, but their violent winds do lots of damage. Tornadoes can tear apart cars, houses, and anything else in their way.

On May 3, 1999, a series of deadly tornadoes ripped across Oklahoma. Weather scientists followed one of the **twisters** in a truck. Using **radar**, the scientists **clocked** the tornado's winds at 484 kilometers (301 miles) an hour. It was the fastest tornado ever recorded.

The Structure of a Tornado

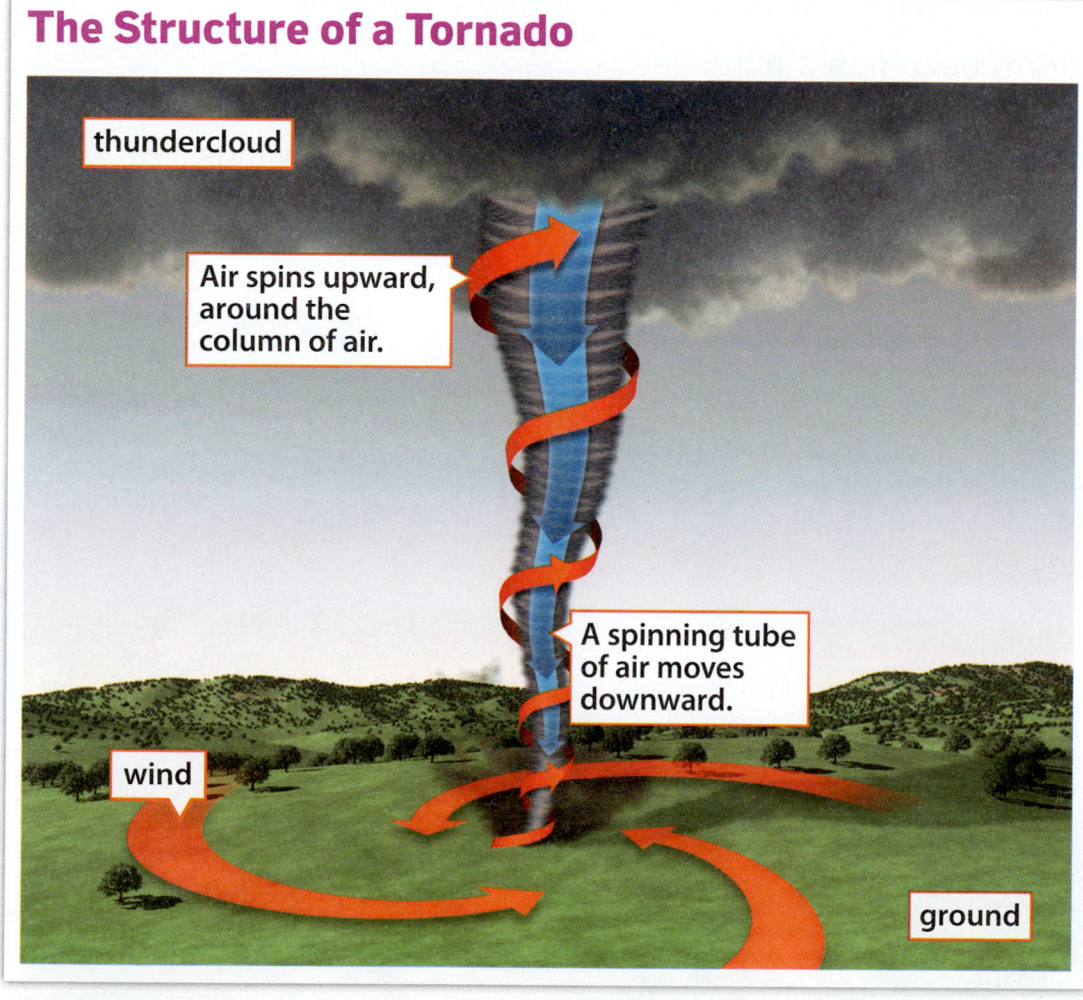

thundercloud

Air spins upward, around the column of air.

A spinning tube of air moves downward.

wind

ground

◄ A tornado's power increases as it spins faster.

In Other Words
twisters tornadoes
radar special technology
clocked measured

▶ **Before You Move On**
1. **Cause/Effect** What is one of the reasons tornadoes form? Which sentences tell you?
2. **Details** Which sentences tell you what weather scientists discovered about the Oklahoma tornado?

Hurricane Force

Tornadoes may be terrifying, but hurricanes are huge and terrifying. A hurricane can easily stretch across three states with winds that **pack a major punch**.

Hurricanes form over tropical oceans. Warm, **moist** air rises. More air moves in underneath and then rises. Big, wet clouds start to gather.

Over a few days, Earth's **rotation** causes the growing **mass** of clouds to spin. When winds reach 119 kilometers (74 miles) an hour, the storm becomes a hurricane.

Once hurricanes hit land, they can do extreme damage. The winds can destroy trees and buildings, and huge waves flood coasts.

▲ As the earth rotates, clouds that gather over the ocean may start to spin, too. Sometimes the spinning clouds become a hurricane.

In Other Words
pack a major punch are very strong
moist wet
rotation motion
mass group

A World of Wind

From gentle breezes to strong gusts, wind is everywhere. It can **sculpt** mountains and tear apart houses. Long ago, wind carried explorers to new places. Now it **helps light** cities.

The next time you are just **shooting the breeze**, think about the many ways that wind changes our world. ❖

In the strongest hurricanes, winds can race at more than 249 kilometers (155 miles) an hour.

In Other Words
sculpt shape
helps light provides electricity for
shooting the breeze relaxing and having fun

▶ **Before You Move On**
1. **Cause/Effect** How does Earth's motion cause hurricanes?
2. **Use Text Features** What does the section heading tell you about the text on this page?

235

Talk About It

1. How can you tell that this is a **science article**? Name two features.

   I can tell this is a science article because _____ .

   It includes _____ and _____ .

2. **Make a comparison** between a tornado and a hurricane.

   A tornado is _____ . But a hurricane is _____ .

3. Choose three section headings from "Wind at Work." Change each heading into a question that the section answers. Look for the answers. How does this help you understand the text better?

Learn test-taking strategies.
🌐 NGReach.com

Write About It

Write a paragraph to describe a very windy day. Use **Key Words** and describing words to tell what it is like. Then revise your draft to include describing words that are even more exact.

The day was _____ . The wind _____ .
It was _____ and _____ .

Cause and Effect

Make a cause-and-effect chart for "Wind at Work."

Cause-and-Effect Chart

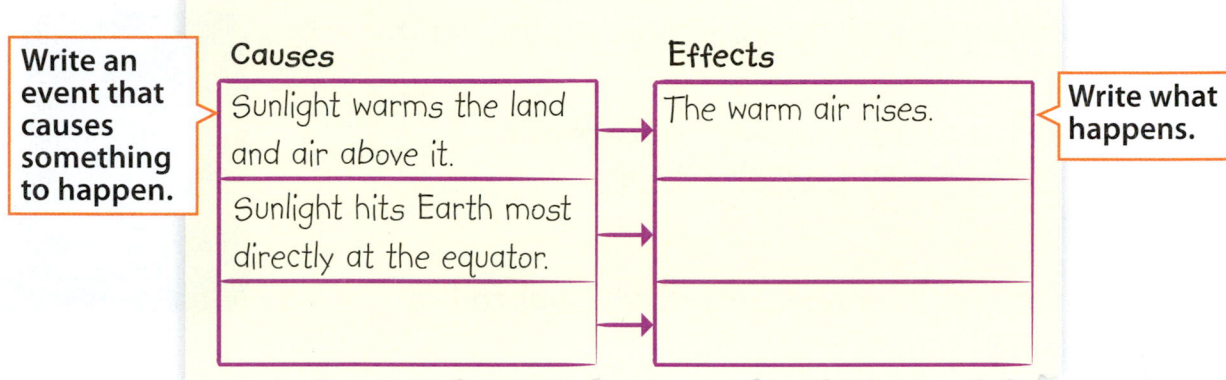

Write an event that causes something to happen.

Causes	Effects
Sunlight warms the land and air above it.	The warm air rises.
Sunlight hits Earth most directly at the equator.	

Write what happens.

Now use your cause-and-effect chart as you explain the important ideas in "Wind at Work" to a partner. Use **Key Words** and words that connect each cause and effect.

_____ happens because _____.
As a result of _____, _____.

Fluency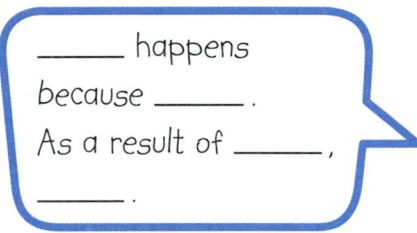

Use the Comprehension Coach to practice reading with intonation. Rate your reading.

Talk Together

How does wind affect you? Draw pictures to show different ways. Use **Key Words** as labels. Share your ideas with the class.

237

Context Clues

When you read, you may come to a word you don't know. Look for **context clues** to help you figure out the meaning.

The sentence may include a definition of the word.

> Energy produced from ocean waves is **renewable** because the waves **can never be used up**.

The word is **defined**.

An example in the sentence may give clues to the word's meaning.

> Things that are **scarce**, such as **diamonds** or **a hand-carved table**, usually cost a lot of money.

Diamonds and a hand-carved table are **examples** of things that are scarce.

Try It Together

Read the passage from "Wind at Work." Then answer the questions.

> Wind **sculpts** rocks and landscapes by tearing away tiny pieces off rocks. Piece by tiny piece, wind can erase a whole mountain. This process of wearing away is called **erosion**.

1. **What does sculpt mean in the first sentence?**

   A to erase

   B to create a mountain

   C to destroy

   D to form shapes

2. **What does erosion mean in the last sentence?**

   A a kind of wind

   B erasing a mountain

   C slowly grinding down

   D making landscapes

Connect Across Texts Read a persuasive essay about another valuable natural **resource**, water.

Genre A **persuasive essay** gives an opinion and tries to get readers to agree with it. The author uses facts to support his or her opinion, along with persuasive words like *must* and *should*.

Water
The Blue Gold

by Alexandra Cousteau, with Carol Verbeeck

▲ Alexandra Cousteau

Imagine that you go to brush your teeth one night. You turn on the faucet, but nothing comes out. Then you try to take a shower. There's no water there, either.

We use water for so many things. It's hard to imagine life without it. However, some scientists believe that **in this century**, clean water may become as highly valued as gold.

In Other Words
in this century during the next 100 years

▶ **Before You Move On**

1. **Ask Questions** What is a question you have about the author's opinion of water?
2. **Fact/Opinion** Identify an opinion in the second paragraph and explain how you know it is an opinion.

My Story

Water has always been an important part of my life. When I was seven years old, my grandfather taught me **to scuba dive**. His name was Jacques-Yves Cousteau. He explored the world's oceans. He made films and wrote books to share his explorations with the world.

My grandfather taught me that all living things, inside and outside the oceans, are connected by water. The future of our planet depends on our water <mark>resources</mark>. We must care for Earth's water by protecting and preserving it. Everything we do makes a difference.

▲ Water helps all living things survive. Here, I examine a frog from the waters of Botswana, a country in Africa.

▲ I often travel around the world and record water issues through film and photographs.

In Other Words
◀ **to scuba dive** how to dive deep in the ocean

Some factories dump chemicals into water systems.

▲ A huge mass of garbage—the world's largest garbage dump—floats in the Pacific Ocean.

Protect Against Pollution

Earth's water **flows** in an endless **cycle** around the planet. If we dump garbage in a river, lake, or ocean, it eventually flows to another body of water.

Pollution from farms and factories can affect the chemistry of water, too. It can change the balance of oxygen and other important elements in water. These changes affect plants and animals that live there. To help protect Earth's water, we must stop polluting our water systems.

In Other Words
cycle pattern; circle

▶ **Before You Move On**

1. **Ask Questions** Look at the photos on this page. What is one question you have about water pollution?
2. **Cause/Effect** Describe some effects of dumping garbage into rivers and lakes.

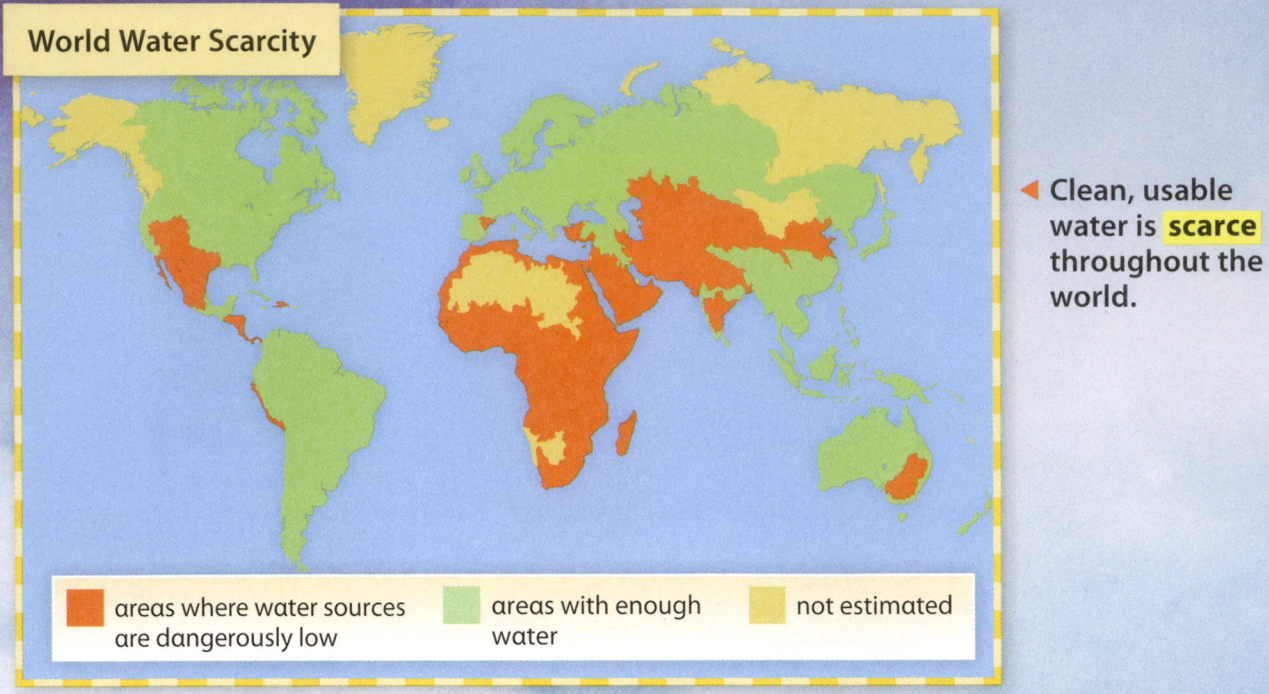

World Water Scarcity

areas where water sources are dangerously low

areas with enough water

not estimated

◄ Clean, usable water is **scarce** throughout the world.

A Scarce Resource

To preserve Earth's water, we must use it wisely. If you look at a world map, you'll see that Earth is mostly covered by water. Most of this water, however, cannot be used by people. In fact, only two percent of Earth's water is **available** to us. Seven billion people depend on this water!

Many cities and countries do not have enough fresh water. Fresh water is water that is not salty like ocean water. Scientists believe that one third of Earth's population will not have enough fresh water by 2025.

In many places, people pump water from underground. ▶

Protect Our Blue Gold

We must all take action to protect water resources. Talk with people about water issues. Encourage people to use cleaning products without **toxic** chemicals. Ask them not to throw garbage into **storm drains**. You should conserve water by turning off the faucet while you brush your teeth. Or you can take shorter showers.

Remember that water flows in an endless cycle. This source of life connects us all. The next time you get a cool drink from the water fountain, think about what life would be like without clean water. We should protect our planet's **precious** blue gold. ❖

Pure, clean water is a valuable resource.

Animals, such as dolphins, need clean water to survive.

People need clean water, too.

We must work together to keep our waterways clean.

In Other Words
toxic dangerous
storm drains water pipes
precious extremely valuable

▶ **Before You Move On**
1. **Ask Questions** Look at the map on page 242. What questions do you have about it?
2. **Use Text Features** How is the last section heading persuasive?

243

Respond and Extend

Compare Genres

A science article and a persuasive essay are different genres. Both give information on a specific topic. In what other ways are they similar? How are they different? How do the authors use language? Work with a partner to complete the comparison chart.

Comparison Chart

	"Wind at Work"	"Water: The Blue Gold"
Topic	wind	water
Point of view: first person or third person?	third person	
Author's purpose		
What statements from the text support the purpose?		
Does the author express a strong opinion about the topic? Give an example. Explain it.		
What did you learn?		

Talk Together

How do wind and water affect your daily life? Think about the science article and the persuasive essay about natural resources. Use **Key Words** to talk about your ideas.

Present-Tense Action Verbs

A **present-tense action verb** tells about an action that happens now or on a regular basis.

<table>
<tr><th colspan="2">**Grammar Rules** Present-Tense Action Verbs</th></tr>
<tr>
<td>• Add **-s** to the action verb if the subject tells about one place, one thing, or one other person.</td>
<td>The wind **blows** the leaves, and it **turns** the umbrella inside out.

She **finds** shelter from the wind.

He **runs** for shelter from the storm.</td>
</tr>
<tr>
<td>• Do not add **-s** if the subject is **I**, **you**, **we**, **they**, or a plural noun.</td>
<td>We **sail** the boat across the lake.

I **use** the wind to move fast.

Wind farms **generate** electricity.

They **make** clean energy.

You **watch** the wind mills.</td>
</tr>
</table>

Read Present-Tense Action Verbs

Read these sentences about a storm. Identify four action verbs. Spell each action verb. Name the subject.

> The storm sweeps over the land, and the wind blows dust and dry leaves everywhere. Dark clouds threaten the sky. A tornado grows.

Write Present-Tense Action Verbs

Write a short paragraph about the power of the wind. Use present-tense action verbs in your sentences. Make sure the verbs agree with the subjects. Share your work with a partner.

Express Needs and Wants

Listen to Seth's chant. Then use **Language Frames** to talk about things in nature that you need or want.

Chant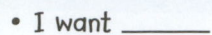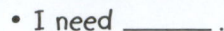

TO THE WOODS

Cars in the street go honk, honk, honk!
I want some peace and calm.
Where can I go? I know!
I'll go to the woods.

Kids in the street go cough, cough, cough!
I need clean air to breathe.
Where can I go? I know!
I'll go to the woods.

Birds in the trees go chirp, chirp, chirp!
I want to stay all day.
Where did I go? You know!
I'm here in the woods.

Key Words

Key Words

atmosphere
element
landscape
material
natural

Look at the picture. Use **Key Words** and other words to talk about the basic parts of the **natural** world.

Elements of Nature

Air makes up the **atmosphere** around us.

Plants bring life to the **landscape**.

Rock and soil are the natural **materials** that form the landscape.

Talk Together

Think about how you relate to the natural world. Imagine that you are in the photo above. What would you need or want? Use **Language Frames** from page 246 and **Key Words** as you tell a partner.

Problem and Solution.

When you tell a story, you may start with a **problem** and then tell what you did to try to solve it. Finally, you may tell about the **solution**.

Look at the pictures of Seth at the park.

Map and Talk

You can make a problem-and-solution chart to tell about a story's problem, the actions taken to solve it, and the solution.

Problem-and-Solution Chart

| Problem: The park is a mess. | Write the problem here. |

↓

| Event 1: Seth picks up the trash. | Write each action in an event box. |
| Event 2: Seth hangs up a sign. | |

↓

| Solution: People are helping to keep the park clean. | State the solution here. |

Talk Together

Think of a problem that you solved. Make a problem-and-solution chart. Add as many event boxes as you need. Tell your partner about your chart.

More Key Words

Use these words to talk about "Doña Flor," "Comida," and "The Sun in Me."

benefit
(**be**-nu-fit) *noun*

A **benefit** is something helpful. One **benefit** of living near school is that you can walk there.

force
(**fors**) *noun*

A **force** is a great power in nature. The **force** of rushing water can break apart roads.

interact
(in-tur-**akt**) *verb*

When you **interact**, you communicate in some way. This girl **interacts** with the horse.

modify
(**mah**-du-fī) *verb*

When you **modify** something, you change it. **Modify** a jar to make a bird feeder.

relate
(ri-**lāt**) *verb*

To **relate** two things, think about how they are connected. You can **relate** these two sports.

Talk Together

Work with a partner to complete a Word Map for each **Key Word**.

Definition	Characteristics
a great power in nature	can move or change things
Example	**Example**
The force of a big river can change land.	A stream does not have a lot of force to change land.

Word: force

Add words to My Vocabulary Notebook.
NGReach.com

Learn to Ask Questions

Watch or listen to a weather report on TV, on the radio, or online. Do you hear words that are new to you? Is there information that you do not understand? Ask yourself questions. They might help you reinforce what you already know or determine what you need to learn. Tell a partner what questions you asked and what you learned.

You **ask questions** when you read, too. Some of your questions will help you look beyond the text to find the meaning.

How to Ask Questions

👁	**1.** As you read, notice if you do not understand something in the text.
❓	**2.** Ask yourself what the author is trying to tell you.
💭	**3.** Think about what you know, to help you figure out the meaning of the text.

I do not understand _____ .

I ask myself, _____ .

I think about _____ to understand _____ .

Talk Together

Read Seth's mystery story. Read the sample question. Then use **Language Frames** to tell a partner about the questions you asked while reading.

Mystery Story

Lights Out

Everything went black! All of a sudden, every light in our apartment turned off, including the TV! We lit candles. Mom flipped the circuit breaker switches. That didn't **modify** things. Still no lights!

We thought of Mr. Acito next door. One **benefit** of living in a high-rise building is that you always have help nearby.

Mr. Acito answered the door, gripping a flashlight. Uh-oh! He didn't have lights either.

We discovered that the whole building was dark. All of our neighbors gathered downstairs in the front lobby. They **interacted** pleasantly, sharing candles and flashlights.

Then we heard a huge crack of thunder. A bright flash of lightning lit up the sky. It started to pour. Rain pounded the roof.

Mr. Acito turned on a battery-powered radio. The announcer said that the **force** of the storm had caused electrical problems. So the rain was directly **related** to our blackout.

The storm hit a tower at the power station before the first crack of thunder reached our building. That's why the lights went out before the rain came. An hour later the lights came back. We applauded. Events in the outside **atmosphere** can affect the atmosphere at home!

Sample Question

"I do not understand what circuit breakers are.

I ask myself, 'What do they have to do with lights?'

I think about how switches work to understand that breakers can turn electricity on."

◀ = A good place to ask a question

251

Read a Story

Genre

A **tall tale** is a funny story. Characters and events are exaggerated. The hero may be based on a real person or may be fictional.

Main Character

Often the main character in a tall tale solves problems in an unusual or exaggerated way.

Doña Flor ▶

Doña Flor

by **Pat Mora** ◆ illustrated by **Raúl Colón**

▶ **Set a Purpose**
Doña Flor is an unusual person.
Find out about her.

Every winter morning when the sun opened one eye, Doña Flor grabbed a handful of snow from the top of a nearby mountain. "*Brrrrrrrr,*" she said, rubbing the snow on her face to wake up.

Long, long ago, when Flor was a baby, her mother sang to her in a voice sweet as river music. When Flor's mother sang to her corn plants, they grew tall as trees. When she sang to her baby, her sweet flower, Flor grew and grew, too.

Some children laughed at her because she was different. "*¡Mira!* Look! Big Foot!" they called when she walked by.

"Flor talks funny," they whispered, because Flor spoke to butterflies and grasshoppers. She spoke every language, even **rattler**.

In Other Words
◀ **rattler** rattlesnake

254

But soon Flor's friends and neighbors asked her for help. Children late for school asked, "***Por favor***, Flor, could you give us a ride?" She took just one of her giant steps and was at the school door.

When Flor finally stopped growing, she built her own house, *una casa* big as a mountain and open as a canyon. She scooped a handful of dirt and made herself a valley for mixing clay, straw, and water. She added some *estrellas*. The stars made the adobe shine. When she worked, Flor sang. Birds came and built nests in her hair. Flor wanted everyone to feel at home in her house. "**Mi casa es su casa**," she said to people, animals, and plants, so they knew they were always welcome. Everyone called her **Doña** Flor because they respected her.

No one needed an alarm clock in Doña Flor's **pueblo**. When her hands, wide as plates, started pat-pat-patting tortillas, everyone in the village woke up. So her neighbors would have plenty to eat, she stacked her tortillas on the huge rock table in front of her house.

Flor's tortillas were the biggest, best tortillas in the whole wide world. People used the extra ones as roofs. *Mmmm*, the houses smelled corn-good when the sun was hot. In the summer, the children floated around the pond on tortilla rafts.

In Other Words

Mi casa es su casa My house is your house (in Spanish)

Doña Lady; Mrs. (a show of respect in Spanish)

pueblo village (in Spanish)

▶ **Before You Move On**

1. **Character** What are three things Doña Flor can do that other people can't?
2. **Ask Questions** Look at the pictures on pages 256 and 257. What questions do you have about the story?

257

One warm spring day, while a family of lizards swept her house, Doña Flor brought out her stacks of fresh tortillas. Nobody came. *Hmmmmmmm,* thought Flor. She started knocking on doors and calling to her neighbors.

"*¿Qué pasa?* What's the matter?" she asked, bending down to **peer** into their small doors to see where they were hiding.

"*¡El puma!*" they whispered. "The children have heard a huge mountain lion circling the village. Listen!"

In Other Words
peer look
◀ *¡El puma!* The mountain lion! (in Spanish)

258

Doña Flor and her animal friends went out looking for the huge **gato**, but they couldn't find it. That night, she carried her tired friends, the coyotes and rabbits, back home. But just as she started to **tuck them in** and read them a good-night story, they all heard, "*Rrrr-oarrr!*"

"Where *is* that darn cat?" asked Flor, but the scared animals were shaking and shivering under their sheets.

That night, the wind got so angry that he blew the trees and houses first to the left and then to the right. Together, the wind and the giant cat roared all night, and nobody got much sleep.

In Other Words
gato cat (in Spanish)
tuck them in put them in their beds

▶ **Before You Move On**

1. **Problem/Solution** What is the problem, and how does Doña Flor try to solve it?
2. **Make Inferences** Why do you think the author describes the wind as if it were a person?

As the sun rose, Flor's neighbors peered out their windows. Tired-looking Flor was giving that wind a big hug to quiet him down. Then she started her morning **chores**.

Doña Flor had work to do. But first she looked around the village. Where were her neighbors? Then she heard, "*Rrrr-oarrr! Rrrr-oarrr!*"

Flor **stomped off** to find the puma that was bothering her **amigos.**

Exhausted by afternoon, Doña Flor still hadn't found that cat, so she sat outside the library for a rest.

In Other Words
chores activities
stomped off walked away angrily
amigos friends (in Spanish)
Exhausted by afternoon Tired from the morning activities

260

What can I do to cheer up my friends? wondered Flor. Now, Flor knew that her village needed *un río*, a river, so to make her neighbors happy, Doña Flor scratched a new riverbed with her thumb. When the water **trickled** down the stones for the first time, Flor called out, "Just listen to that! Isn't that the prettiest sound you've ever heard?" She smiled, but today her neighbors could barely smile back. They were too worried about the mountain lion. Suddenly there was a terrible "*Rrrr-oarrr! Rrrr-oarrr!*"

In Other Words
trickled flowed gently

Where is that big monster gato? Doña Flor wondered. *I know,* thought Flor, *I'll go to my animal friends for help.*

"Go quietly to the tallest **mesa**," said the deer.

Doña Flor walked very, very softly up to the tallest mesa. She looked around carefully for the giant cat. Then right near her she heard, "*Rrrr-oarrr! Rrrr-oarrr!*" Flor jumped so high, she bumped into the sun and gave him a black eye.

Flor looked around. All she saw was the back of a cute little puma.

In Other Words
mesa plateau

Doña Flor began to **tiptoe** toward the puma when all of a sudden he roared into a long, hollow log. The sound became a huge "*Rrrr-oarrr!*" that echoed down into the valley.

Now, the little puma thought the loud noise was so funny that he rolled on his back and started laughing and laughing—until he saw big Doña Flor.

Aha! thought Flor. "Are you the **chico** who's causing all the trouble?" she asked. The little puma tried to look very fierce. "*Rrrr-oarrr!*" he growled, but without the log, the growl wasn't really very fierce.

In Other Words
tiptoe walk quietly
chico little one (in Spanish)

▶ **Before You Move On**

1. **Problem/Solution** How does Doña Flor find the puma?
2. **Ask Questions** What questions do you have about the puma's behavior?

Doña Flor just smiled at that brave cat and said, "Why, you're just a kitten to me, **Pumito**." She bent down and scratched that puma behind the ears, and she whispered to him in cat talk until that cat began to purr.

Suddenly Flor heard a new noise. "Doña Flor, *¿dónde estás?* Where are you?" called her worried neighbors. Even though they were frightened, they had all come, holding hands, looking for her.

"Meet my new *amigo*," said Doña Flor.

That evening, Flor **plucked** a star and **plunked** it on the tallest tree so her friends in the *pueblo* could find their way home.

In Other Words
Pumito Little Puma (in Spanish)
plucked picked
plunked put

264

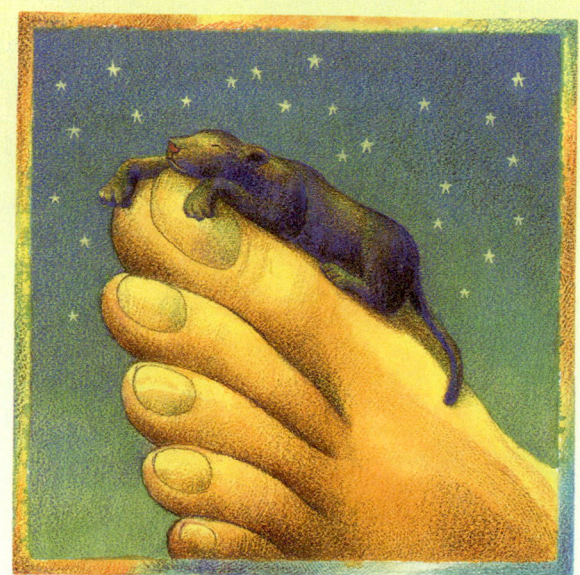

Flor reached up and filled her arms with clouds smelling of flowery breezes. She shaped the clouds into a soft, deep bed and into hills of puffy pillows. "*Mmmm,*" said Flor as she snuggled in the clouds.

"Tonight, I'm very tired after my adventure with the giant cat, right, Pumito?" **chuckled** Doña Flor. All the animals **snuggled** down with her, and Pumito stretched out over her big toes. ❖

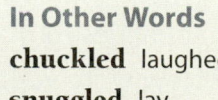

In Other Words
chuckled laughed
snuggled lay

▶ **Before You Move On**

1. **Confirm Prediction** What happens to the puma after Flor discovers his secret?
2. **Ask Questions** Look at the pictures on this page. What questions do you have about the ending of the story?

265

Pat Mora

"I love landscapes," says Pat Mora. Desert landscapes are a huge theme in her work. That's not surprising. She grew up in El Paso, Texas, a city in the middle of a desert.

El Paso is also near the border between the United States and Mexico. "In my house, we spoke both Spanish and English," she says. Today, her books are published in both languages.

Ms. Mora grew up with tall tales about Paul Bunyan and Babe the Blue Ox. She decided to write this tall tale about a woman named Doña Flor.

"The amazing thing about her, was, that she is so connected to the land, and that her heart is so generous," she says.

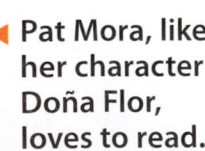

◄ Pat Mora, like her character Doña Flor, loves to read.

Writer's Craft

On page 262, Pat Mora writes that Doña Flor jumped so high, she gave the sun a black eye. Find other parts of the story where the author gives human qualities to non-human things. Now write your own sentence that gives human qualities to an object or animal.

Raúl Colón

What does the wind look like? If you are an illustrator, you ask yourself questions like that. Then you start sketching. Raúl Colón thought a lot about the wind before he began drawing. He says, "I came up with a big open-mouth face, breathing the wind in and breathing the wind out."

Mr. Colón started drawing when he was young. "I learned how to draw the human body using comic books," he says. As a boy, he spent hours copying pictures of superheroes in action.

Today, Raúl Colón makes illustrations with watercolors and colored pencils. He had a lot of fun creating the pictures for *Doña Flor*. "I was fascinated to be able to draw this giant walking around the landscape," he says.

As a young boy, Raúl Colón lived in Puerto Rico. Today he lives in New York City. ▶

267

Talk About It

1. Why is "Doña Flor" a **tall tale**? Give two examples.

   This story is a tall tale because _____ .

   Another example is _____ .

2. Think about how Doña Flor **interacts** with other story characters. **Express** her friends' **needs and wants**.

   Doña Flor's friends need _____ . They want _____ .

3. Were Doña Flor's neighbors wise to be afraid of the puma? What makes you think so? Explain your ideas to a partner.

Learn test-taking strategies.
 NGReach.com

Write About It

How did people's feelings about Doña Flor change when she grew up? Why? Write a paragraph to explain. Use examples from the story and **Key Words** in your writing.

When Doña Flor was a little girl, people _____ .
When she grew up, _____ .

268

Problem and Solution

Make a problem-and-solution chart to show what happens in "Doña Flor."

Problem-and-Solution Chart

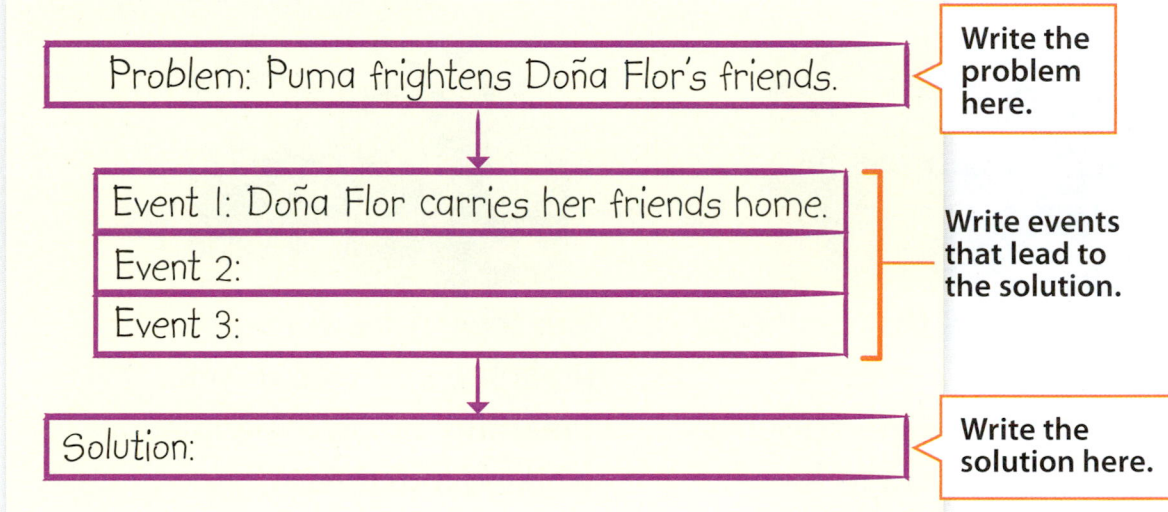

Problem: Puma frightens Doña Flor's friends. — Write the problem here.

Event 1: Doña Flor carries her friends home.
Event 2:
Event 3:
— Write events that lead to the solution.

Solution: — Write the solution here.

Now use your problem-and-solution chart as you retell "Doña Flor" to a partner. Use as many **Key Words** as you can.

The problem is _____ .
First, Doña Flor_____ .
Then, _____ .
The solution is _____ .

Fluency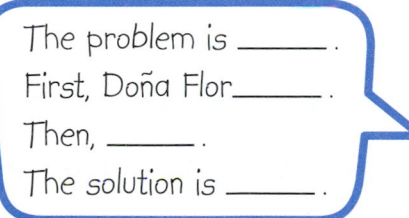

Use the Comprehension Coach to practice reading with expression. Rate your reading.

 Talk Together

How does Doña Flor interact with nature? Choose a favorite illustration in the story. Use **Key Words** as you explain what it shows.

Multiple-Meaning Words

Some words have more than one meaning. You can use context, or other words nearby, to figure out the correct meaning.

Force is a **multiple-meaning word**. Compare these examples.

Water is a **force** that can shape the landscape.

Meaning: something powerful that can cause change

This town has a **force** of firefighters to keep us safe.

Meaning: group of people working together

Try It Together

Read the sentences. Then answer the questions.

> Eli will spend the summer at his uncle's ranch. His uncle will <u>benefit</u> from his help. When Eli returns, he will <u>relate</u> stories of his trip.

1. **What does <u>benefit</u> mean in the second sentence?**

   A to get something good

   B to save money

   C a positive effect

   D a problem

2. **What does <u>relate</u> mean in the third sentence?**

   A to connect

   B to trade

   C to tell

   D to have relatives

Connect Across Texts Read these poems about other ways we **relate** to nature.

Genre **Lyrical poetry** expresses feelings. This form of poetry can be free verse. Some free verse is made up of stanzas, or groups of lines separated by space.

Nature INSIDE Us

Comida
by Victor M. Valle

One eats
the moon in a tortilla
Eat *frijoles*
and you eat the earth
Eat chile
and you eat sun and fire
Drink water
and you drink sky

In Other Words
Comida Food (in Spanish)
frijoles beans (in Spanish) ▶
chile hot peppers

▶ **Before You Move On**

1. **Ask Questions** Think of the objects compared in the poem. What questions do you have about them?

2. **Figurative Language** Which words help you imagine how chile tastes?

The Sun in Me

by **Moira Andrew**

The sun is in me,
pale morning flames
setting my still-sleeping
heart alight.

The wind is in me,
clear blue breath
leading my bare feet
into a new day.

272

The sea is in me,
deep green waves
whispering wild music
  in my ears.

The river is in me,
dark brown waters
swirling its questions
  around my head.

The moon is in me,
sad silver beams
painting my dreams
  with shadows.

In Other Words

setting my still-sleeping heart alight
  waking me up from a deep sleep

silver beams moonlight

▶ **Before You Move On**

1. **Elements of Poetry** How do the stanzas help the poet express her feelings about nature?

2. **Figurative Language** What does the author mean by "The sun is in me"?

Compare Figurative Language

Key Words

atmosphere	landscape
benefit	material
element	modify
force	natural
interact	relate

Writers use words in creative ways. **Figurative language** helps you visualize. It uses words that mean something different from their exact meaning. Figurative language often compares things that are not really alike.

Find examples of figurative language in the story and poems. Compare them. Work with a partner to complete the chart.

Comparison Chart

Title	Example	What It Means	What You Picture
"Doña Flor"	"the houses smelled corn good"	The houses smelled like corn, which smells good.	I picture a kitchen with people eating.
"Comida"			
"The Sun in Me"			

Talk Together

How is nature part of us? Think about the story and poems.
Use **Key Words** to talk about how nature is part of who we are.

Grammar and Spelling

Skills Trace: ▶ Forms of *be*
▶ Forms of *have*
⏵ **Forms of *be* and *have***

Forms of *be* and *have*

The verbs *be* and *have* have irregular forms. The subject and verb must agree. Look at the present tense forms.

Grammar Rules — Irregular Present-Tense Verbs

	be	**have**
• Use for **I**:	*am*	*have*
• Use for **you**:	*are*	*have*
• Use for **he**, **she**, or **it**:	*is*	*has*
• Use for **we**:	*are*	*have*
• Use for **they**:	*are*	*have*

Sometimes you can form a contraction with the subject and the verb. For example, you can change *I am* to *I'm* and *you are* to *you're*. An apostrophe shows where one or more letters are left out.

Read Forms of *be* and *have*

Read these sentences about "Doña Flor." Find present-tense forms of *be* and *have*. Identify the subjects. Find two contractions.

> Flor has many friends. Plants, animals, and even the wind are her friends. They're always welcome at her house. Flor is helpful. She's generous, too.

Write Forms of *be* and *have*

Choose an illustration in the story. Write a short paragraph about it. Include present-tense forms of *be* and *have*.

Write Like an Entertainer

Write a Tall Tale ✏

Write a story about someone who battles a force of nature. Share your tall tale during a storytelling festival.

Study a Model

A tall tale is a story that has a lot of exaggerated details. The details make it funny and impossible to believe.

Slue-Footed Sue and the Tornado

by Isabel Morales

==A monster tornado was headed toward town.== Everyone was scared—but not Slue-Foot Sue!

Sue raced toward the spinning tornado. She jumped up and grabbed the tornado by the tail. She pulled it down to the ground and stomped on its tail. The tornado screamed in pain. It twisted so tightly that it became a skinny piece of string.

==Sue rolled the skinny tornado into a little ball.== "You can forget about this tornado!" she said to the cheering crowd.

The **problem** gets the story started.

The **events** show what the character does to try to solve the problem.

The **solution** tells how the problem is solved.

Prewrite

1. **Choose a Topic** What event in nature will you build your story around? Consider a hurricane, an earthquake, a tornado, or another natural force. Talk with a partner to choose a good idea.

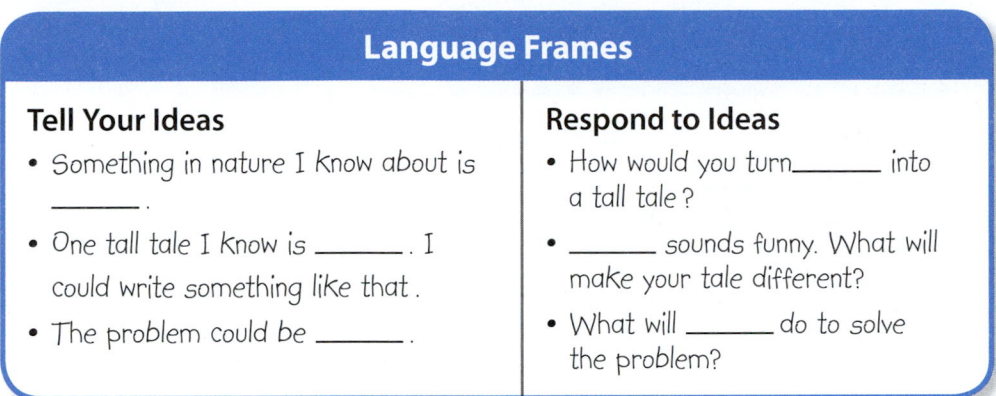

Language Frames	
Tell Your Ideas	**Respond to Ideas**
• Something in nature I know about is _____ .	• How would you turn _____ into a tall tale?
• One tall tale I know is _____ . I could write something like that.	• _____ sounds funny. What will make your tale different?
• The problem could be _____ .	• What will _____ do to solve the problem?

2. **Create Story Elements** Make up a character. Note what's special about the character. How will he or she solve the problem?

3. **Get Organized** Use a problem-and-solution chart to help you organize your details.

Problem-and-Solution Chart

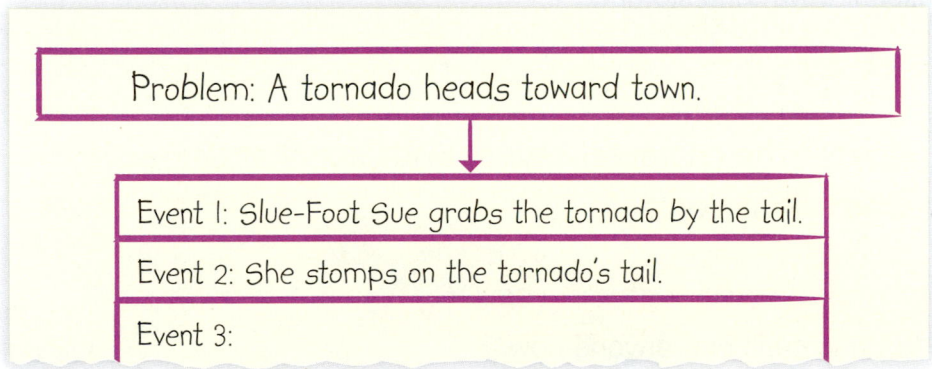

Problem: A tornado heads toward town.

Event 1: Slue-Foot Sue grabs the tornado by the tail.

Event 2: She stomps on the tornado's tail.

Event 3:

Draft

Use your chart to write your draft. Start with the problem and end with the solution. Exaggerate some details. Be sure to use words and sentences that sound like what the character would say and do.

Revise

1. **Read, Retell, Respond** Read your draft aloud to a partner. Your partner listens and then retells the story. Next, talk about ways to improve your writing.

Language Frames	
Retell	**Make Suggestions**
• The story takes place_____ .	• It was hard to picture _____ . You could add more details to _____ .
• The main character's problem is _____ . Then _____ . Finally, _____ .	
	• Your story is _____ in some parts. _____ is one place where you can add _____ .
• The funniest part is when _____ .	

2. **Make Changes** Think about your draft and your partner's suggestions. Then use the Revising Marks on page 585 to mark your changes.

   • Is every event clearly described? If not, add details.

   > on its tail.
   > She pulled it down and stomped.
   > ∧

   • Make sure what the character says sounds like that character. Replace words that don't.

   > "You can forget about this tornado!"
   > ∧ "This tornado can't hurt anyone now."

Edit and Proofread

Work with a partner to edit and proofread your tall tale. Remember to use lots of action verbs. Use verb forms of *have* and *be*. Make sure that each verb agrees with its subject. Use the marks on page 585 to show your changes.

Spelling Tip

✓ When you write a contraction, use an **apostrophe** in place of the letters that are left out.
I have = I've

Publish

1. **On Your Own** Add pictures. Read your story to your classmates. You may even want to use sound effects!

Presentation Tips	
If you are the speaker...	**If you are the listener...**
Read with expression. If your story is funny, make it sound funny.	Try to picture the story in your mind.
Use gestures to help your listeners imagine what the text describes.	Laugh or smile to show the speaker when you think something is funny.

2. **With a Group** Invite family and friends to a storytelling festival. Choose several of your tall tales to act out. Create scenery and assign parts. Practice and perform the stories for your audience.

279

Talk **Together**

In this unit, you found lots of answers to the **Big Question**. Now use your concept map to discuss the **Big Question** with the class.

Concept Map

Ways we relate to nature

We use plants like corn for food.

Write a Description

Use your concept map. Choose one way in which you relate to nature. Write a journal entry about it.

Share Your Ideas

Choose one of these ways to share your ideas about the **Big Question**.

Write It!

Write a Poster

Make a persuasive poster about water conservation. Tell why it's important to protect water resources. You may want to include helpful tips on how to keep from wasting water.

Talk About It!

Talk About Parks

What's your favorite park? Think about the ones in your neighborhood. Think of others you have visited. Choose a favorite park and tell a partner about it. Describe the plants and animals. Describe the activities you can do there.

Do It!

Give a Weather Report

Watch or listen to a weather report on TV, radio, or online. Use this information to plan your own weather report. Use any new weather terms that you learned. Include a diagram or picture to help you explain weather concepts. Then present your report.

Write It!

Write a Poem

Write a poem about how you relate to nature. Use sensory words to help people think of how things look, sound, smell, taste, or feel. Use figurative language, too.

Clouds pass
Like floating thoughts,

Invaders!

BIG Question

When do harmless things become harmful?

Unit at a Glance
- ▶ **Language**: Retell a Story, Define and Explain, Science Words
- ▶ **Literacy**: Make Inferences
- ▶ **Content**: Ecosystems

Unit
5

Share What You Know

Do It!

1. **Think** of a time when you really noticed something in nature. This thing might have surprised you.

2. **Draw** a picture of what you saw.

3. **Tell** the class about what made you notice this thing in nature. What was different about it?

Build Background: Use this interactive resource to learn about living things in their environment.
NGReach.com

Retell a Story

Listen to Diego's song. Then listen as he retells the story. Tell your partner a story about weeds in your neighborhood. Listen to your partner's story. Use **Language Frames** as you retell each other's stories.

Song

Flowers or Weeds?

When Johnny dropped sunflower seeds in the park,

Sprouts grew and grew.

When Johnny dropped sunflower seeds in the park,

Sprouts grew and grew.

They grew on the trails and they grew on the lawn,

By the end of the summer the grass was all gone.

And we all were sorry that Johnny had dropped those seeds.

Tune: "When Johnny Comes Marching Home"

Before Johnny arrived, the park had a beautiful lawn.

Key Words

decompose
experiment
humid
mold
spore

Key Words

Look at the picture. Use **Key Words** and other words to talk about a science **experiment** with food.

Step 1: Put a slice of bread in a **humid**, or damp, place.

Step 2: Check the bread about two weeks later.

mold spores

In this science experiment, **mold** grows on bread and **decomposes** it.

Talk Together

Make up a story about mold. Use **Language Frames** from page 284 and **Key Words** in your story. Tell it to a partner. Then have your partner retell the story and explain if the mold was harmful or harmless.

Plot

The events in a story go together to form the story's **plot**. The events follow a certain order, or sequence. You can summarize the plot. First, think about the most important things that happen. Then, tell these events in sequence.

Look at these pictures of Diego's vine.

Map and Talk

You can use an events chain to summarize the plot. In the first box, write about the first important event. In the next box, write about the next event. Keep writing the most important events in sequence.

Events Chain

| Diego plants a vine. | → | He waters the vine. | → | The vine grows fast. | → | The vine grows indoors and takes over. |

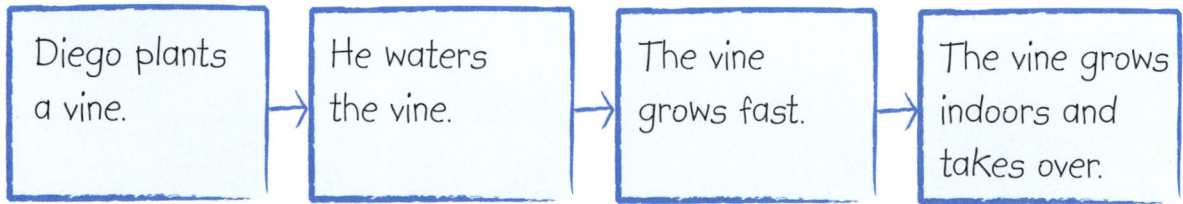

Listen as your partner tells a story about a fast-growing plant. Make an events chain to summarize the events of the story.

More Key Words

Use these words to talk about "The Fungus That Ate My School" and "Mold Terrarium."

contain
(kun-**tān**) *verb*

To **contain** something is to hold it inside. This jar **contains** many coins.

control
(kun-**trōl**) *verb*

To **control** something is to be in charge of it. The driver **controls** where the car goes.

environment
(in-**vi**-run-munt) *noun*

An **environment** is the area where something lives. Plants grow well in a healthy **environment**.

investigate
(in-**ves**-tu-gāt) *verb*

When you **investigate** something, you find out about it. The boy **investigates** the cave.

spread
(**spred**) *verb*

To **spread** is to cover a wider area. Flies can **spread** diseases.

Talk Together

Work with a partner. Make a Word Web for each **Key Word**.

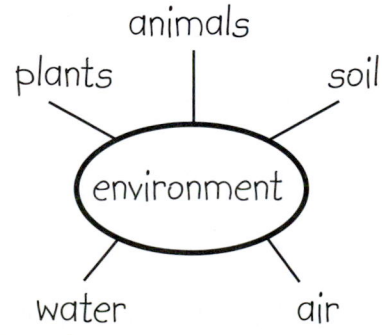

Add words to My Vocabulary Notebook.
NGReach.com

Learn to Make Inferences

Look at the picture. Diego does not say what he forgot to do. Look for clues to figure out, or **make an inference** about, what he forgot.

You can **make inferences** when you read, too.

How to Make Inferences

👁	**1.** Look for details in the text.	*I read_____.*
💭	**2.** Think about what you already know about the details and the topic.	*I know _____.*
🧩	**3.** Put your ideas together. What else can you figure out about the details?	*And so _____.*

Talk Together

Read Diego's retelling of a fairy tale. Read the sample inference. Then use **Language Frames** to tell a partner about the inferences you made while reading.

Fairy Tale

Jack and the Beanstalk

Jack went to buy some food. He met a man on the road.

"Buy my SUPER SEEDS," cried the man. "It's true! In just a week, you can feed your whole family with the food from just one bean seed."

Jack bought the dried seeds and planted them in his backyard. It was a perfect **environment** for growing beans.

In just a few days, the plant had **spread** across the yard. It was out of **control**! The garden wasn't big enough to **contain** the huge stalk, which began to climb high into the sky.

Jack decided to **investigate**. So he climbed the plant lightly, careful not to crush the stalk. Finally he reached a cloud. There, he found a box filled with bright shiny gold. Jack grabbed the gold and climbed quickly down the stalk.

Then Jack heard a rumble in the sky. The beanstalk started to shake.

Jack took an axe and chopped down the stalk. He heard someone shouting in the clouds. Jack sighed with relief. Then he used the gold to buy some real food for his family.

Sample Inference

"<u>I read</u> the man's promises.

<u>I know</u> that plants can't grow that fast.

<u>And so</u> I think the man wants to trick Jack."

◄ = A good place to make an inference

289

Read a Story

Genre

Most **science fiction** stories are based on ideas in science. Even if the events seem realistic, they probably could not really happen.

Narrator's Point of View

The person who tells a story is the narrator. If the narrator is one of the characters, then the story uses the first-person point of view. First-person narrators use the words *we* and *I*.

> A first-person narrator uses the words *we* and *I*.

We told Mr. Harrison our science experiments were **getting out of control**.

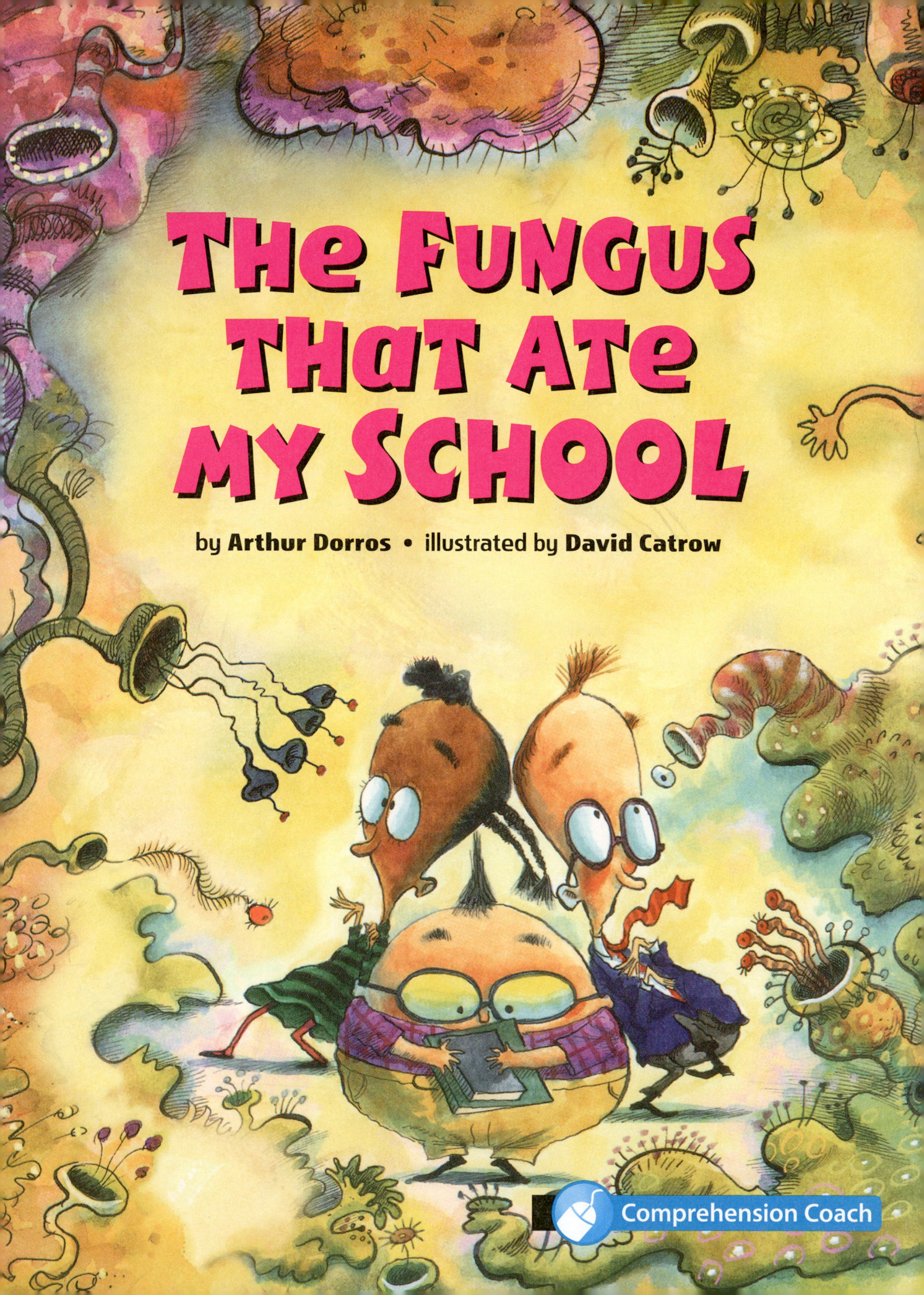

The Fungus That Ate My School

by **Arthur Dorros** • illustrated by **David Catrow**

We told Mr. Harrison our science **experiments** were **getting out of control**.

He didn't believe us, until **IT** ate our school.

IT started before spring vacation. Our class was studying fungus. We were growing fungus in jars.

"Are you sure our experiments will be all right while we're not here?" we asked Mr. Harrison.

"Don't worry," he told us, "fungus can take care of itself."

Mr. Harrison

In Other Words
getting out of control growing too fast

Ms. Moreover

There was rain during the whole vacation. Our first day back at school, Ms. Moreover, the principal, opened the front doors early.

"Come on, children, let's get out of the rain."

We walked into the dark hallway. Ms. Moreover turned on the lights.

"AAAG!" yelled Ellen.

Green, yellow, and purple **fuzz** covered everything.

"What is **IT**?" asked Ms. Moreover.

"**IT**'s big and ugly," said Ellen.

"**IT**'s **fantastic**!" I said.

"**IT** is *not* fantastic," said Ms. Moreover.

"That's true, **IT**'s a fungus!" said Mr. Harrison.

In Other Words
fuzz fungus
fantastic amazing; wonderful

▶ **Before You Move On**

1. **Plot** What happens at school during spring vacation?
2. **Point of View** Is this story written in the first person or third person point of view? Explain how you know.

The bell rang. Actually, the bell went *thud, thud, thud*. **IT** had **smothered** the bell. The **slimy** fuzz covered the floors, walls, bulletin boards, even the lights.

"**IT**'s eating everything!" I said.

"I don't hear **IT** chewing," Ellen **noted**.

"I didn't think fungus had a mouth," said Alex.

"Look! **IT**'s eating our **universe**!" cried Ellen.

In Other Words
smothered covered
slimy wet
noted said
universe models of the planets and sun

294

Mr. Page

IT **squished** under our feet as we **tromped** down the damp hallway. Water splattered on our heads.

"The roof's been leaking," Mr. Harrison said.

"That's definitely a problem," said Ms. Moreover. She opened the office door. "**IT** has taken over my office!"

We **ventured** further through the dark halls. Mr. Page, the librarian, looked into the library.

"Oh, no," said Mr. Page. He fainted.

End of Page.

In Other Words
squished made strange sounds
tromped walked
ventured went

▶ **Before You Move On**
1. **Plot** What does Mr. Harrison discover?
2. **Make Inferences** What does the author mean by "End of Page"?

▶ **Predict**
How will Mr. Harrison solve the
problem of the fungus?

Mr. Harrison let us into our classroom.
"**IT** ate my notebook!" cried Alex.

"**IT**'s eating my homework!" cried Ellen.

"Just as I thought," said Ms. Moreover when she
saw the jars of fungus we'd been growing. "**IT** must
be one of your class's experiments."

"**IT** doesn't look like mine," I said.

"We need **an expert opinion**," said Mr. Harrison.
"I know just who to call."

In Other Words

an expert opinion help from
someone who knows about fungus

Professor Macadamia

We went to the cafeteria.

"Don't let **IT** eat the food!" said Ms. Moreover. Too late.

"Looks like **IT** can eat almost anything," I said.

"Quickly, children, run!" said Ms. Moreover, "I mean *walk* to the nearest **exit**."

A car pulled up.

"Professor Macademia is here," Mr. Harrison said, "she knows fungus."

"She looks like she knows fungus," said Ellen.

"Amazing," said Professor Macademia, "**IT**'s **a jewel, a treasure**!"

"How can we get rid of **IT**?" Ms. Moreover asked. "That's all I want to know."

In Other Words
exit way out
a jewel, a treasure very special

297

The Fungus Unit

"Fresh air, light, **elbow grease**, and a little help from my friends in the Fungus Unit ought to **get rid of IT**," said Professor Macademia.

"Fungus Unit? What's a Fungus Unit?" Ellen asked.

"Special **branch** of the Sanitation Department," said someone dressed in white, pulling a giant hose into the school. Other workers carried in shovels, mops, and big lights.

"Action!" called one of them.

Suddenly the whole school was filled with whirring and clanking, swooshing and scrubbing.

In Other Words
elbow grease hard work
get rid of IT clean up the fungus
branch part

The Fungus Unit **scraped IT** off of
everything in the school and **hauled IT** away.

Professor Macademia kept our fungus
experiments. "I want to see if one of them is **IT**,"
she said. She held up one of the fungus jars. "Aha!"
said Professor Macademia. "This is **IT**!"

"It's not mine," said Alex.

"Uh-oh," I said, "**IT**'s mine."

▶ **Before You Move On**

1. **Plot** Who does Mr. Harrison call? How do
   they clean up the fungus?
2. **Make Inferences** What does the narrator
   mean by "Uh-oh...IT's mine"?

▶ **Predict**
What will happen to the students who grew the fungus?

"**It's not your fault,**" said Professor Macademia. "The wet, closed-up school was the perfect place for a fungus to grow. You have made a great discovery! This fungus belongs in the Museum of Fungus and Industry!"

Our class got a special award from the museum.

"Congratulations, class," Ms. Moreover said. "However, Mr. Harrison, I think you've learned enough about fungus for now."

"Don't worry," said Mr. Harrison. "No more fungus experiments—until next year." ❖

OUR Golden Moldy

▶ **Before You Move On**

1. **Confirm Prediction** Do any students get in trouble? Why or why not?
2. **Plot** Why does the class get an award?

300

Meet the Author

Arthur Dorros

AWARD WINNER

Why did Arthur Dorros write about a fungus that *eats* a school? It might be because he lives in the Pacific Northwest, a damp region where fungus grows easily. "A fungus got my shoe, another started eating its way through my clothes, and there's a fungus in our basement," he says.

Many of Mr. Dorros's book ideas come from things that happened to him. When he was four years old, his parents took him to an alligator farm. They thought it would be nice to take a picture of Arthur and the alligators. They didn't worry that there wasn't a fence between Arthur and the alligators. Fortunately, the alligators didn't *eat* Arthur! That experience later inspired his book *Alligator Shoes*.

▲ Arthur Dorros, as a child, at the alligator farm.

Writer's Craft

Write a brief paragraph about the similarities between Arthur Dorros's life and the characters and events in this story. Then write about the characters and events that are probably different from anything that could happen in the author's life.

Key Words

contain	humid
control	investigate
decompose	mold
environment	spore
experiment	spread

Talk About It

1. How do you know that the story is **science fiction**?

One science idea in this story is _____ .

2. Imagine that you are one of the workers in the Fungus Unit. **Retell the story** of the science **experiment** from your point of view.

Before we arrived, _____ . During spring vacation, _____ .

3. What do the characters in the story think about the fungus? Name two characters. Contrast their opinions of the fungus.

_____ likes the fungus because _____ .

_____ does not like the fungus because _____ .

Learn test-taking strategies.
NGReach.com

Write About It

What do you think will happen in Mr. Harrison's science class next year? Write two paragraphs to continue the story. First write some ideas. Use **Key Words** as you plan your writing. Then organize your ideas as you write your draft.

Another year passed by. Mr. Harrison wondered _____ .

Plot

Make an events chain to summarize the plot of "The Fungus That Ate My School." Tell the events in sequence. Notice how some events influence what happens later in the plot.

Events Chain

The students study fungus.	→	They leave for vacation.	→		→

Write the first important event.   **Write the next important event.**

Now use your events chain as you retell the story to a partner. Use as many **Key Words** as you can. Record your retelling.

First, _____ .
Next, _____ .
Then, _____ .

Fluency  Comprehension Coach

Use the Comprehension Coach to practice reading with expression. Rate your reading.

Talk Together

How is fungus both harmless and harmful? Working in a group, make two lists. Use **Key Words** in your lists.

Antonyms

Antonyms are words with opposite meanings. Writers use them to show contrast: This morning fungus covered **everything**. By noon, **nothing** had any fungus on it.

Sometimes a word like *not* or *but* signals the use of antonyms: The fungus seemed **ordinary** , but I knew it was **special** .

You might see antonyms on tests in **word analogies**. An analogy shows how two words relate to each other.

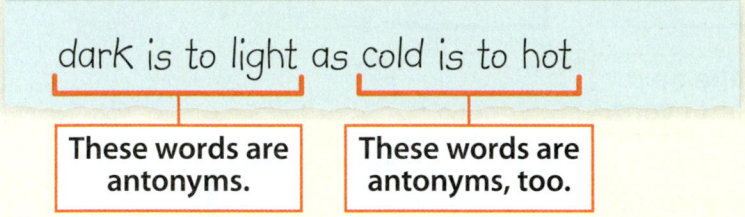

dark is to light as cold is to hot

These words are antonyms.   These words are antonyms, too.

The relationship between both pairs of words is the same. They are opposites.

Try It Together

Read each item. Choose the word that best completes the analogy.

1. **fantastic** is to **terrible** as **special** is to

   A super

   B nasty

   C unique

   D ordinary

2. **treasure** is to **trash** as **expert** is to

   A professional

   B beginner

   C silly

   D unknown

Connect Across Texts In this science **experiment**, you'll **investigate** how fungus grows.

Genre A **science experiment** helps test an idea. It has a list of materials and a list of steps to follow. Sometimes the text explains the results, too.

Mold Terrarium

from *The Science Explorer*

Materials List

leftover bread, fruit, vegetables, or cheese, cut into small pieces

clear plastic container with a lid

water

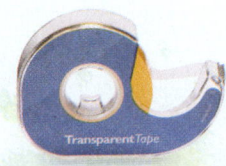

tape

▶ **Before You Move On**

1. **Make Connections** Based on what you know about **mold**, why do you think you need water to do the **experiment**?

2. **Use Text Features** Look at the photos. What do they show you?

Steps to Follow

1. Dip each piece of food into some water and put it into your container. Try to **spread** the pieces out so they are close to each other but not all in a **heap**.

2. Put the lid on the container. Put tape around the edge of the lid to **seal it**.

3. Put the container in a place where no one will **knock it over** or throw it away.

In Other Words
heap pile
seal it make sure no air can get in or out
knock it over spill it

4 Every day, look at the food in your **terrarium**. Do not open the container. After two or three days, you should see blue or green or white **fuzzy stuff** growing on some of the pieces of food. After a few more days, some of the food may start to **rot**. For about two weeks, you can watch how the **mold** spreads and how things rot. After that, it'll get boring, because not much more will happen.

mold

▲ After two or three days, mold will start to appear.

In Other Words
terrarium container
fuzzy stuff mold
rot decompose

▶ **Before You Move On**
1. **Steps in a Process** What might happen if you did not perform step 2 of the **experiment**? Explain.
2. **Use Text Features** Look at the photo on this page. Explain the information it shows.

Here are some things to notice:

- Which food started getting moldy first?

- What color is the mold?

- What texture is the mold? Is it flat, fuzzy, or bumpy?

- Does mold spread from one piece of food to another?

- Do different kinds of mold grow on different types of food?

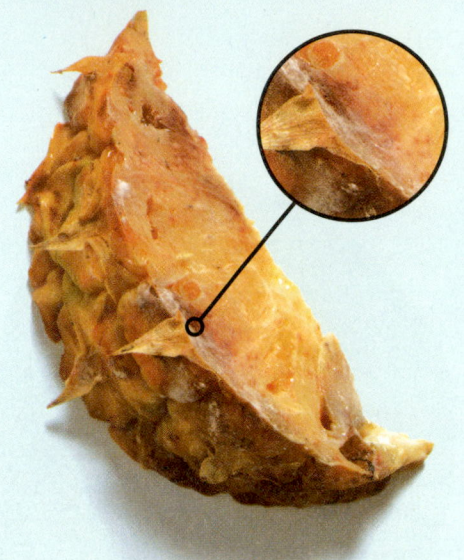

 DANGER!

When you're through with your mold terrarium, throw it in the garbage. Don't reuse the container. Don't even open the lid! Mold is not good for some people to smell or breathe.

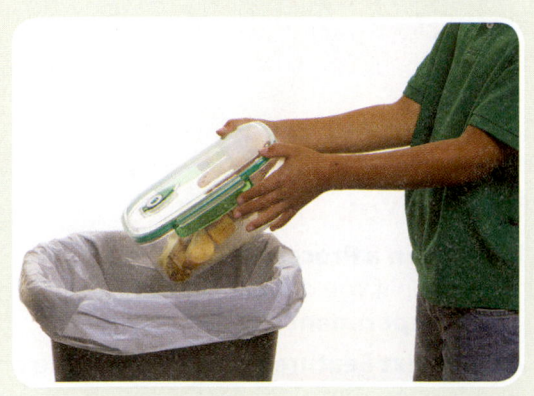

In Other Words
through finished

308

What is mold, anyway?

That fuzzy stuff growing on the food is mold, a kind of fungus. Mushrooms are one kind of fungus. Molds are another.

Unlike plants, molds don't grow from seeds. They grow from tiny **spores** that float in the air. When spores fall onto a piece of damp food, they often grow into mold.

Green plants are green because they **contain** a chemical called chlorophyll (**klor**-uh-fil). Chlorophyll allows green plants to capture the sun's energy and use it to make food from air and water. Unlike green plants, mold and other fungi have no chlorophyll and can't make their own food.

▲ Brown mushrooms are one kind of fungus.

▼ Molds grow from tiny spores like these.

In Other Words
damp slightly wet

▶ **Before You Move On**

1. **Details** Why shouldn't you reuse the plastic container from this **experiment**?

2. **Compare/Contrast** How are **molds** different from plants?

How does mold feed itself?

The mold that grows in a mold terrarium feeds on bread, cheese, and other foods. The mold produces chemicals that make the food break down and start to rot. As the bread rots, the mold grows.

HOW MOLD FEEDS ITSELF

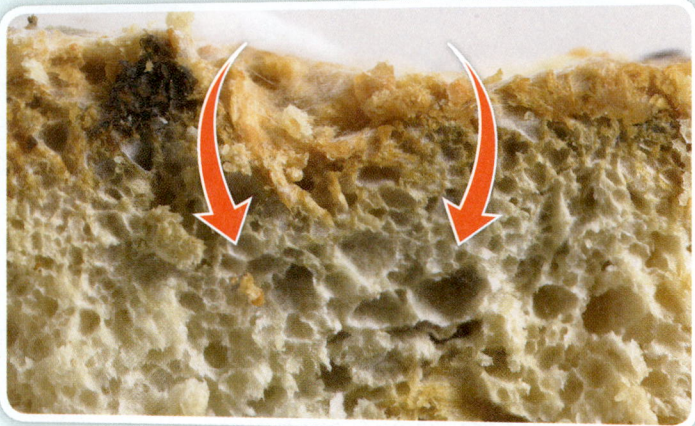

Mold produces chemicals that make the bread start to rot.

The rotting bread releases nutrients that cause the mold to grow.

The mold growth spreads across the bread.

Who wants this stuff around?

It can be annoying to find moldy food in your refrigerator. In nature, though, mold is very useful. It helps break down dead plants and animals. In a natural **environment**, rotting things return to the soil, providing nutrients for other plants. Mold is a natural recycler. ❖

▼ Mold is an important part of the natural environment.

▶ **Before You Move On**

1. **Make Inferences** What might happen in a forest if there were no **mold**?
2. **Use Text Features** Look at the diagram. Explain what it shows.

Key Words

contain	humid
control	investigate
decompose	mold
environment	spore
experiment	spread

Compare Author's Purpose

Each genre, or form of writing, has a certain purpose. An **author's purpose** for writing science fiction is different from the purpose for writing an experiment.

Compare "The Fungus That Ate My School" and "Mold Terrarium." Work with a partner to complete the checklist.

Comparison Chart

Purpose	Science Fiction Story	Science Experiment
Tells about a science idea	✔	
Tests a science idea		✔
Tells how to do something		
Is mostly fun to read		
Describes events that can't really happen		

Write a checkmark if it has this purpose.

Talk Together

When do living things become harmful? Think about the science fiction story and science experiment you just read. Use **Key Words** to talk about your ideas.

Adjectives

An **adjective** tells about a noun. You can use adjectives to describe things or to compare things.

Grammar Rules Adjectives

• Use adjectives to tell about the color, size, or shape or something.	**Round** blobs of **purple** fuzz covered the **long** walls.
• Use adjectives to tell how something sounds, feels, looks, tastes, or smells.	We heard **loud** sounds. We saw **fluffy** puffs of smoke.
• Some adjectives even tell how something is used.	The **cleaning** fluids had a **horrible** smell.
• Add **-er** to a one-syllable adjective when you compare two things.	The fungus in the library was damp**er** than in the hall.
• Add **-est** to a one-syllable adjective to compare three or more things.	The great**est** experiments can happen by accident.

Read Adjectives

Read these sentences from "The Fungus That Ate My School." What adjectives can you find?

> It squished under our feet as we tromped down the damp hallway. We ventured further through the dark halls.

Write Adjectives

What fun experiments have you done? Write a paragraph to tell about one of them. Try to use adjectives in different ways.

Define and Explain

Listen to Mona's poem. Then use **Language Frames** to define and explain what is happening in the animals' environment.

Poem

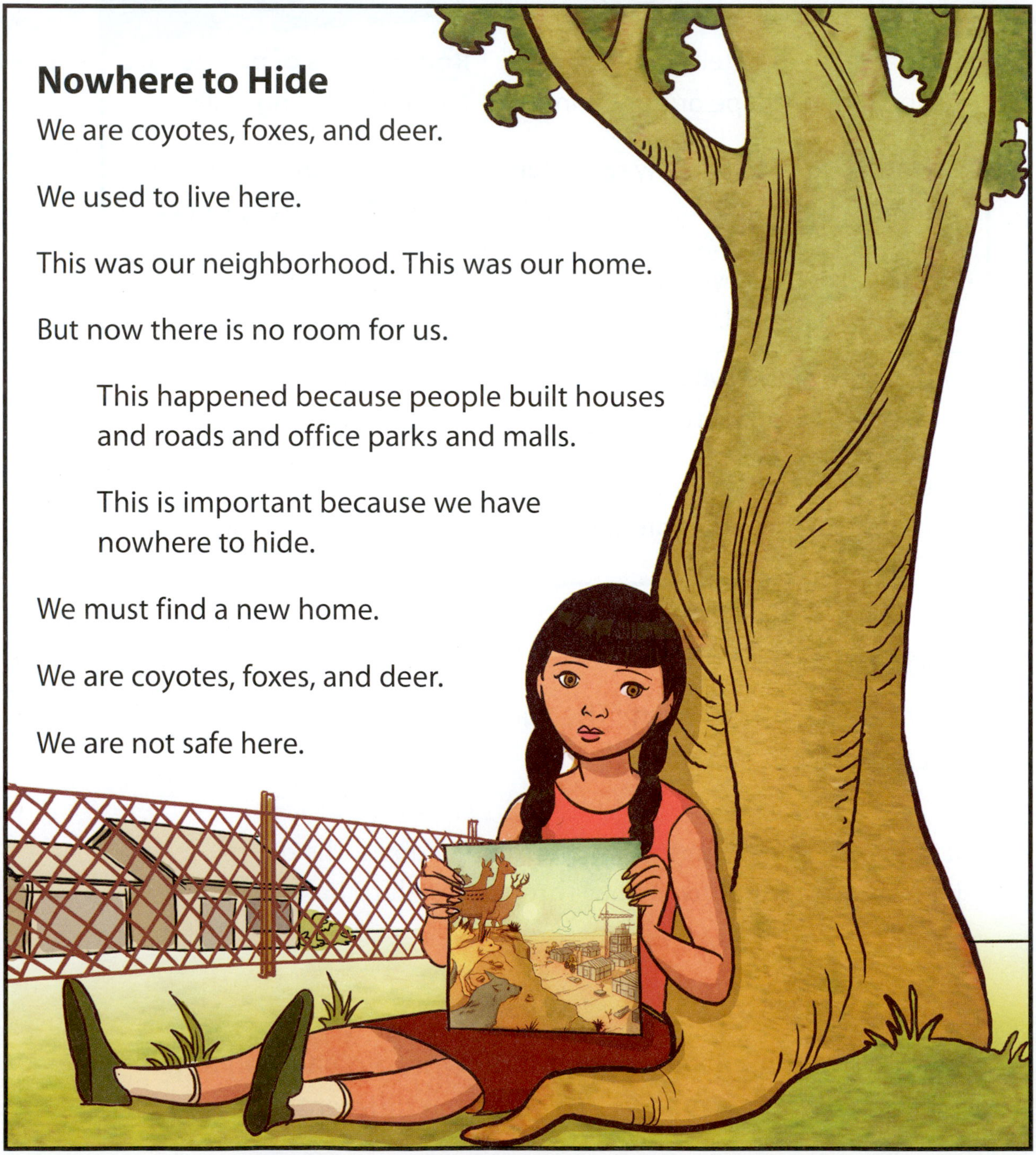

Nowhere to Hide

We are coyotes, foxes, and deer.

We used to live here.

This was our neighborhood. This was our home.

But now there is no room for us.

This happened because people built houses and roads and office parks and malls.

This is important because we have nowhere to hide.

We must find a new home.

We are coyotes, foxes, and deer.

We are not safe here.

Key Words

Look at the picture. Use **Key Words** and other words to talk about how people affect wildlife.

Key Words

habitat
invade
population
species
threatened

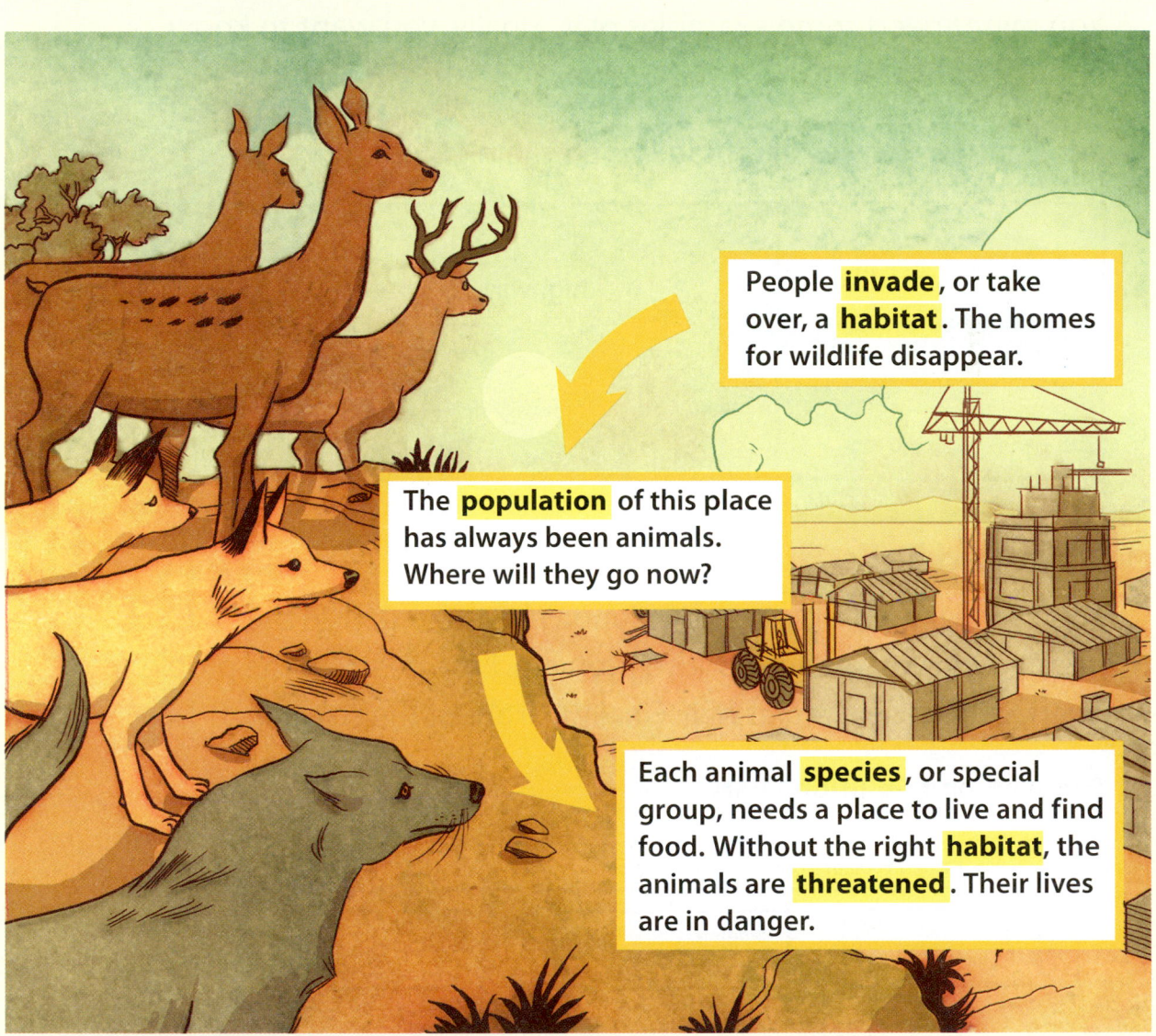

People **invade**, or take over, a **habitat**. The homes for wildlife disappear.

The **population** of this place has always been animals. Where will they go now?

Each animal **species**, or special group, needs a place to live and find food. Without the right **habitat**, the animals are **threatened**. Their lives are in danger.

Talk Together

How do some species become harmful to others? Talk about this question in a small group. Try to use **Language Frames** from page 314 and **Key Words** as you define and explain.

Problem and Solution

When someone describes a **problem**, what information do you expect to learn? First, you need to know what the problem is. You might need some examples of it. Finally, you want to know about a **solution**.

Look at the pictures of armadillos on the highway.

Map and Talk

You can make a problem-and-solution chart to organize the information you receive about a problem. First, describe the problem. Then write any examples of it. Finally, tell about the solution.

Problem-and-Solution Chart

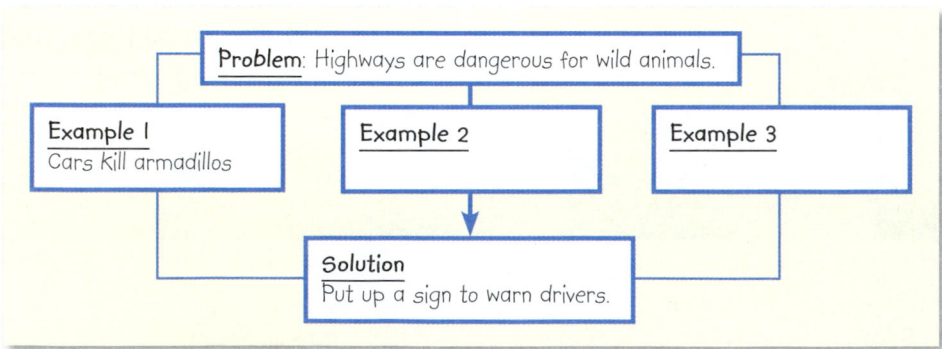

Talk Together

Think of a problem in your environment. Tell your partner about it. Make a problem-and-solution chart together.

More Key Words

Use these words to talk about "Aliens from Earth" and "Island Observations."

balance
(**ba**-luns) *noun*

When something is in **balance**, it is steady. If she keeps her **balance**, she will not fall.

competition
(kom-pu-**ti**-shun) *noun*

A **competition** is a contest. The runners are in **competition** to win the race.

introduce
(in-tru-**düs**) *verb*

When people **introduce** themselves, they meet for the first time.

migration
(mi-**grā**-shun) *noun*

During a **migration**, people or animals move from one place to another.

native
(**nā**-tiv) *adjective*

When living things are **native** to an area, they live and grow there naturally.

Talk Together

Give clues about a **Key Word** until your partner guesses it correctly. Take turns.

The last part of this word sounds like <u>loose</u>.

Add words to My Vocabulary Notebook.
NGReach.com

Learn to Make Inferences

Look at the picture. What kind of animal does it show? Where does it live? Look at the details to figure out, or **make inferences** about, this animal's natural environment.

You also **make inferences** when you read.

How to Make Inferences

👁	**1.** Look for details in the text.	I read _____ .
💭	**2.** Think about what you already know about the details and the topic.	I know _____ .
🧩	**3.** Put your ideas together. What else can you figure out from the details?	And so _____ .

Talk Together

Read this news story about Mona. Read the sample inference. Then use **Language Frames** to tell a partner about the inferences you made while reading.

News Story

Fourth-Grader Rescues Orphan Armadillo

ELGIN, TX—One young armadillo is safe, thanks to local fourth-grader Mona Nighthorse.

While taking part in a highway clean-up, Ms. Nighthorse found a baby armadillo. The animal's mother was dead on the highway. Ms. Nighthorse called the Animal Care Center. Dr. Jay Abasi told her to bring the orphan to the center.

Ms. Nighthorse agreed to help Dr. Abasi care for the baby, which she named Redonda.

"At first, we fed her with an eyedropper," explained Ms. Nighthorse. "Later, we had to be careful to **balance** her diet. We gave her some cat food. But we also fed her things she would find in nature. Redonda loves worms and ants."

Dr. Abasi and Ms. Nighthorse plan to **introduce** Redonda back into the wild.

"We know she will be happier there," said Ms. Nighthorse. "But she has to be able to survive the **competition** with other animals."

Today, armadillos are **native** to Texas, but they were not always found in Elgin. **Migration** brought the beloved **species** to the area during the 19th century.

> **Sample Inference**
>
> "I read that the animal's mother was dead.
>
> I know that armadillos often get hit by cars.
>
> And so I think the mother probably was hit by a car."

◀ = A good place to make an inference

Read a Science Text

Genre

Science texts are nonfiction. They give detailed information about different science topics.

Text Features

The text is divided into sections. The **heading** tells the topic for that section. A **topic sentence** states the main idea about the topic.

heading

What Healthy Ecosystems Need

topic sentence

Aliens are plants or animals that invade another ecosystem, a natural community of plants and animals living in balance with one another. Scientists call these aliens exotics, a word that means "to come from outside."

Aliens from Earth
When Animals and Plants Invade Other Ecosystems

by Mary Batten · illustrated by Dan Burr

Comprehension Coach

▶ **Set a Purpose**
Find out what happens when alien
species **invade** an ecosystem.

Asia

ancient land
bridge

What Healthy Ecosystems Need ~~

Aliens are plants or animals that **invade** another
ecosystem, a natural community of plants and animals
living in **balance** with one another. Scientists call these
aliens *exotics*, a word that means "to come from outside."

A healthy ecosystem needs a variety of **organisms** and a
balance between predators and prey. Alien invaders can
upset the balance of an ecosystem and threaten it.

Pacific Ocean

In Other Words
organisms living things
upset harm

322

For millions of years, living things traveled from one place to another. Animals walked, flew, and crawled across ancient land bridges from one continent to another. Carried by wind, water, birds, and other animals, seeds moved from place to place.

For most of the planet's history, the movement of plants and animals happened very slowly. Ecosystems stayed in balance because they were able to change gradually over time.

North America

▲ An ancient land bridge allowed living things to migrate from Asia to North America.

▶ **Before You Move On**

1. **Problem/Solution** What is an alien invasion? Why is it considered a problem?
2. **Make Inferences** Why do you think the movement of plants and animals across Earth was slow in the past?

How People Change Ecosystems

Humans greatly **sped up the pace** of alien invasions. As human **populations** grew, people needed more natural resources. Eventually they moved into places where human beings had never lived before. They hunted animals, gathered **native** plants, and learned to farm. Wherever people settled, they changed the **habitat**.

Over the centuries, people invented ways to go longer distances and to move around faster. When people began traveling by ship, they took animals such as goats, dogs, cats, and chickens with them. They also took seeds of plants they liked to eat. These **migrations** changed native ecosystems more quickly.

Today, every living thing you can imagine—**viruses, bacteria**, insects, plants, sea creatures—travels on the same planes and ships that carry people and **cargo**. Invaders move quickly all over the globe. It is becoming harder to **maintain** the delicate balance in the world's ecosystems.

In Other Words
sped up the pace increased the speed
viruses, bacteria tiny germs
cargo things
maintain keep

▶ **Before You Move On**

1. **Use Text Features** Read the heading and the first sentence on page 324. What is the topic of this section?
2. **Problem/Solution** What problem was created by human **migration**?

Islands in Danger ~~~

Islands, surrounded by water and **cut off** from other lands, are especially **at risk**. Until recently, few new <mark>species</mark> were able to cross the ocean to reach **distant** islands. Today, any ship or plane that goes to an island could carry an alien invader. Alien invasions can hurt even a large island continent like Australia.

ASIA

INDIAN OCEAN   AUSTRALIA

▲ Ships and planes can carry alien invaders into islands such as Australia.

In Other Words
cut off separated
at risk <mark>threatened</mark>
distant far-off

▲ Today rabbits cause serious problems for Australian farmers.

About 200 years ago, Europeans **colonized** the island of Australia. They took rabbits, foxes, and other animals with them. They also took cats to kill the rats that had arrived on settlers' ships. The cats did not **encounter** any predators, so their numbers grew quickly.

Rabbits also had no natural predators, so the rabbit population also **exploded**. In 2003, Australia had more than 500 million rabbits. These **pests** destroy soil, damage farmers' crops, and wreck the habitat of many native species.

In Other Words
colonized settled on
encounter find
exploded grew quickly
pests animals

▶ **Before You Move On**

1. **Use Text Features** What do the heading and topic sentence on page 326 tell you?
2. **Make Inferences** How could the increase in the rabbit **population** have been prevented?

Starlings ~

You don't have to live on an island to see an alien.
You may find one in your own backyard.

Starlings live throughout the United States, but these
birds are not native. In the 1890s, some people in
New York decided to **import** all of the birds mentioned
in the plays of William Shakespeare, a famous writer. They
brought in some starlings along with the other birds. The
people did not realize the problems the starlings might cause.
These **aggressive** birds compete with native birds for food and
take over the nests of some species. There are now about
200 million starlings in the United States.

▲ starling

In Other Words
import bring to America
aggressive bold and fierce

Killer Bees

In 1956, a scientist brought some African bees to Brazil, a country in South America. Then someone accidentally released the bees from their hive. **Swarms** of bees flew away into the forest.

The scientist thought that the African bees would die in the forest. Instead, they bred with local honeybees. The **offspring** are called Africanized honeybees, or killer bees. These exotic bees defend their hives more fiercely than other honeybees. They have stung to death some farm animals and even a few people.

▼ **Africanized bees**

▶ **Before You Move On**

1. **Problem/Solution** Why are starlings a problem in the United States?
2. **Make Inferences** Why do you think scientists believed that African bees would die in the forest?

Zebra Mussels

Many aliens arrive in the ballast tanks of cargo ships. Filled with seawater, these large tanks help ships stay balanced. The tanks are like **aquariums** in the middle of the ship. When a ship arrives in port, it empties its ballast tank. This action releases thousands of worms, clams, snails, and other sea creatures into an ecosystem where they do not belong.

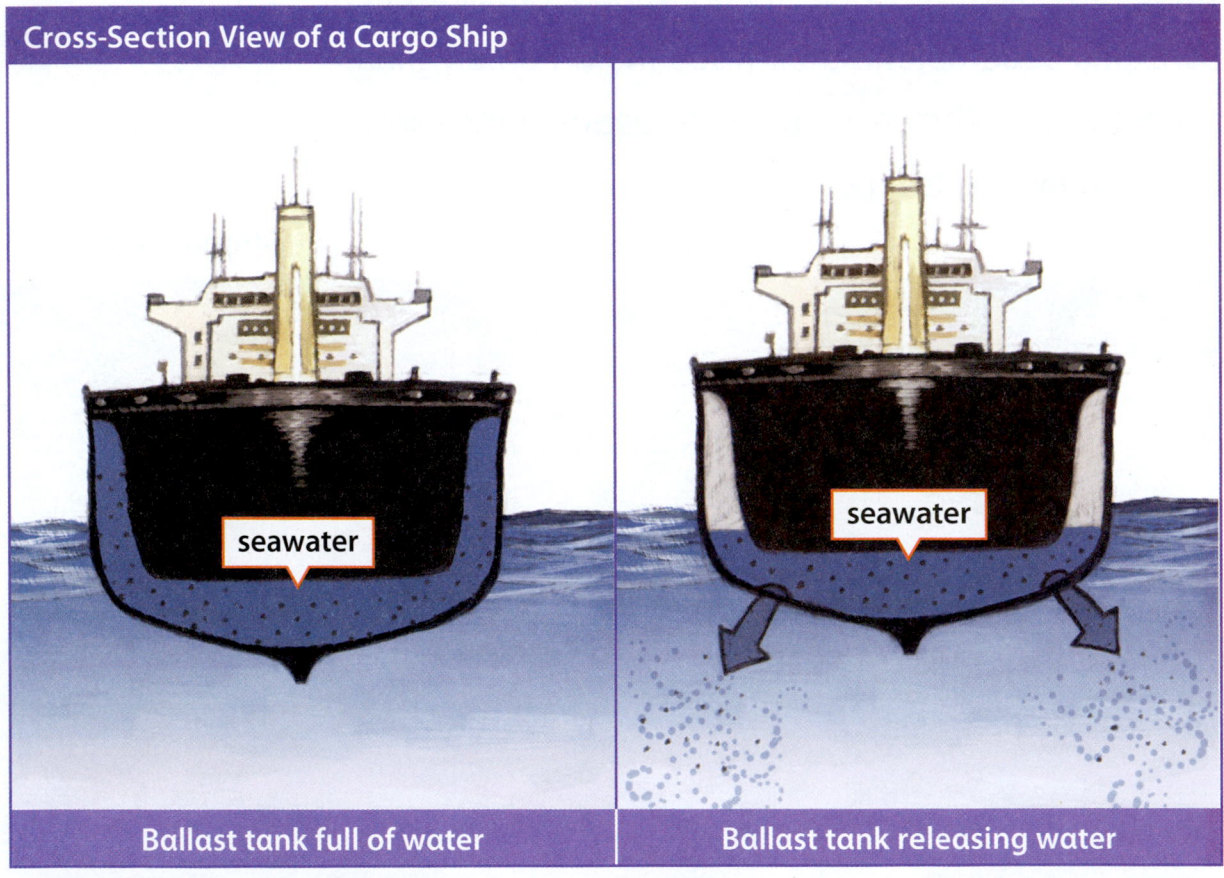

Cross-Section View of a Cargo Ship

seawater

seawater

Ballast tank full of water

Ballast tank releasing water

▲ When a ship empties water from its ballast tank, it may also release alien species into an ecosystem.

◀ zebra mussels

Zebra mussels traveled from Europe to the United States on cargo ships in the late 1980s. Huge populations of these mussels live on **submerged** rocks, concrete, wood, and metal. They sink **buoys** and clog water pipes. They also eat the **plankton** on which local fish depend. There are so many zebra mussels that it is impossible to get rid of them. The United States now has rules to control the dumping of ballast water.

In Other Words
submerged underwater
buoys floating markers
plankton tiny sea animals

▶ **Before You Move On**

1. **Make Inferences** How do you think zebra mussels sink buoys?
2. **Problem/Solution** How did the United States solve the problem of ballast water?

Kudzu 〰️

When people **introduced** kudzu to the United States, they **had good intentions**. Kudzu is a fast-growing green vine. The Japanese brought kudzu into the United States to decorate their **exhibit** at the 1876 Centennial Exposition in Philadelphia, Pennsylvania. Americans liked the beautiful vine with its sweet-smelling blossoms. Many people began planting it in their gardens.

In the 1930s, the U.S. government hired hundreds of workers to plant kudzu. People believed that the vine would help prevent soil from being washed away during rains.

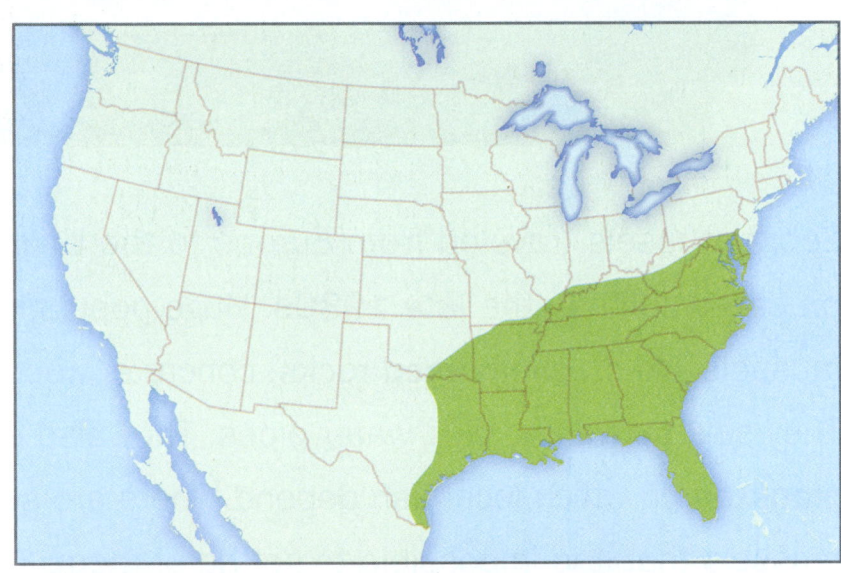

▲ **Kudzu has spread across the southeastern United States.**

No one realized that the warm, humid climate of the southeastern states was **more suitable** for kudzu than that of its native Japan. The vine can grow **up to** a foot a day. It covers millions of acres in the South. Kudzu severely damages forests. It covers trees and prevents them from getting sunlight.

▼ **Kudzu vines compete with native plants.**

kudzu

In Other Words
more suitable better
up to as much as

▶ **Before You Move On**
1. **Make Inferences** Why isn't kudzu a problem in Japan?
2. **Problem/Solution** How did the United States government make the kudzu problem worse?

Protecting Your Habitat ~~

In today's world, travel is easy and quick. Living things can move from one ecosystem to another (or even from one continent to another) in a few hours. No part of our planet is **isolated** anymore. More aliens threaten native species than ever before.

The spread of alien species is a serious problem. People can take some simple steps to help solve it.

port

railway tracks

freeway

▲ Today, ships, cars, and trains can quickly and easily <mark>introduce</mark> alien species into an ecosystem.

In Other Words
isolated alone; separate from the rest

Here are some steps you can take:

- Learn to identify alien species in your area.
- Don't release exotic pets or aquarium plants and fish into the environment.
- Don't **disturb** natural areas.
- Do not send seeds, plants, or animals by mail if they could be harmful to the environment.
- When you travel, do not bring plants, fruits, soil, seeds, or animals from one country to another.

The place where you live is your habitat. You share it with many different kinds of animals and plants. You can help protect them and yourself from alien invaders. ❖

Keep exotic pets in specific areas.	Learn to identify species in your area.	Help keep animals' natural habitats undisturbed.

In Other Words
disturb change things in

▶ **Before You Move On**
1. **Make Inferences** Why are native species threatened more than ever before?
2. **Problem/Solution** What is one way you can protect your habitat from alien invaders?

Talk About It

1. What is the topic of this **science article**? Tell about two interesting details that support the topic.

   The topic is _____. Two details are _____ and _____.

2. How do alien plants and animals upset the **balance** in an ecosystem? **Define** words and phrases as you **explain**.

3. Sometimes people bring in alien species to fix one problem, but it causes another. Give an example from the text. Explain what happened.

Learn test-taking strategies.
 NGReach.com

Write About It

Which **species** from "Aliens from Earth" interests you most? Write four questions that you could research to learn more about this species. Use **Key Words** to help you.

The species that interests me most is _____. My questions are:

1.

2.

3.

4.

Problem and Solution

Make a problem-and-solution chart for "Aliens from Earth." Give examples of the problem. Add boxes for more examples.

Problem-and-Solution Chart

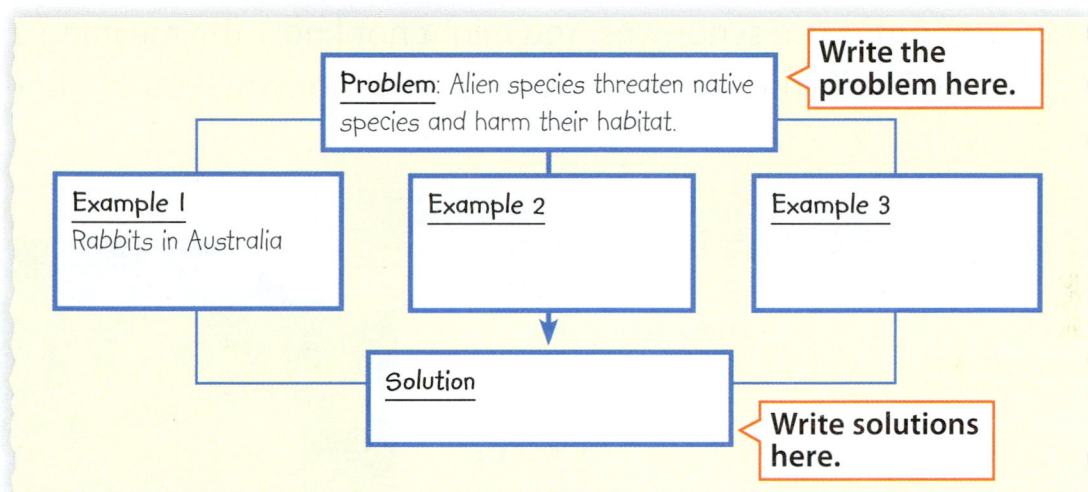

Now use your chart as you summarize for a partner the problems and solutions presented in "Aliens from Earth." Be sure the author's meaning comes through in your summary. Use as many **Key Words** as you can.

The problem is _____ .
One example is _____ .
One solution is _____ .

Fluency Comprehension Coach

Use the Comprehension Coach to practice reading with phrasing. Rate your reading.

Talk Together

What makes some plants and animals harmful? Choose your favorite section of "Aliens from Earth." Make up a rap about that plant or animal. Use **Key Words** to tell how it became harmful.

Synonyms

Synonyms are words that have the same or nearly the same meaning, such as *grow* and *expand*. One word can have several synonyms. For example, *go*, *budge*, and *flow* are all synonyms for *move*.

Some **word analogies** use synonyms. You might not know the meaning of one of the words. But if you see that the words are synonyms, you can figure out an analogy.

humid is to damp as lush is to healthy

These words are synonyms.

These words are synonyms, too.

The relationship between both pairs of words is the same.

Try It Together

Read each item. Choose the word that best completes the analogy.

1. **threaten is to challenge as invade is to**

   A trap

   B species

   C escape

   D attack

2. **population is to people as movement is to**

   A globe

   B population

   C migration

   D species

Connect Across Texts Read about one scientist's work at a place where **native species** are **threatened**.

Genre A **journal** is a written record of what you observe. Dates help you remember what you observe and when. Scientists keep science journals.

Island Observations

by Dr. Christy Finlayson

I am an ecologist, a scientist who studies how organisms interact with their environments. I'm also interested in the ways nonnative **species** affect an ecosystem.

albatross

I'm traveling to Midway Atoll, a group of three small islands in the Pacific Ocean. Midway Atoll is **very isolated**. Nonnative species have recently been **introduced** to the islands.

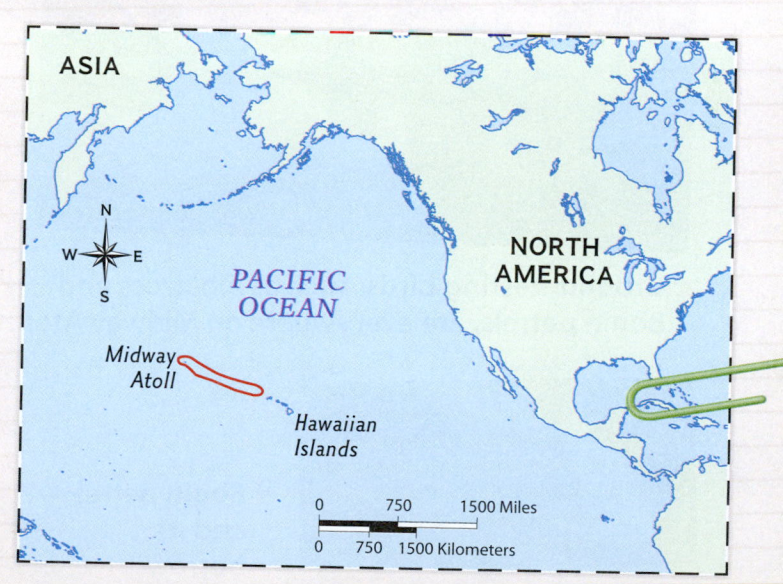

ASIA

N
W · E
S

PACIFIC
OCEAN

NORTH
AMERICA

Midway
Atoll

Hawaiian
Islands

0   750   1500 Miles

0   750   1500 Kilometers

In Other Words

very isolated separated from
other places

▶ **Before You Move On**

1. **Make Inferences** Why do you think Dr. Finlayson is interested in Midway Atoll? What do you think she will study there?

2. **Use Text Features** Using the map, describe Midway Atoll's location.

September 6, 2007

I've arrived on Midway Atoll. Albatross chicks, a **native** seabird, are in nests everywhere! The adult birds feed them. They **regurgitate** partly eaten **squid** into their babies' mouths.

The Bonin petrel is another native seabird. It digs a **burrow** to lay its egg. If I don't pay attention, I could step on a burrow and crush it. So I walk carefully.

albatross

Once more than 250,000 Bonin petrels lived here. Then humans accidentally brought rats to the islands. The rats preyed on the birds, which almost disappeared. Concerned scientists and citizens **eliminated** the rat **population**. Today, there are about 64,000 Bonin petrels on Midway Atoll.

▲ Ground-nesting birds, such as albatross and Bonin petrels, are everywhere on Midway Atoll.

◀ Bonin petrel and its burrow

▲ Adult albatross and chick

September 7, 2007

I've noticed that some areas have many birds. Other areas have few. I also notice a plant called golden crownbeard in the areas with few birds. This plant grows so thick that albatross have trouble walking. It also prevents Bonin petrels from digging their burrows.

golden crownbeard

When golden crownbeard surrounds chicks in nests, adult birds may be unable to find them. The chicks can become trapped in the plant's stems and can **starve**.

People probably brought golden crownbeard to Midway Atoll by accident. The plant's thick growth has decreased the nesting <mark>habitat</mark> for native ground-nesting birds.

▲ Albatross can't walk through the thick growth of the golden crownbeard.

▲ A thick growth of golden crownbeard

In Other Words
starve die of hunger

▶ **Before You Move On**

1. **Problem/Solution** Why were rats such a problem for Bonin petrels? What was the solution?
2. **Make Inferences** Is golden crownbeard <mark>native</mark> to Midway Atoll? Explain.

September 8, 2007

I examined several golden crownbeard plants and noticed that there are many insects living in them. What are these organisms? Do they interact with golden crownbeard and the ground-nesting seabirds?

I decided to **do a survey** of the insects in this plant species. For each plant I examine, I will **record** the name and number of each organism I find. Then I will write notes about the relationship between the organisms.

▲ **Insects on a golden crownbeard plant**

Survey of Insects on Golden Crownbeard

Stem Number	Organism	Number of Organisms	Notes
1	treehopper	6	treehoppers feeding on plant stem
1	crazy ant	13	ants feeding on **treehoppers' honeydew**
2	treehopper	14	treehoppers feeding on plant stem
2	crazy ant	29	ants feeding on treehoppers' honeydew
3	treehopper	2	treehoppers feeding on plant stem

In Other Words

do a survey take a sample

record write down

treehoppers' honeydew feces; waste products from the insect's body

October 25, 2007

I observe three species of nonnative ants on golden crownbeard: crazy ants, tropical fire ants, and bigheaded ants. I know that some ants prey on ground-nesting seabirds. What is their connection with golden crownbeard, though?

golden crownbeard

The golden crownbeard provides food to treehoppers. The treehoppers provide food for the ants. From these observations, I **conclude** that the golden crownbeard is helping the ants that prey on native seabirds.

My next question: How can we prevent the ants from harming the seabird populations on Midway Atoll? ❖

▲ **At work on Midway Atoll**

In Other Words

conclude can tell; believe

▶ **Before You Move On**

1. **Use Text Features** Look at the chart. What relationship does the author observe between ants and treehoppers?

2. **Explain Ideas in the Text** What did the author learn from the survey?

Key Words

balance	migration
competition	native
habitat	population
introduce	species
invade	threatened

Compare Genres

"Aliens from Earth" is a science text. "Island Observations" is a science journal. Think about their text features. How are they the same? How are they different? Work with a partner to complete the Venn diagram.

Venn Diagram

To compare, write what is the same here.

Science Text

Text is divided into sections.

Both

Visuals include informative labels.

Science Journal

Text is divided into daily entries.

To contrast, write what is different here

Talk Together

How can animals and plants become harmful? Think about the science text and science journal you just read. Use **Key Words** to talk about your ideas.

Possessive Nouns and Adjectives

A **possessive noun** is the name of an owner: *the **farmer's** crops*.

A **possessive adjective** can replace an owner's name: ***his** crops*.

Grammar Rules Possessive Nouns/Adjectives

	For One Owner	**More Than One Owner**
Use an **apostrophe** with a possessive noun.	Add **'s**: the starling**'s** nest	Just add an apostrophe if the noun already ends in **-s**: the European**s'** cats Add **'s** if the noun does not end in **-s**: some people**'s** exotic pets
Choose the possessive adjective that matches the number of owners.	my your her, his, its	our your their

Read Possessive Nouns and Adjectives

Read these sentences from "Aliens from Earth." What possessive nouns and adjectives can you find? Show your partner.

> They also took cats to kill the rats that had arrived on settlers' ships. Their numbers grew quickly.

Write Possessive Nouns and Adjectives

Look at the photo on page 327. Write two sentences to describe what you see. Use possessive nouns and adjectives.

Write as a Citizen

Write a Persuasive Essay ✏️

How can you help protect your local ecosystem? Write an essay that persuades people to take action on an important issue. You will publish your essay in a Nature Newsletter.

Study a Model

In a persuasive essay, you give your opinion. You also try to influence what your readers think and do.

Read Kyle's essay about one thing people can do to protect local animals.

Pets as Pests

by Kyle Dushman

What happens when people get tired of pet fish or lizards? Sometimes they release them into a local pond. **They think they're being kind, but they aren't.** **They're actually hurting the ecosystem.**

The freed pets may carry diseases. The pets may also increase in number and eat the food that local animals need. The invaders may even attack or eat the wild animals!

If you have a pet you don't want anymore, don't release it. Instead, **find another owner for it**. You can even donate your pet to a school or daycare. The native animals in your community will thank you!

The essay begins with a description of a **problem**.

Kyle states his **opinion**.

Next, Kyle gives reasons for his opinion.

Finally, Kyle tells what **action** he wants people to take.

Prewrite

1. **Choose a Topic** What problem will you write about? Talk with a partner to choose one that you can help solve.

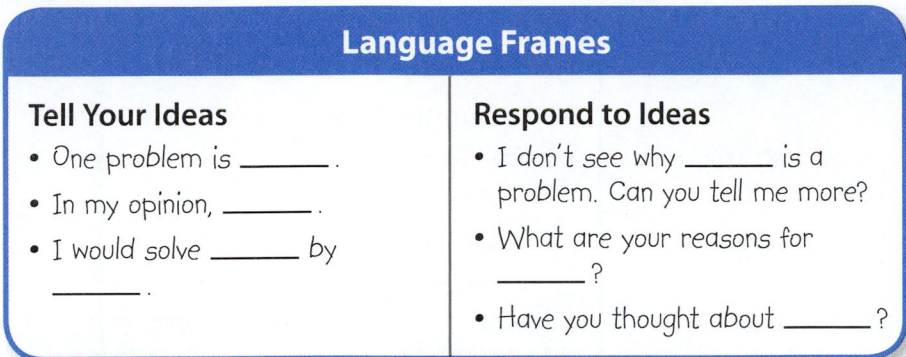

Language Frames

Tell Your Ideas
- One problem is _____ .
- In my opinion, _____ .
- I would solve _____ by _____ .

Respond to Ideas
- I don't see why _____ is a problem. Can you tell me more?
- What are your reasons for _____ ?
- Have you thought about _____ ?

2. **Gather Information** Collect details that describe the problem. Write reasons for your opinion.

3. **Get Organized** Use a problem-and-solution chart to help you organize your ideas.

Problem-and-Solution Chart

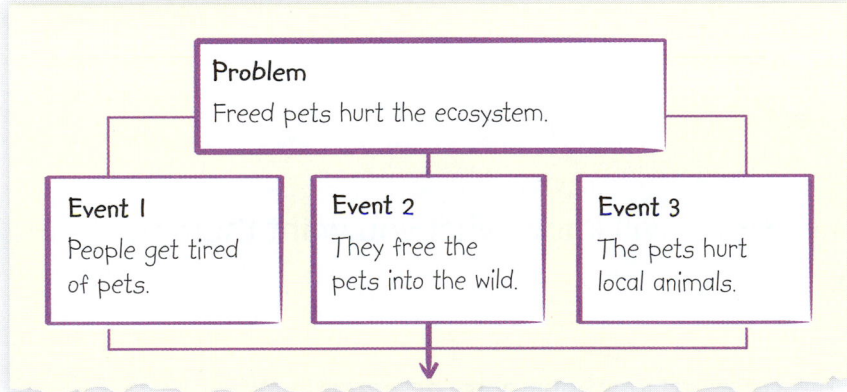

Problem
Freed pets hurt the ecosystem.

Event 1
People get tired of pets.

Event 2
They free the pets into the wild.

Event 3
The pets hurt local animals.

Draft

Use your chart to write your draft.

- Describe the problem and state your opinion.

- Support your opinion with reasons and details.

- End by telling your readers what you want them to do.

Revise

1. **Read, Retell, Respond** Read your draft aloud to a partner. Your partner listens and then retells your main points. Next, talk about ways to improve your writing.

Language Frames	
Retell	**Make Suggestions**
• The problem you're describing is _____ . You think _____ . • Your reasons for your opinion are _____ . • You want people to _____ .	• I don't understand _____ . Can you say it in a different way? • Can you add more details about _____ ? • I'm not sure what you want people to do. Maybe you could _____ .

2. **Make Changes** Think about your draft and your partner's suggestions. Then use the Revising Marks on page 585 to mark your changes.

   • Did you state the problem and your opinion clearly?

   > They think they're being kind, but they aren't. They're actually hurting the ecosystem.
   > ∧ ~~This is a bad idea!~~

   • Make sure your readers will know what you want them to believe or do.

   > If you have a pet you don't want anymore, ~~be careful what you do with it.~~ don't release it. Instead, find another owner for it.

Edit and Proofread

Work with a partner to edit and proofread your persuasive essay. Check that you have used adjectives correctly to show comparison or ownership. Use the marks on page 585 to show your changes.

Use the marks on page 585 to show your changes.

Spelling Tip

✓ Use *more* or *most* in front of longer adjectives instead of adding *-er* or *-est* to the end.

Publish

1. **On Your Own** Make a final copy of your persuasive essay. Put the key points on note cards and present it to your class as a persuasive speech.

Presentation Tips	
If you are the speaker…	**If you are the listener…**
Remember that eye contact is important when you are persuading others.	Notice any persuasive techniques you think the speaker used well.
Be ready to support your opinion with additional reasons and examples.	Listen for specific words or phrases you think the speaker included to persuade you.

2. **In a Group** Collect all of the persuasive essays from your class. Publish them in a Nature Newsletter and share ideas with others in your school. You can also post your newsletter in a blog online.

Nature Newsletter

SPECIAL EDITION: Saving Our Local Ecosystem

Pets as Pests
by Kyle Dushman

What happens when people get tired of pet fish or lizards? Sometimes they release them into a local pond. They think they're being kind, but they aren't. They're actually hurting the ecosystem.

The freed pets may carry diseases. The pets may also increase in number and eat the food that local animals need.

BIG Question ?

When do harmless things become harmful?

Talk Together

In this unit, you found lots of answers to the **Big Question**. Now use your concept map to discuss the **Big Question** with the class.

Concept Map

Harmless Things that Become Harmful

mold

• invade ecosystems
•
•

Write a Paragraph

Look at your concept map. Choose one way that harmless things become harmful. Write a paragraph giving facts and information about it.

Share Your Ideas

Choose one of these ways to share your ideas about the **Big Question**.

Write It!

Write a Play

Write a short play based on "The Fungus That Ate My School." Practice reading the play aloud with a partner.

Talk About It!

Talk About Invasive Plants and Animals

Make up a story about an invasive plant or animal. Tell your story to a partner. Then retell your partner's story to the class.

Do It!

Plant Seeds

Plant different kinds of seeds. Keep a log to see which ones grow fastest.

Write It!

Write about a Science Experiment

Think of a science experiment to test an idea. Write instructions for your experiment. Include drawings.

Treasure Hunters

BIG Question ❓

Why do we seek treasure?

Unit at a Glance
▶ **Language**: Express Intentions,
 Restate an Idea, Social Studies Words
▶ **Literacy**: Determine Importance
▶ **Content**: Exploration

Unit
6

Share What You Know

Do It!

1. **Make** a pirate ship from materials such as a box, construction paper, straws, clay, and colored markers.

2. **Display** your ship so everyone can see it.

3. **Tell** the class about your ship.

Build Background: Watch a video about treasure hunters.
 NGReach.com

Express Intentions

Listen to Zack's chant. Then use **Language Frames** as you express the intention, or plan, to look for treasure.

Chant ((MP3))

My Treasure Hunt

There's treasure hiding here at home.

I'm going to discover it.

There's treasure hiding here at home.

I'm going to uncover it.

I plan to hunt in corners,
    under rugs, and inside drawers.

I plan to hunt on top of shelves
    and open unlocked doors.

I'll move the couch
    and look behind it.

If treasure's there,
    then I will find it!

Key Words

adventure
compass
coastal
navigation
port
treasure

Key Words

Look at the pictures. Use **Key Words** and other words to talk about the explorers who first came to the Americas by sea.

Exploring the New World

pirate

ship

treasure chest

coastal area

compass

Between 1500 and 1700, European explorers came to the Americas. They wanted land, gold, and other **treasure**. They found **adventure**. Some of the adventures involved pirates.

Explorers used tools such as maps and compasses for **navigation**. Some Europeans began to settle along the coasts of the Americas. They looked for good **ports** with deep water for their ships.

Talk Together

Why do you think explorers wanted treasure? With a group, try to use **Language Frames** from page 354 and **Key Words** as you express intentions.

Characters

People grow and change. Story **characters** change, too. People's experiences and relationships can both cause the changes.

Look at the pictures of Zack and his little brother.

Map and Talk

Make a character map to show how a person changes. Think about story events. Think about the character's relationships. Finally, think about how the character changes from beginning to middle to end.

Character Map

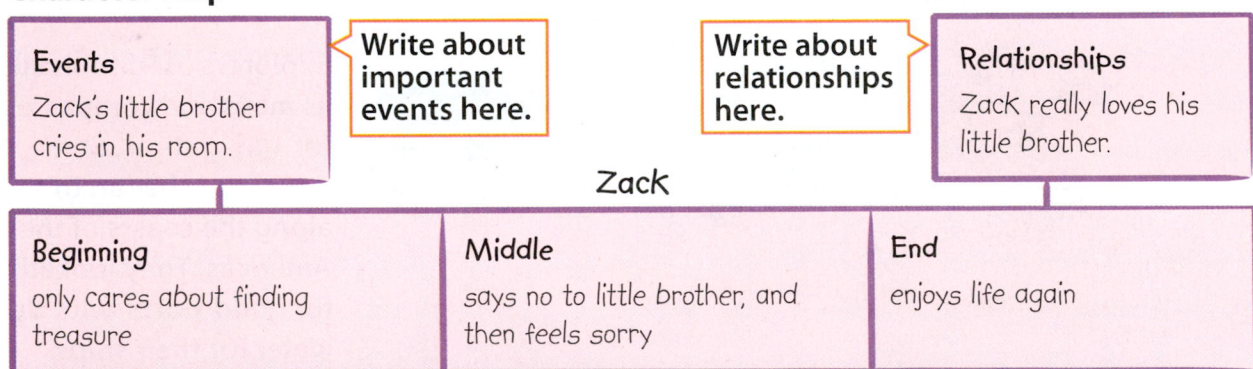

Talk Together

Make a character map for one of your favorite story characters. Use the map to describe to a partner how the character changes.

More Key Words

Use these words to talk about "Treasure Island" and "Make a Treasure Map."

chart
(**chart**) *noun*

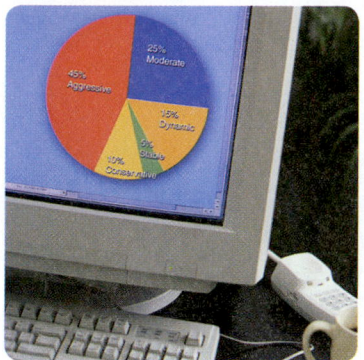

A **chart** shows information with numbers, pictures, and symbols.

discovery
(dis-**ku**-vu-rē) *noun*

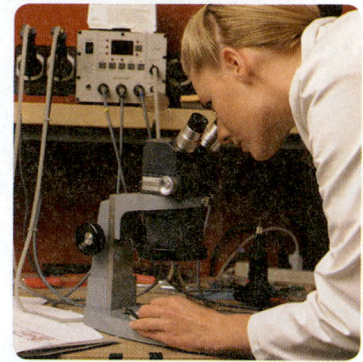

When you find things, you make a **discovery**. Her **discovery** is a new germ.

exploration
(ek-splu-**rā**-shun) *noun*

An **exploration** is a search. Astronauts learn about space from their **exploration**.

interpret
(in-**tur**-prut) *verb*

To **interpret** something is to tell what you think it means. Can you **interpret** the road sign?

legend
(**le**-jund) *noun*

A **legend** explains symbols on a map. This **legend** shows blue lines as rivers.

Talk Together

Work with a partner. Take turns telling a story using **Key Words**.

We are going on an exploration.

We hope to make a big discovery.

Add words to My Vocabulary Notebook.
NGReach.com

Learn to Determine Importance

Look at the picture. What does it show? What details do you notice? Now cover the picture. Think of a sentence or two that briefly tells, or **summarizes**, what the picture shows.

You **summarize** when you read, too.

How to Summarize

1. Identify the topic. Ask, "What is this paragraph mostly about?"

2. Take notes as you read. Note important details.

3. Use your notes to sum up the paragraph. Retell the ideas in a sentence or two.

The topic is _____ .

Important details are _____ .

The paragraph _____ .

Talk Together

Read Zack's essay, "Go for the Gold." Read the
sample summary. Then use **Language Frames** to
summarize each paragraph.

Essay

Go for the Gold

by Zack Jones

One winter, James Marshall made an amazing **discovery**.
He found gold!

In 1847, Marshall began building a sawmill for a man named
Sutter. The next January, Marshall saw some bright flakes in the
water coming from the mill. Many people would have ignored the
flakes. Not Marshall. He knew how to **interpret** the signs. He
thought the flakes were gold. No one believed him at first, but
he was right!

Sutter's sawmill was in California. Word spread fast. About
300,000 people came to California to join the **exploration** for gold.
People called it the Gold Rush. They followed **charts** and maps to
find **treasure**. Of course, not everyone got rich. Marshall never made
any money from his discovery.

You can visit the spot where the Gold Rush started. Today, the area
is a state park. Use the map **legend** to find the way. Visitors can have
their own **adventures**. Maybe you will strike it rich!

Sample Summary

"The topic is James
Marshall.

Important details are
Marshall building a
sawmill and finding
bright flakes in the
water.

The paragraph is
about James Marshall
discovering gold."

◀ = A good place to summarize

Read a Play

Genre
A **play** is a story that actors can perform on a stage. The actors pretend to be characters in the story.

Elements of Drama
The parts of a play are called **scenes**. Each scene describes the setting. **Stage directions** can tell the characters how to talk, act, or move. The words the characters say are called the **dialogue**.

scene → **SCENE ONE**

[**SETTING** *The play begins in a small coastal town in England, around 1740. The Admiral Benbow **Inn**, a common gathering place among sailors. BILLY BONES, looking ill, lies on a couch. MRS. HAWKINS **tends to** him. JIM and DR. LIVESEY enter.*]

JIM [*talks to* DR. LIVESEY, *but points to* BILLY]: He's been here eight months. Billy never gave us any trouble. ← stage directions

dialogue → **MRS. HAWKINS:** Dr. Livesey, thank goodness you've come!

Treasure Island

BASED ON THE NOVEL BY

Robert Louis Stevenson

adapted by Mark Falstein
illustrated by Tim Foley

Characters

NARRATOR

MRS. HAWKINS, owner of the Admiral Benbow Inn

JIM HAWKINS, MRS. HAWKINS' 14-year-old son

DR. LIVESEY, a country doctor

BILLY BONES, a retired sailor, once a pirate

SQUIRE TRELAWNEY, a rich landowner

CAPTAIN SMOLLETT, captain of the ship *Hispaniola*

LONG JOHN SILVER, a sea cook, secretly a pirate

Other **PIRATES**

BEN GUNN, once a pirate

Comprehension Coach

▶ **Set a Purpose**
Find out about a **discovery** that
leads to **adventure**.

SCENE ONE

[**SETTING** *The play begins in a small* **coastal** *town in England, around 1740. The Admiral Benbow* **Inn***, a common gathering place among sailors. BILLY BONES, looking ill, lies on a couch. MRS. HAWKINS* **tends to** *him. JIM and DR. LIVESEY enter.*]

JIM [*talks to* DR. LIVESEY, *but points to* BILLY]: He's been here eight months. Billy never gave us any trouble.

MRS. HAWKINS: Dr. Livesey, thank goodness you've come!

LIVESEY: Let's have a look at him. Young Jim said that a blind man came looking for Billy?

MRS. HAWKINS: Yes, he gave him this paper. Billy **had a fit** when he saw it. Then he **collapsed**.

LIVESEY [*looks at the paper and gasps*]: The black spot! That's a pirate sign!

JIM: Pirates?

BILLY [*weak*]: Jim, is that you?

JIM: Yes, Billy, and Dr. Livesey's here.

In Other Words
Inn Hotel
tends to takes care of
had a fit was very upset
collapsed fell down ill

BILLY: Jim, Flint's **crew is** coming for me! The packet is in my **sea chest**. Don't let them get it!

[BILLY **shudders** *and lies still.* DR. LIVESEY *examines him.*]

LIVESEY: He's dead—frightened to death, most likely. His crimes have caught up with him if he sailed with Captain Flint. They were the most **bloodthirsty** pirates on the seas!

MRS. HAWKINS [*frightened*]: And they're coming here!

In Other Words

crew is sailors are
sea chest box ▶
shudders shakes
bloodthirsty terrible; cruel

[Lights fade, showing that time is passing.]

NARRATOR: That night, pirates *did* come to the inn. They found Billy's sea chest, but Jim had hidden the packet. The next day, Dr. Livesey returned with Squire Trelawney.

[Lights on. JIM, DR. LIVESEY, *and* SQUIRE TRELAWNEY *sit at a table.* JIM *unwraps a packet.]*

TRELAWNEY: You've done a man's job, Jim! Let's see what Captain Flint's men were looking for.

*[*JIM *unfolds a map. They stare at it.]*

LIVESEY: It's a map of an island.

JIM *[pointing]*: Look! It shows a <mark>treasure</mark> here!

TRELAWNEY: This must be Flint's map!

LIVESEY: You're a brave **lad**, Jim! Those pirates would have done anything to get this!

TRELAWNEY: Captain Flint's treasure! There's a fortune in gold and jewels! And we have the map!

LIVESEY: What should we do with it?

TRELAWNEY: Do? Why, I'll hire a ship! Then we're **bound for** Treasure Island! Jim, you and your mother will be rich!

JIM: Us? Rich?

TRELAWNEY: Why, certainly! You're sailing with us, aren't you?

In Other Words
lad boy
bound for going to

▶ **Before You Move On**
1. **Summarize** What important <mark>discovery</mark> do the characters make in Scene One?
2. **Character** Describe the relationship between Jim and Livesey. Explain how you know.

SCENE TWO

[**SETTING** *Aboard the ship* Hispaniola. *JIM, DR. LIVESEY,
SQUIRE TRELAWNEY, and CAPTAIN SMOLLETT are in the
captain's cabin. A large barrel sits on the deck.*]

SMOLLETT: We'll reach the island tomorrow.

JIM: And then we'll be rich!

LIVESEY: We've been lucky. The sea has been calm, and the
crew has been **lively**.

TRELAWNEY: We can thank Long John Silver for finding the
crew. It's a good thing I found *him*! He's only a cook, but
those tough sailors respect him.

JIM: He tells interesting stories, too.

SMOLLETT [*worried*]: Yes, he **favors** you.

LIVESEY: Jim, would you **fetch** me an apple?

JIM: Aye-aye, Doctor.

[*JIM exits the cabin and walks to the barrel. He
reaches into the barrel but can't reach the apples.
He climbs in, just as* LONG JOHN SILVER *and
other* PIRATES *enter.* SILVER *has a wooden leg.
A parrot perches on his shoulder.*]

In Other Words
lively excited and full of energy
favors is very friendly to
fetch get
Aye-aye Yes

SILVER [*talks quietly to* PIRATES]: No, it was Flint. He was captain. I was **second-in-command**. If I knew where the treasure was buried, I'd be dead, like old Ben Gunn!

FIRST PIRATE: I still say we should kill them and take the map!

SILVER: And who will bring the ship home? None of us can **set a course**. No, we should let them dig up the treasure. When we're halfway home, then we'll **strike**!

SECOND PIRATE: Aye! And then we'll live like kings!

[PIRATES *exit, laughing.* JIM *climbs out of the barrel and runs to the cabin.*]

JIM [*excited*]: They're pirates!

SMOLLETT: Who?

JIM: The crew! I heard them talking. Silver is their leader! They plan to **seize** the ship and steal the treasure!

TRELAWNEY [*stunned*]: This is my fault. I never should have told anyone we were **after** treasure.

LIVESEY: That doesn't matter now. We'll have to fight them.

In Other Words
seize take control of
stunned shocked
after looking for

SMOLLETT [*looks at the treasure map*]: Gentlemen, I have a plan. The map shows a **fort** on the island. I'll give the crew some free time on shore. They can take a rowboat. Then *we'll* go **ashore** and **occupy** the fort.

[*Lights fade.*]

NARRATOR: Jim had his own plan. He hid in the rowboat under a piece of sail cloth. The pirates rowed to the island, eager for treasure. As soon as they **touched** land, Jim jumped out of the rowboat.

In Other Words
fort building
ashore to the island
occupy stay in
touched arrived on

▶ **Before You Move On**

1. **Character** What does Jim find out about the crew on the journey to Treasure Island? How does this change him?

2. **Elements of Drama** Where does Scene Two take place? Explain how you know.

▶ **Predict**
If there *is* **treasure**, who will get it, and how?

SCENE THREE

[**SETTING** *The island. Sand and palm trees.*]

[JIM *runs across the stage.*]

SILVER [*from offstage*]: Jim, Jim! Come back!

JIM: No chance of that, you pirate!

[*The* PIRATES *rush onstage, followed by* SILVER.]

FIRST PIRATE: *I'll* fetch him back!

SILVER: Don't hurt him!

JIM [*to himself*]: I thought he was my friend! I'll never trust him again!

[*The* PIRATES *chase* JIM. JIM *runs offstage, followed by the* PIRATES.]

JIM [*enters from offstage, alone and out of breath*]: I think I've lost them. [*hopeless*] I was foolish. Why didn't I stay with my friends? [*points* **upstage**] There's a cave! I'll hide there!

[JIM *goes into the cave.* BEN GUNN *enters the cave from offstage.*]

JIM and BEN [*surprised*]: Oh!

BEN: Are you real, boy? Who are you?

JIM: I'm Jim Hawkins. Who are *you*?

BEN: I'm Ben Gunn. For three years I've been alone here!

JIM: Were you shipwrecked?

BEN: No, I was **marooned**, left here to die. I stayed alive by trapping wild goats. What I wouldn't give for a bit of toasted cheese! [*grabs* JIM's *arm*] Tell me **true**, boy! Is that Flint's ship out there?

In Other Words

upstage   toward the back of the stage
marooned   left on shore alone
true   the truth

JIM: No, Flint's dead. Some of his crew are **on board**, though. They're after Flint's treasure.

BEN: Hee-hee, they won't find it! [*suddenly scared*] I hope they don't find *me*!

JIM: Ben, I have friends here. They are at the fort now. Can we get to the fort without being seen?

BEN: Flint's fort? Hee-hee, I know a secret path. Come, Jim!

[*Lights fade.*]

NARRATOR: Ben led Jim to the fort. That night, the pirates attacked the fort. Jim **slipped away**. But when he returned, the pirates were in control of the fort. Ben Gunn and his friends were gone! The pirates captured Jim.

[*Lights on. Another part of the island.* SILVER *holds the map with one hand. With the other hand, he holds* JIM *by the elbow. Nearby,* PIRATES *are digging.*]

SILVER: Ah, Jim, your friends became as gentle as lambs when they thought I had you. The doctor traded the map for your safety. Well, I didn't have you then, but I do now! [*to the* PIRATES] Dig, you lazy dogs!

SECOND PIRATE: Here, we've struck something!

FIRST PIRATE: It's a treasure chest!

SILVER: **Haul** it up!

In Other Words
on board on the ship
slipped away escaped
Haul Pull

[PIRATES *pull up the treasure chest.* SILVER ***knocks back*** *the lid.*
They stare inside.]

FIRST PIRATE: Two gold coins? That's Flint's treasure?
Two coins?

SILVER: There must be a mistake!

SECOND PIRATE: We trusted you! *That* was *our* mistake!

In Other Words
knocks back opens

[JIM **breaks free** and runs offstage. Lights fade. Sound of pirates fighting. When the lights come back on, SQUIRE TRELAWNEY, DR. LIVESEY, CAPTAIN SMOLLETT–and BEN GUNN–are waiting by a rowboat. They are carrying heavy sacks. JIM enters.]

TRELAWNEY: Jim! Jim, you're safe!

JIM: Hurry! They'll be after me!

[They all climb into the boat.]

LIVESEY: Your friend Ben tells us he had the treasure. I knew the map was useless.

BEN: [holds up a sack] I hid it in my cave! But how could I spend it here?

JIM: You can buy all the toasted cheese you want now!

TRELAWNEY: And those pirates will be **stuck** here!

SMOLLETT: To the ship, now! Row!

JIM: Aye-aye, Captain! ❖

In Other Words
breaks free escapes
stuck trapped

▶ **Before You Move On**

1. **Summarize** In the end, who gets the <mark>treasure</mark>, and how?
2. **Character** How does Ben help Jim? What does this tell you about Ben's character?

Meet the Author

Robert Louis Stevenson

The play "Treasure Island" is based on a book by Robert Louis Stevenson. Stevenson was born in 1850 in Scotland. When he was young, Stevenson was often sick, and Scotland's cold, foggy climate was bad for his health. When he grew up, he traveled to warm islands like the ones he wrote about in his adventure books. Later in his life, Stevenson moved to the island of Upolu, in Samoa. There he was called *Tusitala*, or "Teller of Tales."

The story *Treasure Island* began as a homemade map of a made-up island. The map grew into a story idea, and the story idea grew into a book about buried treasure, pirates, and adventure. The book was a big success.

◀ A portrait of Robert Louis Stevenson appears on a Western Samoan postal stamp.

Writer's Craft

Stevenson created many colorful characters for his story. Look at some of the characters in this play. Then write a short description of a new character that could be part of this play.

Key Words

adventure	interpret
chart	legend
coastal	navigation
compass	port
discovery	treasure
exploration	

Talk About It

1. If you were an actor in this **play**, how would you know how to move or speak on the stage? Use two examples as you explain.

   Actors use _____ to tell them how to speak and move. For example, _____ .

2. Imagine that you are Ben Gunn and that you have just met Jim. **Express intentions** about what you will do.

   Here's my plan, Jim. I am going to _____ . I will _____ .

3. How do you think Long John Silver feels after he opens the **treasure** chest? Why?

   Long John Silver feels _____ because _____ . I think this because _____ .

Learn test-taking strategies.
 NGReach.com

Write About It

Think about Jim's **adventure**. Compare it to the adventures of another story character you have read about. Write a paragraph to compare the adventures. Use **Key Words** and examples to explain your points.

The adventure that Jim experienced was _____ .

Characters

Make a character map for Jim, the main character in "Treasure Island." Show how he changes.

Character Map

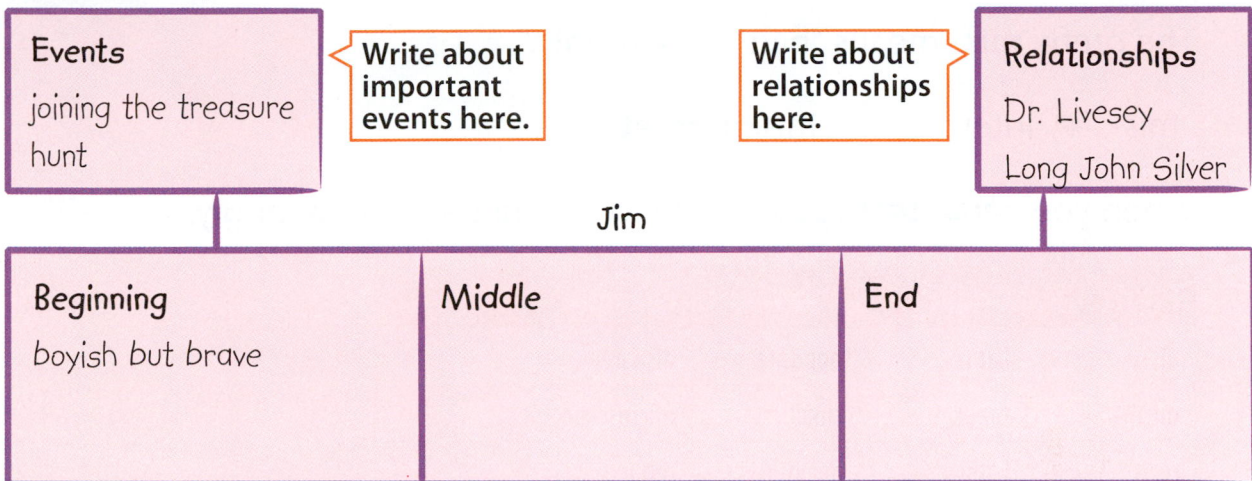

Jim

| Events | | | | | Relationships |
| joining the treasure hunt | Write about important events here. | | Write about relationships here. | | Dr. Livesey
Long John Silver |

| Beginning | Middle | End |
| boyish but brave | | |

Now use your chart as you retell the story to a partner. Focus on Jim and how he changes. Use as many **Key Words** as you can. Record your retelling.

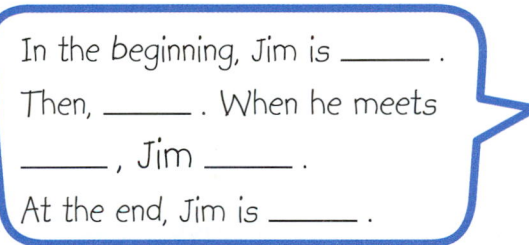

In the beginning, Jim is _____ . Then, _____ . When he meets _____ , Jim _____ . At the end, Jim is _____ .

Fluency    Comprehension Coach

Use the Comprehension Coach to practice reading with expression. Rate your reading.

Talk Together

Why did Jim and his friends seek <mark>treasure</mark>? Role-play an interview with Jim and his friends. Talk about why they left England aboard the ship. Try to use **Key Words**.

Prefixes

A **prefix** is a word part at the beginning of a word. Many prefixes come from other languages such as Latin or Greek. A prefix changes the meaning of the word.

The prefix **mis-** means "bad" or "wrongly."

| mis- | + | interpret | = | misinterpret |

When you **misinterpret** something, you understand wrongly.

Prefix	Origin	Meaning	Example
dis-	Latin	opposite	disagree
micro-	Greek	small	microscope
re-	Latin	again	rebuild
under-	Old English	below	underwater

Try It Together

Read the sentences. Use the chart above to answer the questions.

The explorers told of their <u>misadventures</u>. Their boat had <u>disappeared</u> in a storm. It drifted toward the coast.

1. What does <u>misadventure</u> mean?

    A an adventure that was fun

    B an adventure that went wrong

    C an adventure in the cold

    D an adventure at sea

2. What does <u>disappear</u> mean?

    A to show up again

    B to show up underwater

    C to move out of view

    D to move out of view again

Connect Across Texts Make your own **treasure** map! Read these instructions.

Genre **Instructions** tell how to do something or make something. They usually include steps to follow in a certain order.

Make a Treasure Map

adapted from the
New England Pirate Museum Web Site

Many **adventure** stories tell about pirates who buried chests of **treasure** on uninhabited islands—faraway places where no one lived. The pirates created maps so they could locate the buried treasure. The maps showed details about the island, such as hills, lakes, and trees. A large X marked the spot where the treasure was buried. A line may have shown a path to the treasure.

▶ **Before You Move On**

1. **Summarize** What is a **treasure** map? What is the most important thing it shows?
2. **Use Text Features** Look at the map. Where is the **treasure** buried?

Materials

a pen   a pencil with an eraser   a damp tea bag*   a large sheet of white or brown paper

* You can use brown paper in place of the white paper and tea bag. **Crumple** the brown paper to make it look old and worn.

Steps

1. Use a pencil to **sketch** the shape of your island on the paper.

2. On your island, draw symbols for the following: hills, lakes, trees, water, and your treasure. Then draw a map <mark>legend</mark> that tells what each symbol represents.

In Other Words
sketch lightly draw
◀ **Crumple** Crush

382

3. Draw a **compass** rose in one corner of the map.

4. Make up a name for your island, the ocean that surrounds it, and any coves or bays where ships can land. Write labels for all of these places.

5. Mark the location of the buried treasure with an X.

6. Show a path from the ship to the treasure. Use a dotted line.

7. When your map is finished, trace over the pencil lines with a pen.

8. Rub a damp tea bag over your map to make it look old. Let the map dry. Then fold the map carefully and tear the edges to make it look **worn**. ❖

▶ **Before You Move On**

1. **Summarize** How do you make a **treasure** map?

2. **Steps in a Process** In what order do you use the materials when making the map?

Compare Texts

Some maps show roads and cities. Others show natural features like mountains and oceans. How are the treasure maps in the play and in the instructions similar? How are they different? Work with a partner to complete the Venn diagram.

Venn Diagram

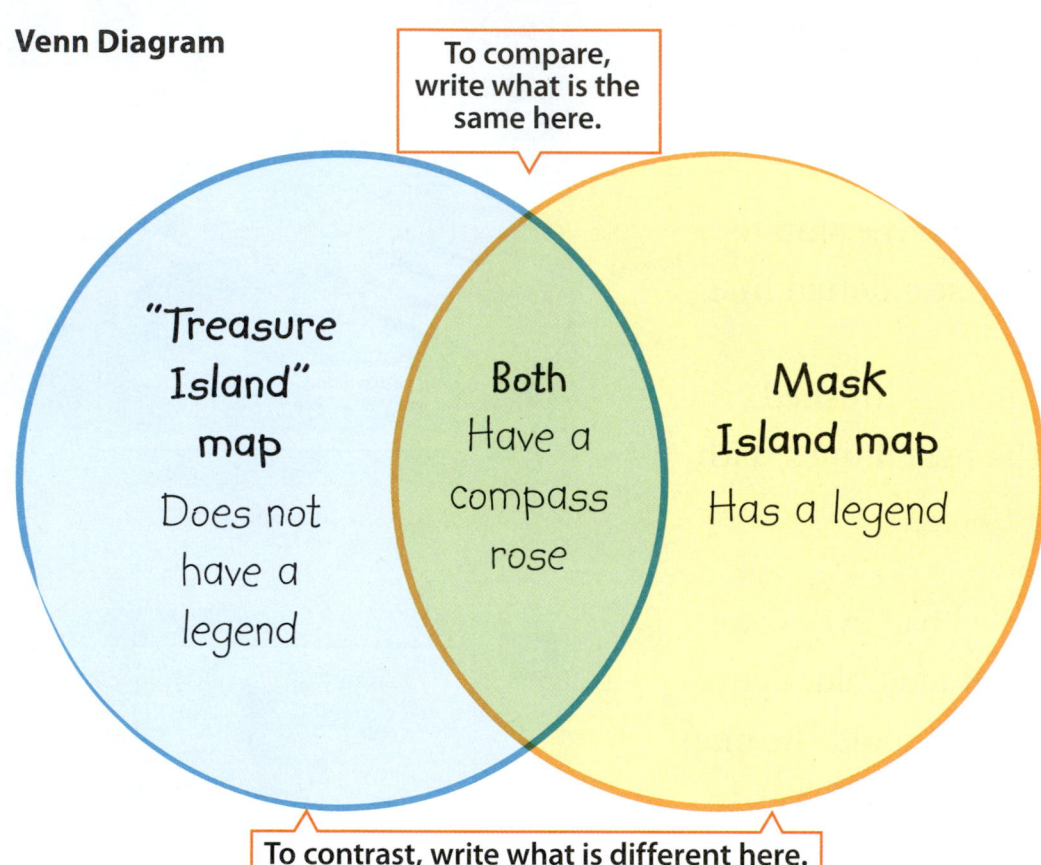

To compare, write what is the same here.

"Treasure Island" map
Does not have a legend

Both
Have a compass rose

Mask Island map
Has a legend

To contrast, write what is different here.

Talk Together

What makes people want to search for **treasure**? Think about the play you read and the treasure map you learned how to make. Use **Key Words** to talk about your ideas.

Pronoun Agreement

Use the right **subject pronoun**, **object pronoun**, or **reflexive pronoun**.

Grammar Rules Pronoun Agreement

	One	More Than One
• Use for yourself.	I, me, myself	
• Use for yourself and one or more persons.		we, us, ourselves
• Use when you speak to one or more persons.	you, you, yourself	you, you, yourselves
• Use for one other person or thing.	he, she, it him, her, it himself, herself, itself	
• Use for more than one other person or thing.		they, them, themselves

Read Pronouns

Read this passage. Find the pronouns.

> SILVER: Don't hurt him!
> JIM [to himself]: I thought he was my friend!

Write Pronouns

What do you own that is a treasure? Write a conversation you might have. Tell about your treasure. Use pronouns.

Restate an Idea

Listen to Lucia's song. Then use **Language Frames** as you restate an idea about looking for treasure.

Song

Bongo's Treasure Hunt

My dog Bongo, my dog Bongo,

Dropped his bone in a hole.

But he is a neat pup,

So he filled the hole up.

Then he ran, off to play.

When my dog returned to find it,

He could not find the bone.

He sniffed all around it.

Finally he found it,

In the ground, in the ground.

Tune: "Frère Jacques"

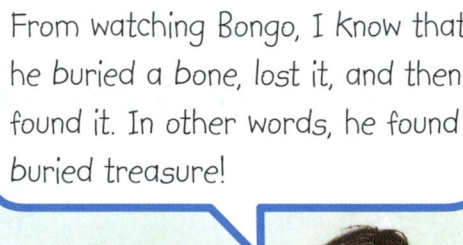

From watching Bongo, I know that he buried a bone, lost it, and then found it. In other words, he found buried treasure!

Key Words

archaeologist
artifact
currency
galleon
merchant

Key Words

Look at the picture. Use **Key Words** and other words to talk about archaeology. This field of study looks at how people lived in the past.

galleon

merchants

archaeologist

An **archaeologist** looks at **artifacts** from a 300-year-old Spanish **galleon**. Long ago, **merchants** sent their goods across the sea on these ships.

Coins tell about **currency** used in the past.

Talk Together

Why do archaeologists look for treasure? Try to use **Language Frames** from page 386 and **Key Words** to restate an idea to a partner.

Sequence

When things happen in a certain order, they are in **sequence**. When you talk about sequence, use

- time-order words: *first, next, then, finally*

- days, months, seasons

- dates

Look at the pictures of a treasure hunt.

Map and Talk

You can make a time line to show the order of events. Here's how you make one. Write the first event beside the first line. At the next line, describe what happens next, and so on.

Time Line

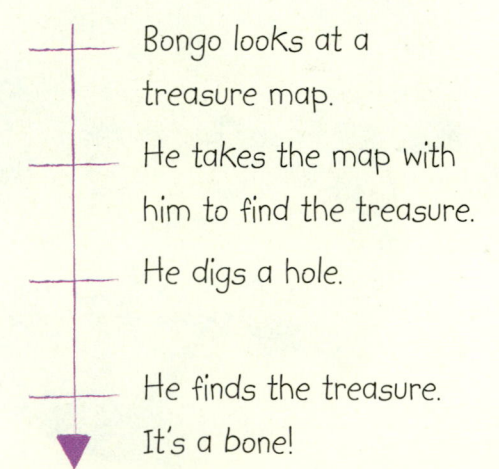

Bongo looks at a treasure map.

He takes the map with him to find the treasure.

He digs a hole.

He finds the treasure. It's a bone!

Talk Together

Did you ever lose an object that was important to you? Make a time line that shows how you tried to find the lost object. Describe the events in order. Tell your partner about your time line.

More Key Words

Use these words to talk about "Real Pirates" and "La Belle Shipwreck."

colony
(**kah**-lu-nē) *noun*

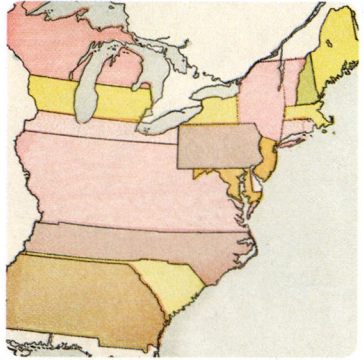

A **colony** is a region that another country controls. These states were **colonies** of Great Britain.

examine
(ig-**za**-mun) *verb*

To **examine** something is to look at it closely. With a hand lens, you can **examine** a butterfly.

preserve
(pri-**zurv**) *verb*

To **preserve** something is to keep it safe from harm. Use scrapbooks to **preserve** old photos.

route
(rūt) *noun*

A **route** is a path to go someplace. Do you take the shortest **route** to school?

trade
(trād) *verb*

To **trade** is to exchange one thing for another. The friends **trade** toys.

Talk Together

Work with a partner. Make a Word Web for each **Key Word**.

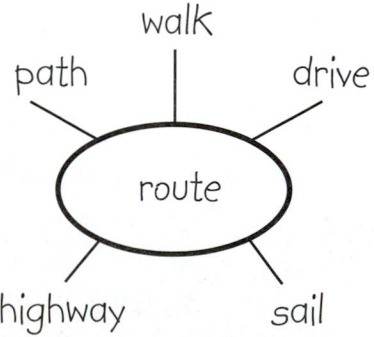

Add words to My Vocabulary Notebook.
NGReach.com

Learn to Determine Importance

Look at the picture. What is it mostly about? Think of a sentence that tells the **main idea**. What **details** support the main idea?

You look for **main ideas** and **details** when you read, too.

How to Identify the Main Idea and Details

 1. Identify the topic. Look at the title, pictures, captions, and repeated words for clues.

2. Read the text. What does it mainly say about the topic?

 3. Look at the details. How do they support the main idea?

The topic is _____ .

The main idea is _____ .

Important details are _____ .

Talk Together

Read the biography that Lucia wrote. Read the sample, too. Then use **Language Frames** as you identify the main idea and details for the other paragraphs in the biography.

Biography

A 16th-Century Treasure Hunter

by Lucia Vargas

Francisco Vázquez de Coronado was born in Spain in 1510. When he was 25, he made an important choice. He went to Spain's **colony** in Mexico. There he heard about seven cities of gold. Coronado wanted to find gold to bring back to Spain.

In 1540, he led a team to find this treasure. The team included 300 Spanish soldiers and more than 1,000 Native Americans. They carried goods to **trade**. Their **route** passed through land that is now Texas, Arizona, New Mexico, Kansas, and Oklahoma.

Coronado never found gold. However, he influenced history. He was a powerful person and part of a government council in Mexico City. A writer kept an account of Coronado's travels in search of gold. This account was **preserved** and later published. Some readers **examined** it for clues about the treasure. So, although he did not get rich, Coronado probably inspired other people to hunt for treasure.

Sample

"The topic is Francisco Vázquez de Coronado.

The main idea is that Coronado looked for gold.

Important details are that he came to Mexico and heard about seven cities of gold."

◄ = A good place to identify the main idea and details

Read a History Article

Genre

A **history article** is nonfiction. It gives facts about people and events from the past.

Text Feature

Illustrations in a history article can help you visualize people and events from long ago, before photography was invented.

The *Whydah Galley* was one ship involved in this terrible business of slavery. The ship was built in London in 1715. It was a fast type of ship known as a "galley." The *Whydah* was also armed with **cannons** in case pirates attacked.

At every port, some goods were unloaded from ships, while other goods were loaded onto ships.

Illustration of a shipping port about 300 years ago

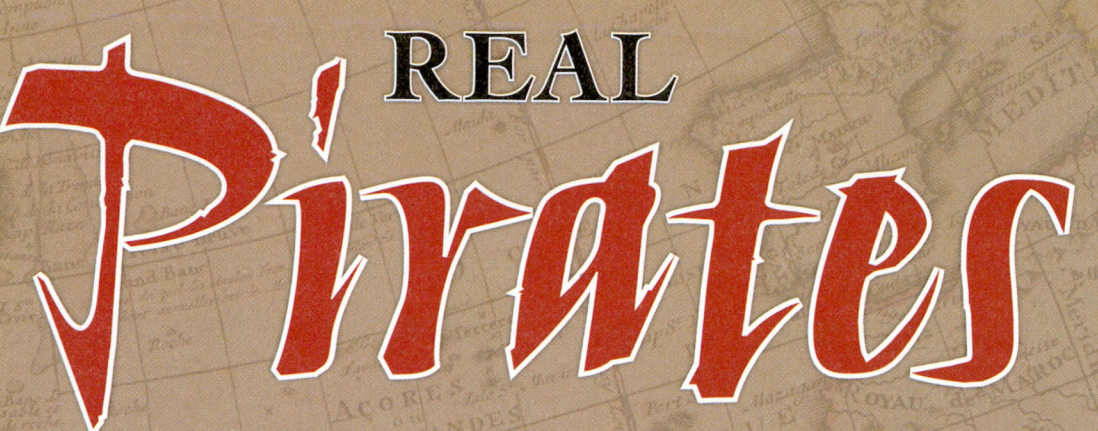

REAL Pirates

THE UNTOLD STORY OF THE WHYDAH

adapted from a book by **Barry Clifford**
with illustrations by **Gregory Manchess**

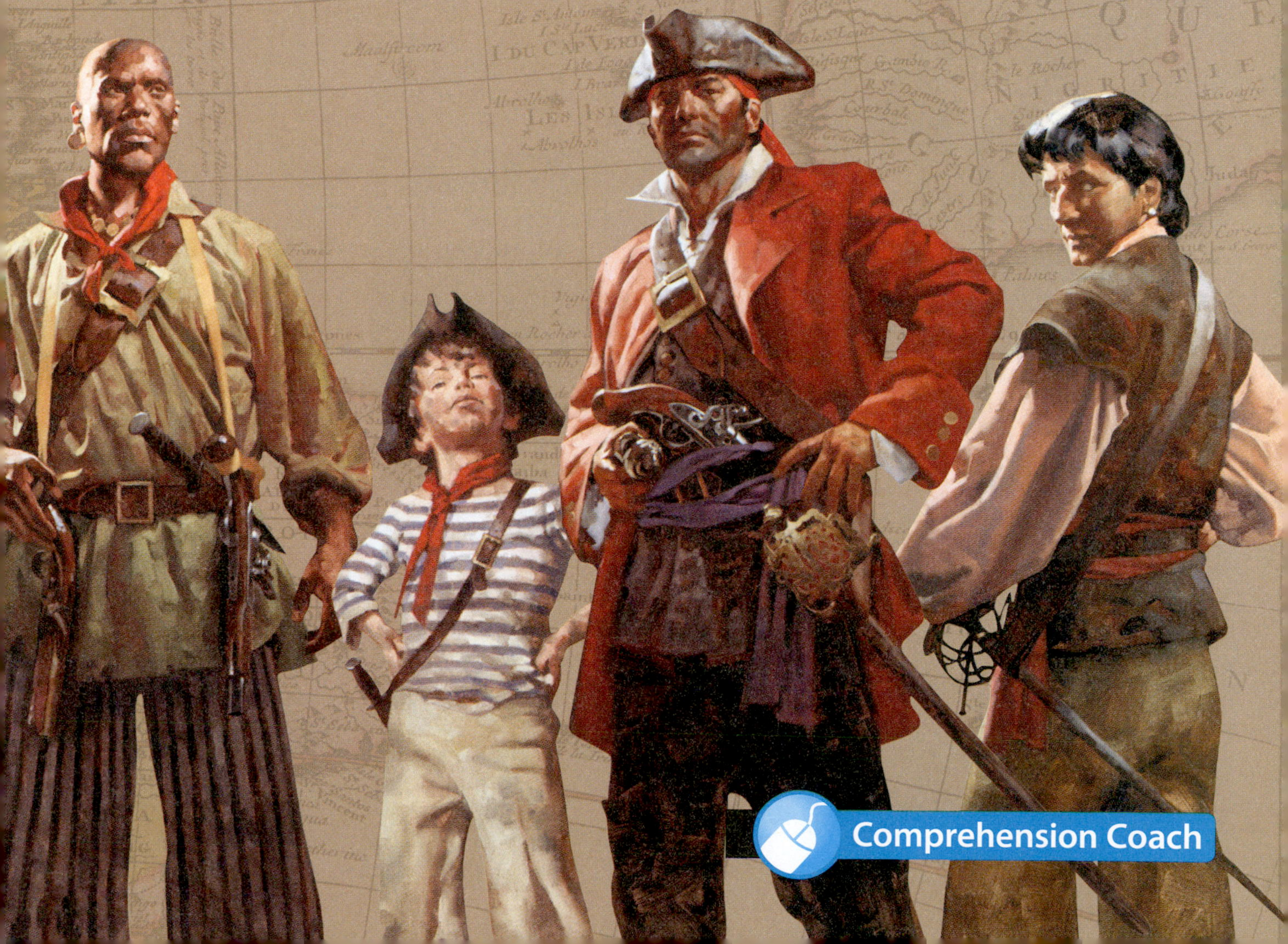

NATIONAL GEOGRAPHIC

▶ **Set a Purpose**
Find out how an explorer
found a sunken pirate ship.

How I Learned About Pirates

When I was a boy growing up on Cape Cod, I spent a lot of
time with my Uncle Bill. He had a **shack** by the Atlantic Ocean
where I would listen to him tell tall tales.

My favorite story was about the pirate ship *Whydah* (**wi**-du)
and her captain, Sam Bellamy. The ship was filled with gold
and silver and jewels. Bellamy hoped that he would live happily
ever after on the **treasure**. Instead, he, his crew, and all of the
treasure sank to the bottom of the sea.

▲ I have always been fascinated by the *Whydah*.

In Other Words
shack tiny house
treasure money he made

From then on, the pirate ship was **never far from my mind**. As I got older, I learned that some of my uncle's stories were true. I also learned how to dive and how to find **shipwrecks**.

After two years of searching, my team and I finally found the *Whydah*. We have been bringing her treasures up from the ocean floor ever since. We've discovered that some stories about pirates are true but that their lives were different from the way books and movies often show them.

◀ My team and I found the shipwrecked *Whydah*.

▼ We discovered many treasures in the shipwreck.

In Other Words
never far from my mind something I thought about often
shipwrecks sunken ships

▶ **Before You Move On**

1. **Details** How did the author learn about pirates?
2. **Sequence** What led to the author's discovery of the *Whydah*? List events in the order they occured.

The Slave Ship Whydah

The European exploration of **the New World** began with Christopher Columbus's first voyage across the Atlantic Ocean. The land he found was rich with gold and silver. It was also rich with crops such as sugarcane and tobacco.

Much labor was needed to gain these riches. People looked to slavery to provide labor.

Europeans soon began sailing to Africa with **goods** to be <mark>traded</mark>. Captive Africans were then taken to America to be sold as slaves. Slave ships then sailed back to Europe with **cargoes** of New World crops. This was known as the "Triangular Trade."

▲ European ships sailed along these <mark>routes</mark> as part of the "Triangular Trade."

In Other Words

the New World North and South America
Much labor A lot of hard work
goods valuable things
cargoes loads

The *Whydah Galley* was one ship involved in this terrible business of slavery. The ship was built in London in 1715. It was a fast type of ship known as a "galley." The *Whydah* was also armed with **cannons** in case pirates attacked.

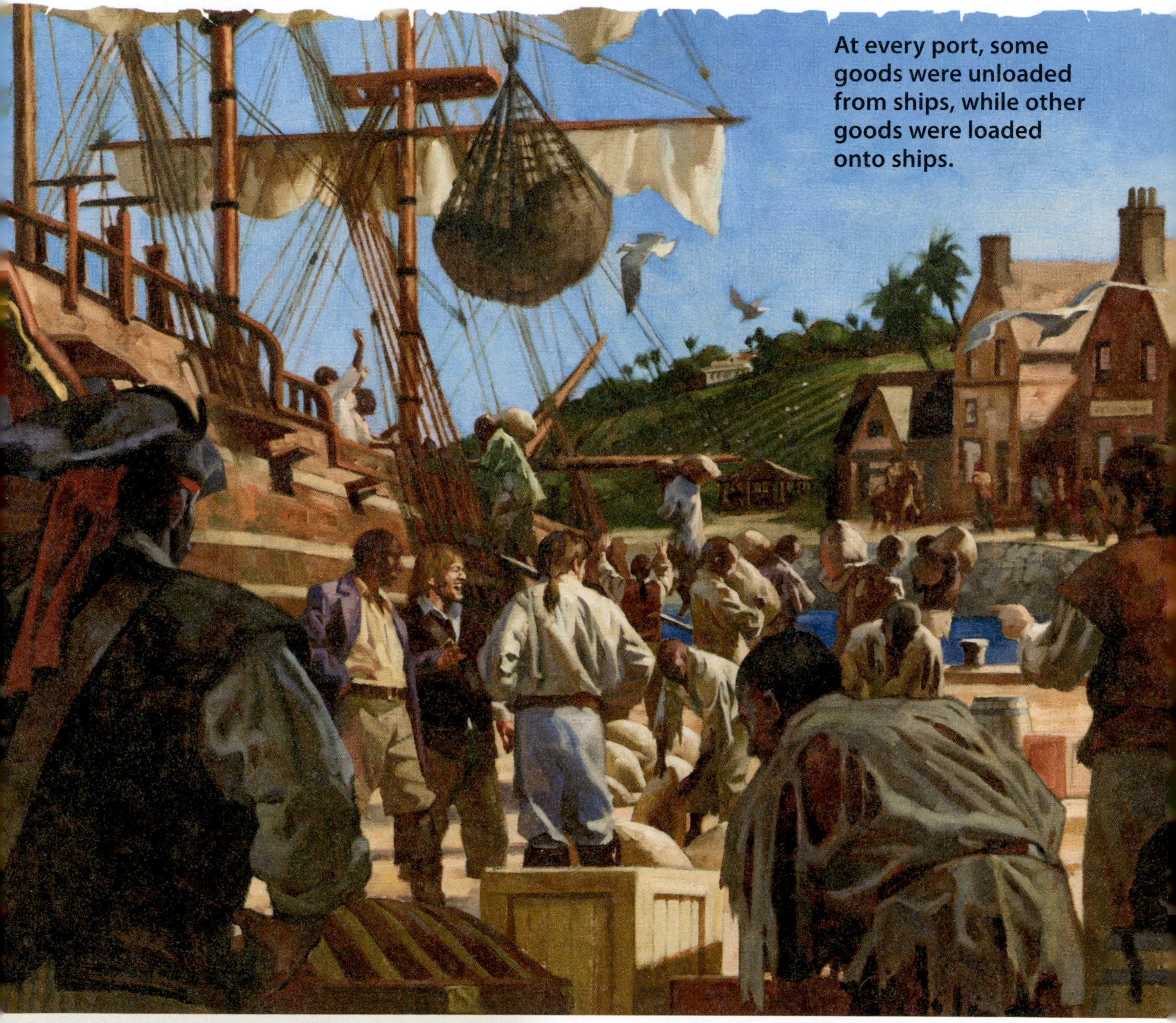

At every port, some goods were unloaded from ships, while other goods were loaded onto ships.

In Other Words

cannons very large guns ▶

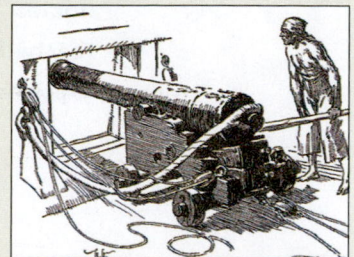

▶ Before You Move On

1. **Determine Importance** What was the *Whydah's* role in the Triangular Trade?
2. **Use Text Features** What does the illustration tell you about life long ago?

The Slave Trade

Lawrence Prince was captain of the *Whydah*. When he came to the coast of Africa, he traded his ship's cargo to local African **nobles** and <mark>merchants</mark>. In exchange, he bought enslaved Africans. Many of the people he bought were prisoners taken by other tribes in war.

The people were loaded aboard the ship, never to see their homes again. Many families were separated forever.

Once the *Whydah* **reached port** in the Caribbean, the **captives** were sold. They would spend the rest of their lives in a strange land as enslaved people in forced labor.

▲ African captives were forced onto ships and then sold as slaves.

In Other Words
nobles chiefs and leaders
reached port arrived
captives enslaved people

The Capture of a Pirate Prize

Captain Prince was probably worried as he set sail from the Caribbean port. The *Whydah* carried treasure and rich cargo from the sale of the captives. Thousands of pirates **swarmed** the Caribbean. They robbed ships wherever they could.

Two pirate ships commanded by Sam Bellamy **caught up to** the *Whydah*. Even though the ship **was well-armed**, Captain Prince quickly surrendered. Bellamy took the *Whydah* as his own.

Bellamy had good reason to be pleased. According to court records, the *Whydah* treasure by itself was worth **a fortune**.

▼ **Pirates often attacked by surprise at night.**

In Other Words
swarmed sailed all around
caught up to reached
was well-armed had guns
a fortune a lot of money

▶ **Before You Move On**
1. **Cite Evidence** Which sentence tells why Prince was worried? Explain.
2. **Sequence** What happened to the *Whydah* after it left Africa? Describe the sequence of events.

Sam Bellamy and His Crew

Sam Bellamy was originally from England. **Legends** say that he came to Cape Cod as a sailor looking for a new start in life. Hearing stories of Spanish shipwrecks, he decided to find their sunken treasure and get rich.

Bellamy and his men didn't find any gold or silver. So they decided to rob ships and become pirates instead.

Bellamy's crew soon grew to about 200 men. Most were British, but there were **many other nationalities** as well. There were French, Dutch, Spanish, American colonists, three Native Americans, at least fifty Africans, and others.

Sam Bellamy, pirate captain ▶

In Other Words
Legends Old stories
many other nationalities people from many other countries

Most crew members were former merchant sailors who were tired of low pay. Others had fled their old lives for political or religious reasons. Many of the black pirates were runaway slaves.

Some of Bellamy's pirates did not even **speak a common** language. Even so, they worked together as equals.

One of the pirates was an eleven-year-old named John King. He had been sailing with his mother when the ship they were on was captured by Sam Bellamy. John decided that he wanted to become a pirate. Bellamy let him join the crew.

◀ Hendrick Quintor, little John King, and John Julian were pirates on the *Whydah*.

In Other Words
speak a common share the same

▶ **Before You Move On**

1. **Main Idea** What is the main reason that people became pirates?
2. **Make Connections** What communication challenges did pirates overcome? How might they have communicated?

The Storm at Sea

After capturing the *Whydah*, the pirates sailed north, robbing more rich ships on the way.

Then the *Whydah* was struck by a storm off Cape Cod on the night of April 26, 1717. Strong winds drove the *Whydah* onto **a sandbar** just 500 feet from shore. The ship was slammed by waves up to twenty feet high. Soon, the mainmast **snapped**. The *Whydah* was pushed off the sandbar and **capsized**.

There were 145 men and at least one boy aboard the *Whydah*. Only two made it to shore alive. The rest died in the dark, cold water.

The *Whydah's* riches quickly sank. They disappeared in the shifting sands of the Cape. There they stayed for nearly three hundred years.

mainmast

hull

In Other Words
a sandbar the sand
snapped broke
capsized turned over

▲ High winds and heavy seas drove the *Whydah* toward shore.

▶ **Before You Move On**

1. **Sequence** How did the *Whydah* sink? Retell the events in the order they happened.

2. **Use Text Features** Look at the illustration. What does it help you to understand?

Three Hundred Years Later

I began searching for the *Whydah* in libraries. I first looked for clues in old records. A chart from 1717 helped a lot. When I felt sure I knew where the *Whydah* was, I **put together** a boat, a crew, and all the **gear** we would need.

We searched for about two years. By July 1984, we were almost ready to **give up**. One day, a diver came to the surface and said there were cannons at the bottom of a pit we had dug. We brought up a coin on the very next dive.

▲ It took two years to find the *Whydah*

Traces of the Whydah

Objects from the *Whydah* have been in the ocean so long that they are completely soaked with seawater. Many objects lose their shape completely. We barely recognize what they are.

As soon as we bring something to the surface, we start work to **conserve** it. Sometimes it takes years to **preserve** a shoe or a tea kettle, but it's worth the work.

Think of a shipwreck as a time capsule, a container that holds history in place. Each object from the time capsule of the *Whydah* tells us a story about what life aboard her was like.

fork

spoon

plate

tea kettle

navigation tools

shoe

▲ Objects from the wreck of the *Whydah*

In Other Words
conserve save

▶ **Before You Move On**
1. **Main Idea** In what way is the *Whydah* a time capsule?
2. **Make Inferences** What do the **artifacts** on this page reveal about pirates' lives?

Pirate Treasure!

Treasure was one of the dreams that led me to search for the *Whydah*. It was one of the best moments in my life when we found our first Spanish silver coin.

Spain controlled most of the silver and gold mines in the New World. A large number of coins stolen by pirates were Spanish. The coins are all different shapes and sizes.

We do not sell the coins or other **artifacts** we find. Each object can tell us a little about what life was like centuries ago. Preserving *Whydah's* history is more important than selling her treasures.

▼ A diver finds coins in the sandy ocean bottom.

◀ Spanish coins were discovered in the wreck of the *Whydah*.

The Work Goes On

Underwater archaeology is not just a matter of finding a shipwreck and bringing up her treasures. First, the recovered objects have to be cleaned, preserved, and studied. We draw and photograph many of the objects.

Then we work to include our new discoveries in public exhibits, as well as to describe them in books and news articles. It's important to share the secret world of the pirates that we're uncovering.

We are still finding many of the *Whydah*'s treasures. There is enough work left for the rest of my lifetime. That excites me most of all! ❖

▼ Objects from the *Whydah*, such as this tea kettle, are carefully preserved.

Workers get ready to clean an anchor from the shipwrecked *Whydah*. ▶

▶ **Before You Move On**

1. **Details** Why do divers find so many Spanish coins in shipwrecks?
2. **Sequence** What do **archaeologists** do after finding objects in a shipwreck?

Talk About It

1. What facts about people and events are in the **history article**? Give three examples.

2. Suppose you are telling a friend about the *Whydah*. **Restate an idea** that you learned about this ship.

   From _____ , I know _____ . In other words, _____ .

3. Pretend you are an **archaeologist** exploring the *Whydah* wreck. Tell a partner about an **artifact** you have just found. Explain what it is and what you can tell from it.

   I just found _____ !. It looks like _____ .

Learn test-taking strategies.
🌐 NGReach.com

Write About It

People often find the adventures of pirates exciting. They may dislike the fact that pirates steal other people's things, though. Decide what you think about pirates. Then write a short essay to persuade readers to agree with you. Use **Key Words** to help you.

I believe that pirates are _____ . I say that because of _____ and _____ . I think you will agree with me because _____ .

Sequence

Make a time line for the *Whydah*, based on "Real Pirates." Put the events in the order they happened.

Time Line

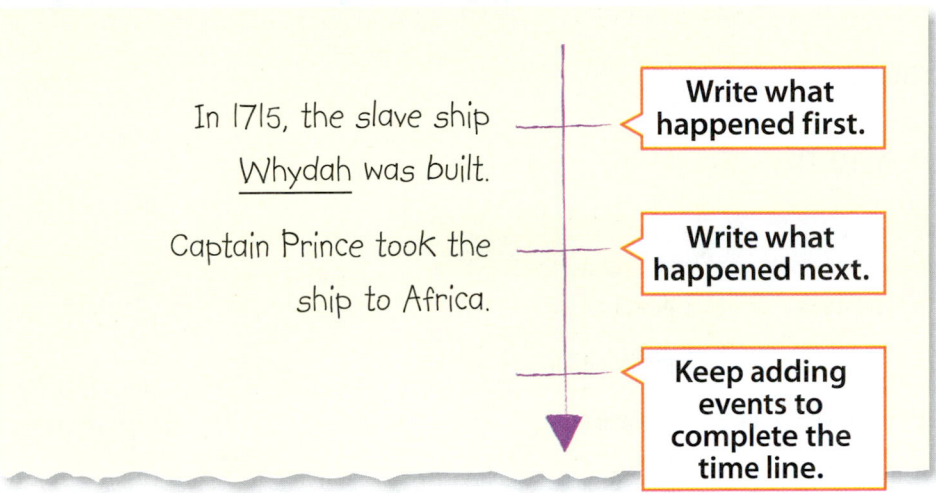

In 1715, the slave ship <u>Whydah</u> was built.

Captain Prince took the ship to Africa.

> Write what happened first.

> Write what happened next.

> Keep adding events to complete the time line.

Now use your time line as you retell "Real Pirates" to a partner. Use dates, time-order words, and **Key Words**.

On April 16, 1717, _____ .

Fluency  Comprehension Coach

Use the Comprehension Coach to practice reading with phrasing. Rate your reading.

Talk Together

Choose an illustration or photograph from "Real Pirates." Use **Key Words** as you tell a partner what the picture shows about searching for treasure.

Suffixes

A suffix is a word part that comes at the end of a word. It changes the meaning of the word.

The suffix **-er** often means "a person who does something."

| trade | + | -er | = | trader |

A **trader** is a person who trades.

Suffix	Origin	Meaning	Example
-al	Latin	belonging to	personal
-ation	Latin	act or process	preservation
-ist	Greek	a person who studies	archaeologist
-ly	Middle English	in a certain way	quickly

Try It Together

Read the sentences. Use the chart above to answer the questions.

> The geologist broke up the rocks and held a stone. At first, he thought it was just a plain rock. On closer examination, he saw a diamond.

1. **What is the work of a geologist?**

   A to crush stones

   B to find diamonds

   C to study rocks

   D to help archaeologists

2. **What does examination mean?**

   A the act of looking

   B the act of finding

   C to look closely

   D a person who finds things

Connect Across Texts Read this Web article to find out about another shipwreck.

Genre A **Web article** is informational text that is posted on the Internet. It may contain links that, when clicked, lead to other Web pages or sites.

La Belle Shipwreck

http://ngreach.com

La Belle Shipwreck

About • Special Exhibits • Prehistoric • Kids • Teachers • Resources   Search ▶

Main

Explore the Shipwreck

Treasures of the *Belle*

ADAPTED FROM THE **TEXAS BEYOND HISTORY WEB SITE**

On a winter day in 1687, the French ship *Belle* **ran aground** off the coast of what is now Texas. The ship was part of an **expedition** led by French explorer René-Robert Cavelier, Sieur de La Salle.

La Salle had come to **establish** a French **colony**. The colony would have been a **base for invading** Mexico, which was controlled by Spain. France and Spain were then at war.

▲ René-Robert Cavelier, Sieur de La Salle (1643–1687)

NEXT ››

In Other Words

ran aground got stuck in land
expedition exploration journey
establish start
base for invading place to prepare for war against

▶ **Before You Move On**

1. **Predict** What do you think the main idea or topic of this selection will be?
2. **Use Text Features** Which link in the Web article would you click to learn about gold and silver found aboard the *Belle*?

411

Main

Explore the Shipwreck

Treasures of the *Belle*

La Belle Shipwreck

The First Expedition

This was not La Salle's first journey to the New World. In 1669 he set out to explore the Great Lakes region of North America. By 1682 he reached Illinois, establishing trading posts along the way.

La Salle's first expedition was a great success. He had claimed about one-third of the land in today's continental United States. He did so in the name of Louis XIV, King of France.

Now La Salle hoped to **conquer** even more **territory**, including the Spanish silver mines in northern Mexico.

▲ **A painting showing LaSalle naming the country 'Louisiana'**

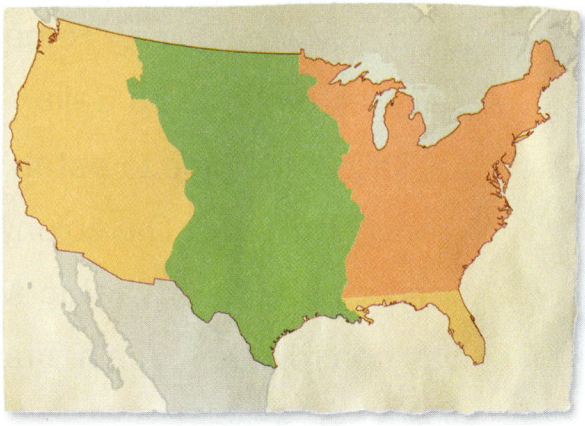

▲ **La Salle claimed about one-third of the continental United States for France.**

In Other Words
conquer take control of
territory land

412

▲ Painting by Theodore Gudin titled *La Salle's Expedition to Louisiana in 1684.*

Headed for Disaster

La Salle set sail from the French port of La Rochelle. The *Belle* was one of four ships in the expedition.

When the expedition reached the Caribbean Sea, it had its first piece of bad luck. Pirates seized one of the ships.

In January 1685, the remaining three ships reached a bay on the Texas coast by mistake. Then La Salle had more bad luck: One of the ships sank. Then another had to return to France. Only the *Belle* was left.

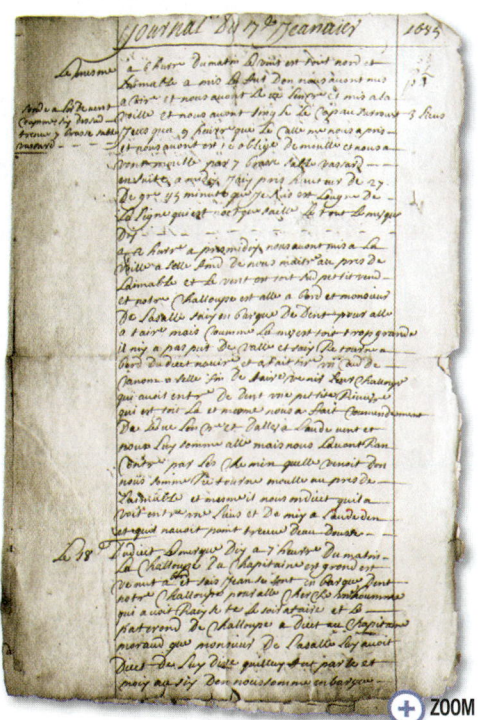

ZOOM

▲ This page from the journal of the *Belle*, dated January 17, 1685, describes what happened on the ship that day.

◀◀ PREVIOUS | NEXT ▶▶

▶ **Before You Move On**

1. **Details** What was the purpose of La Salle's new expedition?

2. **Make Inferences** Look at the journal entry and the caption. How might this journal help **archaeologists** learn more about the *Belle*?

http://ngreach.com

About • Special Exhibits • Prehistoric • Kids • Teachers • Resources

Search

Main

Explore the
Shipwreck

Treasures
of the *Belle*

La Belle Shipwreck

‹‹ PREVIOUS

The Wreck

La Salle left the *Belle* to explore on foot, leaving his sailors in charge of the ship. The *Belle* was not **anchored well**. The sailors were tired and sick.

One day a fierce wind began to push the *Belle* across the bay. The crew could not manage the sails.

The heavy anchor dragged along the bottom of the bay until the ship hit a sandy reef. The reef wrecked the *Belle*, which gradually sank into the mud. The *Belle* remained buried for 310 years, untouched but not forgotten.

The *Belle*'s crew tried to save supplies from the wrecked ship. ▶

In Other Words
anchored well held safely in place

414

The Discovery

Archaeologists from the Texas Historical Commission finally found the *Belle* in 1995. They discovered one of the *Belle* cannons, which **confirmed** the identity of the wreck.

▲ Texas archaeologists slowly uncovered the *Belle*.

Most of the ship's contents were found in good condition. Wooden boxes were **jammed** with goods to **trade**, tools, rope, dishes—everything needed to establish a colony in the New World.

The story of the *Belle* did not end there. The French government claimed that the shipwreck and all its contents belonged to France. In 2003 the French and the American governments signed **a treaty**. France now owns the *Belle*, but the Texas Historical Commission takes care of the ship. ❖

▲ Archaeologists have found more than one million **artifacts** from the *Belle*.

« PREVIOUS

In Other Words
confirmed proved
jammed filled
a treaty an agreement

▶ **Before You Move On**
1. **Cause/Effect** Why did the *Belle* sink?
2. **Clarify** How did **archaeologists** know they had found the *Belle*?

Respond and Extend

Compare Media Texts

"La Belle Shipwreck" is an example of a Web article. A blog is another form of writing on the Internet. Find an example of a blog. Compare it with "La Belle Shipwreck." Complete a comparison chart.

Comparison Chart

Feature	Web article	Blog
Title	"La Belle Shipwreck"	
Name of author	Texas Beyond History	
Date when written?	no	
Is the text in sections?		
Are there pictures?		
Does the information change often?		
Are there mostly facts or mostly opinions?		
Are there links to other articles and websites or definitions?		

Talk Together

Why do **archaeologists** and explorers seek treasure? Think about the two articles. Use **Key Words** to talk about your ideas.

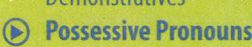

Possessive Pronouns

Possessive pronouns tell who or what owns something. Be sure to use the correct pronoun.

Grammar Rules Possessive Pronouns	
• For yourself, use **mine**.	The treasures are **mine**.
• For yourself and one or more persons, use **ours**.	That ship is **ours**.
• When you speak to one or more persons, use **yours**.	These objects are **yours**.
• For one other person or thing, use **his** or **hers**.	Are those coins **his**? No, I think they are **hers**.
• For two or more persons or things, use **theirs**.	The ship with the tall sails is **theirs**.

Read Pronouns

Read the sentences. Find three possessive pronouns.

The *Whydah* was theirs. After Prince surrendered, the ship was no longer his. "The loss is mine," he said.

Write Pronouns

Imagine that you are exploring a shipwreck. Write a journal entry about what you and the other workers find one day. Use at least two possessive pronouns.

Write as a Storyteller

Write Historical Fiction 🖉

Write an adventure story that takes place when pirates still sailed the seas. You will share your story during a storytelling festival.

Study a Model

Historical fiction is a story that is set in the past. Read Brandon's story about John King, the boy pirate.

Pirate Boy

by Brandon Kelly

I had never thought about being a pirate. But then **Sam Bellamy** and his crew captured the ***Bonetta*, the ship Mother** and **I** were on.

The pirates stayed on the *Bonetta* for fifteen days. They took our valuables and fought with our sailors.

Mother was terrified. For me, it was exciting.

At night, I listened to the pirates tell stories of the fifty ships they had taken and the adventures they'd had. Finally, I went up to the captain himself.

"Captain Bellamy," I said. "I want to join the crew."

The captain laughed. **"Well, well. Young John King, is it? And what if I was to say no?"**

"Then I will jump into the sea," I said. The captain stopped laughing. And I became a pirate.

The beginning introduces the **characters** and **setting** and gives details.

The story stays focused on one event. The **dialogue**, or what the characters say, may sound the way people did long ago.

Prewrite

1. **Choose a Topic** What time and place will you choose for your story? Talk with a partner to find fun ideas.

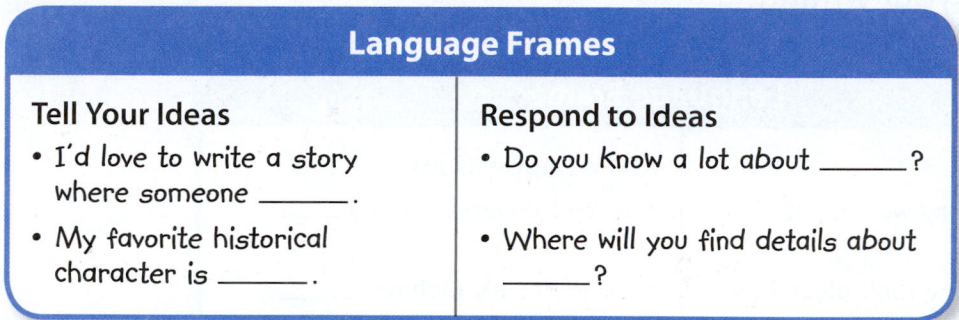

Language Frames	
Tell Your Ideas	**Respond to Ideas**
• I'd love to write a story where someone _____.	• Do you know a lot about _____ ?
• My favorite historical character is _____.	• Where will you find details about _____ ?

2. **Gather Information** For historical fiction, you have to do research. Find the details you need to describe your characters and setting accurately.

3. **Get Organized** Think about the main character in your story. How will the character change? What events and relationships will bring about the changes? Use a character map to plan.

Character Map

Draft

Use your character map and the details you found to write your draft.

- Make sure each event flows logically to the next.

- Use your research to describe your setting and characters accurately.

Revise

1. **Read, Retell, Respond** Read your draft aloud to a partner. Your partner listens and then retells the story. Next, talk about ways to improve your writing.

Language Frames	
Retell	**Make Suggestions**
• Your story was about _____.	• I don't understand why _____.
• The story took place in _____.	• I can't really picture _____. Can you add more details?
• Your main characters were _____.	• Your characters don't seem like _____. What if you _____?

2. **Make Changes** Think about your draft and your partner's suggestions. Then use the Revising Marks on page 585 to mark your changes.

   • Is your story accurate? Check all of your details.

   > I listened to the pirates tell stories of the ~~hundreds of~~ ^fifty^ ships they had taken.

   • Make sure your story is focused. Remove details that don't add to the story.

   > Mother was terrified. ~~She's the kind of person who just likes to read and sew.~~ For me, it was exciting.

Edit and Proofread

Work with a partner to edit and proofread your story. Make sure you use pronouns correctly.

Spelling Tip

✓ Do not confuse the pronoun *its* with the contraction *it's*.

Publish

1. **On Your Own** Make a final copy of your story. Choose a way to share it with your classmates. You can read it aloud, or illustrate it and give it to someone to read.

Presentation Tips	
If you are the speaker . . .	**If you are the listener . . .**
Before you read, practice saying any historical names or terms you may have used.	Connect the story with what you already know about the time period.
Try to listen to yourself read. Adjust your pitch, volume, or speed if you need to.	Listen for details that help you picture the time and place.

2. **In a Group** Hold a storytelling festival! Memorize your story, and practice telling it with gestures and emotion. Dress in a costume that matches the time period. Present your stories to other classes, or invite younger children to hear them.

Why do we seek treasure?

Talk Together

In this unit, you found lots of answers to the **Big Question**. Now use your concept map to discuss the **Big Question** with the class.

Concept Map

Reasons We Seek Treasure

• to get rich

Write a Song

Choose one reason that people seek treasure. Write the lyrics, or words, for a song that describes the reason in detail. You may want to choose the tune first.

Share Your Ideas

Choose one of these ways to share your ideas about the **Big Question**.

Write It!

Make a Comic Book

Form a comic book with eight blank pages. Then plan a story about an explorer or a pirate. Draw pictures to tell the story. Use captions to explain the events. Share your comic book with the class.

Talk About It!

Talk Show

Choose people to represent adventurers such as René-Robert Cavelier. Host a talk show. Ask each adventurer to tell about seeking treasure.

Do It!

Make a Time Capsule

Have everyone in the class bring in one artifact to put in a time capsule. It should be something you can live without for now. Decide when you will open the time capsule in the future. What would people discover about your class?

Write It!

Write a Pirate Journal

Write a journal entry as though you are one of the pirates you read about.

423

MOVING THROUGH
SPACE

BIG Question

What does it take to explore space?

Share What You Know

Do It!

① **Make** a picture of the night sky.

② **Think** about what it would be like to travel to the moon or to a star.

③ **Describe** how you would feel as you left Earth far behind you.

Build Background: Use this interactive resource to learn about space exploration.
🌐 **NGReach.com**

Ask and Answer Questions

Language Frames

• When is _____ ?
• It's _____ .
• Where are _____ ?
• They're _____ .

Listen to the dialogue between Binh and Sofia. Then use **Language Frames** to ask and answer questions with a partner. Talk about objects in space that you wonder about.

Dialogue

Key Words
accelerate
height
measure
motion
speed

Key Words

Look at the pictures. Use **Key Words** and other words to talk about how **motion** makes sports exciting.

Exciting Sports Moments

Listen to the engines roar! The cars **accelerate** quickly to well over 100 miles per hour!

Look at the **height** of that player's jump! He makes touching the rim look easy!

Look at her strong legs! This track star can move at top **speed**.

The fans wait for the officials to **measure**. How far did a player move the ball?

Talk Together

What are some ways to measure how we move through space? Try to use **Language Frames** from page 426 and **Key Words** to ask and answer questions about this topic with a partner.

427

Compare and Contrast

When you **compare** things, you say how they are similar, or alike. When you **contrast** them, you say how they are different.

Look at the pictures of Earth and Mars. Read the text.

Earth has a diameter of 13,000 kilometers. It is 150 million kilometers from the sun.

Mars has a diameter of 6,800 kilometers. It is 228 million kilometers from the sun.

Map and Talk

You can use a comparison chart to show how two things are alike and different. Here's how to make one.

Comparison Chart

Planet	Diameter	Distance from Sun	Characteristics
Earth	13,000 Kilometers	150 million Kilometers	looks blue and green has living things
Mars	6,800 Kilometers	228 million Kilometers	looks red has no living things

> Write headings here.

> Give information in these rows.

Talk Together

Look back at page 427. Choose another sport that requires speed and strength. Compare it to one of the sports shown. Make a comparison chart with a partner.

More Key Words

Use these words to talk about "What's Faster than a Speeding Cheetah?" and "Building for Space Travel."

average
(**a**-vu-rij) *noun*

An **average** is an amount that is usual for a group. Bears have an **average** of two cubs.

distance
(**dis**-tuns) *noun*

Distance is the amount of space between things. Today, we can fly a long **distance** very quickly.

rate
(**rāt**) *noun*

The **rate** of an action is its speed. Turtles move at a slow **rate**.

scale
(**scāl**) *noun*

A **scale** gives size comparisons. The **scale** of this map shows that 1 inch is equal to 1 mile.

solve
(**solv**) *verb*

To **solve** a problem means to figure it out. When you **solve** a puzzle, it's done.

Talk Together

Work with a partner. For each **Key Word**, write a sentence that shows what the word means.

I am going to *solve* a math problem.

Add words to My Vocabulary Notebook.
NGReach.com

Learn to Synthesize

Look at the picture. What do Binh and Sofia plan to do? Look for details. Put the information together to **draw a conclusion**, or decide, what they will do.

You also **draw conclusions** when you read.

How to Draw Conclusions

 1. Notice an important idea in the text.

 2. Look for another idea that you think is important.

 3. How do the ideas go with one another? Put the ideas together to draw a conclusion.

I read _____.

I also read _____.

I connect the ideas and conclude _____.

Talk Together

Read Binh's book report. Read the sample conclusion. Draw your own conclusions. Then use **Language Frames** to tell a partner about them.

Book Report

All About *All About Io*

by Binh Pham

Do you want to know more about the crazy world of outer space? If so, you should read *All About Io* by Jin Park. It is full of interesting facts about Jupiter.

I learned that Jupiter has 63 moons! A lot of them started out as asteroids. Then they got too close to Jupiter, which has a huge mass. That means it also has a lot of gravity. Think about the difference in **scale**: Jupiter is huge, the asteroids are tiny. They got trapped by Jupiter's gravity. Now they orbit Jupiter.

At first, the title of the book confused me. Reading it **solved** the puzzle for me. Io is one of Jupiter's largest moons. It is covered with volcanoes that erupt. The explosions color the moon with yellows and oranges, but I wouldn't want to live there.

The book gives lots of information. It tells how to estimate how much you would weigh on Jupiter. I also learned that Jupiter rotates at a faster **rate** than any other planet in our solar system. On **average**, a day on Jupiter lasts just 9 hours and 55 minutes. Getting to Jupiter would take a very long time, even for the fastest modern space ship. The **distance** between the planets is about 390 million miles.

This book was so much fun to read. I will look for more books by Park when I go to the library.

Sample Conclusion

"I read that this book has a lot of facts.

I also read that it is about the real planet Jupiter.

I connect the ideas and conclude the book is nonfiction. It does not tell a story the author made up."

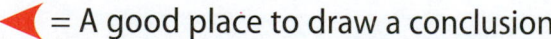

◀ = A good place to draw a conclusion

Read a Math Article

Genre

A **math article** is nonfiction. It gives number facts about people, places, or events.

Text Feature

Graphs show data, or information that uses numbers. A **bar graph** is one kind of graph. Each bar represents one piece of information.

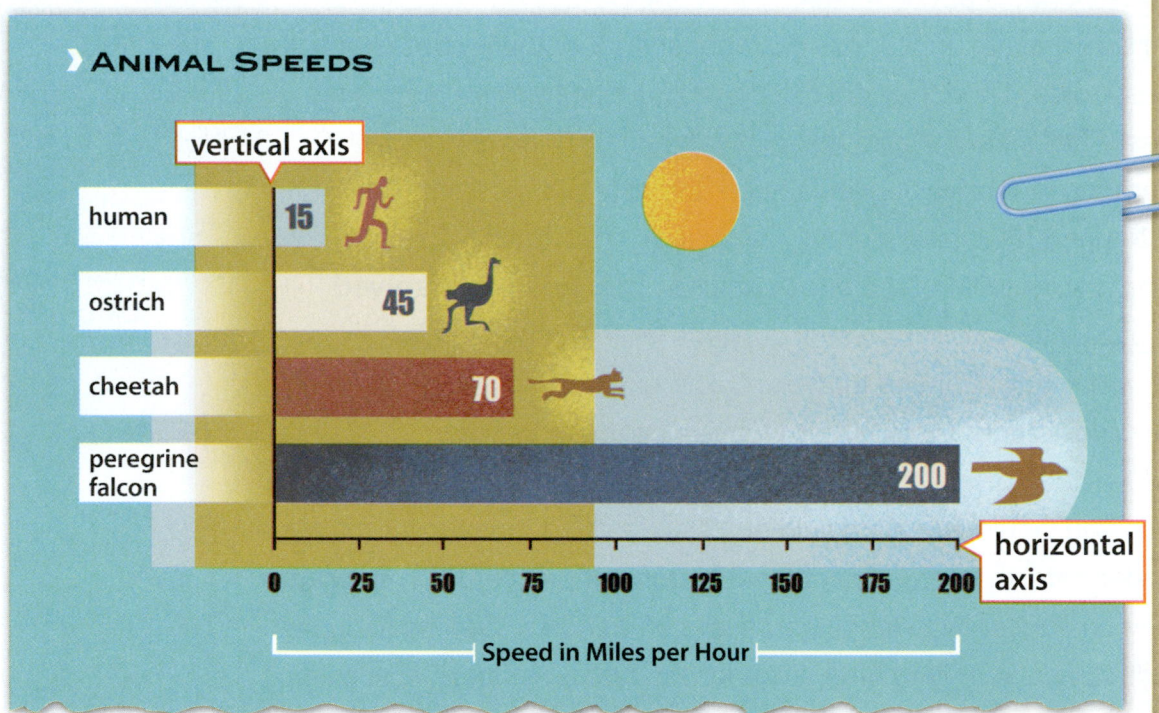

▶ ᴀɴɪᴍᴀʟ Sᴘᴇᴇᴅs

vertical axis

human 15
ostrich 45
cheetah 70
peregrine falcon 200

0   25   50   75   100   125   150   175   200

horizontal axis

Speed in Miles per Hour

▲ The name of the animal is listed on the vertical axis. The animal's speed is on the horizontal axis.

WHAT'S FASTER THAN
A SPEEDING CHEETAH?

>>> by Robert E. Wells

▶ **Set a Purpose**
Learn about the **speeds** of different
animals and objects in our universe.

How Fast Is Fast?

You may be **fast on your feet**, but if you want to win races,
never race a cheetah (or even an ostrich, for that matter).

If you ran very hard, you might reach a **speed** of 24 kilometers
per hour (15 miles per hour). That's not nearly fast enough to
keep up with an ostrich.

An ostrich is the world's fastest two-legged runner. It has a top
speed of about 72 kilometers per hour (45 miles per hour). In a
race, though, the cheetah would certainly be **way out in front**.

▲ **A peregrine falcon in downward
flight is faster than any animal
that lives on land.**

In Other Words

fast on your feet
    a great runner

way out in front first

434

A cheetah can reach a speed of about 113 kilometers per hour (70 miles per hour). That's more than a mile a minute. No animal on Earth can run faster than that.

But a cheetah can't run as fast as a peregrine falcon can **swoop**.

A peregrine falcon can dive through the sky at about 322 kilometers per hour (200 miles per hour). That's three times as fast as a car **zooming** along a highway.

A peregrine falcon is magnificent. It can dive faster than any creature can run. But it can't fly as fast as an airplane.

❯ ANIMAL SPEEDS

Speed in Miles per Hour

▶ **Before You Move On**

1. **Compare/Contrast** How much faster can an ostrich run compared to a person?
2. **Ask Questions** What is one question you have about the information on the graph?

Flight Times

Some propeller planes can fly more than 483 kilometers per hour (300 miles per hour). With a propeller pulling you through the air, you can travel faster than the fastest falcon.

With a jet engine, you can fly faster than the fastest propeller plane. In fact, you can fly even faster than the speed of sound.

Sound travels in waves. **At high altitudes**, where jets fly, sound waves travel about 1,062 kilometers per hour (660 miles per hour). Some very fast jets can fly twice the speed of sound.

jet

sound

propeller plane

peregrine falcon

| 0 | 300 | 600 | 900 | 1200 | 1500 |

Speed in Miles per Hour

▲ **Sound waves travel through the air.**

In Other Words

At high altitudes High in the air; Miles above the ground

◀ **propeller plane** a plane with a propeller

436

If you shouted to someone who was traveling faster than sound, your voice would not go fast enough to catch up to him or her. The person would never hear you.

Faster Still

If you want to travel to the moon, you're going to need something that's much faster than a jet. You'll need a rocket ship.

To escape Earth's gravity and travel into space, a rocket ship must go faster than any jet. To travel to the moon, a rocket ship must reach a speed of about 40,234 kilometers per hour (25,000 miles per hour). That's more than thirty times as fast as sound.

A rocket ship takes off with incredible speed.

▶ **Before You Move On**

1. **Compare/Contrast** Compare the **speed** of a jet with the **speed** of sound. Which travels faster?

2. **Explain** Tell in your own words why a rocket needs to go faster than a jet.

Space Speeders

You can turn off your rockets and **coast** after you're in space. That's because there's little to no drag in space. Drag is a force that acts against objects when they travel through air. Drag slows down moving objects. Now, speeding through space at 40,234 kilometers per hour (25,000 miles per hour) is **mighty** fast.

What's that zooming by, going so much faster that you feel like you are standing still? It's a meteoroid!

A meteoroid is a space rock. Some meteoroids **streak** through space at 241,402 kilometers per hour (150,000 miles per hour). That's six times faster than your rocket ship is traveling.

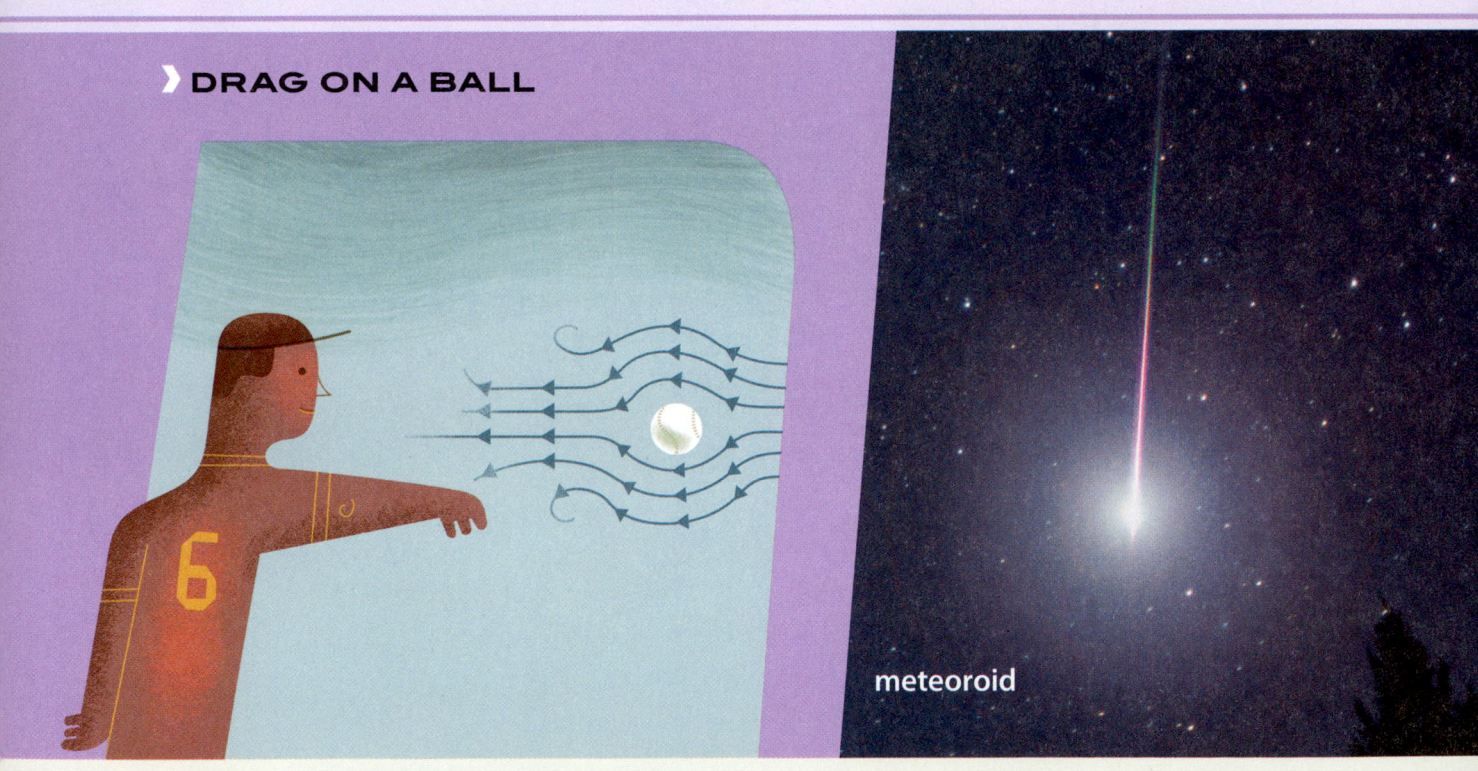

❯ **DRAG ON A BALL**

meteoroid

▲ **The ball pushes against the air as it travels. Air pushes back. The ball slows down.**

In Other Words

coast keep moving without using additional power

mighty very

streak zoom; move

438

As you circle around the moon and head back to Earth, you might be thinking that the meteoroid you saw was the fastest thing you could ever see.

FASTER AND FASTER

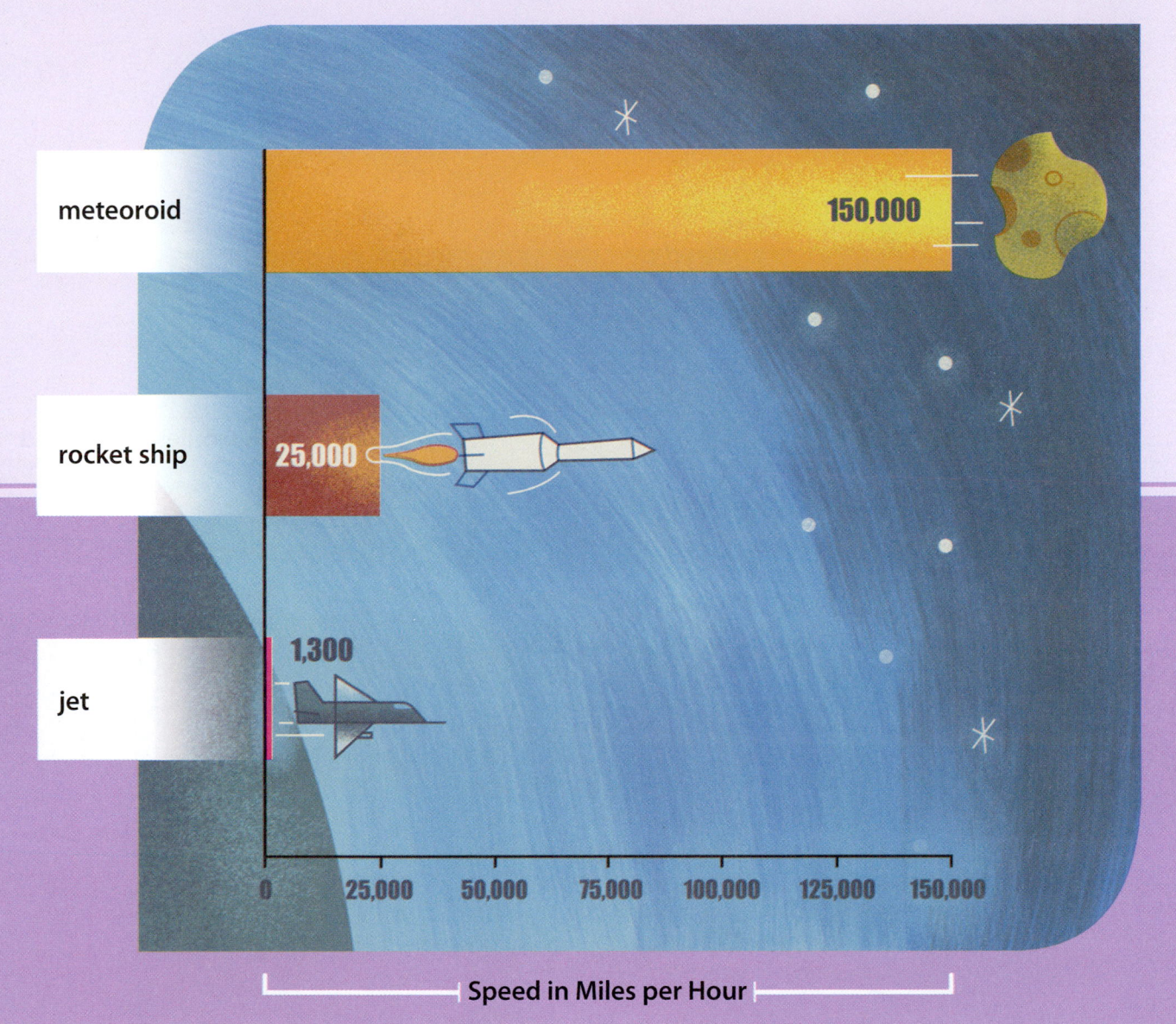

meteoroid 150,000

rocket ship 25,000

jet 1,300

0   25,000   50,000   75,000   100,000   125,000   150,000

Speed in Miles per Hour

▶ **Before You Move On**

1. **Draw Conclusions** What can you conclude about why meteoroids can travel so fast in space?

2. **Use Text Features** What does the bar graph on this page compare?

Fastest of All

Hold on a minute. There's something much faster than even the fastest meteoroid. It's something you see all the time.

Just push the switch on a flashlight. Instantly, a light beam will flash out at the amazing speed of 299,338 kilometers per second (186,000 miles per second).

That's thousands of times faster than a meteoroid. At that speed, a beam of light could circle Earth more than seven times in one second.

186,000 miles per second

In Other Words
Hold on Wait

Most scientists believe that nothing can travel through space faster than light. Who would have thought that the fastest traveling thing in the whole universe could come out of something small enough to hold in your hand?

◄ **A beam of light could circle Earth more than seven times in one second!**

► How Long Would It Take to Travel from Earth to the Moon (239,000 miles)?

AT THIS SPEED...	IT WOULD TAKE ABOUT
Young Runner (15 miles per hour)	1 ¾ years
Ostrich (45 miles per hour)	7 ⅓ months
Cheetah (70 miles per hour)	4 ⅔ months
Peregrine Falcon (200 miles per hour)	7 weeks
Propeller Plane (300 miles per hour)	4 ⅔ weeks
Supersonic Jet (1400 miles per hour)	1 week
Rocket Ship (25,000 miles per hour)	9 ½ hours
Meteoroid (150,000 miles per hour)	1 ½ hours
Light (186,000 miles per second)	1 ⅓ seconds

▶ **Before You Move On**

1. **Draw Conclusions** Identify a detail that supports the conclusion that a light beam travels faster than a meteoroid.

2. **Interpret** Based on the chart, which three objects travel fastest though space?

Some Additional Thoughts on Very Fast Things

Sometimes speeds are hard to **measure**. People often have trouble measuring the speeds of animals. The numbers in this article are the best estimates. It would be much simpler if cheetahs, ostriches, and falcons **came with** speedometers.

The speed of sound through air is easier to measure than the speeds of wild animals. Still, the speed of sound **is not constant**. It's about 1,223 kilometers per hour (760 miles per hour) at sea level. At high altitudes, where the air is thin and cold, it slows to about 1,062 kilometers per hour (660 miles per hour).

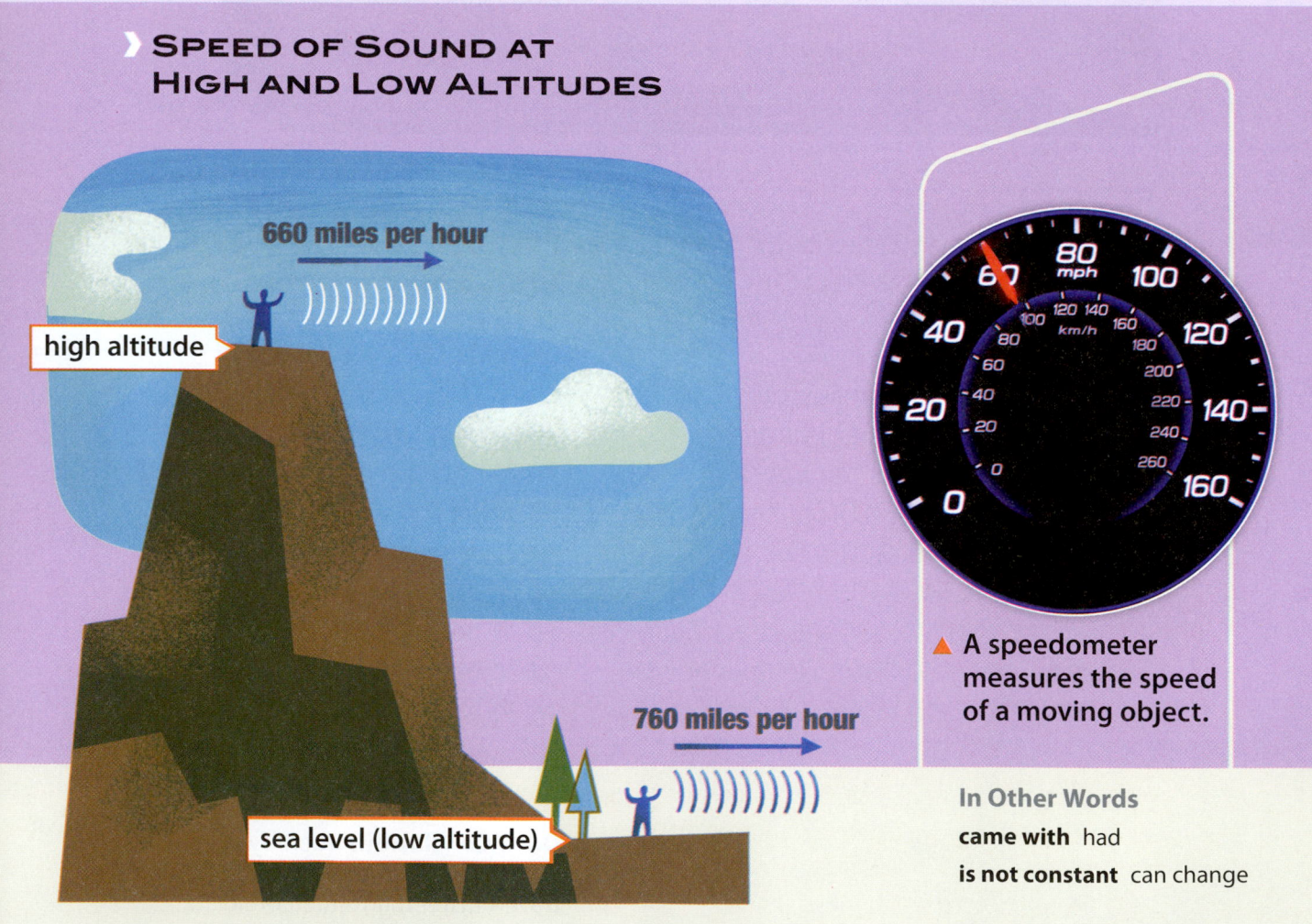

❯ **SPEED OF SOUND AT HIGH AND LOW ALTITUDES**

660 miles per hour

high altitude

760 miles per hour

sea level (low altitude)

▲ A speedometer measures the speed of a moving object.

In Other Words
came with had
is not constant can change

442

Meteoroids zoom through space at different speeds, too. The meteoroid in this article is a fast one.

The amazing speed of light, traveling through space at 299,338 kilometers per second (186,000 miles per second), is one of the few speeds that **is constant**.

Light beams flashing through space are usually shown as bright rays. A real light beam, however, becomes bright and visible only when it hits such things as dust or water particles.

Now you know what the fastest thing in the universe is. The next time you're in a conversation about speed, you'll be able to **shed some light on** the subject! ❖

In Other Words
is constant always stays the same
shed some light on explain

▶ **Before You Move On**

1. **Draw Conclusions** What makes sound easier to <mark>measure</mark> than a racing animal?
2. **Compare/Contrast** Describe one way in which the <mark>speed</mark> of light and the <mark>speed</mark> of sound are different.

Key Words

accelerate	motion
average	rate
distance	scale
height	solve
measure	speed

Talk About It

1. How can you use the graphs in this **math article** to compare and contrast moving objects?

2. How does the **speed** of sound compare to the speed of light? With a partner, **ask and answer questions** about this topic.

   Is _____ faster than _____?

   Yes, _____ travels _____, and _____ travels _____.

3. The author says that researchers have to estimate how fast animals move. Summarize what it means to estimate the **speed** of a moving object.

   When you estimate, you _____ . Researchers have to estimate animal speeds because _____ .

Learn test-taking strategies.
🔵 NGReach.com

Write About It

Who is the fastest runner in your class? How could you find out? Write a set of instructions for a race. In your instructions, tell how you would **measure** each person's running **speed**. Also tell what kind of graph you would use to compare the **rates**. Use **Key Words** in your list.

1. Mark the starting line of the race.
2. Mark the _____ .

Compare and Contrast

Make a comparison chart for "What's Faster Than a Speeding Cheetah?"

In this column, name the things you will compare.

Tell how it moves.

Tell how fast it is.

Tell what speed record it set.

Animal or Object	How It Moves	Fastest Speed	Record
ostrich	runs on two legs	72 km (45 mi) per hour	fastest animal with 2 legs
cheetah	runs on four legs	113 km (70 mi) per hour	fastest land animal
peregrine falcon			
jet plane			

Now use your comparison chart as you tell a partner how the animals and objects are alike and different. Use **Key Words** and words like *but* and *however* to compare.

A _____ is fast, but a _____ is faster.

Fluency  Comprehension Coach

Use the Comprehension Coach to practice reading with intonation. Rate your reading.

Talk Together

Why do we need to be fast to explore space? Use **Key Words** as you talk about space exploration and motion.

Multiple-Meaning Words

Some words have more than one meaning. You can use context to figure out the correct meaning.

Rate is a **multiple-meaning word**. In the sentence below, **rate** means speed. You can use the words *travels* and *slower* as clues to the meaning.

> The **rate** at which sound travels is slower where the air is thin and cold.

> **rate** (rāt) *noun* **1.** the speed at which something moves **2.** a fee charged for a service

Try It Together

Read the passage. Then answer the questions.

> Just push the **switch** on a flashlight. Instantly, a **beam** will flash out at the amazing speed of 299,338 kilometers per second (186,000 miles per second).

1. **What is the best definition for beam in this passage?**

   A a long piece of wood or metal

   B the widest part of a ship

   C the bar on a balance scale

   D a ray of light

2. **What is the best definition for switch in this passage?**

   A a section of railroad track

   B an on/off button

   C a change

   D a fast, jerking motion

Connect Across Texts You read a math article about the **speed** of moving objects such as space ships. Now read a report about designing spacecraft.

Genre A **science report** presents facts about a topic. Most reports have a title and an introduction that tells what the report is about. Often, a conclusion sums up the report.

Building for
SPACE TRAVEL

by Anastasia Suen

Imagine this task: Design a space **vehicle** that will also be a home for astronauts on a **mission** to planet Mars that could take months or years. For **architect** Constance Adams, this job was tough. She designed TransHab—a "transit habitat" where astronauts would live and work. Not surprisingly, Adams faced many challenges along the way.

▲ Constance Adams worked with NASA, the U.S. space agency, to design TransHab.

Earth

Mars

sun

In Other Words
vehicle craft
mission trip
architect building designer

▶ **Before You Move On**

1. **Make Connections** Think about the length of time for this mission. What do you think the TransHab might need?

2. **Make Predictions** What design challenges do you think Adams faced?

NASA did not expect TransHab to launch into space on its own. A space shuttle was supposed to carry it into space. So TransHab had to be small enough to fit inside a shuttle's **cargo** area, and big enough for six astronauts to live in.

How would this be possible? Think about a beach ball. It's flat until you fill it with air. NASA asked Adams to use this idea for TransHab. Therefore, Adams had to design TransHab so it could be carried into space in its flattened state. Once it was in space, TransHab would be **inflated**.

cargo area

◀ A space shuttle was supposed to carry TransHab into space.

In Other Words
cargo storage
inflated filled with air

TransHab's soft outer surface created safety challenges. Space is a very dangerous place. Chunks of ice and rock **speed** along at four miles a second. Some types of radiation, or energy traveling through space, can also hurt astronauts' bodies. Most spacecraft have a hard outside shell to protect it from damage and keep radiation out.

Adams's team had to figure out how strong to make TransHab's soft outer shell. They made a one-foot-thick skin that combined different materials. One very strong material was Kevlar, which is used in convertible cars.

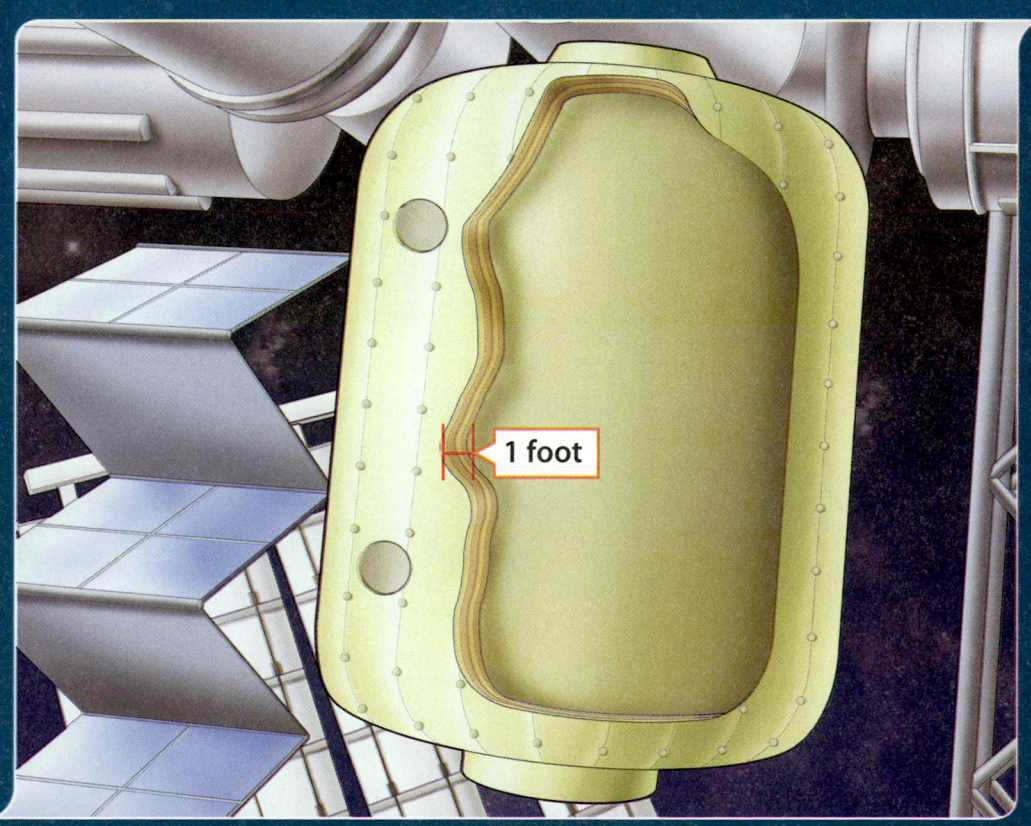

1 foot

◀ TransHab's outer skin is one foot thick.

▶ **Before You Move On**

1. **Draw Conclusions** Based on the text, what can you conclude about the risks of space travel?

2. **Compare/Contrast** How is TransHab different from a traditional spacecraft?

A trip to Mars would take a long time. Astronauts would have to live inside TransHab for years. They would need a real home in space. They would need places to eat, sleep, exercise, get care when sick, and have **privacy**. They also would need a group area for meetings and for celebrating special occasions like birthdays.

"We had to create a design for long-term living," Adams explains.

The diagram below shows Adams's plan for TransHab. There are three levels with living areas. The top level is a tunnel entryway and exit.

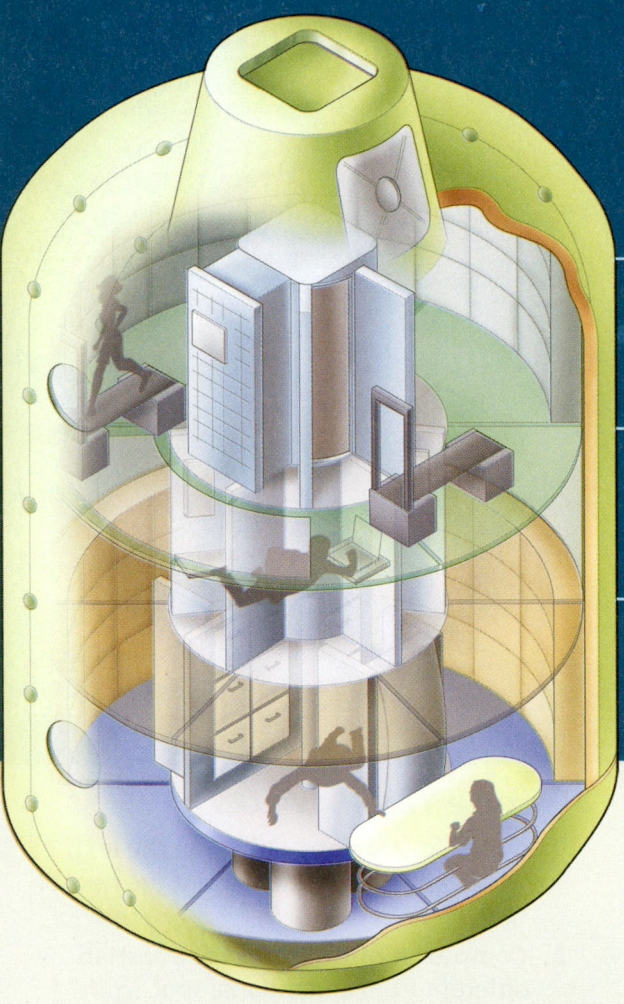

‹ Level Four:
Entry and Exit Tunnel

‹ Level Three:
Exercise Room, Bathroom and Storage

‹ Level Two:
Control Room and Six Bedrooms

‹ Level One:
Kitchen and Dining Room

In Other Words
privacy space to be alone

Gravity is the force that keeps you firmly on the ground. Other forces of **motion** can cancel out the force of gravity. This creates a condition called *zero gravity*. A zero-gravity environment presents a design challenge because it causes objects to "float."

Adams attached furniture and other objects **securely** inside TransHab so astronauts could grab them to help themselves move around. She also used a pattern on the walls to help the astronauts tell up from down.

After years of hard work, Constance Adams met all these challenges. However, space scientists must meet other challenges before they can launch a mission to Mars. Even if TransHab does not go to Mars, it could be a home for astronauts on a future **space station**. ❖

▲ Constance Adams tests what zero gravity is like.

▲ TransHab on a space station

space station

TransHab

In Other Words

securely firmly

space station place in space where astronauts work

▶ **Before You Move On**

1. **Use Text Features** Look at the diagram on page 450. Describe the areas that make TransHab a real home for astronauts.

2. **Draw Conclusions** What can you conclude about zero gravity's effects on astronauts?

Compare Fact and Opinion

Key Words

accelerate	motion
average	rate
distance	scale
height	solve
measure	speed

A **fact** is a statement that can be proved true. An **opinion** tells what someone thinks, feels, or believes. An author may include both facts and opinions, even in nonfiction. Work with a partner to complete the comparison chart. Discuss how you can tell if a statement is fact or opinion.

Write statements of fact in this column.

In this column, write statements that express opinions.

Comparison Chart

	Facts	Opinions
"What's Faster Than a Speeding Cheetah?"	•	• A peregrine falcon is magnificent. •
"Building for Space Travel"	• Constance Adams helped design TransHab. •	•

Talk Together

Think about the math article and the science report. Use **Key Words** to discuss what it takes to explore space. Speak clearly and support your opinion.

Adverbs

Adverbs usually tell more about a verb.

Grammar Rules Adverbs	
• Use an **adverb** to tell how, where, or when something happens.	An eagle flies **smoothly**. (how) It soars **upward**. (where) I watch an eagle **now**. (when)
• For some adverbs, add -**er** to compare two actions. Add -**est** to compare three or more actions.	A marlin swims fast**er** than a shark. A sailfish swims the fast**est** of all fish.
• If an adverb ends in -**ly**, use **more** or **less** to compare two actions. Use **the most** or **the least** to compare three or more actions.	Snakes move more gent**ly** than lizards. Lizards move less gent**ly** than snakes. Sloths move the most gent**ly** of all. Frogs move the least gent**ly** of all.

Read Adverbs

Read this passage with a partner. Find three adverbs.

> If you shouted loudly and clearly to someone who was traveling faster than sound, the person would never hear you.

Write Adverbs

Write a paragraph about objects in motion, such as kites or paper airplanes. Share with your partner. Use at least three adverbs.

Language Frames

- It means _____ .
- For example, _____ .

Clarify

Listen to Francisco's song. Then use **Language Frames** to clarify information about the moon.

Song ((MP3))

Let's Go to the Moon

Look up in the night for a circle that's bright.
Yes, it means you should look for the moon.
There are no creatures there—
   for example, no bears.
Let's all ride in a spaceship there soon.

Chorus
Let's go to the moon.
On our way we can all sing this tune.
If you want some more space,
   then the moon is the place.
We will have lots of room on the moon.

Tune: "Home on the Range"

Key Words

astronaut

launch

orbit

planet

rotation

Key Words

Look at the photos. Use **Key Words** and other words to talk about how you could teach younger children about space.

Tools for Teaching Very Young Children About Space

action figure: astronaut As you talk about modern space travelers, let the children play with this astronaut. They can show the astronaut at work.

globe Use the globe as you teach children that Earth is a **planet**. Show them that planets are round. Demonstrate the Earth's **rotation**, or how it spins.

space shuttle model Tell children that many astronauts travel in the space shuttle. Demonstrate how the space shuttle **launches**, or takes off from Earth. Then use the model and the globe to show how the space shuttle **orbits**, or moves around, Earth.

solar system model Use the model as you tell children about the other planets in the solar system. Demonstrate how the planets orbit around the Sun.

Talk Together

What does it take for astronauts to explore space? Try to use **Language Frames** from page 454 and **Key Words** as you clarify your ideas with a partner.

Plot

The action in a story is the **plot**. Every plot is built around a problem. When you follow the plot, you see:

- one story event leads to the next event

- at the turning point, an important change happens

- at the solution, the problem is solved

Look at the pictures. Follow the plot.

Map and Talk

You can use a plot diagram to retell a story. First, tell what the problem is. Then, tell the events in the order they happen. Next, tell the turning point. Last, tell how the problem is solved.

Plot Diagram

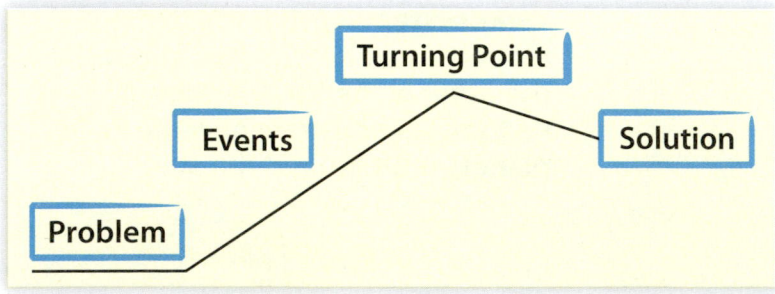

Problem: Francisco's rocket crash lands.

Events: Francisco picks up the rocket. He sees that it is getting banged up.

Turning Point: Francisco and his dad make a parachute.

Solution: The rocket lands softly.

Retell a favorite story to your partner. Use a plot diagram for help.

More Key Words

Use these words to talk about "The Moon Over Star" and "The First Person on the Moon."

capacity
(ku-**pa**-su-tē) *noun*

The **capacity** of an object is the most it can hold. This bucket has a **capacity** of 1 gallon.

constant
(**kon**-stunt) *noun*

Something that never changes is a **constant**. The number of days in a week is a **constant**.

limit
(**li**-mut) *verb*

To **limit** something is to stop it after a a set amount of time. Many parents **limit** TV viewing.

resistance
(ri-**zis**-tunts) *noun*

Resistance is a slowing force. Deep snow creates **resistance** when you walk in it.

technology
(tek-**nah**-lu-jē) *noun*

Technology is the use of science to solve problems. Doctors rely on **technology**.

Talk Together

Work with a partner to complete a Meaning Map for each **Key Word**.

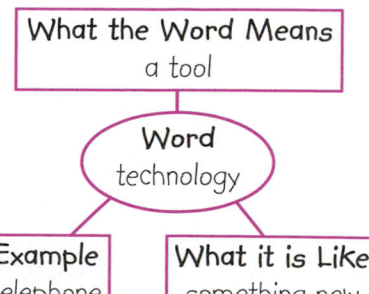

What the Word Means
a tool

Word
technology

Example
telephone

What it is Like
something new

Add words to My Vocabulary Notebook.
NGReach.com

Learn to Synthesize

Look at the photographs. Notice details that show what it takes to be a good astronaut. Think about what you already know about space travel.

From this information, you can **form a generalization** about what most astronauts have in common.

You also **form generalizations** when you read.

How to Form Generalizations

 1. As you read, think about the important ideas in the text.

 2. Think about how the ideas fit together with what you know or have experienced.

 3. Create a statement that seems true for both the text and what you know. Use words like *some*, *many*, *most*, or *all*.

> I read _____ .
>
> I know_____ .
>
> Most of the time, it is true that _____ .

Language Frames

👁 I read _____ .

💭 I know _____ .

💬 Most of the
time, it is true
that _____ .

Talk Together

Read Francisco's story. Read the sample generalization. Then use **Language Frames** to tell a partner about your own generalizations.

Story

Game Over

by Francisco Soto

Ramón gets what he wanted for his birthday: the brand new video game *Planet Surfer*. As soon as he starts playing, his little brother Nico wants to play, too. Ramón ignores him.

Ramón plays the character Zozo in *Planet Surfer*. Zozo is an explorer in outer space. He uses lots of amazing space **technology**.

The game is great, but Nico's nagging is a **constant**. When Zozo **launches** his rocket, Nico tugs on Ramón's arm. "Stop bothering me!" says Ramón, trying to **limit** his little brother's interruptions.

Zozo collects rock samples as he explores the **planets**. The ship is loaded down, near to **capacity**. He wants one more rock. Yes, it fits! Nico claps loudly. "Shhh," says Ramón.

Zozo overcomes a giant space robot. When the battle is over, Nico finally overcomes Ramón's **resistance**. Ramón gives Nico the controller and lets him play.

Sample Generalization

"I read that Ramón is playing a brand new game.

I know I feel excited when I play a new game for the first time.

Most of the time, it is true that people would like to play a new game without being interrupted."

◀ A good place to form a generalization

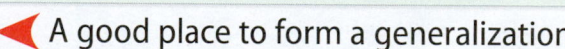

459

Read a Story

Genre

Realistic fiction tells a story about events that really happened or could happen. The characters and setting in this story seem real, but were created by the author.

Dialogue in a Story

The dialogue in a story is what the characters say. Quotation marks signal the beginning or the end of a character's speech. The words that appear between the quotation marks are the speaker's exact words.

quotation marks   **dialogue**   **quotation marks**

"I wonder how many miles it is to the moon," Cousin Carrie said. **the person speaking**

I'd been reading the moon stories in the paper, so I knew.

The Moon over Star

by **Dianna Hutts Aston**

illustrated by **Jerry Pinkney**

▶ **Set a Purpose**
Find out what one family in the
town of Star thinks of space travel.

It was a summer's morning in 1969, in the town of Star, where I lived. If all went well, a spaceship carrying **astronauts** Neil Armstrong, Edwin Aldrin, Jr., and Michael Collins would land on the moon today. I dreamed that maybe one day, I could go to the moon, too.

My **gramps** thought the space program was a **waste** of money, but I knew he still thought about the astronauts. I thought about the astronauts' kids and wondered if they were scared—scared but proud. I knew I'd be.

In Other Words
gramps grandfather
waste bad use

462

Once upon a summer's noon, my cousins and I
scouted **Gran's** watermelon patch for the biggest one.
It took three of us to carry it to a tub of ice—three and
a half, counting my littlest cousin, Lacey.

We decorated the picnic table with pails of
wildflowers. Then, our **chores** done, we built our own
spaceship from **scraps** we found in the barn.

In Other Words
Gran's Grandmother's
chores work
scraps pieces or parts of things

As the oldest grandchild, I got to be **launch controller** and Commander Armstrong.

"**Ignition sequence start** . . . 6, 5, 4, 3, 2, 1, 0. Liftoff, we have liftoff!"

We closed our eyes, imagining **with all our might** the rumble, the roar, and the force of the Saturn rocket, blasting the spaceship into the stars. Then we were rushing through space at 25,000 miles per hour.

In Other Words

launch controller the person in charge of the **launch**

Ignition sequence start Start counting backward

with all our might as hard as we could

"I wonder how many miles it is to the moon," Cousin Carrie said.

I'd been reading the moon stories in the paper, so I knew. "About 240,000 miles," I said. "And some scientists say it's moving away from us—an inch or so farther every year."

I also knew that in May 1961, a month before I was born, President John F. Kennedy had said America would send men to the moon before **the decade was out**.

In Other Words
the decade was out the year 1970

▶ **Before You Move On**
1. **Generalize** What is one thing the narrator thinks about space travel?
2. **Make Comparisons** How is the children's game like a real liftoff?

▶ **Predict**
How will Gramps respond when the
first spacecraft lands on the moon?

That afternoon, we were helping

Gramps with the tractor when Gran **hollered**, "Come
quick! They're landing!"

Gramps kept right on **tinkering with** the engine.
The rest of us ran **pell-mell** for the house and squirmed
around the television screen as it glowed with equal
parts of moon and the spaceship called *Eagle*.

We heard the voice of Commander Armstrong
directing the landing. "Forward . . . forward," he said.

In Other Words
hollered yelled
tinkering with working on
pell-mell in a wild rush

Then the newsman we all knew, Walter Cronkite, exclaimed, "Man on the moon!"

For a **split second** we were silent. The whole universe must have been, as we waited to hear the voice of an astronaut 240,000 miles away.

And then: "Houston, **Tranquility Base here**," Commander Armstrong said. **"The *Eagle* has landed."**

In Other Words

split second short moment

Tranquility Base here I'm calling from Tranquility Base

"The *Eagle* has landed." ▶ The spacecraft has landed on the moon.

467

Boy, did we cheer, all of the cousins and even the grown-ups—all except Gramps. I remembered something he'd once said:

"Why spend all that money to go to the moon when there are so many folks **in need** right here on Earth?"

"Because we can!" I'd almost shouted, but **caught** myself.

I began to wonder then what Gramps's dreams had been. From the time he was little, he had worked the farm, doing the same jobs, **day to day**, season to season.

In Other Words
in need who need money
caught stopped
day to day one day after another

When the **crickets began to sing**, Gramps sat down to rest. I pulled off his **dirt-caked** boots for him and stomped around the porch.

"Gramps, will you watch the moon walk with me tonight?"

"I'm mighty **worn out** today," he said, "but maybe."

Suddenly, I could see how tired he was. Lifetime-tired. There were deep lines in his face—a farmer's face, an old farmer's face.

"All right, Gramps," I said. "It's okay."

In Other Words
crickets began to sing evening came
dirt-caked dirt-covered
worn out tired

▶ **Before You Move On**

1. **Explain** Why isn't Gramps as excited as everyone else about the moon landing?
2. **Plot** What two events are happening in the story at this point?

▶ **Predict**
What will the moon walk mean
to the narrator?

Once upon a summer's night in 1969,
we spread blankets and folding chairs on the edge of the
yard, where the buffalo grass grew thick and soft. The
cornstalks whispered while we **gazed** at the pearly slice
of moon and the stars, which gleamed like spilled sugar.

What were the astronauts seeing, right at this very
second? Could they see beyond the moon, to Mars or
Neptune or Jupiter?

What I could see above me, and what I could see in
my imagination, were better than any **picture** show.

In Other Words
gazed looked
picture movie or television

470

Later on that summer's night, in 1969, the television screen flashed with words that **gave me goose bumps:** **LIVE FROM** THE SURFACE OF THE MOON.

Mr. Cronkite said, ". . . Neil Armstrong, thirty-eight-year-old American, standing on the surface of the moon on this July twentieth, nineteen hundred and sixty-nine!"

In Other Words

gave me goose bumps thrilled me

LIVE FROM THIS IS HAPPENING RIGHT NOW ON

I didn't know it then, but there were 600 million people **the world over** watching with me and listening, when Commander Armstrong said, "That's one small step for man, one giant leap for mankind."

All of us—from New York to Tokyo to Paris to Cairo . . . to Star—watched it together, the astronauts bounding across the moon like ghosts on a **trampoline**. I felt a hand on my shoulder.

"I **reckon** that's something to remember," Gramps said quietly.

trampoline

In Other Words
the world over all over the world
trampoline springy surface
reckon guess

Later, when it was as quiet as the world ever gets, Gramps and I stood together under the moon.

"What's mankind?" I asked him.

"It's all of us," he finally said. "It's all of us who've ever lived, all of us still to come."

I put my hand in his. "Just think, Gramps, if they could go to the moon, maybe one day I could too!"

"Great days," he said, "an astronaut in the family. **Who'd a** thought?"

I smiled in the dark. My gramps was proud of me.

In Other Words
Who'd a Who would have

"The first airplane I ever saw, I was your age. It was right over **yonder**," Gramps said, nodding toward the cornfield. "That was something to see."

A sigh in Gramps's voice made my heart squeeze.

"Keep on dreaming, Mae," he said. "Just remember, we're here now together on the prettiest star in **the heavens**."

Gramps had **looked to** the moon all of his life. It told him when to plant and when to harvest. And once upon a summer's night, it told me to dream. ❖

In Other Words
yonder there
the heavens space
looked to depended on

▶ **Before You Move On**

1. **Visualize** What does Mae see when she looks up at the sky? What does she imagine that the **astronauts** see?
2. **Character** How does Gramps change?

Meet the Illustrator

Jerry Pinkney

As a teenager, Jerry Pinkney worked at a newsstand. Every day he drew pictures of the people walking by. One day, a famous cartoonist stopped and gave him advice. That's when Mr. Pinkney realized he could become a professional artist.

Now when Mr. Pinkney starts drawing, he doesn't know exactly what will happen until his pencil touches the paper. He says, "Then the image comes to life. When I put a line down, the only thing I know is how it should feel."

▲ Jerry Pinkney

Artist's Craft

An illustrator has to use the writer's words to help him picture the characters. How do words like "lifetime-tired" help the artist to draw Gramps?

475

Talk About It

1. What seems **realistic** about the story? Give three examples.

   The story is realistic because _____ .

2. Summarize one theme of the story. Explain why you think this is the author's main message. **Clarify** your ideas.

3. Does this story have a first-person narrator or a third-person narrator? Explain how you can tell.

   The story has a _____ . I can tell because _____ .

Learn test-taking strategies.
🚀 NGReach.com

Write About It

What image does the author use to describe the **astronauts** as they walk on the moon? How does this help you picture what Mae sees? Write a short paragraph. Use **Key Words** to explain your thinking.

The astronauts look like _____ .

Plot

Make a plot diagram to retell the story of "The Moon Over Star." Include the problem, the important events, the turning point, and the solution.

Plot Diagram

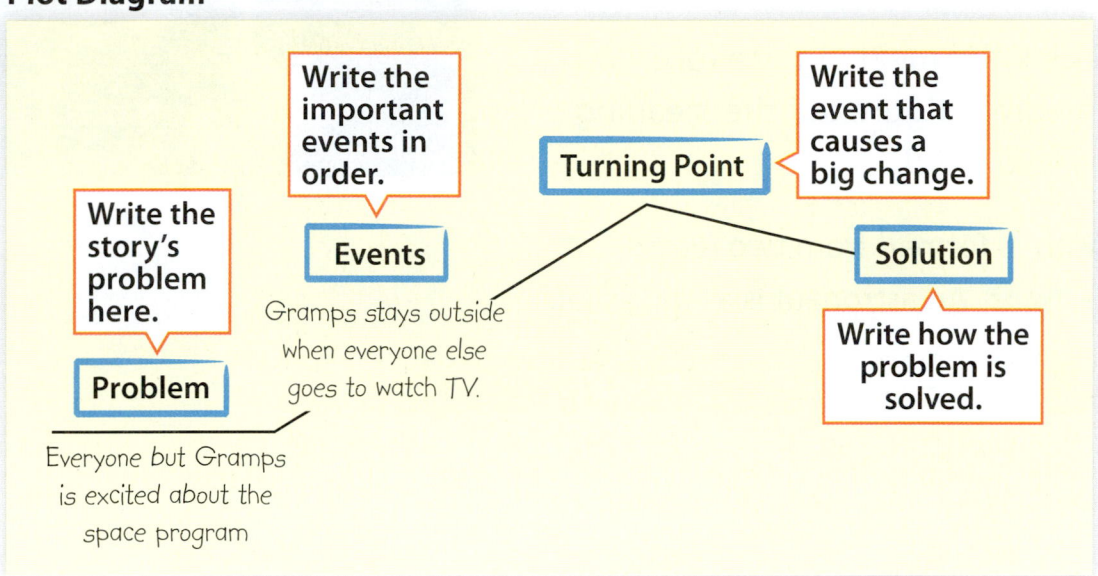

Write the important events in order.

Write the event that causes a big change.

Turning Point

Write the story's problem here.

Events

Solution

Problem

Gramps stays outside when everyone else goes to watch TV.

Write how the problem is solved.

Everyone but Gramps is excited about the space program

Now use your plot diagram as you retell the story to a partner. Use **Key Words** as you tell what the turning point is and how the problem is solved.

The turning point is _____. The problem is solved _____.

Fluency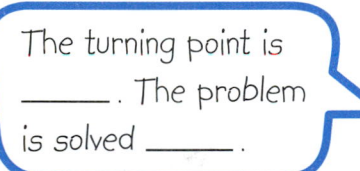

Comprehension Coach

Use the Comprehension Coach to practice reading with expression. Rate your reading.

Talk Together

Role-play a conversation between Mae and Gramps. What does it take to explore space? Use **Key Words** as you answer this question: Is it worth it?

Word Parts

Many English words are made up of word parts. A **root** is a word part that has meaning. Unlike a base word, though, it cannot stand on its own.

If you know the meaning of a root, you can sometimes figure out the meaning of the whole word.

Astronaut is formed from two roots: **astro** + **naut**. An astronaut is a "star sailor."

Root	Origin	Meaning	Example
astro	Greek	star	astronomy
naut	Greek	sailor	nautical
wis	Old English	wise	wisdom
rota	Latin	wheel	rotation

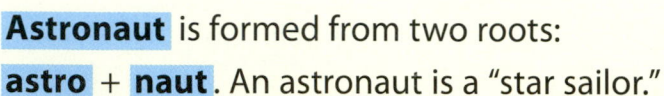
Try It Together

Answer each question. Use the chart above to help you.

1. What do you think <u>wisdom</u> means?

   A a faraway star

   B someone who lives on a ship

   C a good student

   D good sense

2. What do you think <u>rotary</u> means?

   A a large ship

   B something that turns like a wheel

   C something that is rotten

   D a car

Connect Across Texts Read this biography to learn more about Neil Armstrong, the first **astronaut** to walk on the moon.

Genre A **biography** is the true story of a person's life. It tells important facts about the person. It includes dates that tell when events happened.

The astronauts placed an American flag on the moon's surface.

The First Person on the Moon

adapted from the National Aeronautics and Space Administration (NASA) Web site

On July 20, 1969,

astronaut Neil Armstrong became the first person to **set foot** on the moon. As the world watched on television, Armstrong stepped onto the moon's surface and spoke these famous words: "One small step for a man, one giant leap for **mankind**."

In Other Words
set foot step
mankind people everywhere

▶ **Before You Move On**

1. **Explain** Why was July 20, 1969, an important day in human history?
2. **Paraphrase** What does Armstrong's famous quote mean? Restate it.

The Right Pilot for the Job

This amazing day was the result of years of hard work. In 1961, President John F. Kennedy wanted America to be the first nation to land humans on the moon and bring them back safely. NASA space scientists worked toward that goal. At last they were ready to put people on the moon. Neil Armstrong was the perfect person to command the **mission**.

Armstrong was born in 1930 in Wapakoneta, Ohio. He loved flying, and he got his pilot's license at age sixteen. After graduating from college, he became a military pilot. In 1962 Armstrong joined NASA's astronaut program.

▲ Neil Armstrong

◀ The astronauts left a small golden olive branch on the moon as a symbol of peace.

In Other Words
mission project

In 1969 Armstrong became the commander of Apollo 11, the first **lunar** landing mission. He and his crew, Edwin "Buzz" Aldrin and Michael Collins, fulfilled the dream of a nation. When Apollo 11 returned safely to Earth, Armstrong was greeted as a hero.

Armstrong has received many awards, including the Presidential Medal of Freedom. Although he never walked on the moon again, he helped plan other space missions. He also taught spacecraft design at the University of Cincinnati. But he will always be remembered as the first person on the moon. ❖

▲ **The astronauts' return to Earth.**

▲ **The astronauts were greeted as heroes after the success of Apollo 11.**

In Other Words
lunar moon

▶ **Before You Move On**

1. **Generalize** What does it mean to be a hero? How did the **astronauts** fit that meaning?

2. **Goal/Outcome** Compare President Kennedy's goal with the outcome of the Apollo 11 mission.

Compare Fiction and Biography

A story that is fiction is not true, even if it includes events that really happened. A biography is nonfiction. It tells a true story.

Compare the story and the biography. What events and facts do both of them tell about? Work with a partner to complete a comparison chart.

Comparison Chart

> Put a checkmark if it gives the fact.

Event or Fact	"The Moon Over Star"	"The First Person on the Moon"
Neil Armstrong was born in 1930.		✓
In 1961, President Kennedy said that America would send people to the moon.	✓	✓
Armstrong, Aldrin, and Collins flew to the moon in the summer of 1969.		
Armstrong was the commander of the mission.		
The first person to walk on the moon was Armstrong.		
The world watched on television.		
Armstrong said, "One small step for man, one giant leap for mankind."		
The astronauts placed a flag on the moon.		
The moon is 240,000 miles from Earth.		

Talk Together

What did it take for the astronauts to explore the moon? Think about the story and the biography. Use **Key Words** to to talk about your ideas.

Prepositional Phrases

A **prepositional phrase** starts with a **preposition** and ends with a noun or a pronoun. Use prepositional phrases in these ways.

Grammar Rules Prepositional Phrases

• to show where something is	Earth orbits the sun **between Venus and Mars**.
• to show time	**After** sunset, the moon rose.
• to show direction	A meteor flew **across** the sky.
• to add details	The space ship landed **with** a thud. The astronauts worked **as** a team.

Read Prepositional Phrases

Read this passage from "Moon Over Star." Can you find four prepositional phrases? They start with the prepositions *with, of, into,* and *through.*

> We closed our eyes, imagining with all our might the rumble, the roar, and the force of the Saturn rocket, blasting the spaceship into the stars. Then we were rushing through space.

Write Prepositional Phrases

Write a short paragraph about exploring space. Use at least three prepositional phrases to describe the event.

Write About Yourself

Write a Personal Narrative ✏️

Tell about an experience that changed the way you thought about "fast." You and your classmates will collect your stories in a book called *How Fast Is Fast?*

Study a Model

A personal narrative is a true story about something important. Read Stacey's story about her sister's race.

My Sister, the Turtle

by Stacey Allen

My sister Alyssa should never have been a runner. She's got such short legs! But she always loved to run.

In middle school, **Alyssa joined the track team.** She was so slow, even her friends called her "Turtle."

"Why don't you quit?" I asked.

"Because I'm going to get better," she told me. At her first track meet, Alyssa was going to run the 100-meter dash. I almost stayed home. I didn't want to see her lose.

The race began. Alyssa was the last one off the starting blocks. But then she started to pass the other runners.

The Turtle came in third. As for me, **I learned that you should never give up doing what you love.**

The first lines capture the reader's interest.

The **beginning** tells what the experience is all about.

The **middle** gives details to help readers understand the experience.

The **ending** tells why the experience was important.

Prewrite

1. **Choose a Topic** What experience will you write about? Talk with a partner to choose one.

Language Frames	
Tell Your Ideas	**Respond to Ideas**
• One of my favorite memories is _____ .	• Tell me why _____ was important to you.
• I once knew someone who _____ .	• _____ sounds interesting. I'd like to read about it because _____ .
• I never knew what _____ meant until _____ .	• I'm not sure _____ would make a good story. Tell me more.

2. **Gather Information** Recall the details about where and when your event took place. Tell who was involved. Write down how you felt about what happened.

3. **Get Organized** Use a chart or map to help you organize your details. Stacey used a comparison chart to show how her feelings changed.

Comparison Chart

Before the Race	During the Race	After the Race
I thought Alyssa wasn't a good runner.	I didn't want to go to the race.	Alyssa was fast!

Draft

Use your chart and details to write your draft. Tell what happened and how the experience affected you. Think about using dialogue to make the story more interesting.

Revise

1. **Read, Retell, Respond** Read your draft aloud to a partner. Your partner listens and then retells the story. Next, talk about ways to improve your writing.

Language Frames

Retell

- You told about a time when _____ .

- At first, you felt _____ . Later, you felt _____ .

- The experience was important to you because _____ .

Make Suggestions

- I can't really picture _____ .

- Maybe you could say more about how you felt about _____ .

- Some of the sentences don't sound like you. One example is _____ .

---

2. **Make Changes** Think about your draft and your partner's suggestions. Then use the revising marks on page 585 to mark your changes.

- Could dialogue make your story more interesting? See if there are places you could add some.

  > "Why don't you quit?" I asked.
  >
  > ~~Could you please answer some questions?~~

- Does your writing sound like you? Make sure you've used your own voice.

  > She was so slow, even her friends called her "Turtle."
  >
  > Alyssa joined the track team. ~~She wasn't a fast runner.~~

Edit and Proofread

Work with a partner to edit and proofread your personal narrative. Be sure your sentences have meaningful details. Use the marks on page 585 to show your changes.

Publish

1. **On Your Own** Make a final copy of your personal narrative. Choose a way to share it with your classmates. You can read it aloud, or you can have someone videotape you telling it.

Presentation Tips	
If you are the speaker…	**If you are the listener…**
Use gestures to emphasize important parts of your story.	Think about why the writer chose to tell about this event.
If you are retelling your personal narrative, be sure to present events in the right order.	Decide what message the writer is trying to share through this narrative.

2. **In a Group** Collect all of the personal narratives from your class. Bind them into a book called *How Fast Is Fast?* Share the book with friends. You could also choose to videotape your narratives. If you do, include photographs from the real events.

Grammar Tip

✓ Use prepositional phrases to add details. Some common prepositions are *above, between, during,* and *through.*

487

Talk Together

In this unit, you found lots of answers to the **Big Question**. Now, make a concept map to discuss the **Big Question** with the class.

Concept Map

What does it take to explore space?

very fast speed

Write a Note

Use your concept map. Write a note to a friend explaining whether you would like to explore space and why.

Share Your Ideas

Choose one of these ways to share your ideas about the **Big Question**.

Write It!

Write a Story

Write a story about a fast-moving creature. How would the creature use speed to do things? Make the plot exciting! Include details about the setting and characters. Illustrate your story.

Talk About It!

Give an Interview

Imagine you were the first person on the moon. Give an interview to tell about your experiences. Tell how you felt, what you saw, and what people should know about the moon.

Do It!

Model the Earth, Sun, and Moon

With a small group, show how Earth moves around the sun. Then show how the moon revolves around Earth. Give clear, step-by-step instructions so your classmates can follow.

Earth

sun

Write It!

Make a Packing List

Imagine that the space program asked you to travel to the moon for one week. What would you bring? Make a packing list. Include personal things and tools for your moon study.

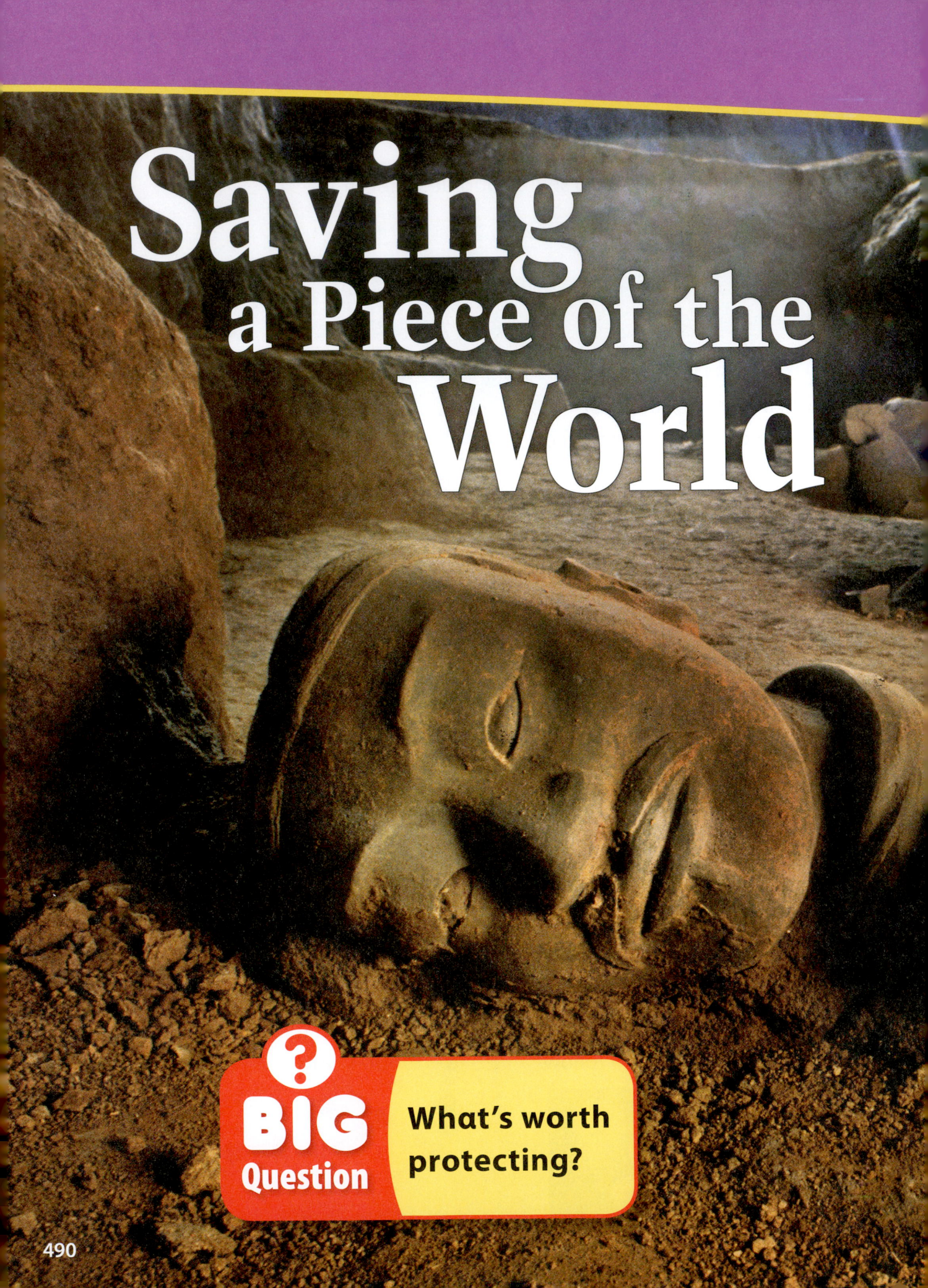

Saving a Piece of the World

BIG Question

What's worth protecting?

Unit at a Glance
▶ **Language**: Express Opinions, Justify, Social Studies, Words
▶ **Literacy**: Review Strategies
▶ **Content**: Preserving Our Heritage

Unit
8

Share What You Know

Do It!

❶ **Think** of a brave character from a movie or TV show.

❷ **Pantomime** a scene that shows how the character might act to help someone in need.

❸ **Take** a vote. Which character does your class think is bravest? Why?

Build Background: Watch a video about heroes.
 NGReach.com

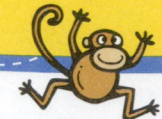

Express Opinions

Language Frames

- I do/don't believe ______.
- I do/don't think ______.

Listen to Beatriz's song. Then use **Language Frames** to express an opinion about a problem that you can help solve.

Song MP3

One Kid Can

When your town has a problem,
Remember this inspiring song.
I don't believe that it's
too difficult
To change something
that's wrong.
One kid can make a difference.
Yes, I do think that
one kid can.
It only takes one
good idea
For us to start a
perfect plan.

Tune: "Give My Regards to Broadway"

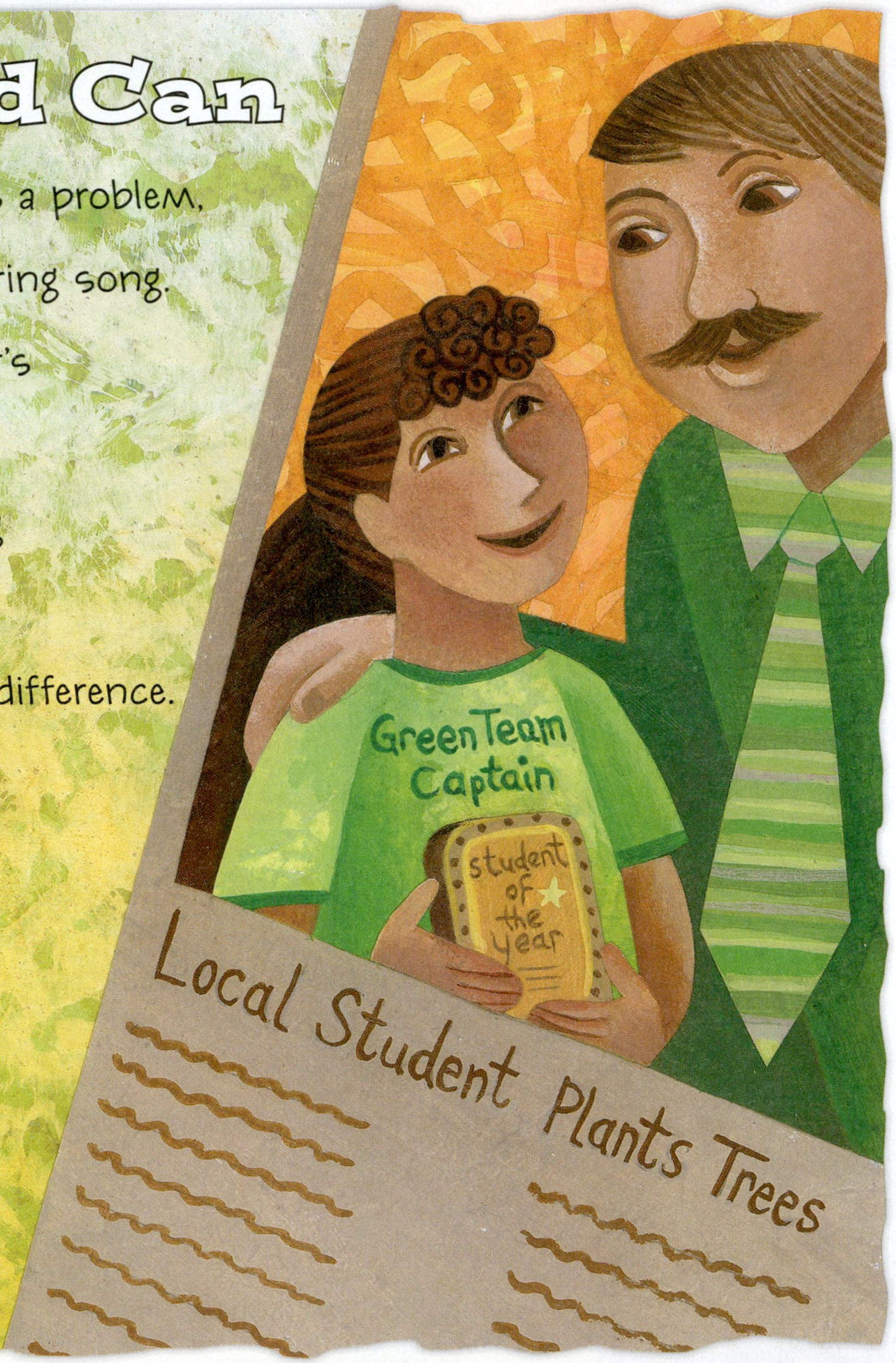
Green Team Captain
student of the year
Local Student Plants Trees

Key Words

Look at the pictures. Use **Key Words** and other words as you talk about what makes someone a **hero**.

Who Is a Hero?

A **volunteer** works without pay. These volunteers serve food to people in need.

This park ranger **protects** animals. She works to keep them safe.

Some workers keep our national **heritage** alive. She teaches about a Native American way of life.

A **president** leads the nation.

Talk Together

What things of value do heroes protect? Try to use **Language Frames** from page 492 and **Key Words** to **express opinions** to a partner.

Goal and Outcome

A **goal** is something you want to achieve. The **outcome** is whether or not you actually reach your goal.

Look at the pictures of Beatriz's project. Keep track of goals and outcomes to understand how and why things happen.

Map and Talk

You can make a goal-and-outcome map to track someone's progress. Write the goal on the first step. Use the next steps to list events that happen on the way to reaching the goal. Write the outcome on the last step.

Goal-and-Outcome Map

Beatriz wants to make her street greener.
Goal

She calls the Green Team.
Event 1

They plant young trees.
Event 2

The trees grow. The street gets very green!
Outcome

Talk Together

Tell your partner about a project you completed. Use a goal-and-outcome map to describe your goal and the steps you followed to reach it.

More Key Words

Use these words to talk about "Buffalo Music" and "Saving Bison from Extinction."

mission
(**mi**-shun) *noun*

A **mission** is a job with a goal. Their **mission** is to rescue people after an earthquake.

motive
(**mō**-tiv) *noun*

A **motive** is a reason for doing something. One **motive** for studying is to get good grades.

responsible
(ri-**spon**-su-bul) *adjective*

A person who is **responsible** is in charge. This dad is **responsible** for his son.

service
(**sur**-vus) *noun*

When something is of **service**, it is useful. A cart is of **service** when you move heavy boxes.

value
(**val**-yū) *verb*

To **value** something is to care about it. Many people **value** saving money.

Talk Together

Talk with a partner. Tell how each **Key Word** makes you feel. Say why.

> *Value* reminds me that I believe my family is valuable. It makes me feel good!

Add words to My Vocabulary Notebook.
NGReach.com

Choose Reading Strategies

Reading Strategies

- Plan and Monitor
- Make Connections
- Visualize
- Ask Questions
- Make Inferences
- Determine Importance
- Synthesize

As you read, you use different strategies to help you understand a text's meaning. Often, you use more than one strategy. You just need to know which strategies to use and when to use them. As you read:

- Think about the different strategies you have in your mental toolbox.

- Know what you are reading. Some strategies are better than others for each type of text.

- Be flexible. Sometimes you need to stop using one strategy and try another. Even the best readers switch and add strategies!

When you read, choose a reading strategy to help you understand.

How to Choose a Reading Strategy

1. Think about what you are trying to understand.

   I don't understand _____ .

2. Decide which strategy you can use to help you understand.

   I can _____ .

3. Think about how the strategy helped you.

   That strategy helped me _____ .

Read Beatriz's poem. Practice the reading strategies. Tell a partner which strategies you used to help you understand the poem.

Poem

A Million Trees

Let's get down on our knees
and plant a million trees!
My **mission** sounds unlikely,
　but I think we can do it.
We only have one planet.
　Planting trees will help renew it.
Our **motive** is simple—
　We want to see more green.
We'll plant from Maine to Oregon
　and everywhere between.
Let's all be **responsible**.
　We'll make the planet greener.
The trees will be of **service**.
　The air will be much cleaner.
Let's show we **value** nature
　by helping to restore it.
Let's plant a million trees—
　The squirrels will adore it!

Read a Story

Genre

Historical fiction is a story that takes place in the past. It is based on real events. The writer adds events that could have happened.

Setting

The setting of a story is where and when the events happen. In historical fiction, the setting is usually tied to the events in the story.

▲ The setting of this story is Palo Duro Canyon in northern Texas, in the late 1800s.

Buffalo Music

by Tracey E. Fern ◆ illustrated by Greg Shed

▶ **Set a Purpose**
Find out what "buffalo music"
means to the narrator of this story.

W hen I first settled here on Palo Duro Canyon, I had no
company except for the animals. I woke to the **reveille** of the
roosters. I did chores to the **choir** of the crows. I dreamed to
the **chorus** of the coyotes. Mostly, though, I lived to the music
of the buffalo.

I stirred the fire to the *huff-huff* of buffalo breath clouding
the chill dawn. I gardened to the *scritch-scritch* of buffalo
scratching themselves against the cottonwoods.

I swept the **dugout** to the thunder of buffalo as they
drifted like a dark cloud across the prairie. That buffalo music
played right to my heart.

In Other Words
reveille morning song
choir singing
chorus howls; cries
◀ **dugout** house

One day, different sounds filled the canyon. They were the boom and blast of rifles.

"What are those shots?" I asked my husband Charlie.

"Buffalo hunters, Molly," he said. "They're trying to **turn a profit** on **hides** and hooves."

It seemed as if every man in Texas was **afire to make a fortune** in the buffalo business. Day after day, the hunters galloped into the heart of the **herd**. Shots echoed over the hills and through the hollows from sunup till sundown. And day after day, another hundred or more buffalo lay dead.

In Other Words

turn a profit make money
hides buffalo skins
afire to make a fortune wanting to get rich
herd group

That summer, the heat fell as heavy as an angry fist. The trails were **deep** with dust. The grass cracked like glass **underfoot**. And everywhere, as far as the eye could see, the bleached bones of the buffalo **glistened** white in the sun.

Within six seasons, the hunters were gone. So was the buffalo music.

Oh, those were lonely, silent days! I was sure the only song left in the canyon was the cold whistle of the north wind.

502

But one spring morning, I was **lugging** wash water up
from the river when a cowhand named Billie came trotting up.

"Howdy, Miss Molly," Billie said. "I've got some **orphans**
for you."

Billie knew I had **a soft spot for critters**. He'd bring me
whatever stray or sickly creature he found on the trail—prairie
dogs, wolf pups, wild turkeys. Once, he even brought me an
antelope.

"What did you bring this time?" I asked Billie as I set
down the water and went to have a look.

Two buffalo calves were trailing after him, as skinny as
hungry snakes.

In Other Words
lugging carrying
orphans young animals that don't have parents
a soft spot for critters always liked animals

▶ **Before You Move On**
1. **Theme** What does "buffalo music" mean
   to Molly?
2. **Figurative Language** What would grass
   that "cracked like glass underfoot" look and
   feel like?

▶ **Predict**
What will Molly do with
the buffalo calves?

"I found them **snoozing** under a **juniper**," Billie said. "Hunters must have figured they were too **puny to fuss with**. Do you think you can fatten them up?"

Right then, one of the calves let out a soft snort. That sound brought back some memories. I didn't need to hear anything else before making up my mind.

"I **can't tell** till I try," I told Billie. "Let's get them inside before the wolves find them."

In Other Words
snoozing sleeping
◀ **juniper** tree
puny to fuss with small to hunt
can't tell won't know

504

I know that some people think I'm as tough as old **beef jerky**. The truth is, I'd seen too many living things **disappear** in the hard struggle for life here. I **wasn't about** to let the buffalo go, too.

Those calves followed me back to the dugout, **strolled** in through the front door, and lay down in front of the fire. I named one Calico, because she was the same faded red as my favorite dress. I called the other one Chester, after a neighbor back home in Tennessee with the same fierce-eyed stare.

calico ▶

In Other Words
beef jerky dried meat
disappear die
wasn't about didn't want
strolled walked

Then I got to work caring for them. I **tucked** hot-water bottles inside flannel cloth and wrapped a cloth around each calf. I fed them like babies, squeezing cow's milk from a rag.

Those calves sure could drink—three gallons a day or more! Feeding them kept me so busy that I hardly had time to blink.

Charlie just shook his head at me. "**Tending to** those two **runts** won't change anything," he told me.

But Charlie knew better than to waste his breath arguing with me. I was determined to hear buffalo music again in this lifetime.

Within a few weeks, Calico and Chester were as **plump** as biscuit dumplings! By then, Charlie was tired of having wild critters in the dugout. He fenced off a section of pasture, and I turned the calves loose with the milking cows.

Pretty soon, word **got out** all over **the Panhandle** that I was tending buffalo calves. Every time a cowhand rode up with another orphan, Charlie would sigh and start **stoking** the dugout fire.

In Other Words
plump fat
got out spread
the Panhandle this part of Texas
stoking stirring

▶ **Before You Move On**
1. **Goal/Outcome** What is Molly's goal? How does she try to achieve it?
2. **Make Connections** How would you feel if you were Charlie?

▶ **Predict**
Will Molly achieve her goal?

Maybe Charlie was right. The wild herds probably were long gone, like dew before the sun. But I knew there was another way to end the silence in the canyon. I could start a herd of my own.

I got to work feeding and watering my orphans, **mending** the sick, and **fending off** wolves and **poachers** with the long end of my rifle. With time and tending, my little herd grew. Soon I had one hundred **head**.

In Other Words
mending healing
fending off scaring away
poachers hunters
head buffalo

508

Then one day, word came that Yellowstone National Park wanted to rebuild its buffalo herd. As soon as I heard that, I got to work.

I drove Calico and Chester and two **yearlings** to the east edge of our **spread**, where the Santa Fe railway line came through. I set Billie to work building four **timber stalls spiked to** the frame of a **boxcar**. We fastened some thick padding to keep the buffalo safe from the swaying and jostling of the train. Then I loaded up the boxcar with bales of hay and barrels of water.

In Other Words

yearlings one-year-old buffalo

spread land

timber stalls spiked to wood containers attached to

boxcar railroad car

I couldn't leave the rest of my herd. Billie would tend these four till they got settled on their new **range**. "Take good care of them," I told Billie as he climbed aboard the train.

I stood watching, till the last hollow echo of the train whistle faded. "Good luck to you, my old friends," I whispered.

When Billie wrote a few months later, he had some big news. Calico had given birth to a healthy calf. That was some day! **To my way of thinking**, it wasn't just the birth of a calf. It was the **rebirth** of our national herd.

In Other Words
range land; home
To my way of thinking
 In my opinion
rebirth new birth

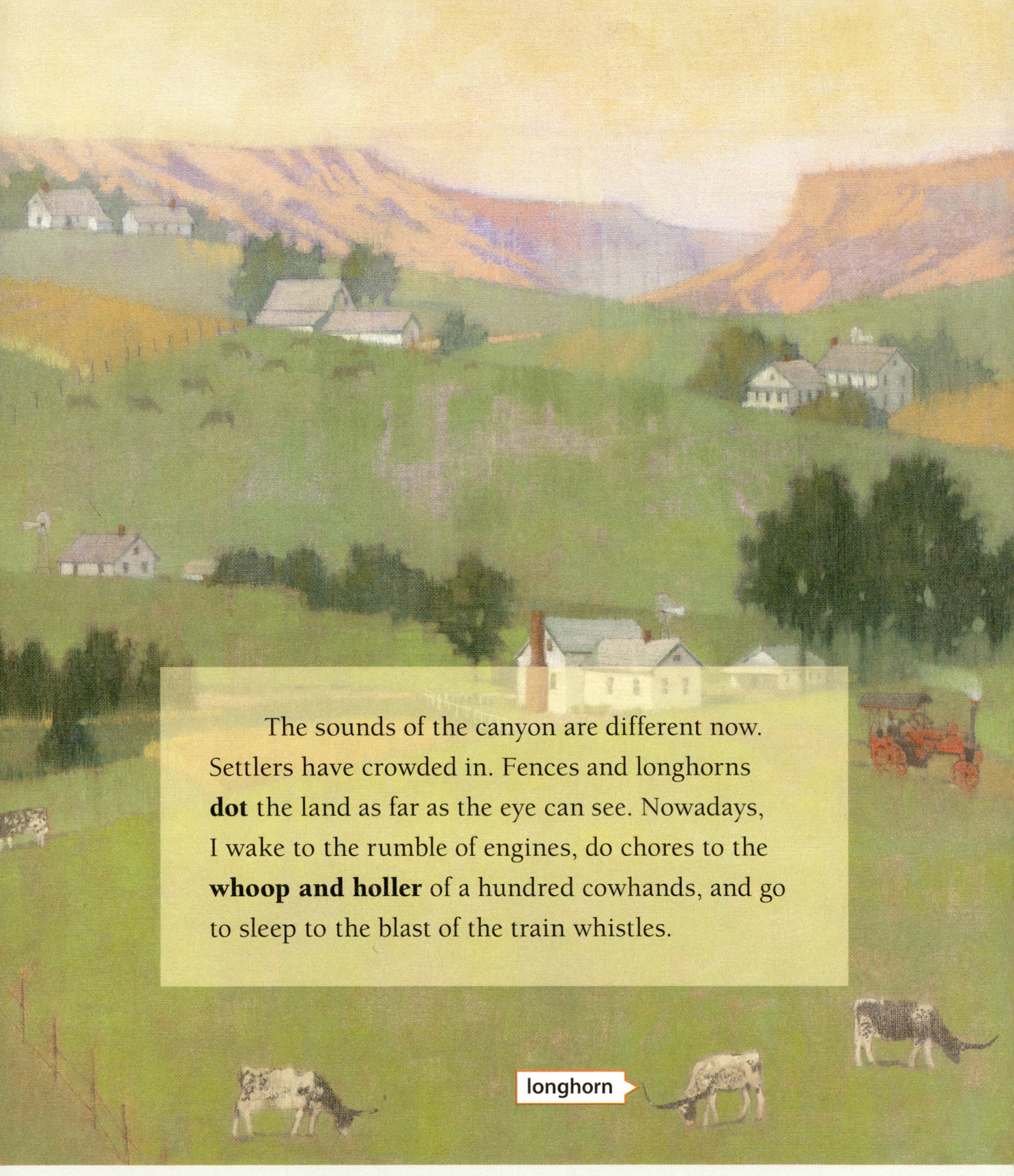

The sounds of the canyon are different now. Settlers have crowded in. Fences and longhorns **dot** the land as far as the eye can see. Nowadays, I wake to the rumble of engines, do chores to the **whoop and holler** of a hundred cowhands, and go to sleep to the blast of the train whistles.

longhorn

In Other Words
dot cover
whoop and holler shouting

But some days when I ride north beyond the last **stand of salt cedar**, I can once again hear the faint chords of the old songs. I hear the clatter of clashing horns. I hear the bellowing of the bulls. I hear the muffled thud of hooves as they hurl up dust. And I live **on the keen edge of** hope that one day the **strains** of that sweet, wild music will echo far beyond these canyon walls. ❖

In Other Words

stand of salt cedar group of trees
on the keen edge of with the
strains sounds

▶ **Before You Move On**

1. **Goal/Outcome** Does Molly achieve her goal? Explain.
2. **Visualize** What do you think the narrator is picturing when she describes the sounds she hopes to hear again?

Meet the Author

Tracey E. Fern

Like Molly, Tracey E. Fern loves the sights and sounds of nature. When she was young, she lived near a beach. She says, "If I walked far enough along that beach, there were no houses and no people—just water and birds and sand and sky. It was the perfect place to dream."

As a child, Tracey E. Fern dreamed of writing books. When she grew up, she did it! Many of her books and stories are historical fiction.

Tracey E. Fern still loves walking along the beach and dreaming. Now she dreams about the books she plans to write.

Tracey E. Fern ▶

Writer's Craft ✏️

Tracey Fern writes: "...the heat fell as heavy as an angry fist." Find other examples of figurative language in "Buffalo Music." Then use figurative language to write your own description of something in nature.

Talk About It

1. What clues tell you that this story is **historical fiction**?

   _____ really happened, but _____ is/are made up.

2. Do you think the main character of this story is a <mark>hero</mark>? **Express** your **opinion** to a partner. Use the text to support your opinion. Speak clearly and check that your partner understands you.

3. How does the story's main message, or theme, relate to <mark>protecting</mark> things that are endangered? Give a brief summary of the story to a partner. Then explain how the story events relate to the theme.

Learn test-taking strategies.
◯ **NGReach.com**

Write About It

This story includes many details about nature. Think of something from nature that you think is worth protecting. Write a short rhyming poem to describe it. Use sensory details and **Key Words**, if possible.

> I'd like to save a _____ .

Goal and Outcome

Make a goal-and-outcome map for "Buffalo Music." Notice how each event leads to the next.

Goal-and-Outcome Map

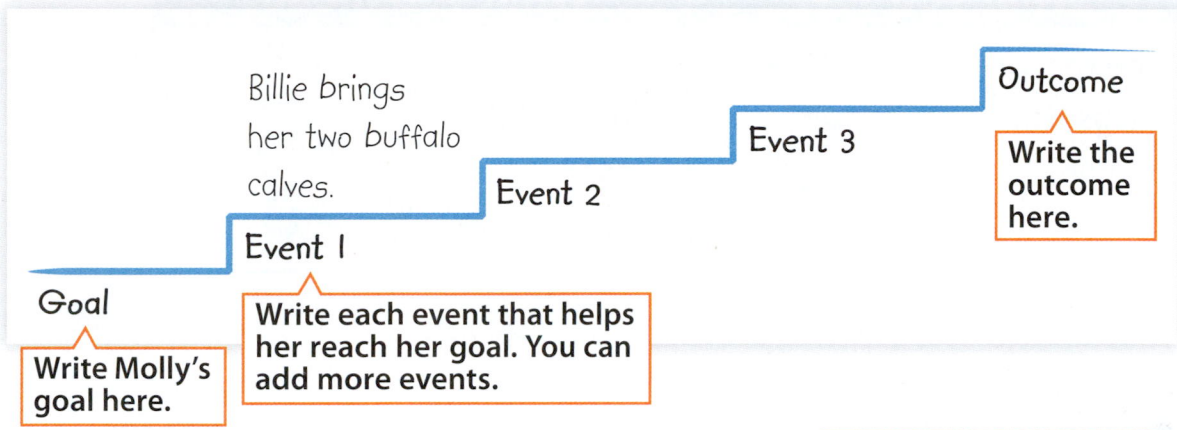

Billie brings her two buffalo calves.

Outcome

Write the outcome here.

Event 3

Event 2

Event 1

Write each event that helps her reach her goal. You can add more events.

Goal

Write Molly's goal here.

Now use your goal-and-outcome map as you retell the story to a partner. Use **Key Words**.

Molly wants to _____.
First, _____ . . . .
The outcome is _____ .

Fluency Comprehension Coach

Use the Comprehension Coach to practice reading with intonation. Rate your reading.

Talk Together

What does Molly think is worth protecting, and why? Do you agree? Use **Key Words** as you discuss your ideas.

More Idioms

An **idiom** is a colorful way to say something. Sometimes you can use context clues to figure out what an idiom means.

What you say:	What you mean:
The mayor **sings Bill's praises**. 	The mayor **thinks Bill deserves recognition**. 

Try It Together

Read the paragraph. Use context clues to figure out the meaning. Then answer the questions.

> My hero is my Uncle Dave. He is a veterinarian, which means he cares for animals. He is <u>as sharp as a tack</u>! He can spot a sick animal <u>in the blink of an eye</u>, and he always knows how to help.

1. **As sharp as a tack most likely means**

   A not very smart.

   B very smart.

   C has pointy fingers.

   D is always sad.

2. **In the blink of an eye probably means**

   A with his eyes open.

   B with his back turned.

   C all day long.

   D very quickly.

Connect Across Texts Read this report about other **heroes** who, like Molly, helped save bison.

Genre A **report** presents facts about a topic. It has a title and an introduction. The last paragraph is usually a conclusion that sums up the report.

SAVING Bison FROM Extinction

by Dorothy Young

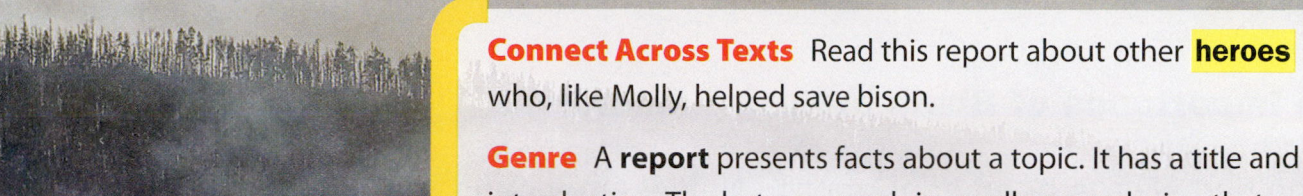

▲ An American bison at Yellowstone National Park

At one time, 25 to 50 million American bison, often called buffalo, lived in North America. Many Native American groups depended on the animals for food, clothing, and shelter. They used almost every part of the animal.

In Other Words
Extinction Dying Out As a Species

▶ **Before You Move On**

1. **Use Text Features** Read the title and look at the photo on this page. Together, what do they tell you about the topic?
2. **Visualize** What do you think clothing made from buffalo feels like? Why?

The Importance of Bison to Native Americans

Bison had always been important to Native Americans of the **Plains**. For hundreds of years, many Native Americans depended on bison for survival. Bison were part of their culture.

Many Native Americans used bison meat for food. They used their hides for gloves, **moccasins**, and **tepee** coverings. They even used the bones for tools and decorations.

▲ Bison provided food, clothing, and shelter for Native Americans of the Plains.

In Other Words
Plains flat lands
◄ **moccasins** shoes
tepee tent

Bison in Danger

European settlers also hunted bison, but not just for food. They wanted to remove bison from the land so they could start farms. They also hunted bison for **sport and profit**. As settlers moved west, they killed more and more bison.

Railroads and Bison

Railroads helped settle the West. But they were not good for the bison. Hunters shot bison to feed the workers who were laying railroad tracks.

Sometimes train operators slowed their engines when they spotted bison. They let passengers shoot the animals from train windows.

Railroads allowed hunters to send bison hides to the cities. People in cities made leather from bison hides.

By 1890 only about 1,000 bison remained.

▲ **Bison hunters in 1882**

▲ **Workers lay new track for the railroad.**

In Other Words
sport and profit fun and to make money

▶ **Before You Move On**

1. **Generalize** How did some Native Americans of the Plains depend on bison?
2. **Summarize** How did railroads affect bison?

Settlers Follow the Railroad

Railroads united the country. They joined the East Coast to the West Coast. Trains also made it easier for people to travel great distances across the Plains. Many settlers traveled to the West by train. As more people traveled to the West, the number of bison decreased.

▲ Ads like this encouraged many settlers to move to the West.

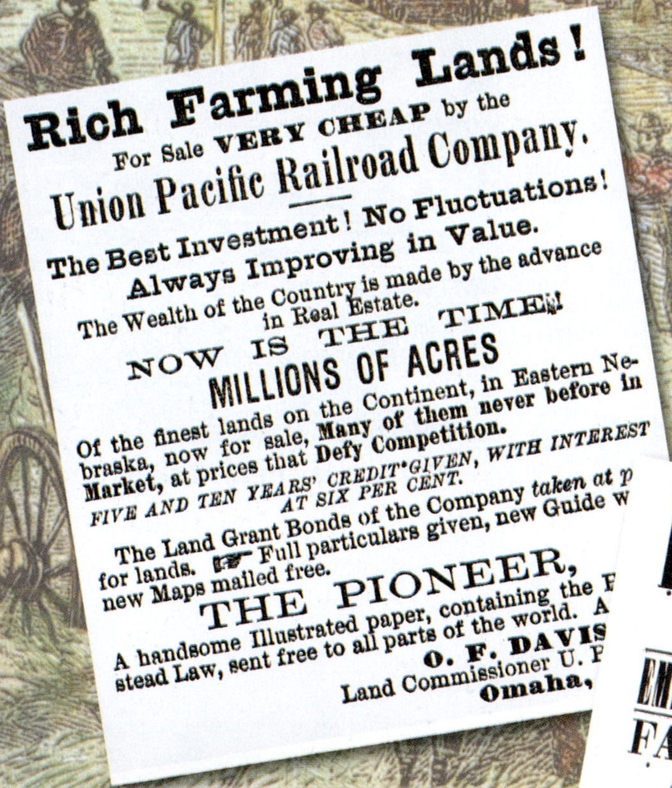

Rich Farming Lands !
For Sale **VERY CHEAP** by the
Union Pacific Railroad Company.
The Best Investment ! No Fluctuations !
Always Improving in Value.
The Wealth of the Country is made by the advance in Real Estate.
NOW IS THE TIME!
MILLIONS OF ACRES
Of the finest lands on the Continent, in Eastern Nebraska, now for sale, Many of them never before in Market, at prices that **Defy Competition.**
FIVE AND TEN YEARS' CREDIT GIVEN, WITH INTEREST AT SIX PER CENT.
The Land Grant Bonds of the Company taken at p for lands. ☞ Full particulars given, new Guide w new Maps mailed free.
THE PIONEER,
A handsome Illustrated paper, containing the F stead Law, sent free to all parts of the world. A
O. F. DAVIS
Land Commissioner U. P
Omaha,

1869. **May 10th.** 1869.
GREAT EVENT
Rail Road from the Atlantic to the Pacific
GRAND OPENING
—— OF THE ——
Union Pacific
RAIL ROAD,
PLATTE VALLEY ROUTE.
PASSENGER TRAINS LEAVE
OMAHA
ON THE ARRIVAL OF TRAINS FROM THE EAST.
THROUGH TO SAN FRANCISCO
In less than Four Days, avoiding the Dangers of the Sea !
Travelers for Pleasure, Health or Business
Will find a Trip over The Rocky Mountains Healthy and Pleasant.
LUXURIOUS CARS & EATING HOUSES
ON THE UNION PACIFIC RAIL ROAD.
PULLMAN'S PALACE SLEEPING CARS
RUN WITH ALL THROUGH PASSENGER TRAINS.
GOLD, SILVER AND OTHER MINERS !
Now is the time to seek your Fortunes in Nebraska, Wyoming, Arizona, Washington, Dakotah Colorado, Utah, Oregon, Montana, New Mexico, Idaho, Nevada or California.
CONNECTIONS MADE AT
CENTRAL CITY & SANTA FE

FARMS AND HOMES
IN KANSAS !
EMIGRANTS, LOOK TO YOUR INTERESTS.
FARMS AT $3 PER ACRE,
AND NOT A FOOT OF WASTE LAND !
Farms on Ten Years Credit !
And on Purchase, no portion of the Principal Required.
Lands not Taxable for Six Years !!
FARMING LANDS IN
EASTERN KANSAS,
But one hour's ride from the city of Atchison and the Missouri river, are offered on terms which guarantee to the Actual Settler larger benefits than can be secured under the Homestead Act.
THE CENTRAL BRANCH UNION PACIFIC R. R. CO.
Offer for Sale their Lands in the
KICKAPOO

▲ William Hornaday, pictured here with a bison calf, believed nature was worth protecting.

▲ In 1899, bison were also kept at the National Zoo in Washington D.C.

In Other Words
promote support

William Hornaday Takes Action

In 1889, William Hornaday from the New York Zoological Society discovered that bison were in danger of becoming extinct. He decided to do something about the problem. "It is the duty of every good citizen," he said, "to **promote** the protection of forests and wildlife."

In 1899, Hornaday brought a small group of bison to the new Bronx Zoo. He got the bison from private herds, not from the wild. These herds were owned by individual ranchers.

In 1905, Hornaday and others formed the American Bison Society to **protect** the remaining bison from hunters. Hornaday's work helped save the bison from becoming extinct.

▶ **Before You Move On**

1. **Evaluate** How would the ads on page 520 prompt people to move to the West? What were negative effects of ads like this?

2. **Clarify** How did Hornaday demonstrate his idea of being a "good citizen"

521

Samuel Walking Coyote Starts a Herd

Samuel Walking Coyote also helped save bison from extinction. Walking Coyote was a Kalispel from the Flathead **Reservation** in Montana. He was hunting buffalo with a group of **Blackfeet** one winter day in 1872. Eight calves wandered into the camp. The calves were orphans.

Walking Coyote took the orphan calves back home and kept them. His small herd grew. Eventually, he sold it. The new owners allowed the herd to roam freely on the Flathead Reservation.

▲ The yellow area shows where bison roamed wild before the 1800s.

Flathead Reservation in 1906 ▶

Starting Supper. Flathead Reservation
Copyright 1908, by N. A. Forsyth, Butte.

In Other Words

Reservation lands set aside for Native Americans

Blackfeet Native Americans from another group

522

Bison Today

For some Native Americans, bison are a symbol of their culture and strength. Many groups, such as the Blackfeet in Montana, are working to bring more bison back to their natural habitat.

▲ The yellow areas show where American bison roam wild today.

Today, the United States has more than 200,000 bison. Many of these are **offspring** from Walking Coyote's original herd.

There are now bison herds in South Dakota, Texas, and several other states. Thanks to the efforts of a few **determined** people, bison are no longer in danger of extinction. ❖

Yellowstone National Park in Wyoming has the largest population of free-roaming plains bison on public land.

In Other Words
offspring animals born
determined hard-working

▶ **Before You Move On**

1. **Make Comparisons** What do the maps on pages 522 and 523 show?
2. **Summarize** What is the conclusion of this report? Explain it in your own words.

Key Words

heritage	protect
hero	responsible
mission	service
motive	value
president	volunteer

Compare Fiction and Nonfiction

"Buffalo Music" and "Saving Bison from Extinction" have a similar topic. Make a Venn diagram to compare the ideas in the story and the report. Work with a partner.

Venn Diagram

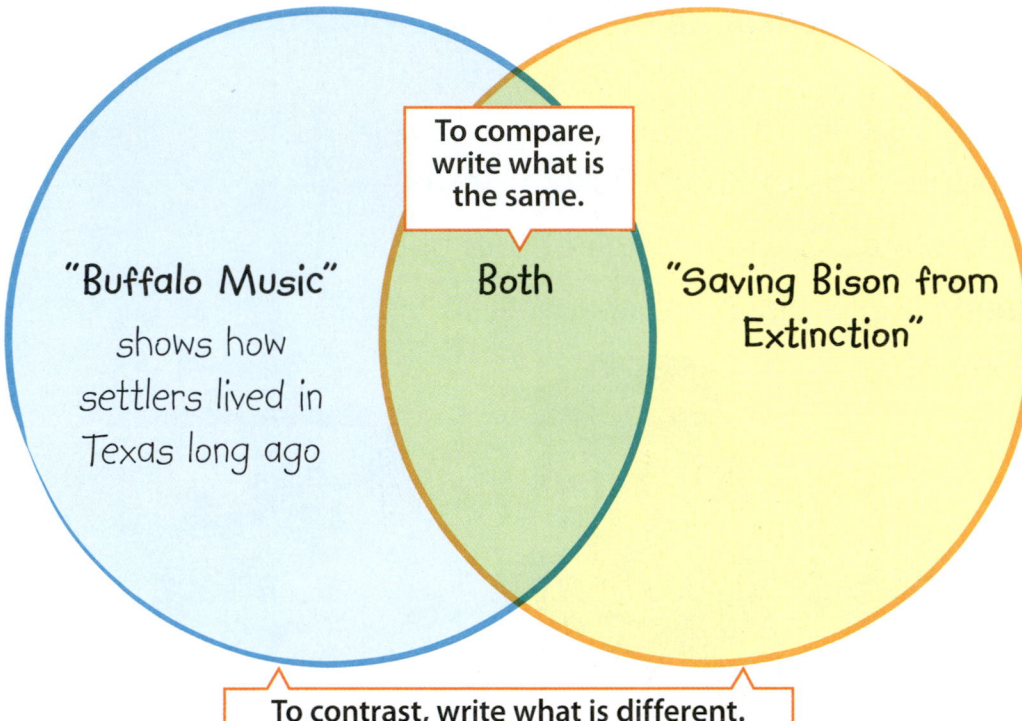

To compare, write what is the same.

"Buffalo Music" shows how settlers lived in Texas long ago

Both

"Saving Bison from Extinction"

To contrast, write what is different.

Talk Together

What do Molly, Samuel Walking Coyote, and William Hornaday think is worth **protecting**? Why? Think about the story and the report. Use **Key Words** to talk about your ideas.

524

Past Tense

Regular past-tense verbs end in *-ed*. However, **irregular** past-tense verbs have other forms.

Grammar Rules Past-Tense Verbs

	Now	In the Past
• To form some regular past-tense verbs, you have to change the base word before you add -**ed**.	car̸e	People **cared** about what happened to endangered animals.
	chop	After people **chopped** down the trees, birds had nowhere to nest.
	tr̸y (i)	We **tried** to help.
• You just have to remember the forms for irregular past tense verbs.	go	The volunteers **went** to help out.
	know	No one **knew** what to do.
	see	Lindsay **saw** the firefighters.

Read Past-Tense Verbs

Read aloud this passage from "Buffalo Music." Find three regular past-tense verbs and two irregular past-tense verbs.

> Those calves followed me back to the dugout, strolled in through the front door, and lay down in front of the fire. I named one Calico, because she was the same red as my favorite dress.

Write Past-Tense Verbs

Write a paragraph about a time in the past when you felt like a **hero**. Use past-tense verbs. Share with a partner.

Justify

Listen to the dialogue between Tierra and Oksana.
Then use **Language Frames** to justify a belief, or to explain why
you think your views on an important topic are right. Be sure to
support your views and speak clearly.

Dialogue

1

Let's give this to someone in our community. Who do you think should get it?

I think firefighters are the bravest people.

2

Why do you think so?

They save people from danger. And they fight fires that could destroy buildings.

3

That's true. They risk their lives.

That's why I believe firefighters deserve our prize.

526

Key Words

Look at the pictures. Use **Key Words** to tell what you know about protecting **ancient** ruins.

Long ago, the Maya culture spread across what is now Mexico and Central America. The Mayans did not create an **empire**, however. Their cities were mostly independent.

Tikal is one of many **sites** from the ancient Maya **civilization**.

Objects such as carvings and drawings provide a **record** of how Mayans lived.

Talk Together

Are ancient ruins worth protecting? Why or why not? Try to use **Language Frames** from page 526 and **Key Words** to **justify** your answer.

Fact and Opinion

A **fact** is something you can check to see if it's true. An **opinion** tells what someone thinks or feels.

Look at the highway poster.

Map and Talk

You can make a fact-and-opinion chart to sort out information you read, see, or hear.

Fact-and-Opinion Chart

Facts	Opinions
Galveston is in Texas.	It's an important historic site.
It was founded in 1839.	The buildings are beautiful.
Historic Galveston covers many blocks.	They need to be taken care of.

List information that you can check as true.

List beliefs or feelings here.

Talk Together

Tell your partner about an advertisement, poster, or flyer. Talk about how the pictures and words tell the message. Use a fact-and-opinion chart to sort the ideas.

More Key Words

Use these words to talk about "The Keyholders of Kabul" and "The Librarian of Basra."

courage

(**kur**-ij) *noun*

If you have **courage**, you are brave. It takes **courage** to do challenging things.

official

(u-**fi**-shul) *adjective*

When something is **official,** it's approved. This **official** seal is from the president's office.

principle

(**prin**-su-pul) *noun*

A **principle** is a rule or law. Some U.S. laws are based on the **principles** of freedom.

project

(**prah**-jekt) *noun*

A **project** is a job or activity. Building a skyscraper is a huge **project**.

risk

(risk) *noun*

Risk is the possibility of harm. Wearing a helmet lowers your **risk** when you ride a bike.

Talk Together

Use a **Key Word** to ask a question. Your partner uses a different **Key Word** to answer.

When do you show courage?

When I take risks.

Add words to My Vocabulary Notebook.
🌐 NGReach.com

Use Reading Strategies

When do you use reading strategies? You can use reading strategies before, during, and after you read. Here's how to read actively:

Reading Strategies

- Plan and Monitor
- Make Connections
- Visualize
- Ask Questions
- Make Inferences
- Determine Importance
- Synthesize

- Look through the text to get an idea of what it will be about. Decide on your purpose, or reason for reading.

- While you read, stop now and then to ask yourself: "Does this make sense?" Use a reading strategy to help you understand better.

- When you are finished reading, spend some time thinking about the text. Decide what you have learned.

How to Use a Reading Strategy

1. Before you open a text, stop and think: What strategies can help me get ready to read?

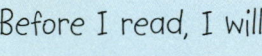
Before I read, I will _____ .

2. During reading, think about what strategies can help you understand.

As I read, I can _____ .

3. After reading, ask yourself: What strategies can I use to help me think about what I read?

Now that I'm done, I think _____ .

Read Tierra's speech. Practice the reading strategies. Tell a partner which strategies you used and how they helped you understand the speech.

Speech

Protect Our Past!

We should save our petroglyphs now. If we do not protect them, we could lose an important part of our past. We should start a **project** to make sure they are safe.

Petroglyphs are **ancient** rock carvings. These amazing pictures are a **record** of an early **civilization**. Many **sites** with petroglyphs are at **risk**.

Some petroglyphs have been destroyed for new highways. There should be an **official** rule: Highways should follow other routes.

People can also cause trouble. Some people paint over the carvings, destroying them. Sometimes they just carve other designs nearby. We must have the **courage** to stop this.

We must stand up for our **principles**! Petroglyphs are more than just incredible **objects**. They are our past.

CENTRAL ASIA

Read a Personal Narrative

Genre

A **personal narrative** is nonfiction. It is written in first person point of view and describes real events in someone's life. Because the narrative is written in first person, it uses *I*, *me*, and *my*.

Text Feature

Maps can show where important events in the narrative took place.

◀ Afghanistan is a country in Central Asia.

▲ **This personal narrative takes place in Afghanistan.**

THE KEY HOLDERS OF KABUL

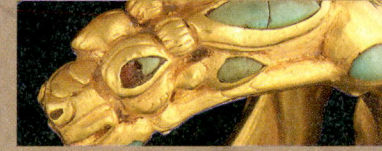

by
Fredrik Hiebert,

with
Ronald Scro

Comprehension Coach

▶ **Set a Purpose**
Find out what it means to be a
key holder of Kabul.

Artifacts Lost...

In 1987, I went to Central Asia to work with
Viktor Sarianidi, a Russian archaeologist. He told
me about some priceless artifacts that he had
discovered almost ten years earlier in Afghanistan.
After hearing Sarianidi's story, I knew the **objects**
he had found were remarkable.

▲ Fredrik Hiebert

I was eager to see these treasures. Sarianidi had placed them
in Afghanistan's National Museum. **Unfortunately**, a civil war
broke out in Afghanistan. The treasures, which Sarianidi had
placed in the museum, were eventually lost in the **chaos** of war.

For years, most people thought that these unique and valuable
artifacts were gone forever, but they were wrong.

◀ **Afghanistan is a
country in Central Asia.**

UZBEKISTAN

TAJIKISTAN

TURKMENISTAN

CHINA

Kabul

AFGHANISTAN

CENTRAL
ASIA

IRAN

PAKISTAN

INDIA

0   150   250 Miles

0   150   250 Kilometers

N
W   E
S

In Other Words

Unfortunately To my
disappointment
broke out started
chaos confusion

…And Found

Many years after my trip to Central Asia, I finally got to see these artifacts. In 2003, I traveled to Kabul, Afghanistan's capital city, as an archaeologist for National Geographic. I learned that the artifacts had survived more than 20 years of war in Afghanistan.

The artifacts had been saved by a few brave workers at the National Museum in Kabul. These workers, called key holders, had hidden many of the museum's most **prized** works of art. To keep these treasures safe, the key holders had risked their lives. This is the story of those Afghan heroes.

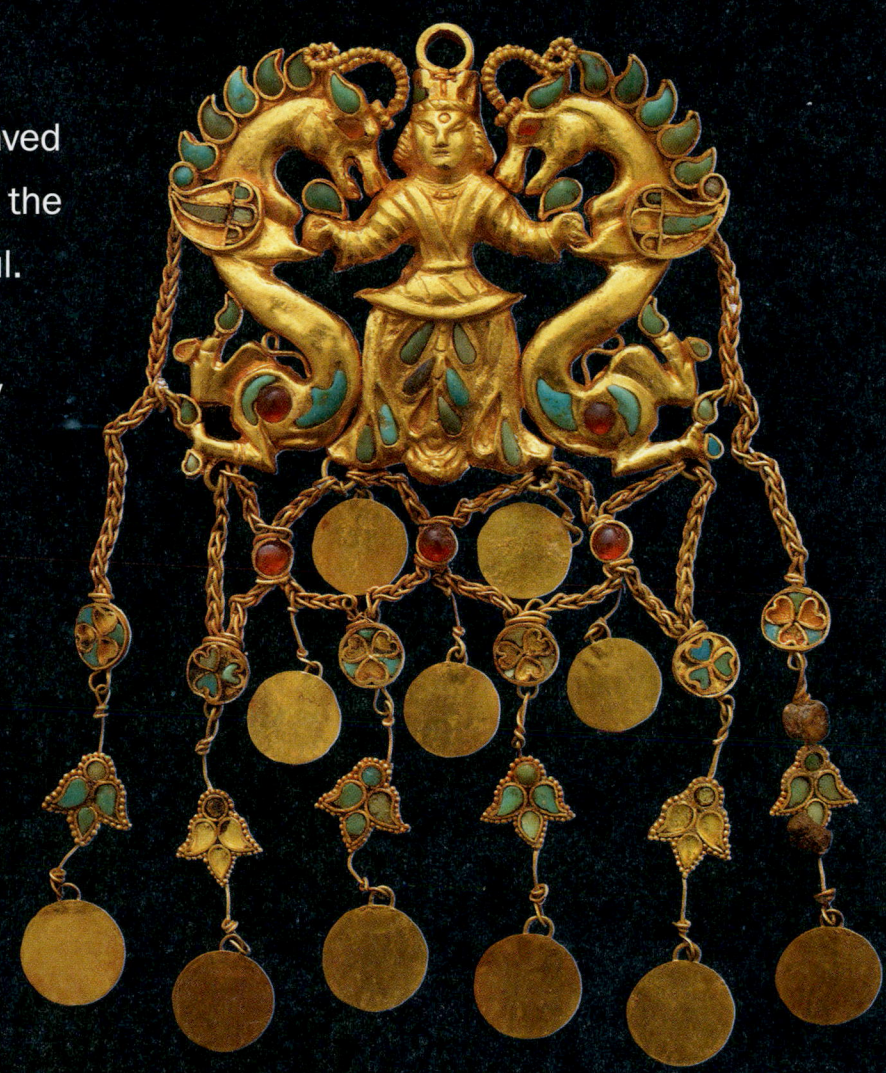

▲ This artifact, saved by the key holders, is about two thousand years old.

In Other Words
prized valued

▶ **Before You Move On**

1. **Fact/Opinion** Which sentence in the first paragraph on page 534 states an opinion? How can you tell?
2. **Determine Importance** What will be the main idea of this selection?

An Ancient Tradition

The museum workers in Kabul follow an **ancient** Afghan tradition. Some workers are chosen as key holders. Those workers are personally responsible for guarding valuable objects. When a key holder dies, his key is passed to his son, who **takes his place**.

During years of war, different groups took control of the region around the National Museum. They sometimes arrested museum workers and tried to make them tell the location of the hidden artifacts. But the key holders refused to tell their secrets. They would not betray their national history. Their silence made them heroes.

▲ **The National Museum in Kabul was damaged during the many years of war.**

In Other Words

takes his place
becomes the new key holder

536

Why did the key holders risk their lives to protect these objects? The artifacts must have contained something more **precious** than the gold and **gems** themselves.

War destroyed much of Afghanistan. But the ancient artifacts protected by the key holders showed a different picture of the country. The artifacts included fine works made with great skill and care. They told the history of the Afghan culture.

Ancient Afghans loved beauty. Their culture was rich and creative. The museum workers did not want Afghanistan's **glorious** past to be lost forever.

gems

gold

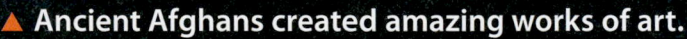
▲ **Ancient Afghans created amazing works of art.**

▶ **Before You Move On**

1. **Ask Questions** If you could ask the authors a question about the key holder tradition, what would you ask?
2. **Synthesize** How did key holders feel about their country and culture?

The Crossroads for East-West Trade

In modern times, Afghanistan has been a poor country. This was true even before 1979, when the Soviet Union invaded Afghanistan. However, Afghanistan was once a trading center of great wealth.

Hundreds of years ago, travelers followed a set of trails called the Silk Road. The trails cross through what is now northern Afghanistan. People used this route to trade goods between Europe and Asia. Some traders became very wealthy.

Often the traders were nomads, people who carry their homes with them as they travel. Six of these nomads—a prince and five princesses—owned what would become Afghanistan's most prized treasures.

▼ The red lines show the various trails people used to trade goods between Europe and Asia.

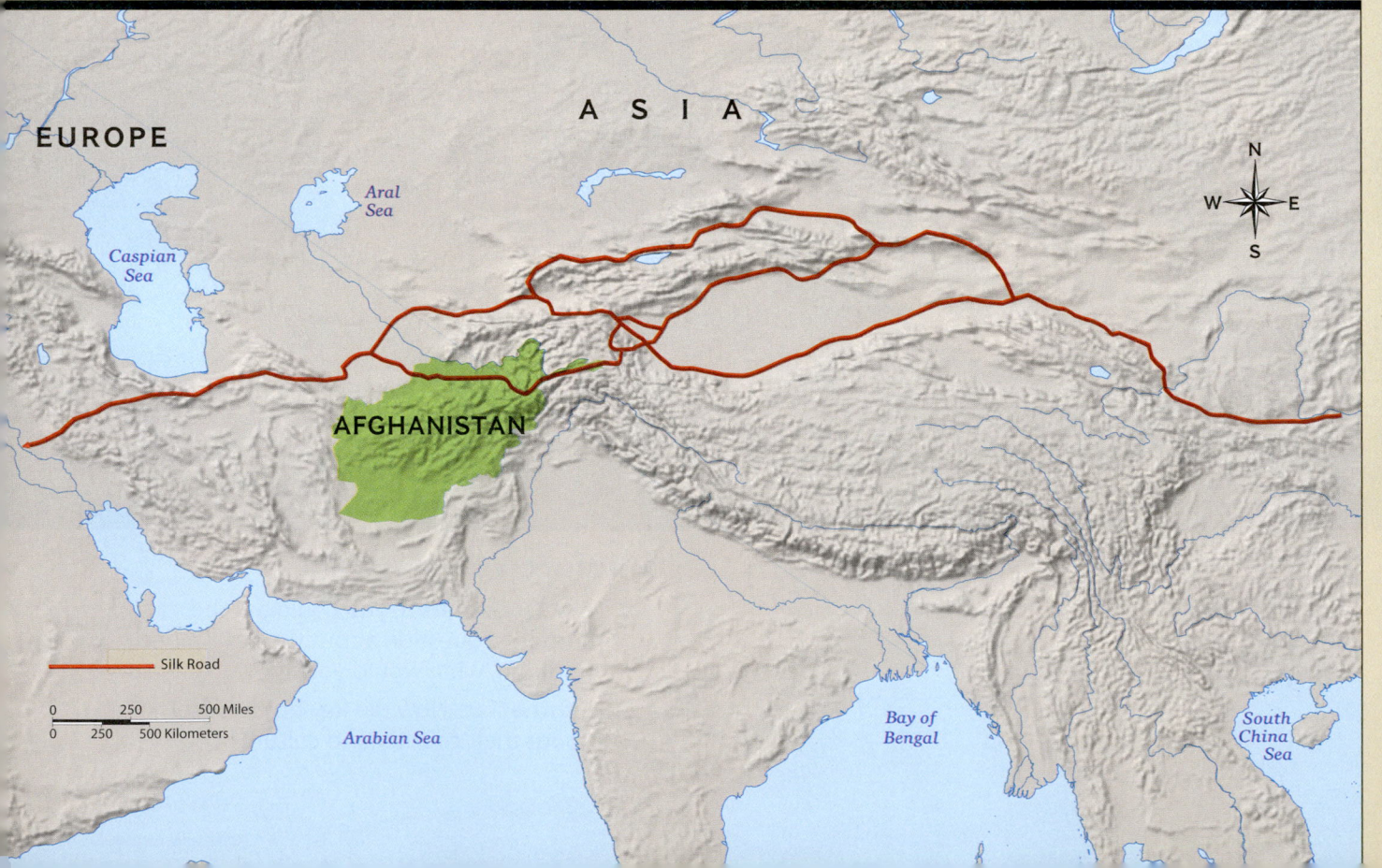

Sarianidi's Discovery

In 1978, Viktor Sarianidi and his team were in northern Afghanistan. They were searching for ancient artifacts at a `site` called Tillya Tepe (which means "hill of gold").

One day, rain interrupted their work. The next day they saw that the rain had uncovered a shining **disk**. It was gold! The workers dug more. They found the skull of a young woman, one of the nomad princesses. Layers of brilliant gold jewelry surrounded her. Sarianidi had found the first of six sites where these royal nomads were buried with their treasures.

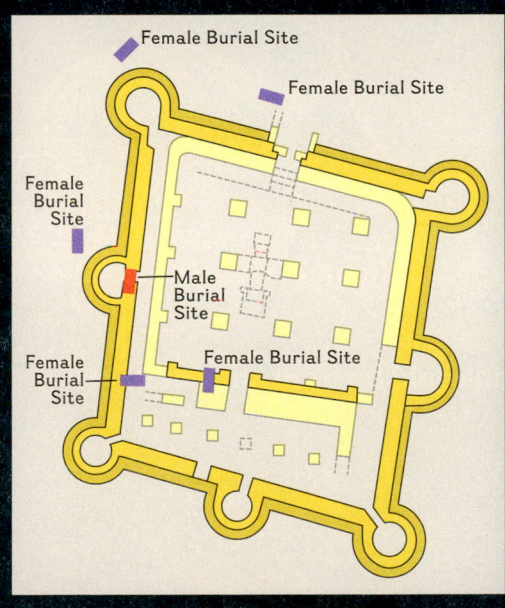

▲ The six nomads at Tillya Tepe were buried on a hill that contained a ruined building.

▲ In 1978, Viktor Sarianidi uncovered artifacts, such as this necklace, at Tillya Tepe.

In Other Words
disk circular `object`

▶ **Before You Move On**

1. **Synthesize** How did the Silk Road help connect Afghanistan with Europe and other parts of Asia? Use the map to explain.

2. **Main Idea** What did the workers discover at Tillya Tepe?

Lost Worlds

The artifacts that Viktor Sarianidi found are beautifully artistic. Some are thousands of years old. By studying the artifacts, archaeologists learn about the culture of the artists who created them. For example, the artifacts can tell about the clothing and jewelry people wore.

The objects also prove that Afghanistan was a place where people from different ancient civilizations met and mixed. Sarianidi's discoveries include a coin from ancient Rome, boot buckles that look Chinese, and knives that seem Siberian. In all, Sarianidi and his team cleaned and listed more than 20,000 gold, silver, and ivory artifacts.

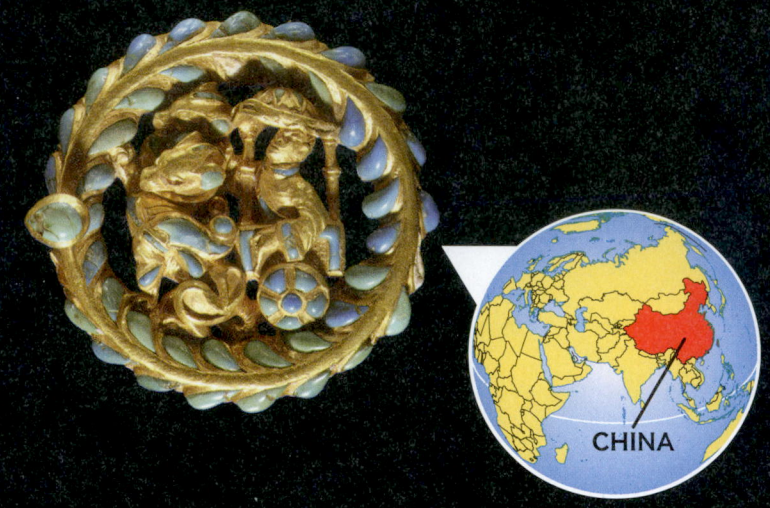

▲ These boot buckles may be from ancient China.

▲ This gold coin could be from ancient Rome.

▲ This ancient dagger looks like it may be from Siberia.

War and Violence

In 1979, the Soviet Union invaded Afghanistan. Sarianidi wanted to protect the treasures he had uncovered. Secretly, he moved them to the National Museum in Kabul.

The fight against the Soviets became a **civil war**. Within two years, a museum in another Afghan city was robbed. Workers at the National Museum did not want their treasures to be lost, too.

In 1988, the museum key holders in Kabul packed and labeled their most valuable objects. They hid them in a **vault** in the presidential palace in Kabul. The key holders kept their secret well. The Afghan people and the rest of the world believed the artifacts had disappeared.

Many Afghan museums were destroyed or badly damaged during the war.

In Other Words
civil war fight between different groups of Afghans
vault locked, well-protected room

▶ **Before You Move On**

1. **Summarize** What do the artifacts tell about ancient Afghanistan?
2. **Make Inferences** How do you know that the key holders believed the artifacts were worth saving?

Artifacts in Danger

In the next few years, thieves broke into the National Museum many times. They stole many objects, including thousands of ancient coins. They even took large sculptures. After every disaster, museum workers repacked and labeled the art that **remained**.

Then in 1996, a group called the Taliban took power in Afghanistan. Museum staff quickly moved 500 crates of art out of the museum. They hid them in an empty hotel in Kabul. When Taliban leaders arrived at the museum, they locked the storage rooms and told the workers to leave and never come back.

▲ **Workers at the National Museum tried to protect the treasures.**

The Taliban's War on Afghan Culture

In 2001, Taliban leaders decided to destroy many works of art. At the National Museum, they opened the storerooms and destroyed 2,500 works of art.

In March of that year, the Taliban traveled to Bamiyan, an Afghan town. There they used dynamite to destroy two world-famous giant statues. This terrible act shocked the world.

In September 2001, terrorists attacked the United States, killing almost 3,000 people. The United States government claimed the terrorists were supporters of the Taliban. Soon afterwards, U.S. and British forces attacked and **defeated** the Taliban. Kabul was free.

▲ The world was horrified by the Taliban's destruction of the giant statues in Bamiyan.

◄ The Taliban destroyed many works of art at the Kabul Museum.

In Other Words
defeated removed power from

▶ **Before You Move On**

1. **Fact/Opinion** The author calls the destruction of the statues a "terrible act." Is this is a fact or an opinion? Explain.
2. **Sequence** Describe the events leading to the Taliban's removal from power.

The Secret Hiding Place

In 2003, Afghan president Hamid Karzai made an important announcement. Someone had found **sealed** boxes inside a vault in the presidential palace. The boxes were from the National Museum. Did they contain the lost artifacts from Tillya Tepe? Only the key holders knew for sure.

As an archaeologist for National Geographic, I was invited to Kabul to watch as museum officials opened the boxes. Viktor Sarianidi, the archaeologist of Tillya Tepe, and Carla Grissmann from the National Museum in Kabul were also present. If the artifacts were in those boxes, we would need to identify each one.

▲ **Afghan president Hamid Karzai in 2003**

◀ **Museum workers carry a box that could contain the lost artifacts.**

In Other Words
sealed tightly closed

On the day of the opening, the palace was **crowded** with officials and reporters. We had to pass through many locked doors to get to the vault. A different key holder unlocked each door.

Then officials brought out the locked boxes. But there was still one problem: the key holders for the boxes were missing. According to law, only the key holders could open their boxes.

Finally, President Hamid Karzai gave permission to break open the locked boxes. Special tools were brought in. Workers began to cut open the boxes.

▲ Workers cut open the locked boxes.

In Other Words
crowded filled

▶ **Before You Move On**

1. **Draw Conclusions** Why do you think Fredrik Hiebert was invited to the opening of the boxes?
2. **Details** Why did the workers have to break open the locked boxes?

545

Recovering the Artifacts of Tillya Tepe

When the first box was finally opened, we saw piles of small plastic bags with old labels. The bags were opened, and Viktor Sarianidi examined several artifacts. He smiled as he examined a pair of gold objects. He pointed out a small repair that he had made with his own hands. The repair proved that these artifacts were the same treasures that Sarianidi had dug up years ago in Tillya Tepe. It was an amazing discovery!

As we examined more artifacts, we became very excited. Many of us had heard about these treasures but had never seen them. Soon, news of the discovery spread.

▲ Carla Grissmann and I examine the long-lost artifacts.

◀ Viktor Sarianidi examines the artifacts.

The World Learns About the Afghan Heroes

The world was amazed to learn what a few brave Afghan heroes had done. Most people had thought that the ancient jewelry, sculptures, gold, and gems had been lost forever. But the key holders had risked their lives to preserve the ancient Afghan artifacts. They saved a part of their cultural history.

The National Museum has now been rebuilt. The remaining artifacts are being identified and listed. The workers use modern techniques and the key holder tradition to protect them. Today people who visit the museum can see its **motto** printed on a wall: "A nation stays alive when its culture stays alive." ❖

▲ **A gold headdress from the National Museum**

▲ **The National Museum in Kabul once again displays its treasures.**

In Other Words
motto main **principle**

▶ **Before You Move On**

1. **Summarize** How did Viktor Sarianidi know that the artifacts were the same ones he had seen years ago?
2. **Analyze** How do the actions of the key holders relate to the museum's motto? Explain.

Key Words	
ancient	principle
civilization	project
courage	record
empire	risk
object	site
official	

Talk About It

1. What did you learn about the author of this **personal narrative**? Give two facts.

   One fact about Fredrik Hiebert is _____ .
   Another fact is _____ .

2. After reading about Afghanistan's key holders, how do you feel about these people? Why? Explain and **justify** your ideas to a partner.

   I think the key holders were _____ , because _____ .

3. Do you think Hamid Karzai made the right decision to break open the locked boxes? Why or why not? Use facts from the story to support your opinion.

Learn test-taking strategies.
🌐 NGReach.com

Write About It ✏️

In your opinion, how did the key holders of Afghanistan show **courage**? Write a paragraph to explain. Include a topic sentence, other sentences that give details, and a conclusion.
Use **Key Words**.

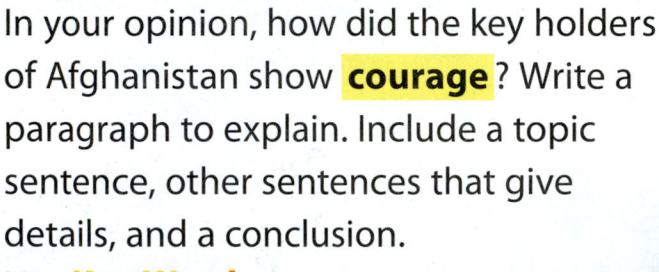
The key holders showed courage by _____ .

Fact and Opinion

Make a fact-and-opinion chart for "Key Holders of Kabul." List examples from the text. Dates are often clues to facts. Words like *think* and *believe* are clues to opinions. So are words like *wonderful*.

Fact-and-Opinion Chart

Facts	Opinions
In 1987, I went to Central Asia.	After hearing Sarianidi's story, I knew the objects he had found were remarkable.
List statements of fact here.	**List statements of opinion here.**

Now use your fact-and-opinion chart as you analyze "Key Holders of Kabul" with a partner. How could you check that the facts are true? Use **Key Words** as you talk about the text.

One fact is _____ .
I could check
by _____ .

Fluency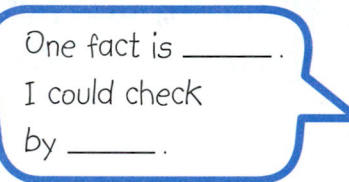

Use the Comprehension Coach to practice reading with phrasing. Rate your reading.

Choose a photo of one of the artifacts. Explain why the **object** was worth protecting. Use **Key Words** as you talk about the key holders' actions.

549

Homographs

Homographs are words that are spelled the same but have different meanings. They might be different parts of speech. You often say the words differently, too. You can use context to figure out the correct meaning.

Compare these examples.

The runner set a new **record** for speed. 	The singer gets ready to **record** a new song. 
Meaning: the best performance written down	**Meaning:** to put information in writing or in another form

Try It Together

Read the paragraph. Then answer the questions.

The archaeologist picked up the <u>object</u> and examined it. She labeled it and put it in a box. The museum director changed the label. The archaeologist did not <u>object</u>, even though she believed he was wrong.

1. What does object mean in the first sentence?

A something you can hold

B a museum

C to agree

D to disagree

2. What does object mean in the fourth sentence?

A something you can hold

B a museum

C to agree

D to disagree

Connect Across Texts Read this story about another hero who saved some other valuable **objects**.

Genre A **historical narrative** tells a story about a real event that happened in the past. The event may follow the plot of a story.

THE LIBRARIAN OF BASRA

Alia Muhammad Baker is the librarian of Basra, a port city in the sand-swept country of Iraq. Her library is a meeting place for all who love books. They discuss **matters** of the world and **matters of the spirit**. Until now—now, they talk only of war.

Alia worries that the fires of war will destroy the books, which are more precious to her than mountains of gold.

WRITTEN AND ILLUSTRATED BY
JEANETTE WINTER

In Other Words
matters news
matters of the spirit what people think and feel

▶ **Before You Move On**

1. **Point of View** Is this narrative written in first or third person? How do you know?
2. **Make Inferences** How does Alia feel about books? How can you tell?

The books are in every language—new books, <mark>ancient</mark> books, even a biography of Muhammad that is seven hundred years old.

She asks the **governor** for permission to move them to a safe place. He refuses. So Alia **takes matters into her own hands**. Secretly, she brings books home every night, filling her car late after work.

In Other Words
governor city's leader
takes matters into her own hands
decides to act

552

The whispers of war grow louder. Government offices are moved into the library. Soldiers with guns wait on the roof. Alia waits—and fears the worst.

Then . . . **rumors** become reality. War reaches Basra. The city is lit with a firestorm of bombs and gunfire.

Alia watches as library workers, government workers, and soldiers **abandon** the library. Only Alia is left to protect the books.

In Other Words
rumors the talk about war
abandon leave

▶ **Before You Move On**

1. **Clarify** Why did Alia remove the books from the library?
2. **Ask Questions** What would you ask Alia about her decision to protect the books in the library?

She calls over the library wall to her friend Anis Muhammad, who owns a restaurant on the other side. "Can you help me save the books?"

"I can use these curtains to wrap them."

"Here are **crates** from my shop."

"Can you use these sacks?"

"The books must be saved."

All through the night, Alia, Anis, his brothers, and shopkeepers and neighbors take the books from the library shelves, pass them over the seven-foot wall, and hide them in Anis's restaurant.

crate

The books stay hidden as the war **rages on**. Then, nine days later, a fire burns the library **to the ground**.

The next day, soldiers come to Anis's restaurant.

They quickly scan the room with their eyes.

The soldiers leave without searching inside.

*They do not know that **the whole of** the library is in my restaurant*, thinks Anis.

In Other Words

rages on continues

to the ground completely

the whole of everything that was in

▶ **Before You Move On**

1. **Draw Conclusions** What kind of person do you think Anis is?
2. **Explain** What <mark>risks</mark> did Anis take? What could have happened to him? Why did he take those <mark>risks</mark>?

At last, the **beast of war moves on**. Alia knows that if the books are to be safe, they must be moved again, while the city is quiet. So she hires a truck to bring all thirty thousand books to her house and to the houses of friends.

In Alia's house, books are everywhere, filling floors and cupboards and windows—leaving barely enough room for anything else.

In Other Words
beast of war moves on fighting stops in Basra

Alia waits. She waits for war to end. She waits, and dreams of peace.

She waits . . . and dreams of a new library. But until then, the books are safe—safe with the librarian of Basra. ❖

▶ **Before You Move On**

1. **Determine Importance** What is the main lesson of Alia's story?
2. **Figurative Language** Why does the author describe war as a "beast"?

Compare Features

Compare different features of a literary text and an informational text. Work with a partner to complete the comparison chart.

Key Words

ancient	principle
civilization	project
courage	record
empire	risk
official	site
object	

Comparison Chart

	"The Key Holders of Kabul"	"The Librarian of Basra"
genre	personal narrative	
real or fiction?	real	
text features	photographs	
point of view		
author's purpose		
how you know the purpose		

Talk Together

Imagine that you are the authors. Explain why you wanted to write these texts. Use **Key Words** as you say what's worth protecting.

Future Tense

There are two ways to show the **future tense**.

Grammar Rules Future Tense

• Use the helping verb **will** along with a **main verb**.	Our town **will** honor the brave heroes next week.
• Use **am going to**, **are going to**, or **is going to** before a **main verb**.	I **am going to** visit the ruins. The government **is going to** build a museum. The archaeologists **are going to** examine the objects.

Read Future Tense

Read these sentences about the National Museum of Kabul. Find two examples of the future tense. Identify the main verb in each example.

> When visitors come to the National Museum in Kabul, they will see a motto on the wall. The museum is going to preserve the culture of Afghanistan.

Write Future Tense

What do you think will happen to the Afghan heroes? Write a paragraph to explain. Use the future tense.

Write as a Reader

Write a Literary Response

Write a response to a story or an article in this unit. Then discuss it with others in your class.

Study a Model

In a literary response, you give your opinion, or personal feelings, about a story or article. You support your opinion with reasons and details.

"The Librarian of Basra"

by Jeanette Winter
Reviewed by Rajit Shah

"The Librarian of Basra" is the true story of Alia, who took risks to protect the library's books during the war in Iraq. **I liked this account for its message, but more details would have made it even better**.

Before I read the account, I did not think of books as treasures. To Alia, though, books were more precious "than mountains of gold." So she and her neighbors risked their lives to smuggle 30,000 books out of the library and hide them.

This account **made me think about all the ideas and information that books contain**. What would happen if they all disappeared? I suddenly understood why Alia thought books were so precious.

Rajit begins with a short **summary** of the literature.

He clearly states his **opinion**.

He gives **reasons** that support his opinion.

He uses **details** from the story to develop ideas.

Prewrite

1. **Choose a Topic** With a partner, review and talk about the literature in this unit. Choose a story or article to write about.

Language Frames	
Tell Your Ideas	**Respond to Ideas**
• I think this story was _____ because _____ .	• What are your reasons for saying _____ ?
• My favorite part of this story was _____ .	• I disagree with you about _____ because _____ .
• Some things I didn't like were _____ .	• What do you mean by _____ ?

2. **Gather Information** What reasons will you give to support your opinion? Reread the literature. Look for details that will help you explain your reasons.

3. **Get Organized** Use a T-Chart to help you organize your thoughts.

T-Chart

What I Liked	What I Didn't Like
The line "books are more precious to her than mountains of gold"	Not enough detail about the war or why she had to hide the books
How Alia took matters into her own hands	Unexciting description—for example, when the soldiers came to Anis's restaurant

Draft

Use your chart to write your draft. State your opinion and reasons clearly. Use details from the selection to develop your ideas.

Revise

1. **Read, Retell, Respond** Read your draft aloud to a partner. Your partner listens and then restates your ideas. Next, talk about ways to improve your writing.

Language Frames	
Retell	**Make Suggestions**
• Your opinion about the story was _____ .	• I don't understand why you said _____ . Could you explain it differently?
• Your main reasons for your opinion were _____ .	• You didn't include many details from the story. Maybe you could add _____ .
• Some details you used to develop your ideas were _____ .	

2. **Make Changes** Think about your draft and your partner's suggestions. Then use the Revising Marks on page 585 to mark your changes.

   • Did you state your opinion clearly? If not, try rewording it

   I liked this account, ~~but it could have been better.~~ for its message, but more details would have made it even better.

   • Use details from the selection to develop your ideas.

   To Alia, though, books were ~~very important.~~ more precious "than mountains of gold."

Edit and Proofread

Work with a partner to edit and proofread your literary response. Pay special attention to irregular verbs. Use the marks on page 585 to show your changes.

the marks on page 585

Spelling Tip

Remember that irregular verbs form the past tense with special spellings: *bring/brought*

Publish

1. **On Your Own** Make a final copy of your literary response. Post it on a class blog, or share it with someone who has read the same selection.

Presentation Tips	
If you are the speaker…	**If you are the listener…**
Speak clearly. Pause slightly before sentences and phrases from the literature.	Be ready to summarize the writer's response to the literature.
Be ready to respond to questions about your opinion and reasons.	Think about whether the writer's opinion is supported by details.

2. **With a Group** Form a Reader's Circle to discuss the selections you read. Be sure to share both positive and negative opinions. You can also share your opinions in an online discussion group.

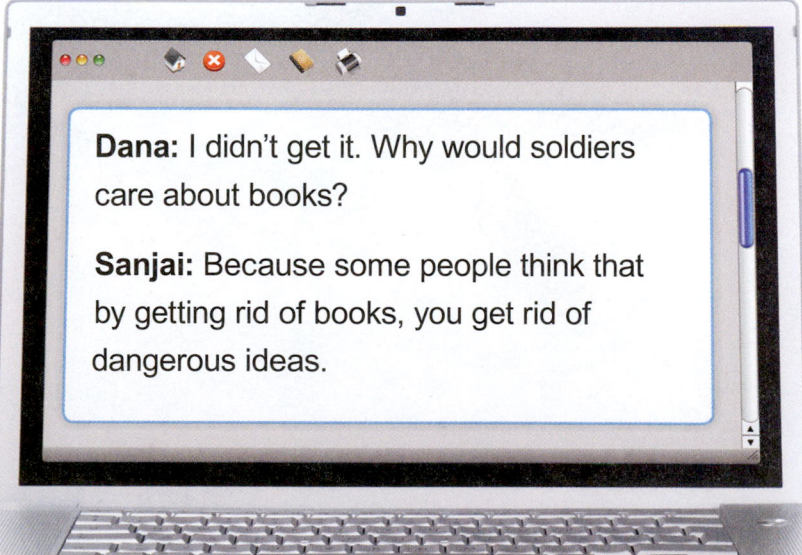

Dana: I didn't get it. Why would soldiers care about books?

Sanjai: Because some people think that by getting rid of books, you get rid of dangerous ideas.

?
BIG
Question

What's worth protecting?

Talk Together

In this unit, you found lots of answers to the **Big Question**. Now make a concept map to discuss the **Big Question** with the class.

Concept Map

records of our history

things that are worth protecting

Write a Persuasive Essay

Choose one thing that's worth protecting. Write a persuasive essay about it. Include details to support your ideas.

Share Your Ideas

Choose one of these ways to share your ideas about the **Big Question**.

Write It!

Write a Letter

What social cause do you care about? What organization would you like to help by volunteering? Write a letter to an organization to learn more. Include all of the parts of a letter.

Do It!

Make an Ad

Design an ad that asks people to support a cause. Share your ad with the class. Talk about how the words and pictures make the meaning clear.

The Oak Street Soup Kitchen needs your support!

Talk About It!

Share a Superhero Fantasy

Imagine that you are a superhero. Tell a partner what you would do as a superhero to protect something important.

I would protect all the animals in the ocean!

Do It!

Have a Debate

Talk with classmates about an issue that you think is important to the lives of people today. Then have a debate about it. Discuss different ways to solve the issue.

Strategies for Learning Language

These strategies can help you learn to use
and understand the English language.

1 Listen actively and try out language.

What to Do	Examples	
Repeat what you hear.	**You hear:** Way to go, Joe! Fantastic catch!	**You say:** Way to go, Joe! Fantastic catch!
Recite songs and poems.	My Family Tree Two grandmas, one brother, Two grandpas, one mother, One father, and then there's me. Eight of us together Make up my family tree.	Two grandmas, one brother,...
Listen to others and use their language.	**You hear:** "When did you know that something was missing?"	**You say:** "I knew that something was missing when I got to class."

2 Ask for help.

What to Do	Examples	
Ask questions about how to use language.	Did I say that right? Did I use that word in the right way?	Which is correct, "bringed" or "brought"?
Use your native language or English to make sure that you understand.	**You say:** "Wait! Could you say that again more slowly, please?"	**Other options:** "Does 'violet' mean 'purple'?" "Is 'enormous' another way to say 'big'?"

3 Use gestures and body language, and watch for them.

What to Do	Examples
Use gestures and movements to help others understand your ideas.	I will hold up five fingers to show that I need five more minutes.
Watch people as they speak. The way they look or move can help you understand the meaning of their words.	Let's give him a hand. — Everyone is clapping. "Give him a hand" must mean to clap for him.

4 Think about what you are learning.

What to Do	Examples
Ask yourself: Are my language skills getting better? How can I improve?	Was it correct to use "they" when I talked about my grandparents? — Did I add 's to show ownership?
Keep notes about what you've learned. Use your notes to practice using English.	How to Ask Questions • I can start a question with "is," "can," or "do": Do you have my math book? • I can start a question with "who," "what," "where," "when," "how," or "why" to get more information: Where did you put my math book?

569

Vocabulary Strategies

When you read, you may find a word you don't know. But, don't worry! There are many things you can do to figure out the meaning of an unfamiliar word.

Use What You Know

Ask yourself "Does this new word look like a word I know?" If it does, use what you know about the familiar word to figure out the meaning of the new word. Think about:

- **word families**, or words that look similar and have related meanings. The words *locate*, *location*, and *relocate* are in the same word family.

- **cognates**, or pairs of words that look the same in English and in another language. The English word *problem* and the Spanish word *problema* are cognates.

On the Top of the World

Mount Everest is the highest mountain in the world. It is 29,028 feet (8,848 meters) high. This **magnificent** mountain is covered in permanently frozen snow and ice. But this doesn't stop **adventurous** climbers from trying to reach its peak.

> This English word looks like **magnifico**. That means "beautiful" in Spanish. I think that meaning makes sense here, too.

> I know that **adventure** means "an exciting event" and that an **adventurer** is "someone who takes risks." So, **adventurous** probably means "willing to be a part of risky activities."

Use Context Clues

Sometimes you can figure out a word's meaning by looking at other words and phrases near the word. Those words and phrases are called **context clues.**

There are different kinds of context clues. Look for signal words such as *means, like, but,* or *unlike* to help you find the clues.

Extremely cold temperatures are hazardous to mountain climbers.

Kind of Clue	Signal Words	Example
Definition Gives the word's meaning.	*is, are, was, refers to, means*	Hazardous *refers to* something that causes harm or injury.
Restatement Gives the word's meaning in a different way, usually after a comma.	*or*	Mountain climbing can be hazardous, *or* result in injuries to climbers.
Synonym Gives a word or phrase that means almost the same thing.	*like, also*	Sudden drops in temperature can be hazardous. *Also* dangerous are very high altitudes that make it hard to breathe.
Antonym Gives a word or phrase that means the opposite.	*but, unlike*	The subzero temperatures can be hazardous, *but* special gear keeps the climbers safe.
Examples Gives examples of what the word means.	*such as, for example, including*	Climbers prepare for hazardous situations. *For example*, they carry extra food, equipment for heavy snowfall, and first-aid kits.

Use Word Parts

Many English words are made up of parts. You can use these parts as clues to a word's meaning.

When you don't know a word, look to see if you know any of its parts. Put the meaning of the word parts together to figure out the meaning of the whole word.

Compound Words

A compound word is made up of two or more smaller words. To figure out the meaning of the whole word:

laptop

keyboard

1. Break the long word into parts.

   keyboard = key + board

2. Put the meanings of the smaller words together to predict the meaning of the whole word.

   key = button
   +
   board = flat surface

   keyboard = flat part of computer with buttons

3. If you can't predict the meaning from the parts, use what you know and the meaning of the other words to figure it out.

   lap + top = laptop

   laptop means "small portable computer," not "the top of your lap"

Prefixes

A prefix comes at the beginning of a word. It changes the word's meaning. To figure out the meaning of an unfamiliar word, look to see if it has a prefix.

1. Break the word into parts. Think about the meaning of each part.

   I need to **rearrange** the files on my computer.

   re- + arrange

   The prefix *re-* means "again." The word *arrange* means "to put in order."

2. Put the meanings of the word parts together.

   The word *rearrange* means "to put in order again."

Some Prefixes and Their Meanings

Prefix	Meaning
anti-	against
dis-	opposite of
In-	not
mis	wrongly
pre-	before
re-	again, back
un-	not

Suffixes

A suffix comes at the end of a word. It changes the word's meaning and part of speech. To figure out the meaning of new word, look to see if it has a suffix.

Some Suffixes and Their Meanings

Suffix	Meaning
-able	can be done
-al	having characteristics of
-ion	act, process
-er, -or	one who
-ful	full of
-less	without
-ly	in a certain way

1. Break the word into parts. Think about the meaning of each part.

My **teacher** helps me find online articles.

teach + -er

verb

The word *teach* means "to give lessons." The suffix *-er* means "one who."

2. Put the meanings of the word parts together.

A *teacher* is "a person who gives lessons."

noun

Greek and Latin Roots

Many words in English have Greek and Latin roots. A root is a word part that has meaning, but it cannot stand on its own.

1. Break the unfamiliar word into parts.

I won't be done in time if there's one more **interruption**!

inter + rupt + ion

prefix   root   suffix

2. Focus on the root. Do you know other words with the same root?

"I've seen the root **rupt** in the words *erupt* and *rupture*.

'rupt' must have something to do with breaking or destroying something."

3. Put the meanings of all the word parts together.

between   act or process

inter + rupt + ion = interruption

break   a break in activity

573

Look Beyond the Literal Meaning

Writers use colorful language to keep their readers interested. They use words and phrases that mean something different from their usual definitions. Figurative language and idioms are kinds of colorful language.

Figurative Language: Similes

A simile compares two things that are alike in some way. It uses the words *like* or *as* to make the comparison.

Simile	Things Compared	How They're Alike
Cory hiked across the desert **as sluggishly as a snail**.	Cory and a snail	They both move very slowly.
His skin was **like sheets of sandpaper.**	skin and sandpaper	They are both rough and very dry.

Figurative Language: Metaphors

A metaphor compares two things without using the words *like* or *as*.

Metaphor	Things Compared	Meaning
The **sun's rays were a thousand bee stings** on his face.	sun's rays and bee stings	The sun's rays blistered his face.
His only **companion was thirst.**	friend and thirst	His thirst was always there with him.

Figurative Language: Personification

When writers use personification they give human qualities to nonhuman things.

Personification	Object	Human Quality
The **angry sun** kept punishing him.	sun	has feelings
A **cactus reached out to** him.	cactus	is able to be friendly

Idioms

An idiom is a special kind of phrase that means something different from what the words mean by themselves.

What you say:

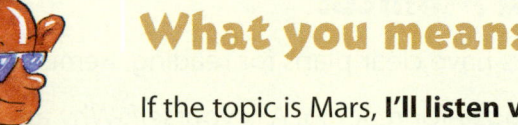

If the topic is Mars, **I'm all ears.**

Break a leg!

Rachel had **to eat her words.**

Give me a break!

Hang on.

I'm **in a jam.**

The joke was so funny, Lisa **laughed her head off.**

Juan was **steamed** when I lost his video game.

Let's **surf the Net** for ideas for report ideas.

I'm so tired, I just want to **veg out**.

Rob and Zak are together **24-seven.**

You can say that again.

Zip your lips!

What you mean:

If the topic is Mars, **I'll listen very carefully**.

Good luck!

Rachel had **to say she was wrong.**

That's ridiculous!

Wait.

I'm **in trouble.**

The joke was so funny, Lisa **laughed very hard.**

Juan was **very angry** when I lost his video game.

Let's **look around the contents of the Internet** for report ideas.

I'm so tired, I just want to **relax and not think about anything.**

Rob and Zak are together **all the time.**

I totally agree with you.

Be quiet!

Reading Strategies

Good readers use a set of strategies before, during, and after reading. Knowing which strategy to use and when will help you understand and enjoy all kinds of text.

Plan and Monitor

Good readers have clear plans for reading. Remember to:

- **Set a purpose** for reading. Ask yourself: Why am I reading this? What do I hope to get from it?

- **Preview** what you are about to read. Look at the title. Scan the text, pictures, and other visuals.

- **Make predictions**, or thoughtful guesses, about what comes next. Check your predictions as you read. Change them as you learn new information.

Monitor, or keep track of, your reading. Remember to:

- **Clarify ideas and vocabulary** to make sure you understand what the words and passages mean. Stop and ask yourself: Does that make sense?

- **Reread, read on,** or **change your reading speed** if you are confused.

Determine Importance

How can you keep track of all the facts and details as you read? Do what good readers do and focus on the most important ideas.

- Identify the **main idea**. Connect details to the main idea.

- **Summarize** as you read and after you read.

Ask Questions

Asking yourself questions as you read keeps your mind active. You'll ask different types of questions, so you'll need to find the answers in different ways.

- Some questions are connected to answers **right there** in the text.

- Others cover more than one part of the text. So, you'll have to **think and search** to find the answers.

Not all answers are found in the book.

- **On your own** questions can focus on your experiences or on the big ideas of the text.

- **Author and you** questions may be about the author's purpose or point of view.

Visualize

Good readers use the text and their own experiences to picture a writer's words. When you **visualize**, use all your senses to see, hear, smell, feel, and taste what the writer describes.

Make Connections

When you make connections, you put together information from the text with what you know from outside the text. As you read, think about:

- **your own ideas and experiences**
- what you know about the **world** from TV, songs, school, and so on
- **other texts** you've read by the same author, about the same topic, or in the same genre.

Make Inferences

Sometimes an author doesn't tell a reader everything. To figure out what is left unsaid:

- Look for what the author emphasizes.
- Think about what you already know.
- Combine what you read with what you know to figure out what the author means.

Synthesize

When you **synthesize**, you put together information from different places and come up with new understandings. You might:

- **Draw conclusions**, or combine what you know with what you read to decide what to think about a topic.
- **Form generalizations**, or combine ideas from the text with what you know to form an idea that is true in many situations.

Writing and Research

Writing is one of the best ways to express yourself. Sometimes you'll write to share a personal experience. Other times, you'll write to give information about a research topic. Whenever you write, use the following steps to help you say want you want clearly, correctly, and in your own special way.

Prewrite

When you prewrite, you choose a topic and collect all the details and information you need for writing.

1. **Choose a Topic and Make a Plan** Think about your writing prompt assignment or what you want to write about.

   - Make a list. Then choose the best idea to use for your topic.

   - Think about your writing role, audience, and form. Add those to a RAFT chart.

   - Jot down any research questions, too. Those will help you look for the information you need.

   RAFT Chart

   Role: scientist

   Audience: my teacher and classmates

   Form: report

   Topic: honeybees

2. **Gather Information** Think about your topic and your plan. Jot down ideas. Or, use resources like those on pages 579–582 to find information that answers your questions. Take notes.

Use Information Resources

Books

A book is a good source of information.

Notecard

Where do honeybees live? — research question

The Honey Makers, by Gail Gibbons, page 6 — name of source

—Many honeybees live in dark places like hollow trees. — notes in your own words

—"Honeybees cared for by today's beekeepers live in box-shaped wooden hives." — author's exact words in **quotation marks**

Read the pages to find information you need. Take notes.

WILD HONEYBEE HIVE

WOODEN BEEHIVE

Many honeybees like to make their homes in dark, enclosed places. Often a colony of wild honeybees builds its hive in a hollow tree. Honeybees cared for by today's beekeepers live in box-shaped wooden hives.

Writing and Research, *continued*

Encyclopedias

Each encyclopedia volume has facts about different topics.

guide words

• Rain forest

Rain forest

Rain forests are thick forests of tall trees. They are found where the weather is warm the year around, and there is plenty of rain. Most rain forests grow near the equator, a make-believe line around Earth's middle. Africa, Asia, and Central and South America have large rain forests. Smaller rain forests are found in Australia and islands in the Pacific.

Tropical rain forests have more kinds of trees than anywhere else in the world. More than half of all the kinds of plants and animals on Earth live in tropical rain forests.

The tallest rain forest trees are as tall as 165 feet (50 meters). The treetops form a leafy covering called the canopy

Tropical rain forests have more kinds of trees than anywhere else in the world.

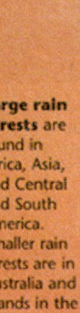

article

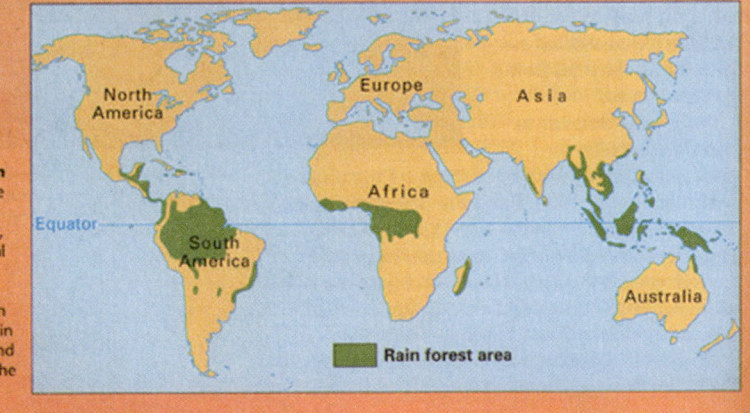

North America   Europe   Asia

Equator

Africa

South America

Australia

Large rain forests are found in Africa, Asia, and Central and South America. Smaller rain forests are in Australia and islands in the Pacific.

■ Rain forest area

180 The World Book Student Discovery Encyclopedia

1. Look up your topic in the correct encyclopedia **volume** or on the **CD-ROM**.

2. Read the **guide words**. Keep turning the pages until you find the article you want. Use alphabetical order.

3. Read the **article** and take notes.

Magazines

The **date** tells when the **issue** was published.

This is the **title** of the magazine.

This is the **main topic** of the issue.

These are some of the **topics** in the issue.

. . . and Experts

Arrange a time to talk to an **expert,** or someone who knows a lot about your topic.

- Prepare questions you want to ask about the topic.

- Conduct the interview. Write down the person's answers.

- Choose the notes you'll use for your writing

Internet

The Internet is a connection of computers that share information through the World Wide Web. It is like a giant library. Check with your teacher for how to access the Internet from your school.

1. Go to a search page. Type in your key words. Click Search.

2. Read the list of Web sites, or pages, that have your key words. The underlined words are links to the Web sites.

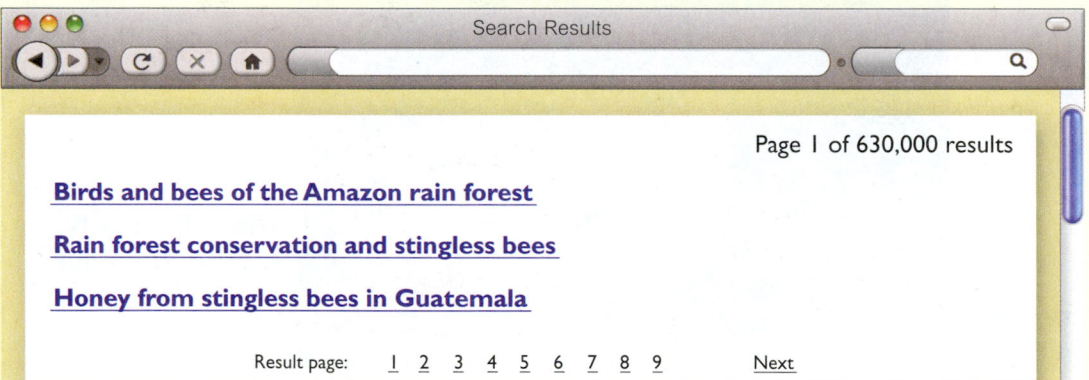

3. Click on a link to go directly to the site, or Web page. Read the article online. Or print it if it is helpful for your research. Later on, you can use the article to take notes.

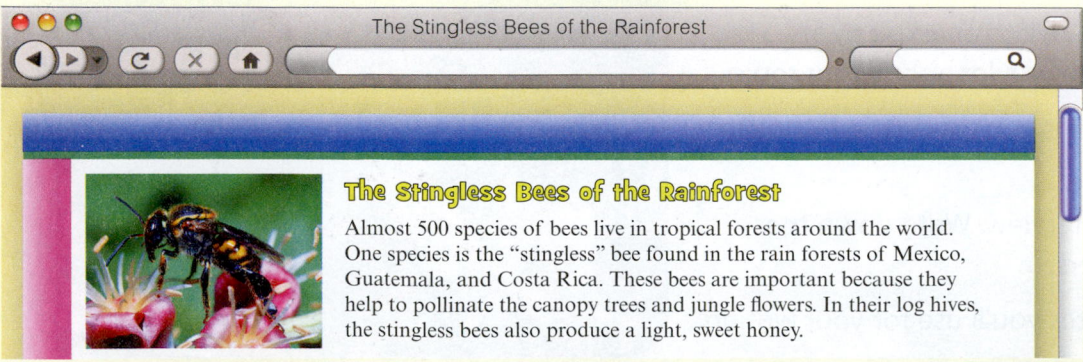

4. **Get Organized** Think about all the details you've gathered about your topic. Use a list, a chart, or other graphic organizer to show what you'll include in your writing. Use the organizer to show the order of your ideas, too.

Cluster

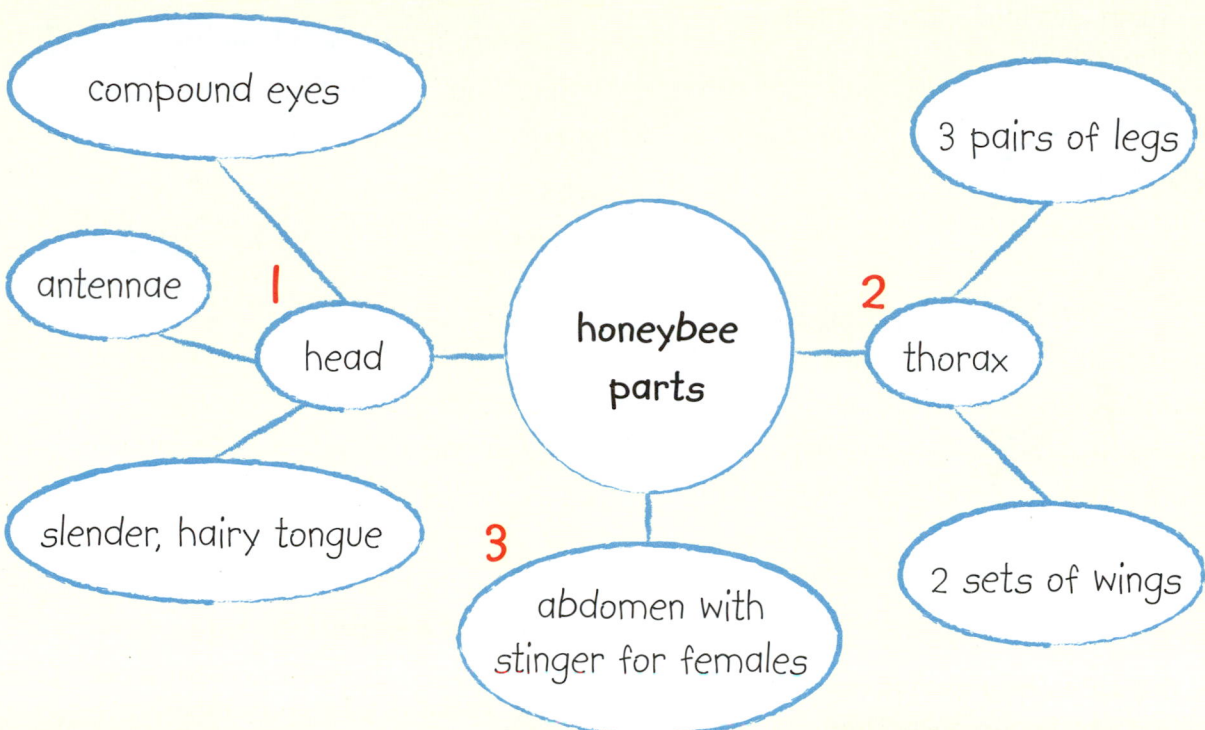

Outline

The Helpful, Sweet Honeybee

I. Important insects

   A. help pollinate plants

      1. flowers and trees

      2. fruits

   B. turn nectar into honey

II. Honeybee homes

   A. around the world

   B. hives

Draft

When you write your first draft, you turn all your ideas into sentences. You write quickly just to get all your ideas down. You can correct mistakes later.

Cluster

Turn your main idea into a topic sentence. Then add the details.

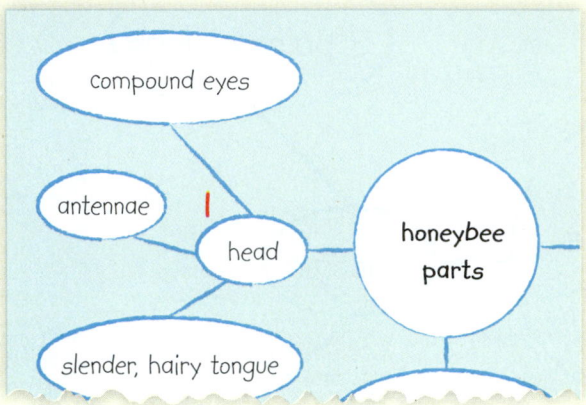

Beginning of a Description

One main part of a honeybee is the head. The bee's head seems to be mostly eyes! They are called compound eyes and have a lot of tiny lenses in them.

Outline

Turn the main idea after each Roman numeral into a topic sentence. Then turn the words next to the letters and numbers into detail sentences that tell more about the main idea.

The Helpful, Sweet Honeybee

I. Important insects
   A. help pollinate plants
      1. flowers and trees
      2. fruits

Beginning of a Report

The Helpful, Sweet Honeybee

You may think that all the honeybee does is make honey. But, believe it or not, this insect is always busy with another important job.

A honeybee helps keep plants growing. It helps to spread the pollen flowers and trees need to start new plants.

Revise

When you revise, you make changes to your writing to make it better and clearer.

❶ Read, Retell, Respond Read your draft aloud to a partner. Your partner listens and then retells your main points.

> You are describing a honeybee's hive. Isn't a bee's nest the same as a hive?

> Yes, it is. I don't need the word "nest," so I'll take it out.

Your partner can help you discover what is unclear or what you need to add. Use your partner's suggestions to decide what you can to do to make your writing better.

❷ Make Changes Think about your draft and what you and your partner discussed. What changes will you make? Use Revising Marks to mark your changes.

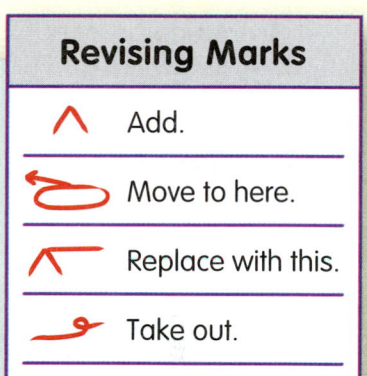

Revising Marks	
∧	Add.
↺	Move to here.
⋀	Replace with this.
⤴	Take out.

In the wild, honeybee scouts look for places to make hives ~~and nests~~. The opening needs to be high off the ground. (They look for openings in hollow tree trunks.) That way the hive will be safe from ~~harmful animals~~ ^predators^. A hive needs to hold thousands of bees and all ^the nectar and pollen^ they gather.

The best bee's nest will also face south so it stays warm.

Edit and Proofread

When you edit and proofread, you look for mistakes in capitalization, grammar, and punctuation.

1 **Check Your Sentences** Check that your sentences are clear, complete, and correct. Add any missing subjects or predicates

2 **Check Your Spelling** Look for any misspelled words. Check their spelling in a dictionary or a glossary.

3 **Check for Capital Letters, Punctuation, and Grammar** Look especially for correct use of

- capital letters in proper nouns
- apostrophes and quotation marks
- subject-verb agreement
- pronouns
- verb tenses

4 **Mark Your Changes** Use the Editing and Proofreading Marks to show your changes.

5 **Make a Final Copy** Make all the corrections you've marked to make a final, clean copy of your writing. If you are using a computer, print out your corrected version.

It is crowded and busy inside a honeybee hive. A hive can have more than 50000 honeybees. Most of them are worker bees. The worker bees create wax from their bodyes to build combs. The combs are layers of Cells, or holes. The cells hold nectar pollen, or larvae.

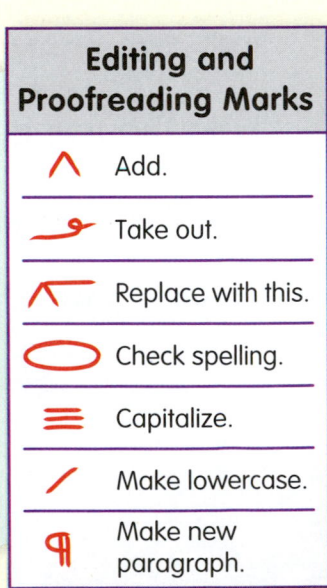

Editing and Proofreading Marks	
∧	Add.
✎	Take out.
⊼	Replace with this.
◯	Check spelling.
≡	Capitalize.
/	Make lowercase.
¶	Make new paragraph.

Publish

When you publish your writing, you share it with others.

1 Add Visuals Visuals can make your writing more interesting and easier to understand. Maybe you will

- import photographs or illustrations
- insert computer clip art
- add graphs, charts, or diagrams

2 Present Your Writing There are a lot of ways to share your finished work. Here are just a few ideas.

- E-mail it to a friend or family member.
- Send it to your favorite magazine or publication.
- Turn it into a chapter for a group book about the topic.
- Make a video clip of you reading it to add to a group presentation.

A Home for the Honeybee

In the wild, honeybee scouts look for places to make hives. They look for openings in hollow tree trunks. The opening needs to be high off the ground. That way the hive will be safe from predators. A hive also needs to be big enough for thousands of bees and all the nectar and pollen they gather. The best hive will also face south so it stays warm.

Writing Traits

Good writing is clear, interesting, and easy to follow. To make your writing as good as it can be, check your writing to be sure it has the characteristics, or traits, of good writing.

Ideas

Writing is well-developed when the message is clear and interesting to the reader. It is supported by details that show the writer knows the topic well.

	Is the message clear and interesting?	Do the details show the writer knows the topic?
4	❑ All of the writing is clear and focused. ❑ The writing is very interesting.	❑ All the details tell about the topic. The writer knows the topic well.
3	❑ Most of the writing is clear and focused. ❑ Most of the writing is interesting.	❑ Most of the details are about the topic. The writer knows the topic fairly well.
2	❑ Some of the writing is not clear. The writing lacks some focus. ❑ Some of the writing is confusing.	❑ Some details are about the topic. The writer doesn't know the topic well.
1	❑ The writing is not clear or focused. ❑ The writing is confusing.	❑ Many details are not about the topic. The writer does not know the topic.

Organization

Writing is organized when it is easy to follow. All the ideas make sense together and flow from one idea to the next in an order that fits the writer's audience and purpose.

	Is the writing organized? Does it fit the audience and purpose?	Does the writing flow?
4	❑ The writing is very well-organized. ❑ It clearly fits both the writer's audience and purpose.	❑ The writing is smooth and logical. Each sentence flows into the next one.
3	❑ Most of the writing is organized. ❑ It mostly fits the writer's audience and purpose.	❑ Most of the writing is smooth. There are only a few sentences that do not flow logically.
2	❑ The writing is not well-organized. ❑ It fits the writer's audience or the writer's purpose, but not both.	❑ Some of the writing is smooth. Many sentences do not flow smoothly.
1	❑ The writing is not organized at all. ❑ It does not fit the writer's audience or purpose.	❑ The sentences do not flow smoothly or logically.

Organized

Not organized

Voice

Every writer has a special way of saying things, or a voice. The voice should sound genuine, or real, and be unique to that writer.

	Does the writing sound genuine and unique ?	Does the tone fit the audience and purpose?
4	❏ The writing is genuine and unique. It shows who the writer is.	❏ The writer's tone, formal or informal, fits the audience and purpose.
3	❏ Most of the writing sounds genuine and unique.	❏ The writer's tone mostly fits the audience and purpose.
2	❏ Some of the writing sounds genuine and unique.	❏ Some of the writing fits the audience and purpose.
1	❏ The writing does not sound genuine or unique.	❏ The writer's tone does not fit the audience or purpose.

Word Choice

Readers can always tell who the writer is by the words the writer uses.

	Do the writer's words fit the message?	Does the language fit the audience? Is it interesting?
4	❏ The writer chose words that really fit the message.	❏ The words and sentences fit the audience and are interesting.
3	❏ Most of the words really fit the writer's message.	❏ Most of the words and sentences fit the audience and are interesting.
2	❏ Some of the words fit the writer's message.	❏ Some of the words and sentences fit the audience and are interesting.
1	❏ Few or no words fit the writer's message.	❏ The language does not fit the audience and lose the readers' attention.

Fluency

Good writers use a variety of sentence types. They also use transitions, or signal words.

	Is there sentence variety? Are there transitions?	Does the writing sound natural and rhythmic?
4	❏ The writer uses lots of different types of sentences. ❏ The writer uses useful transitions.	❏ When I read the writing aloud, it sounds natural and rhythmic.
3	❏ The writer uses many different types of sentences. ❏ Most transition words are useful.	❏ When I read the writing aloud, most of it sounds natural and rhythmic.
2	❏ The writer uses some different kinds of sentences. ❏ Some transition words are useful.	❏ When I read the writing aloud, some of it sounds natural and rhythmic.
1	❏ The writer does not vary sentences. ❏ The writer does not use transitions.	❏ When I read the writing aloud, it sounds unnatural.

Conventions

Good writers always follow the rules of grammar, punctuation, and spelling.

	Is the writing correct?	Are the sentences complete?
4	❏ All the punctuation, capitalization, and spelling is correct.	❏ Every sentence has a subject and a predicate.
3	❏ Most of the punctuation, spelling, and capitalization is correct.	❏ Most of the sentences have a subject and a predicate.
2	❏ Some of the punctuation, spelling, and capitalization is correct.	❏ Some of the sentences are missing subjects or predicates.
1	❏ There are many punctuation, spelling, and capitalization errors.	❏ Several sentences are missing subjects or predicates.

Grammar, Usage, Mechanics, and Spelling

Sentences

A sentence expresses a complete thought.

Kinds of Sentences

There are four kinds of sentences.

A **statement** tells something. It ends with a **period**.	Ned is at the mall now**.** He needs a new shirt**.**
A **question** asks for information. It ends with a **question mark**.	Where can I find the shirts**?**

Kinds of Questions

Some questions ask for "Yes" or "No" answers. They start with words such as **Is**, **Do**, **Can**, **Are**, and **Will**.	**Do** you have a size 10? **Answer:** Yes. **Are** these shirts on sale? **Answer:** No.
Other questions ask for more information. They start with words such as **Who**, **What**, **Where**, **When**, and **Why**.	**What** colors do you have? **Answer:** We have red and blue. **Where** can I try this on? **Answer:** You can use this room.

An **exclamation** shows strong feeling. It ends with an **exclamation mark**.	This is such a cool shirt**!** I love it**!**
A **command** tells you what to do or what not to do. It usually begins with a **verb** and ends with a period. If a command shows strong emotion, it ends with an exclamation mark.	**Please** bring me a size 10. **Don't open** the door yet. Wait until I come out!

Negative Sentences

A negative sentence means "no."	
A **negative sentence** uses a **negative word** to say "no."	That is **not** a good color for me. I **can't** find the right size.

Complete Sentences

A complete sentence has two parts.	
The **subject** tells whom or what the sentence is about.	My friends buy clothes here. The other store has nicer shirts.
The **predicate** tells what the subject is, has, or does.	My friends buy clothes here. The other store has nicer shirts.

Subjects

All the words that tell about a subject is the **complete subject**.	My younger sister loves the toy store.
The **simple subject** is the most important word in the complete subject.	My younger sister loves the toy store.
A **compound subject** has two nouns joined together by the words **and** or **or**.	Terry **and** Brittany never shop at this store. My mom **or** my dad always comes with me.

Predicates

All the words in the predicate is the **complete predicate**.	The stores open today at nine.
The **simple predicate** is the **verb**. It is the most important word in the predicate.	The stores open today at nine.
A **compound predicate** has two or more verbs that tell about the same subject. The verbs are joined by **and** or **or**.	We eat **and** shop at the mall. Sometimes we see a movie **or** just talk with our friends.

Sentences *(continued)*

Compound Sentences

When you join two sentences together, you can make a compound sentence.

Use a comma and the conjunction **and** to combine two similar ideas.	My friends walk to the mall. I go with them. My friends walk to the mall **, and** I go with them.
Use a comma and the conjunction **but** to combine two different ideas.	My friends walk to the mall. I ride my bike. My friends walk to the mall **, but** I ride my bike.
Use a comma and the conjunction **or** to show a choice of ideas.	You can walk to the mall with me. You can ride with Dad. You can walk to the mall with me **, or** you can ride with Dad.

Complex Sentences

When you join independent and dependent clauses, you can make a complex sentence.

An **independent clause** expresses a complete thought. It can stand alone as a sentence.	Mom and her friends walk around the mall for exercise. They walk around the mall.
A **dependent clause** does not express a complete thought. It is not a sentence.	before it gets busy because they want to exercise
To make a **complex sentence**, join an **independent clause** with one or more **dependent clauses**. If the dependent clause comes first, put a **comma** after it.	Before it gets busy **,** Mom and her friends walk around the mall for exercise. They walk around the mall because they want to exercise.

Condensing Clauses

Condense clauses to create precise and detailed sentences.

Condense clauses by combining ideas and using complex sentences.	It's a plant. It's green and red. It's found in the tropical rainforest. ➡ It's a green and red plant that is found in the tropical rainforest.

Nouns

Nouns name people, animals, places, or things.

Common Nouns and Proper Nouns

There are two kinds of nouns.

A **common noun** names any person, animal, place, or thing of a certain type.	I know that **girl**. She rides a **horse**. I sometimes see her at the **park**. She walks her **dog** there.
A **proper noun** names a particular person, animal, place, or thing. ● Start all the important words with a capital letter. ● Start the names of streets, cities, and states with a capital letter. ● Also use capital letters when you abbreviate state names.	 I know **Marissa**. I sometimes see her at **Hilltop Park**. She walks her dog **Chase** there. Her family is from **Dallas, Texas**. They live on **Crockett Lane**.

Abbreviations for State Names in Mailing Addresses

Alabama	AL	Hawaii	HI	Massachusetts	MA	New Mexico	NM	South Dakota	SD
Alaska	AK	Idaho	ID	Michigan	MI	New York	NY	Tennessee	TN
Arizona	AZ	Illinois	IL	Minnesota	MN	North Carolina	NC	Texas	TX
Arkansas	AR	Indiana	IN	Mississippi	MS	North Dakota	ND	Utah	UT
California	CA	Iowa	IA	Missouri	MO	Ohio	OH	Vermont	VT
Colorado	CO	Kansas	KS	Montana	MT	Oklahoma	OK	Virginia	VA
Connecticut	CT	Kentucky	KY	Nebraska	NE	Oregon	OR	Washington	WA
Delaware	DE	Louisiana	LA	Nevada	NV	Pennsylvania	PA	West Virginia	WV
Florida	FL	Maine	ME	New Hampshire	NH	Rhode Island	RI	Wisconsin	WI
Georgea	GA	Maryland	MD	New Jersey	NJ	South Carolina	SC	Wyoming	WY

Nouns *(continued)*

Singular and Plural Count Nouns

Count nouns name things that you can count. A singular count noun shows "one." A plural count noun shows "more than one."

Add **-s** to most singular count nouns to form the plural count noun.	bicycle → bicycle**s** club → club**s**	
Add **-es** to count nouns that end in **x**, **ch**, **sh**, **ss**, **z**, and sometimes **o**.	tax → tax**es** bench → bench**es** wish → wish**es** loss → loss**es** potato → potato**es**	
For count nouns that end in a consonant plus **y**, change the **y** to **i** and then add **-es**. For nouns that end in a vowel plus **y**, just add **-s**.	berr~~y~~ **i** → berri**es** famil~~y~~ **i** → famili**es** boy → boy**s** day → day**s**	
For a few count nouns, use special forms to show the plural.	man → men woman → women foot → feet tooth → teeth child → children	

Noncount Nouns

Noncount nouns name things that you cannot count.
Noncount nouns have one form for "one" and "more than one."

Weather Words	fog heat lightning thunder rain **YES:** **Thunder** and **lightning** scare my dog. **NO:** Thunders and lightnings scare my dog.
Food Words Some food items can be counted by using a measurement word such as **cup, slice, glass,** or **head** plus the word **of**. To show the plural form, make the measurement word plural.	bread corn milk rice soup **YES:** I'm thirsty for **milk.** I want **two glasses of milk.** **NO:** I'm thirsty for milks. I want milks.
Ideas and Feelings	fun help honesty luck work **YES:** I need **help** to finish my homework. **NO:** I need helps to finish my homework.
Category Nouns	clothing equipment mail money time **YES:** My football **equipment** is in the car. **NO:** My football equipments is in the car.
Materials	air gold paper water wood **YES:** Is the **water** in this river clean? **NO:** Is the waters in this river clean?
Activities and Sports	baseball dancing golf singing soccer **YES:** I played **soccer** three times this week. **NO:** I played soccers three times this week.

Nouns *(continued)*

Words That Signal Nouns

The articles *a*, *an*, *some*, and *the* help identify a noun. They often appear before count nouns.

Use **a, an,** or **some** before a noun to talk about something in general.	**Some jokes** are funny. Do you have **a favorite joke**? I have **an uncle** who knows a lot of jokes.
Use **an** instead of **a** before a word that begins with a vowel sound.	It is **an event** when my uncle comes to visit. He lives about **an hour** away from us.
Do <u>not</u> use **a** or **an** before a noncount noun.	He drives in ~~a~~ snow, ~~a~~ fog, or ~~an~~ ice to get here.

Use **the** to talk about something specific.	Uncle Raul is **the** uncle I told you about. **The** jokes he tells make me laugh!
Do <u>not</u> use **the** before the name of:	
• a city or state	Uncle Raul lives in **Dallas**. That's a city in **Texas**.
• most countries	He used to live in **Brazil**.
• a language	He speaks **English** and **Spanish**.
• a day, month, or most holidays	Uncle Raul often visits on **Saturday**. In **February**, he comes up for **President's Day**.
• a sport or activity	Sometimes he'll play **soccer** with me.
• most businesses	Then we go to **Sal's Café** to eat.
• a person's name	He likes to talk to **Sal**, too.

The words *this*, *that*, *these*, and *those* point out nouns. Like other adjectives, they answer the question "Which one?"

Use **this** or **these** to talk about things that are near you.	**This** book has a lot of photographs.
Use **that** or **those** to talk about things that are far from you.	**Those** books on the shelf are all fiction.

	Near	Far
One thing	this	that
More than one thing	these	those

Possessive Nouns

A possessive noun is the name of an owner. An apostrophe (') is used to show ownership.

For one owner, add **'s** to the **singular noun**.	This is Raul**'s** cap. The cap**'s** color is a bright red.
For more than one owner, add just the apostrophe (') to the **plural noun**.	The boys**'** T-shirts are the same. The players**'** equipment is ready.
For plural nouns that have special forms, add **'s** to the **plural noun**.	Do you like the **children's** uniforms? The **men's** scores are the highest.

Pronouns

A pronoun takes the place of a noun or refers to a noun.

Pronoun Agreement

When you use a pronoun, be sure you are talking about the right person.

Use a capital **I** to talk about yourself.	 I am Jack. I want to find out about Mars.   Are **you** interested in Mars, too?
Use **you** to speak to another person.	
Use **she** for a girl or a woman.	Julia thinks Mars is a good topic. **She** will help write a report about the planet.
Use **he** for a boy or a man.	Jack downloaded some photos. **He** added the pictures to the report.
Use **it** for a thing.	The report is almost done. **It** will be interesting to read.

Pronouns *(continued)*

Pronoun Agreement

Be sure you are talking about the right number of people or things.

Use **you** to talk to two or more people.

Use **we** for yourself and one or more other people.

> Are **you** prepared for tomorrow?

> Yes. Sam and I are ready. **We** give a report tomorrow.

Use **they** for other people or things.

Scott and Tyrone set up the video camera. **They** will record each presentation.

Subject Pronouns

Subject pronouns take the place of the subject in the sentence.

Subject pronouns tell who or what does the action.

Julia is a good speaker.

She tells the class about Mars.

The photos show the surface of Mars.

They are images from NASA.

Subject Pronouns	
Singular	**Plural**
I	we
you	you
he, she, it	they

Object Pronouns

Object pronouns replace a noun that comes after a verb or a preposition.

An **object pronoun** answers the question "What" or "Whom."	The class asked **Jack and Julia** about Mars.
Object pronouns come after a verb or a preposition such as **to**, **for**, **at**, **of**, or **with**.	The class asked **them** about Mars.

Jack put **the report** online.

Jack put **it** online.

Object Pronouns	
Singular	**Plural**
me	us
you	you
him, her, it	them

Reciprocal Pronouns

Reciprocal pronouns replace objects that refer back to the subject.

The subject must be plural. It can be a compound subject.	**Jack and Julia** helped **each other** on the report.
The subject can also be a plural noun.	**The students** followed **one another** outside.

Reciprocal Pronouns
Plural
each other
one another

Possessive Pronouns

Like a possessive noun, a possessive pronoun tells who or what owns something.

To show that you own something, use **mine**.	**I** wrote a report about the sun. The report about the sun is **mine**.
Use **ours** to show that you and one or more people own something.	**Meg, Bob, and I** drew diagrams. The diagrams are **ours**.
Use **yours** to show that something belongs to one or more people you are talking to.	Have you seen my report, Matt? Yes, that report is **yours**.

Possessive Pronouns	
Singular	**Plural**
mine	ours
yours	yours
his, hers	theirs

Use **his** for one boy or man. Use **hers** for one girl or woman.	Here is **Carole's** desk. The desk is **hers**.
For two or more people, places, or things, use **theirs**.	**Ross and Clare** made posters. The posters are **theirs**.

Adjectives

An adjective describes, or tells about, a noun.

How Adjectives Work

Usually, an **adjective** comes before the noun it tells about.	You can buy **delicious** fruits at the market.
But, an **adjective** can also appear after verbs such as *is, are, look, feel, smell,* and *taste.*	All the fruit looks **fresh**. The shoppers are **happy**.
Adjectives describe • what something is like	The market is a **busy** place.
• the size, color, and shape of something	The **round, brown** baskets are filled with fruits and vegetables.
• what something looks, feels, sounds, or smells like	The **shiny** peppers are in one basket. Another basket has **crunchy** cucumbers. The pineapples are **sweet** and **juicy**.

Some **adjectives** tell "how many" or "in what order."	The sellers have **two** baskets of beans. The **first** basket is near the limes.

If you can count what you see, use:		If you can't count what you see, use:	
many	several	much	not much
a lot of	only a few	a lot of	only a little
few	not any	a little	not any
some	no	some	no

When you don't know the exact number of things, use the adjectives in the chart.	When there's **a lot of** sun, the sellers sit in the shade.
Possessive adjectives tell who owns something.	**I** pick out some oranges. **My** oranges are in the bag. That basket is **Ryan's**. **His** basket is full of apples. **The sellers'** chairs are in the shade. **Their** chairs are under umbrellas.

Adjectives That Compare

Adjectives can help you make a comparison, or show how things are alike or different.

To compare two things, add **-er** to the adjective. You will often use the word **than** in your sentence, too.	This is a **small** pineapple. The guava is **smaller than** the pineapple.
To compare three or more things, add **-est** to the adjective. Always use **the** before the adjective.	The lime is **the smallest** fruit of them all.
For some adjectives, change the spelling before you add **-er** or **-est**. • If the adjective ends in silent **e**, drop the final **e** and add **-er** or **-est**. • If the adjective ends in **y**, change the **y** to **i** and add **-er** or **-est**. • If the adjective has one syllable and ends in one vowel plus one consonant, double the final consonant and add **-er** or **-est**.	larg~~e~~ nic~~e~~ larg**er** nic**er** larg**est** nic**est** pretty**i** crazy**i** pretti**er** crazi**er** pretti**est** crazi**est** big **g** sad **d** bigg**er** sadd**er** bigg**est** sadd**est**
A few adjectives have special forms for comparing things.	good bad little better worse less best worst least
For adjectives with three or more syllables, do not use **-er** or **-est** to compare. Use **more**, **most**, **less**, or **least**.	**YES:** Of all the fruit, the guavas are the **most colorful**. **NO:** Of all the fruit, the guavas are the colorfulest. **YES:** The oranges are **more delicious** than the pears. **NO:** The oranges are deliciouser than the pears.
When you make a comparison, use either **-er** or **more**; or **-est** or **most**. Do <u>not</u> use both.	The oranges are the ~~most~~ juiciest of all the fruits.

Verbs

Verbs tell what the subject of a sentence is, has, or does. They show if something happened in the past, is happening now, or will happen in the future.

Action Verbs

An **action verb** tells what someone or something does.	The children **ride** bikes. They **wear** helmets for safety. They **pedal** as fast as they can.

The Verbs *Have* and *Be*

The verb **to have** tells what the subject of a sentence has.	I **have** a bicycle. It **has** twelve gears. My friend Pedro **has** a bicycle, too. Sometimes we **have** races.	**Forms of the Verb *have*** have has had
The verb **to be** does not show action. It tells what the subject of a sentence is (a noun) or what it is like (an adjective).	I **am** a fan of bicycle races. Pedro **is** excited about our next race.	**Forms of the Verb *be*** am was are were is

Linking Verbs

A few other verbs work like the verb **to be**. They do not show action. They just connect, or link, the subject to a word in the predicate. Some of these verbs are **look**, **seem**, **feel**, **smell**, and **taste**.	My bicycle **looks** fantastic! Pedro and I **feel** ready for the race.

Helping Verbs

A **helping verb** works together with an action verb. A helping verb comes before a **main verb**. Some helping verbs have special meanings.

- Use **can** to tell that someone is able to do something.
- Use **could, may,** or **might** to tell that something is possible.
- Use **must** to tell that somebody has to do something.
- Use **should** to give an opinion or advice.

Pedro and I **are racing** today.
We **will do** our best.

We **can work** as a team.

We **may reach** the finish line first.

We **must pedal** hard to win!

You **should practice** more.

Contractions with Verbs

You can put a subject and verb together to make a **contraction**. In a contraction, an apostrophe (') shows where one or more letters have been left out.

They are riding fast.
They are riding fast.
They're riding fast.

You can make a contraction with the verbs **am**, **are**, and **is**.

Contractions with *Be*

I + am = **I'm**	she + is = **she's**
you + are = **you're**	where + is = **where's**
we + are = **we're**	what + is = **what's**

You can make a contraction with the helping verbs **have**, **has**, and **will**.

Contractions with *Have* and *Will*

I + have = **I've**	he + has = **he's**
you + have = **you've**	I + will = **I'll**
they + have = **they've**	it + will = **it'll**

In contractions with a verb and **not**, the word **not** is shortened to **n't**.

Contractions with *Not*

do + not = **don't**	have + not = **haven't**
did + not = **didn't**	has + not = **hasn't**
are + not = **aren't**	could + not = **couldn't**
was + not = **wasn't**	should + not = **shouldn't**

The contraction of the verb **can** plus **not** has a special spelling.

| can + not = **can't** |

Verbs, *(continued)*

Actions in the Present

All action verbs show when the action happens.

Verbs in the **present tense** show

- that the action happens now.

Pedro **eats** his breakfast.
Then he **takes** his bike out of the garage.

- that the action happens often.

Pedro and I **love** to ride our bikes on weekends.

To show the present tense for the subjects **he, she,** or **it**, add -**s** to the end of most action verbs.

Pedro **checks** the tires on his bike.

He **finds** a flat tire!

- For verbs that end in **x**, **ch**, **sh**, **ss**, or **z**, add -**es.**

Pedro **fixes** the tire.

A pump **pushes** air into it.

- For verbs that end in a consonant plus **y**, change the **y** to **i** and then add -**es**. For verbs that end in a vowel plus **y**, just add -**s**.

"That should do it," he **says** to himself.

He **carries** the pump back into the garage.

- For the subjects **I, you, we,** or **they**, do <u>not</u> add -**s** or -**es.**

I **arrive** at Pedro's house.

We **coast** down the driveway on our bikes.

The **present progressive** form of a verb tells about an action as it is happening. It uses **am, is,** or **are** and a main verb. The main verb ends in -**ing**.

We **are pedaling** faster.

I **am passing** Pedro!

He **is following** right behind me.

Actions in the Past

Verbs in the **past tense** show that the action happened in the past.	Yesterday, I **looked** for sports on TV.
The past tense form of a **regular verb** ends with **-ed**. <ul><li>For most verbs, just add **-ed**.</li><li>For verbs that end in silent **e**, drop the final **e** before you add **-ed**.</li><li>For one-syllable verbs that end in one vowel plus one consonant, double the final consonant before you add **-ed**.</li><li>For verbs that end in **y**, change the **y** to **i** before you add **-ed**. For verbs that end in a vowel plus **y**, just add **-ed**.</li></ul>	I **watched** the race on TV. The bikers **arrived** from all different countries. They **raced** for several hours. People **grabbed** their cameras. They **snapped** pictures of their favorite racer. I **studied** the racer from Italy. I **stayed** close to the TV.
Irregular verbs do not add **-ed** to show the past tense. They have special forms.	The Italian racer **was** fast. He **broke** the speed record!

Some Irregular Verbs

Present Tense	Past Tense
begin	began
do	did
have	had
make	made
take	took
ride	rode
win	won

Verbs, *(continued)*

Actions in the Future

Verbs in the **future tense** tell what will happen later, or in the future.	Tomorrow, Shelley **will clean** her bike.
To show the future tense, you can • add the helping verb **will** before the **main verb**. • use **am going to**, **are going to**, or **is going to** before the **main verb**.	She **will remove** all the dirt. She **is going to remove** all the dirt. I **am going to help** her.
If the **main verb** is a form of the verb **to be**, use **be** to form the future tense.	The bike **will be** spotless. Shelley **is going to be** pleased!
To make negative sentences in the future tense, put the word **not** just after **will**, **am**, **is**, or **are**.	We are **not** going to stop until the bike shines. Pedro is **not** going to believe it. Her bike will **not** be a mess any longer.

Adverbs

An adverb tells more about a verb, an adjective, or another adverb.

How Adverbs Work

An **adverb** can come before or after a **verb** to tell "how," "where," "when," or "how often."	Josh **walks** **quickly** to the bus stop. (how) He **will travel** **downtown** on the bus. (where) He **will arrive** at school **soon**. (when) Josh **never** **misses** a day of school. (how often)
An **adverb** can make an **adjective** or another adverb stronger.	Josh is **really** **good** at baseball. He plays **very well**.
Some **adverbs** compare actions. Add **-er** to compare two actions. Add **-est** to compare three or more actions.	Josh **runs** **fast**. Josh runs **faster** than his best friend. Josh runs the **fastest** of all the players.
A few adverbs have special forms for comparing things.	well → better → best badly → worse → worst
If the adverb ends in **-ly**, use **more**, **most**, **less**, or **least** to compare the actions.	Josh drops a ball *less* frequently than the other players.
When you use **adverbs** to make a comparison with **-er**, **-est**, or with a special form, do not also use **more** or **most**.	Josh jumps ~~more~~ higher than I do. He is ~~more~~ better than I am at catching the ball.
Make sure to use an **adverb** (not an adjective) to tell about a verb.	I do not catch ~~good~~ *well* at all.

Prepositions

A preposition links a noun or pronoun to other words in a sentence. A preposition is the first word in a prepositional phrase.

Prepositions

Some prepositions tell **where** something is.	above over / under below beneath / beside next to by near / in front of / in back of behind / between / in / out / inside / outside / on / off
Some prepositions show **direction**.	up / down / through / across / around / into
Some prepositions tell **when something happens**.	**before** lunch **in** 2003 **on** September 16 **during** lunch **in** September **at** four o'clock **after** lunch **in** the afternoon **from** noon **to** 3:30
Other prepositions have many uses.	**about** **among** **for** **to** **against** **at** **from** **with** **along** **except** **of** **without**

Prepositional Phrases

A **prepositional phrase** starts with a **preposition** and ends with a **noun** or a **pronoun**. Use prepositional phrases to add information or details to your writing.	**At** our school, we did many activities **for** Earth Day. We picked up the trash **along** the fence. Then we planted some flowers **next to** it.

Capital Letters

A word that begins with a capital letter is special in some way.

How to Use Capital Letters

A word that begins with a capital letter is special in some way.

Use a **capital letter** at the beginning of a sentence.	**O**ur class is taking an exciting field trip. **W**e are going to an airplane museum.
Always use a capital letter for the pronoun **I**.	My friends and **I** can't wait!
Use a capital letter for a person's • first and last name • initials • title	**Matt J. Kelly and Matt Ross will ride with Dr. Bye. M**agdalena and I are going with **Mrs. Liu.**

Use a capital letter for the names of • the days of the week and their abbreviations • the twelve months of the year and their abbreviations	We're going the first **S**aturday in **J**anuary.

Days of the Week

Sunday	**S**un.
Monday	**M**on.
Tuesday	**T**ue.
Wednesday	**W**ed.
Thursday	**T**hurs.
Friday	**F**ri.
Saturday	**S**at.

Months of the Year

January	**J**an.
February	**F**eb.
March	**M**ar.
April	**A**pr.
May	
June	
July	
August	**A**ug.
September	**S**ep.
October	**O**ct.
November	**N**ov.
December	**D**ec.

> These months are not abbreviated.

Use a capital letter for each important word in the names of special days and holidays.	That will be after **C**hristmas, **K**wanzaa, and **N**ew **Y**ear's **D**ay. **E**arth **D**ay **F**ourth of **J**uly **H**anukkah **T**hanksgiving

Capital Letters, *(continued)*

More Ways to Use Capital Letters

Use a capital letter for each important word in the names of	
• public places, buildings, and organizations	The **W**ilson **A**irplane **M**useum is in the **V**eterans **M**emorial **H**all. It's in the middle of **V**eterans **P**ark, right next to the **P**iney **W**oods **Z**oo.
• streets, cities, and states	The museum is on **F**light **A**venue. It is the biggest airplane museum in **F**lorida. It's the biggest in the whole **U**nited **S**tates!
• landforms and bodies of water, continents, and planets and stars	**Landforms and Bodies of Water** **Continents** **Planets and Stars** **R**ocky **M**ountains **A**frica **E**arth **S**ahara **D**esert **A**ntarctica **M**ars **G**rand **C**anyon **A**sia the **B**ig **D**ipper **P**acific **O**cean **A**ustralia the **M**ilky **W**ay **C**olorado **R**iver **E**urope **L**ake **E**rie **S**outh **A**merica **N**orth **A**merica
Use a capital letter for the names of countries and adjectives formed from the names of countries.	My friend Magdalena is **C**hilean. She says they don't have a museum like that in **C**hile.
Use a capital letter for each important word in the title of a book, a story, a poem, or a movie.	We are reading *First Flight* about the Wright brothers. Magdalena wrote a poem about Amelia Earhart. She called it "**V**anished from the **S**ky." What a great title!

Punctuation Marks

Punctuation marks make words and sentences easier to understand.

 period  question mark  exclamation point  comma 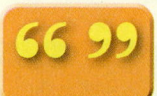 quotation marks  apostrophe

Period

Use a **period** at the end of a statement or a command.	I don't know if I should get a dog or a cat. Please help me decide.
Also use a **period** when you write a decimal, or to separate dollars from cents.	I saw a cute little dog last week. It only weighed 1.3 pounds. But it costs $349.99!
Use a **period** after an initial in somebody's name, and after most abbreviations. But, don't use a period after state abbreviations.	The salesperson gave me this business card: **Kitty B. Perry** **Downtown Pet Sales** **2456 N. Yale Ave.** **Houston, TX 77074** **TX is the abbreviation for the state of Texas.**

Question Mark

Use a **question mark** • at the end of a question • after a question that comes at the end of a statement.	Do you want to go to the pet store with me? You can go right now, can't you?

Exclamation Point

Use an **exclamation point** at the end of a sentence to show strong feelings.	I'm glad you decided to come! This is going to be fun!

Punctuation, *(continued)*

Commas ,

Use a **comma**	
• when you write large numbers	There are more than 1,300 pets at this store.
• to separate three or more things in the same sentence	Should I get a dog, a cat, or a parrot?
• before the words **and**, **but**, or **or** in a compound sentence.	I came to the store last week, and the salesperson showed me some dogs. She was very helpful, but I couldn't make a decision.
Use a **comma** to set off	
• short words like **Oh**, **Yes**, and **Well** that begin a sentence	Oh, what a hard decision! Well, I'd better choose something.
• someone's exact words	The salesperson said, "This little dog wants to go with you." I said, "I like it, but I like those cats, too!"
Use a **comma** between two or more adjectives that tell about the same noun.	Do I get a big, furry puppy? Or do I get a cute, tiny kitten?
Use a **comma** in letters • between the city and state • between the date and the year • after the greeting in a friendly letter • after the closing	177 North Avenue New York, NY 10033 October 3, 2010 Dear Aunt Mia, Can you help me? I want a pet, but don't know which is easier to care for, a cat or a dog? I need your advice. Your niece, Becca

Quotation Marks 66 99

Use quotation marks	
• to show a speaker's exact words	"Ms. Perry, this is the dog for me!" Becca said.
• to show the exact words from a book or other printed material	The ad said "friendly puppies" for sale.
• the title of a magazine or newspaper article	I saw the idea in the article "Keeping Your Pet Happy."
• the title of a chapter from a book.	Now I'm on the chapter "Working Dogs" in my book.
Use periods and commas inside quotation marks.	"Many dogs are good with people," Ms. Perry said. "You just have to decide if you want to big dog or a little one."

> Ms. Perry, this is the dog for me!

Apostrophes ,

Use an **apostrophe** when you write a **possessive noun**.	My **neighbor's** dog is huge. The **Smiths'** yard is just big enough for him.
Use an **apostrophe** to replace the letter or letters left out in a **contraction**.	**Let's** go back to the pet store. **I'll** look some more for the best pet for me.

Picture Dictionary

The definitions are for the words introduced in this book.

Pronunciation Key

Say the sample word out loud to hear how to say, or pronounce, the symbol.

Symbols for Consonant Sounds

b	b<u>o</u>x		p	<u>p</u>an
ch	<u>ch</u>ick		r	<u>r</u>ing
d	<u>d</u>og		s	bu<u>s</u>
f	<u>f</u>ish		sh	<u>f</u>ish
g	<u>g</u>irl		t	<u>h</u>at
h	<u>h</u>at		th	<u>Earth</u>
j	<u>j</u>ar		<u>th</u>	fa<u>th</u>er
k	ca<u>k</u>e		v	<u>v</u>ase
ks	bo<u>x</u>		w	<u>w</u>indow
kw	<u>qu</u>een		hw	<u>wh</u>ale
l	bel<u>l</u>		y	<u>y</u>arn
m	<u>m</u>ouse		z	<u>z</u>ipper
n	pa<u>n</u>		zh	trea<u>s</u>ure
ng	ri<u>ng</u>			

Symbols for Short Vowel Sounds

a	h<u>a</u>t
e	b<u>e</u>ll
i	ch<u>i</u>ck
o	b<u>o</u>x
u	b<u>u</u>s

Symbols for Long Vowel Sounds

ā	c<u>a</u>ke
ē	k<u>e</u>y
ī	b<u>i</u>ke
ō	g<u>oa</u>t
yū	m<u>u</u>le

Symbols for R-controlled Sounds

ar	b<u>ar</u>n
air	ch<u>air</u>
ear	<u>ear</u>
ir	f<u>ire</u>
or	c<u>or</u>n
ur	g<u>ir</u>l

Symbols for Variant Vowel Sounds

ah	f<u>a</u>ther
aw	b<u>a</u>ll
oi	b<u>oy</u>
oo	b<u>oo</u>k
ow	c<u>ow</u>
ü	fr<u>ui</u>t

Miscellaneous Symbols

shun	frac<u>tion</u>	$\frac{1}{2}$
chun	ques<u>tion</u>	?
zhun	divi<u>sion</u>	2)$\overline{100}$ $\frac{50}{}$

Parts of an Entry

The **entry** shows how the word is spelled.

The **pronunciation** shows you how to say the word and how to break it into syllables.

The **picture** helps you understand more about the meaning of the word.

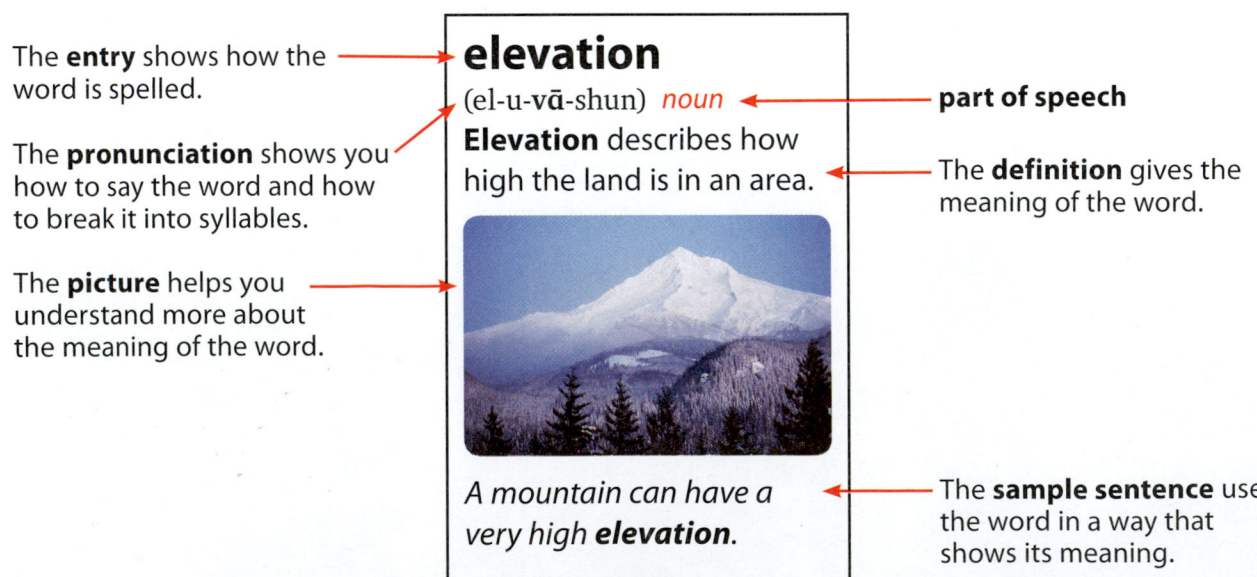

elevation

(el-u-vā-shun) *noun*

Elevation describes how high the land is in an area.

*A mountain can have a very high **elevation**.*

part of speech

The **definition** gives the meaning of the word.

The **sample sentence** uses the word in a way that shows its meaning.

A

ability
(u-**bi**-lu-tē) *noun*
An **ability** is a skill.

*This girl has the **ability** to play the flute.*

accelerate
(ik-**se**-lu-rāt) *verb*
When someone **accelerates** they move faster.

*A racecar **accelerates** to the finish line.*

adaptation
(a-dap-**tā**-shun) *noun*
An **adaptation** is a change that a species develops to live in an environment.

*A giraffe's long neck and legs are **adaptations** so it can eat from tall trees.*

adventure
(ud-**ven**-chur) *noun*
An **adventure** is an exciting experience.

*Early explorers had many **adventures**.*

ancestor
(an-**ses**-tur) *noun*
An **ancestor** is a family member who lived a long time ago.

*The boy is learning about his **ancestors**.*

ancient
(**ānt**-shunt) *adjective*
When something is **ancient**, it is very old or it happened in the past.

*There are **ancient** buildings all around the world.*

a
b
c
d
e
f
g
h
i
j
k
l
m
n
o
p
q
r
s
t
u
v
w
x
y
z

archaeologist

(ar-kē-**ah**-lu-jist) *noun*

An **archaeologist** is someone who studies old buildings and civilizations.

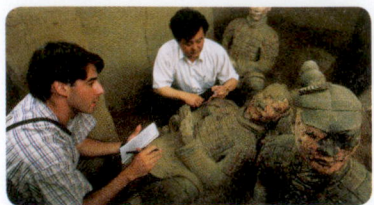

Archaeologists discover new information about ancient cultures.

artifact

(ar-ti-**fakt**) *noun*

An **artifact** is something that a human made long ago, such as a tool or a weapon.

Artifacts such as these arrowheads were used for hunting.

astronaut

(**as**-tru-nawt) *noun*

An **astronaut** is someone who travels in space.

Astronauts wear special equipment so they can breathe in space.

atmosphere

(**at**-mu-sfear) *noun*

The **atmosphere** is the mixture of gases that are all around a planet.

*Clouds form in the **atmosphere**.*

available

(u-**vā**-lu-bul) *adjective*

When something is **available**, it is ready to take.

*Fresh fruit is **available** in summer.*

average

(**a**-vu-rij) *noun*

An **average** is an amount that is usual for a group.

*Bears have an **average** of two cubs.*

balance

(ba-luns) *noun*

When something is in **balance**, it is steady.

*If she keeps her **balance**, she will not fall.*

behavior

(bi-**hā**-vyur) *noun*

Behavior is how a living thing acts.

*You can train an animal to learn a new **behavior**.*

C

belief
(bu-**lēf**) *noun*
A **belief** is a feeling that something is true.

*What is your **belief** about hard work?*

benefit
(**be**-nu-fit) *noun*
A **benefit** is something helpful.

*One **benefit** of living near school is that you can walk there.*

border
(**bor**-dur) *noun*
A **border** is an edge or outline.

*The frame makes a **border** around the art.*

canyon
(**kan**-yun) *noun*
A **canyon** is a very deep valley.

*Most **canyons** are formed by rivers.*

capacity
(ku-**pa**-su-tē) *noun*
The **capacity** of an object is the most it can hold.

*This bucket has a **capacity** of 1 gallon.*

ceremony
(**ser**-u-mō-nē) *noun*
A **ceremony** is a special event where something is celebrated.

*They exchange rings at their wedding **ceremony**.*

characteristic
(kair-ik-tu-**ris**-tik) *noun*
A **characteristic** is a feature.

*White marks are a **characteristic** of this snake.*

chart
(**chart**) *noun*
A **chart** shows information with numbers, pictures, and symbols.

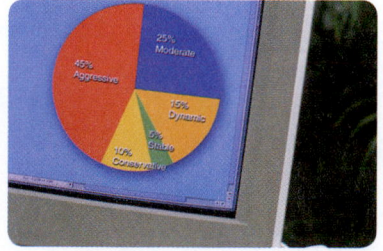

*This **chart** is on a computer screen.*

a
b
c
d
e
f
g
h
i
j
k
l
m
n
o
p
q
r
s
t
u
v
w
x
y
z

a
b
c
d
e
f
g
h
i
j
k
l
m
n
o
p
q
r
s
t
u
v
w
x
y
z

civilization

(si-vu-lu-**zā**-shun) *noun*

A **civilization** is an organized society of people.

*There have been many advanced **civilizations** around the world.*

coastal

(**kōs**-tul) *adjective*

Coastal areas are sections of land next to an ocean.

*Large waves often crash into **coastal** areas.*

colony

(**kah**-lu-nē) *noun*

A **colony** is a region that another country controls.

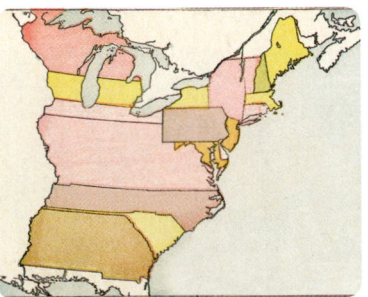

*These states were **colonies** of England.*

command

(ku-**mand**) *noun*

A **command** is an order for what someone wants you to do.

*The general gave a **command** to his troops.*

communication

(ku-myū-nu-**kā**-shun) *noun*

Communication is the sharing of information.

*Cell phones have made **communication** easier.*

compass

(**kum**-pus) *noun*

A **compass** is a tool with a magnet that can show you which direction is north.

***Compasses** help sailors know where to go.*

competition

(kom-pu-**ti**-shun) *noun*

A **competition** is a contest.

*The runners are in **competition** to win the race.*

conservation

(kon-sir-**vā**-shun) *noun*
Conservation means saving or protecting something.

*Through **conservation**, many animals' lives have been saved.*

constant

(**kon**-stunt) *noun*
Something that never changes is a **constant**.

*The number of days in a week is a **constant**.*

contain

(kun-**tān**) *verb*
To **contain** something is to hold it inside.

*This jar **contains** many coins.*

continent

(**kon**-tu-nunt) *noun*
A **continent** is a large body of land.

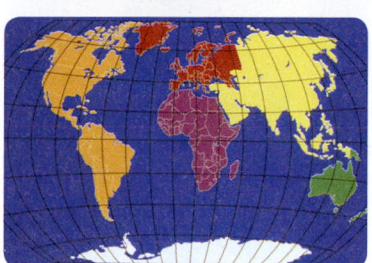

*Africa is one of the seven **continents** on Earth.*

control

(kun-**trōl**) *verb*
To **control** something is to be in charge of it.

*The driver **controls** where the car goes.*

convert

(kun-**vurt**) *verb*
When you **convert** something, you change it from one thing into another.

*A solar panel **converts** sunlight into electricity.*

country

(**kun**-trē) *noun*
A **country** is a nation with its land and people.

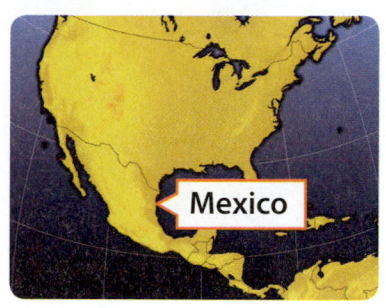

Mexico

*Mexico is a **country** in North America.*

courage

(**kur**-ij) *noun*
If you have **courage**, you are brave.

*It takes **courage** to do challenging things.*

a
b
c
d
e
f
g
h
i
j
k
l
m
n
o
p
q
r
s
t
u
v
w
x
y
z

craft
(kraft) *noun*
Crafts are usually items that you make by hand.

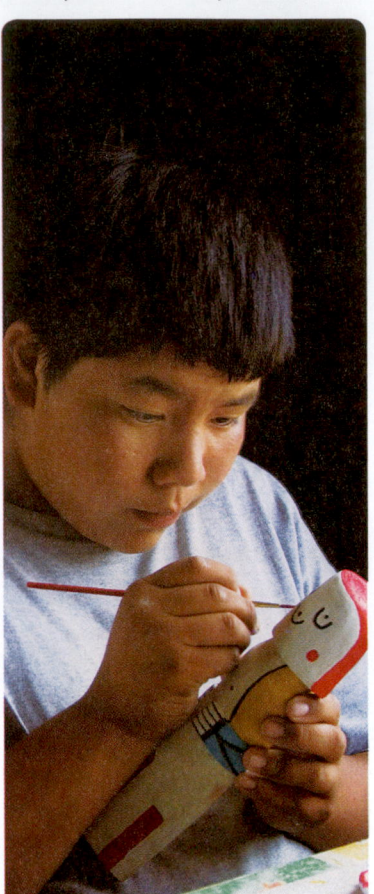

Making dolls by hand is a **craft**.

create
(krē-āt) *verb*
To **create** means to make something new.

The tiles **create** *a pattern on the floor.*

culture
(kul-chur) *noun*
People's ideas and way of life make up a **culture**.

Sports can be part of a **culture**.

currency
(kur-unt-sē) *noun*
Currency is the type of money that is used in an area.

The dollar is the **currency** *in the United States.*

current
(kur-unt) *adjective*
When something is **current**, it is happening now.

You can see **current** *news stories on TV.*

custom
(kus-tum) *noun*
A **custom** is the usual way of doing something.

Their **custom** *is to eat cereal for breakfast.*

decompose
(dē-kum-pōz) *verb*
Something **decomposes** when it breaks down. Living things decompose after they die.

A fallen tree will soon **decompose**.

622

defend

(di-**fend**) *verb*

When something **defends** itself, it protects itself from danger.

*A porcupine can **defend** itself.*

discovery

(dis-**ku**-vu-rē) *noun*

When you find things, you make a **discovery**.

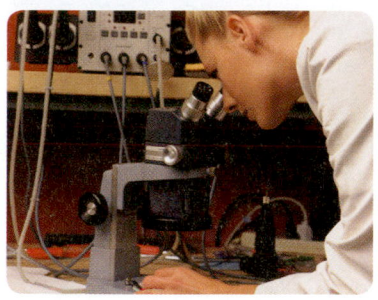

*Her **discovery** is a new germ.*

distance

(**dis**-tuns) *noun*

Distance is the amount of space between two things.

*Today, we can fly a long **distance** very quickly.*

E

electricity

(i-**lek**-tri-su-tē) *noun*

Electricity is a form of energy that can produce light, heat, and power.

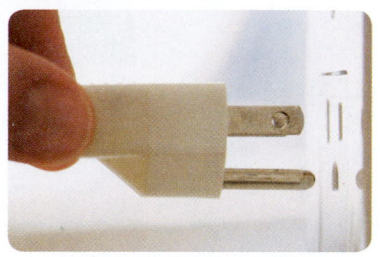

*People use **electricity** to power their appliances.*

element

(**e**-lu-munt) *noun*

An **element** is a simple part of something that is bigger.

*Wind is one **element** in a storm.*

elevation

(el-u-**vā**-shun) *noun*

Elevation describes how high the land is in an area.

*A mountain can have a very high **elevation**.*

empire

(**em**-pīr) *noun*

An **empire** is a group of countries under one ruler.

*As the Roman **Empire** spread, so did the Latin language.*

environment

(in-**vī**-run-munt) *noun*

An **environment** is the area where something lives.

*Plants grow well in a sunny **environment**.*

*Wet **environments**, such as rain forests, are also rich in plant life.*

a b c **d** **e** f g h i j k l m n o p q r s t u v w x y z

623

a b c **d** **e** **f** g h i j k l m n o p q r s t u v w x y z

equator

(i-**kwā**-tur) *noun*

The **equator** is an imaginary line that separates the northern and southern hemispheres of the earth.

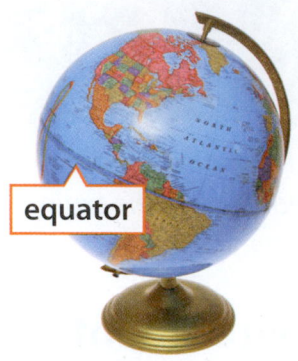

*The **equator** goes all the way around the earth.*

*Countries along the **equator** include Ecuador, Colombia, and Brazil.*

examine

(ig-**za**-mun) *verb*

To **examine** something is to look at it closely.

*With a hand lens, you can **examine** a butterfly.*

experiment

(ik-**sper**-u-munt) *noun*

An **experiment** is a test that people do to find out how things work.

*Her **experiment** on plant growth won first prize.*

exploration

(ek-splu-**rā**-shun) *noun*

An **exploration** is a search.

*Astronauts learn about space from their **exploration**.*

express

(ik-**spres**) *verb*

To **express** yourself means to show how you feel.

*A smile can **express** joy.*

F

feature

(**fē**-chur) *noun*

A **feature** is part of something.

*Sharp teeth are **features** that help sharks hunt.*

flow

(**flō**) *verb*

To **flow** is to move freely.

*Water **flows** from a fountain without stopping.*

force

(**fors**) *noun*

A **force** is a great power in nature.

*The **force** of rushing water can break apart roads.*

G

galleon

(ga-lē-un) *noun*

A **galleon** is a large sailing ship that was used hundreds of years ago.

In the 17th century, people would sail galleons all around the world.

generate

(je-nu-rāt) *verb*

To **generate** something is to make it from other materials.

Windmills are used to generate electricity.

globe

(glōb) *noun*

A **globe** is a ball with the map of the earth on it.

globe

The students studied the globe in their social studies class.

H

habitat

(ha-bu-tat) *noun*

A **habitat** is a place where an organism can live and flourish.

Some snakes live in a hot, desert habitat.

height

(hīt) *noun*

Height is the measurement of how tall someone or something is.

These boys are different heights.

hemisphere

(he-mu-sfear) *noun*

A **hemisphere** is one half of the earth.

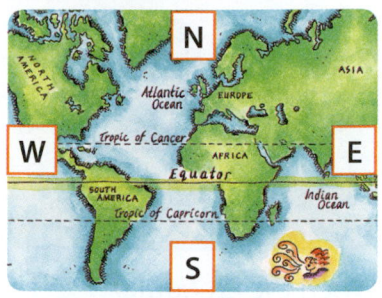

The equator separates the two hemispheres.

heritage

(hair-u-tij) *noun*

Your **heritage** is the traditions, ideas, and language that come from your ancestors.

Playing a traditional instrument is part of his Indonesian heritage.

a
b
c
d
e
f
g
h
i
j
k
l
m
n
o
p
q
r
s
t
u
v
w
x
y
z

a
b
c
d
e
f
g
h
i
j
k
l
m
n
o
p
q
r
s
t
u
v
w
x
y
z

hero

(hēr-ō) *noun*

A **hero** is a person admired by others for being brave.

*When the firefighter rescued the child, everyone said he was a **hero**.*

humid

(hyū-mud) *adjective*

It is **humid** when there is a lot of moisture in the air.

*A hot and **humid** greenhouse is good for plants.*

I

imagine

(i-mɑ-jun) *verb*

To **imagine** something is to picture it in your mind.

*Your art shows others what you **imagine**.*

imitate

(i-mu-tāt) *verb*

When you **imitate** something, you try to copy it.

*Babies will try to **imitate** their mothers' smiles.*

influence

(in-flü-unts) *verb*

To **influence** someone is to affect that person.

*Family members can **influence** your interests.*

inhabitant

(in-hɑ-bu-tunt) *noun*

An **inhabitant** is a person who lives somewhere.

*These people are **inhabitants** of Japan.*

inherit

(in-hair-ut) *verb*

To **inherit** means to get things, usually from parents.

*Skunks **inherit** their stripes.*

interact

(in-tur-ɑkt) *verb*

When you **interact**, you communicate in some way.

*This girl **interacts** with the horse.*

interpret

(in-**tur**-prut) *verb*

To **interpret** something is to tell what you think it means.

*Can you **interpret** these signs?*

introduce

(in-tru-**düs**) *verb*

When people **introduce** themselves, they meet for the first time.

*A handshake is a friendly way to **introduce** yourself.*

invade

(in-**vād**) *verb*

To **invade** something is to take it over without permission.

*Sometimes people **invade** natural habitats.*

investigate

(in-**ves**-tu-gāt) *verb*

When you **investigate** something, you find out about it.

*The boy **investigates** the cave.*

L

landform

(**land**-form) *noun*

A **landform** is the natural shape of a section of land.

*A mountain is a large **landform**.*

landscape

(**land**-skāp) *noun*

A **landscape** is a large area of land.

*These hills are part of this pretty green **landscape**.*

language

(**lang**-gwij) *noun*

Language is a way of sharing ideas.

*Writing is a form of **language**.*

a
b
c
d
e
f
g
h
i
j
k
l
m
n
o
p
q
r
s
t
u
v
w
x
y
z

a
b
c
d
e
f
g
h
i
j
k
l
m
n
o
p
q
r
s
t
u
v
w
x
y
z

launch

(**lawnch**) *verb*

When you **launch** something, you send it up into the air.

*This rocket was **launched** into space.*

learn

(**lurn**) *verb*

To **learn** is to gain new skills and information.

*This calf must **learn** to walk.*

legend

(**le**-jund) *noun*

A **legend** explains symbols on a map.

*This **legend** shows blue lines as rivers.*

limit

(**li**-mut) *verb*

To **limit** something is to stop it after a set time or amount.

*Many parents **limit** TV viewing.*

locate

(**lō**-kāt) *verb*

To **locate** is to find.

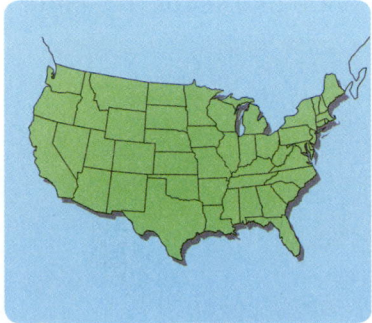

*We use maps to **locate** cities and states.*

M

map

(**map**) *noun*

A **map** is a drawing of Earth's surface, or a part of it.

*The class looks at the world **map**.*

marriage

(**mair**-ij) *noun*

A **marriage** is a wedding ceremony that unites a husband and wife.

*They had a lovely **marriage** ceremony.*

628

material

(mu-**tear**-ē-ul) *noun*

Materials are the small parts that make up something bigger.

*Sand is a **material** used in cement.*

measure

(**me**-zhur) *verb*

When you **measure** something, you find out its size, weight or amount.

*The girl is using a ruler to **measure** her cat.*

*The scale **measures** the weight of the orange.*

medium

(mē-dē-um) *noun*

A **medium** is a form of communication.

*Radio is one **medium** for news.*

memory

(**mem**-rē) *noun*

Memory is the power to recall or remember events.

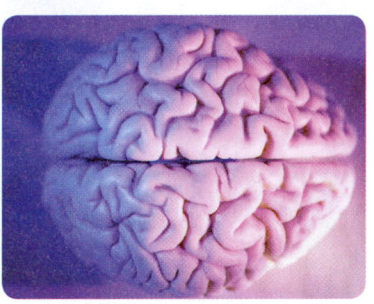

***Memory** is stored in the brain.*

merchant

(**mur**-chunt) *noun*

A **merchant** is someone who buys or sells items.

*People buy fish from this **merchant**.*

migration

(mī-**grā**-shun) *noun*

During a **migration**, people or animals move from one place to another.

*These birds fly south in their yearly **migration**.*

mission

(**mi**-shun) *noun*

A **mission** is a job with a goal.

*Their **mission** is to rescue people after an earthquake.*

modify

(**mah**-du-fī) *verb*

When you **modify** something, you change it.

***Modify** a jar to make a bird feeder.*

a b c d e f g h i j k l **m** n o p q r s t u v w x y z

a
b
c
d
e
f
g
h
i
j
k
l
m
n
o
p
q
r
s
t
u
v
w
x
y
z

mold
(mōld) *noun*
Mold is a fungus that grows on old food.

*This bread has a lot of **mold** on it.*

motion
(mō-shun) *noun*
Motion is movement.

*A racecar's **motion** is very fast!*

motive
(mō-tiv) *noun*
A **motive** is a reason for doing something.

*One **motive** for studying is to get good grades.*

musical
(myū-zi-kul) *adjective*
When someone plays an instrument or sings well, they are **musical**.

*It was a very **musical** performance.*

native
(nā-tiv) *adjective*
When living things are **native** to an area, they live and grow there naturally.

*In many desert regions, the cactus is a **native** plant.*

natural
(na-chu-rul) *adjective*
Something is **natural** if it wasn't made by humans.

*This is a **natural** rock formation.*

navigation
(na-vu-gā-shun) *noun*
Navigation is the process of figuring out how to get somewhere.

*With careful **navigation** the boat can pass through the icebergs safely.*

object
(ob-jekt) *noun*
An **object** is something that isn't alive that you can touch and see.

clock

remote control

ball glove

*These are all **objects**.*

occasion

(u-**kā**-zhun) *noun*

An **occasion** is a special event.

*The birthday party was a fun **occasion**.*

ocean

(**ō**-shun) *noun*

The **ocean** is the salt water that covers almost three-fourths of Earth.

***Oceans** are very large bodies of water.*

official

(u-**fi**-shul) *adjective*

When something is **official**, it's approved.

*This **official** seal is from the president's office.*

orbit

(**or**-but) *verb*

In space, something **orbits** when it moves around a sun, a moon, or a planet in a predictable path.

*The planets **orbit** around the sun.*

P

pattern

(**pa**-turn) *noun*

A **pattern** is a design that repeats more than once.

*This floor has an interesting **pattern**.*

perform

(pur-**form**) *verb*

You **perform** when you put on a show for other people.

*These students **perform** for the school.*

physical

(**fi**-zi-kul) *adjective*

Something you can see and touch is a **physical** object.

*Soccer is a very **physical** sport.*

plain

(**plān**) *noun*

A **plain** is a large area of flat, nearly treeless land.

*Bison live on America's Great **Plains**.*

a
b
c
d
e
f
g
h
i
j
k
l
m
n
o
p
q
r
s
t
u
v
w
x
y
z

planet

(**pla**-nut) *noun*

A **planet** is a large body that orbits around the sun or another star.

*Saturn is one of the **planets** in our solar system.*

plateau

(pla-**tō**) *noun*

A **plateau** is a high, flat area of land.

plateau

*The **plateau** rises above the plains.*

population

(pah-pyū-**lā**-shun) *noun*

The **population** is the number of living things that are in an area.

*China has a very large **population** of people.*

port

(port) *noun*

A **port** is a safe place where boats can dock.

*The boats stay in the **port**.*

pottery

(**pah**-tu-rē) *noun*

Objects made out of clay are called **pottery**.

*This terracotta vase and pitcher are examples of **pottery**.*

power

(**pow**-ur) *noun*

Power is the ability or strength to do something.

*The **power** of the earthquake destroyed the building.*

predator

(**pre**-du-tur) *noun*

A **predator** is an animal that eats other animals.

*Many birds are **predators** to insects.*

preserve

(pri-**zurv**) *verb*

To **preserve** something is to keep it safe from harm.

*Use scrapbooks to **preserve** old photos.*

a b c d e f g h i j k l m n o **p** q r s t u v w x y z

R

president

(**pre**-zu-dunt) *noun*

A **president** is an elected leader of a country.

*George Washington was the first **president** of the United States.*

prey

(**prā**) *noun*

Prey is an animal that is hunted for food.

*The rabbit is **prey** for the bobcat.*

principle

(**prin**-su-pul) *noun*

A **principle** is a rule or law.

*Some U.S. laws are based on the **principles** of freedom.*

project

(**prah**-jekt) *noun*

A **project** is a job or activity.

*Building a skyscraper is a huge **project**.*

protect

(pru-**tekt**) *verb*

You **protect** something when you guard it against harm.

*Seat belts help to **protect** people in cars.*

range

(**rānj**) *noun*

A **range** is a group of things in a certain order.

*The Rocky Mountains are a mountain **range**.*

rate

(**rāt**) *noun*

Rate is the speed at which something is happening.

*Turtles move at a slow **rate**.*

record

(**re**-kurd) *noun*

A **record** of something is the facts about what happened.

clay tablet

*Because many ancient people wrote down information, we have a **record** of their lives.*

a
b
c
d
e
f
g
h
i
j
k
l
m
n
o
p
q
r
s
t
u
v
w
x
y
z

region

(rē-jun) *noun*

A **region** is an area of land.

Oregon

*Oregon is in the northwest **region** of the country.*

relate

(ri-lāt) *verb*

To **relate** two things, think about how they are connected.

*You can **relate** these two sports.*

relationship

(ri-la-shun-ship) *noun*

A **relationship** is the way people or things are connected.

*Friends have a good **relationship**.*

renewable

(ri-nü-u-bul) *adjective*

Something is **renewable** when you can't use up all of it.

*Wind is a **renewable** resource.*

resistance

(ri-zis-tunts) *noun*

Resistance is a slowing force.

*Deep snow creates **resistance** when you walk in it.*

resource

(rē-sors) *noun*

A **resource** is something that people need and use.

*School supplies are **resources** for students.*

response

(ri-spons) *noun*

A **response** is an answer.

*These students want to give a **response** to a question.*

responsible

(ri-spon-su-bul) *adjective*

A person who is **responsible** is in charge.

*This dad is **responsible** for his son.*

risk
(risk) *noun*

Risk is the possibility of harm.

*Wearing a helmet lowers your **risk** when you ride a bike.*

ritual
(ri-chu-wul) *noun*

A **ritual** is a special series of events, often done as a ceremony.

*Many people have **rituals** that use water.*

role
(rōl) *noun*

A **role** is a part or a purpose.

*Each actor plays an important **role** in the school play.*

*The dog's **role** is to lead the blind man safely.*

rotation
(rō-tā-shun) *noun*

The **rotation** of something is how it turns around its axis.

*A globe shows the **rotation** of Earth.*

route
(rüt) *noun*

A **route** is a path to go someplace.

*Do you take the shortest **route** to school?*

S

scale
(skāl) *noun*

A **scale** gives size comparisons.

*The **scale** of this map shows that 1 inch is equal to 1 mile.*

a b c d e f g h i j k l m n o p q r s t u v w x y z

a
b
c
d
e
f
g
h
i
j
k
l
m
n
o
p
q
r
s
t
u
v
w
x
y
z

scarce

(skairs) *adjective*

Something is **scarce** if there is not a lot of it.

*Water can be very **scarce** in the desert.*

service

(**sur**-vus) *noun*

When something is of **service**, it is useful.

*A cart is of **service** when you move heavy boxes.*

site

(sīt) *noun*

A **site** is a special place where something happened.

*People study archeological **sites** to learn about ancient cultures.*

skill

(skil) *noun*

A **skill** is the ability that someone has to do something.

*It takes a lot of **skill** to play soccer well.*

solve

(solv) *verb*

To **solve** a problem means to figure it out.

*When you **solve** a puzzle, it's done.*

species

(spē-shēz) *noun*

A **species** is a group of living things that are very similar and can have offspring.

*Cats and dogs are different **species**.*

speed

(spēd) *noun*

Speed is how fast something is going.

*A racecar travels at a very high **speed**.*

spore

(spor) *noun*

Spores are small, seed-like structures that are made by plants that don't reproduce using flowers.

*A fern reproduces by releasing **spores**.*

spread

(spred) *verb*

To **spread** is to cover a wide area.

*Flies can **spread** diseases.*

strategy

(stra-tu-jē) *noun*

A **strategy** is a careful plan.

*This girl has a **strategy** for winning the game.*

style

(stī-ul) *noun*

A **style** is a special way of doing something.

*These artists have their own **style** of working. She likes to paint and he works in stone.*

suggest

(sug-jest) *verb*

To **suggest** is to give someone an idea.

*These colors **suggest** strong heat.*

surface

(sur-fus) *noun*

The **surface** of something is its top layer or cover.

*A table has a flat **surface**.*

survival

(sur-vī-vul) *noun*

Survival means living.

***Survival** is difficult in very cold places.*

T

technology

(tek-nah-lu-jē) *noun*

Technology is the use of science to solve problems.

*Doctors rely on **technology**, such as X-ray machines.*

a b c d e f g h i j k l m n o p q r **s** **t** u v w x y z

a
b
c
d
e
f
g
h
i
j
k
l
m
n
o
p
q
r
s
t
u
v
w
x
y
z

threatened

(**thre**-tund) *verb*

Something is **threatened** when it is in danger.

Because of habitat destruction, many rainforest animals are threatened.

tool

(**tül**) *noun*

A **tool** is something that helps you do a task.

A hammer is a tool that helps you pound nails into wood.

trade

(**trād**) *verb*

To **trade** is to exchange one thing for another.

The friends trade toys.

tradition

(tru-**di**-shun) *noun*

A **tradition** is a custom or belief shared by a group of people.

It's a tradition to dress up to celebrate the Chinese New Year.

trait

(**trāt**) *noun*

A **trait** is a characteristic that distinguishes one thing from something else.

One trait of a gazelle is that it can run quickly.

transport

(trants-**port**) *verb*

To **transport** something is to carry it.

Large ships transport goods across the ocean.

treasure

(**tre**-zhur) *noun*

A **treasure** is a collection of jewels, money, or other valuable items.

Gold coins are the treasure in this chest.

valley

(**va**-lē) *noun*

A **valley** is a low area of land between two higher areas.

This valley has a river running through it.

value

(val-yū) *verb*

To **value** something is to care about it.

*Many people **value** saving money.*

volunteer

(vah-lun-**tear**) *noun*

A **volunteer** is someone who helps out with a task without being paid.

*This **volunteer** is giving food to people who need it.*

weave

(wēv) *verb*

When you **weave**, you lace threads, grass, or other materials together in a pattern.

*She **weaves** thread into beautiful cloth.*

*A tapestry is something people can **weave**. This one was made in Africa.*

a
b
c
d
e
f
g
h
i
j
k
l
m
n
o
p
q
r
s
t
u
v
w
x
y
z

Handwriting

It's important to use your best **penmanship**, or handwriting. That way your audience will be able to read what you write.

Handwriting Hints

You can **print** your words or write in **cursive**.

Cursive

Cursive is good to use for longer pieces, such as letters or stories, because you can write faster. You don't have to lift your pencil between letters. Also, cursive writing gives your finished pieces a polished look. When you write in cursive, hold the pencil and paper this way.

Left-handed   Right-handed

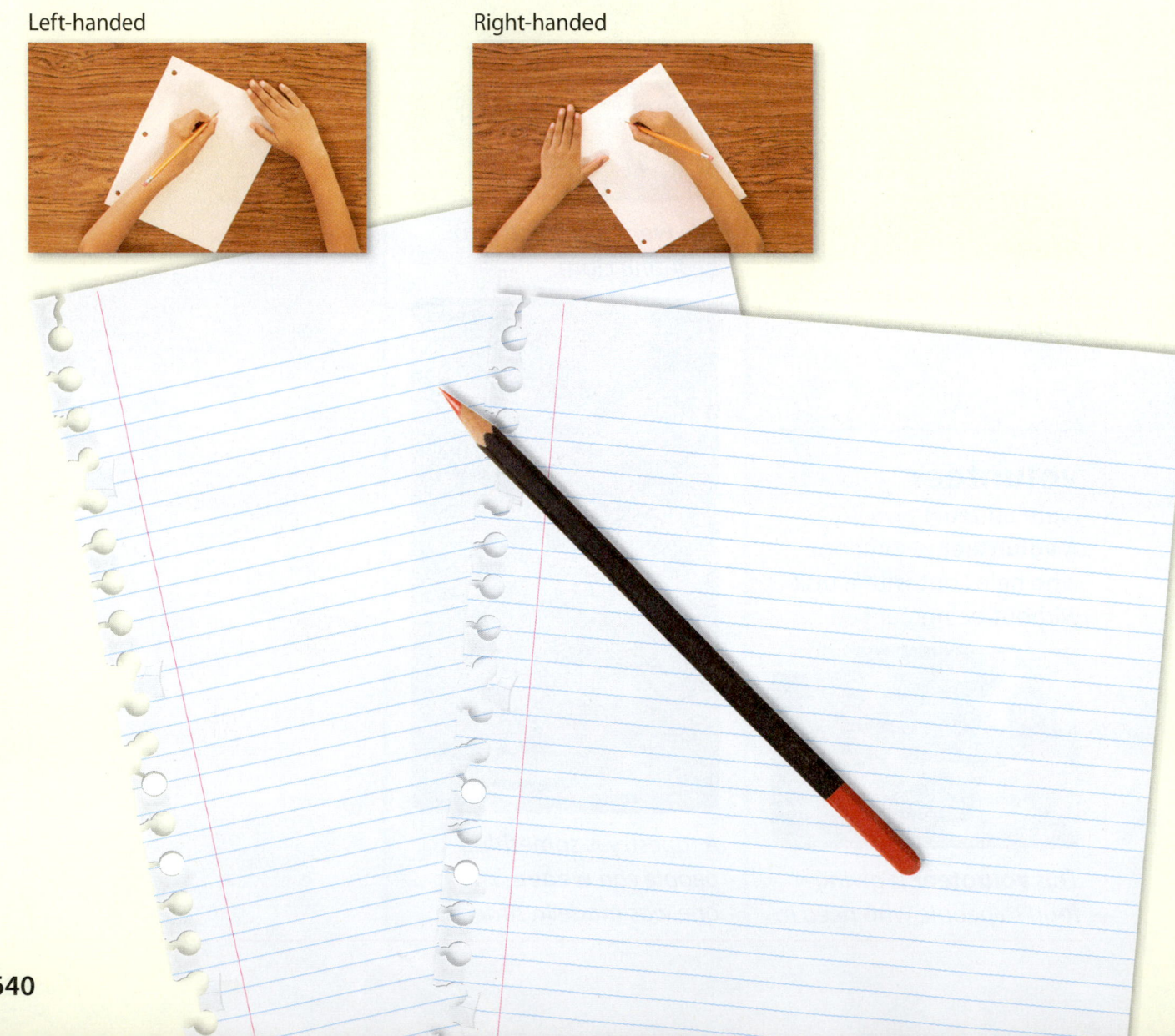

Cursive Alphabet

Capital Letters

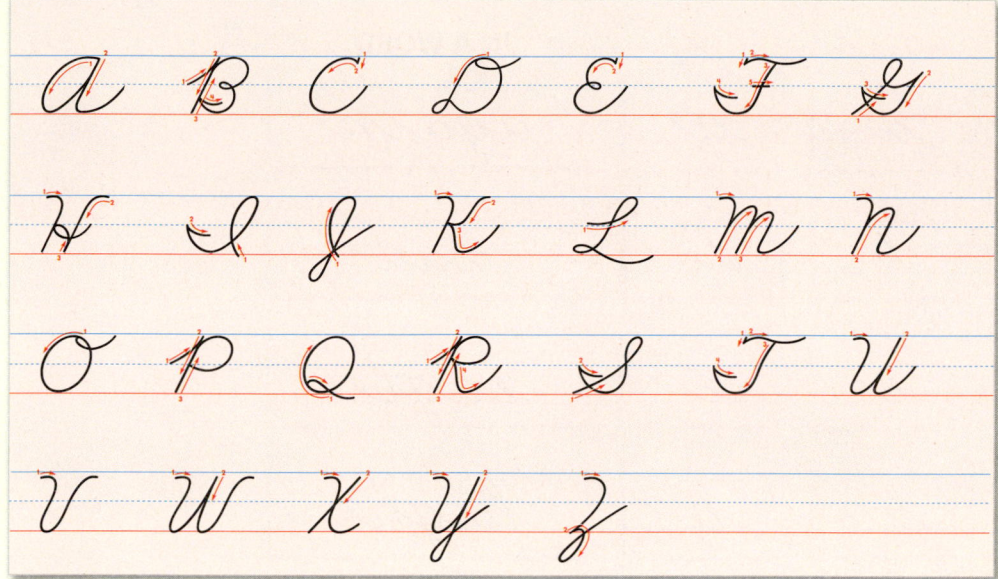

Lowercase Letters

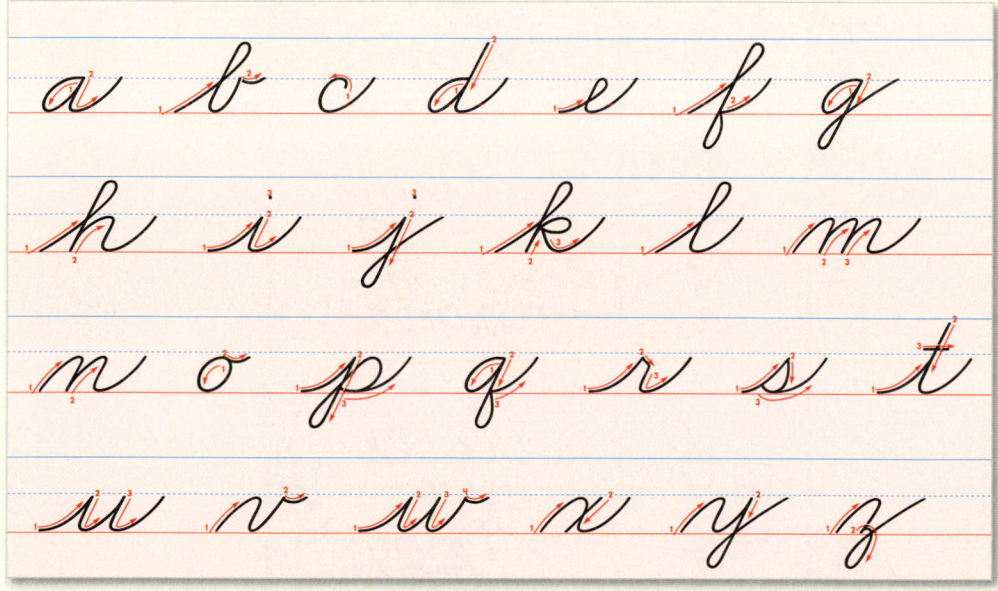

Handwriting, *continued*

Writing Cursive Letters

Be careful not to make these common mistakes when you write in **cursive**.

MISTAKE	NOT OK	OK	IN A WORD
The **a** looks like a **u**.	*u*	*a*	*again*
The **d** looks like a **c** and an **l**.	*d*	*d*	*dad*
The **e** is too narrow.	*e*	*e*	*eagle*
The **h** looks like an **l** and an **i**.	*h*	*h*	*high*
The **i** has no dot.	*i*	*i*	*inside*
The **n** looks like a **w**.	*w*	*n*	*none*
The **o** looks like an **a**.	*a*	*o*	*onion*
The **r** looks like an **i** with no dot.	*r*	*r*	*roar*
The **t** is not crossed.	*l*	*t*	*title*
The **t** is crossed too high.	*t*	*t*	*that*

Writing Words and Sentences

- Slant your letters all the same way.

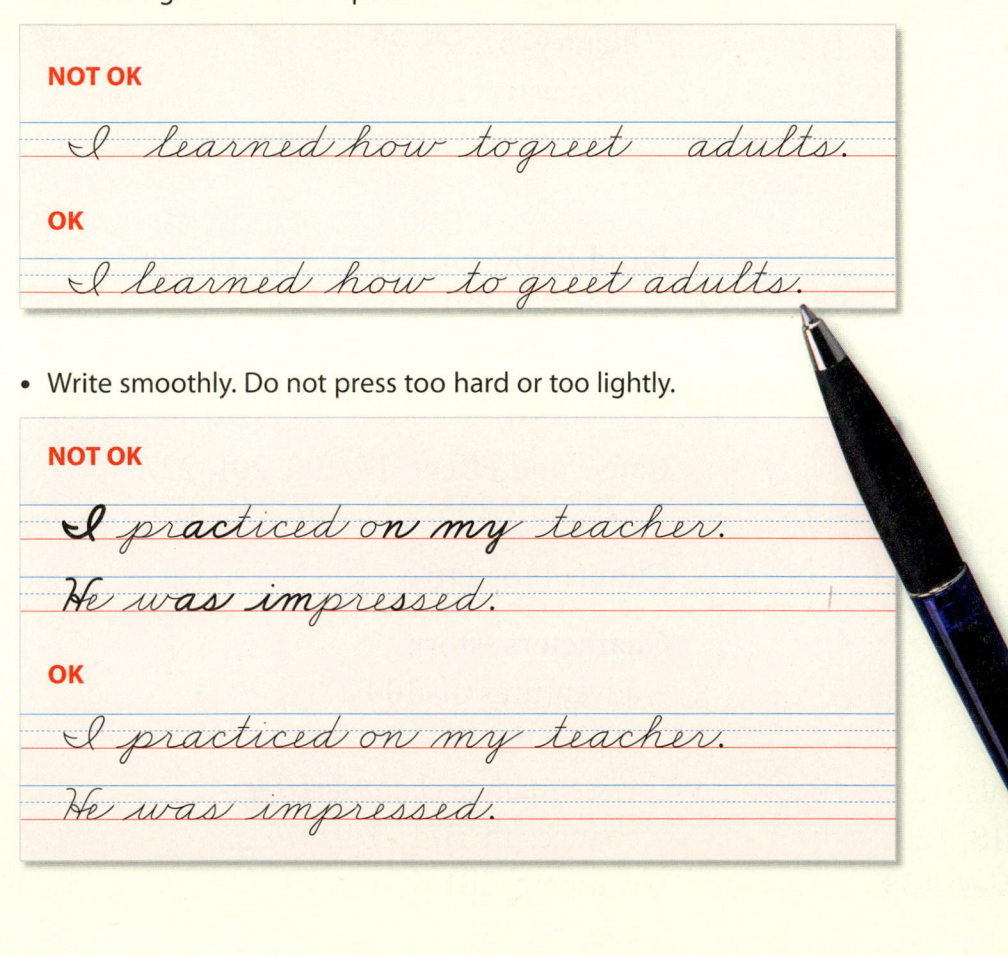

NOT OK

My Chinese-language class today was interesting.

OK

My Chinese-language class today was interesting.

- Put the right amount of space between words.

NOT OK

I learned how togreet   adults.

OK

I learned how to greet adults.

- Write smoothly. Do not press too hard or too lightly.

NOT OK

I practiced on my teacher.
He was impressed.

OK

I practiced on my teacher.
He was impressed.

Index

Acknowledgments, continued

Text Credits

Unit One

Peachtree Publishers: *Martina the Beautiful Cockroach* by Carmen Agra Deedy. Text copyright © 2007 by Carmen Agra Deedy. Reprinted by permission of Peachtree Publishers.

Highlights for Children: "Shaped by Tradition," from *A Touch of Genius* by Patricia Millman, November 2000, Volume 55, Number 11, Issue No. 589. Copyright © 2000 by Highlights for Children, Inc., Columbus, Ohio. Reprinted by permission.

Skipping Stones: Adaptation of "Coming of Age" by Jyotsna Grandhi, from *Skipping Stones*, January/February 2009. Copyright © 2009 by Skipping Stones. Reprinted by permission of Skipping Stones, www.skippingstones.org.

Unit Two

Lerner Publishing Group, Inc.: *Love and Roast Chicken* by Barbara Knutson. Copyright © 2004 by Barbara Knutson. Reprinted with the permission of Carolrhoda Books, a division of Lerner Publishing Group, Inc. All rights reserved. No part of this excerpt may be used or reproduced in any manner whatsoever without the prior written permission of Lerner Publishing Group, Inc.

Shepard Publications: Excerpt adapted from *The Adventures of Mouse Deer: Tales of Indonesia and Malaysia* told by Aaron Shepard from www.aaronshep.com/stories/RO1.html, April 9, 2009. Copyright © 1995 by Shepard Publications. Reprinted by permission.

Unit Three

Farrar Straus & Giroux, LLC: *How I Learned Geography* by Uri Shulevitz. Copyright © 2008 by Uri Shulevitz. Reprinted by permission of Farrar, Straus and Giroux, LLC.

Houghton Mifflin Harcourt: "Tortillas like Africa" from *Canto Familiar* by Gary Soto. Copyright © 1995 by Gary Soto. Reprinted by permission of Houghton Mifflin Harcourt Publishing Company. All rights reserved.

Unit Four

Random House, Inc.: *Doña Flor* by Pat Mora, illustrated by Raúl Colón. Text copyright © 2005 by Pat Mora. Illustrations © 2005 by Raúl Colón. Reprinted by permission of Random House, Inc.

Victor M. Valle: "Comida," by Victor M. Valle from *Fiesta in Aztlan: Anthology of Chicano Poetry*. Text copyright © 1981 by Victor M. Valle. Reprinted by permission of the author. All rights reserved.

Moira Andrew: "The Sun in Me," by Moira Andrew. First published by Barefoot Books. Copyright © 2003 by Moira Andrew. Reprinted by permission of the author. All rights reserved.

Unit Five

Scholastic, Inc.: Adapted from *The Fungus that Ate My School* by Arthur Dorros, illustrated by David Catrow. Text copyright © 2000 by Arthur Dorros. Illustrations © 2000 by David Catrow. Reprinted by permission of Scholastic Inc., Scholastic Press.

Exploratorium: Excerpt from "Mold Terrarium" from www.exploratorium.edu, September 9, 2009. Copyright © 1998 by Exploratorium. Reprinted by permission.

Peachtree Publishers: Excerpt from *Aliens from Earth: When Animals and Plants Invade Other Ecosystems* by Mary Batten. Text © 2003 by Mary Batten. Illustrations © 2003 by Beverly J. Doyle. Permission to reprint granted by Peachtree Publishers.

Unit Six

New England Pirate Museum: Excerpt from "Make a Treasure Map" by the New England Pirate Museum from www.piratemuseum.com, March 5, 2009. Copyright © 2009 by New England Pirate Museum. Reprinted by permission.

National Geographic Books: Adaptation from *Real Pirates: The Untold Story of the Whydah from Slave Ship to Pirate Ship* by Barry Clifford, illustrated by Gregory Manchess. Text copyright © 2008 by Barry Clifford. Illustrations © 2008 by Gregory Manchess. Reprinted with permission.

Texas Archeological Research Laboratory: "La Belle Shipwreck" by the Texas Historical Commission. Copyright © Texas Archeological Research Laboratory, University of Texas, Austin. Original article from the Texas Beyond History website www.texasbeyondhistory.net, March 2009. Reprinted with permission of the Texas Archeological Research Laboratory.

Unit Seven

Albert Whitman & Company: *What's Faster than a Speeding Cheetah?* by Robert E. Wells. Copyright © 1997 by Robert E. Wells. Used by permission of Albert Whitman & Company.

Penguin Group (USA) Inc: Excerpt from *The Moon Over Star* by Diana Hutts Aston, illustrated by Jerry Pinkney. Text copyright © 2008 by Diana Hutts Aston. Illustrations © 2008 by Jerry Pinkney. Used by permission of Dial Books for Young Readers, a division of Penguin Young Readers Group, a member of Penguin Group (USA) Inc., 345 Hudson Street, New York, NY 10014. All rights reserved.

Unit Eight

Houghton Mifflin Harcourt: Abridged from *Buffalo Music* by Tracey E. Fern. Copyright © 2008 by Tracey E. Fern. Used by permission of Clarion Books, an imprint of Houghton Mifflin Harcourt Publishing Company. All rights reserved.

Houghton Mifflin Harcourt Company: Excerpt from *The Librarian of Basra: A True Story from Iraq* by Jeanette Winter. Copyright © 2005 by Jeanette Winter. Reprinted by permission of Houghton Mifflin Harcourt Publishing Company. All rights reserved.

☐ **NATIONAL GEOGRAPHIC SCHOOL PUBLISHING**

National Geographic School Publishing gratefully acknowledges the contributions of the following National Geographic Explorers to our program and to our planet:

Joshua Ponte, 2007 National Geographic Emerging Explorer
Jill Pruetz, 2008 National Geographic Emerging Explorer
Jimmy Chin, 2004 National Geographic Emerging Explorer
Alexandra Cousteau, 2008 National Geographic Emerging Explorer
Christy Finlayson, National Geographic grantee
Constance Adams, 2005 National Geographic Emerging Explorer
Fredrik Hiebert, National Geographic Fellow

Photographic Credits

iv (tl) Jacqui Hurst/Corbis. v (tl) Mattias Klum/National Geographic Image Collection. vi (tc) Jimmy Chin/National Geographic Image Collection. vii (tl) DigitalStock/Corbis. viii (tl) Christy Finlayson, Ph.D.. ix (tc) Bill Curtsinger/National Geographic Image Collection. x (tc) Andy Rouse/Getty Images. xi (tc) Larry Gerbrandt/Getty Images. 2-3 Purestock/Alamy Images. 3 Sankar Rao Grandhi. iv (tl) Jacqui Hurst/Corbis. v (tl) Mattias Klum/National Geographic Image Collection. vi (tc) Jimmy Chin/National Geographic Image Collection. vii (tl) DigitalStock/Corbis. viii (tl) Christy Finlayson, Ph.D.. ix (tc) Bill Curtsinger/National Geographic Image Collection. x (tc) Andy Rouse/Getty Images. xi (tc) Larry Gerbrandt/Getty Images. 2-3 Purestock/Alamy Images. 3 Sankar Rao Grandhi. (inset) Liz Garza Williams/Hampton-Brown/National Geographic School Publishing. 4 Sankar Rao Grandhi. 5 (bl) Clayton Hansen/iStockphoto. (br) Neil Beer/Getty Images. (t) Travelshots.com/Alamy Images. 7 (bl) Image Source/Getty Images. (br) John Lund/Drew Kelly/Blend Images/Corbis. (tc) Doug Menuez/Getty Images. (tl) John Foxx Images/Imagestate. (tr) Jupiterimages. 10-11 Josh Ponte. 12 (inset) Maria Stenzel/National Geographic Image Collection. 12-13 (bg) Michael Nichols/National Geographic Image Collection. 13 (b, t) Josh Ponte. 14 (inset) Desirey Minkoh/AFP/Getty Images. 14-15 (bg) Michael Nichols/National Geographic Image Collection. 15 (b, t) Josh Ponte. 16-17 (bg) Michael Nichols/National Geographic Image Collection. 17 (b) Josh Ponte. (t) Desirey Minkoh/AFP/Getty Images. 18 Josh Ponte. 19 Josh Ponte. (tl) Erik Isakson/RubberBall/Alamy Images. 20 Josh Ponte. 21 (b,t) Martin van der Belen 22-23 (bg) Michael Nichols/National Geographic Image Collection. 23 (inset) Josh Ponte. 24 Sylvain Grandadam/Getty Images. 25 (b) Marion Kaplan/Alamy Images. (t) Josh Ponte. 26 Maria Stenzel/National Geographic Image Collection. 29 (b) Lester Lefkowitz/Corbis. (t) Copyright © November 2000 by Highlights for Children Inc., Columbus, Ohio. Photo credit: Courtesy of the Moxley-Ross-Naranjo Gallery, Santa Fe, NM. 30 Jacqui Hurst/Corbis. (l) Image Source/Getty Images. 31 Toba Tucker. 32 Naranjo Studio. 33 (tl) Clark. Courtesy of the New Mexico Department of Cultural Affairs. (bl, br) Naranjo Studio. (tr) Naranjo Studio. 37 (b) Phillipe Lissac/Godong/Corbis. (tl) Brand X Pictures/Jupiterimages/age fotostock. (tr) Lou Paintin/Getty Images. 39 (bl) Jupiterimages/Getty Images. (br) Adam Taylor/Getty Images. (tc) David Sacks/Getty Images. (tl) Jupiterimages/Creatas/Alamy. (tr) David Young-Wolff/Getty Images. 42 (inset) Martin Child/Getty Images. 57 (l) Ævar Arnfjörð Bjarmason. (r) Carmen Agra Deedy. 60 Stockbyte/Getty Images. 69 Jakub Vacek/iStockphoto. 70 Purestock/Alamy. 71 Jeff Randall/Getty Images. 72-73 (bg) Reuters/Corbis. 73 (inset) Liz Garza Williams/Hampton-Brown/National Geographic School Publishing. 75 (b) Konrad Wothe/Minden Pictures/National Geographic Image Collection. (t) Micheal S. Quinton/National Geographic Image Collection. 77 (bl) Dick Luria/Getty Images. (br) Gordon Wiltsie/National Geographic Image Collection. (tc) John Foxx Images/Imagestate. (tl) Diamond Sky Images/Getty Images. (tr) Richard Lewisohn/Getty Images. 90 Michael Metheny/Shutterstock. 95 (b, t) Courtesy of Chris Jensen. 98 (l) David Pollack/Corbis. (r) PhotoDisc/Getty Images. 99 Anna Sedneva/Shutterstock. 107 (bl) Mark Lovelock/Alamy Images. (br) Juan Silva/Getty Images. (tl) Dennis MacDonald/Alamy Images. (tr) Lee Beel/Alamy Images. 109 (bl) Andrea Chu/Getty Images. (br) T.J. Rich/Nature Picture Library. (tc) Olga Bogatyrenko/Shutterstock. (tr) Jeff Foott/Nature Picture Library. 111 Karine Aigner/National Geographic Image Collection. 112 (inset) Gorilla Foundation/AP Images. 112-113 Darryl Leniuk/Getty Images. 114 Comstock Images/Getty Images. 115 (b) Barbara Strnadova/Photo Researchers, Inc. (t) Anup Shah/Nature Picture Library. 116 (br) Lukasseck / ARCO/Nature Picture Library. (l) Anup Shah/Nature Picture Library. (tr) JH Pete Carmichael/Getty Images. 117 (b) Michael & Patricia Fogden/Corbis. (t) Geoff Brightling/Dorling Kindersley Ltd. Picture Library. 118 Gorilla Foundation/AP Images. 119 (bg) Mattias Klum/National Geographic Image

Illustrator Credits

California Common Core State Standards

Unit 1	Living Traditions		
SE Pages	**Lesson**	**Code**	**Standard**
3	**Unit Launch:** Share What You Know		Engage effectively in a range of collaborative discussions (one-on-one, in groups, and teacher-led) with diverse partners on *grade 4 topics and texts*, building on others' ideas and expressing their own clearly.
4	**Part 1:** **Language:** Express Feelings		Engage effectively in a range of collaborative discussions (one-on-one, in groups, and teacher-led) with diverse partners on *grade 4 topics and texts*, building on others' ideas and expressing their own clearly.
		CA CC.4.SL.1.d	Review the key ideas expressed and explain their own ideas and understanding in light of the discussion.
5	**Social Studies Vocabulary:** Key Words	CA CC.4.Rinf.4	Determine the meaning of general academic and domain-specific words or phrases in a text relevant to a grade 4 topic or subject area. **(See grade 4 Language standards 4–6 for additional expectations.) CA**
6	**Thinking Map:** Main Idea and Details	CA CC.4.Rinf.2	Determine the main idea of a text and explain how it is supported by key details; summarize the text.
7	**Academic Vocabulary:** More Key Words	CA CC.4.Rinf.4	Determine the meaning of general academic and domain-specific words or phrases in a text relevant to a grade 4 topic or subject area. **(See grade 4 Language standards 4–6 for additional expectations.) CA**
8–9	**Strategic Reading:** Learn to Plan and Monitor	CA CC.4.Rlit.1	Refer to details and examples in a text when explaining what the text says explicitly and when drawing inferences from the text.
12	**Selection 1:** Set a Purpose		Read with sufficient accuracy and fluency to support comprehension.
		CA CC.4.Rfou.4.a	Read on-level text with purpose and understanding.
13	**Selection 1:** Before You Move On: Plan and Monitor	CA CC.4.Rlit.1	Refer to details and examples in a text when explaining what the text says explicitly and when drawing inferences from the text.
	Selection 1: Before You Move On: Use Text Features	CA CC.4.Rlit.7	Make connections between the text of a story or drama and a visual or oral presentation of the text, identifying where each version reflects specific descriptions and directions in the text.
15	**Selection 1:** Before You Move On: Main Idea	CA CC.4.Rinf.2	Determine the main idea of a text and explain how it is supported by key details; summarize the text.
	Selection 1: Before You Move On: Clarify	CA CC.4.Rinf.3	Explain events, procedures, ideas, or concepts in a historical, scientific, or technical text, including what happened and why, based on specific information in the text.
			Demonstrate understanding of figurative language, word relationships, and nuances in word meanings.
		CA CC.4.L.5.a	Explain the meaning of simple similes and metaphors (e.g., as pretty as a picture) in context.
17	**Selection 1:** Before You Move On: Cause/Effect	CA CC.4.Rinf.3	Explain events, procedures, ideas, or concepts in a historical, scientific, or technical text, including what happened and why, based on specific information in the text.
		CA CC.4.Rinf.5	Describe the overall structure (e.g., chronology, comparison, cause/effect, problem/solution) of events, ideas, concepts, or information in a text or part of a text.

California Common Core State Standards, *continued*

SE Pages	Lesson	Code	Standard
	Selection 1: Before You Move On: Paraphrase	CA CC.4.Rinf.2	Determine the main idea of a text and explain how it is supported by key details; summarize the text.
19	**Selection 1:** Before You Move On: Confirm Prediction	CA CC.4.Rinf.1	Refer to details and examples in a text when explaining what the text says explicitly and when drawing inferences from the text.
	Selection 1: Before You Move On: Analyze	CA CC.4.Rinf.3	Explain events, procedures, ideas, or concepts in a historical, scientific, or technical text, including what happened and why, based on specific information in the text.
21	**Selection 1:** Before You Move On: Problem/Solution	CA CC.4.Rinf.1	Refer to details and examples in a text when explaining what the text says explicitly and when drawing inferences from the text.
		CA CC.4.Rinf.5	Describe the overall structure (e.g., chronology, comparison, cause/effect, problem/solution) of events, ideas, concepts, or information in a text or part of a text.
	Selection 1: Before You Move On: Clarify	CA CC.4.Rinf.3	Explain events, procedures, ideas, or concepts in a historical, scientific, or technical text, including what happened and why, based on specific information in the text.
			Demonstrate understanding of figurative language, word relationships, and nuances in word meanings.
		CA CC.4.L.5.a	Explain the meaning of simple similes and metaphors (e.g., as pretty as a picture) in context.
23	**Selection 1:** Before You Move On: Details	CA CC.4.Rinf.1	Refer to details and examples in a text when explaining what the text says explicitly and when drawing inferences from the text.
	Selection 1: Before You Move On: Clarify	CA CC.4.Rinf.2	Determine the main idea of a text and explain how it is supported by key details; summarize the text.
25	**Selection 1:** Before You Move On: Clarify	CA CC.4.Rinf.3	Explain events, procedures, ideas, or concepts in a historical, scientific, or technical text, including what happened and why, based on specific information in the text.
			Demonstrate understanding of figurative language, word relationships, and nuances in word meanings.
		CA CC.4.L.5.a	Explain the meaning of simple similes and metaphors (e.g., as pretty as a picture) in context.
	Selection 1: Before You Move On: Paraphrase	CA CC.4.Rinf.2	Determine the main idea of a text and explain how it is supported by key details; summarize the text.
26	**Think and Respond:** Talk About It	CA CC.4.Rinf.10	By the end of year, read and comprehend informational texts, including history/social studies, science, and technical texts, in the grades 4–5 text complexity band proficiently, with scaffolding as needed at the high end of the range.
			Engage effectively in a range of collaborative discussions (one-on-one, in groups, and teacher-led) with diverse partners on *grade 4 topics and texts*, building on others' ideas and expressing their own clearly.
		CA CC.4.SL.1.c	Pose and respond to specific questions to clarify or follow up on information, and make comments that contribute to the discussion and link to the remarks of others.

SE Pages	Lesson	Code	Standard
	Think and Respond: Write About It	CA CC.4.W.10	Write routinely over extended time frames (time for research, reflection, and revision) and shorter time frames (a single sitting or a day or two) for a range of discipline-specific tasks, purposes, and audiences.
		CA CC.4.L.6	Acquire and use accurately grade-appropriate general academic and domain-specific words and phrases, including those that signal precise actions, emotions, or states of being (e.g., quizzed, whined, stammered) and that are basic to a particular topic (e.g., wildlife, conservation, and endangered when discussing animal preservation).
27	**Reread and Retell:** Main Idea and Details	CA CC.4.Rinf.2	Determine the main idea of a text and explain how it is supported by key details; summarize the text.
	Reread and Retell: Fluency		Read with sufficient accuracy and fluency to support comprehension.
		CA CC.4.Rfou.4.b	Read on-level prose and poetry orally with accuracy, appropriate rate, and expression on successive readings.
	Reread and Retell: Talk Together		Engage effectively in a range of collaborative discussions (one-on-one, in groups, and teacher-led) with diverse partners on *grade 4 topics and texts*, building on others' ideas and expressing their own clearly.
		CA CC.4.SL.1.a	Come to discussions prepared, having read or studied required material; explicitly draw on that preparation and other information known about the topic to explore ideas under discussion.
		CA CC.4.L.6	Acquire and use accurately grade-appropriate general academic and domain-specific words and phrases, including those that signal precise actions, emotions, or states of being (e.g., quizzed, whined, stammered) and that are basic to a particular topic (e.g., wildlife, conservation, and endangered when discussing animal preservation).
28	**Word Work:** Use a Dictionary	CA CC.4.Rfou.3	Know and apply grade-level phonics and word analysis skills in decoding words.
		CA CC.4.Rfou.3.a	Use combined knowledge of all letter-sound correspondences, syllabication patterns, and morphology (e.g., roots and affixes) to read accurately unfamiliar multisyllabic words in context and out of context.
			Determine or clarify the meaning of unknown and multiple-meaning words and phrases based on *grade 4 reading and content*, choosing flexibly from a range of strategies.
		CA CC.4.L.4.c	Consult reference materials (e.g., dictionaries, glossaries, thesauruses), both print and digital, to find the pronunciation and determine or clarify the precise meaning of key words and phrases **and to identify alternate word choices in all content areas. CA**
29	**Selection 2 Opener:** Before You Move On: Details	CA CC.4.Rinf.1	Refer to details and examples in a text when explaining what the text says explicitly and when drawing inferences from the text.
	Selection 2 Opener: Before You Move On: Explain	CA CC.4.Rinf.3	Explain events, procedures, ideas, or concepts in a historical, scientific, or technical text, including what happened and why, based on specific information in the text.

California Common Core State Standards, *continued*

SE Pages	Lesson	Code	Standard
31	**Selection 2:** Before You Move On	CA CC.4.Rinf.1	Refer to details and examples in a text when explaining what the text says explicitly and when drawing inferences from the text.
33	**Selection 2:** Before You Move On: Clarify	CA CC.4.Rinf.1	Refer to details and examples in a text when explaining what the text says explicitly and when drawing inferences from the text.
	Selection 2: Before You Move On: Paraphrase	CA CC.4.Rinf.2	Determine the main idea of a text and explain how it is supported by key details; summarize the text.
34	**Respond and Extend:** Compare Author's Purpose	CA CC.4.Rinf.6	Compare and contrast a firsthand and secondhand account of the same event or topic; describe the differences in focus and the information provided.
		CA CC.4.Rinf.9	Integrate information from two texts on the same topic in order to write or speak about the subject knowledgeably.
35	**Grammar and Spelling:** Complete Sentences		Demonstrate command of the conventions of standard English grammar and usage when writing or speaking.
		CA CC.4.L.1.f	Produce complete sentences, recognizing and correcting inappropriate fragments and run-ons.
36	**Part 2:** **Language:** Ask for and Give Information		Engage effectively in a range of collaborative discussions (one-on-one, in groups, and teacher-led) with diverse partners on *grade 4 topics and texts*, building on others' ideas and expressing their own clearly.
		CA CC.4.SL.1.c	Pose and respond to specific questions to clarify or follow up on information, and make comments that contribute to the discussion and link to the remarks of others.
		CA CC.4.SL.1.d	Review the key ideas expressed and explain their own ideas and understanding in light of the discussion.
37	**Social Studies Vocabulary:** Key Words	CA CC.4.Rinf.4	Determine the meaning of general academic and domain-specific words or phrases in a text relevant to a grade 4 topic or subject area. **(See grade 4 Language standards 4–6 for additional expectations.) CA**
38	**Thinking Map:** Plot	CA CC.4.Rlit.3	Describe in depth a character, setting, or event in a story or drama, drawing on specific details in the text (e.g., a character's thoughts, words, or actions).
39	**Academic Vocabulary:** More Key Words	CA CC.4.Rlit.4	Determine the meaning of words and phrases as they are used in a text, including those that allude to significant characters found in mythology (e.g., Herculean). **(See grade 4 Language standards 4–6 for additional expectations.) CA**
40–41	**Strategic Reading:** Learn to Plan and Monitor	CA CC.4.Rlit.1	Refer to details and examples in a text when explaining what the text says explicitly and when drawing inferences from the text.
		CA CC.4.Rlit.3	Describe in depth a character, setting, or event in a story or drama, drawing on specific details in the text (e.g., a character's thoughts, words, or actions).
44	**Selection 1:** Set a Purpose		Read with sufficient accuracy and fluency to support comprehension.
		CA CC.4.Rfou.4.a	Read on-level text with purpose and understanding.

SE Pages	Lesson	Code	Standard
47	**Selection 1:** Before You Move On: Plot	CA CC.4.Rlit.1	Refer to details and examples in a text when explaining what the text says explicitly and when drawing inferences from the text.
	Selection 1: Before You Move On: Character	CA CC.4.Rlit.3	Describe in depth a character, setting, or event in a story or drama, drawing on specific details in the text (e.g., a character's thoughts, words, or actions).
48	**Selection 1:** Predict	CA CC.4.Rlit.1	Refer to details and examples in a text when explaining what the text says explicitly and when drawing inferences from the text.
51	**Selection 1:** Before You Move On: Plot	CA CC.4.Rlit.1	Refer to details and examples in a text when explaining what the text says explicitly and when drawing inferences from the text.
	Selection 1: Before You Move On	CA CC.4.Rlit.3	Describe in depth a character, setting, or event in a story or drama, drawing on specific details in the text (e.g., a character's thoughts, words, or actions).
	Selection 1: Before You Move On: Clarify		Demonstrate understanding of figurative language, word relationships, and nuances in word meanings.
		CA CC.4.L.5.a	Explain the meaning of simple similes and metaphors (e.g., as pretty as a picture) in context.
52	**Selection 1:** Predict	CA CC.4.Rlit.1	Refer to details and examples in a text when explaining what the text says explicitly and when drawing inferences from the text.
56	**Selection 1:** Before You Move On	CA CC.4.Rlit.3	Describe in depth a character, setting, or event in a story or drama, drawing on specific details in the text (e.g., a character's thoughts, words, or actions).
	Selection 1: Before You Move On: Plot	CA CC.4.Rlit.1	Refer to details and examples in a text when explaining what the text says explicitly and when drawing inferences from the text.
57	**Meet the Author:** Writer's Craft	CA CC.4.Rlit.1	Refer to details and examples in a text when explaining what the text says explicitly and when drawing inferences from the text.
		CA CC.4.W.10	Write routinely over extended time frames (time for research, reflection, and revision) and shorter time frames (a single sitting or a day or two) for a range of discipline-specific tasks, purposes, and audiences.
58	**Think and Respond:** Talk About It	CA CC.4.Rinf.10	By the end of year, read and comprehend informational texts, including history/social studies, science, and technical texts, in the grades 4–5 text complexity band proficiently, with scaffolding as needed at the high end of the range.
			Engage effectively in a range of collaborative discussions (one-on-one, in groups, and teacher-led) with diverse partners on *grade 4 topics and texts*, building on others, ideas and expressing their own clearly.
		CA CC.4.SL.1.c	Pose and respond to specific questions to clarify or follow up on information, and make comments that contribute to the discussion and link to the remarks of others.
	Think and Respond: Write About It		Draw evidence from literary or informational texts to support analysis, reflection, and research.
		CA CC.4.W.9.a	Apply *grade 4 Reading standards* to literature (e.g., "Describe in depth a character, setting, or event in a story or drama, drawing on specific details in the text [e.g., a character's thoughts, words, or actions].").

California Common Core State Standards, *continued*

SE Pages	Lesson	Code	Standard
		CA CC.4.L.6	Acquire and use accurately grade-appropriate general academic and domain-specific words and phrases, including those that signal precise actions, emotions, or states of being (e.g., quizzed, whined, stammered) and that are basic to a particular topic (e.g., wildlife, conservation, and endangered when discussing animal preservation).
59	**Reread and Retell:** Plot	CA CC.4.Rlit.1	Refer to details and examples in a text when explaining what the text says explicitly and when drawing inferences from the text.
		CA CC.4.Rlit.2	Determine a theme of a story, drama, or poem from details in the text; summarize the text.
		CA CC.4.Rlit.3	Describe in depth a character, setting, or event in a story or drama, drawing on specific details in the text (e.g., a character's thoughts, words, or actions).
	Reread and Retell: Fluency		Read with sufficient accuracy and fluency to support comprehension.
		CA CC.4.Rfou.4.b	Read on-level prose and poetry orally with accuracy, appropriate rate, and expression on successive readings.
	Reread and Retell: Talk Together		Engage effectively in a range of collaborative discussions (one-on-one, in groups, and teacher-led) with diverse partners on *grade 4 topics and texts*, building on others' ideas and expressing their own clearly.
		CA CC.4.SL.1.a	Come to discussions prepared, having read or studied required material; explicitly draw on that preparation and other information known about the topic to explore ideas under discussion.
		CA CC.4.SL.1.c	Pose and respond to specific questions to clarify or follow up on information, and make comments that contribute to the discussion and link to the remarks of others.
		CA CC.4.SL.1.d	Review the key ideas expressed and explain their own ideas and understanding in light of the discussion.
		CA CC.4.L.6	Acquire and use accurately grade-appropriate general academic and domain-specific words and phrases, including those that signal precise actions, emotions, or states of being (e.g., quizzed, whined, stammered) and that are basic to a particular topic (e.g., wildlife, conservation, and endangered when discussing animal preservation).
60	**Word Work:** Idioms and Expressions	CA CC.4.Rlit.4	Determine the meaning of words and phrases as they are used in a text, including those that allude to significant characters found in mythology (e.g., Herculean). **(See grade 4 Language standards 4–6 for additional expectations.) CA**
			Demonstrate understanding of figurative language, word relationships, and nuances in word meanings.
		CA CC.4.L.5.b	Recognize and explain the meaning of common idioms, adages, and proverbs.
61	**Selection 2:** Before You Move On: Use Text Features	CA CC.4.Rinf.7	Interpret information presented visually, orally, or quantitatively (e.g., in charts, graphs, diagrams, time lines, animations, or interactive elements on Web pages) and explain how the information contributes to an understanding of the text in which it appears.

SE Pages	Lesson	Code	Standard
	Selection 2 Opener: Before You Move On: Main Idea	CA CC.4.Rinf.2	Determine the main idea of a text and explain how it is supported by key details; summarize the text.
63	**Selection 2 Opener:** Before You Move On: Clarify	CA CC.4.Rinf.1	Refer to details and examples in a text when explaining what the text says explicitly and when drawing inferences from the text.
	Selection 2 Opener: Before You Move On: Clarify	CA CC.4.Rinf.3	Explain events, procedures, ideas, or concepts in a historical, scientific, or technical text, including what happened and why, based on specific information in the text.
	Selection 2: Before You Move On: Details	CA CC.4.Rinf.1	Refer to details and examples in a text when explaining what the text says explicitly and when drawing inferences from the text.
64	**Respond and Extend:** Compare Content	CA CC.4.Rlit.9	Compare and contrast the treatment of similar themes and topics (e.g., opposition of good and evil) and patterns of events (e.g., the quest) in stories, myths, and traditional literature from different cultures.
		CA CC.4.Rinf.9	Integrate information from two texts on the same topic in order to write or speak about the subject knowledgeably.
	Respond and Extend: Talk Together		Engage effectively in a range of collaborative discussions (one-on-one, in groups, and teacher-led) with diverse partners on *grade 4 topics and texts*, building on others' ideas and expressing their own clearly.
		CA CC.4.SL.1.a	Come to discussions prepared, having read or studied required material; explicitly draw on that preparation and other information known about the topic to explore ideas under discussion.
		CA CC.4.L.6	Acquire and use accurately grade-appropriate general academic and domain-specific words and phrases, including those that signal precise actions, emotions, or states of being (e.g., quizzed, whined, stammered) and that are basic to a particular topic (e.g., wildlife, conservation, and endangered when discussing animal preservation).
65	**Grammar and Spelling:** Subject-Verb Agreement	CA CC.4.L.1	Demonstrate command of the conventions of standard English grammar and usage when writing or speaking.
66–67	**Writing Project:** Interview Study a Model Prewrite Draft		Write informative/explanatory texts to examine a topic and convey ideas and information clearly.
		CA CC.4.W.2.a	Introduce a topic clearly and group related information in paragraphs and sections; include formatting (e.g., headings), illustrations, and multimedia when useful to aiding comprehension.
		CA CC.4.W.2.b	Develop the topic with facts, definitions, concrete details, quotations, or other information and examples related to the topic.
		CA CC.4.W.2.d	Use precise language and domain-specific vocabulary to inform about or explain the topic.
		CA CC.4.W.2.e	Provide a concluding statement or section related to the information or explanation presented.

California Common Core State Standards, *continued*

SE Pages	Lesson	Code	Standard
		CA CC.4.W.4	Produce clear and coherent writing **(including multiple-paragraph texts)** in which the development and organization are appropriate to task, purpose, and audience. (Grade-specific expectations for writing types are defined in standards 1–3 above.) **CA**
68	**Writing Project:** Interview Revise	CA CC.4.W.5	With guidance and support from peers and adults, develop and strengthen writing as needed by planning, revising, and editing. (Editing for conventions should demonstrate command of Language standards 1–3 up to and including grade 4.)
69	**Writing Project: Interview** Edit and Proofread	CA CC.4.W.5	With guidance and support from peers and adults, develop and strengthen writing as needed by planning, revising, and editing. (Editing for conventions should demonstrate command of Language standards 1–3 up to and including grade 4.)
	Writing Project: Interview Publish	CA CC.4.W.6	With some guidance and support from adults, use technology, including the Internet, to produce and publish writing as well as to interact and collaborate with others; demonstrate sufficient command of keyboarding skills to type a minimum of one page in a single sitting.
		CA CC.4.SL.5	Add audio recordings and visual displays to presentations when appropriate to enhance the development of main ideas or themes.
70	**Talk Together**		Engage effectively in a range of collaborative discussions (one-on-one, in groups, and teacher-led) with diverse partners on *grade 4 topics and texts*, building on others' ideas and expressing their own clearly.
		CA CC.4.SL.1.a	Come to discussions prepared, having read or studied required material; explicitly draw on that preparation and other information known about the topic to explore ideas under discussion.
		CA CC.4.SL.1.c	Pose and respond to specific questions to clarify or follow up on information, and make comments that contribute to the discussion and link to the remarks of others.
		CA CC.4.SL.1.d	Review the key ideas expressed and explain their own ideas and understanding in light of the discussion.
	Write a Description	CA CC.4.W.10	Write routinely over extended time frames (time for research, reflection, and revision) and shorter time frames (a single sitting or a day or two) for a range of discipline-specific tasks, purposes, and audiences.
71	**Unit Wrap-Up:** Share Your Ideas	CA CC.4.W.10	Write routinely over extended time frames (time for research, reflection, and revision) and shorter time frames (a single sitting or a day or two) for a range of discipline-specific tasks, purposes, and audiences.
			Engage effectively in a range of collaborative discussions (one-on-one, in groups, and teacher-led) with diverse partners on *grade 4 topics and texts*, building on others' ideas and expressing their own clearly.
		CA CC.4.SL.1.d	Review the key ideas expressed and explain their own ideas and understanding in light of the discussion.
		CA CC.4.SL.4	Report on a topic or text, tell a story, or recount an experience in an organized manner, using appropriate facts and relevant, descriptive details to support main ideas or themes; speak clearly at an understandable pace.

SE Pages	Lesson	Code	Standard
73	**Unit Launch:** Share What You Know		Engage effectively in a range of collaborative discussions (one-on-one, in groups, and teacher-led) with diverse partners on *grade 4 topics* and *texts*, building on others' ideas and expressing their own clearly.
74	**Part 1: Language:** Express Ideas		Engage effectively in a range of collaborative discussions (one-on-one, in groups, and teacher-led) with diverse partners on *grade 4 topics and texts*, building on others' ideas and expressing their own clearly.
		CA CC.4.SL.1.a	Come to discussions prepared, having read or studied required material; explicitly draw on that preparation and other information known about the topic to explore ideas under discussion.
75	**Science Vocabulary:** Key Words	CA CC.4.Rinf.4	Determine the meaning of general academic and domain-specific words or phrases in a text relevant to a grade 4 topic or subject area. **(See grade 4 Language standards 4–6 for additional expectations.) CA**
76	**Thinking Map:** Analyze Characters	CA CC.4.Rlit.3	Describe in depth a character, setting, or event in a story or drama, drawing on specific details in the text (e.g., a character's thoughts, words, or actions).
77	**Academic Vocabulary:** More Key Words	CA CC.4.Rlit.4	Determine the meaning of words and phrases as they are used in a text, including those that allude to significant characters found in mythology (e.g., Herculean). **(See grade 4 Language standards 4–6 for additional expectations.) CA**
78–79	**Strategic Reading:** Learn to Make Connections	CA CC.4.Rlit.1	Refer to details and examples in a text when explaining what the text says explicitly and when drawing inferences from the text.
		CA CC.4.Rlit.7	Make connections between the text of a story or drama and a visual or oral presentation of the text, identifying where each version reflects specific descriptions and directions in the text.
82	**Selection 1:** Set a Purpose		Read with sufficient accuracy and fluency to support comprehension.
		CA CC.4.Rfou.4.a	Read on-level text with purpose and understanding.
83	**Selection 1:** Before You Move On: Plot	CA CC.4.Rlit.3	Describe in depth a character, setting, or event in a story or drama, drawing on specific details in the text (e.g., a character's thoughts, words, or actions).
	Selection 1: Before You Move On: Character	CA CC.4.Rlit.1	Refer to details and examples in a text when explaining what the text says explicitly and when drawing inferences from the text.
84	**Selection 1:** Predict	CA CC.4.Rlit.1	Refer to details and examples in a text when explaining what the text says explicitly and when drawing inferences from the text.
85	**Selection 1:** Before You Move On	CA CC.4.Rlit.1	Refer to details and examples in a text when explaining what the text says explicitly and when drawing inferences from the text.
	Selection 1: Before You Move On: Make Connections	CA CC.4.Rlit.3	Describe in depth a character, setting, or event in a story or drama, drawing on specific details in the text (e.g., a character's thoughts, words, or actions).
86	**Selection 1:** Predict	CA CC.4.Rlit.1	Refer to details and examples in a text when explaining what the text says explicitly and when drawing inferences from the text.

California Common Core State Standards, *continued*

SE Pages	Lesson	Code	Standard
89	**Selection 1:** Before You Move On	CA CC.4.Rlit.1	Refer to details and examples in a text when explaining what the text says explicitly and when drawing inferences from the text.
	Selection 1: Before You Move On: Make Connections	CA CC.4.Rlit.3	Describe in depth a character, setting, or event in a story or drama, drawing on specific details in the text (e.g., a character's thoughts, words, or actions).
90	**Selection 1:** Predict	CA CC.4.Rlit.1	Refer to details and examples in a text when explaining what the text says explicitly and when drawing inferences from the text.
94	**Selection 1:** Before You Move On: Confirm Prediction	CA CC.4.Rlit.1	Refer to details and examples in a text when explaining what the text says explicitly and when drawing inferences from the text.
	Selection 1: Before You Move On: Character	CA CC.4.Rlit.3	Describe in depth a character, setting, or event in a story or drama, drawing on specific details in the text (e.g., a character's thoughts, words, or actions).
95	**Meet the Author:** Writer's Craft		Draw evidence from literary or informational texts to support analysis, reflection, and research.
		CA CC.4.W.9.a	Apply *grade 4 Reading standards* to literature (e.g., "Describe in depth a character, setting, or event in a story or drama, drawing on specific details in the text [e.g., a character's thoughts, words, or actions].").
96	**Think and Respond:** Talk About It	CA CC.4.Rlit.3	Describe in depth a character, setting, or event in a story or drama, drawing on specific details in the text (e.g., a character's thoughts, words, or actions).
		CA CC.4.Rlit.10	By the end of the year, read and comprehend literature, including stories, dramas, and poetry, in the grades 4–5 text complexity band proficiently, with scaffolding as needed at the high end of the range.
			Engage effectively in a range of collaborative discussions (one-on-one, in groups, and teacher-led) with diverse partners on *grade 4 topics and texts,* building on others' ideas and expressing their own clearly.
		CA CC.4.SL.1.d	Review the key ideas expressed and explain their own ideas and understanding in light of the discussion.
	Think and Respond: Write About It		Draw evidence from literary or informational texts to support analysis, reflection, and research.
		CA CC.4.W.9.a	Apply *grade 4 Reading standards* to literature (e.g., "Describe in depth a character, setting, or event in a story or drama, drawing on specific details in the text [e.g., a character's thoughts, words, or actions].").
		CA CC.4.L.6	Acquire and use accurately grade-appropriate general academic and domain-specific words and phrases, including those that signal precise actions, emotions, or states of being (e.g., quizzed, whined, stammered) and that are basic to a particular topic (e.g., wildlife, conservation, and endangered when discussing animal preservation).
97	**Reread and Analyze:** Analyze Characters	CA CC.4.Rlit.1	Refer to details and examples in a text when explaining what the text says explicitly and when drawing inferences from the text.
	Reread and Analyze: Analyze Characters	CA CC.4.Rlit.3	Describe in depth a character, setting, or event in a story or drama, drawing on specific details in the text (e.g., a character's thoughts, words, or actions).

SE Pages	Lesson	Code	Standard
	Reread and Analyze: Fluency		Read with sufficient accuracy and fluency to support comprehension.
		CA CC.4.Rfou.4.b	Read on-level prose and poetry orally with accuracy, appropriate rate, and expression on successive readings.
	Reread and Analyze: Talk Together	CA CC.4.Rlit.1	Refer to details and examples in a text when explaining what the text says explicitly and when drawing inferences from the text.
		CA CC.4.Rlit.3	Describe in depth a character, setting, or event in a story or drama, drawing on specific details in the text (e.g., a character's thoughts, words, or actions).
		CA CC.4.L.6	Acquire and use accurately grade-appropriate general academic and domain-specific words and phrases, including those that signal precise actions, emotions, or states of being (e.g., quizzed, whined, stammered) and that are basic to a particular topic (e.g., wildlife, conservation, and endangered when discussing animal preservation).
98	**Word Work:** Homophones		Read with sufficient accuracy and fluency to support comprehension.
		CA CC.4.Rfou.4.c	Use context to confirm or self-correct word recognition and understanding, rereading as necessary.
			Determine or clarify the meaning of unknown and multiple-meaning words and phrases based on *grade 4 reading and content,* choosing flexibly from a range of strategies.
		CA CC.4.L.4.a	Use context (e.g., definitions, examples, or restatements in text) as a clue to the meaning of a word or phrase.
99	**Selection 2 Opener:** Before You Move On: Character's Motive	CA CC.4.Rlit.3	Describe in depth a character, setting, or event in a story or drama, drawing on specific details in the text (e.g., a character's thoughts, words, or actions).
	Selection 2 Opener: Before You Move On: Setting	CA CC.4.Rlit.1	Refer to details and examples in a text when explaining what the text says explicitly and when drawing inferences from the text.
		CA CC.4.Rlit.7	Make connections between the text of a story or drama and a visual or oral presentation of the text, identifying where each version reflects specific descriptions and directions in the text.
101	**Selection 2:** Before You Move On: Character's Motive	CA CC.4.Rlit.3	Describe in depth a character, setting, or event in a story or drama, drawing on specific details in the text (e.g., a character's thoughts, words, or actions).
	Selection 2: Before You Move On: Make Connections	CA CC.4.Rlit.9	Compare and contrast the treatment of similar themes and topics (e.g., opposition of good and evil) and patterns of events (e.g., the quest) in stories, myths, and traditional literature from different cultures.
103	**Selection 2:** Before You Move On: Make Connections	CA CC.4.Rlit.9	Compare and contrast the treatment of similar themes and topics (e.g., opposition of good and evil) and patterns of events (e.g., the quest) in stories, myths, and traditional literature from different cultures.
	Selection 2: Before You Move On: Connect Characters	CA CC.4.Rlit.3	Describe in depth a character, setting, or event in a story or drama, drawing on specific details in the text (e.g., a character's thoughts, words, or actions).

California Common Core State Standards, continued

SE Pages	Lesson	Code	Standard
104	**Respond and Extend:** Compare Characters' Adventures	CA CC.4.Rlit.9	Compare and contrast the treatment of similar themes and topics (e.g., opposition of good and evil) and patterns of events (e.g., the quest) in stories, myths, and traditional literature from different cultures.
105	**Grammar and Spelling:** Kinds of Sentences		Demonstrate command of the conventions of standard English grammar and usage when writing or speaking.
		CA CC.4.L.1.a	Use **interrogative**, relative pronouns (who, whose, whom, which, that) and relative adverbs (where, when, why). **CA**
		CA CC.4.L.1.f	Produce complete sentences, recognizing and correcting inappropriate fragments and run-ons.
106	**Part 2:** **Language:** Engage in Conversation		Engage effectively in a range of collaborative discussions (one-on-one, in groups, and teacher-led) with diverse partners on *grade 4 topics and texts*, building on others' ideas and expressing their own clearly.
		CA CC.4.SL.1.a	Come to discussions prepared, having read or studied required material; explicitly draw on that preparation and other information known about the topic to explore ideas under discussion.
		CA CC.4.SL.1.c	Pose and respond to specific questions to clarify or follow up on information, and make comments that contribute to the discussion and link to the remarks of others.
		CA CC.4.SL.1.d	Review the key ideas expressed and explain their own ideas and understanding in light of the discussion.
			Write narratives to develop real or imagined experiences or events using effective technique, descriptive details, and clear event sequences.
		CA CC.4.W.3.b	Use dialogue and description to develop experiences and events or show the responses of characters to situations.
107	**Science Vocabulary:** Key Words	CA CC.4.Rinf.4	Determine the meaning of general academic and domain-specific words or phrases in a text relevant to a grade 4 topic or subject area. **(See grade 4 Language standards 4–6 for additional expectations.) CA**
108	**Thinking Map:** Main Idea and Details	CA CC.4.Rinf.2	Determine the main idea of a text and explain how it is supported by key details; summarize the text.
109	**Academic Vocabulary:** More Key Words	CA CC.4.Rinf.4	Determine the meaning of general academic and domain-specific words or phrases in a text relevant to a grade 4 topic or subject area. **(See grade 4 Language standards 4–6 for additional expectations.) CA**
110–111	**Strategic Reading:** Learn to Make Connections	CA CC.4.Rinf.1	Refer to details and examples in a text when explaining what the text says explicitly and when drawing inferences from the text.
		CA CC.4.Rinf.7	Interpret information presented visually, orally, or quantitatively (e.g., in charts, graphs, diagrams, time lines, animations, or interactive elements on Web pages) and explain how the information contributes to an understanding of the text in which it appears.
114	**Selection 1:** Set a Purpose		Read with sufficient accuracy and fluency to support comprehension.
		CA CC.4.Rfou.4.a	Read on-level text with purpose and understanding.

SE Pages	Lesson	Code	Standard
115	**Selection 1:** Before You Move On: Main Idea	CA CC.4.Rinf.2	Determine the main idea of a text and explain how it is supported by key details; summarize the text.
	Selection 1: Before You Move On: Make Connections	CA CC.4.Rinf.1	Refer to details and examples in a text when explaining what the text says explicitly and when drawing inferences from the text.
		CA CC.4.Rinf.6	Compare and contrast a firsthand and secondhand account of the same event or topic; describe the differences in focus and the information provided.
117	**Selection 1:** Before You Move On: Use Text Features	CA CC.4.Rinf.7	Interpret information presented visually, orally, or quantitatively (e.g., in charts, graphs, diagrams, time lines, animations, or interactive elements on Web pages) and explain how the information contributes to an understanding of the text in which it appears.
	Selection 1: Before You Move On: Details	CA CC.4.Rinf.1	Refer to details and examples in a text when explaining what the text says explicitly and when drawing inferences from the text.
119	**Selection 1:** Before You Move On	CA CC.4.Rinf.1	Refer to details and examples in a text when explaining what the text says explicitly and when drawing inferences from the text.
	Selection 1: Before You Move On: Make Connections	CA CC.4.Rinf.9	Integrate information from two texts on the same topic in order to write or speak about the subject knowledgeably.
121	**Selection 1:** Before You Move On: Make Connections	CA CC.4.Rinf.1	Refer to details and examples in a text when explaining what the text says explicitly and when drawing inferences from the text.
		CA CC.4.Rinf.6	Compare and contrast a firsthand and secondhand account of the same event or topic; describe the differences in focus and the information provided.
	Selection 1: Before You Move On: Main Idea	CA CC.4.Rinf.2	Determine the main idea of a text and explain how it is supported by key details; summarize the text.
123	**Selection 1:** Before You Move On: Details	CA CC.4.Rinf.1	Refer to details and examples in a text when explaining what the text says explicitly and when drawing inferences from the text.
	Selection 1: Before You Move On: Use Text Features	CA CC.4.Rinf.7	Interpret information presented visually, orally, or quantitatively (e.g., in charts, graphs, diagrams, time lines, animations, or interactive elements on Web pages) and explain how the information contributes to an understanding of the text in which it appears.
125	**Selection 1:** Before You Move On	CA CC.4.Rinf.1	Refer to details and examples in a text when explaining what the text says explicitly and when drawing inferences from the text.
	Selection 1: Before You Move On: Make Connections	CA CC.4.Rinf.3	Explain events, procedures, ideas, or concepts in a historical, scientific, or technical text, including what happened and why, based on specific information in the text.
127	**Selection 1:** Before You Move On: Main Idea	CA CC.4.Rinf.2	Determine the main idea of a text and explain how it is supported by key details; summarize the text.

California Common Core State Standards, *continued*

SE Pages	Lesson	Code	Standard
	Selection 1: Before You Move On: Use Text Features	CA CC.4.Rinf.7	Interpret information presented visually, orally, or quantitatively (e.g., in charts, graphs, diagrams, time lines, animations, or interactive elements on Web pages) and explain how the information contributes to an understanding of the text in which it appears.
128	**Think and Respond:** Talk About It	CA CC.4.Rinf.10	By the end of year, read and comprehend informational texts, including history/social studies, science, and technical texts, in the grades 4–5 text complexity band proficiently, with scaffolding as needed at the high end of the range.
			Engage effectively in a range of collaborative discussions (one-on-one, in groups, and teacher-led) with diverse partners on *grade 4 topics and texts,* building on others' ideas and expressing their own clearly.
		CA CC.4.SL.1.a	Come to discussions prepared, having read or studied required material; explicitly draw on that preparation and other information known about the topic to explore ideas under discussion.
	Think and Respond: Write About It		Draw evidence from literary or informational texts to support analysis, reflection, and research.
		CA CC.4.W.9.b	Apply *grade 4 Reading standards* to informational texts (e.g., "Explain how an author uses reasons and evidence to support particular points in a text").
		CA CC.4.L.6	Acquire and use accurately grade-appropriate general academic and domain-specific words and phrases, including those that signal precise actions, emotions, or states of being (e.g., quizzed, whined, stammered) and that are basic to a particular topic (e.g., wildlife, conservation, and endangered when discussing animal preservation).
129	**Reread and Explain:** Main Idea and Details	CA CC.4.Rinf.2	Determine the main idea of a text and explain how it is supported by key details; summarize the text.
		CA CC.4.L.6	Acquire and use accurately grade-appropriate general academic and domain-specific words and phrases, including those that signal precise actions, emotions, or states of being (e.g., quizzed, whined, stammered) and that are basic to a particular topic (e.g., wildlife, conservation, and endangered when discussing animal preservation).
	Reread and Explain: Fluency		Read with sufficient accuracy and fluency to support comprehension.
		CA CC.4.Rfou.4.b	Read on-level prose and poetry orally with accuracy, appropriate rate, and expression on successive readings.
	Reread and Explain: Talk Together	CA CC.4.Rinf.1	Refer to details and examples in a text when explaining what the text says explicitly and when drawing inferences from the text.
			Engage effectively in a range of collaborative discussions (one-on-one, in groups, and teacher-led) with diverse partners on *grade 4 topics and texts,* building on others' ideas and expressing their own clearly.
		CA CC.4.SL.1.d	Review the key ideas expressed and explain their own ideas and understanding in light of the discussion.
130	**Word Work:** Use a Dictionary		Determine or clarify the meaning of unknown and multiple-meaning words and phrases based on *grade 4 reading and content,* choosing flexibly from a range of strategies.

Unit 2   Animal Intelligence, continued

SE Pages	Lesson	Code	Standard
		CA CC.4.L.4.c	Consult reference materials (e.g., dictionaries, glossaries, thesauruses), both print and digital, to find the pronunciation and determine or clarify the precise meaning of key words and phrases **and to identify alternate word choices in all content areas. CA**
131	**Selection 2 Opener:** Before You Move On: Make Connections	CA CC.4.Rinf.1	Refer to details and examples in a text when explaining what the text says explicitly and when drawing inferences from the text.
		CA CC.4.Rinf.9	Integrate information from two texts on the same topic in order to write or speak about the subject knowledgeably.
	Selection 2 Opener: Before You Move On: Use Text Features	CA CC.4.Rinf.7	Interpret information presented visually, orally, or quantitatively (e.g., in charts, graphs, diagrams, time lines, animations, or interactive elements on Web pages) and explain how the information contributes to an understanding of the text in which it appears.
133	**Selection 2:** Before You Move On: Compare/Contrast	CA CC.4.Rinf.3	Explain events, procedures, ideas, or concepts in a historical, scientific, or technical text, including what happened and why, based on specific information in the text.
	Selection 2: Before You Move On: Make Connections	CA CC.4.Rinf.1	Refer to details and examples in a text when explaining what the text says explicitly and when drawing inferences from the text.
		CA CC.4.Rinf.4	Determine the meaning of general academic and domain-specific words or phrases in a text relevant to a grade 4 topic or subject area. **(See grade 4 Language standards 4–6 for additional expectations.) CA**
135	**Selection 2:** Before You Move On	CA CC.4.Rinf.3	Explain events, procedures, ideas, or concepts in a historical, scientific, or technical text, including what happened and why, based on specific information in the text.
	Selection 2: Before You Move On: Draw Conclusions	CA CC.4.Rinf.1	Refer to details and examples in a text when explaining what the text says explicitly and when drawing inferences from the text.
136	**Respond and Extend:** Compare Facts	CA CC.4.Rinf.6	Compare and contrast a firsthand and secondhand account of the same event or topic; describe the differences in focus and the information provided.
		CA CC.4.Rinf.9	Integrate information from two texts on the same topic in order to write or speak about the subject knowledgeably.
	Respond and Extend: Talk Together	CA CC.4.Rinf.1	Refer to details and examples in a text when explaining what the text says explicitly and when drawing inferences from the text.
		CA CC.4.Rinf.9	Integrate information from two texts on the same topic in order to write or speak about the subject knowledgeably.
			Engage effectively in a range of collaborative discussions (one-on-one, in groups, and teacher-led) with diverse partners on *grade 4 topics and texts,* building on others' ideas and expressing their own clearly.
		CA CC.4.SL.1.a	Come to discussions prepared, having read or studied required material; explicitly draw on that preparation and other information known about the topic to explore ideas under discussion.

California Common Core State Standards, *continued*

SE Pages	Lesson	Code	Standard
137	**Grammar and Spelling:** Compound Sentences		Demonstrate command of the conventions of standard English grammar and usage when writing or speaking.
		CA CC.4.L.1.f	Produce complete sentences, recognizing and correcting inappropriate fragments and run-ons.
			Demonstrate command of the conventions of standard English capitalization, punctuation, and spelling when writing.
		CA CC.4.L.2.c	Use a comma before a coordinating conjunction in a compound sentence.
138–139	**Writing Project:** Business Letter Study a Model Prewrite Draft	CA CC.4.W.4	Produce clear and coherent writing **(including multiple-paragraph texts)** in which the development and organization are appropriate to task, purpose, and audience. (Grade-specific expectations for writing types are defined in standards 1–3 above.) **CA**
140	**Writing Project:** Business Letter Revise	CA CC.4.W.5	With guidance and support from peers and adults, develop and strengthen writing as needed by planning, revising, and editing. (Editing for conventions should demonstrate command of Language standards 1–3 up to and including grade 4.)
			Use knowledge of language and its conventions when writing, speaking, reading, or listening.
		CA CC.4.L.3.a	Choose words and phrases to convey ideas precisely.
141	**Writing Project:** Business Letter Edit and Proofread	CA CC.4.W.5	With guidance and support from peers and adults, develop and strengthen writing as needed by planning, revising, and editing. (Editing for conventions should demonstrate command of Language standards 1–3 up to and including grade 4.)
			Demonstrate command of the conventions of standard English grammar and usage when writing or speaking.
		CA CC.4.L.1.a	Use **interrogative**, relative pronouns (*who, whose, whom, which, that*) and relative adverbs (*where, when, why*). **CA**
		CA CC.4.L.1.f	Produce complete sentences, recognizing and correcting inappropriate fragments and run-ons.
	Writing Project: Business Letter Publish	CA CC.4.W.6	With some guidance and support from adults, use technology, including the Internet, to produce and publish writing as well as to interact and collaborate with others; demonstrate sufficient command of keyboarding skills to type a minimum of one page in a single sitting.
		CA CC.4.SL.1	Engage effectively in a range of collaborative discussions (one-on-one, in groups, and teacher-led) with diverse partners on grade 4 topics and texts, building on others' ideas and expressing their own clearly.
		CA CC.4.SL.1.a	Come to discussions prepared, having read or studied required material; explicitly draw on that preparation and other information known about the topic to explore ideas under discussion.
		CA CC.4.SL.1.b	Follow agreed-upon rules for discussions and carry out assigned roles.
		CA CC.4.SL.1.c	Pose and respond to specific questions to clarify or follow up on information, and make comments that contribute to the discussion and link to the remarks of others.

SE Pages	Lesson	Code	Standard
		CA CC.4.SL.1.d	Review the key ideas expressed and explain their own ideas and understanding in light of the discussion.
		CA CC.4.SL.6	Differentiate between contexts that call for formal English (e.g., presenting ideas) and situations where informal discourse is appropriate (e.g., small-group discussion); use formal English when appropriate to task and situation. (See grade 4 Language standards 1 and 3 for specific expectations.)
142	**Talk Together**		Engage effectively in a range of collaborative discussions (one-on-one, in groups, and teacher-led) with diverse partners on *grade 4 topics and texts,* building on others' ideas and expressing their own clearly.
		CA CC.4.SL.1.a	Come to discussions prepared, having read or studied required material; explicitly draw on that preparation and other information known about the topic to explore ideas under discussion.
	Write an E-Mail		Draw evidence from literary or informational texts to support analysis, reflection, and research.
		CA CC.4.W.9.b	Apply *grade 4 Reading standards* to informational texts (e.g., "Explain how an author uses reasons and evidence to support particular points in a text").
		CA CC.4.W.10	Write routinely over extended time frames (time for research, reflection, and revision) and shorter time frames (a single sitting or a day or two) for a range of discipline-specific tasks, purposes, and audiences.
143	**Unit Wrap-Up:** Share Your Ideas	CA CC.4.Rlit.5	Explain major differences between poems, drama, and prose, and refer to the structural elements of poems (e.g., verse, rhythm, meter) and drama (e.g., casts of characters, settings, descriptions, dialogue, stage directions) when writing or speaking about a text.
		CA CC.4.W.7	Conduct short research projects that build knowledge through investigation of different aspects of a topic.
		CA CC.4.W.10	Write routinely over extended time frames (time for research, reflection, and revision) and shorter time frames (a single sitting or a day or two) for a range of discipline-specific tasks, purposes, and audiences.
		CA CC.4.SL.1	Engage effectively in a range of collaborative discussions (one-on-one, in groups, and teacher-led) with diverse partners on *grade 4 topics and texts,* building on others' ideas and expressing their own clearly.
		CA CC.4.SL.1.a	Come to discussions prepared, having read or studied required material; explicitly draw on that preparation and other information known about the topic to explore ideas under discussion.
		CA CC.4.SL.1.b	Follow agreed-upon rules for discussions and carry out assigned roles.
		CA CC.4.SL.1.c	Pose and respond to specific questions to clarify or follow up on information, and make comments that contribute to the discussion and link to the remarks of others.
		CA CC.4.SL.1.d	Review the key ideas expressed and explain their own ideas and understanding in light of the discussion.

California Common Core State Standards, continued

SE Pages	Lesson	Code	Standard
		CA CC.4.SL.4	Report on a topic or text, tell a story, or recount an experience in an organized manner, using appropriate facts and relevant, descriptive details to support main ideas or themes; speak clearly at an understandable pace.
		CA CC.4.SL.4.a	**Plan and deliver a narrative presentation that: relates ideas, observations, or recollections; provides a clear context; and includes clear insight into why the event or experience is memorable. CA**
145	**Unit Launch:** Share What You Know		Engage effectively in a range of collaborative discussions (one-on-one, in groups, and teacher-led) with diverse partners on *grade 4 topics and texts*, building on others' ideas and expressing their own clearly.
146	**Part 1:** **Language:** Give and Follow Directions		Engage effectively in a range of collaborative discussions (one-on-one, in groups, and teacher-led) with diverse partners on *grade 4 topics and texts*, building on others' ideas and expressing their own clearly.
		CA CC.4.SL.1.c	Pose and respond to specific questions to clarify or follow up on information, and make comments that contribute to the discussion and link to the remarks of others.
147	**Social Studies Vocabulary:** Key Words	CA CC.4.Rinf.4	Determine the meaning of general academic and domain-specific words or phrases in a text relevant to a grade 4 topic or subject area. **(See grade 4 Language standards 4–6 for additional expectations.) CA**
148	**Thinking Map:** Theme	CA CC.4.Rlit.2	Determine a theme of a story, drama, or poem from details in the text; summarize the text.
149	**Academic Vocabulary:** More Key Words	CA CC.4.Rlit.4	Determine the meaning of words and phrases as they are used in a text, including those that allude to significant characters found in mythology (e.g., Herculean). **(See grade 4 Language standards 4–6 for additional expectations.) CA**
150–151	**Strategic Reading:** Learn to Visualize	CA CC.4.Rlit.1	Refer to details and examples in a text when explaining what the text says explicitly and when drawing inferences from the text.
154	**Selection 1:** Set a Purpose		Read with sufficient accuracy and fluency to support comprehension.
		CA CC.4.Rfou.4.a	Read on-level text with purpose and understanding.
155	**Selection 1:** Before You Move On	CA CC.4.Rlit.3	Describe in depth a character, setting, or event in a story or drama, drawing on specific details in the text (e.g., a character's thoughts, words, or actions).
	Selection 1: Before You Move On: Setting	CA CC.4.Rlit.7	Make connections between the text of a story or drama and a visual or oral presentation of the text, identifying where each version reflects specific descriptions and directions in the text.
	Selection 1: Before You Move On: Figurative Language	CA CC.4.Rlit.4	Determine the meaning of words and phrases as they are used in a text, including those that allude to significant characters found in mythology (e.g., Herculean). **(See grade 4 Language standards 4–6 for additional expectations.) CA**
			Demonstrate understanding of figurative language, word relationships, and nuances in word meanings.
		CA CC.4.L.5.a	Explain the meaning of simple similes and metaphors (e.g., *as pretty as a picture*) in context.

SE Pages	Lesson	Code	Standard
156	**Selection 1:** Predict	CA CC.4.Rlit.1	Refer to details and examples in a text when explaining what the text says explicitly and when drawing inferences from the text.
159	**Selection 1:** Before You Move On	CA CC.4.Rlit.1	Refer to details and examples in a text when explaining what the text says explicitly and when drawing inferences from the text.
160	**Selection 1:** Predict	CA CC.4.Rlit.1	Refer to details and examples in a text when explaining what the text says explicitly and when drawing inferences from the text.
161	**Selection 1:** Before You Move On: Theme	CA CC.4.Rlit.2	Determine a theme of a story, drama, or poem from details in the text; summarize the text.
	Selection 1: Before You Move On: Visualize	CA CC.4.Rlit.1	Refer to details and examples in a text when explaining what the text says explicitly and when drawing inferences from the text.
		CA CC.4.Rlit.4	Determine the meaning of words and phrases as they are used in a text, including those that allude to significant characters found in mythology (e.g., Herculean). **(See grade 4 Language standards 4–6 for additional expectations.) CA**
		CA CC.4.Rlit.5	Explain major differences between poems, drama, and prose, and refer to the structural elements of poems (e.g., verse, rhythm, meter) and drama (e.g., casts of characters, settings, descriptions, dialogue, stage directions) when writing or speaking about a text.
162	**Selection 1:** Predict	CA CC.4.Rlit.1	Refer to details and examples in a text when explaining what the text says explicitly and when drawing inferences from the text.
164	**Selection 1:** Before You Move On: Confirm Prediction	CA CC.4.Rlit.1	Refer to details and examples in a text when explaining what the text says explicitly and when drawing inferences from the text.
	Selection 1: Before You Move On: Theme	CA CC.4.Rlit.2	Determine a theme of a story, drama, or poem from details in the text; summarize the text.
		CA CC.4.Rlit.4	Determine the meaning of words and phrases as they are used in a text, including those that allude to significant characters found in mythology (e.g., Herculean). **(See grade 4 Language standards 4–6 for additional expectations.) CA**
165	**Meet the Author and Illustrator:** Writer's Craft	CA CC.4.Rlit.3	Describe in depth a character, setting, or event in a story or drama, drawing on specific details in the text (e.g., a character's thoughts, words, or actions).
166	**Think and Respond:** Talk About It	CA CC.4.Rlit.1	Refer to details and examples in a text when explaining what the text says explicitly and when drawing inferences from the text.
		CA CC.4.Rlit.10	By the end of the year, read and comprehend literature, including stories, dramas, and poetry, in the grades 4–5 text complexity band proficiently, with scaffolding as needed at the high end of the range.
			Engage effectively in a range of collaborative discussions (one-on-one, in groups, and teacher-led) with diverse partners on *grade 4 topics and texts*, building on others' ideas and expressing their own clearly.
		CA CC.4.SL.1.a	Come to discussions prepared, having read or studied required material; explicitly draw on that preparation and other information known about the topic to explore ideas under discussion.

California Common Core State Standards, *continued*

SE Pages	Lesson	Code	Standard
	Think and Respond: Write About It	CA CC.4.W.10	Write routinely over extended time frames (time for research, reflection, and revision) and shorter time frames (a single sitting or a day or two) for a range of discipline-specific tasks, purposes, and audiences.
		CA CC.4.L.6	Acquire and use accurately grade-appropriate general academic and domain-specific words and phrases, including those that signal precise actions, emotions, or states of being (e.g., quizzed, whined, stammered) and that are basic to a particular topic (e.g., wildlife, conservation, and endangered when discussing animal preservation).
167	**Reread and Summarize:** Theme	CA CC.4.Rlit.2	Determine a theme of a story, drama, or poem from details in the text; summarize the text.
	Reread and Summarize: Fluency		Read with sufficient accuracy and fluency to support comprehension.
		CA CC.4.Rfou.4.b	Read on-level prose and poetry orally with accuracy, appropriate rate, and expression on successive readings.
	Reread and Summarize: Talk Together	CA CC.4.Rlit.1	Refer to details and examples in a text when explaining what the text says explicitly and when drawing inferences from the text.
		CA CC.4.Rlit.4	Determine the meaning of words and phrases as they are used in a text, including those that allude to significant characters found in mythology (e.g., Herculean). **(See grade 4 Language standards 4–6 for additional expectations.) CA**
		CA CC.4.Rlit.5	Explain major differences between poems, drama, and prose, and refer to the structural elements of poems (e.g., verse, rhythm, meter) and drama (e.g., casts of characters, settings, descriptions, dialogue, stage directions) when writing or speaking about a text.
168	**Word Work:** Word Origins		Know and apply grade-level phonics and word analysis skills in decoding words.
		CA CC.4.Rfou.3.a	Use combined knowledge of all letter-sound correspondences, syllabication patterns, and morphology (e.g., roots and affixes) to read accurately unfamiliar multisyllabic words in context and out of context.
			Determine or clarify the meaning of unknown and multiple-meaning words and phrases based on *grade 4 reading and content*, choosing flexibly from a range of strategies.
		CA CC.4.L.4.b	Use common, grade-appropriate Greek and Latin affixes and roots as clues to the meaning of a word (e.g., telegraph, photograph, autograph).
169	**Selection 2 Opener:** Before You Move On	CA CC.4.Rlit.1	Refer to details and examples in a text when explaining what the text says explicitly and when drawing inferences from the text.
	Selection 2 Opener: Before You Move On: Poetry	CA CC.4.Rlit.5	Explain major differences between poems, drama, and prose, and refer to the structural elements of poems (e.g., verse, rhythm, meter) and drama (e.g., casts of characters, settings, descriptions, dialogue, stage directions) when writing or speaking about a text.
171	**Selection 2:** Before You Move On	CA CC.4.Rlit.1	Refer to details and examples in a text when explaining what the text says explicitly and when drawing inferences from the text.

SE Pages	Lesson	Code	Standard
	Selection 2: Before You Move On: Figurative Language	CA CC.4.Rlit.4	Determine the meaning of words and phrases as they are used in a text, including those that allude to significant characters found in mythology (e.g., Herculean). **(See grade 4 Language standards 4–6 for additional expectations.) CA**
	Selection 2: Before You Move On		Demonstrate understanding of figurative language, word relationships, and nuances in word meanings.
		CA CC.4.L.5.a	Explain the meaning of simple similes and metaphors (e.g., *as pretty as a picture*) in context.
172	**Respond and Extend:** Compare Figurative Language	CA CC.4.Rlit.4	Determine the meaning of words and phrases as they are used in a text, including those that allude to significant characters found in mythology (e.g., Herculean). **(See grade 4 Language standards 4–6 for additional expectations.) CA**
			Demonstrate understanding of figurative language, word relationships, and nuances in word meanings.
		CA CC.4.L.5.a	Explain the meaning of simple similes and metaphors (e.g., *as pretty as a picture*) in context.
173	**Grammar and Spelling:** Plural Nouns	CA CC.4.L.1	Demonstrate command of the conventions of standard English grammar and usage when writing or speaking.
			Demonstrate command of the conventions of standard English capitalization, punctuation, and spelling when writing.
		CA CC.4.L.2.d	Spell grade-appropriate words correctly, consulting references as needed.
174	**Part 2: Language:** Describe Places		Engage effectively in a range of collaborative discussions (one-on-one, in groups, and teacher-led) with diverse partners on grade 4 topics and texts, building on others' ideas and expressing their own clearly.
		CA CC.4.SL.1.a	Come to discussions prepared, having read or studied required material; explicitly draw on that preparation and other information known about the topic to explore ideas under discussion.
175	**Social Studies Vocabulary:** Key Words	CA CC.4.Rinf.4	Determine the meaning of general academic and domain-specific words or phrases in a text relevant to a grade 4 topic or subject area. **(See grade 4 Language standards 4–6 for additional expectations.) CA**
176	**Thinking Map:** Main Idea and Details	CA CC.4.Rinf.2	Determine the main idea of a text and explain how it is supported by key details; summarize the text.
177	**Academic Vocabulary:** More Key Words	CA CC.4.Rinf.4	Determine the meaning of general academic and domain-specific words or phrases in a text relevant to a grade 4 topic or subject area. **(See grade 4 Language standards 4–6 for additional expectations.) CA**
178–179	**Strategic Reading:** Learn to Visualize	CA CC.4.Rlit.1	Refer to details and examples in a text when explaining what the text says explicitly and when drawing inferences from the text.
182	**Selection 1:** Set a Purpose		Read with sufficient accuracy and fluency to support comprehension.
		CA CC.4.Rfou.4.a	Read on-level text with purpose and understanding.
183	**Selection 1:** Before You Move On: Visualize	CA CC.4.Rlit.1	Refer to details and examples in a text when explaining what the text says explicitly and when drawing inferences from the text.

California Common Core State Standards, *continued*

SE Pages	Lesson	Code	Standard
	Selection 1: Before You Move On: Use Text Features	CA CC.4.Rinf.7	Interpret information presented visually, orally, or quantitatively (e.g., in charts, graphs, diagrams, time lines, animations, or interactive elements on Web pages) and explain how the information contributes to an understanding of the text in which it appears.
185	**Selection 1:** Before You Move On: Details	CA CC.4.Rinf.1	Refer to details and examples in a text when explaining what the text says explicitly and when drawing inferences from the text.
	Selection 1: Before You Move On: Use Text Features	CA CC.4.Rinf.7	Interpret information presented visually, orally, or quantitatively (e.g., in charts, graphs, diagrams, time lines, animations, or interactive elements on Web pages) and explain how the information contributes to an understanding of the text in which it appears.
187	**Selection 1:** Before You Move On: Visualize	CA CC.4.Rlit.1	Refer to details and examples in a text when explaining what the text says explicitly and when drawing inferences from the text.
	Selection 1: Before You Move On: Use Text Features	CA CC.4.Rinf.7	Interpret information presented visually, orally, or quantitatively (e.g., in charts, graphs, diagrams, time lines, animations, or interactive elements on Web pages) and explain how the information contributes to an understanding of the text in which it appears.
189	**Selection 1:** Before You Move On: Use Text Features	CA CC.4.Rinf.7	Interpret information presented visually, orally, or quantitatively (e.g., in charts, graphs, diagrams, time lines, animations, or interactive elements on Web pages) and explain how the information contributes to an understanding of the text in which it appears.
	Selection 1: Before You Move On: Visualize	CA CC.4.Rlit.1	Refer to details and examples in a text when explaining what the text says explicitly and when drawing inferences from the text.
191	**Selection 1:** Before You Move On	CA CC.4.Rlit.1	Refer to details and examples in a text when explaining what the text says explicitly and when drawing inferences from the text.
193	**Selection 1:** Before You Move On: Make Inferences	CA CC.4.Rlit.1	Refer to details and examples in a text when explaining what the text says explicitly and when drawing inferences from the text.
	Selection 1: Before You Move On: Summarize	CA CC.4.Rinf.2	Determine the main idea of a text and explain how it is supported by key details; summarize the text.
195	**Selection 1:** Before You Move On	CA CC.4.Rlit.1	Refer to details and examples in a text when explaining what the text says explicitly and when drawing inferences from the text.
196	**Think and Respond:** Talk About It	CA CC.4.Rinf.5	Describe the overall structure (e.g., chronology, comparison, cause/effect, problem/solution) of events, ideas, concepts, or information in a text or part of a text.
		CA CC.4.Rinf.10	By the end of year, read and comprehend informational texts, including history/social studies, science, and technical texts, in the grades 4–5 text complexity band proficiently, with scaffolding as needed at the high end of the range.
			Engage effectively in a range of collaborative discussions (one-on-one, in groups, and teacher-led) with diverse partners on *grade 4 topics and texts*, building on others' ideas and expressing their own clearly.

SE Pages	Lesson	Code	Standard
	Think and Respond: Write About It	CA CC.4.SL.1.a	Come to discussions prepared, having read or studied required material; explicitly draw on that preparation and other information known about the topic to explore ideas under discussion.
		CA CC.4.W.8	Recall relevant information from experiences or gather relevant information from print and digital sources; take notes, **paraphrase,** and categorize information, and provide a list of sources. **CA**
		CA CC.4.W.10	Write routinely over extended time frames (time for research, reflection, and revision) and shorter time frames (a single sitting or a day or two) for a range of discipline-specific tasks, purposes, and audiences.
		CA CC.4.L.6	Acquire and use accurately grade-appropriate general academic and domain-specific words and phrases, including those that signal precise actions, emotions, or states of being (e.g., quizzed, whined, stammered) and that are basic to a particular topic (e.g., wildlife, conservation, and endangered when discussing animal preservation).
197	**Reread and Summarize:** Main Idea and Details	CA CC.4.Rinf.2	Determine the main idea of a text and explain how it is supported by key details; summarize the text.
	Reread and Summarize: Fluency		Read with sufficient accuracy and fluency to support comprehension.
		CA CC.4.Rfou.4.b	Read on-level prose and poetry orally with accuracy, appropriate rate, and expression on successive readings.
	Reread and Summarize: Talk Together	CA CC.4.Rinf.2	Determine the main idea of a text and explain how it is supported by key details; summarize the text.
			Engage effectively in a range of collaborative discussions (one-on-one, in groups, and teacher-led) with diverse partners on *grade 4 topics and texts*, building on others' ideas and expressing their own clearly.
		CA CC.4.SL.1.a	Come to discussions prepared, having read or studied required material; explicitly draw on that preparation and other information known about the topic to explore ideas under discussion.
198	**Word Work:** Compound Words	CA CC.4.Rfou.3	Know and apply grade-level phonics and word analysis skills in decoding words.
		CA CC.4.Rfou.3.a	Use combined knowledge of all letter-sound correspondences, syllabication patterns, and morphology (e.g., roots and affixes) to read accurately unfamiliar multisyllabic words in context and out of context.
199	**Selection 2 Opener:** Before You Move On: Cause/Effect	CA CC.4.Rinf.5	Describe the overall structure (e.g., chronology, comparison, cause/effect, problem/solution) of events, ideas, concepts, or information in a text or part of a text.
	Selection 2 Opener: Before You Move On: Analyze	CA CC.4.Rinf.1	Refer to details and examples in a text when explaining what the text says explicitly and when drawing inferences from the text.
201	**Selection 2:** Before You Move On: Cause/Effect	CA CC.4.Rinf.5	Describe the overall structure (e.g., chronology, comparison, cause/effect, problem/solution) of events, ideas, concepts, or information in a text or part of a text.

California Common Core State Standards, *continued*

SE Pages	Lesson	Code	Standard
	Selection 2: Before You Move On: Visualize	CA CC.4.Rinf.1	Refer to details and examples in a text when explaining what the text says explicitly and when drawing inferences from the text.
203	**Selection 2:** Before You Move On	CA CC.4.Rinf.3	Explain events, procedures, ideas, or concepts in a historical, scientific, or technical text, including what happened and why, based on specific information in the text.
204	**Respond and Extend:** Compare Text Features	CA CC.4.Rinf.6	Compare and contrast a firsthand and secondhand account of the same event or topic; describe the differences in focus and the information provided.
	Respond and Extend: Talk Together	CA CC.4.Rinf.7	Interpret information presented visually, orally, or quantitatively (e.g., in charts, graphs, diagrams, time lines, animations, or interactive elements on Web pages) and explain how the information contributes to an understanding of the text in which it appears.
			Engage effectively in a range of collaborative discussions (one-on-one, in groups, and teacher-led) with diverse partners on *grade 4 topics and texts*, building on others' ideas and expressing their own clearly.
		CA CC.4.SL.1.a	Come to discussions prepared, having read or studied required material; explicitly draw on that preparation and other information known about the topic to explore ideas under discussion.
		CA CC.4.SL.1.d	Review the key ideas expressed and explain their own ideas and understanding in light of the discussion.
		CA CC.4.L.6	Acquire and use accurately grade-appropriate general academic and domain-specific words and phrases, including those that signal precise actions, emotions, or states of being (e.g., quizzed, whined, stammered) and that are basic to a particular topic (e.g., wildlife, conservation, and endangered when discussing animal preservation).
205	**Grammar and Spelling:** More Plural Nouns	CA CC.4.L.1	Demonstrate command of the conventions of standard English grammar and usage when writing or speaking.
			Demonstrate command of the conventions of standard English capitalization, punctuation, and spelling when writing.
		CA CC.4.L.2.d	Spell grade-appropriate words correctly, consulting references as needed.
206–207	**Writing Project:** Research Report Study a Model		Write informative/explanatory texts to examine a topic and convey ideas and information clearly.
		CA CC.4.W.2.a	Introduce a topic clearly and group related information in paragraphs and sections; include formatting (e.g., headings), illustrations, and multimedia when useful to aiding comprehension.
		CA CC.4.W.2.b	Develop the topic with facts, definitions, concrete details, quotations, or other information and examples related to the topic.
		CA CC.4.W.7	Conduct short research projects that build knowledge through investigation of different aspects of a topic.
		CA CC.4.W.8	Recall relevant information from experiences or gather relevant information from print and digital sources; take notes, **paraphrase,** and categorize information, and provide a list of sources. **CA**

SE Pages	Lesson	Code	Standard
208–209	**Writing Project:** Research Report Prewrite Gather Information		Write informative/explanatory texts to examine a topic and convey ideas and information clearly.
		CA CC.4.W.2.a	Introduce a topic clearly and group related information in paragraphs and sections; include formatting (e.g., headings), illustrations, and multimedia when useful to aiding comprehension.
		CA CC.4.W.2.b	Develop the topic with facts, definitions, concrete details, quotations, or other information and examples related to the topic.
		CA CC.4.W.5	With guidance and support from peers and adults, develop and strengthen writing as needed by planning, revising, and editing. (Editing for conventions should demonstrate command of Language standards 1–3 up to and including grade 4.)
		CA CC.4.W.7	Conduct short research projects that build knowledge through investigation of different aspects of a topic.
		CA CC.4.W.8	Recall relevant information from experiences or gather relevant information from print and digital sources; take notes, **paraphrase,** and categorize information, and provide a list of sources. **CA**
210	**Writing Project:** Research Report Get Organized Draft	CA CC.4.Rinf.2	Determine the main idea of a text and explain how it is supported by key details; summarize the text.
			Write informative/explanatory texts to examine a topic and convey ideas and information clearly.
		CA CC.4.W.2.b	Develop the topic with facts, definitions, concrete details, quotations, or other information and examples related to the topic.
		CA CC.4.W.8	Recall relevant information from experiences or gather relevant information from print and digital sources; take notes, **paraphrase,** and categorize information, and provide a list of sources. **CA**
211	**Writing Project:** Research Report Revise		Write informative/explanatory texts to examine a topic and convey ideas and information clearly.
		CA CC.4.W.2.b	Develop the topic with facts, definitions, concrete details, quotations, or other information and examples related to the topic.
		CA CC.4.W.5	With guidance and support from peers and adults, develop and strengthen writing as needed by planning, revising, and editing. (Editing for conventions should demonstrate command of Language standards 1–3 up to and including grade 4.)
	Writing Project: Research Report Edit and Proofread	CA CC.4.W.5	With guidance and support from peers and adults, develop and strengthen writing as needed by planning, revising, and editing. (Editing for conventions should demonstrate command of Language standards 1–3 up to and including grade 4.)
	Writing Project: Research Report Publish	CA CC.4.W.6	With some guidance and support from adults, use technology, including the Internet, to produce and publish writing as well as to interact and collaborate with others; demonstrate sufficient command of keyboarding skills to type a minimum of one page in a single sitting.

California Common Core State Standards, *continued*

SE Pages	Lesson	Code	Standard
212	**Talk Together**		Engage effectively in a range of collaborative discussions (one-on-one, in groups, and teacher-led) with diverse partners on grade 4 topics and texts, building on others' ideas and expressing their own clearly.
		CA CC.4.SL.1.a	Come to discussions prepared, having read or studied required material; explicitly draw on that preparation and other information known about the topic to explore ideas under discussion.
		CA CC.4.SL.1.c	Pose and respond to specific questions to clarify or follow up on information, and make comments that contribute to the discussion and link to the remarks of others.
		CA CC.4.SL.1.d	Review the key ideas expressed and explain their own ideas and understanding in light of the discussion.
		CA CC.4.SL.4	Report on a topic or text, tell a story, or recount an experience in an organized manner, using appropriate facts and relevant, descriptive details to support main ideas or themes; speak clearly at an understandable pace.
	Write a Poem	CA CC.4.Rlit.5	Explain major differences between poems, drama, and prose, and refer to the structural elements of poems (e.g., verse, rhythm, meter) and drama (e.g., casts of characters, settings, descriptions, dialogue, stage directions) when writing or speaking about a text.
		CA CC.4.W.10	Write routinely over extended time frames (time for research, reflection, and revision) and shorter time frames (a single sitting or a day or two) for a range of discipline-specific tasks, purposes, and audiences.
213	**Unit Wrap-Up:** Share Your Ideas	CA CC.4.W.10	Write routinely over extended time frames (time for research, reflection, and revision) and shorter time frames (a single sitting or a day or two) for a range of discipline-specific tasks, purposes, and audiences.
		CA CC.4.SL.1	Engage effectively in a range of collaborative discussions (one-on-one, in groups, and teacher-led) with diverse partners on *grade 4 topics and texts,* building on others' ideas and expressing their own clearly.
		CA CC.4.SL.1.a	Come to discussions prepared, having read or studied required material; explicitly draw on that preparation and other information known about the topic to explore ideas under discussion.
		CA CC.4.SL.1.b	Follow agreed-upon rules for discussions and carry out assigned roles.
		CA CC.4.SL.1.c	Pose and respond to specific questions to clarify or follow up on information, and make comments that contribute to the discussion and link to the remarks of others.
		CA CC.4.SL.1.d	Review the key ideas expressed and explain their own ideas and understanding in light of the discussion.
		CA CC.4.SL.4	Report on a topic or text, tell a story, or recount an experience in an organized manner, using appropriate facts and relevant, descriptive details to support main ideas or themes; speak clearly at an understandable pace.
		CA CC.4.SL.4.a	**Plan and deliver a narrative presentation that: relates ideas, observations, or recollections; provides a clear context; and includes clear insight into why the event or experience is memorable. CA**

SE Pages	Lesson	Code	Standard
215	**Unit Launch:** Share What You Know	CA CC.4.SL.1	Engage effectively in a range of collaborative discussions (one-on-one, in groups, and teacher-led) with diverse partners on *grade 4 topics and texts,* building on others' ideas and expressing their own clearly.
216	**Part 1: Language:** Make Comparisons		Engage effectively in a range of collaborative discussions (one-on-one, in groups, and teacher-led) with diverse partners on *grade 4 topics and texts,* building on others' ideas and expressing their own clearly.
		CA CC.4.SL.1.a	Come to discussions prepared, having read or studied required material; explicitly draw on that preparation and other information known about the topic to explore ideas under discussion.
217	**Science Vocabulary:** Key Words	CA CC.4.Rinf.4	Determine the meaning of general academic and domain-specific words or phrases in a text relevant to a grade 4 topic or subject area. **(See grade 4 Language standards 4–6 for additional expectations.) CA**
218	**Thinking Map:** Cause and Effect	CA CC.4.Rinf.5	Describe the overall structure (e.g., chronology, comparison, cause/effect, problem/solution) of events, ideas, concepts, or information in a text or part of a text.
			Write informative/explanatory texts to examine a topic and convey ideas and information clearly.
		CA CC.4.W.2.c	Link ideas within categories of information using words and phrases (e.g., *another, for example, also, because*).
219	**Academic Vocabulary:** More Key Words	CA CC.4.Rinf.4	Determine the meaning of general academic and domain-specific words or phrases in a text relevant to a grade 4 topic or subject area. **(See grade 4 Language standards 4–6 for additional expectations.) CA**
220–221	**Strategic Reading:** Learn to Ask Questions	CA CC.4.Rinf.1	Refer to details and examples in a text when explaining what the text says explicitly and when drawing inferences from the text.
224	**Selection 1:** Set a Purpose		Read with sufficient accuracy and fluency to support comprehension.
		CA CC.4.Rfou.4.a	Read on-level text with purpose and understanding.
225	**Selection 1:** Before You Move On: Use Text Features	CA CC.4.Rinf.7	Interpret information presented visually, orally, or quantitatively (e.g., in charts, graphs, diagrams, time lines, animations, or interactive elements on Web pages) and explain how the information contributes to an understanding of the text in which it appears.
	Selection 1: Before You Move On: Ask Questions	CA CC.4.Rinf.1	Refer to details and examples in a text when explaining what the text says explicitly and when drawing inferences from the text.
		CA CC.4.Rinf.1	Interpret information presented visually, orally, or quantitatively (e.g., in charts, graphs, diagrams, time lines, animations, or interactive elements on Web pages) and explain how the information contributes to an understanding of the text in which it appears.
227	**Selection 1:** Before You Move On: Cause/Effect	CA CC.4.Rinf.5	Describe the overall structure (e.g., chronology, comparison, cause/effect, problem/solution) of events, ideas, concepts, or information in a text or part of a text.

California Common Core State Standards, *continued*

SE Pages	Lesson	Code	Standard
	Selection 1: Before You Move On: Ask Questions	CA CC.4.Rinf.1	Refer to details and examples in a text when explaining what the text says explicitly and when drawing inferences from the text.
229	**Selection 1:** Before You Move On	CA CC.4.Rinf.1	Refer to details and examples in a text when explaining what the text says explicitly and when drawing inferences from the text.
	Selection 1: Before You Move On: Cause/Effect	CA CC.4.Rinf.5	Describe the overall structure (e.g., chronology, comparison, cause/effect, problem/solution) of events, ideas, concepts, or information in a text or part of a text.
	Selection 1: Before You Move On: Ask Questions	CA CC.4.Rinf.7	Interpret information presented visually, orally, or quantitatively (e.g., in charts, graphs, diagrams, time lines, animations, or interactive elements on Web pages) and explain how the information contributes to an understanding of the text in which it appears.
231	**Selection 1:** Before You Move On: Ask Questions	CA CC.4.Rinf.1	Refer to details and examples in a text when explaining what the text says explicitly and when drawing inferences from the text.
	Selection 1: Before You Move On: Cause/Effect	CA CC.4.Rinf.3	Explain events, procedures, ideas, or concepts in a historical, scientific, or technical text, including what happened and why, based on specific information in the text.
		CA CC.4.Rinf.5	Describe the overall structure (e.g., chronology, comparison, cause/effect, problem/solution) of events, ideas, concepts, or information in a text or part of a text.
233	**Selection 1:** Before You Move On: Cause/Effect	CA CC.4.Rinf.5	Describe the overall structure (e.g., chronology, comparison, cause/effect, problem/solution) of events, ideas, concepts, or information in a text or part of a text.
	Selection 1: Before You Move On: Details	CA CC.4.Rinf.1	Refer to details and examples in a text when explaining what the text says explicitly and when drawing inferences from the text.
235	**Selection 1:** Before You Move On: Cause/Effect	CA CC.4.Rinf.1	Refer to details and examples in a text when explaining what the text says explicitly and when drawing inferences from the text.
		CA CC.4.Rinf.5	Describe the overall structure (e.g., chronology, comparison, cause/effect, problem/solution) of events, ideas, concepts, or information in a text or part of a text.
	Selection 1: Before You Move On: Use Text Features	CA CC.4.Rinf.7	Interpret information presented visually, orally, or quantitatively (e.g., in charts, graphs, diagrams, time lines, animations, or interactive elements on Web pages) and explain how the information contributes to an understanding of the text in which it appears.
236	**Think and Respond:** Talk About It	CA CC.4.Rinf.3	Explain events, procedures, ideas, or concepts in a historical, scientific, or technical text, including what happened and why, based on specific information in the text.
		CA CC.4.Rinf.10	By the end of year, read and comprehend informational texts, including history/social studies, science, and technical texts, in the grades 4–5 text complexity band proficiently, with scaffolding as needed at the high end of the range.
			Engage effectively in a range of collaborative discussions (one-on-one, in groups, and teacher-led) with diverse partners on *grade 4 topics and texts*, building on others' ideas and expressing their own clearly.

Unit 4 Power of Nature, *continued*

SE Pages	Lesson	Code	Standard
		CA CC.4.SL.1.a	Come to discussions prepared, having read or studied required material; explicitly draw on that preparation and other information known about the topic to explore ideas under discussion.
	Think and Respond: Write About It	CA CC.4.W.10	Write routinely over extended time frames (time for research, reflection, and revision) and shorter time frames (a single sitting or a day or two) for a range of discipline-specific tasks, purposes, and audiences.
		CA CC.4.L.6	Acquire and use accurately grade-appropriate general academic and domain-specific words and phrases, including those that signal precise actions, emotions, or states of being (e.g., quizzed, whined, stammered) and that are basic to a particular topic (e.g., wildlife, conservation, and endangered when discussing animal preservation).
237	**Reread and Explain:** Cause and Effect	CA CC.4.Rinf.5	Describe the overall structure (e.g., chronology, comparison, cause/effect, problem/solution) of events, ideas, concepts, or information in a text or part of a text.
	Reread and Explain: Fluency		Read with sufficient accuracy and fluency to support comprehension.
		CA CC.4.Rfou.4.b	Read on-level prose and poetry orally with accuracy, appropriate rate, and expression on successive readings.
	Reread and Explain: Talk Together	CA CC.4.Rinf.3	Explain events, procedures, ideas, or concepts in a historical, scientific, or technical text, including what happened and why, based on specific information in the text.
			Engage effectively in a range of collaborative discussions (one-on-one, in groups, and teacher-led) with diverse partners on grade 4 topics and texts, building on others' ideas and expressing their own clearly.
		CA CC.4.SL.1.a	Come to discussions prepared, having read or studied required material; explicitly draw on that preparation and other information known about the topic to explore ideas under discussion.
238	**Word Work:** Context Clues		Read with sufficient accuracy and fluency to support comprehension.
		CA CC.4.Rfou.4.c	Use context to confirm or self-correct word recognition and understanding, rereading as necessary.
			Determine or clarify the meaning of unknown and multiple-meaning words and phrases based on *grade 4 reading and content*, choosing flexibly from a range of strategies.
		CA CC.4.L.4.a	Use context (e.g., definitions, examples, or restatements in text) as a clue to the meaning of a word or phrase.
239	**Selection 2 Opener:** Before You Move On	CA CC.4.Rinf.1	Refer to details and examples in a text when explaining what the text says explicitly and when drawing inferences from the text.
241	**Selection 2:** Before You Move On: Ask Questions	CA CC.4.Rinf.1	Refer to details and examples in a text when explaining what the text says explicitly and when drawing inferences from the text.
	Selection 2: Before You Move On: Cause/Effect	CA CC.4.Rinf.3	Explain events, procedures, ideas, or concepts in a historical, scientific, or technical text, including what happened and why, based on specific information in the text.

California Common Core State Standards, continued

Unit 4	Power of Nature, continued		
SE Pages	**Lesson**	**Code**	**Standard**
		CA CC.4.Rinf.5	Describe the overall structure (e.g., chronology, comparison, cause/effect, problem/solution) of events, ideas, concepts, or information in a text or part of a text.
243	**Selection 2:** Before You Move On: Ask Questions	CA CC.4.Rinf.1	Refer to details and examples in a text when explaining what the text says explicitly and when drawing inferences from the text.
	Selection 2: Before You Move On	CA CC.4.Rinf.7	Interpret information presented visually, orally, or quantitatively (e.g., in charts, graphs, diagrams, time lines, animations, or interactive elements on Web pages) and explain how the information contributes to an understanding of the text in which it appears.
244	**Respond and Extend:** Compare Genres	CA CC.4.Rinf.6	Compare and contrast a firsthand and secondhand account of the same event or topic; describe the differences in focus and the information provided.
		CA CC.4.Rinf.9	Integrate information from two texts on the same topic in order to write or speak about the subject knowledgeably.
245	**Grammar and Spelling:** Present-Tense Action Verbs	CA CC.4.L.1	Demonstrate command of the conventions of standard English grammar and usage when writing or speaking.
			Demonstrate command of the conventions of standard English capitalization, punctuation, and spelling when writing.
		CA CC.4.L.2.d	Spell grade-appropriate words correctly, consulting references as needed.
246	**Part 2:** **Language:** Express Needs and Wants	CA CC.4.Rinf.4	Determine the meaning of general academic and domain-specific words or phrases in a text relevant to a grade 4 topic or subject area. **(See grade 4 Language standards 4–6 for additional expectations.) CA**
			Engage effectively in a range of collaborative discussions (one-on-one, in groups, and teacher-led) with diverse partners on grade 4 topics and texts, building on others' ideas and expressing their own clearly.
		CA CC.4.SL.1.a	Come to discussions prepared, having read or studied required material; explicitly draw on that preparation and other information known about the topic to explore ideas under discussion.
247	**Science Vocabulary:** Key Words	CA CC.4.Rinf.4	Determine the meaning of general academic and domain-specific words or phrases in a text relevant to a grade 4 topic or subject area. **(See grade 4 Language standards 4–6 for additional expectations.) CA**
248	**Thinking Map:** Problem and Solution	CA CC.4.Rinf.5	Describe the overall structure (e.g., chronology, comparison, cause/effect, problem/solution) of events, ideas, concepts, or information in a text or part of a text.
249	**Academic Vocabulary:** More Key Words	CA CC.4.Rlit.4	Determine the meaning of words and phrases as they are used in a text, including those that allude to significant characters found in mythology (e.g., Herculean). **(See grade 4 Language standards 4–6 for additional expectations.) CA**
250–251	**Strategic Reading:** Learn to Ask Questions	CA CC.4.Rlit.1	Refer to details and examples in a text when explaining what the text says explicitly and when drawing inferences from the text.

SE Pages	Lesson	Code	Standard
254	**Selection 1:** Set a Purpose		Read with sufficient accuracy and fluency to support comprehension.
		CA CC.4.Rfou.4.a	Read on-level text with purpose and understanding.
257	**Selection 1:** Before You Move On: Character	CA CC.4.Rlit.3	Describe in depth a character, setting, or event in a story or drama, drawing on specific details in the text (e.g., a character's thoughts, words, or actions).
	Selection 1: Before You Move On: Ask Questions	CA CC.4.Rlit.1	Refer to details and examples in a text when explaining what the text says explicitly and when drawing inferences from the text.
258	**Selection 1:** Predict	CA CC.4.Rlit.1	Refer to details and examples in a text when explaining what the text says explicitly and when drawing inferences from the text.
259	**Selection 1:** Before You Move On	CA CC.4.Rlit.1	Refer to details and examples in a text when explaining what the text says explicitly and when drawing inferences from the text.
	Selection 1: Before You Move On: Problem/Solution	CA CC.4.Rinf.5	Describe the overall structure (e.g., chronology, comparison, cause/effect, problem/solution) of events, ideas, concepts, or information in a text or part of a text.
	Selection 1: Before You Move On: Make Inferences	CA CC.4.Rlit.3	Describe in depth a character, setting, or event in a story or drama, drawing on specific details in the text (e.g., a character's thoughts, words, or actions).
260	**Selection 1:** Predict	CA CC.4.Rlit.1	Refer to details and examples in a text when explaining what the text says explicitly and when drawing inferences from the text.
263	**Selection 1:** Before You Move On	CA CC.4.Rlit.1	Refer to details and examples in a text when explaining what the text says explicitly and when drawing inferences from the text.
	Selection 1: Before You Move On: Problem/Solution	CA CC.4.Rinf.5	Describe the overall structure (e.g., chronology, comparison, cause/effect, problem/solution) of events, ideas, concepts, or information in a text or part of a text.
264	**Selection 1:** Predict	CA CC.4.Rlit.1	Refer to details and examples in a text when explaining what the text says explicitly and when drawing inferences from the text.
265	**Selection 1:** Before You Move On	CA CC.4.Rlit.1	Refer to details and examples in a text when explaining what the text says explicitly and when drawing inferences from the text.
	Selection 1: Before You Move On: Ask Questions	CA CC.4.Rlit.7	Make connections between the text of a story or drama and a visual or oral presentation of the text, identifying where each version reflects specific descriptions and directions in the text.
266	**Meet the Author:** Writer's Craft	CA CC.4.Rlit.1	Refer to details and examples in a text when explaining what the text says explicitly and when drawing inferences from the text.
		CA CC.4.L.5	Demonstrate understanding of figurative language, word relationships, and nuances in word meanings.
268	**Think and Respond:** Talk About It	CA CC.4.Rlit.10	By the end of the year, read and comprehend literature, including stories, dramas, and poetry, in the grades 4–5 text complexity band proficiently, with scaffolding as needed at the high end of the range.
			Engage effectively in a range of collaborative discussions (one-on-one, in groups, and teacher-led) with diverse partners on *grade 4 topics and texts*, building on others' ideas and expressing their own clearly.

California Common Core State Standards, *continued*

SE Pages	Lesson	Code	Standard
	Think and Respond: Write About It	CA CC.4.SL.1.a	Come to discussions prepared, having read or studied required material; explicitly draw on that preparation and other information known about the topic to explore ideas under discussion.
		CA CC.4.W.10	Write routinely over extended time frames (time for research, reflection, and revision) and shorter time frames (a single sitting or a day or two) for a range of discipline-specific tasks, purposes, and audiences.
		CA CC.4.L.6	Acquire and use accurately grade-appropriate general academic and domain-specific words and phrases, including those that signal precise actions, emotions, or states of being (e.g., quizzed, whined, stammered) and that are basic to a particular topic (e.g., wildlife, conservation, and endangered when discussing animal preservation).
269	**Reread and Retell :** Problem and Solution	CA CC.4.Rinf.5	Describe the overall structure (e.g., chronology, comparison, cause/effect, problem/solution) of events, ideas, concepts, or information in a text or part of a text.
	Reread and Retell: Fluency		Read with sufficient accuracy and fluency to support comprehension.
		CA CC.4.Rfou.4.b	Read on-level prose and poetry orally with accuracy, appropriate rate, and expression on successive readings.
	Reread and Retell: Talk Together	CA CC.4.Rlit.7	Make connections between the text of a story or drama and a visual or oral presentation of the text, identifying where each version reflects specific descriptions and directions in the text.
		CA CC.4.L.6	Acquire and use accurately grade-appropriate general academic and domain-specific words and phrases, including those that signal precise actions, emotions, or states of being (e.g., quizzed, whined, stammered) and that are basic to a particular topic (e.g., wildlife, conservation, and endangered when discussing animal preservation).
270	**Word Work:** Multiple-Meaning Words		Read with sufficient accuracy and fluency to support comprehension.
		CA CC.4.Rfou.4.c	Use context to confirm or self-correct word recognition and understanding, rereading as necessary.
			Determine or clarify the meaning of unknown and multiple-meaning words and phrases based on *grade 4 reading and content*, choosing flexibly from a range of strategies.
		CA CC.4.L.4.a	Use context (e.g., definitions, examples, or restatements in text) as a clue to the meaning of a word or phrase.
271	**Selection 2 Opener:** Before You Move On	CA CC.4.Rlit.1	Refer to details and examples in a text when explaining what the text says explicitly and when drawing inferences from the text.
			Demonstrate understanding of figurative language, word relationships, and nuances in word meanings.
		CA CC.4.L.5.a	Explain the meaning of simple similes and metaphors (e.g., as pretty as a picture) in context.
273	**Selection 2:** Before You Move On: Elements of Poetry	CA CC.4.Rlit.5	Explain major differences between poems, drama, and prose, and refer to the structural elements of poems (e.g., verse, rhythm, meter) and drama (e.g., casts of characters, settings, descriptions, dialogue, stage directions) when writing or speaking about a text.

SE Pages	Lesson	Code	Standard
	Selection 1: Before You Move On: Figurative Language	CA CC.4.Rlit.3	Describe in depth a character, setting, or event in a story or drama, drawing on specific details in the text (e.g., a character's thoughts, words, or actions).
			Demonstrate understanding of figurative language, word relationships, and nuances in word meanings.
		CA CC.4.L.5.a	Explain the meaning of simple similes and metaphors (e.g., *as pretty as a picture*) in context.
274	**Respond and Extend:** Compare Figurative Language	CA CC.4.Rlit.4	Determine the meaning of words and phrases as they are used in a text, including those that allude to significant characters found in mythology (e.g., Herculean). **(See grade 4 Language standards 4–6 for additional expectations.) CA**
			Demonstrate understanding of figurative language, word relationships, and nuances in word meanings.
		CA CC.4.L.5.a	Explain the meaning of simple similes and metaphors (e.g., *as pretty as a picture*) in context.
	Respond and Extend: Talk Together		Engage effectively in a range of collaborative discussions (one-on-one, in groups, and teacher-led) with diverse partners on *grade 4 topics and texts*, building on others' ideas and expressing their own clearly.
		CA CC.4.SL.1.d	Review the key ideas expressed and explain their own ideas and understanding in light of the discussion.
		CA CC.4.L.6	Acquire and use accurately grade-appropriate general academic and domain-specific words and phrases, including those that signal precise actions, emotions, or states of being (e.g., quizzed, whined, stammered) and that are basic to a particular topic (e.g., wildlife, conservation, and endangered when discussing animal preservation).
275	**Grammar and Spelling:** Forms of *be* and *have*	CA CC.4.L.1	Demonstrate command of the conventions of standard English grammar and usage when writing or speaking.
276–277	**Writing Project:** Tall Tale Study a Model Prewrite Draft		Write narratives to develop real or imagined experiences or events using effective technique, descriptive details, and clear event sequences.
		CA CC.4.W.3.a	Orient the reader by establishing a situation and introducing a narrator and/or characters; organize an event sequence that unfolds naturally.
		CA CC.4.W.3.b	Use dialogue and description to develop experiences and events or show the responses of characters to situations.
		CA CC.4.W.3.e	Provide a conclusion that follows from the narrated experiences or events.
278	**Writing Project:** Tall Tale Revise		Write narratives to develop real or imagined experiences or events using effective technique, descriptive details, and clear event sequences.
		CA CC.4.W.3.d	Use concrete words and phrases and sensory details to convey experiences and events precisely.
279	**Writing Project:** Tall Tale Edit and Proofread	CA CC.4.W.5	With guidance and support from peers and adults, develop and strengthen writing as needed by planning, revising, and editing. (Editing for conventions should demonstrate command of Language standards 1–3 up to and including grade 4.)

California Common Core State Standards, continued

SE Pages	Lesson	Code	Standard
	Writing Project: Tall Tale Publish		Read with sufficient accuracy and fluency to support comprehension.
		CA CC.4.Rfou.4.b	Read on-level prose and poetry orally with accuracy, appropriate rate, and expression on successive readings.
		CA CC.4.W.6	With some guidance and support from adults, use technology, including the Internet, to produce and publish writing as well as to interact and collaborate with others; demonstrate sufficient command of keyboarding skills to type a minimum of one page in a single sitting.
		CA CC.4.SL.4	Report on a topic or text, tell a story, or recount an experience in an organized manner, using appropriate facts and relevant, descriptive details to support main ideas or themes; speak clearly at an understandable pace.
		CA CC.4.SL.4.a	**Plan and deliver a narrative presentation that: relates ideas, observations, or recollections; provides a clear context; and includes clear insight into why the event or experience is memorable. CA**
280	**Talk Together**		Engage effectively in a range of collaborative discussions (one-on-one, in groups, and teacher-led) with diverse partners on *grade 4 topics and texts*, building on others' ideas and expressing their own clearly.
		CA CC.4.SL.1.a	Come to discussions prepared, having read or studied required material; explicitly draw on that preparation and other information known about the topic to explore ideas under discussion.
		CA CC.4.L.6	Acquire and use accurately grade-appropriate general academic and domain-specific words and phrases, including those that signal precise actions, emotions, or states of being (e.g., quizzed, whined, stammered) and that are basic to a particular topic (e.g., wildlife, conservation, and endangered when discussing animal preservation).
	Write a Description	CA CC.4.W.9	Draw evidence from literary or informational texts to support analysis, reflection, and research.
281	**Unit Wrap-Up:** Share Your Ideas	CA CC.4.Rlit.5	Explain major differences between poems, drama, and prose, and refer to the structural elements of poems (e.g., verse, rhythm, meter) and drama (e.g., casts of characters, settings, descriptions, dialogue, stage directions) when writing or speaking about a text.
		CA CC.4.W.7	Conduct short research projects that build knowledge through investigation of different aspects of a topic.
		CA CC.4.W.10	Write routinely over extended time frames (time for research, reflection, and revision) and shorter time frames (a single sitting or a day or two) for a range of discipline-specific tasks, purposes, and audiences.
			Engage effectively in a range of collaborative discussions (one-on-one, in groups, and teacher-led) with diverse partners on *grade 4 topics and texts*, building on others' ideas and expressing their own clearly.

SE Pages	Lesson	Code	Standard
		CA CC.4.SL.1.a	Come to discussions prepared, having read or studied required material; explicitly draw on that preparation and other information known about the topic to explore ideas under discussion.
		CA CC.4.SL.4	Report on a topic or text, tell a story, or recount an experience in an organized manner, using appropriate facts and relevant, descriptive details to support main ideas or themes; speak clearly at an understandable pace.
		CA CC.4.SL.4.a	**Plan and deliver a narrative presentation that: relates ideas, observations, or recollections; provides a clear context; and includes clear insight into why the event or experience is memorable. CA**
283	**Unit Launch:** Share What You Know		Engage effectively in a range of collaborative discussions (one-on-one, in groups, and teacher-led) with diverse partners on grade 4 topics and texts, building on others' ideas and expressing their own clearly.
284	**Part 1:** **Language:** Retell a Story		Engage effectively in a range of collaborative discussions (one-on-one, in groups, and teacher-led) with diverse partners on grade 4 topics and texts, building on others' ideas and expressing their own clearly.
		CA CC.4.SL.1.a	Come to discussions prepared, having read or studied required material; explicitly draw on that preparation and other information known about the topic to explore ideas under discussion.
		CA CC.4.SL.1.c	Pose and respond to specific questions to clarify or follow up on information, and make comments that contribute to the discussion and link to the remarks of others.
		CA CC.4.SL.1.d	Review the key ideas expressed and explain their own ideas and understanding in light of the discussion.
		CA CC.4.SL.4	Report on a topic or text, tell a story, or recount an experience in an organized manner, using appropriate facts and relevant, descriptive details to support main ideas or themes; speak clearly at an understandable pace.
285	**Science Vocabulary:** Key Words	CA CC.4.Rinf.4	Determine the meaning of general academic and domain-specific words or phrases in a text relevant to a grade 4 topic or subject area. **(See grade 4 Language standards 4–6 for additional expectations.) CA**
286	**Thinking Map:** Plot	CA CC.4.Rlit.2	Determine a theme of a story, drama, or poem from details in the text; summarize the text.
		CA CC.4.Rlit.3	Describe in depth a character, setting, or event in a story or drama, drawing on specific details in the text (e.g., a character's thoughts, words, or actions).

California Common Core State Standards, *continued*

SE Pages	Lesson	Code	Standard
287	**Academic Vocabulary:** More Key Words	CA CC.4.Rlit.4	Determine the meaning of words and phrases as they are used in a text, including those that allude to significant characters found in mythology (e.g., Herculean). **(See grade 4 Language standards 4–6 for additional expectations.) CA**
		CA CC.4.Rinf.4	Determine the meaning of general academic and domain-specific words or phrases in a text relevant to a grade 4 topic or subject area. **(See grade 4 Language standards 4–6 for additional expectations.) CA**
288–289	**Strategic Reading:** Learn to Make Inferences	CA CC.4.Rlit.1	Refer to details and examples in a text when explaining what the text says explicitly and when drawing inferences from the text.
		CA CC.4.SL.1	Engage effectively in a range of collaborative discussions (one-on-one, in groups, and teacher-led) with diverse partners on grade 4 topics and texts, building on others' ideas and expressing their own clearly.
292	**Selection 1:** Set a Purpose		Read with sufficient accuracy and fluency to support comprehension.
		CA CC.4.Rfou.4.a	Read on-level text with purpose and understanding.
293	**Selection 1:** Before You Move On: Plot	CA CC.4.Rlit.1	Refer to details and examples in a text when explaining what the text says explicitly and when drawing inferences from the text.
	Selection 1: Before You Move On: Point of View	CA CC.4.Rlit.6	Compare and contrast the point of view from which different stories are narrated, including the difference between first- and third-person narrations.
294	**Selection 1:** Predict	CA CC.4.Rlit.1	Refer to details and examples in a text when explaining what the text says explicitly and when drawing inferences from the text.
295	**Selection 1:** Before You Move On	CA CC.4.Rlit.1	Refer to details and examples in a text when explaining what the text says explicitly and when drawing inferences from the text.
	Selection 1: Before You Move On: Plot	CA CC.4.Rlit.3	Describe in depth a character, setting, or event in a story or drama, drawing on specific details in the text (e.g., a character's thoughts, words, or actions).
	Selection 1: Before You Move On: Make Inferences	CA CC.4.Rlit.4	Determine the meaning of words and phrases as they are used in a text, including those that allude to significant characters found in mythology (e.g., Herculean). **(See grade 4 Language standards 4–6 for additional expectations.) CA**
296	**Selection 1:** Predict	CA CC.4.Rlit.1	Refer to details and examples in a text when explaining what the text says explicitly and when drawing inferences from the text.
299	**Selection 1:** Before You Move On	CA CC.4.Rlit.1	Refer to details and examples in a text when explaining what the text says explicitly and when drawing inferences from the text.
	Selection 1: Before You Move On: Plot	CA CC.4.Rlit.3	Describe in depth a character, setting, or event in a story or drama, drawing on specific details in the text (e.g., a character's thoughts, words, or actions).
	Selection 1: Before You Move On: Make Inferences	CA CC.4.Rlit.4	Determine the meaning of words and phrases as they are used in a text, including those that allude to significant characters found in mythology (e.g., Herculean). **(See grade 4 Language standards 4–6 for additional expectations.) CA**

SE Pages	Lesson	Code	Standard
300	**Selection 1:** Predict	CA CC.4.Rlit.1	Refer to details and examples in a text when explaining what the text says explicitly and when drawing inferences from the text.
	Selection 1: Before You Move On	CA CC.4.Rlit.1	Refer to details and examples in a text when explaining what the text says explicitly and when drawing inferences from the text.
	Selection 1: Before You Move On: Plot	CA CC.4.Rlit.2	Determine a theme of a story, drama, or poem from details in the text; summarize the text.
301	**Meet the Author:** Writer's Craft	CA CC.4.Rlit.3	Describe in depth a character, setting, or event in a story or drama, drawing on specific details in the text (e.g., a character's thoughts, words, or actions).
		CA CC.4.Rlit.9	Compare and contrast the treatment of similar themes and topics (e.g., opposition of good and evil) and patterns of events (e.g., the quest) in stories, myths, and traditional literature from different cultures.
302	**Think and Respond:** Talk About It	CA CC.4.Rlit.3	Describe in depth a character, setting, or event in a story or drama, drawing on specific details in the text (e.g., a character's thoughts, words, or actions).
		CA CC.4.Rlit.6	Compare and contrast the point of view from which different stories are narrated, including the difference between first- and third-person narrations.
		CA CC.4.Rlit.10	By the end of the year, read and comprehend literature, including stories, dramas, and poetry, in the grades 4–5 text complexity band proficiently, with scaffolding as needed at the high end of the range.
			Engage effectively in a range of collaborative discussions (one-on-one, in groups, and teacher-led) with diverse partners on *grade 4 topics and texts,* building on others' ideas and expressing their own clearly.
		CA CC.4.SL.1.a	Come to discussions prepared, having read or studied required material; explicitly draw on that preparation and other information known about the topic to explore ideas under discussion.
	Think and Respond: Write About It	CA CC.4.W.10	Write routinely over extended time frames (time for research, reflection, and revision) and shorter time frames (a single sitting or a day or two) for a range of discipline-specific tasks, purposes, and audiences.
		CA CC.4.L.6	Acquire and use accurately grade-appropriate general academic and domain-specific words and phrases, including those that signal precise actions, emotions, or states of being (e.g., quizzed, whined, stammered) and that are basic to a particular topic (e.g., wildlife, conservation, and endangered when discussing animal preservation).
303	**Reread and Retell:** Plot	CA CC.4.Rlit.2	Determine a theme of a story, drama, or poem from details in the text; summarize the text.
	Reread and Retell: Plot	CA CC.4.Rlit.3	Describe in depth a character, setting, or event in a story or drama, drawing on specific details in the text (e.g., a character's thoughts, words, or actions).
		CA CC.4.SL.2	Paraphrase portions of a text read aloud or information presented in diverse media and formats, including visually, quantitatively, and orally.

California Common Core State Standards, *continued*

SE Pages	Lesson	Code	Standard
	Reread and Retell: Fluency		Read with sufficient accuracy and fluency to support comprehension.
		CA CC.4.Rfou.4.b	Read on-level prose and poetry orally with accuracy, appropriate rate, and expression on successive readings.
	Reread and Retell: Talk Together	CA CC.4.Rlit.1	Refer to details and examples in a text when explaining what the text says explicitly and when drawing inferences from the text.
			Engage effectively in a range of collaborative discussions (one-on-one, in groups, and teacher-led) with diverse partners on *grade 4 topics and texts,* building on others' ideas and expressing their own clearly.
		CA CC.4.SL.1.a	Come to discussions prepared, having read or studied required material; explicitly draw on that preparation and other information known about the topic to explore ideas under discussion.
		CA CC.4.L.6	Acquire and use accurately grade-appropriate general academic and domain-specific words and phrases, including those that signal precise actions, emotions, or states of being (e.g., quizzed, whined, stammered) and that are basic to a particular topic (e.g., wildlife, conservation, and endangered when discussing animal preservation).
304	**Word Work:** Antonyms		Demonstrate understanding of figurative language, word relationships, and nuances in word meanings.
		CA CC.4.L.5.c	Demonstrate understanding of words by relating them to their opposites (antonyms) and to words with similar but not identical meanings (synonyms).
305	**Selection 2 Opener:** Before You Move On: Make Connections	CA CC.4.Rinf.3	Explain events, procedures, ideas, or concepts in a historical, scientific, or technical text, including what happened and why, based on specific information in the text.
	Selection 2 Opener: Before You Move On: Use Text Features	CA CC.4.Rinf.7	Interpret information presented visually, orally, or quantitatively (e.g., in charts, graphs, diagrams, time lines, animations, or interactive elements on Web pages) and explain how the information contributes to an understanding of the text in which it appears.
307	**Selection 2:** Before You Move On: Steps in a Process	CA CC.4.Rinf.1	Refer to details and examples in a text when explaining what the text says explicitly and when drawing inferences from the text.
	Selection 2: Before You Move On: Use Text Features	CA CC.4.Rinf.7	Interpret information presented visually, orally, or quantitatively (e.g., in charts, graphs, diagrams, time lines, animations, or interactive elements on Web pages) and explain how the information contributes to an understanding of the text in which it appears.
309	**Selection 2:** Before You Move On: Details	CA CC.4.Rinf.1	Refer to details and examples in a text when explaining what the text says explicitly and when drawing inferences from the text.
	Selection 2: Before You Move On: Compare/Contrast	CA CC.4.Rinf.3	Explain events, procedures, ideas, or concepts in a historical, scientific, or technical text, including what happened and why, based on specific information in the text.

SE Pages	Lesson	Code	Standard
311	**Selection 2:** Before You Move On: Make Inferences	CA CC.4.Rinf.1	Refer to details and examples in a text when explaining what the text says explicitly and when drawing inferences from the text.
	Selection 2: Before You Move On: Use Text Features	CA CC.4.Rinf.7	Interpret information presented visually, orally, or quantitatively (e.g., in charts, graphs, diagrams, time lines, animations, or interactive elements on Web pages) and explain how the information contributes to an understanding of the text in which it appears.
312	**Respond and Extend:** Compare Author's Purpose	CA CC.4.Rinf.6	Compare and contrast a firsthand and secondhand account of the same event or topic; describe the differences in focus and the information provided.
313	**Grammar and Spelling:** Adjectives	CA CC.4.Rfou.3	Know and apply grade-level phonics and word analysis skills in decoding words.
		CA CC.4.Rfou.3.a	Use combined knowledge of all letter-sound correspondences, syllabication patterns, and morphology (e.g., roots and affixes) to read accurately unfamiliar multisyllabic words in context and out of context.
			Demonstrate command of the conventions of standard English grammar and usage when writing or speaking.
		CA CC.4.L.1.d	Order adjectives within sentences according to conventional patterns (e.g., *a small red bag* rather than *a red small bag*).
			Demonstrate command of the conventions of standard English capitalization, punctuation, and spelling when writing.
		CA CC.4.L.2.d	Spell grade-appropriate words correctly, consulting references as needed.
314	**Part 2:** **Language:** Define and Explain		Engage effectively in a range of collaborative discussions (one-on-one, in groups, and teacher-led) with diverse partners on *grade 4 topics and texts*, building on others' ideas and expressing their own clearly.
		CA CC.4.SL.1.a	Come to discussions prepared, having read or studied required material; explicitly draw on that preparation and other information known about the topic to explore ideas under discussion.
315	**Science Vocabulary:** Key Words	CA CC.4.Rinf.4	Determine the meaning of general academic and domain-specific words or phrases in a text relevant to a grade 4 topic or subject area. **(See grade 4 Language standards 4–6 for additional expectations.) CA**
316	**Thinking Map:** Problem and Solution	CA CC.4.Rinf.5	Describe the overall structure (e.g., chronology, comparison, cause/effect, problem/solution) of events, ideas, concepts, or information in a text or part of a text.
317	**Academic Vocabulary:** More Key Words	CA CC.4.Rinf.4	Determine the meaning of general academic and domain-specific words or phrases in a text relevant to a grade 4 topic or subject area. **(See grade 4 Language standards 4–6 for additional expectations.) CA**
318–319	**Strategic Reading:** Learn to Make Inferences	CA CC.4.Rinf.1	Refer to details and examples in a text when explaining what the text says explicitly and when drawing inferences from the text.

California Common Core State Standards, continued

SE Pages	Lesson	Code	Standard
322	**Selection 1:** Set a Purpose		Read with sufficient accuracy and fluency to support comprehension.
		CA CC.4.Rfou.4.a	Read on-level text with purpose and understanding.
323	**Selection 1:** Before You Move On	CA CC.4.Rinf.1	Refer to details and examples in a text when explaining what the text says explicitly and when drawing inferences from the text.
	Selection 1: Before You Move On: Problem/Solution	CA CC.4.Rinf.5	Describe the overall structure (e.g., chronology, comparison, cause/effect, problem/solution) of events, ideas, concepts, or information in a text or part of a text.
325	**Selection 1:** Before You Move On: Use Text Features	CA CC.4.Rinf.7	Interpret information presented visually, orally, or quantitatively (e.g., in charts, graphs, diagrams, time lines, animations, or interactive elements on Web pages) and explain how the information contributes to an understanding of the text in which it appears.
	Selection 1: Before You Move On: Problem/Solution	CA CC.4.Rinf.5	Describe the overall structure (e.g., chronology, comparison, cause/effect, problem/solution) of events, ideas, concepts, or information in a text or part of a text.
327	**Selection 1:** Before You Move On: Use Text Features	CA CC.4.Rinf.7	Interpret information presented visually, orally, or quantitatively (e.g., in charts, graphs, diagrams, time lines, animations, or interactive elements on Web pages) and explain how the information contributes to an understanding of the text in which it appears.
	Selection 1: Before You Move On: Make Inferences	CA CC.4.Rinf.1	Refer to details and examples in a text when explaining what the text says explicitly and when drawing inferences from the text.
329	**Selection 1:** Before You Move On Problem/Solution	CA CC.4.Rinf.5	Describe the overall structure (e.g., chronology, comparison, cause/effect, problem/solution) of events, ideas, concepts, or information in a text or part of a text.
	Selection 1: Before You Move On Make Inferences	CA CC.4.Rinf.1	Refer to details and examples in a text when explaining what the text says explicitly and when drawing inferences from the text.
331	**Selection 1:** Before You Move On	CA CC.4.Rinf.1	Refer to details and examples in a text when explaining what the text says explicitly and when drawing inferences from the text.
	Selection 1: Before You Move On: Problem/Solution	CA CC.4.Rinf.5	Describe the overall structure (e.g., chronology, comparison, cause/effect, problem/solution) of events, ideas, concepts, or information in a text or part of a text.
333	**Selection 1:** Before You Move On	CA CC.4.Rinf.1	Refer to details and examples in a text when explaining what the text says explicitly and when drawing inferences from the text.
	Selection 1: Before You Move On: Problem/Solution	CA CC.4.Rinf.5	Describe the overall structure (e.g., chronology, comparison, cause/effect, problem/solution) of events, ideas, concepts, or information in a text or part of a text.
335	**Selection 1:** Before You Move On	CA CC.4.Rinf.1	Refer to details and examples in a text when explaining what the text says explicitly and when drawing inferences from the text.
	Selection 1: Before You Move On: Problem/Solution	CA CC.4.Rinf.5	Describe the overall structure (e.g., chronology, comparison, cause/effect, problem/solution) of events, ideas, concepts, or information in a text or part of a text.
336	**Think and Respond:** Talk About It	CA CC.4.Rinf.1	Refer to details and examples in a text when explaining what the text says explicitly and when drawing inferences from the text.

SE Pages	Lesson	Code	Standard
		CA CC.4.Rinf.5	Describe the overall structure (e.g., chronology, comparison, cause/effect, problem/solution) of events, ideas, concepts, or information in a text or part of a text.
		CA CC.4.Rlit.10	By the end of the year, read and comprehend literature, including stories, dramas, and poetry, in the grades 4–5 text complexity band proficiently, with scaffolding as needed at the high end of the range.
		CA CC.4.L.6	Acquire and use accurately grade-appropriate general academic and domain-specific words and phrases, including those that signal precise actions, emotions, or states of being (e.g., quizzed, whined, stammered) and that are basic to a particular topic (e.g., wildlife, conservation, and endangered when discussing animal preservation).
	Think and Respond: Write About It	CA CC.4.W.10	Write routinely over extended time frames (time for research, reflection, and revision) and shorter time frames (a single sitting or a day or two) for a range of discipline-specific tasks, purposes, and audiences.
		CA CC.4.L.6	Acquire and use accurately grade-appropriate general academic and domain-specific words and phrases, including those that signal precise actions, emotions, or states of being (e.g., quizzed, whined, stammered) and that are basic to a particular topic (e.g., wildlife, conservation, and endangered when discussing animal preservation).
337	**Reread and Summarize:** Problem and Solution	CA CC.4.Rinf.1	Refer to details and examples in a text when explaining what the text says explicitly and when drawing inferences from the text.
		CA CC.4.Rinf.5	Describe the overall structure (e.g., chronology, comparison, cause/effect, problem/solution) of events, ideas, concepts, or information in a text or part of a text.
		CA CC.4.SL.2	Paraphrase portions of a text read aloud or information presented in diverse media and formats, including visually, quantitatively, and orally.
	Reread and Summarize: Fluency		Read with sufficient accuracy and fluency to support comprehension.
		CA CC.4.Rfou.4.b	Read on-level prose and poetry orally with accuracy, appropriate rate, and expression on successive readings.
	Reread and Summarize: Talk Together		Engage effectively in a range of collaborative discussions (one-on-one, in groups, and teacher-led) with diverse partners on *grade 4 topics and texts,* building on others' ideas and expressing their own clearly.
		CA CC.4.SL.1.a	Come to discussions prepared, having read or studied required material; explicitly draw on that preparation and other information known about the topic to explore ideas under discussion.
		CA CC.4.L.6	Acquire and use accurately grade-appropriate general academic and domain-specific words and phrases, including those that signal precise actions, emotions, or states of being (e.g., quizzed, whined, stammered) and that are basic to a particular topic (e.g., wildlife, conservation, and endangered when discussing animal preservation).

California Common Core State Standards, *continued*

SE Pages	Lesson	Code	Standard
338	**Word Work:** Synonyms		Demonstrate understanding of figurative language, word relationships, and nuances in word meanings.
		CA CC.4.L.5.c	Demonstrate understanding of words by relating them to their opposites (antonyms) and to words with similar but not identical meanings (synonyms).
339	**Selection 2 Opener:** Before You Move On: Make Inferences	CA CC.4.Rinf.1	Refer to details and examples in a text when explaining what the text says explicitly and when drawing inferences from the text.
	Selection 2 Opener: Before You Move On: Use Text Features	CA CC.4.Rinf.7	Interpret information presented visually, orally, or quantitatively (e.g., in charts, graphs, diagrams, time lines, animations, or interactive elements on Web pages) and explain how the information contributes to an understanding of the text in which it appears.
341	**Selection 2:** Before You Move On: Problem/Solution	CA CC.4.Rinf.5	Describe the overall structure (e.g., chronology, comparison, cause/effect, problem/solution) of events, ideas, concepts, or information in a text or part of a text.
	Selection 2: Before You Move On: Make Inferences	CA CC.4.Rinf.1	Refer to details and examples in a text when explaining what the text says explicitly and when drawing inferences from the text.
343	**Selection 2:** Before You Move On	CA CC.4.Rinf.1	Refer to details and examples in a text when explaining what the text says explicitly and when drawing inferences from the text.
	Selection 2: Before You Move On: Use Text Features	CA CC.4.Rinf.7	Interpret information presented visually, orally, or quantitatively (e.g., in charts, graphs, diagrams, time lines, animations, or interactive elements on Web pages) and explain how the information contributes to an understanding of the text in which it appears.
344	**Respond and Extend:** Compare Genres	CA CC.4.Rinf.6	Compare and contrast a firsthand and secondhand account of the same event or topic; describe the differences in focus and the information provided.
		CA CC.4.Rinf.7	Interpret information presented visually, orally, or quantitatively (e.g., in charts, graphs, diagrams, time lines, animations, or interactive elements on Web pages) and explain how the information contributes to an understanding of the text in which it appears.
	Respond and Extend: Talk Together	CA CC.4.Rinf.6	Compare and contrast a firsthand and secondhand account of the same event or topic; describe the differences in focus and the information provided.
			Engage effectively in a range of collaborative discussions (one-on-one, in groups, and teacher-led) with diverse partners on *grade 4 topics and texts,* building on others' ideas and expressing their own clearly.
		CA CC.4.SL.1.d	Review the key ideas expressed and explain their own ideas and understanding in light of the discussion.
		CA CC.4.L.6	Acquire and use accurately grade-appropriate general academic and domain-specific words and phrases, including those that signal precise actions, emotions, or states of being (e.g., quizzed, whined, stammered) and that are basic to a particular topic (e.g., wildlife, conservation, and endangered when discussing animal preservation).

SE Pages	Lesson	Code	Standard
345	**Grammar and Spelling:** Possessive Nouns and Adjectives	CA CC.4.Rfou.3	Know and apply grade-level phonics and word analysis skills in decoding words.
		CA CC.4.Rfou.3.a	Use combined knowledge of all letter-sound correspondences, syllabication patterns, and morphology (e.g., roots and affixes) to read accurately unfamiliar multisyllabic words in context and out of context.
		CA CC.4.L.1	Demonstrate command of the conventions of standard English grammar and usage when writing or speaking.
			Demonstrate command of the conventions of standard English capitalization, punctuation, and spelling when writing.
		CA CC.4.L.2.d	Spell grade-appropriate words correctly, consulting references as needed.
346–347	**Writing Project:** Persuasive Essay Study a Model Prewrite Draft		Write opinion pieces on topics or texts, supporting a point of view with reasons and information.
		CA CC.4.W.1.a	Introduce a topic or text clearly, state an opinion, and create an organizational structure in which related ideas are grouped to support the writer's purpose.
		CA CC.4.W.1.b	Provide reasons that are supported by facts and details.
		CA CC.4.W.1.d	Provide a concluding statement or section related to the opinion presented.
348	**Writing Project:** Persuasive Essay Revise	CA CC.4.W.5	With guidance and support from peers and adults, develop and strengthen writing as needed by planning, revising, and editing. (Editing for conventions should demonstrate command of Language standards 1–3 up to and including grade 4.)
349	**Writing Project:** Persuasive Essay Edit and Proofread	CA CC.4.W.5	With guidance and support from peers and adults, develop and strengthen writing as needed by planning, revising, and editing. (Editing for conventions should demonstrate command of Language standards 1–3 up to and including grade 4.)
	Writing Project: Persuasive Essay Publish	CA CC.4.W.6	With some guidance and support from adults, use technology, including the Internet, to produce and publish writing as well as to interact and collaborate with others; demonstrate sufficient command of keyboarding skills to type a minimum of one page in a single sitting.
	Writing Project: Persuasive Essay Publish	CA CC.4.SL.3	Identify the reasons and evidence a speaker **or media source** provides to support particular points. **CA**
350	**Talk Together**		Engage effectively in a range of collaborative discussions (one-on-one, in groups, and teacher-led) with diverse partners on *grade 4 topics and texts,* building on others' ideas and expressing their own clearly.
		CA CC.4.SL.1.a	Come to discussions prepared, having read or studied required material; explicitly draw on that preparation and other information known about the topic to explore ideas under discussion.

California Common Core State Standards, *continued*

SE Pages	Lesson	Code	Standard
		CA CC.4.L.6	Acquire and use accurately grade-appropriate general academic and domain-specific words and phrases, including those that signal precise actions, emotions, or states of being (e.g., quizzed, whined, stammered) and that are basic to a particular topic (e.g., wildlife, conservation, and endangered when discussing animal preservation).
	Write a Paragraph	CA CC.4.W.9	Draw evidence from literary or informational texts to support analysis, reflection, and research.
		CA CC.4.W.10	Write routinely over extended time frames (time for research, reflection, and revision) and shorter time frames (a single sitting or a day or two) for a range of discipline-specific tasks, purposes, and audiences.
351	**Unit Wrap-Up:** Share Your Ideas	CA CC.4.Rlit.5	Explain major differences between poems, drama, and prose, and refer to the structural elements of poems (e.g., verse, rhythm, meter) and drama (e.g., casts of characters, settings, descriptions, dialogue, stage directions) when writing or speaking about a text.
		CA CC.4.W.7	Conduct short research projects that build knowledge through investigation of different aspects of a topic.
		CA CC.4.W.10	Write routinely over extended time frames (time for research, reflection, and revision) and shorter time frames (a single sitting or a day or two) for a range of discipline-specific tasks, purposes, and audiences.
			Engage effectively in a range of collaborative discussions (one-on-one, in groups, and teacher-led) with diverse partners on *grade 4 topics and texts,* building on others' ideas and expressing their own clearly.
		CA CC.4.SL.1.a	Come to discussions prepared, having read or studied required material; explicitly draw on that preparation and other information known about the topic to explore ideas under discussion.
		CA CC.4.SL.1.c	Pose and respond to specific questions to clarify or follow up on information, and make comments that contribute to the discussion and link to the remarks of others.
		CA CC.4.SL.1.d	Review the key ideas expressed and explain their own ideas and understanding in light of the discussion.
		CA CC.4.SL.4	Report on a topic or text, tell a story, or recount an experience in an organized manner, using appropriate facts and relevant, descriptive details to support main ideas or themes; speak clearly at an understandable pace.
		CA CC.4.SL.4.a	**Plan and deliver a narrative presentation that: relates ideas, observations, or recollections; provides a clear context; and includes clear insight into why the event or experience is memorable. CA**

SE Pages	Lesson	Code	Standard
353	**Unit Launch:** Share What You Know		Engage effectively in a range of collaborative discussions (one-on-one, in groups, and teacher-led) with diverse partners on *grade 4 topics and texts,* building on others' ideas and expressing their own clearly.
354	**Part 1:** **Language:** Express Intentions		Engage effectively in a range of collaborative discussions (one-on-one, in groups, and teacher-led) with diverse partners on *grade 4 topics and texts*, building on others' ideas and expressing their own clearly.
		CA CC.4.SL.1.a	Come to discussions prepared, having read or studied required material; explicitly draw on that preparation and other information known about the topic to explore ideas under discussion.
355	**Social Studies Vocabulary:** Key Words	CA CC.4.Rinf.4	Determine the meaning of general academic and domain-specific words or phrases in a text relevant to a grade 4 topic or subject area. **(See grade 4 Language standards 4–6 for additional expectations.) CA**
356	**Thinking Map:** Characters	CA CC.4.Rlit.3	Describe in depth a character, setting, or event in a story or drama, drawing on specific details in the text (e.g., a character's thoughts, words, or actions).
357	**Academic Vocabulary:** More Key Words	CA CC.4.Rlit.4	Determine the meaning of words and phrases as they are used in a text, including those that allude to significant characters found in mythology (e.g., Herculean). **(See grade 4 Language standards 4–6 for additional expectations.) CA**
		CA CC.4.Rinf.4	Determine the meaning of general academic and domain-specific words or phrases in a text relevant to a grade 4 topic or subject area. **(See grade 4 Language standards 4–6 for additional expectations.) CA**
358–359	**Strategic Reading:** Learn to Determine Importance	CA CC.4.Rinf.2	Determine the main idea of a text and explain how it is supported by key details; summarize the text.
362	**Selection 1:** Set a Purpose		Read with sufficient accuracy and fluency to support comprehension.
		CA CC.4.Rfou.4.a	Read on-level text with purpose and understanding.
365	**Selection 1:** Before You Move On: Summarize	CA CC.4.Rlit.2	Determine a theme of a story, drama, or poem from details in the text; summarize the text.
357	**Academic Vocabulary:** More Key Words	CA CC.4.Rlit.4	Determine the meaning of words and phrases as they are used in a text, including those that allude to significant characters found in mythology (e.g., Herculean). **(See grade 4 Language standards 4–6 for additional expectations.) CA**
		CA CC.4.Rinf.4	Determine the meaning of general academic and domain-specific words or phrases in a text relevant to a grade 4 topic or subject area. **(See grade 4 Language standards 4–6 for additional expectations.) CA**
358–359	**Strategic Reading:** Learn to Determine Importance	CA CC.4.Rinf.2	Determine the main idea of a text and explain how it is supported by key details; summarize the text.
362	**Selection 1:** Set a Purpose		Read with sufficient accuracy and fluency to support comprehension.
		CA CC.4.Rfou.4.a	Read on-level text with purpose and understanding.

California Common Core State Standards, *continued*

SE Pages	Lesson	Code	Standard
365	**Selection 1:** Before You Move On: Summarize	CA CC.4.Rlit.2	Determine a theme of a story, drama, or poem from details in the text; summarize the text.
	Selection 1: Before You Move On: Character	CA CC.4.Rlit.3	Describe in depth a character, setting, or event in a story or drama, drawing on specific details in the text (e.g., a character's thoughts, words, or actions).
366	**Selection 1:** Predict	CA CC.4.Rlit.1	Refer to details and examples in a text when explaining what the text says explicitly and when drawing inferences from the text.
371	**Selection 1:** Before You Move On: Character	CA CC.4.Rlit.3	Describe in depth a character, setting, or event in a story or drama, drawing on specific details in the text (e.g., a character's thoughts, words, or actions).
	Selection 1: Before You Move On: Elements of Drama	CA CC.4.Rlit.5	Explain major differences between poems, drama, and prose, and refer to the structural elements of poems (e.g., verse, rhythm, meter) and drama (e.g., casts of characters, settings, descriptions, dialogue, stage directions) when writing or speaking about a text.
372	**Selection 1:** Predict	CA CC.4.Rlit.1	Refer to details and examples in a text when explaining what the text says explicitly and when drawing inferences from the text.
376	**Selection 1:** Before You Move On: Summarize	CA CC.4.Rlit.2	Determine a theme of a story, drama, or poem from details in the text; summarize the text.
	Selection 1: Before You Move On: Character	CA CC.4.Rlit.3	Describe in depth a character, setting, or event in a story or drama, drawing on specific details in the text (e.g., a character's thoughts, words, or actions).
377	**Meet the Author:** Writer's Craft	CA CC.4.Rlit.3	Describe in depth a character, setting, or event in a story or drama, drawing on specific details in the text (e.g., a character's thoughts, words, or actions).
			Write narratives to develop real or imagined experiences or events using effective technique, descriptive details, and clear event sequences.
		CA CC.4.W.3.b	Use dialogue and description to develop experiences and events or show the responses of characters to situations.
378	**Think and Respond:** Talk About It	CA CC.4.Rlit.3	Describe in depth a character, setting, or event in a story or drama, drawing on specific details in the text (e.g., a character's thoughts, words, or actions).
		CA CC.4.W.10	Write routinely over extended time frames (time for research, reflection, and revision) and shorter time frames (a single sitting or a day or two) for a range of discipline-specific tasks, purposes, and audiences.
			Engage effectively in a range of collaborative discussions (one-on-one, in groups, and teacher-led) with diverse partners on grade 4 topics and texts, building on others' ideas and expressing their own clearly.
		CA CC.4.SL.1.a	Come to discussions prepared, having read or studied required material; explicitly draw on that preparation and other information known about the topic to explore ideas under discussion.

SE Pages	Lesson	Code	Standard
	Think and Respond: Write About It		Draw evidence from literary or informational texts to support analysis, reflection, and research.
		CA CC.4.W.9.a	*Apply grade 4 Reading standards* to literature (e.g., "Describe in depth a character, setting, or event in a story or drama, drawing on specific details in the text [e.g., a character's thoughts, words, or actions].").
		CA CC.4.W.10	Write routinely over extended time frames (time for research, reflection, and revision) and shorter time frames (a single sitting or a day or two) for a range of discipline-specific tasks, purposes, and audiences.
379	**Reread and Retell:** Characters	CA CC.4.Rlit.3	Describe in depth a character, setting, or event in a story or drama, drawing on specific details in the text (e.g., a character's thoughts, words, or actions).
		CA CC.4.SL.4	Report on a topic or text, tell a story, or recount an experience in an organized manner, using appropriate facts and relevant, descriptive details to support main ideas or themes; speak clearly at an understandable pace.
	Reread and Retell: Fluency		Read with sufficient accuracy and fluency to support comprehension.
		CA CC.4.Rfou.4.b	Read on-level prose and poetry orally with accuracy, appropriate rate, and expression on successive readings.
	Reread and Retell: Talk Together	CA CC.4.SL.1	Engage effectively in a range of collaborative discussions (one-on-one, in groups, and teacher-led) with diverse partners on grade 4 topics and texts, building on others' ideas and expressing their own clearly.
		CA CC.4.SL.1.a	Come to discussions prepared, having read or studied required material; explicitly draw on that preparation and other information known about the topic to explore ideas under discussion.
		CA CC.4.SL.1.b	Follow agreed-upon rules for discussions and carry out assigned roles.
		CA CC.4.SL.1.c	Pose and respond to specific questions to clarify or follow up on information, and make comments that contribute to the discussion and link to the remarks of others.
		CA CC.4.SL.1.d	Review the key ideas expressed and explain their own ideas and understanding in light of the discussion.
		CA CC.4.L.6	Acquire and use accurately grade-appropriate general academic and domain-specific words and phrases, including those that signal precise actions, emotions, or states of being (e.g., quizzed, whined, stammered) and that are basic to a particular topic (e.g., wildlife, conservation, and endangered when discussing animal preservation).
380	**Word Work:** Prefixes	CA CC.4.Rfou.3	Know and apply grade-level phonics and word analysis skills in decoding words.
		CA CC.4.Rfou.3.a	Use combined knowledge of all letter-sound correspondences, syllabication patterns, and morphology (e.g., roots and affixes) to read accurately unfamiliar multisyllabic words in context and out of context.

California Common Core State Standards, *continued*

SE Pages	Lesson	Code	Standard
			Determine or clarify the meaning of unknown and multiple-meaning words and phrases based on *grade 4 reading and content,* choosing flexibly from a range of strategies.
		CA CC.4.L.4.b	Use common, grade-appropriate Greek and Latin affixes and roots as clues to the meaning of a word (e.g., telegraph, photograph, autograph).
381	**Selection 2 Opener:** Before You Move On: Summarize	CA CC.4.Rinf.1	Refer to details and examples in a text when explaining what the text says explicitly and when drawing inferences from the text.
		CA CC.4.Rinf.2	Determine the main idea of a text and explain how it is supported by key details; summarize the text.
	Selection 2 Opener: Before You Move On: Use Text Features	CA CC.4.Rinf.7	Interpret information presented visually, orally, or quantitatively (e.g., in charts, graphs, diagrams, time lines, animations, or interactive elements on Web pages) and explain how the information contributes to an understanding of the text in which it appears.
383	**Selection 2:** Before You Move On: Summarize	CA CC.4.Rinf.2	Determine the main idea of a text and explain how it is supported by key details; summarize the text.
	Selection 2: Before You Move On: Steps in a Process	CA CC.4.Rinf.1	Refer to details and examples in a text when explaining what the text says explicitly and when drawing inferences from the text.
384	**Respond and Extend:** Compare Texts	CA CC.4.Rlit.5	Explain major differences between poems, drama, and prose, and refer to the structural elements of poems (e.g., verse, rhythm, meter) and drama (e.g., casts of characters, settings, descriptions, dialogue, stage directions) when writing or speaking about a text.
		CA CC.4.Rlit.9	Compare and contrast the treatment of similar themes and topics (e.g., opposition of good and evil) and patterns of events (e.g., the quest) in stories, myths, and traditional literature from different cultures.
		CA CC.4.Rinf.9	Integrate information from two texts on the same topic in order to write or speak about the subject knowledgeably.
385	**Grammar and Spelling:** Pronoun Agreement	CA CC.4.L.1	Demonstrate command of the conventions of standard English grammar and usage when writing or speaking.
386	**Part 2:** **Language:** Restate an Idea		Engage effectively in a range of collaborative discussions (one-on-one, in groups, and teacher-led) with diverse partners on grade 4 topics and texts, building on others' ideas and expressing their own clearly.
		CA CC.4.SL.1.a	Come to discussions prepared, having read or studied required material; explicitly draw on that preparation and other information known about the topic to explore ideas under discussion.
		CA CC.4.SL.1.c	Pose and respond to specific questions to clarify or follow up on information, and make comments that contribute to the discussion and link to the remarks of others.
		CA CC.4.SL.1.d	Review the key ideas expressed and explain their own ideas and understanding in light of the discussion.

SE Pages	Lesson	Code	Standard
387	**Social Studies Vocabulary:** Key Words	CA CC.4.Rinf.4	Determine the meaning of general academic and domain-specific words or phrases in a text relevant to a grade 4 topic or subject area. **(See grade 4 Language standards 4–6 for additional expectations.) CA**
388	**Thinking Map:** Sequence	CA CC.4.Rinf.1	Refer to details and examples in a text when explaining what the text says explicitly and when drawing inferences from the text.
		CA CC.4.Rinf.5	Describe the overall structure (e.g., chronology, comparison, cause/effect, problem/solution) of events, ideas, concepts, or information in a text or part of a text.
			Write narratives to develop real or imagined experiences or events using effective technique, descriptive details, and clear event sequences.
		CA CC.4.W.3.c	Use a variety of transitional words and phrases to manage the sequence of events.
		CA CC.4.SL.5	Add audio recordings and visual displays to presentations when appropriate to enhance the development of main ideas or themes.
389	**Academic Vocabulary:** More Key Words	CA CC.4.Rinf.4	Determine the meaning of general academic and domain-specific words or phrases in a text relevant to a grade 4 topic or subject area. (See grade 4 Language standards 4–6 for additional expectations.) CA
390–391	**Strategic Reading:** Learn to Determine Importance	CA CC.4.Rinf.2	Determine the main idea of a text and explain how it is supported by key details; summarize the text.
394	**Selection 1:** Set a Purpose		Read with sufficient accuracy and fluency to support comprehension.
		CA CC.4.Rfou.4.a	Read on-level text with purpose and understanding.
395	**Selection 1:** Before You Move On	CA CC.4.Rinf.1	Refer to details and examples in a text when explaining what the text says explicitly and when drawing inferences from the text.
	Selection 1: Before You Move On: Sequence	CA CC.4.Rinf.5	Describe the overall structure (e.g., chronology, comparison, cause/effect, problem/solution) of events, ideas, concepts, or information in a text or part of a text.
397	**Selection 1:** Before You Move On: Determine Importance	CA CC.4.Rinf.2	Determine the main idea of a text and explain how it is supported by key details; summarize the text.
	Selection 1: Before You Move On: Use Text Features	CA CC.4.Rinf.7	Interpret information presented visually, orally, or quantitatively (e.g., in charts, graphs, diagrams, time lines, animations, or interactive elements on Web pages) and explain how the information contributes to an understanding of the text in which it appears.
399	**Selection 1:** Before You Move On	CA CC.4.Rinf.1	Refer to details and examples in a text when explaining what the text says explicitly and when drawing inferences from the text.
	Selection 1: Before You Move On: Sequence	CA CC.4.Rinf.5	Describe the overall structure (e.g., chronology, comparison, cause/effect, problem/solution) of events, ideas, concepts, or information in a text or part of a text.

California Common Core State Standards, *continued*

Unit 6 Treasure Hunters, continued

SE Pages	Lesson	Code	Standard
401	**Selection 1:** Before You Move On: Main Idea	CA CC.4.Rinf.2	Determine the main idea of a text and explain how it is supported by key details; summarize the text.
	Selection 1: Before You Move On: Make Connections	CA CC.4.Rinf.3	Explain events, procedures, ideas, or concepts in a historical, scientific, or technical text, including what happened and why, based on specific information in the text.
403	**Selection 1:** Before You Move On: Sequence	CA CC.4.Rinf.1	Refer to details and examples in a text when explaining what the text says explicitly and when drawing inferences from the text.
		CA CC.4.Rinf.5	Describe the overall structure (e.g., chronology, comparison, cause/effect, problem/solution) of events, ideas, concepts, or information in a text or part of a text.
	Selection 1: Before You Move On: Use Text Features	CA CC.4.Rinf.7	Interpret information presented visually, orally, or quantitatively (e.g., in charts, graphs, diagrams, time lines, animations, or interactive elements on Web pages) and explain how the information contributes to an understanding of the text in which it appears.
405	**Selection 1:** Before You Move On	CA CC.4.Rinf.1	Refer to details and examples in a text when explaining what the text says explicitly and when drawing inferences from the text.
	Selection 1: Before You Move On: Main Idea	CA CC.4.Rinf.2	Determine the main idea of a text and explain how it is supported by key details; summarize the text.
407	**Selection 1:** Before You Move On	CA CC.4.Rinf.1	Refer to details and examples in a text when explaining what the text says explicitly and when drawing inferences from the text.
	Selection 1: Before You Move On: Sequence	CA CC.4.Rinf.5	Describe the overall structure (e.g., chronology, comparison, cause/effect, problem/solution) of events, ideas, concepts, or information in a text or part of a text.
408	**Think and Respond:** Talk About It	CA CC.4.Rinf.1	Refer to details and examples in a text when explaining what the text says explicitly and when drawing inferences from the text.
		CA CC.4.Rinf.2	Determine the main idea of a text and explain how it is supported by key details; summarize the text.
		CA CC.4.SL.4	Report on a topic or text, tell a story, or recount an experience in an organized manner, using appropriate facts and relevant, descriptive details to support main ideas or themes; speak clearly at an understandable pace.
	Think and Respond: Write About It	CA CC.4.W.9	Draw evidence from literary or informational texts to support analysis, reflection, and research.
		CA CC.4.W.10	Write routinely over extended time frames (time for research, reflection, and revision) and shorter time frames (a single sitting or a day or two) for a range of discipline-specific tasks, purposes, and audiences.
409	**Reread and Retell:** Sequence	CA CC.4.Rinf.1	Refer to details and examples in a text when explaining what the text says explicitly and when drawing inferences from the text.

SE Pages	Lesson	Code	Standard
		CA CC.4.Rinf.5	Describe the overall structure (e.g., chronology, comparison, cause/effect, problem/solution) of events, ideas, concepts, or information in a text or part of a text.
	Reread and Retell: Fluency		Read with sufficient accuracy and fluency to support comprehension.
		CA CC.4.Rfou.4	Read with sufficient accuracy and fluency to support comprehension.
	Reread and Retell: Talk Together	CA CC.4.Rinf.7	Interpret information presented visually, orally, or quantitatively (e.g., in charts, graphs, diagrams, time lines, animations, or interactive elements on Web pages) and explain how the information contributes to an understanding of the text in which it appears.
		CA CC.4.L.6	Acquire and use accurately grade-appropriate general academic and domain-specific words and phrases, including those that signal precise actions, emotions, or states of being (e.g., quizzed, whined, stammered) and that are basic to a particular topic (e.g., wildlife, conservation, and endangered when discussing animal preservation).
410	**Word Work:** Suffixes	CA CC.4.Rfou.3	Know and apply grade-level phonics and word analysis skills in decoding words.
		CA CC.4.Rfou.3.a	Use combined knowledge of all letter-sound correspondences, syllabication patterns, and morphology (e.g., roots and affixes) to read accurately unfamiliar multisyllabic words in context and out of context.
			Determine or clarify the meaning of unknown and multiple-meaning words and phrases based on *grade 4 reading and content,* choosing flexibly from a range of strategies.
		CA CC.4.L.4.b	Use common, grade-appropriate Greek and Latin affixes and roots as clues to the meaning of a word (e.g., telegraph, photograph, autograph).
411	**Selection 2 Opener:** Before You Move On: Predict	CA CC.4.Rinf.1	Refer to details and examples in a text when explaining what the text says explicitly and when drawing inferences from the text.
	Selection 2 Opener: Before You Move On: Use Text Features	CA CC.4.Rinf.7	Interpret information presented visually, orally, or quantitatively (e.g., in charts, graphs, diagrams, time lines, animations, or interactive elements on Web pages) and explain how the information contributes to an understanding of the text in which it appears.
413	**Selection 2:** Before You Move On	CA CC.4.Rinf.1	Refer to details and examples in a text when explaining what the text says explicitly and when drawing inferences from the text.
415	**Selection 2:** Before You Move On: Cause/Effect	CA CC.4.Rinf.5	Describe the overall structure (e.g., chronology, comparison, cause/effect, problem/solution) of events, ideas, concepts, or information in a text or part of a text.
	Selection 2: Before You Move On: Clarify	CA CC.4.Rinf.3	Explain events, procedures, ideas, or concepts in a historical, scientific, or technical text, including what happened and why, based on specific information in the text.
416	**Respond and Extend:** Compare Media Texts	CA CC.4.Rinf.6	Compare and contrast a firsthand and secondhand account of the same event or topic; describe the differences in focus and the information provided.

California Common Core State Standards, *continued*

SE Pages	Lesson	Code	Standard
	Respond and Extend: Talk Together	CA CC.4.Rinf.9	Integrate information from two texts on the same topic in order to write or speak about the subject knowledgeably.
		CA CC.4.Rinf.9	Integrate information from two texts on the same topic in order to write or speak about the subject knowledgeably.
		CA CC.4.L.6	Acquire and use accurately grade-appropriate general academic and domain-specific words and phrases, including those that signal precise actions, emotions, or states of being (e.g., quizzed, whined, stammered) and that are basic to a particular topic (e.g., wildlife, conservation, and endangered when discussing animal preservation).
417	**Grammar and Spelling:** Possessive Pronouns	CA CC.4.L.1	Demonstrate command of the conventions of standard English grammar and usage when writing or speaking.
418–419	**Writing Project:** Historical Fiction Study a Model Prewrite Draft	CA CC.4.W.9.a	Draw evidence from literary or informational texts to support analysis, reflection, and research. Apply *grade 4 Reading standards* to literature (e.g., "Describe in depth a character, setting, or event in a story or drama, drawing on specific details in the text [e.g., a character's thoughts, words, or actions].").
		CA CC.4.W.3.a	Write narratives to develop real or imagined experiences or events using effective technique, descriptive details, and clear event sequences. Orient the reader by establishing a situation and introducing a narrator and/or characters; organize an event sequence that unfolds naturally.
		CA CC.4.W.3.b	Use dialogue and description to develop experiences and events or show the responses of characters to situations.
420	**Writing Project:** Historical Fiction Revise	CA CC.4.W.5	With guidance and support from peers and adults, develop and strengthen writing as needed by planning, revising, and editing. (Editing for conventions should demonstrate command of Language standards 1–3 up to and including grade 4.)
421	**Writing Project:** Historical Fiction Edit and Proofread	CA CC.4.W.5	With guidance and support from peers and adults, develop and strengthen writing as needed by planning, revising, and editing. (Editing for conventions should demonstrate command of Language standards 1–3 up to and including grade 4.)
	Writing Project: Historical Fiction Publish	CA CC.4.W.6	With some guidance and support from adults, use technology, including the Internet, to produce and publish writing as well as to interact and collaborate with others; demonstrate sufficient command of keyboarding skills to type a minimum of one page in a single sitting.
		CA CC.4.SL.1	Engage effectively in a range of collaborative discussions (one-on-one, in groups, and teacher-led) with diverse partners on grade 4 topics and texts, building on others' ideas and expressing their own clearly.
		CA CC.4.SL.1.a	Come to discussions prepared, having read or studied required material; explicitly draw on that preparation and other information known about the topic to explore ideas under discussion.
		CA CC.4.SL.1.b	Follow agreed-upon rules for discussions and carry out assigned roles.

SE Pages	Lesson	Code	Standard
		CA CC.4.SL.1.c	Pose and respond to specific questions to clarify or follow up on information, and make comments that contribute to the discussion and link to the remarks of others.
		CA CC.4.SL.1.d	Review the key ideas expressed and explain their own ideas and understanding in light of the discussion.
422	**Talk Together**		Engage effectively in a range of collaborative discussions (one-on-one, in groups, and teacher-led) with diverse partners on *grade 4 topics* and texts, building on others' ideas and expressing their own clearly.
		CA CC.4.SL.1.a	Come to discussions prepared, having read or studied required material; explicitly draw on that preparation and other information known about the topic to explore ideas under discussion.
		CA CC.4.SL.1.d	Review the key ideas expressed and explain their own ideas and understanding in light of the discussion.
	Write a Song	CA CC.4.W.10	Write routinely over extended time frames (time for research, reflection, and revision) and shorter time frames (a single sitting or a day or two) for a range of discipline-specific tasks, purposes, and audiences.
423	**Unit Wrap-Up:** Share Your Ideas	CA CC.4.W.7	Conduct short research projects that build knowledge through investigation of different aspects of a topic.
		CA CC.4.W.10	Write routinely over extended time frames (time for research, reflection, and revision) and shorter time frames (a single sitting or a day or two) for a range of discipline-specific tasks, purposes, and audiences.
		CA CC.4.SL.1	Engage effectively in a range of collaborative discussions (one-on-one, in groups, and teacher-led) with diverse partners on grade 4 topics and texts, building on others' ideas and expressing their own clearly.
		CA CC.4.SL.1.b	Follow agreed-upon rules for discussions and carry out assigned roles.
		CA CC.4.SL.1.c	Pose and respond to specific questions to clarify or follow up on information, and make comments that contribute to the discussion and link to the remarks of others.
		CA CC.4.SL.1.d	Review the key ideas expressed and explain their own ideas and understanding in light of the discussion.
		CA CC.4.SL.4	Report on a topic or text, tell a story, or recount an experience in an organized manner, using appropriate facts and relevant, descriptive details to support main ideas or themes; speak clearly at an understandable pace.
435	**Selection 1:** Before You Move On: Compare/Contrast	CA CC.4.Rinf.5	Describe the overall structure (e.g., chronology, comparison, cause/effect, problem/solution) of events, ideas, concepts, or information in a text or part of a text.
	Selection 1: Before You Move On: Ask Questions	CA CC.4.Rinf.1	Refer to details and examples in a text when explaining what the text says explicitly and when drawing inferences from the text.

California Common Core State Standards, *continued*

SE Pages	Lesson	Code	Standard
	Selection 1: Before You Move On: Use Text Features	CA CC.4.Rinf.7	Make connections between the text of a story or drama and a visual or oral presentation of the text, identifying where each version reflects specific descriptions and directions in the text.
441	**Selection 1:** Before You Move On: Draw Conclusions	CA CC.4.Rinf.2	Determine the main idea of a text and explain how it is supported by key details; summarize the text.
		CA CC.4.Rinf.3	Explain events, procedures, ideas, or concepts in a historical, scientific, or technical text, including what happened and why, based on specific information in the text.
	Selection 1: Before You Move On: Interpret	CA CC.4.Rinf.7	Interpret information presented visually, orally, or quantitatively (e.g., in charts, graphs, diagrams, time lines, animations, or interactive elements on Web pages) and explain how the information contributes to an understanding of the text in which it appears.
443	**Selection 1:** Before You Move On: Draw Conclusions	CA CC.4.Rinf.2	Determine the main idea of a text and explain how it is supported by key details; summarize the text.
	Selection 1: Before You Move On: Draw Conclusions	CA CC.4.Rinf.3	Explain events, procedures, ideas, or concepts in a historical, scientific, or technical text, including what happened and why, based on specific information in the text.
	Selection 1: Before You Move On: Compare/Contrast	CA CC.4.Rinf.5	Describe the overall structure (e.g., chronology, comparison, cause/effect, problem/solution) of events, ideas, concepts, or information in a text or part of a text.
444	**Think and Respond:** Talk About It	CA CC.4.Rinf.3	Explain events, procedures, ideas, or concepts in a historical, scientific, or technical text, including what happened and why, based on specific information in the text.
		CA CC.4.Rinf.5	Describe the overall structure (e.g., chronology, comparison, cause/effect, problem/solution) of events, ideas, concepts, or information in a text or part of a text.
			Engage effectively in a range of collaborative discussions (one-on-one, in groups, and teacher-led) with diverse partners on *grade 4 topics and texts*, building on others' ideas and expressing their own clearly.
		CA CC.4.SL.1.d	Review the key ideas expressed and explain their own ideas and understanding in light of the discussion.
	Think and Respond: Write About It	CA CC.4.W.4	**Produce clear and coherent writing (including multiple-paragraph texts) in which the development and organization are appropriate to task, purpose, and audience. (Grade-specific expectations for writing types are defined in standards 1–3 above.) CA**
			Draw evidence from literary or informational texts to support analysis, reflection, and research.
		CA CC.4.W.9.b	Apply *grade 4 Reading standards* to informational texts (e.g., "Explain how an author uses reasons and evidence to support particular points in a text").
		CA CC.4.L.6	Acquire and use accurately grade-appropriate general academic and domain-specific words and phrases, including those that signal precise actions, emotions, or states of being (e.g., quizzed, whined, stammered) and that are basic to a particular topic (e.g., wildlife, conservation, and endangered when discussing animal preservation).
445	**Reread and Compare:** Compare and Contrast	CA CC.4.Rinf.3	Explain events, procedures, ideas, or concepts in a historical, scientific, or technical text, including what happened and why, based on specific information in the text.

California Common Core State Standards, *continued*

SE Pages	Lesson	Code	Standard
		CA CC.4.Rinf.5	Describe the overall structure (e.g., chronology, comparison, cause/effect, problem/solution) of events, ideas, concepts, or information in a text or part of a text.
		CA CC.4.L.6	Acquire and use accurately grade-appropriate general academic and domain-specific words and phrases, including those that signal precise actions, emotions, or states of being (e.g., quizzed, whined, stammered) and that are basic to a particular topic (e.g., wildlife, conservation, and endangered when discussing animal preservation).
	Reread and Compare: Fluency		Read with sufficient accuracy and fluency to support comprehension.
		CA CC.4.Rfou.4.b	Read on-level prose and poetry orally with accuracy, appropriate rate, and expression on successive readings.
	Reread and Compare: Talk Together		Engage effectively in a range of collaborative discussions (one-on-one, in groups, and teacher-led) with diverse partners on *grade 4 topics and texts*, building on others' ideas and expressing their own clearly.
		CA CC.4.SL.1.c	Pose and respond to specific questions to clarify or follow up on information, and make comments that contribute to the discussion and link to the remarks of others.
		CA CC.4.L.6	Acquire and use accurately grade-appropriate general academic and domain-specific words and phrases, including those that signal precise actions, emotions, or states of being (e.g., quizzed, whined, stammered) and that are basic to a particular topic (e.g., wildlife, conservation, and endangered when discussing animal preservation).
446	**Word Work:** Multiple-Meaning Words		Determine or clarify the meaning of unknown and multiple-meaning words and phrases based on *grade 4 reading and content*, choosing flexibly from a range of strategies.
		CA CC.4.L.4.a	Use context (e.g., definitions, examples, or restatements in text) as a clue to the meaning of a word or phrase.
447	**Selection 2 Opener:** Before You Move On: Make Connections	CA CC.4.Rinf.3	Explain events, procedures, ideas, or concepts in a historical, scientific, or technical text, including what happened and why, based on specific information in the text.
	Selection 2 Opener: Before You Move On: Make Predictions	CA CC.4.Rinf.1	Refer to details and examples in a text when explaining what the text says explicitly and when drawing inferences from the text.
449	**Selection 2:** Before You Move On: Draw Conclusions	CA CC.4.Rinf.3	Explain events, procedures, ideas, or concepts in a historical, scientific, or technical text, including what happened and why, based on specific information in the text.
	Selection 2: Before You Move On: Compare/Contrast	CA CC.4.Rinf.5	Describe the overall structure (e.g., chronology, comparison, cause/effect, problem/solution) of events, ideas, concepts, or information in a text or part of a text.
451	**Selection 2:** Before You Move On: Use Text Features	CA CC.4.Rinf.7	Interpret information presented visually, orally, or quantitatively (e.g., in charts, graphs, diagrams, time lines, animations, or interactive elements on Web pages) and explain how the information contributes to an understanding of the text in which it appears.
	Selection 2: Before You Move On: Draw Conclusions	CA CC.4.Rinf.3	Explain events, procedures, ideas, or concepts in a historical, scientific, or technical text, including what happened and why, based on specific information in the text.
452	**Respond and Extend:** Compare Fact and Opinion	CA CC.4.Rinf.6	Compare and contrast a firsthand and secondhand account of the same event or topic; describe the differences in focus and the information provided.

724

SE Pages	Lesson	Code	Standard
		CA CC.4.Rinf.9	Integrate information from two texts on the same topic in order to write or speak about the subject knowledgeably.
			Engage effectively in a range of collaborative discussions (one-on-one, in groups, and teacher-led) with diverse partners on *grade 4 topics and texts*, building on others' ideas and expressing their own clearly.
		CA CC.4.SL.1.a	Come to discussions prepared, having read or studied required material; explicitly draw on that preparation and other information known about the topic to explore ideas under discussion.
		CA CC.4.L.6	Acquire and use accurately grade-appropriate general academic and domain-specific words and phrases, including those that signal precise actions, emotions, or states of being (e.g., quizzed, whined, stammered) and that are basic to a particular topic (e.g., wildlife, conservation, and endangered when discussing animal preservation).
453	**Grammar and Spelling:** Adverbs	CA CC.4.L.1	Demonstrate command of the conventions of standard English grammar and usage when writing or speaking.
454	**Part 2:** **Language:** Clarify	CA CC.4.Rinf.2	Determine the main idea of a text and explain how it is supported by key details; summarize the text.
			Engage effectively in a range of collaborative discussions (one-on-one, in groups, and teacher-led) with diverse partners on grade 4 topics and texts, building on others' ideas and expressing their own clearly.
		CA CC.4.SL.1.a	Come to discussions prepared, having read or studied required material; explicitly draw on that preparation and other information known about the topic to explore ideas under discussion.
		CA CC.4.SL.1.c	Pose and respond to specific questions to clarify or follow up on information, and make comments that contribute to the discussion and link to the remarks of others.
		CA CC.4.SL.1.d	Review the key ideas expressed and explain their own ideas and understanding in light of the discussion.
455	**Science Vocabulary:** Key Words	CA CC.4.Rinf.4	Determine the meaning of general academic and domain-specific words or phrases in a text relevant to a grade 4 topic or subject area. **(See grade 4 Language standards 4–6 for additional expectations.) CA**
456	**Thinking Map:** Plot	CA CC.4.Rlit.1	Refer to details and examples in a text when explaining what the text says explicitly and when drawing inferences from the text.
		CA CC.4.Rlit.3	Describe in depth a character, setting, or event in a story or drama, drawing on specific details in the text (e.g., a character's thoughts, words, or actions).
457	**Academic Vocabulary:** More Key Words	CA CC.4.Rlit.4	Determine the meaning of words and phrases as they are used in a text, including those that allude to significant characters found in mythology (e.g., Herculean). **(See grade 4 Language standards 4–6 for additional expectations.) CA**
		CA CC.4.Rinf.4	Determine the meaning of general academic and domain-specific words or phrases in a text relevant to a grade 4 topic or subject area. **(See grade 4 Language standards 4–6 for additional expectations.) CA**
458–459	**Strategic Reading:** Learn to Synthesize (Form Generalizations)	CA CC.4.Rlit.1	Refer to details and examples in a text when explaining what the text says explicitly and when drawing inferences from the text.
		CA CC.4.Rlit.2	Determine a theme of a story, drama, or poem from details in the text; summarize the text.

California Common Core State Standards, *continued*

SE Pages	Lesson	Code	Standard
462	**Selection 1:** Set a Purpose		Read with sufficient accuracy and fluency to support comprehension.
		CA CC.4.Rfou.4.a	Read on-level text with purpose and understanding.
465	**Selection 1:** Before You Move On	CA CC.4.Rlit.1	Refer to details and examples in a text when explaining what the text says explicitly and when drawing inferences from the text.
	Selection 1: Before You Move On: Generalize	CA CC.4.Rlit.2	Determine a theme of a story, drama, or poem from details in the text; summarize the text.
466	**Selection 1:** Predict	CA CC.4.Rlit.1	Refer to details and examples in a text when explaining what the text says explicitly and when drawing inferences from the text.
469	**Selection 1:** Before You Move On	CA CC.4.Rlit.1	Refer to details and examples in a text when explaining what the text says explicitly and when drawing inferences from the text.
	Selection 1: Before You Move On: Plot	CA CC.4.Rlit.3	Describe in depth a character, setting, or event in a story or drama, drawing on specific details in the text (e.g., a character's thoughts, words, or actions).
470	**Selection 1:** Predict	CA CC.4.Rlit.1	Refer to details and examples in a text when explaining what the text says explicitly and when drawing inferences from the text.
474	**Selection 1:** Before You Move On	CA CC.4.Rlit.1	Refer to details and examples in a text when explaining what the text says explicitly and when drawing inferences from the text.
	Selection 1: Before You Move On: Character	CA CC.4.Rlit.3	Describe in depth a character, setting, or event in a story or drama, drawing on specific details in the text (e.g., a character's thoughts, words, or actions).
475	**Meet the Illustrator:** Artist's Craft	CA CC.4.Rlit.4	Determine the meaning of words and phrases as they are used in a text, including those that allude to significant characters found in mythology (e.g., Herculean). **(See grade 4 Language standards 4–6 for additional expectations.) CA**
476	**Think and Respond:** Talk About It	CA CC.4.Rlit.1	Refer to details and examples in a text when explaining what the text says explicitly and when drawing inferences from the text.
		CA CC.4.Rlit.2	Determine a theme of a story, drama, or poem from details in the text; summarize the text.
		CA CC.4.Rlit.6	Compare and contrast the point of view from which different stories are narrated, including the difference between first- and third-person narrations.
			Engage effectively in a range of collaborative discussions (one-on-one, in groups, and teacher-led) with diverse partners on *grade 4 topics and texts*, building on others' ideas and expressing their own clearly.
		CA CC.4.SL.1.c	Pose and respond to specific questions to clarify or follow up on information, and make comments that contribute to the discussion and link to the remarks of others.
	Think and Respond: Write About It	CA CC.4.Rlit.1	Refer to details and examples in a text when explaining what the text says explicitly and when drawing inferences from the text.
		CA CC.4.W.9	Draw evidence from literary or informational texts to support analysis, reflection, and research.
		CA CC.4.L.6	Acquire and use accurately grade-appropriate general academic and domain-specific words and phrases, including those that signal precise actions, emotions, or states of being (e.g., quizzed, whined, stammered) and that are basic to a particular topic (e.g., wildlife, conservation, and endangered when discussing animal preservation).
477	**Reread and Retell:** Plot	CA CC.4.Rlit.1	Refer to details and examples in a text when explaining what the text says explicitly and when drawing inferences from the text.

SE Pages	Lesson	Code	Standard
		CA CC.4.Rlit.3	Describe in depth a character, setting, or event in a story or drama, drawing on specific details in the text (e.g., a character's thoughts, words, or actions).
	Reread and Retell: Fluency		Read with sufficient accuracy and fluency to support comprehension.
		CA CC.4.Rfou.4.b	Read on-level prose and poetry orally with accuracy, appropriate rate, and expression on successive readings.
	Reread and Retell: Talk Together	CA CC.4.Rlit.3	Describe in depth a character, setting, or event in a story or drama, drawing on specific details in the text (e.g., a character's thoughts, words, or actions).
		CA CC.4.SL.4	Report on a topic or text, tell a story, or recount an experience in an organized manner, using appropriate facts and relevant, descriptive details to support main ideas or themes; speak clearly at an understandable pace.
		CA CC.4.SL.4.a	**Plan and deliver a narrative presentation that: relates ideas, observations, or recollections; provides a clear context; and includes clear insight into why the event or experience is memorable. CA**
	Reread and Retell: Talk Together	CA CC.4.L.6	Acquire and use accurately grade-appropriate general academic and domain-specific words and phrases, including those that signal precise actions, emotions, or states of being (e.g., quizzed, whined, stammered) and that are basic to a particular topic (e.g., wildlife, conservation, and endangered when discussing animal preservation).
478	**Word Work:** Word Parts	CA CC.4.Rfou.3	Know and apply grade-level phonics and word analysis skills in decoding words.
		CA CC.4.Rfou.3.a	Use combined knowledge of all letter-sound correspondences, syllabication patterns, and morphology (e.g., roots and affixes) to read accurately unfamiliar multisyllabic words in context and out of context.
			Determine or clarify the meaning of unknown and multiple-meaning words and phrases based on *grade 4 reading and content*, choosing flexibly from a range of strategies.
		CA CC.4.L.4.b	Use common, grade-appropriate Greek and Latin affixes and roots as clues to the meaning of a word (e.g., telegraph, photograph, autograph).
479	**Selection 2 Opener:** Before You Move On: Explain	CA CC.4.Rinf.3	Explain events, procedures, ideas, or concepts in a historical, scientific, or technical text, including what happened and why, based on specific information in the text.
	Selection 2 Opener: Before You Move On: Paraphrase	CA CC.4.Rinf.2	Determine the main idea of a text and explain how it is supported by key details; summarize the text.
481	**Selection 2:** Before You Move On: Generalize	CA CC.4.Rinf.1	Refer to details and examples in a text when explaining what the text says explicitly and when drawing inferences from the text.
		CA CC.4.Rinf.2	Determine a theme of a story, drama, or poem from details in the text; summarize the text.
	Selection 2: Before You Move On: Goal/Outcome	CA CC.4.Rinf.3	Explain events, procedures, ideas, or concepts in a historical, scientific, or technical text, including what happened and why, based on specific information in the text.
		CA CC.4.Rinf.5	Describe the overall structure (e.g., chronology, comparison, cause/effect, problem/solution) of events, ideas, concepts, or information in a text or part of a text.

California Common Core State Standards, *continued*

SE Pages	Lesson	Code	Standard
482	**Respond and Extend:** Compare Fiction and Biography	CA CC.4.Rlit.9	Compare and contrast the treatment of similar themes and topics (e.g., opposition of good and evil) and patterns of events (e.g., the quest) in stories, myths, and traditional literature from different cultures.
		CA CC.4.Rlit.10	By the end of the year, read and comprehend literature, including stories, dramas, and poetry, in the grades 4–5 text complexity band proficiently, with scaffolding as needed at the high end of the range.
		CA CC.4.Rinf.10	By the end of year, read and comprehend informational texts, including history/social studies, science, and technical texts, in the grades 4–5 text complexity band proficiently, with scaffolding as needed at the high end of the range.
	Respond and Extend: Talk Together	CA CC.4.Rinf.9	Integrate information from two texts on the same topic in order to write or speak about the subject knowledgeably.
			Engage effectively in a range of collaborative discussions (one-on-one, in groups, and teacher-led) with diverse partners on *grade 4 topics and texts*, building on others' ideas and expressing their own clearly.
		CA CC.4.SL.1.a	Come to discussions prepared, having read or studied required material; explicitly draw on that preparation and other information known about the topic to explore ideas under discussion.
		CA CC.4.L.6	Acquire and use accurately grade-appropriate general academic and domain-specific words and phrases, including those that signal precise actions, emotions, or states of being (e.g., quizzed, whined, stammered) and that are basic to a particular topic (e.g., wildlife, conservation, and endangered when discussing animal preservation).
483	**Grammar and Spelling:** Prepositional Phrases		Demonstrate command of the conventions of standard English grammar and usage when writing or speaking.
		CA CC.4.L.1.e	Form and use prepositional phrases.
484–485	**Writing Project:** Personal Narrative Study a Model Prewrite Draft		Write narratives to develop real or imagined experiences or events using effective technique, descriptive details, and clear event sequences.
		CA CC.4.W.3.a	Orient the reader by establishing a situation and introducing a narrator and/or characters; organize an event sequence that unfolds naturally.
		CA CC.4.W.3.b	Use dialogue and description to develop experiences and events or show the responses of characters to situations.
		CA CC.4.W.3.e	Provide a conclusion that follows from the narrated experiences or events.
486	**Writing Project:** Personal Narrative Revise		Write narratives to develop real or imagined experiences or events using effective technique, descriptive details, and clear event sequences.
		CA CC.4.W.3.b	Use dialogue and description to develop experiences and events or show the responses of characters to situations.
		CA CC.4.W.5	With guidance and support from peers and adults, develop and strengthen writing as needed by planning, revising, and editing. (Editing for conventions should demonstrate command of Language standards 1–3 up to and including grade 4.)

SE Pages	Lesson	Code	Standard
487	**Writing Project:** Personal Narrative Edit and Proofread	CA CC.4.W.5	With guidance and support from peers and adults, develop and strengthen writing as needed by planning, revising, and editing. (Editing for conventions should demonstrate command of Language standards 1–3 up to and including grade 4.)
			Demonstrate command of the conventions of standard English grammar and usage when writing or speaking.
		CA CC.4.L.1.e	Form and use prepositional phrases.
	Writing Project: Personal Narrative Publish	CA CC.4.W.6	With some guidance and support from adults, use technology, including the Internet, to produce and publish writing as well as to interact and collaborate with others; demonstrate sufficient command of keyboarding skills to type a minimum of one page in a single sitting.
		CA CC.4.SL.4	Report on a topic or text, tell a story, or recount an experience in an organized manner, using appropriate facts and relevant, descriptive details to support main ideas or themes; speak clearly at an understandable pace.
		CA CC.4.SL.4.a	**Plan and deliver a narrative presentation that: relates ideas, observations, or recollections; provides a clear context; and includes clear insight into why the event or experience is memorable. CA**
488	**Talk Together**		Engage effectively in a range of collaborative discussions (one-on-one, in groups, and teacher-led) with diverse partners on *grade 4 topics and texts*, building on others' ideas and expressing their own clearly.
		CA CC.4.SL.1.a	Come to discussions prepared, having read or studied required material; explicitly draw on that preparation and other information known about the topic to explore ideas under discussion.
		CA CC.4.SL.1.d	Review the key ideas expressed and explain their own ideas and understanding in light of the discussion.
	Write a Note	CA CC.4.W.10	Write routinely over extended time frames (time for research, reflection, and revision) and shorter time frames (a single sitting or a day or two) for a range of discipline-specific tasks, purposes, and audiences.
489	**Unit Wrap-Up:** Share Your Ideas	CA CC.4.Rlit.3	Describe in depth a character, setting, or event in a story or drama, drawing on specific details in the text (e.g., a character's thoughts, words, or actions).
		CA CC.4.W.4	Produce clear and coherent writing **(including multiple-paragraph texts)** in which the development and organization are appropriate to task, purpose, and audience. (Grade-specific expectations for writing types are defined in standards 1–3 above.) **CA**
		CA CC.4.W.7	Conduct short research projects that build knowledge through investigation of different aspects of a topic.
		CA CC.4.W.10	Write routinely over extended time frames (time for research, reflection, and revision) and shorter time frames (a single sitting or a day or two) for a range of discipline-specific tasks, purposes, and audiences.
		CA CC.4.SL.1	Engage effectively in a range of collaborative discussions (one-on-one, in groups, and teacher-led) with diverse partners on grade 4 topics and texts, building on others' ideas and expressing their own clearly.
		CA CC.4.SL.1.a	Come to discussions prepared, having read or studied required material; explicitly draw on that preparation and other information known about the topic to explore ideas under discussion.

California Common Core State Standards, *continued*

SE Pages	Lesson	Code	Standard
496–497	**Strategic Reading:** Choose Reading Strategies	CA CC.4.Rlit.1	Refer to details and examples in a text when explaining what the text says explicitly and when drawing inferences from the text.
		CA CC.4.Rinf.1	Refer to details and examples in a text when explaining what the text says explicitly and when drawing inferences from the text.
500	**Selection 1:** Set a Purpose		Read with sufficient accuracy and fluency to support comprehension.
		CA CC.4.Rfou.4.a	Read on-level text with purpose and understanding.
503	**Selection 1:** Before You Move On: Theme	CA CC.4.Rlit.2	Determine a theme of a story, drama, or poem from details in the text; summarize the text.
	Selection 1: Before You Move On: Figurative Language	CA CC.4.Rlit.4	Determine the meaning of words and phrases as they are used in a text, including those that allude to significant characters found in mythology (e.g., Herculean). **(See grade 4 Language standards 4–6 for additional expectations.) CA**
			Demonstrate understanding of figurative language, word relationships, and nuances in word meanings.
		CA CC.4.L.5.a	Explain the meaning of simple similes and metaphors (e.g., as pretty as a picture) in context.
504	**Selection 1:** Predict	CA CC.4.Rlit.1	Refer to details and examples in a text when explaining what the text says explicitly and when drawing inferences from the text.
507	**Selection 1:** Before You Move On: Goal/Outcome	CA CC.4.Rlit.2	Determine a theme of a story, drama, or poem from details in the text; summarize the text.
	Selection 1: Before You Move On	CA CC.4.Rlit.3	Describe in depth a character, setting, or event in a story or drama, drawing on specific details in the text (e.g., a character's thoughts, words, or actions).
508	**Selection 1:** Predict	CA CC.4.Rlit.1	Refer to details and examples in a text when explaining what the text says explicitly and when drawing inferences from the text.
512	**Selection 1:** Before You Move On: Goal/Outcome	CA CC.4.Rlit.2	Determine a theme of a story, drama, or poem from details in the text; summarize the text.
		CA CC.4.Rlit.3	Describe in depth a character, setting, or event in a story or drama, drawing on specific details in the text (e.g., a character's thoughts, words, or actions).
	Selection 1: Before You Move On: Visualize	CA CC.4.Rlit.1	Refer to details and examples in a text when explaining what the text says explicitly and when drawing inferences from the text.
513	**Meet the Author:** Writer's Craft	CA CC.4.Rlit.4	Determine the meaning of words and phrases as they are used in a text, including those that allude to significant characters found in mythology (e.g., Herculean). **(See grade 4 Language standards 4–6 for additional expectations.) CA**
			Demonstrate understanding of figurative language, word relationships, and nuances in word meanings.
		CA CC.4.L.5.a	Explain the meaning of simple similes and metaphors (e.g., *as pretty as a picture*) in context.

California Common Core State Standards, *continued*

SE Pages	Lesson	Code	Standard
			Draw evidence from literary or informational texts to support analysis, reflection, and research.
		CA CC.4.W.9.a	Apply *grade 4 Reading standards* to literature (e.g., "Describe in depth a character, setting, or event in a story or drama, drawing on specific details in the text [e.g., a character's thoughts, words, or actions].").
514	**Think and Respond:** Talk About It	CA CC.4.Rlit.1	Refer to details and examples in a text when explaining what the text says explicitly and when drawing inferences from the text.
		CA CC.4.Rlit.2	Determine a theme of a story, drama, or poem from details in the text; summarize the text.
		CA CC.4.Rlit.3	Describe in depth a character, setting, or event in a story or drama, drawing on specific details in the text (e.g., a character's thoughts, words, or actions).
	Think and Respond: Write About It	CA CC.4.W.4	Produce clear and coherent writing **(including multiple-paragraph texts)** in which the development and organization are appropriate to task, purpose, and audience. (Grade-specific expectations for writing types are defined in standards 1–3 above.) **CA**
		CA CC.4.L.6	Acquire and use accurately grade-appropriate general academic and domain-specific words and phrases, including those that signal precise actions, emotions, or states of being (e.g., quizzed, whined, stammered) and that are basic to a particular topic (e.g., wildlife, conservation, and endangered when discussing animal preservation).
515	**Reread and Retell:** Goal and Outcome	CA CC.4.Rlit.2	Determine a theme of a story, drama, or poem from details in the text; summarize the text.
	Reread and Retell: Goal and Outcome	CA CC.4.Rlit.3	Describe in depth a character, setting, or event in a story or drama, drawing on specific details in the text (e.g., a character's thoughts, words, or actions).
	Reread and Retell: Fluency		Read with sufficient accuracy and fluency to support comprehension.
		CA CC.4.Rfou.4.b	Read on-level prose and poetry orally with accuracy, appropriate rate, and expression on successive readings.
	Reread and Retell: Talk Together		Engage effectively in a range of collaborative discussions (one-on-one, in groups, and teacher-led) with diverse partners on *grade 4 topics and texts*, building on others' ideas and expressing their own clearly.
		CA CC.4.SL.1.c	Pose and respond to specific questions to clarify or follow up on information, and make comments that contribute to the discussion and link to the remarks of others.
		CA CC.4.L.6	Acquire and use accurately grade-appropriate general academic and domain-specific words and phrases, including those that signal precise actions, emotions, or states of being (e.g., quizzed, whined, stammered) and that are basic to a particular topic (e.g., wildlife, conservation, and endangered when discussing animal preservation).
516	**Word Work:** More Idioms		Demonstrate understanding of figurative language, word relationships, and nuances in word meanings.
		CA CC.4.L.5.b	Recognize and explain the meaning of common idioms, adages, and proverbs.

SE Pages	Lesson	Code	Standard
517	**Selection 2 Opener:** Before You Move On: Use Text Features	CA CC.4.Rinf.7	Interpret information presented visually, orally, or quantitatively (e.g., in charts, graphs, diagrams, time lines, animations, or interactive elements on Web pages) and explain how the information contributes to an understanding of the text in which it appears.
	Selection 2 Opener: Before You Move On: Visualize	CA CC.4.Rinf.1	Refer to details and examples in a text when explaining what the text says explicitly and when drawing inferences from the text.
519	**Selection 2:** Before You Move On: Summarize	CA CC.4.Rinf.2	Determine the main idea of a text and explain how it is supported by key details; summarize the text.
	Selection 2: Before You Move On: Generalize	CA CC.4.Rinf.3	Explain events, procedures, ideas, or concepts in a historical, scientific, or technical text, including what happened and why, based on specific information in the text.
521	**Selection 2:** Before You Move On: Clarify	CA CC.4.Rinf.3	Explain events, procedures, ideas, or concepts in a historical, scientific, or technical text, including what happened and why, based on specific information in the text.
	Selection 2: Before You Move On: Evaluate	CA CC.4.Rinf.7	Interpret information presented visually, orally, or quantitatively (e.g., in charts, graphs, diagrams, time lines, animations, or interactive elements on Web pages) and explain how the information contributes to an understanding of the text in which it appears.
523	**Selection 2:** Before You Move On: Make Comparisons	CA CC.4.Rinf.7	Interpret information presented visually, orally, or quantitatively (e.g., in charts, graphs, diagrams, time lines, animations, or interactive elements on Web pages) and explain how the information contributes to an understanding of the text in which it appears.
	Selection 2: Before You Move On: Summarize	CA CC.4.Rinf.2	Determine the main idea of a text and explain how it is supported by key details; summarize the text.
524	**Respond and Extend:** Compare Fiction and Nonfiction	CA CC.4.Rlit.6	Compare and contrast the point of view from which different stories are narrated, including the difference between first- and third-person narrations.
		CA CC.4.Rinf.9	Integrate information from two texts on the same topic in order to write or speak about the subject knowledgeably.
			Engage effectively in a range of collaborative discussions (one-on-one, in groups, and teacher-led) with diverse partners on *grade 4 topics and texts*, building on others' ideas and expressing their own clearly.
		CA CC.4.SL.1.a	Come to discussions prepared, having read or studied required material; explicitly draw on that preparation and other information known about the topic to explore ideas under discussion.
		CA CC.4.L.6	Acquire and use accurately grade-appropriate general academic and domain-specific words and phrases, including those that signal precise actions, emotions, or states of being (e.g., quizzed, whined, stammered) and that are basic to a particular topic (e.g., wildlife, conservation, and endangered when discussing animal preservation).

California Common Core State Standards, continued

SE Pages	Lesson	Code	Standard
525	**Grammar and Spelling:** Past-Tense	CA CC.4.L.1	Demonstrate command of the conventions of standard English grammar and usage when writing or speaking.
	Grammar and Spelling: Past-Tense		Demonstrate command of the conventions of standard English capitalization, punctuation, and spelling when writing.
		CA CC.4.L.2.d	Spell grade-appropriate words correctly, consulting references as needed.
526	**Part 2: Language:** Justify	CA CC.4.SL.1	Engage effectively in a range of collaborative discussions (one-on-one, in groups, and teacher-led) with diverse partners on grade 4 topics and texts, building on others' ideas and expressing their own clearly.
		CA CC.4.SL.1.a	Come to discussions prepared, having read or studied required material; explicitly draw on that preparation and other information known about the topic to explore ideas under discussion.
		CA CC.4.SL.1.b	Follow agreed-upon rules for discussions and carry out assigned roles.
		CA CC.4.SL.1.c	Pose and respond to specific questions to clarify or follow up on information, and make comments that contribute to the discussion and link to the remarks of others.
		CA CC.4.SL.1.d	Review the key ideas expressed and explain their own ideas and understanding in light of the discussion.
527	**Social Studies Vocabulary:** Key Words	CA CC.4.Rinf.4	Determine the meaning of general academic and domain-specific words or phrases in a text relevant to a grade 4 topic or subject area. **(See grade 4 Language standards 4–6 for additional expectations.) CA**
528	**Thinking Map:** Fact and Opinion	CA CC.4.Rinf.1	Refer to details and examples in a text when explaining what the text says explicitly and when drawing inferences from the text.
		CA CC.4.Rinf.2	Determine the main idea of a text and explain how it is supported by key details; summarize the text.
529	**Academic Vocabulary:** More Key Words	CA CC.4.Rinf.4	Determine the meaning of general academic and domain-specific words or phrases in a text relevant to a grade 4 topic or subject area. **(See grade 4 Language standards 4–6 for additional expectations.) CA**
530–531	**Strategic Reading:** Use Reading Strategies	CA CC.4.Rlit.1	Refer to details and examples in a text when explaining what the text says explicitly and when drawing inferences from the text.
		CA CC.4.Rinf.1	Refer to details and examples in a text when explaining what the text says explicitly and when drawing inferences from the text.
534	**Selection 1:** Set a Purpose		Read with sufficient accuracy and fluency to support comprehension.
		CA CC.4.Rfou.4.a	Read on-level text with purpose and understanding.
535	**Selection 1:** Before You Move On: Fact/Opinion	CA CC.4.Rinf.1	Refer to details and examples in a text when explaining what the text says explicitly and when drawing inferences from the text.
	Selection 1: Before You Move On: Determine Importance	CA CC.4.Rinf.2	Determine the main idea of a text and explain how it is supported by key details; summarize the text.

SE Pages	Lesson	Code	Standard
537	**Selection 1:** Before You Move On: Ask Questions		Engage effectively in a range of collaborative discussions (one-on-one, in groups, and teacher-led) with diverse partners on *grade 4 topics and texts*, building on others' ideas and expressing their own clearly.
		CA CC.4.SL.1.c	Pose and respond to specific questions to clarify or follow up on information, and make comments that contribute to the discussion and link to the remarks of others.
	Selection 1: Before You Move On: Synthesize	CA CC.4.Rinf.3	Explain events, procedures, ideas, or concepts in a historical, scientific, or technical text, including what happened and why, based on specific information in the text.
539	**Selection 1:** Before You Move On: Synthesize	CA CC.4.Rinf.3	Explain events, procedures, ideas, or concepts in a historical, scientific, or technical text, including what happened and why, based on specific information in the text.
		CA CC.4.Rinf.7	Interpret information presented visually, orally, or quantitatively (e.g., in charts, graphs, diagrams, time lines, animations, or interactive elements on Web pages) and explain how the information contributes to an understanding of the text in which it appears.
	Selection 1: Before You Move On: Main Idea	CA CC.4.Rinf.2	Determine the main idea of a text and explain how it is supported by key details; summarize the text.
541	**Selection 1:** Before You Move On: Summarize	CA CC.4.Rinf.2	Determine the main idea of a text and explain how it is supported by key details; summarize the text.
	Selection 1: Before You Move On: Make Inferences	CA CC.4.Rinf.1	Refer to details and examples in a text when explaining what the text says explicitly and when drawing inferences from the text.
543	**Selection 1:** Before You Move On: Fact/Opinion	CA CC.4.Rinf.2	Determine the main idea of a text and explain how it is supported by key details; summarize the text.
	Selection 1: Before You Move On: Sequence	CA CC.4.Rinf.5	Describe the overall structure (e.g., chronology, comparison, cause/effect, problem/solution) of events, ideas, concepts, or information in a text or part of a text.
545	**Selection 1:** Before You Move On: Draw Conclusions	CA CC.4.Rinf.3	Explain events, procedures, ideas, or concepts in a historical, scientific, or technical text, including what happened and why, based on specific information in the text.
	Selection 1: Before You Move On: Details	CA CC.4.Rinf.1	Refer to details and examples in a text when explaining what the text says explicitly and when drawing inferences from the text.
547	**Selection 1:** Before You Move On: Summarize	CA CC.4.Rinf.2	Determine the main idea of a text and explain how it is supported by key details; summarize the text.
	Selection 1: Before You Move On: Analyze	CA CC.4.Rinf.3	Explain events, procedures, ideas, or concepts in a historical, scientific, or technical text, including what happened and why, based on specific information in the text.

California Common Core State Standards, continued

Unit 8	Saving a Piece of the World, continued		
SE Pages	**Lesson**	**Code**	**Standard**
548	**Think and Respond:** Talk About It	CA CC.4.Rinf.2	Determine the main idea of a text and explain how it is supported by key details; summarize the text.
		CA CC.4.Rinf.3	Explain events, procedures, ideas, or concepts in a historical, scientific, or technical text, including what happened and why, based on specific information in the text.
			Engage effectively in a range of collaborative discussions (one-on-one, in groups, and teacher-led) with diverse partners on *grade 4 topics and texts*, building on others' ideas and expressing their own clearly.
		CA CC.4.SL.1.d	Review the key ideas expressed and explain their own ideas and understanding in light of the discussion.
	Think and Respond: Write About It		Write opinion pieces on topics or texts, supporting a point of view with reasons and information.
		CA CC.4.W.1.a	Introduce a topic or text clearly, state an opinion, and create an organizational structure in which related ideas are grouped to support the writer's purpose.
		CA CC.4.W.1.b	Provide reasons that are supported by facts and details.
		CA CC.4.W.1.d	Provide a concluding statement or section related to the opinion presented.
		CA CC.4.W.4	Produce clear and coherent writing **(including multiple-paragraph texts)** in which the development and organization are appropriate to task, purpose, and audience. (Grade-specific expectations for writing types are defined in standards 1–3 above.) **CA**
		CA CC.4.L.6	Acquire and use accurately grade-appropriate general academic and domain-specific words and phrases, including those that signal precise actions, emotions, or states of being (e.g., quizzed, whined, stammered) and that are basic to a particular topic (e.g., wildlife, conservation, and endangered when discussing animal preservation).
549	**Reread and Analyze:** Fact and Opinion	CA CC.4.Rinf.1	Refer to details and examples in a text when explaining what the text says explicitly and when drawing inferences from the text.
		CA CC.4.Rinf.2	Determine the main idea of a text and explain how it is supported by key details; summarize the text.
	Reread and Analyze: Fluency		Read with sufficient accuracy and fluency to support comprehension.
		CA CC.4.Rfou.4.b	Read on-level prose and poetry orally with accuracy, appropriate rate, and expression on successive readings.
	Reread and Analyze: Talk Together	CA CC.4.Rinf.7	Interpret information presented visually, orally, or quantitatively (e.g., in charts, graphs, diagrams, time lines, animations, or interactive elements on Web pages) and explain how the information contributes to an understanding of the text in which it appears.
			Engage effectively in a range of collaborative discussions (one-on-one, in groups, and teacher-led) with diverse partners on *grade 4 topics and texts*, building on others' ideas and expressing their own clearly.
		CA CC.4.SL.1.d	Review the key ideas expressed and explain their own ideas and understanding in light of the discussion.

SE Pages	Lesson	Code	Standard
	Reread and Analyze: Talk Together	CA CC.4.L.6	Acquire and use accurately grade-appropriate general academic and domain-specific words and phrases, including those that signal precise actions, emotions, or states of being (e.g., quizzed, whined, stammered) and that are basic to a particular topic (e.g., wildlife, conservation, and endangered when discussing animal preservation).
550	**Word Work:** Homographs		Read with sufficient accuracy and fluency to support comprehension.
		CA CC.4.Rfou.4.c	Use context to confirm or self-correct word recognition and understanding, rereading as necessary.
			Determine or clarify the meaning of unknown and multiple-meaning words and phrases based on *grade 4 reading and content*, choosing flexibly from a range of strategies.
		CA CC.4.L.4.a	Use context (e.g., definitions, examples, or restatements in text) as a clue to the meaning of a word or phrase.
551	**Selection 2 Opener:** Before You Move On: Point of View	CA CC.4.Rinf.6	Compare and contrast a firsthand and secondhand account of the same event or topic; describe the differences in focus and the information provided.
	Selection 2 Opener: Before You Move On: Make Inferences	CA CC.4.Rinf.1	Refer to details and examples in a text when explaining what the text says explicitly and when drawing inferences from the text.
553	**Selection 2:** Before You Move On: Clarify	CA CC.4.Rinf.3	Explain events, procedures, ideas, or concepts in a historical, scientific, or technical text, including what happened and why, based on specific information in the text.
	Selection 2: Before You Move On: Ask Questions	CA CC.4.Rinf.1	Refer to details and examples in a text when explaining what the text says explicitly and when drawing inferences from the text.
			Engage effectively in a range of collaborative discussions (one-on-one, in groups, and teacher-led) with diverse partners on *grade 4 topics and texts*, building on others' ideas and expressing their own clearly.
		CA CC.4.SL.1.c	Pose and respond to specific questions to clarify or follow up on information, and make comments that contribute to the discussion and link to the remarks of others.
555	**Selection 2:** Before You Move On: Draw Conclusions	CA CC.4.Rinf.2	Determine the main idea of a text and explain how it is supported by key details; summarize the text.
	Selection 2: Before You Move On: Explain	CA CC.4.Rinf.3	Explain events, procedures, ideas, or concepts in a historical, scientific, or technical text, including what happened and why, based on specific information in the text.
557	**Selection 2:** Before You Move On: Determine Importance	CA CC.4.Rinf.2	Determine the main idea of a text and explain how it is supported by key details; summarize the text.
	Selection 2: Before You Move On: Figurative Language	CA CC.4.Rinf.1	Refer to details and examples in a text when explaining what the text says explicitly and when drawing inferences from the text.

California Common Core State Standards, continued

SE Pages	Lesson	Code	Standard
			Demonstrate understanding of figurative language, word relationships, and nuances in word meanings.
		CA CC.4.L.5.a	Explain the meaning of simple similes and metaphors (e.g., *as pretty as a picture*) in context.
558	**Respond and Extend:** Compare Features	CA CC.4.Rinf.6	Compare and contrast a firsthand and secondhand account of the same event or topic; describe the differences in focus and the information provided.
		CA CC.4.Rinf.9	Integrate information from two texts on the same topic in order to write or speak about the subject knowledgeably.
	Respond and Extend: Talk Together		Engage effectively in a range of collaborative discussions (one-on-one, in groups, and teacher-led) with diverse partners on *grade 4 topics and texts*, building on others' ideas and expressing their own clearly.
		CA CC.4.SL.1.a	Come to discussions prepared, having read or studied required material; explicitly draw on that preparation and other information known about the topic to explore ideas under discussion.
		CA CC.4.L.6	Acquire and use accurately grade-appropriate general academic and domain-specific words and phrases, including those that signal precise actions, emotions, or states of being (e.g., quizzed, whined, stammered) and that are basic to a particular topic (e.g., wildlife, conservation, and endangered when discussing animal preservation).
559	**Grammar and Spelling:** Future Tense	CA CC.4.L.1	Demonstrate command of the conventions of standard English grammar and usage when writing or speaking.
560–561	**Writing Project:** Literary Response Study a Model Prewrite Draft	CA CC.4.W.1	Write opinion pieces on topics or texts, supporting a point of view with reasons and information.
		CA CC.4.W.1.a	Introduce a topic or text clearly, state an opinion, and create an organizational structure in which related ideas are grouped to support the writer's purpose.
		CA CC.4.W.1.b	Provide reasons that are supported by facts and details.
562	**Writing Project:** Literary Response Revise		Draw evidence from literary or informational texts to support analysis, reflection, and research.
		CA CC.4.W.9.b	Apply *grade 4 Reading standards* to informational texts (e.g., "Explain how an author uses reasons and evidence to support particular points in a text").
563	**Writing Project:** Literary Response Edit and Proofread	CA CC.4.W.5	With guidance and support from peers and adults, develop and strengthen writing as needed by planning, revising, and editing. (Editing for conventions should demonstrate command of Language standards 1–3 up to and including grade 4.)
			Demonstrate command of the conventions of standard English capitalization, punctuation, and spelling when writing.
		CA CC.4.L.2.d	Spell grade-appropriate words correctly, consulting references as needed.

SE Pages	Lesson	Code	Standard
	Writing Project: Literary Response Publish	CA CC.4.W.6	With some guidance and support from adults, use technology, including the Internet, to produce and publish writing as well as to interact and collaborate with others; demonstrate sufficient command of keyboarding skills to type a minimum of one page in a single sitting.
		CA CC.4.SL.3	Identify the reasons and evidence a speaker **or media source** provides to support particular points. **CA**
		CA CC.4.SL.4	Report on a topic or text, tell a story, or recount an experience in an organized manner, using appropriate facts and relevant, descriptive details to support main ideas or themes; speak clearly at an understandable pace.
564	**Talk Together**		Engage effectively in a range of collaborative discussions (one-on-one, in groups, and teacher-led) with diverse partners on *grade 4 topics and texts*, building on others' ideas and expressing their own clearly.
		CA CC.4.SL.1.a	Come to discussions prepared, having read or studied required material; explicitly draw on that preparation and other information known about the topic to explore ideas under discussion.
		CA CC.4.SL.1.d	Review the key ideas expressed and explain their own ideas and understanding in light of the discussion.
	Write a Persuasive Essay	CA CC.4.W.1	Write opinion pieces on topics or texts, supporting a point of view with reasons and information.
		CA CC.4.W.1.a	Introduce a topic or text clearly, state an opinion, and create an organizational structure in which related ideas are grouped to support the writer's purpose.
		CA CC.4.W.1.b	Provide reasons that are supported by facts and details.
		CA CC.4.W.1.c	Link opinion and reasons using words and phrases (e.g., *for instance, in order to, in addition*).
		CA CC.4.W.1.d	Provide a concluding statement or section related to the opinion presented.
		CA CC.4.W.4	Produce clear and coherent writing **(including multiple-paragraph texts)** in which the development and organization are appropriate to task, purpose, and audience. (Grade-specific expectations for writing types are defined in standards 1–3 above.) **CA**
565	**Unit Wrap-Up:** Share Your Ideas	CA CC.4.Rlit.3	Describe in depth a character, setting, or event in a story or drama, drawing on specific details in the text (e.g., a character's thoughts, words, or actions).
		CA CC.4.W.4	Produce clear and coherent writing **(including multiple-paragraph texts)** in which the development and organization are appropriate to task, purpose, and audience. (Grade-specific expectations for writing types are defined in standards 1–3 above.) **CA**
		CA CC.4.W.7	Conduct short research projects that build knowledge through investigation of different aspects of a topic.
		CA CC.4.W.10	Write routinely over extended time frames (time for research, reflection, and revision) and shorter time frames (a single sitting or a day or two) for a range of discipline-specific tasks, purposes, and audiences.

California Common Core State Standards, *continued*

SE Pages	Lesson	Code	Standard
		CA CC.4.SL.1	Engage effectively in a range of collaborative discussions (one-on-one, in groups, and teacher-led) with diverse partners on grade 4 topics and texts, building on others' ideas and expressing their own clearly.
		CA CC.4.SL.1.a	Come to discussions prepared, having read or studied required material; explicitly draw on that preparation and other information known about the topic to explore ideas under discussion.
		CA CC.4.SL.1.b	Follow agreed-upon rules for discussions and carry out assigned roles.
		CA CC.4.SL.1.c	Pose and respond to specific questions to clarify or follow up on information, and make comments that contribute to the discussion and link to the remarks of others.
		CA CC.4.SL.1.d	Review the key ideas expressed and explain their own ideas and understanding in light of the discussion.
		CA CC.4.SL.4	Report on a topic or text, tell a story, or recount an experience in an organized manner, using appropriate facts and relevant, descriptive details to support main ideas or themes; speak clearly at an understandable pace.